# Immigration Law and Practice in the United Kingdom

Supplement to the Ninth Edition, Volume 1

**General Editors**

**Ian A Macdonald QC**
Garden Court Chambers

**Ronan Toal**
Garden Court Chambers

and a team of specialist Contributing Editors

Members of the LexisNexis Group worldwide

| | |
|---|---|
| United Kingdom | RELX (UK) Limited trading as LexisNexis, 1-3 Strand, London WC2N 5JR and 9-10 St Andrew Square, Edinburgh EH2 2AF |
| Australia | Reed International Books Australia Pty Ltd trading as LexisNexis, Chatswood, New South Wales |
| Austria | LexisNexis Verlag ARD Orac GmbH & Co KG, Vienna |
| Benelux | LexisNexis Benelux, Amsterdam |
| Canada | LexisNexis Canada, Markham, Ontario |
| China | LexisNexis China, Beijing and Shanghai |
| France | LexisNexis SA, Paris |
| Germany | LexisNexis GmbH, Dusseldorf |
| Hong Kong | LexisNexis Hong Kong, Hong Kong |
| India | LexisNexis India, New Delhi |
| Italy | Giuffrè Editore, Milan |
| Japan | LexisNexis Japan, Tokyo |
| Malaysia | Malayan Law Journal Sdn Bhd, Kuala Lumpur |
| New Zealand | LexisNexis New Zealand Ltd, Wellington |
| Singapore | LexisNexis Singapore, Singapore |
| South Africa | LexisNexis, Durban |
| USA | LexisNexis, Dayton, Ohio |

First edition 1983, Second edition 1987, Third edition 1991, Fourth edition 1995, Fifth edition 2001, Sixth edition 2005, Seventh edition 2008, Eighth edition 2010, Ninth edition 2014

© 2017 RELX (UK) Limited

Published by LexisNexis

ISBN 978-1-4743-0698-0

9 781474 306980

ISBN for this volume: 9781474306980

ISBN for the set: Z000050746675

Printed and bound by CPI Group (UK) Ltd, Croydon, CRO 4YY

VISIT LEXISNEXIS AT WWW.LEXISNEXIS.CO.UK

# Contributors

**General Editors**

**Ian A Macdonald QC**
Garden Court Chambers

**Ronan Toal**
Garden Court Chambers


**Contributors**

**Ali Bandegani**
Garden Court Chambers

**Michelle Brewer**
Garden Court Chambers

**Grace Brown**
Garden Court Chambers

**Rebecca Chapman**
Garden Court Chambers

**Kathryn Cronin**
Garden Court Chambers

**Andrew Eaton**
Garden Court Chambers

**Emma Fitzsimons**
Garden Court Chambers

**Helen Foot**
Garden Court Chambers

**Alex Grigg**
Garden Court Chambers

**Stephanie Harrison QC**

Garden Court Chambers

**Peter Jorro**

Garden Court Chambers

**Gemma Loughran**

Garden Court Chambers

**Shu Shin Luh**

Garden Court Chambers

**Joseph Markus**

Garden Court North Chambers

**Richard McKee**

Barrister and former judge of the Upper Tribunal

**Chris McWatters**

Garden Court Chambers

**Sonali Naik**

Garden Court Chambers

**David Neale**

Garden Court Chambers

**Greg O'Ceallaigh**

Garden Court Chambers

**Desmond Rutledge**

Garden Court Chambers

**Sadat Sayeed**

Garden Court Chambers

**David Sellwood**

Garden Court Chambers

**Mark Symes**

Garden Court Chambers

**Anthony Vaughan**

Garden Court Chambers

**Amanda Weston**

Garden Court Chambers

**Natalie Wilkins**
Garden Court North Chambers
**Colin Yeo**
Garden Court Chambers

# Preface

By and large, writing this supplement has been a miserable experience because it has mainly entailed describing the features of the ever more hostile environment that the government has been creating for migrants, immigrants and refugee seekers and all those associated with them. Politically all three of these different categories of persons are bundled into one great group of undifferentiated scapegoats.

The centerpiece of this supplement is the Immigration Act 2016 which has carried on with a vengeance from where the Immigration Act 2014 left off. Together, they seek to make social and economic life impossible for those without the requisite immigration status by criminalising basic activities such as working and driving and by criminalising basic dealings with migrants lacking requisite status such as employing them or renting accommodation to them.

As with previous Immigration Acts, more and more state apparatuses are required to perform functions relating to the control of immigration. They range from naval and air force personnel being empowered to engage in hot pursuit of vessels, thought to be carrying asylum seekers or illegal entrants, to schools being required to provide documents that might assist in establishing a person's nationality.

On the other hand, the increasingly Byzantine immigration rules make the achievement and retention of leave to enter or remain far more difficult both procedurally and substantively. Meanwhile, the courts and tribunals would seem to have lost a great deal of their will or their power or both to provide real protection.

Much of the harm was done by the stripping away of rights of appeal by the Immigration Act 2014. The absence of a right opens the door to the most arbitrary kind of action by the government of the day and against whom there is less and less hope of redress by legal means, especially as so many decisions in immigration law are fact specific. In the words of a famous Victorian judge, speaking of the actions of parochial officers:[1]

'In a free country the very essence of the system must be that there should be an appeal to somebody who can say whether those officers are doing what is

---

[1]    *R v Justices of the County of London* [1893] 2 QB 617, at p 492, per Bowen LJ.

just. If no appeal were possible, I have no great hesitation in saying that this would not be a desirable country to live in, or every parochial officer might do as he liked in this matter. It is quite true that there is enough difficulty in appealing as it is, but if there is no appeal at all possible the system would be intolerable. Therefore, it is of the essence, the pivot of the system, that there should be a right of appeal.'

The lack of appeal has been compounded by the readiness of the court of appeal to accept that where there is a right of appeal, there is generally no objection to it being exercised after the appellant has been removed from the country.[2] Hopefully the Supreme Court which will shortly be addressing this issue will not display the same striking insouciance.

One area in which the court of appeal has been especially active is in overturning decisions by the tribunal to allow appeals against deportation on Article 8 grounds. Generally, the law relating to Article 8 in the immigration context, whilst never straightforward, has become impossibly complicated by the claims of the immigration rules, primary legislation and judicial decision making, none of which are entirely congruent, to map out the Article 8 terrain.

Another area of concern is the manner in which applications in Tier 1 of the Points Based System (PBS) to set up in business, and in Tier 2 to obtain visas for foreign workers to come to the UK. The PBS has now become over-regulated and so complicated as to be unworkable, but has also been effectively pushed aside and taken over by the introduction of the genuineness test – is the caseworker or entry clearance officer satisfied that the applicant genuinely intends to, and is able to, establish the proposed business? Or in the case of employment, that the vacancy is genuine one. This is the easy road to refusal, thereby helping to keep the numbers down. If European free movement comes to an end, and EU workers and their UK employers have to become subjected to the existing regulatory mess, the omens are not good, except for the lawyers.

However, it is not all gloom and doom. A very welcome development is the decision of the Grand Chamber of the European Court of Human Rights in *Paposhvili v Belgium*[3] which revisited the question of whether the consequences for health of removal resulting in loss of treatment could breach Article 3. The court held that the 'exceptional circumstances' required to establish a breach of Article 3 may be established by 'a real risk, on account of the absence of appropriate treatment in the receiving country or the lack of access to such treatment, of being exposed to a serious, rapid and irreversible decline in his or her state of health resulting in intense suffering or to a significant reduction in life expectancy'. If *N v Secretary of State for the Home Department*[4] remains binding as a matter of domestic law, it may be

---

[2]   *Kiarie and Byndloss v Secretary of State for the Home Department* [2015] EWCA Civ 1020.

[3]   [2016] ECHR 1113.

[4]   [2005] UKHL 31, [2005] 2 AC 296.

appropriate in this area to use the new power to leap-frog a case from the Upper Tribunal to the Supreme Court.[5]

Finally, we would like to pay tribute to the team of contributors, almost entirely from Garden Court Chambers South and North. Sometimes the difficulties of updating an immigration text book in the midst of carrying on a busy practice have been quite daunting. We at Garden Court are proud to be able to put our collective skills and experience of immigration law into the production of successive editions and updates of this work. In chambers, we work with massive support for our Bar work from our administration and clerks and we are beginning to realise that, as *Macdonald* grows bigger and more necessary, we increasingly need more support from our publisher and we are grateful for their help and the resources they have provided.

The law is stated as it was at 28 February 2017, though there have been one or two references to later law changes. We do not deal with the latest changes in the Immigration Rules, HC 1078, most of which will come into force on 6 April 2017.

Ian Macdonald QC

Ronan Toal

---

[5] Tribunals, Courts and Enforcement Act 2007, ss 14A–14C, inserted by the Criminal Justice and Courts Act 2015, s 64.

# Contents

# Contents

# Table of Statutes

# Table of Statutory Instruments

**M**

**N**

# Table of Immigration Rules

# Table of Conventions and Agreements

# Table of European Legislation

# Table of Cases

*Table of Cases*

**B**

## J

## K

## L

## M

## O

## P

## R

T

V

# Table of Cases

Decisions of the European Court of Justice are listed below numerically. These decisions are also included in the preceding alphabetical list.

l

# Chapter 2

# RIGHT OF ABODE AND CITIZENSHIP

## BECOMING A BRITISH CITIZEN

### Immigration Act 2014 changes

**2.50** *[N.B.]*

On 6 April 2015 s 65 of the Immigration Act 2014 came into force. This made a change to the British Nationality Act 1981, whereby people born before July 2006 who did not acquire British citizenship through their fathers because of illegitimacy became entitled to registration as British citizens – provided they satisfy the 'good character' requirement.

*In R (on the application of Johnson) v Secretary of State for the Home Department,*[1] the appellant, who had been born in 1985 to an unmarried British father, would have been eligible for registration but for his serious criminal record. Indeed, he was facing deportation as a 'foreign criminal', and was trying to resist this on human rights grounds. But the Secretary of State certified his human rights claim as 'clearly unfounded', so that he could only appeal against the decision after his removal from the UK. He sought judicial review to quash the certificate, and succeeded at the Administrative Court. But this was reversed by the Court of Appeal, and the matter eventually came before the Supreme Court.

Lady Hale explained that 'the denial of citizenship, having such an important effect upon a person's social identity, is sufficiently within the ambit of article 8 to trigger the application of the prohibition of discrimination in article 14' of the ECHR, birth outside wedlock being a 'status' for the purpose of Article 14. Had there been unlawful discrimination in the present case?

A difference in treatment is discriminatory if it has no objective and reasonable justification. Her Ladyship noted that people who are born illegitimate, but are legitimated by the subsequent marriage of their parents, do not have to pass the 'good character' test in s 41A of the British Nationality Act 1981 in order to register as British citizens, no matter how bad their behaviour has been. That the appellant did not have an automatic entitlement to British citizenship, just because his parents had not got married after his birth, was indeed unjustifiable discrimination.

The Court has therefore quashed the 'clearly unfounded' certificate, and made a declaration under s 4 of the Human Rights Act 1998 that the provisions which apply the 'good character' test to applications for registration made by people born out of wedlock are incompatible with human rights. The British Nationality Act 1981 has not yet, however, been amended to give effect to this declaration.

¹    [2016] UKSC 56, [2016] 3 WLR 1267, 166 NLJ 7720.

**Adoption in the British Overseas Territories**

*Registration*

**2.66  [N.B.]**

A child born in the UK, who does not become a British citizen by birth because neither of his parents is settled in the UK is entitled to register as a British citizen under the British Nationality Act 1981, s 1(4), but must pay a fee. On the application of *Ric Williams*¹ the court of Appeal held that the adoption of a scheme for citizenship applications that did not include a fee exemption for those who were unable to pay the fee because of impecuniosity did not exceed the Secretary of State's powers under the British Nationality Act 1981, s 1(4) and the Immigration, Asylum and Nationality Act 2006, s 51. Although a denial of nationality was sufficiently within the ambit of Article 8 to engage Article 14, there was no authority for the proposition that impecuniosity could be a status under Article 14 (paras 70-75).

¹    *R (on the application of Ric Williams (by his Litigation Friend Richard Williams)) v Secretary of State for the Home Department* [2017] EWCA Civ 98.

**NATURALISATION**

**2.67  [N.B.]**

The British Nationality (General) (Amendment No 3) Regulations 2015,¹ in force from 12 November 2015, have imposed a new requirement on citizens of other EU Member States who want to acquire British nationality on the basis of residence in the United Kingdom. This can be done after five years' lawful residence, with the last year being free from any time limit on one's stay. When lawful residence means 'with leave', this usually requires six years' residence, since it most often takes five years with limited leave for a Tier 1 or Tier 2 Migrant to achieve settlement. Six years' residence is also required by citizens of Member States of the European Economic Area.

Unlike other migrants, however, EEA nationals do not require leave to enter or remain, and do not have to obtain any official document to prove their right to reside in the UK. They obtain a permanent right to reside here after five years' residence in accordance with European law, ie by exercising 'Treaty rights' such as the right to take employment. Family members, including 'third country nationals', who have resided with them also obtain a permanent right of residence.

Strictly speaking, this does not have to be evidenced by obtaining a document certifying permanent residence or a permanent residence card issued by the Home Office under reg 19 of the Immigration (European Economic Area) Regulations 2016.² But in applications for citizenship one of these must now be produced to the Nationality Directorate, which is thereby relieved of the burden of establishing that the applicant has been exercising Treaty rights for the requisite period. That will already have been established by another part of UK Visas & Immigration.

1    SI 2015/1806.
2    SI 2016/1052.

## Good character

**2.69** *[N.B.]*

The Nationality Instructions, which guide caseworkers in dealing with naturalisation applications, now say that the requirement to be of good character is unlikely to be met for 15 years after the end of their sentence when applicants have been given prison sentences of between twelve months and four years (regardless of how long they have actually spent in prison). For prison sentences of less than twelve months, seven years must have passed, while for sentences of four years or more, citizenship will not normally be granted, ever.

People who have been given a non-custodial sentence, or who have accepted a police caution, normally have to wait three years before applying for naturalisation, before they can satisfy the 'good character' requirement. If they apply too early, their application will be refused and only £80 (for the citizenship ceremony) will be returned out of the application fee of £1,236.

When filling in an application form for naturalisation, non-disclosure of a conviction, even if it did not merit a custodial sentence, can result not just in refusal but in a ten-year moratorium on any further applications. Oddly, however, there is a loophole reported by the Upper Tribunal in *Omenma (Conditional discharge – not a conviction of an offence)*.[1] The strapline says it all. A guilty plea at the magistrates' court, followed by a conditional (or indeed unconditional) discharge, does not count as a conviction for most purposes. So an applicant for citizenship does not have to disclose it, whereas someone who keeps quiet about, say, a suspended sentence will have a bad character imputed to him.

Applicants sometimes do not appreciate that they have done something that will show up on a criminal record check (or perhaps they assume that no check will be made), and therefore omit to mention on their application form that they once received a fine for such things as a motoring offence or, as a licensee, for selling alcohol to someone who they should have known was under 18. They will then get a letter back from the Home Office to say that, for ten years after the date of the letter, any further application for citizenship is likely to be refused, as their failure to declare a conviction means that the 'good character' requirement has not been satisfied. Excuses by applicants who say that they did not realise they had a criminal conviction which had to be disclosed usually fall on deaf ears, even when *AA (Nigeria)*[2] is cited (this is the case which holds that 'deception', leading to mandatory refusal under the Immigration Rules, does not include innocent misrepresentation).

1    [2014] UKUT 314 (IAC).

² *Adedoyin v Secretary of State for the Home Department*[2010] EWCA Civ 773, [2011] 1 WLR 564, [2010] NLJR 1013.

### Deprivation of citizenship

**2.92** *[N.B.]*

A person can be deprived of British citizenship under s 40 of the British Nationality Act 1981, but can appeal against deprivation under s 40A. In *Deliallisi (British citizenship: deprivation appeal: scope)*¹ the Upper Tribunal held that, in assessing the proportionality of deprivation, European Union law must be involved, because deprivation of British citizenship entails loss of Union citizenship as well. This finding was reached *per incuriam*, as noted now in *AB (British citizenship: deprivation: Deliallisi considered) Nigeria*.² In the earlier case, the Upper Tribunal had not referred to *G1 v Secretary of State for the Home Department*,³ in which Laws LJ explained that European law would only be applicable if there was a 'cross-border element', ie if the British citizen had exercised Treaty rights in another Member State.

In *AB*, the Tribunal held that the reasonably foreseeable consequences of deprivation had to be considered. If the appellant had a strong human rights case against removal, it was less likely that removal would be effected, and hence the consequences of deprivation would be less severe. That was relevant to the assessment of whether deprivation would be disproportionate.

The Tribunal also noted that a person who had indefinite leave to remain before becoming a British citizen does not resume that status when deprived of citizenship. Leave to remain is effectively extinguished by the acquisition of British citizenship.

In *Secretary of State for the Home Department v Pham*⁴ the Supreme Court corrected the view expressed by Jackson LJ in *B2*⁵ about the court only being concerned with *de jure*, not *de facto*, statelessness. It was held instead that, in answering the question posed by Article 1(1) of the 1954 Convention on Statelessness, ie whether a person should be considered a national of a state under the operation of its own law, the UNHCR guidance ought to be followed. Article 1(1) refers not to the letter of the law, but to the operation of the law in practice, including where the government of a state makes executive decisions ignoring its own laws. In the instant case, however, the Vietnamese government had not actually decided to refuse to accept the appellant as one of its nationals, and so it was premature to regard him as stateless.

Lord Carnwath saw considerable force in the criticism of *Rottmann*⁶ by Laws LJ in *G1*⁷ on the question of whether European law has a bearing on the decision whether to deprive a British national of his citizenship, in the absence of a 'cross-border element'. Indeed, since Union citizenship is parasitic on the citizenship of a Member State, and since it is up to each Member State to decide who its own citizens are, the Supreme Court took the view *obiter* that deprivation of citizenship is not within the purview of the CJEU. If the European Court appears to be exceeding its jurisdiction, the municipal court is not bound to follow its judgment.

On the other hand, the effect of deprivation on the individual concerned does play an important role in ascertaining whether the decision is proportionate. The assessment of proportionality should, suggested Lord Carnwath, be much the same whether it is being considered under judicial review principles, under EU law, or under the ECHR.

Apart from its guidance when British citizens are facing deprivation of their citizenship, *Pham* is useful in determining whether persons seeking protection in the UK are stateless, as they claim. In *R (on the application of Seneda) v Secretary of State for the Home Department (statelessness: Pham [2015] UKSC 19 applied) IJR*,[8] the President of the Upper Tribunal has confirmed that the requirements of para 403 of the Immigration Rules for a grant of leave to remain as a stateless person must be given effect in tandem with the United Nations Convention Relating to the Status of Stateless Persons. In deciding whether '*the person concerned is considered as* . . . *a national* . . . *by any state* . . . *under the operation of its law*', the guidance in *Pham* should be applied.

1   [2013] UKUT 439 (IAC).
2   [2016] UKUT 451 (IAC).
3   [2012] EWCA Civ 867, [2013] QB 1008, [2012] 4 All ER 987.
4   [2015] UKSC 19, [2015] 3 All ER 1015, [2015] 1 WLR 1591.
5   *B2 v Secretary of State for the Home Department* [2013] EWCA Civ 616, at [156].
6   *Rottmann (Rottmann (Janko) v Freistaat Bayern* C-135/08 [2010] QB 761, [2010] ECR I-1449, [2010] 3 WLR 1166,ECJ.
7   *G1 v Secretary of State for the Home Department* [2012] EWCA Civ 867.
8   [2015] UKUT 658 (IAC).

# Chapter 3

# CONTROL OF ENTRY AND STAY

**Part I COMMON FEATURES OF LEAVE**

**Biometric Documents and information**

**3.7** *[In the text at line 2 delete: 'five further regulations' and replace with 'seven further regulations'.]*

*[At the end of footnote 1 add:]*

Biometric information has now been specifically defined as 'photographs or fingerprints provided under regulation 5': reg 3 of the Immigration (Biometric Registration) (Amendment) Regulations 2015, SI 2015/433.

*[At the end of footnote 2 add:]*

Immigration (Biometric Registration) (Amendment) Regulations 2015, SI 2015/433 and Immigration (Biometric Registration) (Amendment) (No 2) Regulations 2015, SI 2015/897.

**3.9** *[At the end of the paragraph insert:]*

A new reg 3A was inserted by reg 5 of the Immigration (Biometric Registration) (Amendment) Regulations 2015,[3] which extended the requirement to apply for a biometric immigration document to overseas applicants applying for entry clearance from certain specified countries as set out in a schedule to the regulations.

[3]   SI 2015/433.

**3.10** *[Delete the text starting 'Under reg 9 the government can use this biometric information for seven specified government functions including the prevention, investigation or prosecution of crime,' and insert:]*

Under reg 9 the government can use this biometric information for five specified government functions in connection with the prevention of crime; protection of national security; identification in the case of death or illness; in ascertaining whether a person has acted or obtained something unlawfully and identification of family members of EU citizens entitled to reside in the UK,

*[At the end of the paragraph insert:]*

The Immigration (Biometric Registration) (Amendment) Regulations 2015, SI 2015/433 have inserted new regs 3A, 13A and 13B into the Regulations. The new reg 3A extends the requirement to apply for a BID to certain kinds of overseas applications. Regulation 13A allows the Secretary of State to issue a biometric immigration document in accordance with an application under reg 3A. Regulation 13A also introduces a short-term biometric entry clearance document which allows a person with entry clearance to travel to the UK in order to collect their BID. Regulation 13B allows the Secretary of State to issue a short-term biometric document for grants of leave to enter or remain of six months or less.

*[In footnote 3 delete the text 'regs 11 and 12' and insert:]*

reg 10. A new regulation 11 inserted by the Immigration (Biometric Registration) (Amendment) Regulations 2015, SI 2015/433, requires the Secretary of State to destroy the fingerprint record after a period of 10 years. There are exceptions to this rule however: where the person has either a permanent right to reside in the UK; or are subject to a deportation order; have previously been in breach of UK immigration laws; or are deemed to be a threat to national security.

**3.11** *[At the end of footnote 1 add:]*

A new code of practice came into force in March 2015 following the Immigration (Biometric Registration) (Civil Penalty Code of Practice) Order 2015, SI 2015/565. The new guidance addresses changes consequent to the repeal of the Identity Cards Act 2006 and the use of Biometric Immigration Documents.

**3.12** *[At the end of footnote 1 add:]*See also footnote 6 of paragraph **3.67**.

**3.17** *[The main text for this paragraph is deleted. Insert:]*

See now, **3.18** below.

### On line applications

**3.18** *[Delete paragraph text and footnotes and insert:]*

HC 667, which was laid before Parliament on 3 November 2016, removed paragraphs A34–34l regarding online and valid applications. The statement of changes acknowledged that 'The rules relating to specified forms and procedures for applications or claims in connection with immigration, previously A34–34I, were complicated and difficult to interpret in places'. Under a new heading of 'How to make a valid application for leave to remain in the UK', a new paragraph 34 has been inserted. Paragraph A34 has not been replaced as the most significant change is that the new rules no longer distinguished between 'online and 'specified' forms. The reference to 'specified' in the new rules has been changed to reflect that a specified form is one which has been posted on the visa and immigration pages of the GOV.UK website.[1] A specified form for the purpose of the new rules can be either an online or paper form. A valid application under the new rules will need to be on the specified form; with all mandatory sections completed; that pays the applicable fee (including the Immigration Health Surcharge); has a required form of identity; passport photographs and biometric information.[2] The amended rules also set out what the Secretary of State may do if it is in receipt of an invalid application. A notice of invalidity will be served in accordance with Appendix SN of the Immigration Rules. The Secretary of State can either choose to request that the applicant submits the missing information or document or in certain specified cases waive the requirement. In all circumstances where biometric information is not provided, that application will be treated as invalid.[3]

1   HC 395, para 34(1)(b), as amended.
2   HC 395, para 34(2)–(10), as amended.
3   HC 395, para 34B, as amended.

## Compulsory application forms

**3.22** *[Replace footnote 3 with:]*

Modern Guidance – Specified application forms and procedures – Version 18, 18 March 2016, p 87.

## Fees

**3.29** *[N.B.]*

The changes in the fees regime pursuant to the Immigration Act 2014, set out at **3.38–3.39,** came into force on 15 December 2014. The previous fees regime described in paragraphs 3.29–3.37 of the 9th edition no longer apply; however, these paragraphs do provide relevant historical commentary.

**3.30** *[N.B.]*

The changes in the fees regime pursuant to the Immigration Act 2014, set out at **3.38–3.39,** came into force on 15 December 2014. The previous fees regime described in paragraphs 3.29–3.37 of the 9th edition no longer apply; however, these paragraphs do provide relevant historical commentary.

**3.31** *[N.B.]*

The changes in the fees regime pursuant to the Immigration Act 2014, set out at **3.38–3.39,** came into force on 15 December 2014. The previous fees regime described in paragraphs 3.29–3.37 of the 9th edition no longer apply; however, these paragraphs do provide relevant historical commentary.

**3.32** *[N.B.]*

The changes in the fees regime pursuant to the Immigration Act 2014, set out at **3.38–3.39,** came into force on 15 December 2014. The previous fees regime described in paragraphs 3.29–3.37 of the 9th edition no longer apply; however, these paragraphs do provide relevant historical commentary.

**3.33** *[N.B.]*

The changes in the fees regime pursuant to the Immigration Act 2014, set out at **3.38–3.39,** came into force on 15 December 2014. The previous fees regime described in paragraphs 3.29–3.37 of the 9th edition no longer apply; however, these paragraphs do provide relevant historical commentary.

**3.34** *[N.B.]*

The changes in the fees regime pursuant to the Immigration Act 2014, set out at **3.38–3.39,** came into force on 15 December 2014. The previous fees regime described in paragraphs 3.29–3.37 of the 9th edition no longer apply; however, these paragraphs do provide relevant historical commentary.

**3.35** *[N.B.]*

The changes in the fees regime pursuant to the Immigration Act 2014, set out at **3.38–3.39**, came into force on 15 December 2014. The previous fees regime described in paragraphs 3.29–3.37 of the 9th edition no longer apply; however, these paragraphs do provide relevant historical commentary.

*Fees Regs SI 2014/92, reduction and waiver*

**3.36** *[N.B.]*

The changes in the fees regime pursuant to the Immigration Act 2014, set out at **3.38–3.39**, came into force on 15 December 2014. The previous fees regime described in paragraphs 3.29–3.37 of the 9th edition no longer apply; however, these paragraphs do provide relevant historical commentary.

**3.37** *[N.B.]*

The changes in the fees regime pursuant to the Immigration Act 2014, set out at **3.38–3.39**, came into force on 15 December 2014. The previous fees regime described in paragraphs 3.29–3.37 of the 9th edition no longer apply; however, these paragraphs do provide relevant historical commentary.

## Immigration Act 2014 changes

**3.39** *[At the end of the paragraph add:]*

Section 86 of the Immigration Act 2016, which came in to force on 12 July 2016, empowered the Secretary of State to make similar regulations setting out the fees to be charged for applications for passports or other travel documents.

## Medical examinations and Tuberculosis tests

**3.41** *[Replace footnote 3 with:]*

The Modernised Guidance: General Grounds for Refusal, Version 26.0, section 1 in circumstances where the entrant may have a mental disorder or senility; a conduct disorder; lice infestation; bodily dirty; or suffering from scabies; or they have a serious or terminal illness.

## Registration with the police

**3.50** *[Replace footnote 7 with:]*

Modern Guidance – Police registration – Version 11.0, valid from 9 June 2015, p 4.

*[Replace footnote 8 with:]*

Modern Guidance – Police registration – Version 11.0, valid from 9 June 2015, p 4.

*[Replace footnote 9 with:]*

Modern Guidance – Police registration – Version 11.0, valid from 9 June 2015, p 5.

**3.51** *[In footnote 1 delete the final reference 'Modern Guidance . . . ' and replace with:]*

Modern Guidance – Police registration – Version 11.0, valid from 9 June 2015, p 6.

*[Replace footnote 2 with:]*

Modern Guidance – Police registration – Version 11.0, valid from 9 June 2015.

*[At the end of footnote 4 before the full stop insert:]*

(this IDI is not currently on the Home Office's website and either has been withdrawn or is currently being updated)

**Notice of decisions to grant or refuse leave to enter or remain**

**3.53** *[At the end of footnote 4 add:]*

Regulation 7(3) was amended by Immigration (Notices) (Amendment) Regulations 2014, SI 2014/2768, reg 2(6)(a) to state that the time limit for an appeal will be calculated from the date the notice is deemed to have been served on the file.

*[At the end of footnote 6 add:]*

For the purpose of art 8ZA(2), a notice will not be deemed to have been sent to a correspondence address provided by the applicant, if the address was provided by a third party who is not an authorised agent of the applicant. However, where no other address has been provided, this address may be the 'last-known address or usual place of abode' for the purpose of art 8ZA(3)(a), see *Khurram, R (on the application of) v Secretary of State for the Home Department* [2016] UKUT 281 (IAC).

**Part II – ENTRY**

**Who needs entry clearance**

**3.60** *[In the text delete the sentence starting 'The list of visa countries . . . ' and replace with:]*

Appendix 1 was deleted from the Immigration Rules by HC 1025. The definitions and lists of visa countries, formally set out in Appendix 1, are now in appendix 2 to Appendix V (Visitor rules).

*[Delete subparagraph (iii) and footnote reference 5.]*

*[In subparagraph (vii) delete 'Kuwait and Bahrain' and insert:]*

Kuwait, Bahrain, South Africa, Vietnam and Indonesia.

*[Delete subparagraph (viii) and footnote 10.]*

*[In subparagraph (ix) delete text 'in accordance with Appendix 1 paragraphs 3 to 9' and insert new footnote reference 10 after 'Document'.]*

*[Replace footnote 3 with:]*

HC 395 as amended, para 18A.

*[In footnote 4 delete the text 'HC 395, as amended, Appendix 1, para 2(b). See also'.]*

*[Footnote 5 is deleted.]*

*[Replace footnote 7 with:]*

HC 395 as amended, Appendix V (Visitor rules), Appendix 2, para 2(a), (b), as amended.

*[Replace footnote 8 with:]*

HC 395 as amended, Appendix V (Visitor rules), Appendix 2, para 2(c).

*[Replace footnote 9 with:]*

HC 395 as amended, Appendix V (Visitor rules), Appendix 2, para 2(e)–m).

*[Delete current footnote 10 and in new footnote 10 insert:]*

HC 395 as amended, Appendix V (Visitor rules), Appendix 2, para 2.

*[Replace footnote 11 with:]*

HC 395 as amended, Appendix V (Visitor rules), Appendix 2, paras 4–18.

*[At the end of footnote 12 add:]*

This IDI is not currently on the Home Office's website and either has been withdrawn or is currently being updated.

### The application

**3.67** *[At the end of footnote 6 add:]*

The 2006 Regulations have been further amended by the Immigration (Provision of Physical Data) (Amendment) Regulations 2015, SI 2015/737 in response to changes made under the Immigration Act 2014. They amend the 2006 Regulations to revise the list of applications that an authorised person can require to be accompanied by specified biometric information, the process by which this information is provided and the provisions about the use and retention of biometric information. The amendment also makes provision for the use, retention and destruction of biometric information.

### Entry clearance as leave to enter

**3.72** *[At the end of the paragraph insert:]*

The 2000 order has more recently been amended by SI 2015/434 and SI 2016/1132. The most significant changes include art 4 of the 2000 Order being amended, so that an entrant with a visa for private medical treatment or for entry as an academic visitor, that visa will have effect for a period of 11 or

12 months respectively. Articles 13–13B now allow certain categories to leave the common travel area without leave lapsing for a period up to two years. This includes family members of HM Forces and certain Crown servants such as employees of the British Council; DFID; the Home Office or the Diplomatic Service.

*[At the end of footnote 7 before the full stop add:]*

(this IDI is not currently on the Home Office's website and either has been withdrawn or is currently being updated)

**3.73** *[At the end of footnote 4 before the full stop add:]*

(this IDI is not currently on the Home Office's website and either has been withdrawn or is currently being updated)

*[At the end of footnote 5 before the full stop add:]*

(this IDI is not currently on the Home Office's website and either been withdrawn or is currently being updated)

*[In footnote 6 delete 'Immigration Act 1971, Sch 2, para 2A(8), (9)' and substitute:]*

Immigration Act 1971, Sch 2, para 2A(8)

*[In footnote 6 at the end of the text add:]*

Paragraph 2A(9) was repealed by the Immigration Act 2016, s 65(1). However, there is a saving provision under s 65 for a person who had an appealing pending, under s 104 of the Nationality, Immigration and Asylum Act 2002 at the time of repeal.

## Examination at the port of entry

*Who is examined*

**3.81** *[In footnote 11 before the final sentence insert:]*

This IDI is not currently on the Home Office's website and either has been withdrawn or is currently being updated.

**3.83** *[Delete paragraph and footnotes and insert:]*

The provisions for passengers in transit within the Immigration Rules have been moved to Appendix V, Part V7, under a heading of 'Transit Visitor'.

## Examination, decision and the 24-hour rule

**3.89** *[Replace footnote 4 with:]*

Article 8 was amended by art 2(3) of the Immigration (Leave to Enter and Remain) Amendment Order 2016, SI 2016/1132. Oral refusals or grants of leave can be given to visitors; short-term students or parents of a Tier 4 (child) student who are seeking leave to enter for no more than six months.

## Part IV– LEAVE TO REMAIN

### Leave to remain

**3.103** *[Delete the last sentence but retain footnote 13, and insert:]*

From February 2004, leave to remain which extended stay to more than six months took the form of a UK residence permit stuck into the passport.

### Variation of leave to enter or remain

**3.107** *[Delete second sub paragraph (ii) and insert:]*

(ii) the right of appeal would, prior to amendments to section 82 of NIAA 2002, have been lost;[2] only an application made during the currency of existing leave would under that regime have given the applicant a right of appeal;

*[In the second paragraph, delete the second sentence beginning 'First, as indicated above . . . ' and substitute:]*

First, as indicated above, prior to changes to appeal rights introduced by the Immigration Act 2014, it was essential to apply before the current leave expired if the person was to have a right of appeal under section 82 of the Nationality, Immigration and Asylum Act 2002.

*[At the end of footnote 4 before the full stop, insert:]*

, see, for instance, HC 395, para 276ADE

[2] Section 82(2)(d) and (e) of the NIAA 2002, like the IA 1971, s 14, requires extant leave in order to appeal against refusal to extend it. See now the amendments to section 82 by IA 2014, s 15.

**3.109** *[At the end of footnote 2, add:]*

It must be clear from the form which information is mandatory: see *R (Mombeshora) v Secretary of State for the Home Department* [2013] EWHC 1252 (Admin).

*[At the end of footnote 3, add:]*

See *R (Kisuule) v Secretary of State for the Home Department* [2011] EWHC 2966 (Admin), where a challenge was made to the Secretary of State's assertion that no photographs were supplied with the application. Edwards-Stuart J made a declaration that the photographs had been supplied with the application and, thus, that it had been validly made.

**3.111** *[In the main text, after footnote reference 1, insert:]*

The application will be treated as having been invalid from the outset, although a question-mark still exists in respect of other bases for invalidity, such as a failure to enrol biometric details.[1a]

[1a] *R (Iqbal) v Secretary of State for the Home Department* [2016] UKSC 63, [2017] 1 WLR 85.

**Consideration and variation of an application for leave to remain**

**3.112** *[Delete the text for footnote 1 and substitute:]*

Modernised Guidance: Specified application forms and procedures (version 18), p 91.

**3.113** *[In the main text, after footnote reference 3, delete the duplicated full stop and the sentence beginning 'In the UK . . . ' and substitute:]*

In the UK an applicant can pay £500 extra on top of the normal fees and get a premium service[4] or pay even more (£8,750) and get a super premium service.[5]

*[At the end of footnote 2, add:]*

However, see now *TN (Afghanistan) v Secretary of State for the Home Department* [2015] UKSC 40; [2015] 1 WLR 3083, which overrules the Court of Appeal's judgment, affirming the decision of Davis J, in *Rashid* [2005] Imm AR 608. Practitioners should approach this line of cases with caution.

*[Delete the text of footnote 7 and substitute:]*

See Modernised Guidance: Specified application forms and procedures (version 18), p 101: 'An applicant can also withdraw their application by sending a written request. If the request is ambiguous, you must confirm the withdrawal request with the applicant. The case of *Qadeer* clarified that the SSHD does not have to agree to the withdrawal of an application but may consider and decide the application even where that might lead to an adverse decision. The most common reason to reject a withdrawal request from an applicant and decide an application is where we suspect that deception has been exercised by the applicant.'

[4] Applicants should check if you're eligible to apply for the premium service. If they are eligible, they need to choose which of the seven premium service centres they want to visit, book an appointment in advance and pay the fee online when they book: https://www.gov.uk/ukvi-pr emium-service-centres/overview. Premium service centres were previously called public enquiry offices (PEOs).

[5] The super premium service is an at-home service. It means that a courier will collect the applicant's application forms and documents; then someone will visit him or her to get the person's biometric information (fingerprints and photo) and their signature. A decision on the application will usually be made within 24 hours: for more detail see https://www.gov.uk/uk vi-premium-service-centres/use-the-super-premium-service.

**3.116** *[Delete the third sentence beginning 'Hence once that application has been decided . . . ' and substitute:]*

Hence once that application has been decided, and the case has gone to an appeal, any new information will have to be included in the grounds of appeal (made timeously or given permission to be varied); otherwise they could not be raised on appeal.[1]

*[Following the sentence 'There is a duty . . . original grounds of appeal,' insert:]*

Following amendments to NIAA 2002 by the IA 2014:

- there is no longer a general right of appeal against an 'immigration decision'. A right of appeal arises only in relation to the three forms of decision listed in section 82(1), namely refusal of a protection claim, refusal of a human rights claim and revocation of protection status;
- while an appellant remains able to raise a 'new matter', being defined as something which would constitute a ground of appeal within the meaning of section 84, on appeal, the tribunal is barred by section 85(5) from considering it unless the Secretary of State consents to it doing so.[3a]

*[Delete the sentence 'So, not only do the IDI state . . . they go further.' and substitute:]*

So, not only does the Modernised Guidance state that there may be little difference in practice between a fresh application and a request to vary an existing application, they go further.

*[Delete the text for footnote 3 and substitute:]*

There is no reported guidance from the tribunal on the interpretation of 'new matter'. The Modernised Guidance: Rights of appeal (version 4) distinguishes between 'new matter' and 'new evidence'. The guidance suggests that the new matter must be wholly different to what has already been considered, for instance a human rights claim is raised on appeal where an applicant had only previously made a protection claim. The unreported decision of the Upper Tribunal with appeal reference IA/23638/2015 substantially aligns with that guidance.

*[Delete the text for footnote 4 and substitute:]*

Modernised Guidance: Specified application forms and procedures (v 18), pp 57–58.

[1] The Court of Appeal in *AS (Afghanistan) v Secretary of State for the Home Department* [2009] EWCA 1076, [2010] 2 All ER 21 upheld this interpretation, which was originally contained in now discontinued IDIs. There was a duty on the Tribunal to consider matters raised by an appellant in so far as they provided grounds for challenging a substantive decision of a kind identified in s 82 that affected the immigration status. Sections 96(2) and 120 and reinforced that interpretation.

[3a] There is no reported guidance from the tribunal on the interpretation of 'new matter'. The Modernised Guidance: Rights of appeal (version 4) distinguishes between 'new matter' and 'new evidence'. The guidance suggests that the new matter must be wholly different to what has already been considered, for instance a human rights claim is raised on appeal where an applicant had only previously made a protection claim. The unreported decision of the Upper Tribunal with appeal reference IA/23638/2015 substantially aligns with that guidance.

### Withdrawal of an application

**3.117** *[At the end of the first paragraph delete the words: 'Modern Guidance Specified forms and procedure p 58'.]*

*[Delete the text for footnotes 1, 2, 4, 6, 8 and 9 and substitute the following new text for the respective footnote numbers:]*

Fn 1: Under HC 395, para 34(5) (the *vires* for which can be found in section 50 IAN 2006).

Fn 2: See Modernised Guidance: Specified application forms and procedures, p 99.

Fn 4: Modernised Guidance: Specified application forms and procedures (v 18), pp 99–100.

Fn 6: Modernised Guidance: Specified application forms and procedures (v 18), pp 90–91. The instructions are to void such applications: p 90.

Fn 8: Modernised Guidance: Specified application forms and procedures (v 18), p 90.

Fn 9: Modernised Guidance: Specified application forms and procedures (v 18), p 101.

**3.118** *[Delete the text for footnote 2 and substitute:]*

Paragraph 34J of HC 395. Section 3C leave will end at the point the Secretary of State treats the application as withdrawn: see Modernised Guidance: Specified application forms and procedures (v 18), p 100.


## Variation of leave

**3.119** *[Delete the last sentence of footnote 5.]*


## Variation of leave by statute

**3.120** *[Delete the sentence beginning 'Under section 82' and substitute:]*

Under section 82 of the Nationality, Immigration and Asylum Act 2002,[1] there is, in general, a right of appeal where one of three types of decision is made in respect of a person, including a refusal of a protection claim, a refusal of a human rights claim and a decision to revoke protection status.

*[In footnote 6 amend the reference to the Nationality, Immigration and Asylum Act 2002 to read:]*

Nationality, Immigration and Asylum Act 2002, s 104(1)–(4B) as amended by Asylum and Immigration (Treatment of Claimants, etc) Act 2004, Sch 2, para 20 and IA 2014, Sch 9(4), para 47(2)–(5).

*[Delete the text of footnote 9 and substitute:]*

Immigration Act 1971, s 3C(4). Leave cannot be extended by operation of section 3C in the event that an application is refused prior the expiry of leave and an appeal is then lodged which is not determined prior to expiry: see wording of subsection (1) for the cases to which the provision applies.

[1]  Appeal rights under the version of section 82 in force prior to amendment by IA 2014, s 15, may still exist in respect of transitional cases but are likely to be increasingly uncommon.

**3.121** *[Delete the first sentence of the paragraph and substitute:]*

Section 3C(2), as amended by section 11 of IAN 2006 and section 62 of IA 2016,[1] lays down the periods during which leave can be extended in cases to which section 3C (1) applies.

*[After the first sentence of the second paragraph, insert:]*

Section 3C(3) enacts that leave extended by virtue of the section shall lapse if the applicant leaves the UK. Section 3C(3A) provides that the Secretary of State can cancel leave extended by virtue of the section if the applicant fails to comply with a condition attached to the leave, or used or uses deception in seeking leave to remain (whether successfully or not).

[1]   By virtue of the Immigration Act 2016 (Commencement No 2 and Transitional Provisions) Regulations 2016, SI 2016/1037.

**3.122** *[Footnote 1 is deleted.]*

*[Delete the text in footnote 4 and insert:]*

Immigration Act 1971, ss 8(2), (3), and 8A, as amended by the 1999 Act, ss 6 and 7: s 8A(2)(b). This concession by s 8A(4) does not apply to those who cease to be exempt by operation of IA 1971, s 8B(3): both provisions inserted by IA 2016, s 76, brought into force by SI 2016/603.

## Notifying leave decisions

**3.123** *[Delete the two sentences 'First there are the visitors, here for a period of no more than six months. Notice can be given orally instead of in writing' including the footnote reference 3, and substitute:]*

First, there are the visitors, short-term students and parents of Tier 4 (child) students, here for a period of no more than six months. Notice can be given orally, including by telephone, instead of in writing.[3]

[3]   SI 2000/1161, art 8(1) and (2), as substituted by the Immigration (Leave to Enter and Remain) (Amendment) Order 2016, SI 2016/1132.

## Cancellation, curtailment and revocation of leave

**3.126** *[Delete the text in footnote 3 and substitute:]*

Immigration Act 1971, s 8B, inserted by the Immigration and Asylum Act 1999, s 8 (war criminals). Where the Secretary of State purports to grant leave to remain to a person who is excluded, that leave will be 'invalid': IA 1971, s 8B(1), as amended by IA 2016, s 76(4).

## Curtailment, revocation and section 3D

**3.127** *[Delete the text from the sentence commencing 'When leave to enter or remain is curtailed or revoked . . . ' to the end of the paragraph and substitute:]*

When leave to enter or remain was curtailed or revoked, section 3D extended the leave (in much the same way as section 3C does for applications to vary leave) while an appeal could be brought or was pending. Since the changes to the structure of appeal rights brought about by the amendment of section 82 of 2002 Act by section 15 of the Immigration Act 2014, it is no longer possible to appeal against a curtailment decision. Given that a curtailment decision does not constitute an eligible decision for the purpose of Appendix AR, which deals with administrative review, section 3D was repealed by section 64 of the Immigration Act 2016 with effect from 1 December 2016, subject to transitional provisions contained in subsection (5).

*[Footnotes 2, 3, 4 and 5 are deleted.]*

## Part V – GENERAL GROUNDS FOR REFUSAL, CANCELLATION AND CURTAILMENT OF LEAVE

### Introduction

**3.133** *[Delete the text in footnote 1 and substitute:]*

See Modernised Guidance: General Grounds for Refusal, Section 1: 'About this guidance, general grounds for refusal and checks' (v 26), p 2.

**3.134** *[Delete the text of footnote 1 and substitute:]*

See the Modernised Guidance which makes it clear that even the 'mandatory' grounds are not wholly mandatory: General Grounds for Refusal, Section 2: Considering entry clearance (v 26), p 4. In *JC (Part 9 HC 395, burden of proof) China* [2007] UKAIT 00027, the AIT drew this distinction, but also pointed out that in all paragraph 320 cases the burden of proof is on the decision maker to establish the facts relied on, their common thread being that the decision maker must establish a precedent fact. The application of the concept of precedent fact to cases concerning dishonesty as a general ground for refusal has, however, been disapproved by the Court of Appeal in *R (Giri) v Secretary of State for the Home Department* [2015] EWCA Civ 784, [2016] 1 WLR 4418. In that light, practitioners should be cautious of invoking earlier tribunal authorities that suggested a different approach should apply.

*[Delete the text of footnote 3 and substitute:]*

Modernised Guidance: General Grounds for Refusal, Section 2: Considering entry clearance (v 26), p 4.

*[Delete last sentence of footnote 4 and substitute:]*

An Immigration Judge dealing with an appeal under the pre-Immigration Act 2014 appellate regime would, therefore, be entitled, depending on the facts, to allow an appeal even if he or she considered that one (or more) of the later subparagraphs apply to the case.

### The texts – Setting out the rules

*E. Curtailment of leave*

CURTAILMENT UNDER THE IMMIGRATION ACT 1971 AND PARAGRAPHS 322, 323 AND 323A

**3.142** *[In the main text after sub-paragraph (i) insert new sub-para (ia):]*

(ia) if he uses deception in seeking (whether successfully or not) leave to remain or a variation of leave to remain;[1]

*[After sub-paragraph (vi) insert new sub-para (vii):]*

(vii) if, without a reasonable explanation, he fails to comply with a request made by or on behalf of the Secretary of State under paragraph 39D.[2]

[1]   Inserted by HC 1138 with effect from 20 October 2014.
[2]   Inserted by HC 1025 with effect from 6 April 2015.

**3.143** *[At end of the paragraph add:]*

Tier 1 (Graduate Entrepreneurs) can have their leave curtailed under para 323C if his or her endorsing body loses its status as an endorsing institution, ceases to be a sponsor with Tier 4 Sponsor status, ceases to be an A-rated sponsor under Tiers 2 or 5 because its sponsor licence is downgraded or revoked or because the endorsing body withdraws its endorsement.[6]

[6]   Inserted by HC 1888 with effect from 6 April 2012.

**3.144** *[At the end of the paragraph after footnote reference 4, delete the last two sentences and substitute:]*

A decision to curtail leave made on or after 6 April 2015 will not attract a right of appeal or administrative review. The only remedy in those circumstances will be a claim for judicial review.[5]

*[Delete the text for footnote 1 and substitute:]*

See HC 395, para 323. See also Home Office policy, Curtailment (v 16).

*[Delete the text for footnote 2 and substitute:]*

Curtailment is generally discretionary and should not follow automatically when the basis of stay no longer exists: Home Office policy, Curtailment (v 16), pp 21-22, 62, though it will be considered where a relationship, which formed the basis of stay, breaks down (Curtailment policy, p 45). It may not be appropriate where a migrant claimed public funds short term in an emergency.

*[Footnote 6 is deleted.]*

[5]   Home Office policy, Curtailment (v 16), p 100. See too Appendix AR dealing with administrative review.

## Comment on the Texts

*A.   Deceivers*

**3.145**  *[Delete the text in footnote 3 and substitute:]*

*R (on the application of Giri) v Secretary of State for the Home Department* [2014] EWHC 1832 (Admin); affirmed on different grounds by the Court of Appeal, [2015] EWCA Civ 784, [2016] 1 WLR 4418.

*[At the end of footnote 4, insert:]*

See also *Shen (Paper Appeals: Proving Dishonesty)* [2014] UKUT 236 (IAC) and *Muhandiramge (section S-LTR 1.7)* [2015] UKUT 675 (IAC) (the latter case was one in which McCloskey J memorably described the nature of the legal and evidential burdens of proof in fraud or dishonesty cases). See also in the context of the ETS cases, *SM and Qadir (ETS – Evidence – Burden of Proof)* [2016] UKUT 229 (IAC).

### D. *Criminal convictions*

Non-custodial sentences under paragraphs 320(18A), (18B) and 322 (5A)

**3.158** *[Delete the first sentence of the paragraph and substitute:]*

The rules now contain paras 320(18A) and (18B) and 322(5A) which provide for discretionary exclusion on the basis of conviction for, or admission of, an offence within the last 12 months which is recorded on the criminal record albeit with a non-custodial or out of court disposal or on the basis that the person's offending has caused serious harm or that he or she is a persistent offender who shows particular disregard for the law.

### E. *Deportees*

Barriers to getting leave

**3.160** *[After the sentence ending ' . . . not invalidated by leave to enter granted in error.' insert:]*

Where a deportation order is in force, entry clearance will only be granted in exceptional circumstances, or where refusal would be contrary to the ECHR or Refugee Convention.[4]

*[At the end of the next sentence, delete footnote reference 4 and corresponding footnote text which is replaced by new footnote 4.]*

4   HC 395, para 320(2); Modernised Guidance: General Grounds for Refusal, Section 2: Considering entry clearance (v 26), pp 12-13 (see **3.132**, fn 1 above).

### F. *Frustrating the intentions of immigration rules*

Discretion to refuse under Paragraph 320(11)

**3.161** *[Delete the text of footnote 1 and substitute:]*

Modernised Guidance: General Grounds for Refusal, Section 2: Considering entry clearance (v 26), p 55.

### G. Other mandatory grounds for refusal of leave

#### SEEKING LEAVE FOR A PURPOSE NOT COVERED BY THE RULES

**3.162** *[At the end of the paragraph add:]*

Such an applicant would, following changes made by to the Nationality, Immigration and Asylum Act 2002 by the Immigration Act 2014 would ordinarily now have a right of appeal following the refusal of a human rights claim, subject to certification under sections 94, 94B or 96 of the 2002 Act.

**3.163** *[Footnote 3 should be amended to read:]*

Immigration Act 1971, Sch 2, para 4 (persons arriving in the UK) (as amended by IA 2014, Sch 8(1), para 3(2)); Immigration (Leave to Enter and Remain) Order 2000, SI 2000/1161, art 7(2), (4) (persons seeking leave to enter abroad).

#### THE DISCRETIONARY GROUNDS

**3.164** *[At the end of footnote 1, add:]*

Under the new appellate structure, the discretion would fall for review on traditional judicial review grounds. See further **21.67**, below.

#### UNACCEPTABLE PASSPORTS

**3.165** *[Delete the text in footnote 2 and substitute:]*

Entry Clearance Guidance, ECB08 (Entry Clearance Basics) sets out in full those travel documents acceptable for the purposes of entry clearance.

#### RESTRICTED RETURNABILITY

**3.166** *[Delete the text in footnote 5 and substitute:]*

Modernised Guidance: General grounds for refusal, Section 2: Considering entry clearance, (v 26), p 58.

#### FAILURE TO COMPLY WITH CONDITIONS ATTACHED TO STAY: FURTHER LEAVE

**3.167** *[Delete the first sentence in the paragraph and insert:]*

A failure to comply with conditions attached to stay[1] will lead to a refusal of further leave.[2]

*[Delete the text of footnote 7 and substitute:]*

See fn 2 above.

[1] HC 395, para 322(3).
[2] Modernised Guidance: General Grounds for Refusal, Section 4: Considering leave to remain (v 26), p 27. In previous editions of this work, Ch 9 of the IDI (now deleted) was cited for the proposition that a failure to comply with conditions attached to stay would lead to refusal of

further leave only where a person has shown by his or her conduct that he or she has deliberately and consistently breached conditions of stay.

## Recourse to public funds: further leave

**3.168** *[Delete the text of footnote 2 and substitute:]*

HC 395, para 6, as amended.

*[Delete the text of footnote 5 and substitute:]*

Modernised Guidance: Public Funds (v 13), p 49.

## Breach of undertakings: further leave

**3.169** *[Delete the text of footnote 3 and substitute:]*

Modernised Guidance: General grounds for refusal, Section 4: 'Considering leave to remain' (v 26), p 48.

## Medical grounds for refusal

**3.170** *[Delete the text from the start of the paragraph up to and including the sentence ending with footnote reference 4, and substitute:]*

We have already dealt with the requirements to submit to medical examination at **3.87** above. Entry clearance officers abroad have a discretion to refer intending travellers for medical examination and a power to require a medical report, and leave to enter may be refused if examination is declined or such a report is not produced.[1] Where the medical inspector at the port advises that for medical reasons it is undesirable to admit someone, the immigration officer must refuse leave to enter unless the person is settled here or there are 'strong compassionate reasons justifying admission'.[2] According to the Modernised Guidance, the medical inspector will only certify that it is undesirable to admit a passenger if his or her condition is a significant risk to public health. An inspector may certify that it is undesirable to admit a passenger who is found or suspected to be suffering from pulmonary tuberculosis, venereal disease, leprosy or trachoma.[3] An entry clearance officer must seek medical clearance where, *inter alia*, a passenger presents with a heavy infestation of lice, is bodily dirty or is suffering from scabies.[3a] The Modernised Guidance also indicates that an entry clearance officer must seek medical clearance where the nature of the person's condition would interfere with his or her ability to support themselves and any dependents.[4]

*[Delete the text in footnote 5 and substitute:]*

Ibid, as in fn 4.

---

[1]  Immigration (Leave to Enter and Remain) Order 2000, SI 2000/1161, art 7(3) and (4); HC 395, paras 39 and 320(17).

[2]  HC 395, para 320(7).

[3]  Modernised Guidance: General grounds for refusal, Section 4: Considering leave to remain (v 26), p 48.

[3a]  Modernised Guidance: General grounds for refusal, Section 1: About this guidance, general grounds for refusal and checks (v 26), p 113.

[4] Modernised Guidance: General grounds for refusal, Section 1: About this guidance, general grounds for refusal and checks (v 26), p 113.

REFUSAL OF LEAVE TO REMAIN: CHARACTER, CONDUCT OR ASSOCIATIONS AND REFUSAL OF FURTHER LEAVE OR CURTAILMENT

**3.176** *[Delete the text of footnote 2 and substitute:]*

Modernised Guidance: General Grounds for Refusal, Section 4: 'Considering leave to remain' (v 26), p 30.

*H. EC joint list of persons to be refused entry*

EXCLUDED PERSONS UNDER INTERNATIONAL OBLIGATIONS

**3.178** *[Amend the prefix letter in the heading from 'F' to 'H'. In the main text after footnote reference 4, insert:]*

The same exemption has now been given the force of primary legislation in section 8B(5A) of the Immigration Act 1971 (inserted by section 76(8) of the Immigration Act 2016).

*[Amend the text in footnote 4 to read:]*

The Schedule in the original Order of 2000 and its amendments have now been replaced by the Schedule to the Immigration (Designation of Travel Bans) (Amendment No 2) Order 2015, SI 2015/1994. This Order amends the Immigration (Designation of Travel Bans) Order 2000 ('the 2000 Order') by substituting the Schedule 1 to this Order for the Schedule to the 2000 Order. Any person named by or under an instrument listed in the new Schedule or falling within a description in such an instrument will be excluded from the United Kingdom (subject to the exceptions specified in art 3 of the 2000 Order and s 8B(5A) of IA 1971). Article 3 of this Order revokes the previous amendment order. The orders are amended frequently, reflecting changes in UN and EU resolutions.

FAILURE TO PAY NHS CHARGES

**3.181** *[Delete the whole paragraph including footnotes and insert:]*

With effect from 31 October 2011, HC 1511 amended the General Grounds for Refusal, by inserting new discretionary grounds for refusal of entry clearance under para 320(22), or refusal of leave to remain, variation of leave to enter or remain or curtailment of leave under para 322(12) on the grounds that one or more relevant NHS bodies has notified the Secretary of State that the person seeking entry, leave to enter, leave to remain or a variation of leave to enter or remain, as the case may be, has failed to pay a charge or charges with a total value of at least £1,000 in accordance with the relevant NHS regulations on charges to overseas visitors.[1] In relation to applications for entry clearance or leave to remain made on or after 6 April 2016, the threshold was lowered by HC 877 to £500.[2] Refusal by reference to these provisions is discretionary. Accordingly, consideration must in all cases be given to whether there are compelling or compassionate circumstances or human rights consider-ations.[3] Where the debts relate to the main applicant, dependants should also be refused on the same ground. Where the debt relates to a dependant, only the dependant and not the main applicant should be refused, but where the charges relate to a child, the parents are the debtors and so would fall for refusal. Before such a refusal is made, however, the application must be referred to a HEO to consider the best interests of the child.[4] Where debts have been paid the paragraph does not apply, although where the debt was paid within the six months prior to the making of the application consideration must be given to whether the applicant can meet any other requirement of the rules in the application category in which he or she has applied.[5] In contrast to the previous regime, there is now an obligation imposed on the relevant NHS body (ordinarily an NHS trust or foundation trust) to make charges where satisfied, having made reasonable inquiries, that a patient is not exempt.[6]

[1]   These Regulations are the National Health Service (Charges to Overseas Visitors) Regulations 2015, SI 2015/238 (in force from 6 April 2015), revoking and replacing the equivalent set of regulations from 2011 (SI 2011/1556, in force from 1 August 2011), which themselves revoked and replaced the regulations from 1989 (SI 1989/306). See further **8.29**, below. The countries whose nationals are exempt from charges include Anguilla, Armenia, Australia, Azerbaijan, Barbados, Belarus, Bosnia, British Virgin Islands, Croatia, Falkland Islands, Georgia, Gibraltar, Isle of Man, Israel, Jersey, Kazakhstan, Kyrgyzstan, Macedonia, Moldova, Montenegro, Montserrat, New Zealand, Russia, Serbia, St Helena, Tajikistan, Turkmenistan, Turks and Caicos Islands, Ukraine, and Uzbekistan.

[2]   The threshold remains set at £1,000 for applicants under Appendix FM and Appendix Armed Forces.

[3]   Modernised Guidance: General Grounds for refusal, Section 2: Considering entry clearance (v 26), pp 69–70; Modernised Guidance: General Grounds for refusal, Section 4: Considering leave to remain (v 26), p 55.

[4]   Modernised Guidance: General Grounds for refusal, Section 2: Considering entry clearance (v 26), p 72; Section 4, p 55; Modernised Guidance: General Grounds for refusal, Section 4: Considering leave to remain (v 26), pp 57–58.

[5]   Modernised Guidance: General Grounds for refusal, Section 2: Considering entry clearance (v 26), p 73; Modernised Guidance: General Grounds for refusal, Section 4: Considering leave to remain (v 26), p 59.

[6]   National Health Service (Charges to Overseas Visitors) Regulations 2015, SI 2015/238, reg 3.

### FAILURE TO PAY LITIGATION DEBT

**3.181A** *[Insert new heading above and new paragraph:]*

With effect from 6 April 2016, HC 877 amended the General Grounds for Refusal to insert paras 320(23) and 322(13), which provide a discretionary basis for the refusal of application for entry clearance and leave to remain, respectively, where an applicant has failed to pay 'litigation costs' awarded to the Home Office. The rules do not provide any sort of threshold of relevant litigation costs, in contrast to the provisions dealing with NHS charges (see **3.181** above). The Home Office has published guidance. It is apparent that the power in the rules will not be used in relation to protection claims, EEA applications or applications in relation to nationality.[1] While the rule cannot be applied in relation to applications made prior to 6 April 2016, for applications made after that date the guidance obliges the case worker to consider all litigation debts, whenever accrued.[2] The rule does not apply to applications made under Appendix Armed Forces or Appendix FM, which have their own provisions (S-EC.3.1 of Appendix FM; and para 10A of

Appendix Armed Forces).[3] The debt should not be taken into account if the Litigation Finance Team confirm that the applicant has entered into an arrangement to pay it off in instalments and the applicant is making payments as agreed.[4] Relevant factors in considering whether to exercise discretion not to refuse an application include assessing how the debt was built up (for instance, did the applicant pursue repeated and unmeritorious litigation), the level of cooperation with Home Office debt recovery efforts, the location of the applicant (the suggestion is that discretion would be less likely to be exercised in an entry clearance case), the purpose of the application, the applicant's ability to pay, how long the debt has been outstanding, the amount of the debt, as well as any other relevant factors.[5]

1   Home Office policy, Litigation debt (v 1), p 4.
2   Ibid.
3   Ibid, p 5.
4   Ibid, p 9.
5   Ibid, pp 9–11.

## Part VI- CONTROL OF DEPARTURE AND MISCELLANEOUS POWERS

### Right to depart – immigration officers' powers

**3.185** *[Delete the paragraph and footnotes and substitute:]*

Following amendments by the Immigration Acts of 2014 and 2016,[1] paragraphs 3 and 16 of Schedule 2 to the Immigration Act 1971 now provide that an immigration officer or designated person – which by paragraph 5A of Schedule 2 is defined to mean a person designated by the Secretary of State for the purposes of that schedule; in principle, such a person could work for a private contractor – is empowered to examine any person embarking or seeking to embark from the UK for the purpose of determining whether he is a British citizen and, if not, for the purpose of establishing:

*   his identity;
*   whether the passenger's entry to the UK was lawful;
*   whether the passenger has complied with any conditions of his or her leave in the UK;
*   whether the passenger's return to the UK is prohibited or restricted.[2]

If a cursory investigation into these matters is not enough, the immigration officer can require the passenger to submit to further examination by giving him or her written notice, and can detain him or her for a maximum of 12 hours pending the completion of that further examination.[3] Section 42(4) states that paragraph 21 of Schedule 2 to the 1971 Act, which makes provision for temporary admission, does not apply to the detention of departing passengers. This has presumably been done on the basis that a maximum of 12 hours' detention does not make temporary admission necessary. These powers must be so exercised as not to infringe EEA national right to free movement under community law.

1   IA 2014, Sch 8(1), para 2(2); subject to transitional provisions specified in Sch 9, para 72.

2  Previously an examination could only focus on determining whether the departing person was a British citizen. Amendments made by IAN 2006, s 42(2) added the power to examine for additional purposes.

3  IAN 2006, s 42(3); amended by IA 2014, Sch 8(1), para 2(3) to include cover an examination initially conducted by a 'designated person'.

# Chapter 4
# SETTLEMENT AND RETURN

## SETTLEMENT

### Definition

*No restriction on the period of stay*

**4.4** *[Delete the following text in the first sentence ', which is a valuable document to keep'. Delete the footnote reference and the text for footnote 1.]*

*Ordinary and habitual residence and domicile*

**4.5** *[At end of paragraph add:]*

On appeal, the Supreme Court[7] overturned the finding by the Court of Appeal that requiring an applicant for a student loan to have indefinite leave to remain was justified and not incompatible with human rights. The Supreme Court held by a 3:2 majority that such a provision is incompatible with Art 14 of the European Convention on Human Rights, read with Protocol 1, art 2, and cannot be justified as the criteria of 'settlement' was not a rational link to the aim of limiting the availability of resources to those students likely to remain in the United Kingdom, a fair balance between the rights of the community and the rights of the individual had not been struck, and it could not be said that a less intrusive measure could not be used to achieve the same aim. However, the Supreme Court did not interfere with the Court of Appeal findings regarding the requirement of 'ordinary residence' to be eligible to access public services.

*[Delete footnote 2 and insert:]*

The power to make charges for medical services given to non-residents was first exercised in 1982 and the current exceptions are set out in the National Health Service (Charges to Overseas Visitors) Regulations 2011, SI 2011/1556, as subsequently amended in 2012. For the purposes of those regulations, overseas visitors are defined as persons 'not ordinarily resident in the United Kingdom'. The phrase 'ordinarily resident' is interpreted by the Department of Health as meaning 'for the time being, living lawfully in the UK on a properly settled basis'. See also Immigration Act 2014, s 39.

---

[7]  *R (on the application of Tigere) v Secretary of State for Business, Innovation and Skills* [2015] UKSC 57.

## 4.7  [At the end of the paragraph add:]

It is possible for a parent to unilaterally change a child's place of habitual residence, though the knowledge and intentions of the other parent may be highly relevant to the assessment[5] and, habitual residence does not require a child's full integration into the environment of the new state, but only a degree of integration.[6] The Supreme Court jurisprudence was considered and applied in *Re B (A Minor: Habitual Residence*[7] noting that the clear message emerging from those cases, and from European case law is that the child is at the centre of the exercise when evaluating her habitual residence. The Court issued important guidance.

[5]  *Re R (children)* [2015] UKSC 35 and *Re B (A Child)* [2016] UKSC 4.
[6]  *Re B (A Child)* [2016] UKSC 4, para 39.
[7]  [2016] EWHC 2174 (Fam).

## Consequence of being settled

### 4.10  [Delete paragraph and substitute:]

Settlement brings many advantages. Persons subject to immigration control who are 'settled' have in general a right to permanent residence in the UK, provided they continue living here, although they are potentially liable to deportation, unless they have an exemption,[1] and may be deported if they commit serious crimes or their presence is no longer conducive to the public good for this or some other reason.[2] The Supreme Court have held that anterior indefinite leave to remain is not revived upon the revocation of a deportation order.[3] Revocation of indefinite leave is possible for a number of reasons under the Nationality, Immigration and Asylum Act 2002 (NIAA 2002).[4] Through amendments introduced by the IA 2014, from 20 October 2014, revocation of indefinite leave no longer attracts an in-country right of appeal under s 82 or 92 of the NIAA 2002.

[1]  IA 1971, s 7.
[2]  IA 1971, s 3(5)(a) and (6), and UK Borders Act 2007, s 32.
[3]  *R (on the application of George (Fitzroy)) v Secretary of State for the Home Department* [2014] UKSC 28, [2014] 3 All ER 365, [2014] 1 WLR 1831: The Supreme Court held section 76(1) of the NIAA 2002 (the power to revoke indefinite leave to remain) does not inform the construction of s 5 of the IA 1971. In that case the Secretary of State had made successive grants of time-limited leave.
[4]  See NIAA 2002, s 76.

## Knowledge of English and British way of life

### 4.13  [Replace footnote 1 with:]

Qualifications covering speaking and listening at B1 or above from the Secure English Language Test (SELT) list in the Immigration Rules, Appendix O. The SELT list is available at www.ukba.homeoffice.gov.uk/sitecontent/application forms/new-approved-english-tests.pdf; Qualifications in English for Speakers of Other Languages (ESOL) at Entry level 3, Level 1 or Level 2, that include speaking and listening and that have been regulated by the Office of Qualifications and Examinations Regulation (Ofqual). The qualification must be listed as an ESOL qualification on the Ofqual Register of Regulated Qualifications and have been taken in England, Wales or Northern Ireland. The Ofqual register is available at: register.ofqual.gov.uk; a National Qualification in ESOL at Scottish Qualifications Framework (SCQF) levels 4, 5 or 6 awarded by the Scottish Qualifications Authority (SQA) and taken in Scotland.

## Position of EEA nationals

**4.15** *[Replace footnote 1 with:]*

Or less in certain circumstances, see reg 15 of the EEA Regulations, SI 2006/1003; Directive 2004/38/EC, arts 16–18. Note from 1 February 2017, the EEA Regulations will be repealed and the Immigration (European Economic Area) Regulations 2016, SI 2016/1052 will be in force, see reg 15 regarding right of permanent residence.

*[Replace footnote 3 with:]*

SI 2006/1003. These have been extensively amended since 2006. See Appendix 5 – Statutory Instruments in Volume 2. From 1 February 2017, see SI 2016/1052.

*[Replace footnote 4 with:]*

Guidance notes for applying for residence documentation as a European Economic Area (EEA) national or as the family member of an EEA national (Version 04/2016).

## Settlement for Refugees and Persons in need of Humanitarian Protection

**4.16** *[Replace footnote 3 with:]*

Any applications received by the Secretary of State after the applicant's extant leave has expired will be considered 'out of time', leading to the applicant becoming an overstayer. For applications decided on or after 24 November 2016, the application may be considered to be 'in time' where it is made within 14 days of the applicant's leave expiring and the Secretary of State considers that there is a good reason beyond the control of the applicant or their representative, provided in or with the application, why the application could not be made in-time; para 39E of HC 395 as amended by HC667, para 1.13.

*[Replace footnote 5 with:]*

A summary of relevant considerations can be found at section 5 of the API: Settlement Protection, 2 February 2016.

*[Replace footnote 6 with:]*

API; Settlement Protection, p 18.

## Travellers on temporary leave

**4.20** *[In the third line delete the word 'Tempory' and replace with 'Temporary'.]*

*[Delete the sentence commencing 'Article 4 provides that . . . ' and substitute:]*

Article 4 provides that a visit visa, other than visit visas granted pursuant to the ADS Agreement with China, for private medical treatment, or for entry as an academic, permit, unless endorsed as a 'single entry' visa, leave to enter the UK on an unlimited number of occasions during their period of validity, unless endorsed as a 'single entry' visa.

*[Replace footnote 4 with:]*

SI 2000/1161, art 4(1), as amended by the Immigration (Leave to Enter and Remain) (Amendment) Order 2016, SI 2016/1132.

*[Add the following text to footnote 5:]*

Note also that this rule does not apply to visas granted pursuant to the ADS Agreement with China or those issued for private medical treatment or entry as an academic visitor. For those visas, refer to SI 2000/1161, art 4(2A), (2B), (2C) and (2D) added by SI 2005/1159 and SI 2016/1132.

*[Delete footnote 6 and substitute:]*

SI 2000/1161, art 4(3)(b), subject to the provisions for visits under the ADS agreement with China under art 4(3A) (added by SI 2005/1159), and subject to provisions for visas issued for short-term biometric entry clearance under art 4(3B) (added by SI 2015/434).

**4.21** *[Delete the sentence:]*

If leave is cancelled, the passenger will have an in-country right of appeal (until section 15 of the Immigration Act 2014 does away with these appeal rights) against cancellation, unless cancellation is on the ground that the passenger seeks entry for a different purpose from that on the entry clearance.

*[And substitute the above sentence with:]*

An immigration officer may, on the completion of an examination of a person, cancel his leave to enter.

*[Delete footnotes 12 and 13.]*

**4.22** *[Replace footnote 7 with:]*

SI 2000/1161, art 13(4)(a) subject to arts 13A and 13B.


**Return within two years**

**4.27** *[Replace footnote 1 with:]*

Immigration (Leave to Enter and Remain) Order 2000, SI 2000/1161, art 13(4)(a) subject to arts 13A and 13B.

**4.28** *[Delete text and substitute:]*

Under the Immigration Rules,[1] returning residents must satisfy the immigration officer that they had indefinite leave to enter or remain in the UK when they last left, they have not been away longer than two years, they did not receive public assistance towards the cost of leaving, and they now seek admission for the purpose of settlement.[2] Under the Immigration (Leave to Enter and Remain) Order 2000[3] a passenger with continuing leave who does not intend to resume ordinary residence may have leave cancelled. Cancellation will not attract an in-country right of appeal,[4] however, such decisions will be amenable to challenge by way of judicial review proceedings.[5] The onus is on the immigration officer to justify cancelling leave by reference to a change in circumstances. In the vast majority of cases little examination should be necessary. Returning residents may have their leave cancelled if on inquiry it is discovered that the original leave to enter was secured by their deception.[6]

[1] HC 395, para 18. By para 19A, added by Cm 4851, spouses accompanying members of HM Forces, of British diplomats and of comparable UK-based staff members of the British Council who are serving overseas are exempt from the two-year rule and from the rule preventing travel at public expense (sub-paras (ii) and (iii)).

[2] In *Cawte* (HX 00639) the Tribunal held, following *R v Immigration Appeal Tribunal, ex p Coomasaru* [1983] 1 All ER 208, that an appellant could qualify as a returning resident if she intended to return as such, even if she did not tell the immigration officer on arrival. See fn 5 below. See also *Ali Yazidi* (16387) (16 April 1998, unreported), IAT.

[3] SI 2000/1161.

[4] See s 82 of NIAA 2002 as amended by ss 15 and 17 of the Immigration Act 2014.

[5] *R (on the application of B) v Secretary of State for the Home Department (recording of leave – date stamps) IJR* [2016] UKUT 00135 (IAC).

[6] Immigration Act 1971, Sch 2, para 2A(2)(b); see *Sattar v Secretary of State for the Home Department* [1988] Imm AR 190, CA; *Ali (Mohammed Fazor) v Secretary of State for the Home Department* [1988] Imm AR 274, CA; *R v Secretary of State for the Home Department, ex p Musk* (CO 3956/1996) (26 March 1996, unreported), QBD. However, the dicta on the standard of proof may not apply to this situation, since leave is not being merely refused, but cancelled.

## Return after two years

**4.29** *[Delete the third sentence beginning 'One example . . . ' to the end of the fourth sentence ending ' . . . under this paragraph' , including footnotes, and insert:]*

An application for a Returning Resident Visa must be made where the claimant has either: (a) lost their relevant documentation; or (b) been away from the UK for more than two years. To be eligible for a Returning Resident Visa, the claimant must: (a) plan to return to live in the UK permanently; (b) have been settled in the UK before the claimant last left the UK; and (c) not have been given public funds in order to leave the UK. A claimant must also show that 'exceptional circumstances' have led to them being out of the country for the period that they have been outside of the UK. A claimant must provide evidence with the application demonstrating: (a) their strong family ties in the United Kingdom; (b) that they have lived most of their life in the United Kingdom;[3] and (c) their current circumstances and why they have lived outside of the United Kingdom.

*[At the end of the text add:]*

A request for discretion to be exercised pursuant to paragraph 19 of HC 395 will also likely need to be made by way of a paid application, supported by evidence.[5] With regard to partners and children of members of HM Forces who are accompanying their partner or parent, as the case may be, any period of time spent outside of the United Kingdom during the member of HM Forces posting outside of the United Kingdom, is not counted towards the two-year period. This is the same for partners and children of certain Crown servants who have indefinite or limited leave to remain under Appendix FM to the immigration rules or on the basis of family life under article 8 of the European Convention on Human Rights.[6]

*[In footnote 2, delete the sentence beginning 'Annex K of the . . . ' and substitute:]*

Chapter 1, section 3, Annex K of the IDIs: returning residents and British passport holders was withdrawn on 23 June 2016. The guidance on applying for a Returning Resident Visa is now set out on the Gov.UK website (https://www.gov.uk/ – last updated on 06 January 2017).

*[Delete current footnotes 4 and 5 and current footnote 6 is renumbered as footnote 4]*

[3]  HC 395, para 19. The phrase 'most of his life' does not mean 'most of his adult life': Entry clearance officer, *Kingston, Jamaica v Peart* [1979–80] Imm AR 41.
[5]  *R (on the application of B) v Secretary of State for the Home Department (recording of leave – date stamps) IJR* [2016] UKUT 00135 (IAC).
[6]  HC 395, paragraph 19A and Immigration (Leave to Enter and Remain) Order 2000, SI 2000/1161, art 13(4), as amended by the Immigration (Leave to Enter and Remain) (Amendment) Order 2015, SI 2015/434, art 2(4)(b) and by the Immigration (Leave to Enter and Remain) (Amendment) Order 2016, SI 2016/1132, art 2(5)(b).

**4.30** *[Delete the entire paragraph.]*

**4.31** *[Delete text and substitute:]*

Tribunal cases, where there has been absence from the United Kingdom beyond two years and which have been decided under the previous policy of the Home Office, are likely to remain of relevance. Cases where the outcome has been favourable to the applicant include where a passport had to be surrendered because of legal proceedings abroad, and delay caused by illness[1] and accident or civil disturbance.[2] On the other hand, the longer the period which an applicant has remained out of the United Kingdom the more difficult it will be to qualify for admission under paragraph 19 or 19A of the Immigration Rules.[3]

[1]  *Khokhar v Visa Officer, Islamabad* [1981] Imm AR 56n.
[2]  *Gokulsing* (1632) (1978, unreported). See also *Gomez (Joffrey)* (00TH02294) (parental obstruction).
[3]  *R v Secretary of State for the Home Department, ex p Ademuyiwa* [1986] Imm AR 1, DC; *Agyen-Frempong* [1986] Imm AR 108; *R v Immigration Appeal Tribunal, ex p Saffiullah (Muhammad)* [1986] Imm AR 424, DC. An appellant who had been out of the country for six years and acquired citizenship of another country on marriage succeeded in *Cawte* (HX00639) (8 February 2000, unreported); another away for nearly seven years succeeded because of his four children in the UK (*Forou* (00TH01101)).

**4.32** *[Delete text and substitute:]*

Refusal of leave to enter to a returning resident away for over two years does not attract an in-country right of appeal in the absence of entry clearance[1] but is challengeable by way of judicial review. However, an appeal, albeit outside the country, is often preferable because of the power of the appellate authority to reverse decisions to refuse entry on the merits in what are often finely balanced cases.[2]

1   Section 82, NIAA 2002 as amended by ss 15 and 17 of the Immigration Act 2014.
2   See comments of Carnwath J in *R v Secretary of State for the Home Department, ex p Musk* (CO 3956/1996) (26 March 1996, unreported).

# Chapter 5

# COMMON TRAVEL AREA, CREW MEMBERS AND EXEMPTED GROUPS

## COMMON TRAVEL AREA

**5.2** *[At the end of the paragraph insert:]*

The Common Travel Area could be about to assume more significance as a result of Brexit. The UK exit from the EU, however it happens, will result in a land border between the UK and an EU Member State. The British government have indicated that the Common Travel Area will still remain and will enable free passage of Irish and British citizens and of those others who can cross the border without any frontier immigration or passport control, but may nevertheless be subject to immigration control, as at present. This would enable the border to be kept open in the manner operating since the Good Friday agreement. However, although the Common Travel Area is expressly mentioned in British legislation (see Immigration Act 1971), it may be seen in a different perspective in Ireland. In the Irish case of *Pachero*,[10] Hogan J said that the Common Travel Area was something of a misnomer. It was not an agreement which would be governed by international law nor a treaty for the purposes of Article 2(1)(a) of the Vienna Convention (1969). Rather, it is essentially a mutual understanding between the two countries to synchronise their mutual immigration laws and administrative practices so as to facilitate freedom of travel for Irish and British nationals as between the two countries. As we shall also see, it is full of anomalies and, if it is going to be the guarantee of such free travel, as the British government are suggesting, it needs to be updated and given better status than a mutual understanding.

[10] *Pachero and Another v Minister for Justice and Equality, Ireland* [2011] IEHC 491, at para 14; see also para 7 and 18, describing in what ways the Common Travel Area has long ceased to be a genuine passport-free travel area in the way that the Schengen system is and is administratively flawed. He says 'The practical result . . . is that all persons arriving by air from the United Kingdom face Irish immigration controls. While in theory both Irish and British citizens are entitled to arrive here free from immigration control . . . , increasingly in practice such passengers who arrive by air from the United Kingdom are required to produce their passports (or, at least, some other form of acceptable identity document) in order to prove to immigration officers that they are either Irish or British citizens who can avail of the common travel area' (at para 18).

**5.6** *[At the end of subparagraph (iv) change the semi colon to a full stop and insert:]*

In *the* Irish High Court case of *Pachero*, a Bolivian couple had entered Ireland without a visa (because they did not need one) and had been admitted to the Republic. They then attempted to go to London via Northern Ireland and were stopped when they landed on the mainland and were detained and sent back to Northern Ireland. Hogan J somewhat reluctantly concluded that their permission to enter Ireland had lapsed under s 4 of the [Irish] Immigration Act 2004 when they crossed the border into Northern Ireland *and* so they had entered the UK unlawfully and were not entitled to re-entry to Ireland without more permission (although *the* judge seemed to be encouraging Irish authorities to grant that);

## THE BRITISH IRISH VISA SCHEME

**5.7** *[N.B.]*

No more nationalities have been added and there are no further amendments to the 1972 Order.

### The Irish exceptions

*Situations where leave required*

**5.9** *[At the end of Footnote 4 add:]*

See *Da Silveira, Re Judicial Review* [2008] NIQB 58 (05 June 2008), where permission to enter Ireland was gained by deception (saying coming to visit for five days but in fact going straight to NI); even if this is not detected and leave revoked before the individual crosses to the UK, he or she still falls foul of Article 3(b)(ii) of the 1972 Order as a person who has entered the Republic of Ireland unlawfully from a place outside the Common Travel Area.

*Automatic time limit and conditions prohibiting employment*

**5.10** *[Delete the sentence starting 'Secondly, a refusal to vary . . . ' and insert:]*

Secondly, a refusal to vary or extend the period of leave no longer attracts a right of appeal under s 82 of the Nationality Immigration and Asylum Act 2002.

*[Retain footnote reference 2 in text and replace the text in footnote 2 with:]*

The effect of the Immigration Act 2014 is that there is no longer a right of appeal against the refusal to vary or extend the period of leave.

### Immigration laws in the Islands

**5.14** *[Delete the first paragraph up to footnote reference 2, which should be retained, and insert:]*

The Channel Islands and the Isle of Man have the same nationality laws as the UK, but have nominally separate immigration laws. In practice, the Immigration Acts of 1971 extend to the Islands, with modifications, by the Immigration and Asylum Act 1991 and the British Nationality Act 1981. Although the Islands have their own immigration rules (called Directions in Jersey), they closely follow the UK ones.

*[Delete footnote 1 and renumber footnote 2 accordingly.]*

**5.14A** *[Insert new paragraph:]*

Since the 9th edition there have been the following Orders in Council:

- The Immigration (Isle of Man) (Amendment) Order 2015, SI 2015/1765, made 8 October 2015. This Order came into force: (a) on the day after the Order was made to enable regulations and orders which needed to be made by virtue of the amendments made to the principal Order by this Order; and (b) on 6 April 2016 for all other purposes.
- The Immigration (Isle of Man) (Amendment) Order 2016, SI 2016/156, made on 10 February 2016, coming into force on the day after the day on which it was made.
- The Immigration (Isle of Man) (Amendment) (No 2) Order 2016, SI 2016/755, made 13 July 2016 coming into force on the day after the day on which it is made.
- The Immigration (Guernsey) Order 2015, SI 2015/1533, made 15 July 2015, coming into force seven days after the day on which it is registered by the Royal Court of Guernsey.
- The Immigration (Guernsey) Order 2016, SI 2016/996, made on 12 October 2016, coming comes into force the day after the day on which it is registered by the Royal Court of Guernsey.
- The Immigration (Jersey) Order 2015, SI 2015/1532, made 15 July 2015, coming into force seven days after the day on which it is registered by the Royal Court of Jersey.
- The Immigration (Jersey) Order 2016, SI 2016/994, made 12 October 2016, coming into force on the seventh day after the day on which it is registered by the Royal Court of Jersey.

**Isle of Man**

**5.19** *[At the end of the paragraph add:]*

The Isle of Man Amendment Order 2015[3] amends the Immigration (Isle of Man) Order 2008[4] so as to apply the provisions on the charging of fees for immigration and nationality services under the Immigration Act 2014 (c. 22) in place of those applying under the Immigration, Asylum and Nationality Act 2006 (c. 13). The Order also limited the power of the Lieutenant Governor of the Isle of Man to prescribe fees under the Immigration Acts to functions exercised within the Isle of Man, and restored the power of the Secretary of State to prescribe those fees where the functions are exercised outside the Isle of Man by the Secretary of State on behalf of the Governor.

Further amendments were made to the 2008 Order by the Isle of Man Amendment (No 2) Order 2016, in order to ensure that once a person is listed by the Security Council of the United Nations or the Council of the European

Union as being subject to a travel ban that person becomes an 'excluded person' within the meaning of subsection (4) of section 8B of the 1971 Act.[5]

3    SI 2015/1765.
4    SI 2008/680.
5    This Order amends the Immigration (Isle of Man) Order 2008 (S.I. 2008/680) so as to make equivalent amendments to the Immigration Act 1971 (c. 77) as it has effect in the Isle of Man, following the amendments to the Immigration Act 1971 by section 76 of the Immigration Act 2016. Section 8B(5) of the 1971 Act was amended to reflect that resolutions of the Security Council of the United Nations and instruments made by the Council of the European Union have direct application upon the United Kingdom rather than directly upon the Isle of Man.

**5.21** *[N.B.]*

The (Isle of Man) (Amendment) (No 2) Order 2016, SI 2016/755, is intended to correct a drafting error in the 2008 Order. Its effect is to grant the Lieutenant Governor the power by order to exclude the Republic of Ireland from section 1(3) of the 1971 Act for such purposes as may be specified in the Order.

## Guernsey

**5.23** *[At the end of the paragraph add:]*

The Guernsey Order 2015[2] extends, subject to exceptions and modifications, ss 27 and 42 (documents and information, respectively) of the Immigration, Asylum and Nationality Act 2006 to Guernsey. The Order also extends to Guernsey ss 67 and 73(6) of, and Schs 8 and 9 to, the Immigration Act 2014 (which pertain to embarkation checks). The effect in both cases is to amend paras 3 and 4 of Sch 2 to the Immigration Act 1971 (c. 77) as extended to Guernsey. These pertain to fees for immigration or nationality applications or claims.

The Guernsey Order 2016,[3] which is not yet in force, will extend subject to exceptions and modifications, ss 68 and 70 of the Immigration Act 2014 to Guernsey. These pertain to fees for immigration or nationality applications or claims. The sections in their extended form make provision as regards the respective powers of the States of Guernsey Committee for Home Affairs and the Secretary of State to provide for these fees to be charged.

2    SI 2015/1533.
3    SI 2016/996.

## Jersey

**5.27** *[At the end of the paragraph add:]*

The Immigration (Jersey) Order 2015 and Immigration (Jersey) Order 2016 extend the embarkation checks and fee provisions of the Immigration Act 2014, respectively, to Jersey although the latter is not yet in force.[3]

3    SI 2015/1532 and SI 2016/994.

### Entering UK en route to another part of common travel area

**5.30** *[In footnote 9 replace the sentence starting 'A full text of the Act . . . '*
*with:]*

A full text of the Isle of Man Control of Employment Act 1975 can be found at www.legislation.gov.im.

## CONTROL OF SHIP, AIRCRAFT AND TRAIN CREWS

**5.34** *[In footnote 1 replace the penultimate sentence starting 'A list of countries . . . ' with:]*

A list of countries which have ratified the ILO Convention is available on the ILO website through NORMLEX: http://www.ilo.org/.

### Meaning of crew member

**5.35** *[At end of the paragraph add:]*

The Modernised Guidance allows Immigration Officers to 'apply a limited concessionary visa waiver for a dependent spouse, partner or child under 18 years (each as defined in the relevant Immigration Rules) who is accompanying a crew member on board ship where: the dependant will remain with the ship, and leave the UK with the ship'.[4]

*[In the penultimate sentence of footnote 2, after the colon replace the text beginning 'see IDI Ch 16 . . . Annex B' with:]*

see Modernised Guidance, Seamen, 7 July 2014, pp 4–5. For detailed guidance on special classes of seamen, see the same Modernised Guidance, pp 27–36.

*[In footnote 3 replace the final sentence with:]*

See Modernised Guidance, Seamen, 7 July 2014, p 31.

[4] Modernised Guidance, Seamen, 7 July 2014, p 31.

### Coming to join a ship or aircraft

**5.38** *[At the end of the paragraph add:]*

Now the requirement applies to other types of vessel, subject to exemptions for non-scheduled domestic freight services, vessels operating from UK ports but working wholly in international waters outside the UK 12-mile limit, and EEA (but not UK, Isle of Man or Channel Islands) registered vessels over 650 gross tonnage exercising EEA 'cabotage' (the transporting of good or persons) rights between mainland ports, or island cabotage, but only where the voyage is immediately before or after an international voyage.

*[In footnote 3 replace 'IDI, CH 16, Annex B.' with:]*

Modernised Guidance, Seamen, 7 July 2014, pp 21–22.

*[In footnote 5 add at the outset:]*

Modernised Guidance, Seamen, 7 July 2014, pp 35–36.

*[In footnote 5 delete the last sentence.]*

## Discharged seamen

**5.39** *[N.B.]*

The Modernised Guidance – Seamen – has replaced the earlier IDI, referred to in the 9th edition of this work. It was last updated on 7 July 2014. It is a more comprehensive document. The guidance is for Immigration Officers responsible for the enforcement of immigration control of seamen arriving in the UK as operational crew of a ship or as passengers coming to join a ship as operational crew. The guidance is based on:

- the Immigration Act 1971, Part 1, sections 8, 10 and 11, Part 3, sections 24 and 27, Part 4, section 33 and Schedule 2;
- the Immigration Rules, paragraphs 128 and 324;
- the International Labour Organisation Convention No 108 on Seafarers' Identity Documents;
- the Maritime Labour Convention 2006.

It should be referred to before any advice is given or representations made by immigration practitioners.

*[Replace footnote 1 with:]*

Modernised Guidance, Seamen, 7 July 2014, p 16.

*[Replace footnote 2 with:]*

Modernised Guidance, Seamen, 7 July 2014, pp 19–20.

*[Replace footnote 3 with:]*

Modernised Guidance, Seamen, 7 July 2014, p 17.

*[Replace footnote 4 with:]*

Modernised Guidance, Seamen, 7 July 2014, pp 29–30.

## Arrest, detention and removal of crew members

**5.40** *[Replace the sentence beginning 'The right of appeal . . . ' to ' . . . but then reinstated' with:]*

There is no right of appeal following the coming into force of the Immigration Act 2014, which amended section 82 of the Nationality, Immigration and Asylum Act 2002.

## Shipwrecked seamen

**5.41** *[Delete paragraph and replace with:]*

Whereas Chapter 16 of the Immigration Directorate Instructions, before its withdrawal on 15 December 2014, stated that shipwrecked seamen should 'normally be given leave to enter', the Modernised Guidance on Seamen published on 7 July 2014 says that 'shipwrecked seamen, professional or otherwise, discretionary leave to enter outside the Immigration Rules'. No clear guidance is given on when granting leave to enter might be inappropriate but the only example given is when a deportation order is in force and there is need to refer to a senior officer before refusing leave is mandatory.[1]

[1]  Modernised Guidance, Seamen, 7 July 2014, p 33.

### Seamen's documents

**5.42** *[Replace the text for footnote 1 with:]*

See Modernised Guidance, Seamen, 7 July 2014, p 22.

*[Replace the text for footnote 2 with:]*

Modernised Guidance, Seamen, 7 July 2014, p 22.

### The British Seamen's Card

**5.43** *[Delete the text from 'According to the IDI . . . ' to the end of the paragraph including footnote 2.]*

*[In footnote 1 delete the text from 'See further IDI Ch 16 . . . ' to the end.]*

## GROUPS COVERED BY EXEMPTION ORDER

**5.44** *[At the end of the text for footnote 2, replace the full stop with a semi-colon and add:]*

SI/2004/317; SI/2015/1866.

### Members of the diplomat's family

**5.52** *[In footnote 4 replace text with:]*

IDI, Ch 14, s 1, para 9.

*[In footnote 5 replace text with:]*

IDI, Ch 14, s 1, para 6.

Chapter 6

# EUROPEAN UNION FREE MOVEMENT LAW AND RELATED OBLIGATIONS

## BREXIT

**6.0** *[New paragraph and heading – insert the following as a preface before existing text at para 6.1:]*

Any update to European Union free movement law would be remiss not to refer to the potential impact of the EU Referendum on UK immigration control. On 23 June 2016, the UK held a referendum on its membership of the EU, with a majority of 51.9% voting in favour of leaving the UK. Negotiations will now take place to agree the terms of the UK's withdrawal, though the exact time frame is as yet unknown.

On 24 January 2017, the Supreme Court gave judgment in the historic *Miller*[1] case. It was held that an Act of Parliament is required to authorise ministers to give Notice of the decision of the UK to withdraw from the European Union. In response, the government has published a short bill, the *European Union (Notification of Withdrawal) Bill 2016–2017*, which confers a power on the Prime Minister to notify withdrawal from the EU. At the time of writing, the bill is making its way through the House of Commons. The bill is accompanied by a white paper, *The UK's exit from new partnership with the European Union*,[2] which sets out the strategy for negotiations.

The Government's stated aims going into the negotiations include the maintenance of the Common Travel Area with Ireland;[3] controlling the number of people coming in the UK from the EU,[4] and securing the rights of EU citizens already in the UK, and those of UK nationals in other Member States as early as possible.[5]

[1]  *R (on the application of Miller & Dos Santos) v Secretary of State for Exiting the European Union* [2017] UKSC 5.
[2]  Cm 9417.
[3]  Ibid, paras 4.1–4.10.
[4]  Ibid, paras 5.1–5.10.
[5]  Ibid, paras 6.1–6.4.

## INSTITUTIONS OF EU AND SOURCES OF LAW

### The Schengen Agreements and abolition of internal borders

*Schengen acquis*

**6.44** *[Add the following text at footnote 3:]*

See also *Spain v Parliament and Council (Judgment)* [2015] EUECJ C-44/14 (8 September 2015) in which the CJEU held that limited forms of cooperation do not constitute taking part within the meaning of Article 4 of the Schengen Protocol; Ireland and the UK can take part in those provisions in force in the Schengen *acquis* relating to external borders only after the Council accepts a request by the Member State concerned.

## PERSONAL SCOPE (1) NATIONALS

### UK nationals for EU purposes

*The Surinder Singh situation*

**6.73** *[At the end of the paragraph add:]*

In *Osoro (Surinder Singh)* [2015] UKUT 00593 (IAC), the President of the Upper Tribunal sought to express 'the principle in *Surinder Singh*' as consisting of 'the principle of efficacious enjoyment of Community law rights and the principle of non-discrimination'. The Tribunal did not address the lawfulness of the 'centre of life' concept in reg 9.

**6.73A** *[Insert new paragraph:]*

On 25 November 2016, a new version of reg 9 of the 2006 Regulations came into force.[1] The most significant difference between the new and previous versions is the introduction of the 'genuine residence' and 'purpose of residence' tests. Under the new reg 9, the factors that are relevant in determining whether the residence in the other EEA state is genuine are whether the centre of the UK citizen's life transferred to the EEA state; the length of the UK citizen and his/her family member's joint residence in the EEA state; the nature and quality of their accommodation in the EEA state and whether that state is or was the UK citizen's principal residence; the degree of their integration in the EEA state; and whether the first lawful residence in the EU of the family member with his/her UK sponsor was in the EEA state. The new reg 9 explicitly states it does not apply, 'where the purpose of the residence in the EEA state was a means for circumventing any immigration laws applying to non-EEA nationals to which [the family member] would otherwise be subject'. These new provisions are very clearly in tension with the CJEU's judgment in *O and B v Minister voor Immigratie, Integratie en Asiel*,[2] in which the Court indicated that an obstacle to free movement and residence arises when the residence of the Union citizen in the host Member State has been sufficiently genuine, which is simply when residence is pursued for more than three months, in accordance with the Citizens' Directive 2004/38/EC, art 7. The Commission had already expressed its disquiet with the previous version of reg 9, which introduced a 'centre of life' test, which treated integration and the person's principal residence as being material, notwithstanding that this was 'not contemplated' by *O and B*. The new reg 9 also expressly excludes extended family members from benefitting from the regulation. It also extends the regulation to UK nationals who are resident in the EEA state not just as a worker or self-employed person, but also as a self-sufficient person, student or because he/she has acquired the right of permanent residence in the EEA state.

The 25 November 2016 version of reg 9 of the 2006 Regulations is carried over into reg 9 of the 2016 Regulations,[3] which came into force on 1 February 2017.

1    Immigration (European Economic Area) Regulations 2016, SI 2016/1052, regs 1(2)(a), 44 and Sch 5, para 1. The new reg 9 even applies to applications that were made before 25 November 2016: see Sch 5, para 2 of the 2016 Regulations.
2    (C-456/12), [2014] QB 1163.
3    Immigration (European Economic Area) Regulations 2016, SI 2016/1052.

## Non-nationals and derivative rights of residence

**6.74** *[In footnote 1, at the end of the first sentence, insert:]*

, which is materially the same as the new reg 13 of the Immigration (European Economic Area) Regulations 2016, SI 2016/1052, in force from 1 February 2017.

*[At the end of footnote 2 insert:]*

, which is materially the same as the identically numbered provision in the 2016 Regulations (see footnote 1).

*[At the end of footnote 3 insert:]*

, which is the same as the identically numbered provision in the 2016 Regulations (see footnote 1).

## Iida and O, S & L

**6.83A** *[Insert new paragraph after paragraph 6.83:]*

Three further cases decided by the CJEU have shed light on the scope of the *Zambrano* principle.

In *NA v Secretary of State for the Home Department*,[1] NA was a national of Pakistan who married a German national (KA) in Germany and, following the couple's move to the UK to work, had two daughters in the UK, who were German nationals. The relationship broke down due to domestic violence and the couple divorced. However, since this occurred after KA had left the UK, and was not at the point of divorce exercising Treaty rights, NA did not retain the right of residence under Art 13(2) of the Citizens' Directive/reg 10 of the 2006 EEA Regulations. NA was the primary carer of the two children. The UT held that it would violate Article 8 of the ECHR to expect the children to move to Germany. The Court of Appeal referred a number of questions to the CJEU[2] which revolved around the children's and NA's entitlement to reside in the UK based on the *Zambrano* principle. The FTT's approach to the retained rights aspect of the case was upheld by the CJEU (addressed below). The CJEU did, however, accept that NA and the children enjoyed rights of residence under Art 12 of Regulation 1612/68 since the German national husband, KA, had worked in the UK, and even though he had ceased to reside there before the children had started to attend school in the UK (at [52]–[68]) (see also **6.86** below). In relation to Article 20 of TFEU, the CJEU held that that article does not confer a right of residence in the host Member State either on a minor Union citizen who has resided since birth in that Member State but is not a national of that State, or on a parent who is a third-country national and who has sole custody of that minor, where they qualify for a right of residence in that Member State under a provision of secondary EU law (at [74] (referring to the absence of a right of residence as the fact on which the derived right in *Zambrano* was dependent) and [81]). The Court also held that Art 21 does, however, confer on a minor Union citizen a right of residence in the host Member State provided that that citizen satisfies the conditions set out in Art 7(1) of the Citizens' Directive (sufficient resources not to become a burden on the social assistance system of the host Member State etc), which was for the referring court to determine. If so, that same provision allows the parent who is the primary carer of that Union citizen to reside with that citizen in the host Member State (at [75]–[81]). It did not matter whether the children satisfied the Art 7(1) conditions by themselves or through their mother, or through any other source (at [77]).

In *Rendon Marin v Administración del Estado*,[3] Mr Marin, a Colombian national, was the sole carer parent of two children, a son who was a Spanish national and a daughter who was a Polish national through her mother. Both children were born in Spain and had always resided there with Mr Marin. Mr Marin's application for a residence card was refused due to his criminal record, although no expulsion action was taken against him. The question for the CJEU was essentially whether a non-EU national parent, who is the primary carer of an EU national child, could be refused a residence permit on the basis of a previous criminal conviction, if that would force the children to leave the territory of the Union. In *Marin*, had it not been for his criminal conviction, Mr Marin would have been entitled to a residence permit on the basis of the *Zambrano* principle. The CJEU held that Article 20 of TFEU precluded national legislation automatically nullifying this right in consequence of a criminal conviction alone, and that such an interference would only be consistent with EU law where, in exceptional circumstances, the individual poses a genuine, present and sufficiently serious threat to a fundamental interest of society, namely public policy or public security, and the decision would be proportionate and in accordance with fundamental rights. Although such wording substantially mirrors that in Articles 27 and 28 of the Citizens' Directive, the protections derive in law from Arts 20/21 themselves. The Court made clear that these provisions should be interpreted restrictively, and the child's best interests were central to their application.

Mr Marin could enjoy a derived right of residence under Art 21 if the self-sufficiency provisions in Article 7(1) of the Citizens' Directive were made out, with regard to Mr Marin's Polish daughter, which was a matter for the referring court.

The CJEU also found in *Marin* that the question whether Mr Marin and the children should be expected to relocate to Poland was a matter for the referring court; but, in circumstances where there were no family ties to Poland and neither of the three spoke Polish, the Court observed that it was 'clear' that this was capable of resulting in the children being deprived of the genuine enjoyment of their rights under Article 20 of TFEU (at [80]). This reasoning suggests that being practically required to leave the EU, or being hindered in the exercise of free movement rights, are not necessarily the only ways in which Art 20 may be infringed.

The CJEU's decision in *Marin* is inconsistent with the decision of the UT in the *Amirteymour*[4] case, in which the UT declined to accept that refusal of a residence card should be regarded as forcing a person to leave the UK.

The Court reached similar conclusions in *CS v Secretary of State for the Home Department*,[5] which was handed down simultaneously with *Marin*. CS, a Moroccan national, had been convicted of smuggling a mobile phone SIM card into prison. CS's son was British and had always resided in the UK. CS became subject to the automatic deportation provisions in s 32 of the UK Borders Act 2007. CS argued that her deportation would deprive her son of the effective enjoyment of his rights to Union citizenship. The CJEU held that criminal offending was capable of excluding the *Zambrano*-derived right on which CS relied, but only where the public policy proviso, as set out in the same terms as in *Marin*, was satisfied, which would only be in exceptional circumstances, and paying close regard to the best interests of the child. The UK's automatic deportation regime was therefore unlawful for the category of appellants who would otherwise be entitled to a *Zambrano* right of residence. The Court did not contradict the approach of Advocate General Szpunar who rejected the notion that protection against expulsion under the Directive (where the minor EU citizen was self-sufficient) differed from that derived under Article 20 of TFEU.

1  Case C-115/15, [2016] 3 WLR 1439, 30 June 2016. In *R (Zewdu) v Secretary of State for the Home Department* [2015] EWHC 2148 (Admin), a *Zambrano* right was recognised even where the claimant held DLR.
2  [2014] EWCA Civ 995 and [2015] EWCA Civ 140.
3  Case C-165/14, GC, 13 September 2016.
4  [2015] UKUT 466 (IAC), eg at [74].
5  Case C-304/14, GC, 13 September 2016.

## Domestic cases on Article 20 of TFEU

**6.84** *[Add at the end, as a new paragraph:]*

The approach in *Harrison*,[6] and the UK domestic authorities more broadly as to when the *Zambrano* right arises, may need to be aligned with the approach to *Zambrano*-derived rights in *Rendon Marin* and *CS*. Those cases make it clear that a distinct public interest provisio stage is now required in cases in which the SSHD relies on criminality/conduct to support deportation action or refusal of a residence card etc. Even in cases where criminality does not feature, it is arguable that being physically forced to leave the Union is not a necessary condition for engagement of *Zambrano* derived rights. As noted at **6.83A** above, the CJEU in *Rendon Marin* held that, in circumstances where there were no family ties to Poland and neither Mr Marin, nor his Spanish son and Polish daughter spoke Polish, and none had ever been there, it was 'clear' that this was *capable* of resulting in the children being deprived of the genuine enjoyment of their rights (at [80]). This reasoning suggests that being required to leave the EU, or being hindered in the exercise of free movement rights, are not necessarily the only ways in which Article 20 of TFEU may be infringed. Therefore, the *Harrison* focus on compulsion[7]/whether constructive removal of the Union citizen would occur 'as a matter of reality', may need to give way to the issue of the 'practical effect' of expulsion, particularly the nature and severity of the impact of expulsion on the minor Union citizen.

[6]   See **6.84**, footnote 1.
[7]   For an example of the compulsion test in action, see *FZ (China) v Secretary of State for the Home Department* [2015] EWCA Civ 550, [2015] 3 CMLR 12, in which the Court held that there was no compulsion for the deportee's (FZ's) wife to leave the UK in the event of his deportation, given that she owned a business and had been the sole breadwinner for the family and the carer of the child while FZ had been in prison. However, 'If the father were the sole carer of the child with United Kingdom citizenship, the position might be different' (at [14]–[16]). See also *Secretary of State for the Home Department v AQ (Nigeria)* [2015] EWCA Civ 250 at [73]–[74], [77].

**6.85**   *[At the end of the second bullet point add:]*

But see the addition to **6.84** above.

**6.85A**   *[Insert new paragraph:]*

In *Sanneh*[1] the Court of Appeal held that the *Zambrano* status is a positive right which arises as soon as the necessary conditions are satisfied; there is no need to wait until the carer is destitute or threatened with actual removal from the EU. However, the Court went on to rule that *Zambrano* carers are not entitled to the same level of social assistance as EU citizens lawfully residing in the EU. The *Zambrano* obligation is limited to providing sufficient support to meet the carer's basic needs, which includes the need to be able to care for the EU citizen child. The UT stressed the importance of proving that removal of a carer would in fact cause the British citizen to leave the territory of the Union;[2] the UT's refusal to accept that the reasonableness of the carer leaving the UK was irrelevant is inconsistent with the approach of the CJEU in *Rendon Marin*; see also *Secretary of State for the Home Department v AQ (Nigeria)* [2015] EWCA Civ 250 at [76].

[1]   *Sanneh and Others v Secretary of State for Work and Pensions and Others* [2015] EWCA Civ 49, [2016] QB 455.
[2]   *Ayinde and Thinjom (Carers – Reg 15A – Zambrano)* [2015] UKUT 560 (IAC).

**6.86**   *[In the final paragraph, delete the last two sentences after footnote reference 12 and substitute:]*

Those benefiting from a derived right of residence may only exceptionally be expelled, or refused a right of residence, and only where the individual poses a genuine, present and sufficiently serious threat to a fundamental interest of society, namely public policy or public security, and the decision would be proportionate and in accordance with fundamental rights: *Rendon Marin* and *CS*: see **6.83A** above. Although such wording substantially mirrors that in Arts 27 and 28 of the Citizens' Directive, the protections derive in law from Arts 20/21 themselves in *Zambrano* cases. The Court made clear that these provisions should be interpreted restrictively, and the child's best interests were central to their application. The fact of a criminal conviction is insufficient to meet this test. The Court did not contradict the approach of Advocate General Szpunar who rejected the notion that protection against expulsion under the Directive (where the minor EU citizen was self-sufficient) from that derived under Article 20 of TFEU. It follows that reg 21A(3) of the 2006 EEA Regulations, which disapplies the public policy provision to derived rights cases is unlikely to be lawful. From 6 April 2015, reg 15A(9) was amended so as to include reference, at reg 15(9)(a) to reg 23A (revocation of the right of admission which had been granted under reg 11), and to include immigration officers as decision makers (Immigration (European Economic Area) (Amendment) Regulations 2015, SI 2015/694, Sch 1, para 7).

*[At the end of footnote 2 insert:]*

The same conclusion was reached by the CJEU: see fn 8 below.

*[In footnote 8 delete the second sentence starting 'Note that the case has been referred . . . ' and insert in its place:]*

*NA v Secretary of State for the Home Department* (Case C-115/15), [2016] 3 WLR 1439, 30 June 2016 at [52]–[68]. This requirement has been removed in the new reg 16(3) of the 2016 Regulations. As explained above at **6.83A**, NA and her German national children enjoyed rights of residence in the UK under Art 12 of Regulation 1612/68 since the German national husband, KA, had worked in the UK, although he had ceased to reside there before the children had started to attend school in the UK. The Court of Appeal judgments referring the matter to the CJEU are [2014] EWCA Civ 995 and [2015] EWCA Civ 140. The UT had also, correctly, taken the same approach as the CJEU.

**6.86A** *[Insert new paragraph:]*

Under the 2016 EEA Regulations, it is reg 16 which sets out the criteria for derivative rights of residence, which is substantially, although not entirely, the same as reg 15A of the 2006 Regulations. The material differences are:

- Subparagraph (2) (in both versions) (the *Chen* situation): reg 16(2)(b)(c) says that the relevant EEA national 'would be unable to remain in the UK if "P" were required to leave for an indefinite period' (the underlining is the addition).
- Subparagraphs (3) and (4) (in both versions) (the *Ibrahim/ Teixeira* situation): reg 16(3)(c) deletes the requirement that the child of the EEA national was in education in the UK 'at a time when the EEA national parent was in the United Kingdom', which was held to be unlawful in *NA v Secretary of State for the Home Department* (see **6.86** at footnote 8). 'Education' is defined in reg 16(7)(a) as, 'excluding nursery education but does not exclude education received before the compulsory school age where that education is equivalent to the education received at or after the compulsory school age' (see on this point, **6.86** footnote 7). Subparagraph (4), the corresponding provision for the child's carer, also adds 'for an indefinite period' as in subparagraph (2).
- Subparagraph (5) in the new reg 16 is the equivalent to reg 15(4A) in the 2006 Regulations (the *Zambrano* situation), and is materially the same as the old sub-para (4A), save that 'for an indefinite period' is added in relation to the carer's absence.

- Subparagraph (6) in the new reg 16 adds a further category of eligibility for a child who is under 18; does not have leave under the Immigration Act 1971; the child's primary carer is entitled to a derivative right of residence under paragraphs (2), (4) or (5); and the primary carer would be prevented from residing in the UK if the person left the United Kingdom for an indefinite period.

**6.88** *[Add at the end of the paragraph:]*

No doubt for this reason, in *FZ (China)* [2015] EWCA Civ 550 the appellant did not rely on reg 15(7A) and (7B) and instead framed the submissions as to the scope of the *Zambrano* principle with reference to Art 20 directly. The Court of Appeal did not dissent from this approach (at [20]).

*[At the end of footnote 1 add:]*

See also *Secretary of State for the Home Department v AQ (Nigeria)* [2015] EWCA Civ 250.

## PERSONAL SCOPE (2) WORKERS

### Definition of workers

**6.93** *[Insert at the start of the paragraph:]*

From 1 February 2017, the Immigration (European Economic Area) Regulations 2016, SI 2016/1052 come into force. The definitions of a worker and a jobseeker (etc) which are still contained in regs 5 and 6 are materially the same as in the 2006 Regulations. The 2016 Regulations version of those provisions includes simplified language and updated numbering.

### Jobseekers sickness, illness and retirement

**6.95** *[At the end of the first sentence, add a new footnote reference 4a and for the text of the footnote insert:]*

See also *Yusuf (EEA - ceasing to be a jobseeker; effect)* [2015] UKUT 00433 (IAC).

*[At the end of footnote 7 add:]*

The UT(IAC) considered *St Prix* in the case of *Weldemichael and another (St Prix* [2014] EUECJ C-507/12; effect) [2015] UKUT 540 (IAC), the summary of which reads: 'An EEA national woman will retain continuity of residence for the purposes of the Immigration (European Economic Area) Regulations 2006 ('the 2006 EEA Regulations') for a period in which she was absent from working or job-seeking owing to the physical constraints of the late stages of pregnancy and the aftermath of childbirth if, in line with the decision of the CJEU in *Jessy St Prix*: (a) at the beginning of the relevant period she was either a worker or seeking employment; (b) the relevant period commenced no more than 11 weeks before the expected date of confinement (absent cogent evidence to the contrary that the woman was physically constrained from working or seeking work); (c) the relevant period did not extend beyond 52 weeks; and, (d) she returned to work. So long as these requirements are met, there will be no breach of the continuity of residence for the purposes of regulation 15. Time spent in the United Kingdom during such periods counts for the purposes of acquiring permanent residence.' In *Secretary of State for Work and Pensions v SFF* [2015] UKUT 502 (AAC), the UT (Administrative Appeals Chamber) observed that a woman was protected by her worker status until such time, not exceeding the 'reasonable period' contemplated by *Saint Prix*, as she showed an intention not to be part of the employment market. In practice, the Secretary of State had accepted that a woman retained worker status until there was reason to suppose otherwise and, on a practical and a legal level, the UT considered that to be the right approach.

**6.96** *[Add at the end of the paragraph:]*

However, the lawfulness of at least part of these provisions, notably reg 6(2A), which restricts the retention of worker status to six months in the case of a person to whom paragraph 2(ba) applies, is supported by two recent decisions of the CJEU. In *Dano*[11] the CJEU held that Member States may refuse to grant social assistance to EU citizens who enter their territory without intending to find a job and without being able to support themselves by their own resources. Ms Dano had never been a worker or a jobseeker. In *Alimanovic*[12] the CJEU effectively extended this principle to the case of an EU citizen who had worked for less than one year in a host Member State, who, after becoming unemployed, applied for subsistence benefits in the host State. The CJEU held that Ms Alimanovic had ceased to be a worker, and thereby ceased to be entitled to such benefits, after six months of claiming them while retaining the status of worker. The basis for the Court's ruling was that the non-discrimination principle could only be relied upon by Ms Alimanovic if her residence in the host State, Germany, complied with the conditions of the Citizens' Directive, ie she had the right to reside. It is concerning that the Court did not address the relevance of the fact that the minor children were attending school in Germany and appeared to have been doing so at the time that Alimanovic was a worker, which ought to have led to a right to reside on the basis of the *Ibrahim/Teixeira* principles. Applying *Dano* and *Alimanovic*, the UK Supreme Court held in *R (Mirga) v SSWP & SSHD*[13] that since M had not worked for 12 months in the UK, she could not claim to be a worker, and, since she was not a jobseeker, self-employed, a student or self-sufficient, she could validly be denied a right of residence and thus could be excluded from social assistance without infringing her rights under Article 21(1) of TFEU; and that Article 18 of TFEU did not assist the second claimant since it did not confer a broad or general right not to be discriminated against, but only came into play when there was discrimination in connection with a right in a European Union treaty (which had not been established): see [42]–[48], [54]–[57], [72]. See also *Garcia Nieto v Vestische Arbeit Jobcenter Kreis Recklinghausen*,[14] in which the CJEU held that EU law did not preclude legislation of a Member State under which nationals of other Member States who were in a situation such as that referred to in Art 6(1) of the Directive (right of residence of up to three months, and not a worker etc) were excluded from entitlement to certain 'special non-contributory cash benefits' within the meaning of Art 70(2) of Regulation 883/2004, which also constituted 'social assistance' within the meaning of Art 24(2) of the Citizens' Directive.

[11] *Dano v Jobcenter Leipzig* (C-333/12), ECLI:EU:C:2014:2358, [2015] 1 WLR 2519, [2015] All ER (EC) 1,

12   *Neukolln v Alimanovic*: C-67/14, ECLI:EU:C:2015:597, [2016] QB 308, [2016] 2 WLR 208.
13   *Mirga v Secretary of State for Work and Pensions; Samin v Westminster City Council (Secretary of State for Communities and Local Government and another intervening)* [2016] UKSC 1, [2016] 2 All ER 447, [2016] 1 WLR 481.
14   C-299/14, [2016] 3 CMLR 5, [2016] 1 WLR 3089, [2016] 3 CMLR 77, [2016] All ER (D) 257 (Feb).

## PERSONAL SCOPE (3) ESTABLISHMENT

**6.99** *[In the final sentence after 'Regulations', add:]*

and, from 1 February 2017, the Immigration (European Economic Area) Regulations 2016, SI 2016/1052, also by regs 4(1)(b) and 6,

*[At the end of the paragraph add:]*

The equivalent provision in the 2016 Regulations is reg 6(4).

## PERSONAL SCOPE (4) SERVICES

### Posted workers

**6.106** *[At the end of the paragraph add:]*

Laval was followed by the CJEU in *Sähköalojen ammattiliitto ry v Elektrobudowa Spółka akcyjna.*[5] Also, in Criminal Proceedings against *De Clercq*,[6] the CJEU held that Member States could, on certain conditions, require the recipient of services performed by workers posted by a service provider established in another Member State to forward to the competent authorities, before those workers begin to work, the data identifying those persons, where they have been unable to submit proof of the declaration which their employer should have made to the competent authorities of that host Member State prior to the commencement of their provision of services.

5   C-396/13,, [2015] 3 CMLR 255, [2015] IRLR 407, [2015] All ER (D) 183 (Feb).
6   C-315/13, [2015] 2 CMLR 6.

## PERSONAL SCOPE (5) STUDENTS, THE SELF-SUFFICIENT, RETIRED AND INCAPACITATED

### Students

**6.109** *[In the text before footnote reference 2, change the full stop to a comma, and after footnote reference 2 add:]*

and now by the Immigration (European Economic Area) Regulations 2016, SI 2016/1052, from 1 February 2017, where students are also defined in reg 4(1)(d) in materially the same terms as under the 2006 Regulations, and are qualified persons under reg 6, and are entitled to extended free movement rights under reg 14.

**6.110** *[In the text before footnote reference 5, change the full stop to a comma, and after footnote reference 5 add:]*

and from 1 February 2017, the 2016 Regulations, SI 2016/1052, which adopts materially the same wording and the same principal numbering as the 2006 Regulations, ie regs 4(1)(d), (4), 6(1)(e) and 14 as explained in the following text.

**6.111** *[At the end of the paragraph add:]*

and, from 1 February 2017, by the 2016 Regulations, SI 2016/1052, reg 7(1) and (2) which are in simplified terms but of the same practical effect as the equivalent provision in the 2006 Regulations.

## Students with derived free movement rights

**6.112** *[At the end of the third sentence, ending 'comprehensive sickness insurance', insert a footnote reference 0.]*

*[At the end of the paragraph add:]*

From 1 February 2017, the equivalent provision in the 2016 Regulations (SI 2016/1052) is reg 16.

*[Insert above footnote 1 the text for new footnote 0:]*

In Joined Cases C-401/15 to C-403/15, *Depesme and others v Ministre de l'Enseignement supérieur et de la Recherche*, the CJEU held that Article 45 of TFEU and Article 7(2) of Regulation (EU) No 492/2011 must be interpreted as meaning that a child of a frontier worker, who is able to benefit indirectly from the social advantages referred to in the latter provision, such as study finance granted by a Member State to the children of workers pursuing or who have pursued an activity in that Member State, means not only a child who has a child-parent relationship with that worker, but also a child of the spouse or registered partner of that worker, where that worker supports that child. See also *Martens v Minister van Onderwijs, Cultuur en Wetenschap* (C-359/13), [2015] 3 CMLR 79, [2015] All ER (D) 274 (Mar), in which the CJEU held that Articles 20 and 21 of TFEU must be interpreted as precluding legislation of a Member State which made the continued grant of funding for higher education outside that State subject to the rule that the student applying for such funding had resided in that Member State for a period of at least three out of the six years preceding his enrolment, on the grounds, inter alia, that it would deter free movement; and *Commission v Netherlands* (C-233/14), [2017] 1 CMLR 5.

## The self-sufficient

**6.113** *[In the text after footnote reference 3 add:]*

From 1 February 2017, the equivalent provisions in the 2016 Regulations are also regs 4(1)(c), (4), 6(1)(e) and 14, which are materially the same.

**6.114** *[In the text after footnote reference 2 add:]*

From 1 February 2017, the equivalent provisions in the 2016 Regulations are also regs 7(1) and 7(3).

*[In the text after 'see above at 6.81.' add:]*

From 1 February 2017, the equivalent provision in the 2016 Regulations is reg 16.

*[In the text after footnote reference 4 add:]*

However, in the light of the CJEU's rulings in *NA* and *Rendon Marin*, the UK domestic approach on this issue may need to be revised: see **6.83A** above (and, in particular, *NA* at [76]–[79], and *Rendon Marin* at [48]–[49]).

### The retired and incapacitated

**6.115** *[In the first paragraph, after the penultimate sentence (ending 'UK law'), add:]*

Under the 2016 EEA Regulations (SI 2016/1052), in force from 1 February 2017, the relevant provisions are also contained in reg 5, which are materially the same and adopt substantially the same numbering as the 2006 Regulations (the key conditions are also numbered as subparagraphs (2), (3), (4) and (5)). The following text should be read subject to this insertion. Reference to the Accession and EU2 Regulations is removed.

## MEMBERS OF THE FAMILY

### Right of entry and residence of family groups

**6.118** *[In the text before footnote reference 1 insert:]*

and in the 2016 Regulations (SI 2016/1052), reg 8,

**6.119** *[At the end of the second sentence, before the full stop and footnote reference 1, insert:]*

as they are also termed in the 2016 Regulations (SI 2016/1052), reg 10

**6.120** *[At the end of the paragraph insert:]*

In *Confederazione Generale Italiana del Lavoro v Presidenza del Consiglio dei Ministri*,[7]2 September 2015, the CJEU held that Council Directive 2003/109/EC of 25 November 2003 concerning the status of third-country nationals who are long-term residents, as amended, precludes national legislation which requires third-country nationals, when applying for the issue or renewal of a residence permit in the Member State concerned, to pay a fee which varies in amount between EUR 80 and EUR 200, in as much as such a fee is disproportionate and is liable to create an obstacle to the exercise of the rights conferred by that Directive.

*[At the end of the text in footnote 6 add:]*

In *AS (Ghana) v Secretary of State for the Home Department* [2016] EWCA Civ 133, [2016] Imm AR 637, the Court of Appeal recalled that the residence permits of third country national family members were, like those of the EU national, declaratory rather than constitutive of the right to reside (at [20]–[23]), and drew a distinction with the approach under the Immigration

Act 1971.

7   C-309/14, ECLI:EU:C:2015:523, [2015] All ER (D) 19 (Sep).

### Third country national family members

**6.122** *[After each reference to the '2006 Regulations', add:]*

(and the 2016 Regulations (SI 2016/1052), from 1 February 2017)

*[After 'regulation 16(5) and (6)', add:]*

(and, under the 2016 Regulations (SI 2016/1052), reg 17(5) and (6))

**6.123** *[After each reference to the '2006 Regulations', add:]*

(and the 2016 Regulations (SI 2016/1052), from 1 February 2017)

*[After '(Regulation 12(2)' and before the closing bracket', add:]*

, or, from 1 February 2017, reg 12(4) of the 2016 Regulations

*[In footnote 2 add:]*

*Cudjoe (Proxy marriages: burden of proof)* [2016] UKUT 180 (IAC).

### SPOUSES AND CIVIL PARTNERS

**6.126** *[In the second paragraph after 'regulation 10(5) of the 2006 Regulations', insert:]*

, or, from 1 February 2017, the 2016 Regulations (SI 2016/1052),

*[After 'in the 2006 Regulations', insert:]*

, and in the 2016 Regulations,

*[In footnote 2, add after the first sentence:]*

The definition is identically numbered in the 2016 Regulations.

### Marriages and partnerships of convenience

**6.127** *[In the text after footnote reference 5 add:]*

which are mirrored in the 2016 Regulations,

**6.128** *[Delete the penultimate sentence (starting 'The position . . . ' and replace with the following:]*

*Papajorgi* was approved in *Rosa v Secretary of State for the Home Department*,[4] in which the Court of Appeal reasoned at [24], that 'the legal burden lies on the Secretary of State to prove that an otherwise valid marriage is a marriage of convenience so as to justify the refusal of an application for a residence card under the EEA Regulations'. The Court of Appeal also held that the definition of 'marriage of convenience' in Council Resolution 97/C 382/01 of 4 December 1997 on measures to be adopted on the combating of marriages of convenience was 'difficult to improve upon' (at [10]). The Court disapproved *IS (Serbia)* at [29], describing para 14 of *IS* as 'seriously confused' and reasoning that the result intended by the UT in that case would be achieved if, 'the legal burden of proof lies on the Secretary of State throughout but the evidential burden can shift, as explained in *Papajorgji*'. *Papajorgi* had earlier been approved, *obiter*, in *Agho v Secretary of State for the Home Department*,[5] in which the Court of Appeal observed that the formulation of the UT in that case 'clearly places the burden of proof on the Secretary of State (or ECO)' (at [11]–[14]) and went on to apply those principles to the facts. The Court of Appeal found that the SSHD's evidence was not capable of undermining the documentary evidence of cohabitation adduced by the appellants.

4   [2016] EWCA Civ 14,[2016] 1 WLR 1206, [2016] 2 CMLR 464, 166 NLJ 7684.
5   [2015] EWCA Civ 1198, [2016] INLR 411.

**6.129** *[In footnote 10 add:]*

In *R (Aziz Ait-Rabah) v Secretary of State for the Home Department* [2016] EWHC 1099 (Admin), [2016] All ER (D) 93 (May), Garnham J addressed a number of complaints about the conduct of an interview in relation to a suspected marriage of convenience, including the significance of not cautioning the interviewee and asking whether the couple had had sexual intercourse: see [53]–[60].

## Cohabitating couples

**6.131** *[In the 4th sentence, after 'the 2006 Regulations', add:]*

, and from 1 February 2017, in the identically numbered 2016 EEA Regulations,

## Retained rights (i) divorce/termination

**6.132** *[In the text after 'The 2006 Regulations', which follows footnote reference 8, add:]*

, and, from 1 February 2017, the 2016 Regulations,

*[In the text after footnote reference 11 add:]*

However, the CJEU upheld the lawfulness of Regulation 10(5)(b) in determining the reference, in *NA v Secretary of State for the Home Department* (Case C-115/15), [2016] 3 WLR 1439, 30 June 2016, at [50]–[51], applying *Singh v Minister for Justice and Equality* (Case C-218/14), [2016] 1 CMLR 12, GC, ECLI:EU:C:2015:476, [2016] QB 208, [2015] 3 WLR 1311, [2016] 1 CMLR 416 (see [63]–[66]).

*[In footnote 6 after each instance of '2006 Regulations' add:]*

, and the 2016 Regulations (SI 2016/1052),

*[In footnote 7 add:]*

This is also the case in the new reg 10(5)(d)(iii), within the 2016 Regulations.

**6.133** *[In line 1, after 'the 2006 Regulations', add:]*

or the 2016 Regulations (SI 2016/1052)

*[In the first sentence, after 'Regulation 15A(2) or (4A) of the 2006 Regulations', add:]*

/ Regulation 16(2) or (5) of the 2016 Regulations,

*[In the final sentence of the main text, after '2006 Regulations', add:]*

/ Regulation 16 of the 2016 Regulations,

*[In footnote 2, before the first comma, add:]*

/ Regulation 16 of the 2016 Regulations,

**Retained rights (ii) death and departure**

**6.134** *[Add at the start of the paragraph:]*

All paragraph numbering in the 2006 Regulations is the same in the 2016 Regulations (SI 2016/1052), in force from 1 February 2017, and all references to the 2006 Regulations in this paragraph should be taken to include reference to the 2016 Regulations.

## DESCENDANTS: CHILDREN

**6.135** *[In line 1, after '2006' add:]*

or 2016

*[In footnote 1, before the full stop, add:]*

; SI 2016/1052

**6.136** *[After 'Regulation 15A of the 2006 Regulations', add:]*

/ Regulation 16 of the 2016 Regulations (SI 2016/1052)

*[In footnote 3, at the end, add:]*

See also the cases in the new footnote 0 to **6.112**, above.

*[In footnote 5, add at the end:]*

See also *NA v Secretary of State for the Home Department* (C-115/15), [2016] 3 WLR 1439, 30 June 2016, at [62]–[68].

**6.137** *[In the text after footnote reference 9, add:]*

The CJEU's decision in *NA v Secretary of State for the Home Department* (C-115/15), [2016] 3 WLR 1439, 30 June 2016 applies these authorities, at [62]–[68].

## RELATIVES IN THE ASCENDING LINE

**6.139** *[In the penultimate sentence after 'Under Regulation 15A(4A) of the 2006 Regulations', add:]*

and under Regulation 16 of the 2016 Regulations,

**Extended family members**

**6.140** *[In the first sentence before the full stop and footnote reference 1, add:]*

which, from 1 February 2017, are replaced by the 2016 Regulations (SI 2016/1052)

*[In sub-para (b) after 'Regulation 8 of the 2006 Regs' add:]*

/ 2016 Regs

*[Delete the next sentence, starting 'Save for durable relationships . . . ', and also delete the indented text, and replace with the following:]*

Save for durable relationships and relatives with serious health issues, Regulation 8(2) of the 2016 Regulations, in force from 1 February 2017 (which is materially the same as its predecessor in the 2006 Regulations), provides, in relation to dependent relatives generally:

> '(2)  The condition in this paragraph is that the person is—
> (a)  a relative of an EEA national; and
> (b)  residing in a country other than the United Kingdom and is dependent upon the EEA national or is a member of the EEA national's household; and either—
> (i)  is accompanying the EEA national to the United Kingdom or wants to join the EEA national in the United Kingdom; or
> (ii)  has joined the EEA national in the United Kingdom and continues to be dependent upon the EEA national, or to be a member of the EEA national's household.'

*[In the tenth bullet point, at the end of the first sentence, add:]*

of the 2006 Regulations, and regulation 12(4)(c)/regulation 18(4)(c) of the 2016 Regulations (SI 2016/1052).

*[In the last bullet point, after both instances of '2006 Regs', add:]*

/ 2016 Regs

*[In footnote 11, add at the end:]*

*Soares* was applied in *AA (Algeria) v Secretary of State for the Home Department* [2014] EWCA Civ 1741, [2015] 2 CMLR 14.

**6.141** *[At the end of the paragraph add:]*

As is noted above, the 2016 Regulations (SI 2016/1052) are materially the same as the equivalent provisions in the 2006 Regulations relating to the definition and basis for entry and residence of 'extended family members'. It follows that the observations made in this paragraph in relation to the 2006 Regulations apply with equal force to those equivalent provisions in the 2016 Regulations.

## Dependency

**6.142** *[Delete the third sentence starting 'There is no need to establish . . . ' and replace with:]*

This question of fact is answered by reference to the question whether the claimant is in fact in a position to support him or herself or not; if he/she can support themselves, there is no dependency, even if he/she is given financial material support by the EU citizen, since those additional resources are not necessary to enable him/her to meet their basic needs. If, on the other hand, he/she cannot support themselves from their own resources, the court will not ask why that is the case, save perhaps where there is an abuse of rights .[1] In *Lim* the Court of Appeal dismissed the appeal, applying the legal approach set out by the Court, since the appellant had savings which she was able to live off, and did not need the regular financial support paid to her by the EEA national to meet her basic needs. The fact that she had decided not to live off her savings, since she wanted to pass them on to her children, did not obviate the fact that she was financially independent.

[1] *Lim v Entry Clearance Officer, Manila* [2015] EWCA Civ 1383 at [32], applying *Reyes v Migrationsverket* (C-423/12),, ECLI:EU:C:2014:16, [2014] QB 1140, [2014] 3 WLR 1101, [2014] All ER (EC) 657. In so holding, the Court of Appeal overruled UTJ Storey's decision in *Lim (EEA – dependency)* [2013] UKUT 00437 (IAC).

## MATERIAL SCOPE (1) DISCRIMINATION AND FREE MOVEMENT

### Non-discrimination

**6.144** *[At the end of the paragraph, add:]*

In the context of popular concern about 'benefit tourism', the CJEU has adopted a similarly stringent approach and has declined to permit claimants to rely on the non-discrimination principle to obviate restrictions on access to social benefits. Notably, in *Dano v Jobcenter Leipzig*,[14] the CJEU ruled that the non-discrimination principle, which was given context-specific effect via Article 24 of the Citizens' Directive, could not even be relied upon, so far as access to social benefits were concerned, since her residence in the host Member State did not comply with the Directive (at [69]). The same applied to the non-discrimination provision within another relevant provision in that case, Art 4 of Reg 883/2004 (at [83]). A similarly restrictive approach was applied by the CJEU in other benefits cases excluding the application of the non-discrimination principle absent the establishment of a right to reside, in *Jobcenter Berlin Leipzig v Alimanovic*[15] and *Garcia Nieto v Vestische Arbeit Jobcenter Kreis Recklinghausen*[16], which are discussed at **6.96** above.[17]Further, in *Commission v UK*,[18] the CJEU upheld the lawfulness of the 'right to reside test' as a gateway to child benefit and child tax credit, inter alia on the basis that, although the national legislation in issue gave rise to unequal treatment between United Kingdom nationals and those of other Member States, such indirect discrimination was lawful and justified by the need to protect the finances of the host Member State.

[14] Case C-333/12, ECLI:EU:C:2014:2358, [2015] 1 WLR 2519, [2015] All ER (EC) 1.
[15] C-67/14, ECLI:EU:C:2015:597, [2016] QB 308, [2016] 2 WLR 208..
[16] Case C-299/14, C-299/14, [2016] 3 CMLR 5, [2016] 1 WLR 3089, [2016] 3 CMLR 77, [2016] All ER (D) 257 (Feb)..
[17] See also *Mirga v Secretary of State for Work and Pensions; Samin v Westminster City Council (Secretary of State for Communities and Local Government and another intervening)* [2016] UKSC 1, [2016] 2 All ER 447,[2016] 1 WLR 481 which is also addressed there.
[18] C-308/14, [2016] 1 WLR 5049.

### Non-discriminatory obstacles to free movement

**6.148** *[In the text after footnote reference 5, insert:]*

In *Commission v Belgium*,[5a] the CJEU held that Belgian language requirements for certain public sector jobs amounted to disproportionate, discriminatory and unlawful obstacles to free movement.

[5a] C-317/14,[2015] 2 CMLR 1347.


## MATERIAL SCOPE (2) RIGHT TO ENTER AND RESIDE

### Right to arrive, enter and reside

**6.152** *[In footnote 4, at the end of the sentence, add:]*

; also reg 6 in the 2016 EEA Regulations (SI 2016/1052)

**6.153** *[Insert at the end of the first sentence:]*

, as in the 2016 Regulations (reg 2(1))

*[At the end of the second sentence, insert:]*

, which are superseded by the 2016 Regulations (SI 2016/1052) from 1 February 2017 (all references to the 2006 Regulations in this paragraph remain the same in the 2016 Regulations)

**6.154** *[In the first sentence before the first comma, add:]*

, which are superseded by the 2016 Regulations (SI 2016/1052) from 1 February 2017

*[In footnotes 1, 5, 6 and 7, at the end of each footnote text add:]*

The numbering is the same in the 2016 Regulations.

*[At the end of footnote 3 add:]*

There are transitional provisions in place for the family members of dual nationals under para 9 of Sch 6 to the 2016 Regulations, inserted by SI 2017/1, amending the 2016 Regulations.

*[In footnote 8 add:]*

Regulations 16–20 of the 2016 Regulations.

*[In the main text, after footnote reference 9, and after the words 'Under Regulation 19', add:]*

of the 2006 Regulations, and reg 23 of the 2016 Regulations,

*[In the following sentence, starting 'Regulations 22 and 24', add after '24':]*

of the 2006 Regulations, and regs 29 and 32 of the 2016 Regulations,


### Right of residence

**6.155** *[At the end of the fourth sentence after '(reg 18)' add:]*

; in the 2016 Regulations (SI 2016/1052), the relevant provisions are regs 17 (registration certificates), 18 (family permits/residence cards for family and extended family members) and 19 (document certifying permanent residence).

The 2016 Regulations' requirements in this respect also match the requirements of the Citizens' Directive.

*[At the end of footnote 2 add:]*

See *R (Santos) v Secretary of State for the Home Department* [2016] EWHC 609 (Admin), [2016] 3 CMLR 251, 166 NLJ 7695 for a case in which damages were awarded for the UK's breach of EU law in failing to issue a residence card to an EEA family member, who was also unlawfully detained and removed in breach of EU law. It is understood that an appeal is pending to the Court of Appeal at the time of writing.

**6.156** *[At the end of the second paragraph, insert:]*

Under the 2016 Regulations (SI 2016/1052), extended family members are also dealt with at reg 8; while revocation is dealt with under reg 24.

## Types of residence

**6.157**

*[In the last paragraph, the reference to 'Regulation 15A of the EEA Regulations' should be replaced with:]*

reg 15A of the 2006 Regulations/ reg 16 of the 2016 Regulations (SI 2016/1052)

**6.158** *[In the second substantive paragraph, after 'Regulation 4(4) of the 2006 Regulations', add:*

/ 2016 Regulations (SI 2016/1052)

*[In the final paragraph, first sentence, after 'reg 16 of the 2006 Regulations', add:]*

/ reg 17 of the 2016 Regulations

*[In footnote 3, before the first full stop, add:]*

/ reg 17(5) and (6) of the 2016 Regulations

*[In footnote 5, add:]*

; also reg 6(2) in the 2016 Regulations.

## Permanent residence in the UK

**6.159**

*[At the end of footnote 1 add:]*

, and in regulation 15 of the 2016 EEA Regulations (SI 2016/1052)

*[At the end of footnote 3 add:]*

The derived rights of residence are contained in regulation 16 of the 2016 Regulations.

**Ziolkowski and Szeja**

**6.164** *[Add a fifth bullet point as follows:]*

- In *Oyekan v Secretary of State for the Home Department*,[6] the Court of Appeal upheld the UT's decision that the deportation of V would be unlawful. The CA accepted that V, a national of another Member State, could rely on residence in a host state, the UK, before the host state's accession to the EU, in the same way that they could rely on residence in a host state before the home Member State's accession, applying *Ziolkowski* at [45]. Furthermore, the CA held that the Immigration (European Economic Area) Regulations 2006, Sch 4, para 6, providing that an EU national's period of residence in the UK could not count towards the five years' continuous residence entitling them to a right of permanent residence if they then spent over two years not undertaking qualifying activities within Sch 4, para 6, did not fail to accurately transpose Directive 2004/38/EC.

[6]   [2016] EWCA Civ 1352.

**6.165** *[At the end of the paragraph add:]*

In *AA (Nigeria) v Secretary of State for the Home Department*,[4] the Court of Appeal held that AA had not lost his right of permanent residence in the UK by the commission of an offence of drug importation and a six-year sentence of imprisonment. The Court held that, to interpret Directive 2004/38/EC, Art 16(4) as allowing for the right of permanent residence to be lost by reason of criminality or a resulting sentence of imprisonment, so that serious grounds of public policy no longer had to be shown in order to justify expulsion, would be to subvert the legislative scheme.

[4]   [2015] EWCA Civ 1249, 2015] All ER (D) 76 (Dec).

**Retained right of residence**

**6.166** *[At the end of footnote 1 add:]*

; and regs 15 and 19 of the 2016 Regulations.

**6.167** *[Insert as a new paragraph after the bullet points:]*

In *NA v Secretary of State for the Home Department*,[4] the CJEU held that it was necessary that the EEA national former spouse be residing lawfully in accordance with the Directive at the time of divorce in order that the non-EEA party may retain the right of residence thereunder.

[4]   Case C-115/15, [2016] 3 WLR 1439.

**Appeals against adverse decisions**

**6.168** *[Replace entire paragraph:]*

The Immigration (European Economic Area) Regulations 2016 (SI 2016/1052) are in force from 1 February 2017.[1]

The right of appeal against an adverse 'EEA decision'[2] is contained in Part 6 of the 2016 Regulations.[3] The appeal lies to the First-tier Tribunal (Immigration and Asylum Chamber), except where it raises national security issues; or the interests of the relationship between the UK and another country, when it lies to the Special Immigration Appeals Commission. Jurisdiction arises from reg 36; it does not arise from s 82 of the Nationality, Immigration and Asylum Act 2002 (NNIA 2002). EEA nationals may only appeal if they produce a valid national identity card/EEA passport: reg 36(2).[4] If a person claims to be in a durable relationship with an EEA national he may only appeal if he produces: (a) a passport; and (b) either (i) an EEA family permit; or (ii) sufficient evidence to satisfy the Secretary of State that he is in a *relationship* with that EEA national (ie it will be necessary to see whether in the refusal letter the SSHD accepts that there is at least a relationship even if it is not accepted to be a durable one). Regulation 36(3)–(6) imposes on family members the burden of satisfying the tribunal of their relationship to the EEA national as a fact precedent to the existence of jurisdiction (although tribunals will in practice hear the appeal substantively on all issues and determine the jurisdictional issues first). Regulation 36(7) empowers the SSHD to certify a ground, thereby preventing them from bringing an appeal, if it has been considered in a previous appeal brought under the 2006 EEA Regulations or under s 82 of the 2002 Act. Regulation 36(10) incorporates specified provisions of the Nationality Immigration and Asylum Act 2002 that are listed in Sch 2 to the 2016 Regulations, which relate to the tribunal's powers in the exercise of the appellate jurisdiction.

Note that, in a departure from generally accepted practice, the Upper Tribunal had ruled in *Sala* that under the 2006 Regulations, there was no statutory right of appeal against the decision of the SSHD to refuse to grant a residence card to a person claiming to be an Extended Family Member.[5] In *Sala*, the SSHD had accepted that the relationship was genuine, although not 'durable' under reg 8(5). An 'Extended Family Member' is defined in both the 2006 and 2016 Regulations at reg 8 in materially the same terms. The appropriate means of challenge is therefore currently judicial review. Post-*Sala* the Home Office updated its policy guidance for the 2006 Regulations, so as to reflect the Upper Tribunal's ruling that there are no appeal rights for such persons.[6]

Now, reg 2 of the 2016 Regulations makes it unambiguously clear that the decision to refuse to issue an EEA family permit, registration certificate or issue of residence card to an Extended Family Member does not constitute an 'EEA decision' for the purposes of the Regulations, and therefore is not subject to the appellate jurisdiction of the First-tier Tribunal.

In *Bilal Ahmed*[7] the Upper Tribunal held that where an applicant had made an application for a residence card as the spouse EEA national, but had no other form of leave in his own right, and had been refused a residence card on grounds that the SSHD suspected that the marriage was one of convenience, he could be removed while his appeal against that refusal was pending. The fact that such a person had a right of appeal under the EEA Regulations did not prevent the SSHD from removing him under s 10 of the Immigration and Asylum Act 1999, such that the appeal had to be exercised from abroad. The Upper Tribunal confirmed that the factual issue as to whether the Appellant is indeed a family member (ie whether the marriage is a genuine one in the case of *Bilal Ahmed)* is to be determined on appeal to the First-tier Tribunal, but such an appeal can be pursued out of country. The rationale for that was said to derive from reg 2 of the 2006 Regulations which provided that a spouse does not include a party to a marriage of convenience; the same is reproduced in the 2016 Regulations. Accordingly, a person alleged to have been part of a sham marriage is not entitled to an in-country right of appeal, since they are no longer within the scope of EU law.[8] The decision has since been upheld by the Court of Appeal.[9]

In *Shehu*,[10] the Upper Tribunal was invited to revisit *Ahmed*, on the basis that the Court of Appeal had failed adequately to consider Article 31 of the Citizens' Directive and the question of procedural safeguards. It declined to do so on the basis that the redress procedure required by Articles 31 and 35 of the Directive do not make it necessary to treat EEA appeals of any kind as suspensive, since arrangements can be made, on the conditions set out in Article 31.4 for re-admission of a person for the purposes of submitting his defence.[11]

Where an individual raises both EEA and Article 8 grounds to challenge an EEA removal decision, the correct approach is first to determine if the person satisfied the requirements under the EEA requirements; here ss 117A–117D of NIAA 2002 has no application. If Article 8 is raised as a ground, then sections 117A–117D of NIAA 2002 falls to be considered.[12]

[1] The Immigration (European Economic Area) (Amendment) Regulations 2017 (SI 2017/1) insert a new para 3 into Sch 4 to the 2016 Regulations, to address savings in respect of appeals and rights of appeal under the 2006 Regulations. Paragraph 3 provides that nothing in the 2016 Regulations affects an appeal against, or a person's right to appeal against, an EEA decision taken under the 2006 Regulations.

[2] An 'EEA decision' is defined in reg 2(1) as a decision under these Regulations that concerns—
   (a)   a person's entitlement to be admitted to the United Kingdom;
   (b)   a person's entitlement to be issued with or have renewed, or not to have revoked, a registration certificate, residence card, derivative residence card, document certifying permanent residence or permanent residence card (but does not include a decision that an application for the above documentation is invalid);
   (c)   a person's removal from the United Kingdom; or
   (d)   the cancellation, under regulation 25, of a person's right to reside in the United Kingdom, but does not include a decision to refuse to issue a document under regulation 12(4) (issue of an EEA family permit to an extended family member), 17(5) (issue of a registration certificate to an extended family member) or 18(4) (issue of a residence card to an extended family member), a decision to reject an application under regulation 26(4) (misuse of a right to reside: material change of circumstances), or any decisions under regulation 33 (human rights considerations and interim orders to suspend removal) or 41 (temporary admission to submit case in person).

[3] SI 2016/1052.

[4] Note SSHD's discretion to accept alternative evidence of identity and nationality if a person is unable to produce the required evidence due to circumstances beyond their control: reg 42.

[5] *Sala (EFMs: Rights of Appeal)* [2016] UKUT 00411 (IAC).

[6] See Home Office, *Extended Family Members of EEA Nationals*, v 3.0, published 22 September 2016, p 14, available online at: https://www.gov.uk/government/uploads/system/uploads/attac hment_data/file/554777/Extended_family_members_of_EEA_nationals_v3.pdf accessed on 11 Dec 2016.

[7] *R (on the application of Bilal Ahmed) v Secretary of State for the Home Department [EEA/s10 appeal rights: effect] IJR* [2015] UKUT 436 (IAC), [2015] All ER (D) 47 (Aug). See also *R (on the application of Rajput) v Secretary of State for the Home Department* [2015] EWHC 2051 (Admin) (21 July 2015) in which the High Court also held that the EEA Regulations do not guarantee an in-country right of appeal in cases involving an allegation of marriage of convenience.

[8] Note, however, that the appellant in *Bilal Ahmed* fell to be considered under s 10 of the Immigration and Asylum Act 1999, which has since been amended by the Immigration Act

2014. In *Bilal Ahmed*, the relevant version of s 10 in force at the time provided: '(1) A person who is not a British citizen may be removed from the United Kingdom, in accordance with directions given by an immigration officer, if— . . . .'. By contrast, s 10 as amended by the Immigration Act 2014 now reads: '(1) A person may be removed from the United Kingdom under the authority of the Secretary of State or an immigration officer if the person requires leave to enter or remain in the United Kingdom but does not have it'. A person who is the direct family member of an EEA national exercising Treaty rights (eg a spouse) does not require leave to enter or remain in the UK. It may therefore be possible to distinguish the position in *Bilal Ahmed* from cases where the removal decision is made under the amended s 10. However, given that the Court of Appeal has refused permission to appeal, it remains the case that an appeal against the allegation of a sham marriage is non-suspensive and will be pursued out of country.

⁹  [2016] EWCA Civ 303, [2016] All ER (D) 106 (Jun), [2016] All ER (D) 106 (Jun).

¹⁰ *R (on the application of Shehu) v Secretary of State for the Home Department (Citizens' Directive – no suspensive appeals) IJR* [2016] UKUT 00287 (IAC).

¹¹ See also *Re Judicial Review Pana (AP)* [2016] CSOH 16, 2016 SLT 523, Ct of Sess (19 January 2016), in which the Court of Session discusses the Commission's commentary on suspensive appeals in respect of an earlier draft of the Directive, which interestingly is cited at para 24 of the decision per Lady Scott: 'that "Giving appeals automatic suspensory effect would not be a suitable solution, since it would lay the arrangements open to abuse" and (b) the Recital (28) which specifically states that in order to guard against abuse, notably by marriages of convenience, Member States would have the possibility of adopting "necessary measures". I agree with the respondent that this further underlines that the intention of the Directive was to allow for restriction of the rights conferred and the limitation of procedural safeguards, in order to prevent abuse.'

¹² *Badewa (ss 117A-D and EEA Regulations)* [2015] UKUT 00329 (IAC).

### 6.169 *[Replace entire paragraph:]*

An appeal can be brought 'in-country' unless specified to the contrary by reg 37(1), which lists as out of country the following EEA decisions:

(a)    to refuse to admit that person to the United Kingdom;

(b)    to revoke that person's admission to the United Kingdom;

(c)    to make an exclusion order against that person;

(d)    to refuse to revoke a deportation or exclusion order made against the person;

(e)    to refuse to issue the person with an EEA family permit;

(f)    to revoke, or to refuse to issue or renew any document under these Regulations where that decision is taken at a time when the person is outside the United Kingdom; or

(g)    to remove the person from the United Kingdom following entry to the United Kingdom in breach of a deportation or exclusion order, or in circumstances where that person was not entitled to be admitted pursuant to reg 23(1), (2), (3) or (4).

Regulation 37(2) provides that paragraphs 37(1)(a) to (c) do not apply where the person is in the United Kingdom and:

(a)    the person holds a valid EEA family permit, registration certificate, residence card, derivative residence card, document certifying permanent residence, permanent residence card or qualifying EEA State residence card on arrival in the United Kingdom or the person can otherwise prove that the person is resident in the United Kingdom; or

(b)    the person is deemed not to have been admitted to the United Kingdom under reg 29(3) but at the date on which notice of the decision to refuse admission is given the person has been in the United Kingdom for at least three months.

Note that where no notice under s 120 of NIAA 2002 has been served and where no EEA decision to remove has been made, an appellant cannot bring Human Rights challenge to removal in an appeal under the EEA Regulations: *Amirteymour and others (EEA appeals; human rights)*.[1]

In *TY (Sri Lanka) v Secretary of State for the Home Department*,[2] the Court of Appeal considered the position where the claim is one for asylum, finding that the immigration tribunal cannot consider an appeal on asylum grounds against an application and decision made under EU law. If a section 120 notice is served by the SSHD, then the situation would be different.[1]

[1]   [2015] UKUT 00466 (IAC).
[2]   [2015] EWCA Civ 1233 (1 December 2015).
[1]   See *JM (Liberia) v Secretary of State for the Home Department* [2006] EWCA Civ 1402, [2006] INLR 548, which both the Court of Appeal and Upper Tribunal distinguished from *Amiteymour* and *TY*, because a one-stop notice had been served on the appellant in that case.


## EXCLUSION, TERMINATION OF THE RIGHT TO RESIDE AND EXPULSION

### Cessation and public policy

**6.170** *[Replace 'the 2006 Regulations' with 'the 2016 Regulations' in the main text.]*

**6.171** *[Insert new paragraph after main text:]*

The unique position of Irish nationals is worth noting and was considered by the High Court of Northern Ireland in *Re Doherty's application for Judicial Review* .[3] A dual British and Irish citizen was convicted in the UK of sexual offences against a minor. The conditions of his licence, which extended until 2018, included that he not travel outside the UK without prior permission of his probation officer. After he served his custodial sentence, the applicant sought to live with his Irish partner in the Republic of Ireland, which he regarded as his permanent home. He renounced his British citizenship, and unusually, requested that the SSHD deport him to the Republic of Ireland. That request was refused on the basis that while Irish nationality does not provide automatic exemption from deportation, as a matter of policy, deportation of Irish nationals is only in the public interest in exceptional circumstances. Typically, this must involve an offence involving national security or crime that poses a serious risk to the safety or the public or a section of the public, where they had received a custodial sentence of 10 years or more for a terrorist offence, murder or a serious sexual or violent offence. The Applicant did not meet the policy criteria because he was sentenced to less than 10 years albeit for a sexual offence. He sought to challenge the decision by way of judicial review. The High Court of Northern Ireland held that the challenge on the basis of discrimination was misconceived: the central issue was whether it was lawful for the SSHD to compel the applicant to remain within the UK until the expiry of his licence in 2018. The real reason for the restriction on the applicant's free movement rights was not his nationality, but rather because he was subject to a lawful sentence imposed by the courts in this jurisdiction. Further, the special agreement made between the UK and Irish governments in respect with Irish FNOs was held to be both lawful and proportionate. There was a reasonable and objective justification for treating Irish offenders differently from others, given that an Irish national would find it relatively easy to return to the UK meaning that the Secretary of State was entitled to aim to achieve their rehabilitation before they did so.

[3]   [2016] NIQB 62.

### Enforcement powers under domestic law

**6.172** *[Delete and replace the paragraph with:]*

As in the previous 2006 Regulations,[1] the relevant provisions of which are set out in the principal text of the 9th Edition of this work (in which the associated case law will remain relevant to the operation of the similarly worded provisions in the 2016 Regulations), Parts 4 and 5 of the 2016 Regulations (SI 2016/1052) provide for a range of discretionary enforcement powers to deprive a person of documentary proof of EU residence right, to remove such persons, to 'verify' residence rights, and to restrict appeal rights:

(1)   Regulation 24(1) empowers the Secretary of State to revoke, or refuse to issue or renew proof of an EU residence right (ie a registration certificate, residence card, a document certifying permanent residence or a permanent residence card) where such action is justified on the grounds of public policy, public security or public health, or on grounds of abuse of rights in accordance with reg 26(3) (which is addressed below). Regulation 24(3)–(5) makes provision for the revocation/refusal to issue residence documentation where the holder 'ceases to have, or never had, a right to reside under these Regulations'. As to the revocation of residence rights of EEA nationals, see **6.175** below.

(2)   Regulation 23 provides for:
   •   refusal of entry on the grounds of public policy, public security or public health (reg 23(1));
   •   refusal of entry to a person subject to a deportation or exclusion order, unless they are temporarily admitted under reg 41 (reg 23(2));
   •   refusal of entry if the Secretary of State has reasonable grounds to suspect that the person's admissions would lead to a misuse of a right to reside under reg 26(1) (reg 23(3));
   •   refusal of entry as a family member of an EEA national under reg 11(2) unless at the time of the arrival that person is accompanying the EEA national or joining the EEA national in the UK, and the EEA national has a right to reside (reg 23(4));
   •   the making of an exclusion order prohibiting a person from entering the UK where the public policy proviso is satisfied (reg 23(5));
   •   the removal of persons:

- who do not have, or cease to have, a right to reside under the Regulations (reg 23(6)(a));
- whose removal the SSHD has decided is justified on grounds of public policy, public security or public health in accordance with reg 27 (reg 23(6)(b));
- whose removal the SSHD has decided is justified on grounds of misuse of rights under reg 26(3) (reg 23(6)(c));

• a person must not be removed under reg 23(6) as the automatic consequence of having recourse to the social assistance system of the UK (reg 23(7)(a)). A person must not be removed under the same provision if the person has leave to remain under the 1971 Act unless removal is justified on the grounds of public policy, public security or public health in accordance with reg 27 (reg 23(7)(b));

• a deportation order made in pursuance of a decision under para (6)(b) must state that the relevant person is prohibited from entering the UK under the order is revoked (reg 23(8)(a)) or for the period specified in the order (reg 23(8)(b));

• decisions taken under para (6)(b) or (c) has the effect of terminating any right to reside otherwise enjoyed by the individual concerned (reg 23(9)).

Regulation 27 regulates decisions taken on the basis of public policy, public security and public health: see **6.176** onwards. Regulation 27 is the equivalent of the former regulation 21 of the 2006 Regulations. Regulation 27 provides the existing 'enhanced protection' provisions ('serious' and 'imperative' grounds) in subsections (3) and (4). The list of principles by which such decisions should comply are also listed in subsection (5), save that the following underlined text is new:

(a) the decision must comply with the principle of proportionality;
(b) the decision must be based exclusively on the personal conduct of the person concerned;
(c) the personal conduct of the person must represent a genuine, present and sufficiently serious threat affecting one of the fundamental interests of society, taking into account past conduct of the person and that the threat does not need to be imminent;
(d) matters isolated from the particulars of the case or which relate to considerations of general prevention do not justify the decision;
(e) a person's previous criminal convictions do not in themselves justify the decision;
(f) the decision may be taken on preventative grounds, even in the absence of a previous criminal conviction, provided the grounds are specific to the person.

The underlined provisions clearly are an attempt to lower the applicable hurdle; however, the additions do not appear to be entirely compatible with the need for 'present' risk as recognised in reg 27 and in the equivalent wording of the Citizens' Directive. The Upper Tribunal had previously held that there is no hierarchy of weight or importance in these various considerations when considering the analogous provision in the 2006 Regulations.[2]

[1]   See Parts 4 and 5 of the 2006 Regulations for the previous enforcement provisions.

2    *Abdul (Section 55 – Article 24(3) Charter)* [2016] UKUT 106, in which the Upper Tribunal considered reg 21(6) of the 2006 Regulations.

**6.173**  *[After footnote reference 2 in the text, delete the text starting 'Furthermore . . . ' to the end of the paragraph and replace with:]*

Furthermore, the EEA Regulations provide[3] that a person is not to be removed as an automatic consequence of having recourse to the social assistance system in the UK. They also provide that when a decision to remove is made under reg 23(6)(a) because the person ceases to be qualified, the person is to be treated as if he or she were a person to whom s 10(1)(a) of the Immigration and Asylum Act 1999 Act applied, and s 10 of that Act (removal of certain persons unlawfully in the UK) is to apply accordingly.[4] Where the decision to remove is taken under reg 26(6)(b) under the public policy proviso, that person is to be treated as if he were a person to whom s 3(5)(a) of the 1971 Act (liability to deportation) applied, and s 5 of that Act (procedure for deportation) and Sch 3 to that Act (supplementary provision as to deportation) are to apply accordingly.[5] Normally the person is given one month in which to leave, before removal is carried out.[6]

3    SI 2016/1052, reg 23(7)(a).
4    SI 2016/1052, reg 32(2).
5    SI 2016/1052, reg 32(3).
6    SI 2016/1052, reg 32(6).

**6.174**  *[N.B.]*

A decision to remove an individual under reg 26(3) (public policy proviso) or (4) (following entry in breach of a deportation order) or to revoke a person's admission under reg 31 where they were never entitled to be admitted, has the effect of invalidating a residence document: reg 24(2).

**6.175**  *[Replace 'the 2006 Regulations' with 'the 2016 Regulations' in the main text.]*

*[Replace footnote 1 with:]*

SI 2016/1052, Sch 1, para 6.

## Public policy, security and health

**6.176**  *[Replace 'the 2006 EEA Regulations' with 'the 2016 Regulations' in the main text.]*

## Implementing the public policy proviso

**6.177**  *[Replace footnote 4 with:]*

SI 2016/1052, reg 26 and Sch 1, para 6. Regulation 27 deals with decisions on the grounds of public policy, public security and public health.

**6.179**  *[Replace '2006 Regulations' with '2016 Regulations' in the main text.]*

*[In footnote 2 replace the first sentence with:]*

Reproduced in the 2016 Regulations, reg 27(6).

*[Replace footnote 4 with:]*

2016 Regulations (SI 2016/1052), reg 27(3). In *Bulale v Secretary of State for the Home Department* [2008] EWCA Civ 806, [2009] QB 536, [2009] 2 WLR 992 the Court of Appeal said that there was no need to refer questions going to the meaning or effect of the word 'serious', as that would be to invite an attempt at definition of a concept that the legislation treats either as indefinable or as sufficient in itself to guide the decisions of Member States. Note that the right to permanent residence would not be lost merely by reason of criminality or a resulting sentence of imprisonment: *AA (Nigeria) v Secretary of State for the Home Department* [2015] EWCA Civ 1249, [2015] All ER (D) 76 (Dec).

*[Replace footnote 7 with:]*

2016 Regulations, reg 27(4).

*[At the end of footnote 8 add:]*

The decision in *MG (Portugal)* was applied by the Court of Appeal in *Warsame v Secretary of State for the Home Department* [2016] EWCA Civ 16, [2016] 4 WLR 77, [2016] 2 CMLR 861 in which it was held that a sentence of imprisonment in the ten years must in principle prevent the accrual of ten years' relevant residence for the purposes of Article 28. If the migrant had been present for ten years, albeit without continuity due to imprisonment, then an overall assessment must be made when considering if they are integrated. The view in *FV (Italy)* [2013] 1 WLR 339, that periods of imprisonment could be included when calculating length of residence, could not be sustained in light of *MG (Portugal)*.

*[At the end of footnote 9 add:]*

On *Essa* principles in general, see also updated discussion at **6.187** below and the Court of Appeal decision in *R (on the application of Dumliauskas and others) v Secretary of State for the Home Department* [2015] EWCA Civ 145, in which the principles have been significantly recast.

*[Insert the following new paragraph at the end of the main text:]*

The issue of enhanced protection and permanent residence has recently been considered by the Supreme Court in *Secretary of State for the Home Department v Franco Vomero (Italy)* .[11] FV had served four years in prison for manslaughter. Eight months after his release from prison, the SSHD decided to deport him under regs 9(3)(b) and 21 of the 2006 Regulations, which gave effect to Article 28 of the Citizens' Directive. The respondent did not have a right of permanent residence under Article 16, as he had not legally resided in the UK for a continuous five-year period prior to the Directive's entry into force. He had, however, resided in the UK for 10 years prior to the deportation decision, notwithstanding his imprisonment. This point was accepted by the Court of Appeal, and accordingly, he enjoyed the enhanced protection of Article 28(3)(a) of the Directive: only imperative grounds of public security could justify expulsion. The SSHD appealed.

Interestingly, while a majority of the Supreme Court favoured the view that possession of a right of permanent residence is not needed in order to enjoy enhanced protection under Article 28(3)(a), a minority regarded the position as unclear. Accordingly, the following question was referred to the Court of Justice:

(1)     *Whether enhanced protection under article 28(3)(a) depends upon the possession of a right of permanent residence within article 16 and article 28(2).*

If the answer to question 1 is negative, the Supreme Court also considered it appropriate to refer two further questions:

(2)     *Whether the period of residence for the previous ten years, to which Article 28(3)(a) refers, is (a) a simple calendar period looking back from the relevant date (here that of the decision to deport), including in it any periods of absence or imprisonment, (b) a potentially non-continuous period, derived by looking back from the relevant date and adding together period(s) when the relevant person was not absent or in prison, to arrive, if possible, at a total of ten years' previous residence.*

(3)     *What the true relationship is between the ten-year residence test to which Article 28(3(a) refers and the overall assessment of an integrative link.*

Any future ruling by the CJEU may bring further much needed clarity to the interpretation of Article 28 of the Directive, albeit in a political environment which is growing increasingly hostile with respect to the rights of EEA offenders with lengthy residence in the UK. That much is evident from the fact that the new 2016 Regulations expressly provide that continuity of residence is broken when a person serves a sentence of imprisonment.[12]

Note that reg 3(4) provides that this applies in principle to an EEA national who has resided in the UK for at least 10 years, but does not apply where the SSHD considers that:

(a)     prior to serving a sentence of imprisonment, the EEA national had forged integrating links with the United Kingdom;

(b)     the effect of the sentence of imprisonment was not such as to break those integrating links;

(c)     taking into account an overall assessment of the EEA national's situation, it would not be appropriate to apply para (3)(a) to the assessment of that EEA national's continuity of residence.

[11]   [2016] UKSC 49 (27 July 2016).
[12]   SI 2016/1052, reg 2(3)(a). In addition, reg 2(3) provides continuity of residence is broken when a deportation or exclusion order is made (para (b)) or when a person is removed from the UK (para (c)). No such discretion applies in those cases, as does where continuity is broken by means of a prison sentence.

## Early case law on the public policy proviso

**6.186** *[After the main text add:]*

Save in exceptionally serious cases, it is difficult to see how the desire to reflect public revulsion has any application in EEA expulsions on public or-der grounds: *Straszevwski*[6] disapproving of the view in certain older cases like

*Bouchereau* and *Marchon* that particularly horrifying crimes might themselves justify deportation; the Court of Appeal observed that EEA law was distinct from UK domestic law on this point.

6   [2015] EWCA Civ 1245 (3 December 2015)

*Proportionality*

**6.187** *[In footnote 9 add:]*

The *Essa* principles on rehabilitation have been the subject of discussion in subsequent case law. In *R (on the application of Dumliauskas and others) v Secretary of State for the Home Department* [2015] EWCA Civ 145, [2015] All ER (D) 307 (Feb), the Court of Appeal significantly recast the *Essa* principles. Whereas the Upper Tribunal in *Essa* had concluded that the prospects of rehabilitation in the offender's home state are relevant to the decision to deport only if he acquired a permanent right of residence, the Court of Appeal disagreed. Once proportionality is engaged, the factors to be taken into account do not vary with the qualifications of the individual. However, what is affected by length of legal residence (in the sense used in Article 16.1) is the weight to be given to the respective prospects of rehabilitation. In the case of an offender with no permanent right of residence, substantial weight should not be given to rehabilitation.

The Upper Tribunal considered *Dumliauskas* in *MC (Essa principles recast) Portugal* [2015] UKUT 520 (IAC), summarising the principles as follows:

(a)   *Essa* rehabilitation principles are specific to decisions taken on public policy, public security and public health grounds under reg 21 of the 2006 EEA Regulations;

(b)   it is only if the personal conduct of the person concerned is found to represent a genuine, present and sufficiently serious threat affecting one of the fundamental interests of society (reg 21(5)(c)) that it becomes relevant to consider whether the decision is proportionate taking into account all the considerations identified in reg 21(5)–(6);

(c)   there is no specific reference in the expulsion provisions of either Directive 2004/38/EC or the 2006 EEA Regulations to rehabilitation, but it has been seen by the Court of Justice as an aspect of integration, which is one of the factors referred to in Article 28(1) and reg 21(6) (*Essa* (2013) at [23]);

(d)   rehabilitation is not an issue to be addressed in every EEA deportation or removal decision taken under reg 21; it will not be relevant, for example, if rehabilitation has already been completed (*Essa* (2013) at [32]–[33]);

(e)   reference to prospects of rehabilitation concerns reasonable prospects of a person ceasing to commit crime (*Essa* (2013) at [35]), not the mere possibility of rehabilitation;

(f)   where relevant (see (d) above) such prospects are a factor to be taken into account in the proportionality assessment required by reg 21(5) and (6) (*Dumliauskas* at [41]);

(g)   such prospects are to be taken into account even if not raised by the offender (*Dumliauskas* at [52]);

(h)     gauging such prospects requires assessing the relative prospects of rehabilitation in the host Member State as compared with those in the Member State of origin, but, in the absence of evidence, it is not to be assumed that prospects are materially different in that other Member State (*Dumliauskas* at [46], [52], [53] and [59]);

(i)     matters that are relevant when examining the prospects of the rehabilitation of offenders include family ties and responsibilities, accommodation, education, training, employment, active membership of a community and the like (*Essa* (2013) at [34]). However, lack of access to a Probation Officer or equivalent in the other Member State should not, in general, preclude deportation (*Dumliauskas* at [55]);

(j)     in the absence of integration and a right of permanent residence, the future prospects of integration cannot be a weighty factor (*Dumliauskas* at [44] and [54]). Even when such prospects have significant weight they are not a trump card, as what the Directive and the 2006 EEA Regulations require is a wide-ranging holistic assessment. Both recognise that the more serious the risk of reoffending, and the offences that a person may commit, the greater the right to interfere with the right of residence (*Dumliauskas* at [46] and [54]).

### Abuse of Rights/Misuse of Rights

**6.191** *[Replace entire paragraph:]*

The 2016 Regulations (SI 2016/1052) includes a provision at reg 26, 'Misuse of a right to reside,' (as opposed to 'abuse' which appeared in the 2006 Regulations) which defines the concept as occurring where a person:

(a)     observes the requirements of the Regulations in circumstances which do not achieve the purpose of the Regulations (as determined by reference to the Citizens' Directive and the Treaties); and

(b)     intends to obtain an advantage from these Regulations by engaging in conduct which artificially creates the conditions required to satisfy the criteria set out in these Regulations.

Regulation 26(2) provides that such misuse 'includes' attempting to enter the UK within 12 months of being removed under reg 23(6)(a), where the person attempting to do so is unable to provide evidence that upon re-entry to the UK, the conditions for a right to reside, other than the initial right of residence under reg 13, will be met.

Regulation 26(3) gives the Secretary of State a discretion to take an EEA decision on the grounds of abuse of rights 'where there are reasonable grounds to suspect the misuse of a right to reside and it is proportionate to do so'. Regulation 26(6) states that 'this regulation may not be involved systematically'. A misuse of rights' decision under reg 26 can be the basis for revocation/denial of a residence document (reg 24(1)), denial of entry (reg 23(3)), a decision to remove (reg 23(6)(c)), and cancellation of a right of residence (reg 25).

Regulation 26(4) provides that where a person is removed pursuant to reg 23(6)(a) – ie that they do not have or cease to have a right to reside – then that person may apply during the 12-month period after removal, to the

Secretary of State to have the decision set aside on the basis that there has been a material change in circumstances. Such an application may only be made when the individual is outside the UK: reg 26(5).

*Appeal to the First-tier Tribunal*

**6.195** *[Replace entire paragraph:]*

Regulation 36 of the 2016 EEA Regulations (SI 2016/1052) establishes the jurisdiction of the FTT to hear appeals against 'EEA decisions,' which are defined in reg 2(1) and include removal for the UK under reg 23, removals justified on public policy etc grounds: see **6.169** above. In 2014, the Home Office amended the 2006 Regulations to allow deportation to proceed before the completion of an EEA national's appeal to the Tribunal – commonly referred to as the 'deport first, appeal later' rules. Regulation 33 in the 2016 Regulations is drafted in near identical terms to reg 24AA in the 2006 Regulations. Under reg 33(2), the SSHD may only make removal directions before an appeal is begun or finally determined if she certifies that removal pending the outcome of that appeal would not be unlawful under s 6 of the Human Rights Act 1998. Regulation 33(3) provides that the grounds upon which the SSHD 'may certify a removal include (in particular) that P would not, before the appeal is finally determined, face a real risk of serious irreversible harm if removed to the country or territory to which P is proposed to be removed'. Where a person's removal on the basis of reg 23(6)(b) is enforced, they are entitled to pursue their appeal against removal outside of the UK, but may apply to the SSHD for temporary admission to re-enter the UK, for the purposes of attending their appeal under reg 41. A very similar provision was contained at reg 29AA of the 2006 Regulations. 'Appearance' refers to the person's formal presence at his appeal.[1] Note that the right to temporary admission does not extend to the pre-hearing stages of the appeal.[2] Under reg 41(3), the SSHD must grant the person temporary admission unless his appearance 'may cause serious troubles to public policy or public security'. This reflects the wording of Article 31.4 of the Citizens Directive. In ascertaining whether the exception applies, the possibility of managing the risk by detention or conditions is a factor to be taken into account.[3]

After the person's attendance at their appeal, reg 41(5) states that the person 'may be removed' pending determination of their appeal, but they may return to the UK to make submissions in person during the remaining stages of the redress procedure under reg 41. Regulation 34(3) governs applications to revoke a deportation order by a person who is outside the UK following a material change in circumstances.

The upshot then, as with the 2006 Regulations, is that an appeal will not automatically suspend removal,[4] unless the SSHD has *not* certified the appeal (reg 33(3)) or where the person has applied for an interim order to suspend removal (reg 33(4)). Note, however, that an application for an interim order will not suspended removal where the removal decision is based on a previous judicial decision (reg 33(4)(a)); where the person has had previous access to a judicial review (reg 33(4)(b)) or where the removal decision is based on imperative grounds of public security (reg 33(4)(c)). As in the 2006

Regulations, these three categories mirror the words used in Article 31(2) of the Citizens Directive.

The equivalent provisions under the s 94B of the Nationality Immigration and Asylum Act are discussed in detail at CHAPTER 19. Section 94B was considered by the Court of Appeal in R *(on the application of Kiarie) v Secretary of State for the Home Department*.[5] The Home Office argued that the correct test for certification was real risk of serious irreversible harm if removed, rather than removal being unlawful under s 6 of the Human Rights Act 1998. Indeed, this position was reflected in the policy guidance on section 94B. However, the Court of Appeal found that this was incorrect: the proper approach is to consider whether removal is unlawful under the 1998 Act. The avoidance of 'serious or irreversible harm' is therefore properly construed as an example of a ground on which the SSHD may rely on for the purposes of certification, rather than the test. At the time of writing, the Supreme Court has granted permission for Mr Kiarie to argue that the requirement that he conduct his appeal against deportation from abroad is procedurally unfair and breaches his rights under Article 8 of ECHR.

In R *(on the application) Masalska v Secretary of State for the Home Department (Regulations 24AA and 29AA EEA) IJR*[6] the Upper Tribunal considered for the first time the parallel EEA 'deport first, appeal later' provisions. The decision was handed down one day after the Court of Appeal gave judgment in *Kiarie*. It adopts the same approach in respect of the test for certification. Hence, the avoidance of 'serious or irreversible harm' is not the sole or overriding test; it is also necessary for the SSHD to assess whether removal would be unlawful under s 6 of the Human Rights Act 1998. While the assessment under s 6 requires a proportionality assessment, it is limited to the proportionality of removal for the period during which any appeal can be brought in time or is pending. At para 31, the Upper Tribunal cite, by way of example lifted from a Home Office policy document, a person who has a genuine and subsisting relationship with a partner or parental relationship with a child who is seriously ill and requires full-time care, and there is credible evidence that no one could provide that care. The Upper Tribunal itself remarks that in light of *Kiaire* that such cases are likely to be relatively rare.

In terms of when the SSHD exercises the discretion to certify an appeal, in *Gheorghiu (Reg 24AA EEA Regs – relevant factors)*,[7] the Upper Tribunal held that the decision maker should take into account, inter alia: (i) the status of the EEA national; (ii) the impact of removal on members of family members; (iii) evidence of continuing risk to the public; and (iv) the role oral evidence may play in the appeal. Other relevant factors might include strong prospects of rehabilitation and the risk that destitution in the proposed removee's country of origin would set that back.[8] The relevant counter veiling public interest is that in temporary removal, which is not to be confused with the public interest in permanent exclusion as justification for deportation itself.[9]

A decision to make a deportation order is not a decision to transfer a serving prisoner to another Member State to serve his prison sentence there and so in any appeal against a decision to make a deportation order the Tribunal is not concerned with whether there is any legal impediment to such a transfer taking place.[10]

1  R (on the application Kaiscky) v Secretary of State for the Home Department (Reg 29AA: interpretation) IJR [2006] UKUT 00107 (IAC).
2  R (on the application) Masalska v Secretary of State for the Home Department (Regulations 24AA and 29AA EEA) IJR [2015] UKUT 00677 (IAC), para 6 of the official headnote.
3  R (on the application Kaiscky) v Secretary of State for the Home Department (Reg 29AA: interpretation) IJR [2006] UKUT 00107 (IAC).
4  A point clarified by the Upper Tribunal in R (on the application) Masalska v Secretary of State for the Home Department (Regulations 24AA and 29AA EEA) IJR [2015] UKUT 00677 (IAC), [2015] All ER (D) 121 (Dec), at para 22.
5  [2015] EWCA Civ 1020, 2016] 3 All ER 741, [2016] 1 WLR 1961.
6  [2015] UKUT 00677 (IAC), [2015] All ER (D) 121 (Dec).
7  [2016] UKUT 00024 (IAC).
8  R (on the application of X) v Secretary of State for the Home Department [2016] EWHC 1997 (Admin) (29 July 2016),
9  R (on the application of X) v Secretary of State for the Home Department [2016] EWHC 1997 (Admin) (29 July 2016), [2016] All ER (D) 41 (Aug),
10  Restivo (EEA – prisoner transfer) [2016] UKUT 00449 (IAC),

## National security cases

**6.196** *[Replace entire paragraph:]*

An appeal against an EEA decision lies to the Special Immigration Appeals Commission (SIAC) where:

- Regulation 38(2): the SSHD certifies that the EEA decision was taken: (a) by the SSHD wholly or partly on a ground listed in paragraph 3; or (b) in accordance with a direction of the SSHD which identifies the person to whom the decision relates and which is given wholly or partly on a ground listed in paragraph 3;
- Regulation 38(3): those grounds referred to in reg 38(2) are (a): in the interests of national security; or (b) in the interests of the relationship between the United Kingdom and another country;
- Regulation 38(4): the SSHD certifies the EEA decision was taken wholly or partly in reliance on information which the SSHD considers must not be made public: (a) in the interests of national security; (b) in the interests of the relationship between the UK and another country; or (c) otherwise in the public interest.

Following the CJEU's decision in *ZZ v United Kingdom*,[1] it is necessary in SIAC proceedings for the SSHD to provide the essence of the grounds against an appellant, notwithstanding the interests of national security, in order to comply inter alia with the procedural requirements of the Citizens' Directive and the principle of effective judicial protection of EU rights. For more details of appeals to SIAC, see CHAPTER 22.

1  ZZ (France) v Secretary of State for the Home Department (Case C-300/11), CJEU 4 June 2013, [2013] QB 1136, [2013] 3 WLR 813, [2014] All ER (EC) 56, [2013] 3 CMLR 46, applied by the Court of Appeal in ZZ (France) v Secretary of State for the Home Department [2014] EWCA Civ 7, [2014] 2 WLR 791, [2014] 3 All ER 587, [2014] 2 CMLR 49.

**6.203** *[At the end of footnote 20 add:]*

In *Raad van bestuur van het Uitvoeringsinstituut werknemersverzekeringen (UWV) v Demirci* (C-171/13), CLI:EU:C:2015:8, [2015] 2 CMLR 1055,

[2015] All ER (D) 123 (Jan), the CJEU held that Turkish workers who had been registered as belonging to the Netherlands labour force, and who had acquired Netherlands nationality while retaining their Turkish nationality, were not able to rely on Decision 3/80 of the EEC-Turkey Association Agreement art.6 to object to a residence requirement provided for by Netherlands law in order to receive a non-contributory benefit after they became incapacitated for work and returned to Turkey.

## TURKISH ASSOCIATION AGREEMENT

### Turkish workers

**6.207** *[At the end of the paragraph add:]*

Applying *Dogan*, this was the conclusion reached in *Genc v Integrationsministeriet (European Commission and Austria, intervening)*,[10] in which the CJEU held that national measure making family reunification between a Turkish worker residing lawfully in Denmark and his minor child subject to the condition that the latter have, or have the possibility of establishing, ties sufficient to enable successful integration, when the child concerned and his other parent resided in the State of origin or in another State, constituted a 'new restriction', within the meaning of Article 13 of Decision 1/80.

[10] C-561/14, ECLI:EU:C:2016:247, [2016] 3 CMLR 571, [2016] All ER (D) 81 (Apr).

Chapter 7

# HUMAN RIGHTS LAW

## EC, ECHR AND THE CHARTER OF FUNDAMENTAL RIGHTS

**7.9** *[At the end of the paragraph, add:]*

Article 24 of the Charter, bearing the title 'The Rights of the Child' is inspired by the UN Convention on the Rights of the Child (UNCRC).[17] The critical driver of Article 24 is the perception that 'children are no longer considered as mere recipients of services or beneficiaries of protective measures but rather as rights-holders and participants in actions affecting them'.[18] Article 24(3) provides that 'every child shall have the right to maintain on a regular basis a personal relationship and direct contact with both his or her parents, unless this is contrary to his or her interests'.[19] In *Abdul (section 55 – Article 24(3) Charter)* [2016] UKUT 106 (IAC), McCloskey J, the President of the Tribunal, described Article 24(3) as a 'discrete' and 'free standing right'.[20]

[17] The word 'inspired' and its cognates, is used several times in the context of Article 24 of the Charter and the UNCRC, pp 207–215, Commentary of the Charter of Fundamental Rights of the European Union (June 2006).

[18] Commentary, p 207.

[19] Subject to Article 52 of the Charter, which sets out general principles of scope and interpretation similar to those applied to the qualified ECHR rights.

[20] McCloskey J held (para 30) that ' . . . I consider it clear that Article 24(3) was designed to create a discrete right, an analysis which is harmonious with general principles of EU law. These include the well-known principle that every part of a measure of EU law is presumed to have a separate and individual effect and impact. Article 24(3) may also be viewed through the prism of the principle that where one has an amalgam of specific and general provisions, the former should normally be considered in advance of the latter'.

## THE ECHR RIGHTS

### Shared burden in establishing the facts

**7.47A** *[Add new heading as above and paragraph:]*

To ensure that any decision made pursuant to the ECHR is effective, State authorities must co-operate with the applicant to ascertain all relevant facts: *JK v Sweden* (Application no 59166/12) *(Grand Chamber)* (para 101):

(i)     In practical terms, this means that if, 'for any reason whatsoever', the elements provided by an Applicant for international protection are not complete, up to date, or relevant, it is necessary for the State 'to cooperate actively with the Applicant so that all the elements needed to substantiate the application may be assembled' and this may include gaining access to certain types of documents (para 49).

(ii)     Take into account facts known or that ought to be known and all other relevant facts in the case under examination (paras 87, 96, 98). Where necessary, obtain relevant COI materials *proprio motu* because the State has 'full access' to COI and ' . . . it may be difficult, if not impossible, for the person concerned to supply evidence within a short time' (paras 92, 90, 96–98).[1]

(iii)     Ensure the assessment is adequate and sufficiently supported by (a) domestic COI materials, 'compared with' (b) COI materials from other sources (eg other Contracting or non-Contracting States, agencies of the United Nations and reputable NGOs) that are (c) reliable and objective (paras 84, 88).[2]

(iv)     Assess the weight to be attached to COI by reference to the source of such material, in particular its independence, reliability and objectivity. In respect of reports, the authority and reputation of the author, the seriousness of the investigations by means of which they were compiled, the consistency of their conclusions and their corroboration by other sources are all relevant considerations (para 88).

In *Sharifi and Others v Italy and Greece*, 16643/09 the court held that Member States of the EU cannot eschew from their obligations under the ECHR when implementing EU law, the European Court of Human Rights (ECtHR) has unanimously found Italy to be in violation of the prohibition of collective expulsion of aliens (Article 4 of Protocol 4 of ECHR) as well as the prohibition of inhumane and degrading treatment (Article 3) and the right to an effective remedy (Article 13) by returning a group of Afghan asylum applicants to Greece. In turn, the Court has ruled that Greece had also breached Articles 2 and 13 read in conjunction with Article 3 given the lack of access to the asylum procedure in Greece and the risk of deportation to Afghanistan.

[1]     It must use all the means at its disposal 'to produce the necessary evidence' in support of the application: *FG v Sweden* (Application no 43611/11), 23 March 2016 (para 122).

[2]     See also *FG v Sweden* at paras 90 and 117.

## Exposure to torture or inhuman or degrading treatment or punishment

**17.48** *[At the end of footnote 11, add:]*

A single impulsive slap by a police officer to the face of a suspect, during interrogation at a police station, amounted to degrading but not inhuman treatment under Article 3: *Bouyid v Belgium* (Application no 23380/09), 28 September 2015 (GC). One of the suspects was a minor at the time; the other (they were brothers) was not.

*[At the end of footnote 17, add:]*

When determining whether detention conditions breach Article 3, a simple calculation of floor space allocated to each detainee is generally insufficient; a comprehensive assessment is required. However, where personal space falls below three square metres in multi-occupancy accommodation there exists a strong presumption of an Article 3 violation. It is then for the government in question to rebut the presumption by showing there are compensatory factors. Space remains a weighty factor where three to four square metres are allocated; and where in excess of four metres, other conditions will need to be evaluated: *Mursic v Croatia* (Application no 7334/13) 20 October 2016 (GC); *Georgia v Russia*, (Application no 13255/07), 3 July 2014 at para 200. As reiterated in *Yarashonen v Turkey* (Application no 72710/11) 24 June 2014, [2014] ECHR 72710/11, ECtHR, compensatory factors can include the freedom to spend time outside of a cell. See also *Alimov v Turkey* (Application no 14344/13), 6 September 2016 at paras 68–85 and *Mahamad Jama v Malta* (Application no 10290/13), 26 November 2015, in which the court held that compensatory factors and improvements to the detention regime did not breach Article 3.

The age of the detainee is highly relevant. The reception conditions for children seeking asylum must be adapted to their age, to ensure that those conditions do not 'create . . . for them a situation of stress and anxiety, with particularly traumatic consequences': *Tarakhel v Switzerland* (GC) (Application no 29217/12, para 99, ECHR 2014. In *Popov v France* (Application no 39472/07), 19 January 2012, (2012) 63 EHRR 362, ECtHR, the ECtHR found a violation of Article 3 where two children (aged five months and three years respectively) were detained with their parents for a period of 15 days, in an adult environment with a strong police presence. Whilst the duration was not deemed to violate Article 3 in and of itself, the court noted for children that period of time could have been perceived as never ending. In *Abdullahi Elmi and Aweys Abubakar v Malta* (Application nos 25794/13 and 28151/13), at paras 110-115 the Court concluded that since the applicants were minors, who were detained for a period of around eight months, the cumulative effect of the conditions complained of amounted to degrading treatment in violation of Article 3 of ECHR. The conditions included, inter alia, limited light and ventilation, deplorable sanitary facilities, lack of organised (entertainment) activities for minors, lack of proper counselling and educational assistance, a violent atmosphere and a lack of support mechanisms for the minors, as well as lack of information concerning their situation.

In *Abdi Mahamud v Malta* (Application no 56796/13), 3 May 2016, at para 89, the Court held that cumulative effect of circumstances including the female applicant's vulnerability as a result of her health, the lack of female staff, and the little privacy she was offered in the detention centre, which persisted for over 16 months, diminished the applicant's human dignity.

*[After the penultimate sentence of footnote 20, insert:]*

To comply with Article 3, life sentences must be reducible, including a prospect of release and a possibility of review. To comply with international standards a review must take place no later than 25 years into the sentence, and periodically thereafter. Life prisoners must also be given the possibility of rehabilitating themselves. The sentence must not be grossly disproportionate to the gravity of the offence(s): *Murray v The Netherlands* (Application no 10511/10), 26 April 2016 (GC). See also *Harakchiev and Tolumov v Bulgaria* (Application no 15018/11), 8 July 2014 where a life sentence with inadequate opportunities to rehabilitate was found to breach Article 3.

*[At the end of footnote 26, insert:]*

In *RBAB and Others v The Netherlands* (Application no 7211/06), the Grand Chamber held at paras 54–56 although there is no dispute that subjecting a child or adult to FGM amounts to treatment proscribed by Article 3, and that a considerable majority of girls and women in Sudan have traditionally been subjected to FGM and continue to be, in general there is no real risk of a girl or woman being subjected to FGM at the instigation of persons who are not family members. In the case of an unmarried woman, the risk of FGM being practised will depend on the attitude of her family, most particularly her parents, but also her extended family and, if a woman's parents are opposed to FGM, they will normally be in a position to ensure that she does not marry a man who (or whose family) is in favour of it, regardless of the attitude of other relatives of the woman concerned.

### Degrading treatment

**7.49** *[At the end of the third sentence after footnote reference 4, add:]*

Degrading treatment may arise simply from the victim being humiliated in their own eyes.[4a]

*[At the end of footnote 2, add:]*

In *Svinarenko and Slyadnev v Russia* (Application nos 32541/08 and 43441/08), 17 July 2014 (GC), (2014) 37 BHRC 628, [2014] ECHR 32541/08, ECtHR, the applicants were subjected to degrading treatment through being held in a metal courtroom cage during the course of their trial. The hearings were attended by up to 70 witnesses, over the course of one year. The court concluded, contrary to previous decisions, the use of cages in that a context could never be justified; it was an affront to human dignity.

*[At end of footnote 6, add:]*

Attempts to re-argue whether national security concerns affect an Article 3 assessment have been repeatedly rejected by the court. See, for example, *Labsi v Slovakia* (Application no 33809/08), 24 September 2012, [2012] ECHR 33809/08, ECtHR (it was not the court's role to determine whether the applicant posed a national security threat, only whether his deportation was compatible with rights under the Convention).

[4a] *Bouyid v Belgium* (Application no 23380/09), 28 September 2015, (CG). See **7.48** above.

**7.50** *[At the end of footnote 9, add:]*

This was reaffirmed in *Aden Ahmed v Malta* (Application no 55352/12), 23 July 2013, at para 90, notwithstanding the court's awareness of the State's difficulty in coping with an increasing influx of migrants and asylum seekers.

**7.51** *[At the end of the fourth sentence after footnote reference 7, insert:]*

Where an asylum claim is based on a well-known general risk, identified in freely available sources, this requires the authorities to make an assessment of risk of their own motion.[7a]

Assurances by the receiving state must be carefully scrutinised. Consideration needs to be given to the quality of the assurance given, and whether it can be relied on. Relevant factors in that assessment include: (i) whether it is specific or vague; (ii) the source of the assurance; (iii) whether it concerns legal or illegal treatment; (iv) whether compliance can be objectively verified; (v) whether there is an effective system of protection against torture; and (vi) whether the reliability of such assurances has been tested in the courts of the sending/receiving states.[7b]

*[At the end of footnote 7, add:]*

Unlike the Refugee Convention, Article 3 protection is not compromised by the commission of a 'particularly serious crime', making the exact definition of that term of little relevance in removal cases: *Bajsultanov v Austria* (Application no 54131/10), 12 June 2012.

*[At the end of footnote 9, add:]*

In *RH v Sweden* (Application no 4601/44), 10 September 2015, [2015] ECHR 4601/14, ECtHR, the court considered, it noted for the third time, whether the general situation had worsened since its finding in *KAB v Sweden* in September 2013. It held that although the general security situation remained serious and fragile the situation had not deteriorated since that judgment. It attached weight to the Upper Tribunal decision of *MOJ and Others (Return to Mogadishu) Somalia CG* [2014] UKUT 00442 (IAC) which concluded that there had been an improvement. The general conditions in Iraq (*JK and Others v Sweden* (Application no 59166/12), 23 August 2016 (GC)) and Afghanistan (*H and B v The United Kingdom* (Application nos 70073/10 and 44539/11) 9 April 2013, [2013] ECHR 70073/10, [2013] All ER (D) 142 (Apr), ECtHR) are not deemed to currently breach Article 3 (although in neither of the cases before the ECtHR was it positively asserted they did). (In five cases: *AGR v The Netherlands* (Application no 13442/08); *AWQ and DH v The Netherlands* (Application no 25077/06); *MRA and Others v The Netherlands* (Application no 46856/07); *SDM v The Netherlands* (Application no 8161/07); *SS v The Netherlands* (Application no 39575/06), the court held that men who held senior positions during the communist regime in the Afghan government (army and security services), would not be at real risk of Article 3 harm due to their former roles, or because of the general situation.) Given the scale of violence in Syria, expulsion to Aleppo would give rise to breach of Articles 2 and 3 (*LM and Others v Russia* (Application nos 40081/14, 40088/14, and 40127/14), at paras 123–126) (although there is no risk for Kurds based on the evidence dated no later than 2010: *KF v Cyprus* (Application no 41858/10); *HS and Others v Cyprus* (Application no 41753/10), 21 July 2015, and *AH and JK v Cyprus* (Application nos 41903/10 and 41911/10)). Similarly, extradition to Uzbekistan, on charges of religiously or politically motivated crimes, runs a real risk of treatment contrary to Article 3 because the use of torture is 'systematic' and 'indiscriminate', eg *Khalikov v Russia* (Application no 66373/13), 26 Feb 2015 at paras 51–54; *Eshonkulov v Russia* (Application no 68900/13), 15 January 2015, [2015] ECHR 68900/13, ECtHR, at paras 44–49; and *Rakhimov v Russia* (Application no 50552/13), 10 July 2014 at paras 98–103.

*[At the end of footnote 11, add:]*

Personal circumstances include disabilities, taking into account the UN Convention of Rights of Persons with Disabilities: *SHH v United Kingdom* (Application no 60367/10), 29 January 2013.

*[At the end of footnote 13, add:]*

The ECtHR has also held the rejection of an asylum claim on the basis it was made too late can be relevant to credibility, but cannot absolve a state from determining whether Article 3 would be breached on return: *Ismilov v Russia* (Application no 20110/13), 17 April 2014, at para 80. In the same case the suggestion the applicant needed to produce 'indisputable' evidence of risk was flatly rejected; it was impossible to do so, and would place a disproportionate burden on the applicant (see para 81).

7a    *FG v Sweden* (Application no 43611/11), 23 March 2016 (GC). In that case the applicant was a low profile political activist from Iran who had subsequently converted to Christianity whilst in Sweden. He initially refused to rely on his conversion to prevent removal. As a result, the authorities did not thoroughly investigate whether he would be at risk on return for that reason. Finding a breach of Article 3, the ECtHR noted the positive duty to assess risk arose in particular where the state is made aware an asylum seeker may plausibly belong to a group systematically exposed to ill treatment in the country of return. The same duty arises under Article 2 of ECHR.

7b    *Labsi v Slovakia* (Application no 33809/08), 24 September 2012, [2012] ECHR 33809/08, ECtHR. In that case the ECtHR drew from previous jurisprudence when assurances from Algeria had been scrutinised. The applicant's removal was ultimately found to breach Article 3.

## 7.52 *[At the end of the paragraph, add:]*

More recently, the Court of Appeal in *NA (Sudan)*[12] concluded the return of asylum seekers and beneficiaries of international protection (BIPs) with vulnerabilities to Italy, under Dublin III, would not breach Article 3.

12    *NA (Sudan) v Secretary of State for the Home Department* [2016] EWCA Civ 1060. At the time of writing. an application for permission to appeal to the Supreme Court was pending. It is noteworthy that the appeals were dismissed on the basis of the country situation in Italy in 2015. When such cases are considered by the ECtHR an assessment is made at the time the proceedings are before the court, on the understanding that the situation may change over time: *Mohammadi v Austria* (Application no 71932/12), 3 July 2014.

## 7.53 *[At the end of the first sentence, after footnote reference 2, insert:]*

Similarly, Article 3 encompasses the right to an effective investigation where ill treatment is alleged.[2a]

*[At the end of footnote 9, add:]*

The ECtHR has relied on internal relocation on a number of occasions; see, for example, *AAM v Sweden* (Application no 68519), 3 April 2014 (relocation to the Kurdistan region of Iraq was deemed a viable option for an asylum seeker at risk in his home area); and *MYH and Others v Sweden* (Application no 50859/10), 27 June 2013 (again relocation to the Kurdistan region for the applicant, a Christian, was found to be available).

2a    See, for example, *Jeronovics v Latvia* (Application no 44898/10), 5 July 2016 (GC), where the ECtHR found a breach of Article 3 on account of the state refusing to reopen criminal proceedings against police officers accused of ill treatment.

## Application of Article 3 to illness

**7.54** *[At the end of the final paragraph, add:]*

The Grand Chamber of the ECtHR has, however, clarified these principles recently, in *Paposhvili v Belgium*.[11] In that case, the applicant, who died before proceedings were concluded, had been diagnosed with chronic lymphocytic leukaemia and related illnesses. He began treatment in 2008, when his life expectancy was three and a half years. By 2011 it had reduced to 24 months. With continued treatment, his prognosis became more favourable, although a discontinuation of treatment would have resulted in his death. Considering N and D, the court noted the possibility for 'other very exceptional circumstances' where humanitarian considerations would be equally compelling; that term:

> '[S]hould be understood to refer to situations involving the removal of a seriously ill person in which substantial grounds have been shown for believing that he or she, although not at imminent risk of dying, would face a real risk, on account of the absence of appropriate treatment in the receiving country or the lack of access to such treatment, of being exposed to a serious, rapid and irreversible decline in his or her state of health resulting in intense suffering or to a significant reduction in life expectancy. The Court points out that these situations correspond to a high threshold for the application of Article 3 of the Convention in cases concerning the removal of aliens suffering from serious illness.'[12]

Further principles underlined in *Paposhvili* include: (i) Article 3 cases by their very nature require a degree of speculation, meaning there can be no requirement to provide 'clear proof' of future exposure to ill treatment; (ii) a comparison of the individual's health prior and post removal is required, as is; (iii) an individual assessment of whether the care available in the receiving state is sufficient and appropriate in practice; and (iv) whether the individual will be able to access the requisite care and facilities, including an assessment of the cost of medication and treatment, the extent of any social and family network, the distance to be travelled to access care; (v) if serious doubts arise, the returning state must secure individual and sufficient assurances from the receiving state that the required treatment will be available and accessible.

On the facts, the decision to remove the applicant in *Paposhvili* was held to breach Articles 3 and 8: the domestic courts had not properly considered the extent of his ill health and poor prognosis. The treatment he was receiving in the removing state was not available in the receiving state, and there was no guarantee he would have access to other forms of treatment there.[13]

[11] *Paposhvili v Belgium* (Application no 41738/10), 13 December 2016, (CG).
[12] *Paposhvili v Belgium*, para 184.
[13] *Compare Tatar v Switzerland* (Application no 65692/12), 14 April 2015.

**7.56** *[In the text after footnote reference 3, delete 'In GS and EO (Article 3 – health cases) India . . . ' up to including ' . . . in the receiving State' and substitute:]*

In *GS (India) and Others*,[4] the Court of Appeal summarised the key principles in such cases, including; (i) those subject to immigration control cannot in principle claim an entitlement to remain in the UK to benefit from medical, social or other forms of assistance and services, but; (ii) the decision to remove someone with serious mental or physical illness, to a country where their treatment would be inferior, may raise an issue under Article 3; (iii) such cases would be exceptional, where the humanitarian grounds against the removal are compelling; (iv) in the case of *D* the applicant was critically ill, close to death, could not be guaranteed medical care, and had no family or support in the country of removal; (v) there may be other exceptional cases that are equally compelling; (vi) such principles apply equally in cases where the individual suffers from a serious, naturally occurring physical or mental illness that may cause suffering, pain and reduced life expectancy, and require medical treatment which may not be so readily available in the country of origin, or available at a substantial cost. The precise application of these principles following *Paposhvili* remains to be seen.

*[After footnote reference 7, delete the remaining text from 'It is noteworthy . . . ' to the end of the paragraph, including the quotation.]*

*[Delete footnotes 5, 8 and 9 and remaining footnotes are renumbered accordingly.]*

⁴ GS (India) and Others v Secretary of State for the Home Department [2015] EWCA Civ 40, at para 50.

### 7.58 *[At the end of the paragraph, add:]*

In *VM and Others v Belgium*[7] at paras 133-138 the court summarised[8] the relevant ECHR cases concerning the vulnerability of asylum seekers as a category of persons relevant to an assessment of the relative Article 3 threshold in the context of living conditions in the receiving State. At para 162 the court held:

> '[T]he situation experienced by the applicants calls for the same conclusion as in the case of MSS v Belgium and Greece . . . the Belgian authorities did not duly take account of the vulnerability of the applicants as asylum-seekers or of that of their children. Notwithstanding the fact that the reception crisis was an exceptional situation, the Court finds that the Belgian authorities should be considered to have failed to satisfy their obligation not to expose the applicants to conditions of extreme poverty for four weeks – barring two nights – having left them out on the streets with no resources, no access to sanitary facilities, and no means of providing for their essential needs. The Court considers that the applicants were thus victims of treatment which failed to respect their dignity and that this situation undoubtedly aroused in them feelings of fear, anguish or inferiority capable of inducing desperation. It finds that such living conditions, combined with the lack of any prospects of their situation improving, attained the level of severity required to fall within the scope of Article 3 of the Convention and amounted to degrading treatment.'

⁷ Application no 60125/11, 7 July 2015.
⁸ '134. Applying those criteria to the question of living conditions, the Court had found – prior to *M.S.S. v Belgium and Greece*, cited above – that it could not be excluded that the responsibility of the State might be engaged under Article 3 in respect of treatment where an applicant, who was wholly dependent on State support, found him or herself faced with official indifference in a situation of serious deprivation or want incompatible with human dignity. However, none of the factual situations examined had been considered by the Court to reach the threshold of severity required by Article 3 (see, for example, *Budina v Russia*, (dec), no. 45603/05, 18 June 2009).
135. With regard to an Iraqi national who had obtained provisional refugee status from the Office of the United Nations High Commissioner for Refugees and complained that he had

been unable to provide for his essential needs in Turkey, the Court held that Articles 3 and 8 of the Convention could not be interpreted as entailing any general obligation to give refugees financial assistance to enable them to maintain a certain standard of living (see *Müslim v Turkey*, no. 53566/99, § 85, 26 April 2005).

136. With *M.S.S. v Belgium and Greece*, cited above, which concerned an Afghan asylum-seeker who had been sent back to Greece by the Belgian authorities in accordance with the Dublin II Regulation, the Court initiated a change in its case-law. After noting that, unlike in the Müslim case, the obligation to provide decent material conditions to impoverished asylum-seekers had entered into positive law, the Court held that, in determining whether the threshold of severity required by Article 3 had been attained, particular importance had to be attached to the applicant's status as an asylum seeker. Accordingly, he belonged to a particularly underprivileged and vulnerable population group in need of special protection. It noted the existence of a broad consensus at the international and European level concerning this need for special protection (see *M.S.S. v Belgium and Greece*, cited above, § 251).

137. When assessing the applicant's individual situation, the Court held that the national authorities had not had due regard to that vulnerability and that the seriousness of the impoverished situation in which the applicant had found himself, having remained for several months with no means of providing for his essential needs, combined with the inertia on the part of the asylum authorities, had amounted to a violation of Article 3 of the Convention (see *M.S.S. v Belgium and Greece*, cited above, §§ 262–63; see, following *M.S.S.*, *Sufi and Elmi v the United Kingdom*, nos. 8319/07 and 11449/07, § 283, 28 June 2011, and *F.H. v Greece*, no. 78456/11, §§ 107 11, 31 July 2014).

138. In cases concerning the reception of accompanied or unaccompanied minors, the Court has also established that the relevant authorities should consider that the status of child prevailed over that of illegal immigrant (see *Muskhadzhiyeva and Others v Belgium*, no. 41442/07, §§ 55 and 63, 19 January 2010; *Kanagaratnam v Belgium*, no. 15297/09, § 62, 13 December 2011; and *Popov v France*, nos. 39472/07 and 39474/07, § 91, 19 January 2012). Recently, the *Tarakhel* case, which concerned the planned return to Italy by the Swiss authorities under the Dublin II Regulation of a family of Afghan nationals, gave the Court the opportunity to rule that the vulnerability of asylum-seekers was accentuated in the case of families with children and that the reception conditions for children seeking asylum must be appropriate for their age, to ensure that those conditions did not create for them a situation of stress and anxiety, with particularly traumatic consequences (see *Tarakhel*, cited above, § 119).'

## Detention

**7.62** *[At the end of the paragraph, add:]*

There however remains a presumption, under Article 5, in favour of liberty.[4]

4   Reiterated in *Buzadji v The Republic of Moldova* (Application no 23755/07), 5 July 2016 (GC), at para 89.

**7.63** *[At the end of footnote 1, add:]*

Reiterating the fundamental importance of Article 5, the ECtHR in *Buzadji v The Republic of Moldova* (Application no 23755/07), 5 July 2016 (GC), highlighted at para 84 the three recurring themes in the case law: (i) the exhaustive nature of exceptions to liberty, which must be strictly determined; (ii) the need for detention to be lawful (procedurally and substantively); and (iii) the need for prompt or speedy judicial control. See also the Grand Chamber in *Austin and Others v UK* (Applications nos 39692/09, 40713/09 and 41008/09) (Grand Chamber) 15 March 2012, at para 57 (concerning the UK police practice of 'kettling'). At para 59 the Court held the requirement to take account of the 'type' and 'manner of implementation' of the measure in question enables it to have regard to 'the specific context and circumstances surrounding types of restriction' other than the paradigm of confinement in a cell, emphasising that 'the context in which action is taken' is an 'important factor': see also paras 64–68.

In *Creanga v Reanga v Romania* (Application no 29226/03), 13 March 2012, the Grand Chamber held at para 92: 'the characterisation or lack of characterisation given by a State to a factual situation cannot decisively affect the Court's conclusion as to the existence of a deprivation of liberty'.

Further, in *Stanev v Bulgaria* (Application no 36760/06) 17 January 2012, the Grand Chamber rejected the idea that purporting to act in someone's best interests means that it cannot be a deprivation of liberty.

*[At the end of footnote 4, add:]*

In *Nada v Switzerland* (Application no 10593/08), 12 September 2012, the Court distinguished *Guzzardi* holding that the applicant's confinement to the 1,6 sq km of the Campione enclave did not constitute a deprivation of liberty under Article 5 of ECHR (paras 227-234):

'227. The Court observes that, in support of his argument that Article 5 must apply in the present case, the applicant relied particularly on the above-cited Guzzardi case. In that case, the application had been lodged by an individual who, being suspected of belonging to a "band of Mafiosi", had been forced to live on an island within an (unfenced) area of 2.5 sq. km, together with other residents in a similar situation and supervisory staff. The Court found that the applicant had been "deprived of his liberty" within the meaning of Article 5 and that he could therefore rely on the guarantees under that provision (see also *Giulia Manzoni v Italy*, 1 July 1997, §§ 18 25, Reports 1997 IV).

228. By contrast, in the *S.F. v Switzerland* case (cited above), where the applicant complained about not being authorised to leave Campione d'Italia for several years, the Commission declared the complaint inadmissible, finding that Article 5 was not applicable in that case. The Grand Chamber finds it appropriate in the present case to opt for the latter approach, for the following reasons.

229. In the applicant's concrete situation, the Court acknowledges that the restrictions were maintained for a considerable length of time. However, it observes that the area in which the applicant was not allowed to travel was the territory of a third country, Switzerland, and that, under international law, that country had the right to prevent the entry of an alien (see paragraph 164 above). The restrictions in question did not prevent the applicant from freely living and moving within the territory of his permanent residence, where he had chosen, of his own free will, to live and carry on his activities. The Court considers that, in these circumstances, his case differs radically from the factual situation in *Guzzardi* (cited above) and that the prohibition imposed upon the applicant does not raise an issue under Article 5 of the Convention.

230. The Court further recognises that Campione d'Italia represents a small area of territory. However, it observes that the applicant was not, strictly speaking, in a situation of detention, nor was he actually under house arrest: he was merely prohibited from entering or transiting through a given territory, and as a result of that measure he was unable to leave the enclave.

231. In addition, the Court notes that the applicant did not dispute before it the Swiss Government's assertion that he had not been subjected to any surveillance by the Swiss authorities and had not been obliged to report regularly to the police

(contrast *Guzzardi*, cited above, § 95). Nor does it appear, moreover, that he was restricted in his freedom to receive visitors, whether his family, his doctors or his lawyers (ibid.).

232. Lastly, the Court would point out that the sanctions regime permitted the applicant to seek exemptions from the entry or transit ban and that such exemptions were indeed granted to him on two occasions but he did not make use of them.

233. Having regard to all the circumstances of the present case, and in accordance with its case-law, the Court, like the Federal Court (see paragraph 48 above), finds that the applicant was not "deprived of his liberty" within the meaning of Article 5 § 1 by the measure prohibiting him from entering and transiting through Switzerland.

234. It follows that the complaints under Article 5 of the Convention are manifestly ill-founded and must be rejected pursuant to Article 35 §§ 3 and 4.'

*[At the end of footnote 7, add:]*

The ECtHR recently reiterated that house arrest amounts to a deprivation of liberty, due to the degree and intensity of the restriction it places on the individual: *Buzadji v The Republic of Moldova* (Application no 23755/07), 5 June 2016 (GC), at para 104.

*[At the end of footnote 9, add:]*

The right to liberty cannot be waived in any event, bearing in mind its importance in a democratic society; see *Buzadji v The Republic of Moldova* (Application no 23755/07), 5 July 2016 (GC), at para 107–109, where previous cases are also discussed.

## Purpose

**7.64** *[At the end of footnote 1, add:]*

The detention of a minor who was under the age of criminal responsibility, for a period of 30 days to 'correct his behaviour' did not fall within any of the permissible grounds under Article 5: *Blokhin v Russia* (Application no 47152/06), 23 March 2016 (GC).

## Action with a view to deportation

**7.65** *[At the end of footnote 3, add:]*

In *Kim v Russia* (Application no 44260/13), 17 July 2014, the applicant was released from detention after two years, the maximum time allowed for enforcing expulsion orders under domestic law. The court concluded the Russian authorities had failed to vigorously pursue enquiries for the issuance of a travel document via the Uzbek authorities (having written to the Embassy on five occasions during the period of detention). See also *Suso Musa v Malta* (Application no 42337/12), 23 July 2013, where continued detention for a relatively short period of time after being made aware there was no prospect of deportation breached Article 5(1)(f), at para 100.

*[At the end of the main text, add:]*

However, the Supreme Court confirmed in *Lumba and Mighty*[7] that a refusal to return voluntarily did not always carry an inference of a risk of absconding. A distinction was required between cases where return was possible and where it was not, for reasons beyond the individual's control. In the latter cases, a refusal to return voluntarily had no causal effect. In the former cases, consideration was required as to whether proceedings challenging removal were pending. If there were, it was reasonable for someone to seek to remain until they were concluded, meaning a refusal to voluntarily return in those circumstances would be irrelevant. Where neither scenario applied, a refusal to voluntarily return could not, however, be used by the government as a 'trump card' to continued detention, which still needed to be reasonable.

[7] *Lumba and Mighty v Secretary of State for the Home Department* [2011] UKSC 12, discussed and endorsed by the ECtHR in *Abdi v The United Kingdom* (Application no 27770/08), 9 April 2013, in particular at paras 73–74.

## Legality

**7.66** *[At the end of footnote 4, add:]*

The applicant in *Del Rio Prada v Spain* (Application no 42750/09) could not have reasonably foreseen that the method used to apply remissions of sentence for work done in detention would change as a result of a departure from case law by the Spanish Supreme Court. The application of the unforeseen approach resulted in her release being delayed by almost nine years. That period that was not lawful in breach of Article 5(1). In *Abdullahi Elmi and Aweys Abubakar v Malta* (Application nos 25794/13 and 28151/13) at para 146–148 the court held that delays in the processing of an asylum claim, having already been determined to be a child, generated 'serious doubts as to the authorities' good faith' and together with other factors (inadequate safeguards and poor conditions) breached Article 5(1).

*[At the end of footnote 7, add:]*

See also *Abdi v The United Kingdom* (Application no 27770/08) 9 July 2013, where the government accepted a period of detention was unlawful because of a failure to carry out regular reviews, as per published policy.

*[In the main text, at the end of the paragraph, add:]*

In *OM v Hungary*, (Application no 9912/15), 5 July 2016 at para 53, the Court considered that, in the course of detaining an asylum seeker claiming to be a part of a vulnerable group in the country he had to leave, ' . . . the authorities should exercise particular care in order to avoid situations which may reproduce the plight that forced the person to flee in the first place'. In the present case, the authorities failed to do so when they ordered the applicant's detention without considering the extent to which vulnerable individuals – such as LGBT people like the applicant – were safe or unsafe in custody among other detained persons, many of whom had come from countries with widespread cultural or religious prejudice against such persons. The decisions of the authorities did not contain any adequate reflection on the individual circumstances of the applicant, member of a vulnerable group by virtue of belonging to a sexual minority in Iran.[10] In *JN v United Kingdom*,[11] the Grand Chamber held that the failure to prescribe a maximum period of detention was, in light of the other procedural safeguards against arbitrariness, not in violation of Article 5(1), and that the entitlement to review detention, albeit not automatic (para 94), was also not a breach.

10 This appears to be part of the court's reasoning for finding a breach of Article 5(2)(b), ie one among other failures, on the part of the State, to undertake an individualised assessment as required by domestic law.
11 Application no 37289/12, at paras 90–93.

## Proportionate

**7.67** *[At the end of footnote 6, add:]*

There will be a breach of Article 5, para 1 if the justification for detention is that the person 'might frustrate their expulsion' and there are no or insufficient reasons are adduced to show that an asylum seeker is actually a flight risk, and moreover, if the decision does not deal with the possibility of alternative measures or the impact of the on-going asylum procedure: *Nabil and Others v Hungary* (Application no 62116/12), 22 Sept 2015.

**7.70** *[Immediately before the last sentence of the paragraph, add:]*

In certain circumstances, it may require the authorities to transfer a prisoner to special facilities to access treatment; examination and diagnosis is not sufficient, proper treatment is also required.[2a] In the case of minors, their best interests require proper care and protection, including a medical assessment prior to determining whether to detain at all.[2b]

Private and family life factors also remain relevant to conditions of detention, including the need for authorities to enable and, if necessary, assist those detained in maintaining contact with their close family.[2c] Severe restrictions on visiting rights and telephone calls can in themselves breach Article 8, depending on the circumstances.[2d]

2a *Murray v The Netherlands* (Application no 10511/10), 26 April 2016 (GC). See also *Mozer v Republic of Moldova and Russia* (Application no 11138/10), 23 February 2016 (GC) where Article 3 was found to be breached in part due to the lack of adequate medical treatment. The doctors within the detention centre noted the applicant's declining health and the lack of the necessary equipment at the detention centre, yet refused to transfer him to a civilian hospital.
2b *Blokhin v Russia* (Application no 47152/06), 23 March 2016 (GC). The applicant in that case was a 12-year old child with attention deficit hyperactivity disorder (ADHD). The state's failure to provide him with adequate medical treatment over a 30-day period breached Article 3.
2c This long-standing principle was reiterated in *Khoroshenko v Russia* (Application no 41418/04), 30 June 2015 (GC), at para 106.
2d *Khoroshenko v Russia* (Application no 41418/04), 30 June 2015 (GC). In that particular case the applicant was subjected to severe restrictions on visitation rights (duration, frequency and conditions therein) for a period of ten years, during which time he was not allowed telephone contact, except in emergencies. The regime was applied to all prisoners serving life sentences. The restrictions were deemed a disproportionate breach of Article 8.

## Articles 5(2) and (4)

**7.72** *[After the penultimate sentence of this paragraph, add:]*

In *Alimov v Turkey*[5] the Court held notification of the reasons for detention made two weeks after the start of the detention period was not made sufficiently promptly to satisfy the requirements of Article 5(2) of the Convention: ' . . . anyone entitled to take proceedings to have the lawfulness of his detention speedily decided cannot make effective use of that right unless he or she is promptly and adequately informed of the reasons relied on to deprive him or her of his or her liberty' (paras 44–46). That, 'in itself', meant the applicant's right of appeal against his detention under Article 5(4) was deprived of all substance (Paras 51–52).

In *Sharma v Latvia*[6] the Court found there to be no breach of Article 5(2) in circumstances where the applicant was aware of the decision to withdraw his residence permit because of his entry on a 'black list' and accordingly that he expected to leave the territory. That information was contained in the detention records, which the applicant signed, and there was no evidence he did not understand the information, eg due to language difficulties (paras 87–90).

[5] Application no 14344/13, 6 September 2016.
[6] Application no 28026/05, 24 June 2016.

### 7.73 *[At the beginning of footnote 1, insert:]*

A legal system that does not provide detained persons with a remedy to review the lawfulness of their detention, within the meaning of Article 5(4), constitutes a plain breach. A number of countries have been repeatedly been held to be in breach including but not limited to: (i) Turkey: eg *Alimov v Turkey* (Application no 14344/13); *Abdolkhani and Karimnia v Turkey* (Application no 30471/08), 22 September 2009, and *Yarashonen v Turkey* (Application no 72710/11), 24 June 2014; (ii) Russia: eg *LM and Others v Russia* (Application nos 40081/14, 40088/14, and 40127/14) at paras 141–142; *Khalikov v Russia* (Application no 66373/13), 26 Feb 2015 at paras 65–66, and (iii) Cyprus: eg *AH and JK v Cyprus*; *HS and Others v Cyprus* (Application no 41753/10), 21 July 2015 and (iv) Malta: eg *Mahamad Jama v Malta* (Application no 10290/13), 26 November 2015; *Suso Musa v Malta* (Application no 42337/12), 23 July 2013, and *Aden Ahmed v Malta* (Application no 55352/12), 9 December 2013.

### Fair trial

### 7.78 *[At the end of footnote 4, add:]*

In *Margus v Croatia* (Application no 4455/10), 27 May 2014 (GC), the ECtHR concluded it was not incompatible with the impartiality requirement for a judge to terminate proceedings on the basis of an amnesty, only to then sit as part of a panel in subsequent proceedings against the same individual, which were wider in scope. No guilt or innocence had been assessed in the first set of proceedings.

### Family and private life

### 7.85 *[After the first sentence in footnote 1, add]*

In *AS v Switzerland* (Application no 39350/13), 30 June 2015, at para 49 the Court reiterated there would be no family life between parents and adult children or between adult siblings unless they would demonstrate additional elements of dependence. The court in *AS* cited *FN v United Kingdom* (dec), (Application no 3202/09), 17 September 2013, at para 36, which said:

> 'The Court has previously held that there will be no family life, within the meaning of Article 8, between parents and adult children or between adult siblings unless they can demonstrate additional elements of dependence (*Slivenko v Latvia* (GC), no 48321/99, § 97, ECHR 2003 X; *Kwakye-Nti and Dufie v The Netherlands* (dec.), no. 31519/96, 7 November 2000), and similar considerations apply to other familial relations such as that between aunt and niece. However, the Court accepts, as did the domestic authorities, that the applicant lived with and was more than usually dependent on her aunt as a result of her vulnerable mental state and thus that family life existed between the two. Although the applicant has been able to remain in close contact with her aunt since her removal to Uganda, the Court accepts that her removal did interfere, to an extent, with the family life she and her aunt enjoyed, since the two were no longer able to live together or enjoy the close contact that such cohabitation entailed. The Court further notes that the applicant's aunt appears to be her only surviving relation. The Court also accepts that the applicant's removal to Uganda interfered with the private life which she had unquestionably established in the United Kingdom (see *Miah v the United Kingdom* (dec.), no. 53080/07, § 17, 27 April 2010).'

*[In the main text, after footnote reference 4, insert:]*

In *ZH and RH v Switzerland*, the Court held that Switzerland was under no obligation to recognise the marriage of a child[4a] either by reference to Article 8 or 12 of the Convention, emphasising that Article 12 expressly provides for regulation of marriage by national law, and ' . . . given the sensitive moral choices concerned and the importance to be attached to the protection of children and the fostering of secure family environments, this Court must not rush to substitute its own judgment in place of the authorities who are best placed to assess and respond to the needs of society' (para 44).

In *Van der Heijden v The Netherlands*, the Grand Chamber held[4b] that when deciding whether a relationship can amount to 'family life', a number of factors may be relevant, including whether the couple live together, the length of their relationship and whether they have demonstrated their commitment to each other by having children together or by any other means.[4c]

[4a] Application no 60119/12: see para 44. No such obligation is imposed.
[4b] Application no 42857/05: see para 50.
[4c] Cited by the ECtHR in *ZH and RH v Switzerland* (Application no 60119/12) at para 42.

### 7.87 *[At the end of footnote 4, add:]*

This was further highlighted by the Supreme Court in *Hesham Ali v Secretary of State for the Home Department* [2016] UKSC 60, where Lord Reed confirmed at para 32, albeit in relation to deportation:

> 'Whether the situation is analysed in terms of positive or negative obligations is, however, unlikely to be of substantial importance. Whether the person concerned enjoys private or family life in the UK depends on the facts relating to his relationships with others: whether, for example, he is married or has children. Where he does enjoy private or family life in the UK, he has a right under Article 8 to

respect for that life, whatever his immigration status may be (although that status may greatly affect the weight to be given to his Article 8 right, as *Jeunesse* makes clear).'

**7.92** *[After the final sentence, insert:]*

The distinction, or lack thereof, between private and family life also arises in the right to mourn. Reviewing a number of Strasbourg authorities, the President of the Upper Tribunal confirmed in *Abbasi and Another* that the refusal to grant entry clearance for the purpose of visiting a family member's grave can disproportionately interfere with Article 8 rights.[11]

[11]  *Abbasi and Another (Visits – Bereavement – Article 8)* [2015] UKUT 00463.

## Article 8 in the domestic courts

**7.101** *[At end of main text add:]*

The Court of Appeal in *Singh and Khalid*[9] approved Mr Fordham QC's formulation in *Ganesabalan*, but with certain caveats. There is always a 'second stage' in which the Secretary of State must consider the exercise of discretion outside the Rules and must be in a position to demonstrate that she has done so, but this does not qualify what Sales J said at para 30 of his judgment in *Nagre*: the 'second stage' can, in an appropriate case, be satisfied by the decision-maker concluding that any family life or private life issues raised by the claim have already been addressed at the first stage – in which case there is no need to go through it all again. The extent of the consideration and reasoning called for will depend on the circumstances of the individual case. In *SS (Congo)*,[10] the Court of Appeal agreed with the Court in *MF (Nigeria)* that it is a 'sterile question' whether one is dealing with a 'complete code' case or a case falling to be addressed in the context of a part of the Immigration Rules which does not constitute a 'complete code'. The basic, two-stage analysis will apply in both contexts. In paragraph 398 of the Rules, Statement of Changes HC 532 substituted 'very compelling circumstances' for the 'exceptional circumstances' considered in *MF (Nigeria)*. This does not seem to have affected the two-stage approach in deportation cases: the Upper Tribunal has held that the purpose of paragraph 398 is to recognise circumstances that are sufficiently compelling to outweigh the public interest in deportation but do not fall within paras 399 and 399A, and that judges should carry out a proportionality assessment.[11] More recently, the Supreme Court has given important guidance in *Hesham Ali*[12] as to the nature of the appellate tribunal's task, in the context of paras 398–399A of the Rules. Lord Reed observed that the idea that the new rules comprise a 'complete code' appears to have been mistakenly interpreted in some later cases as meaning that the Rules, and the Rules alone, govern appellate decision-making. The Rules are not law and therefore do not govern the determination of appeals, other than appeals brought on the ground that the decision is not in accordance with the Rules. The policies adopted by the Secretary of State, and given effect by the Rules, are nevertheless a relevant and important consideration for tribunals determining appeals brought on Convention grounds, because they reflect the assessment of the general public interest made by the responsible minister and endorsed by Parliament. In particular, tribunals should accord respect to the Secretary of State's assessment of the strength of the general public interest in the deportation of foreign offenders, and also consider all factors relevant to the specific case before them.

⁹  *Singh and Khalid v Secretary of State for the Home Department* [2015] EWCA Civ 74.
¹⁰  *SS (Congo) v Secretary of State for the Home Department* [2015] EWCA Civ 387.
¹¹  *Chege (section 117D – Article 8 – approach)* [2015] UKUT 00165 (IAC).
¹²  *Hesham Ali v Secretary of State for the Home Department* [2016] UKSC 60.

**7.105** *[At end of main text add:]*

A Panel of the Upper Tribunal has expressed the view that a person's immigration status will be 'precarious' if their continued presence in the UK will be dependent upon their obtaining a further grant of leave. Further, the Panel held that in some circumstances it may also be that even a person with indefinite leave to remain, or a person who has obtained citizenship, enjoys a status that is 'precarious' either because that status is revocable by the Secretary of State as a result of their deception, or because of their criminal conduct.⁶ This wide formulation is open to question, since it would bring the vast majority of litigants likely to come before the Tribunal within the ambit of section 117B(5) and thereby significantly reducing the scope for an evaluation of individual circumstances. The correctness of this formulation was doubted, albeit obiter, by Sales LJ in *Rhuppiah*⁷ who observed that:

> '[T]here is a very wide range of cases in which some form of leave to remain short of ILR may have been granted, and the word "precarious" seems to me to convey a more evaluative concept, the opposite of the idea that a person could be regarded as a settled migrant for Article 8 purposes, which is to be applied having regard to the overall circumstances in which an immigrant finds himself in the host country.'

⁶  *AM (S 117B) Malawi* [2015] UKUT 0260 (IAC).
⁷  *Rhuppiah v Secretary of State for the Home Department* [2016] EWCA Civ 803.

**7.106** *[In the main text delete the penultimate sentence beginning 'The reference to . . . ' and substitute:]*

The Court of Appeal has held that the reference to 'reasonable to expect the child to leave the UK' requires the court or tribunal to have regard to the conduct of the applicant and any other matters relevant to the public interest, and not only to the interests of the child.⁴ Elias LJ doubted whether this was correct, but considered himself bound by the decision of a differently constituted Court of Appeal in *MM (Uganda)*⁵ in respect of the expression 'unduly harsh' in section 117C(5).⁶ Significantly, the Court in *MA (Pakistan)* was concerned with appellants whose children were 'qualifying children' by virtue of seven years' residence in the UK, not by virtue of citizenship. Where the 'qualifying child' is a British citizen, established law pre-dating the 2014 Act would suggest that it cannot be reasonable to expect the British child to relocate to a country outside the European Union.⁷ This position is reflected in the most recent edition of the Home Office's Immigration Directorate Instructions, which, at the time of writing, state:

> 'Save in cases involving criminality, the decision maker must not take a decision in relation to the parent or primary carer of a British Citizen child where the effect of that decision would be to force that British child to leave the EU, regardless of the age of that child. This reflects the European Court of Justice judgment in

> Zambrano . . . Where a decision to refuse the application would require a parent
> or primary carer to return to a country outside the EU, the case must always be
> assessed on the basis that it would be unreasonable to expect a British Citizen child
> to leave the EU with that parent or primary carer.'[8]

The same Instructions go on to suggest that family separation might nonetheless be justified by a particularly poor immigration history or by criminality
falling short of the deportation threshold. It is submitted, however, that where
a court or tribunal is faced with a British citizen child and with a non-citizen
parent who is not liable to deportation, and the hypothetical removal would be
to a country outside the European Union, the only tenable construction of
section 117B(6) is that there is per se no public interest in the non-citizen
parent's removal.

*[At end of main text add:]*

It is not necessary for a person to have parental responsibility in law for there
to exist a parental relationship, and a person who is not a biological parent
may have a parental relationship with a child if they have 'stepped into the
shoes' of a parent. However, the relationships between a child and professional
or voluntary carers or family friends are not 'parental relationships'.[9] Part 5A
has a complex interrelationship with the Immigration Rules. The Upper
Tribunal has held that Part 5A has not altered the need for a two-stage
approach to Article 8 claims. Ordinarily a court or tribunal will, as a first
stage, consider an appellant's Article 8 claim by reference to the Immigration
Rules that set out substantive conditions, without any direct reference to
Part 5A considerations. Such considerations have no direct application to
rules of this kind. Part 5A considerations only have direct application at the
second stage of the Article 8 analysis.[10] It remains to be seen whether this
approach will be altered by the Supreme Court's decision in *Hesham Ali*, at
7.101 above, as to the approach that appellate tribunals should take to the
Rules.

*[Delete the current footnote 4.]*

4    *MA (Pakistan) v Secretary of State for the Home Department* [2016] EWCA Civ 705.
5    *MM (Uganda) v Secretary of State for the Home Department* [2016] EWCA Civ 450.
6    See **7.107** below.
7    *Sanade and Others (British children – Zambrano – Dereci)* [2012] UKUT 00048 (IAC).
8    Immigration Directorate Instructions, Appendix FM 1.0 Family Life (as a Partner or Parent)
     and Private Life: 10-Year Routes, August 2015.
9    *R (on the application of RK) v Secretary of State for the Home Department (s 117B(6);
     'parental relationship')* IJR [2016] UKUT 00031 (IAC).
10   *Bossade (ss.117A-D-interrelationship with Rules)* [2015] UKUT 00415 (IAC).

**7.107**  *[After the first sentence of main text insert:]*

It has been confirmed by the Upper Tribunal that section 117C only applies to
cases involving deportation; it does not apply in a non-deportation case,
irrespective of whether or not an appellant may fall within the definition of a
'foreign criminal' in section 117D(2).[0]

*[In the main text delete the sentence 'The 'unduly harsh' test . . . will be
weighed.' and substitute:]*

Although a Panel of the Upper Tribunal held that the phrase 'unduly harsh' did
not import a balancing exercise and that the focus was solely on an evaluation

of the consequences and impact for the individual concerned,[5a] this has now been disapproved by the Court of Appeal in *MM (Uganda)*[5b] which confirmed that the expression requires regard to be had to all the circumstances including the criminal's immigration and criminal history. The Court also confirmed that the expression 'unduly harsh' plainly means the same in section 117C(5) as in paragraph 399.

*[At end of main text add:]*

In a number of recent decisions the Court of Appeal has emphasised that in cases where the sentence exceeds four years, it will only be rarely that the 'exceptional circumstances' or 'very compelling circumstances' requirement is met, and the fact that deportation is contrary to the best interests of the foreign criminal's British children will not necessarily be sufficient.[7] These decisions do not appear to draw any clear distinction between the 'exceptional circumstances' requirement in section 117C and that in paragraph 398. Where a foreign criminal's sentence is between twelve months and four years and they cannot meet 'Exception 1' or 'Exception 2' in section 117C, the Court of Appeal has confirmed that it is open to them to rely upon 'very compelling circumstances' under section 117C(6), despite the drafting of section 117C(3) suggesting the contrary.[8] A foreign criminal is not disentitled from seeking to rely on matters falling within the scope of the circumstances described in Exceptions 1 and 2 when seeking to contend that there are 'very compelling circumstances' over and above Exceptions 1 and 2.[9]

*[Insert new footnotes in correct sequential order.]*

[0] Clarke ('Section 117C – limited to deportation') [2015] UKUT 00628 (IAC).

[5a] MAB (para 399; 'unduly harsh') USA [2015] UKUT 00435 (IAC).

[5b] MM (Uganda) v Secretary of State for the Home Department [2016] EWCA Civ 450.

[7] LC (China) v Secretary of State for the Home Department [2014] EWCA Civ 1310:

> '[I]n cases where the person to be deported has been sentenced to a term of imprisonment for less than 4 years and has a genuine and subsisting parental relationship with a child under the age of 18 years who enjoys British nationality and is in the UK, less weight is to be attached to the pubic [*sic*] interest in deportation if it would not be reasonable to expect the child to leave the UK and there is no one else here to look after him. By contrast, however, where the person to be deported has been sentenced to a term of 4 years' imprisonment or more, the provisions of paragraph 399 do not apply and accordingly the weight to be attached to the public interest in deportation remains very great despite the factors to which that paragraph refers. It follows that neither the fact that the appellant's children enjoy British nationality nor the fact that they may be separated from their father for a long time will be sufficient to constitute exceptional circumstances of a kind which outweigh the public interest in his deportation' [para 24].

CT (Vietnam) v Secretary of State for the Home Department [2016] EWCA Civ 488:

> 'The starting point in considering exceptional circumstances is not neutral . . . Rather, the scales are heavily weighted in favour of deportation and something very compelling is required to swing the outcome in favour of a foreign criminal whom Parliament has said should be deported' [para 18];

and:

> 'The best interests of the child, always a primary consideration, are not sole or paramount but to be balanced against other factors, in this case that only the strongest Article 8 claims will outweigh the public interest in deporting someone sentenced to at least four years' imprisonment. It will almost always be proportionate to deport, even taking into account as a primary consideration the best interests of a child' [para 19].

[8] NA (Pakistan) v Secretary of State for the Home Department [2016] EWCA Civ 662:

> 'A curious feature of section 117C(3) is that it does not make any provision for medium offenders who fall outside Exceptions 1 and 2. One would have expected that sub-section to say that they too can escape deportation if "there are very compelling circumstances, over

and above Exceptions 1 and 2". It would be bizarre in the extreme if the statute gave this right to serious offenders, but not to medium offenders. Furthermore, the new rule 398 (which came into force on the same day as section 117C) proceeds on the basis that medium offenders do have this right [para 24] . . . Something has obviously gone amiss with the drafting of section 117C(3) . . . In our view the lacuna in section 117C(3) is an obvious drafting error. Parliament must have intended medium offenders to have the same fall back protection as serious offenders [para 25].'

9    *NA (Pakistan)* above, at para 29.

### 7.108 *[At end of main text add:]*

The recent Upper Tribunal decision in *Chen*[7] gives guidance on the application of the *Chikwamba* principle where an applicant cannot succeed under Appendix FM. The Tribunal acknowledged, in the headnote to the decision, that 'there may be cases in which there are no insurmountable obstacles to family life being enjoyed outside the UK but where temporary separation to enable an individual to make an application for entry clearance may be disproportionate'. However, it went on to emphasise that 'In all cases, it will be for the individual to place before the Secretary of State evidence that such temporary separation will interfere disproportionately with protected rights' and that '[i]t will not be enough to rely solely upon the case-law concerning *Chikwamba*'. This Upper Tribunal decision cannot be taken to have undermined anything said by their Lordships in *Chikwamba*, nor the guidance issued by the Court of Appeal in *MA(Pakistan)* or *Hayat*[8]

7    *R (on the application of Chen) v Secretary of State for the Home Department (Appendix FM – Chikwamba – temporary separation – proportionality) IJR* [2015] UKUT 00189 (IAC).
8    See fn 8 at 7.107 above.

### 7.110 *[In the main text, after footnote reference 7, insert:]*

In *El Ghatet v Switzerland*,[8] the Swiss courts examined the best interests of the applicant's son ' . . . in a brief manner and put forward a rather summary reasoning in that regard . . . '. His best interests were not sufficiently placed ' . . . at the centre of its balancing exercise and its reasoning, contrary to the requirements under the Convention'.[9] On that basis there was a violation of Article 8.[10]

In *X v Latvias*[11] the Grand Chamber affirmed that the ECHR and the Hague Convention[12] are to be applied in a 'combined and harmonious' manner (para 94),[13] reiterating that in all decisions concerning children, their best interests must be 'a paramount consideration' (paras 95–97).[14] Thus, factors capable of constituting an exception to the child's immediate return per The Hague Convention[15] must be properly taken into account in a sufficiently reasoned decision. Those factors must then be evaluated in the light of Article 8 of the Convention (para 104]. A failure to do either breaches the procedural requirements of Article 8.[16] In the present case, by refusing to examine a psychologist's report disclosing a 'serious risk'[17] of trauma to 'X' if immediately separated from her mother (para 117), the Latvian authorities perpetrated a procedural breach of Article 8.

In a different context, in *Nada v Switzerland*,[18] the court avoided conflict between Article 8 of ECHR and state obligations under the UN sanctions regime[19] through a 'harmonious interpretation'.[20]

8    Application no 56971/10, 8 November 2016.

[9] '52. . . . Had the domestic authorities engaged in a thorough balancing of the interests in issue, particularly taking into account the child's best interests, and put forward relevant and sufficient reasons for their decision, the Court would, in line with the principle of subsidiarity, consider that the domestic authorities neither failed to strike a fair balance between the interests of the applicants and the interest of the State, nor to have exceeded the margin of appreciation available to them under the Convention in the domain of immigration.'

[10] See para 54.

[11] Application no 27853/09, 26 November 2013.

[12] Hague Convention on the Civil Aspects of International Child Abduction, 25 October 1980.

[13] See para 94: 'This approach involves a combined and harmonious application of the international instruments, and in particular in the instant case of the Convention and the Hague Convention, regard being had to its purpose and its impact on the protection of the rights of children and parents. Such consideration of international provisions should not result in conflict or opposition between the different treaties, provided that the Court is able to perform its task in full, namely 'to ensure the observance of the engagements undertaken by the High Contracting Parties' to the Convention (see, among other authorities, *Loizidou v Turkey* (preliminary objections), 23 March 1995, § 93, Series A no. 310), by interpreting and applying the Convention's provisions in a manner that renders its guarantees practical and effective (see, in particular, *Artico v Italy*, 13 May 1980, § 33, Series A no. 37, and *Nada*, cited above, § 182).' See also § 92, citing §168–170 of *Nada v Switzerland* ((GC), no. 10593/08, § 167, ECHR 2012).

[14] See paras 95–97. At para 96, the Court says: 'The Court reiterates that there is a broad consensus – including in international law – in support of the idea that in all decisions concerning children, their best interests must be paramount (see paragraphs 37–39 above)'.

[15] The exceptions: Articles 12, 13 and 20 of the Hague Convention.

[16] See paras 107 and 115: para 107 states: ' . . . when assessing an application for a child's return, the courts must not only consider arguable allegations of a 'grave risk' for the child in the event of return, but must also make a ruling giving specific reasons in the light of the circumstances of the case. Both a refusal to take account of objections to the return capable of falling within the scope of Articles 12, 13 and 20 of the Hague Convention and insufficient reasoning in the ruling dismissing such objections would be contrary to the requirements of Article 8 of the Convention and also to the aim and purpose of the Hague Convention. Due consideration of such allegations, demonstrated by reasoning of the domestic courts that is not automatic and stereotyped, but sufficiently detailed in the light of the exceptions set out in the Hague Convention, which must be interpreted strictly (see *Maumousseau* and *Washington*, cited above, § 73), is necessary. This will also enable the Court, whose task is not to take the place of the national courts, to carry out the European supervision entrusted to it.'

[17] Within the meaning of Article 13(b) of the Hague Convention.

[18] Application no 10593/08.

[19] Ibid, at para 22.

[20] Ibid, see para 197. This interpretation was reached without resort to the supremacy clause in Article 103 of the UN Charter. See also para 170.

## 7.112 *[At the end of main text add:]*

Section 55 requires the decision-maker to be properly informed of the position of a child affected by the discharge of an immigration function. Thus equipped, the decision maker must conduct a careful examination of all relevant information and factors. The question whether the duties imposed by section 55 have been duly performed in any given case will invariably be an intensely fact sensitive and contextual one. In the real world of litigation, the tools available to the court or tribunal considering this question will frequently be confined to the application or submission made to Secretary of State and the ultimate letter of decision.[12] Where it is contended in an appeal that either of the section 55 duties has been breached, the onus rests on the appellant to establish this on the balance of probabilities. The second duty under section 55, to have regard to statutory guidance, does not require that the decision letter must make specific reference to the statutory guidance.[13] Where the Tribunal decides that there has been a breach by the Secretary of State of either of the section 55 duties, it is empowered, in its final determination of the appeal, to assess the best interests of any affected child and determine the appeal accordingly. This exercise will be appropriate in cases where the evidence is sufficient to enable the Tribunal to conduct a properly informed assessment of the child's best interests. In cases where the Tribunal forms the view that the assembled evidence is insufficient for this purpose, two options arise: the first is to consider such further relevant evidence as the Appellant can muster and/or to exercise case management powers in an attempt to augment the available evidence; the second is to determine the appeal in a manner which requires the Secretary of State to make a fresh decision.[14] It would now appear that in non-deportation cases where the appellant's child is a British citizen, the Article 8 balancing exercise will in general be resolved decisively in favour of the child's interests by s 117B(6) of the NIAA 2002: see **7.106** above.[15] Conversely, very different considerations will apply in deportation cases involving serious criminality, where the public interest in deportation will be given great weight: see **7.107** above.

[12] *JO and Others (section 55 duty) Nigeria* [2014] UKUT 00517 (IAC).

[13] *MK (section 55 – Tribunal options) Sierra Leone* [2015] UKUT 00223 (IAC).

[14] *MK*, above, at para 39. See also *Greenwood (No 2) (para 398 considered)* [2015] UKUT 00629 (IAC) to the effect that, although 'remittal' is no longer a power available to the Tribunal under the new appeals regime (brought in by amendments to Part 5 of the Nationality, Immigration and Asylum Act 2002 by the Immigration Act 2014), the Tribunal may still 'make a decision the effect whereof is that the Secretary of State either must, or may, make a fresh decision' (headnote, para (iv)).

[15] See also *Treebhawon and Others (section 117B(6))* [2015] UKUT 00674 (IAC):

'Section 117B(6) is a reflection of the distinction which Parliament has chosen to make between persons who are, and who are not, liable to deportation. In any case where the conditions enshrined in section 117B(6) of the Nationality, Immigration and Asylum Act 2002 are satisfied, the section 117B(6) public interest prevails over the public interests identified in section 117B (1)–(3).'

**7.113** *[In the main text delete the sentence: 'What amounts to lengthy residence is not clear cut but past and present policies have identified seven years as a relevant period.' , retain footnote 4, and substitute:]*

As regards the meaning of 'lengthy residence', the threshold of seven years has now been enshrined in section 117B(6) of the NIAA 2002 and paragraph 276ADE of the Rules: see **7.106** above. However, it should not be assumed that shorter periods of residence by a child cannot carry weight in the assessment of proportionality.

**7.114** *[At end of main text add:]*

Stanley Burnton LJ in *Miah* distinguished, at [12], the so-called 'near miss' principle – whose existence he rejected – from the *de minimis* principle, stating: '[i]f a departure from a rule is truly *de minimis*, the rule is considered to have been complied with'. The same was suggested *obiter* by Dyson LJ at [27] in *MD (Jamaica)*.[13] However, a Panel of the Upper Tribunal recently held in *Chau Le*[14] that there is no *de minimis* principle applicable to the Immigration Rules. The Court of Appeal in *SS(Congo)*,[15] while endorsing the conclusion in *Miah* that there is no 'near miss' principle, appeared to develop the Supreme Court's reasoning in *Patel* on this topic, concluding that the fact that a case is a 'near miss' case may, in appropriate circumstances, 'tip the balance under Article 8' in an applicant's favour.

[13] *MD (Jamaica) v Secretary of State for the Home Department* [2010] EWCA Civ 213.

[14] *Chau Le (Immigration Rules – de minimis principle)* [2016] UKUT 00186 (IAC).

[15] *SS (Congo) v Secretary of State for the Home Department* [2015] EWCA Civ 387 at para 56:

'However, it cannot be said that the fact that a case involves a "near miss" in relation to the requirements set out in the Rules is wholly irrelevant to the balancing exercise required under Article 8. If an applicant can show that there are individual interests at stake covered by Article 8 which give rise to a strong claim that compelling circumstances may exist to justify the grant of LTE outside the Rules, the fact that their case is also a "near miss" case may be a relevant consideration which tips the balance under Article 8 in their favour. In such a case, the applicant will be able to say that the detrimental impact on the public interest in issue if LTE is granted in their favour will be somewhat less than in a case where the gap between the applicant's position and the requirements of the Rules is great, and the risk that they may end up having recourse to public funds and resources is therefore greater.'

**7.115** *[At the end of the main text add:]*

As a corollary of the Court of Appeal's observation, at [17] of *JA (Ivory Coast)*, that Article 8 'is not simply a more easily accessed version' of Article 3, the Court of Appeal has held in *GS (India) and Others*[6] that, in a 'health' claim which cannot succeed under Article 3, 'Article 8 cannot prosper without some separate or additional factual element which brings the case within the Article 8 paradigm – the capacity to form and enjoy relationships – or a state of affairs having some affinity with the paradigm' (at [86]). The Court remitted the appeal of one appellant, *GM*, to the Upper Tribunal for further consideration of his claim under Article 8, with the consent of the Secretary of State who accepted that the Upper Tribunal's consideration of Article 8 was inadequate. The other appellants' claims under Article 8 were not substantively considered by the Court because Article 8 had not been argued in the Upper Tribunal.

[6] *GS (India) and Others v Secretary of State for the Home Department* [2015] EWCA Civ 40.

**7.116** *[At end of main text add:]*

In non-deportation cases, private life claims will now be considered in the first instance under para 276ADE of the Rules. At this stage, sections 117A–117D have no direct relevance.[14] Paragraph 276ADE(1)(vi), which applies in respect of adults who have lived in the UK for less than 20 years, has taken on increasing importance. Until 7 August 2014, para 276ADE(1)(vi) provided for the grant of leave to a person who 'has no ties (including social, cultural or family) with the country to which he would have to go if required to leave the UK'. This required a rounded assessment as to whether a person's familial ties could result in support to him in the event of his return, an assessment taking into account both subjective and objective considerations and also consideration of what lies within the choice of a claimant to achieve.[15] Statement of Changes HC 532 (7 August 2014) substituted those words with the phrase 'there would be very significant obstacles to the applicant's integration into the country to which he would have to go if required to leave the UK'. There is as yet little clear authority on the meaning of this provision. In deportation cases, the 'very significant obstacles' wording is also found in the new version of para 399A, which applies where 'the person has been lawfully resident in the UK for most of his life', 'is socially and culturally integrated in the UK', and 'there would be very significant obstacles to his integration into the country to which it is proposed he is deported'. In deportation cases, if the claim does not succeed under paras 399 and 399A, the decision-maker will go on to consider whether there are 'very compelling circumstances' applying established Article

8 standards: see **7.107** above. In non-deportation cases, if the private life claim does not succeed under the Rules, the decision-maker will proceed to the second stage and consider Article 8 outside the Rules: see **7.101** above. In this regard, where the decision-maker is a court or tribunal, section 117B of the 2002 Act now mandates that a person's private life be given 'little weight' if it was established while their status was 'precarious'. For the meaning of 'precarious', see **7.105** above. The term 'established' is not confined to the initiation, or creation, of the private life in question but also includes its continuation or development.[16] The meaning of the instruction to attach 'little weight' to private life has been considered in a trio of Upper Tribunal decisions. In *Forman*[17] the Tribunal held that the list of considerations in section 117B is 'not exhaustive' and that a court or tribunal is entitled to have regard to other factors, provided that they properly bear on the public interest question. Nonetheless, in *Deelah*,[18] the Tribunal emphasised that 'in giving effect to section 117B(4) and (5), the court or tribunal concerned is not, in truth, performing the exercise of *having regard* to these statutory provisions. Rather, the Judge is complying with a statutory obligation, unconditional and unambiguous, to give effect to a parliamentary instruction that the considerations in question are to receive little weight'. In *Miah*[19] the Tribunal emphasised that the statutory factors in section 117B(1) to (5) apply to all including children, but also observed in its headnote that those factors 'are not however an exhaustive list, and all other relevant factors must also be weighed in the balance. These may include age, vulnerability and immaturity'.[20]

[14] *Bossade (ss 117A-D-interrelationship with Rules)* [2015] UKUT 00415 (IAC).
[15] *Bossadi (paragraph 276ADE; suitability; ties)* [2015] UKUT 00042 (IAC).
[16] *Deelah and Others (section 117B – ambit)* [2015] UKUT 00515 (IAC).
[17] *Forman (ss 117A-C considerations)* [2015] UKUT 00412 (IAC).
[18] *Deelah*, above.
[19] *Miah (section 117B NIAA 2002 – children)* [2016] UKUT 00131 (IAC).
[20] See also *Miah* at para 24:

> '[T]he obligatory statutory considerations will be weighed by the Tribunal with all other facts and factors which have a legitimate bearing on the issue of proportionality. In the case of a child it is possible to envisage, in the abstract, a series of considerations which could potentially outweigh the public interest. These might include matters such as parental dominance and influence; trafficking; other forms of compulsion; and the absence of any flagrant, repeated or persistent breaches of the United Kingdom's immigration regime by the child concerned. Furthermore, the child's age and personal circumstances at the commencement of the period under scrutiny and thereafter will be obviously material considerations. Viewed panoramically, it seems uncontroversial to suggest that an Article 8(2) proportionality exercise which strikes the balance in a manner which overcomes the public interests engaged is more likely to occur in the case of a child than that of an adult.'

## Freedom of thought, conscience and religion

**7.118** *[At the end of footnote 5, add:]*

Similarly, refusing to allow a prisoner access to a Pastor where there was no clear legal basis for doing so, and where the interference showed no legitimate aim or proportionality, breached Article 9: *Mozer v Republic of Moldova and Russia* (Application no 11138/10), 23 February 2016 (GC).

*[At the end of footnote 7, add:]*

In *SAS v France* (Application no 43835/11), 1 July 2014 (GC) the ECtHR concluded the French ban on wearing a full-face veil in public did not breach

Article 9. The ECtHR had previously considered other circumstances relating to the wearing of religious symbols, in relation to teaching staff in state schools; for pupils and students; in respect of security checks; and where there was a requirement to appear bareheaded in identity photos on official documents. In none of those cases was a breach of Article 9 found (see para 133).

### Freedom of expression

**7.120** *[After the final sentence, insert:]*

More recently, in *Sehwerert*, the Court of Appeal held a decision to refuse entry clearance to one of the 'Cuban Five' (a group of Cuban intelligence agents convicted in the US of related activities) breached Article 10.[4] The appellant had been invited by a number of Members of Parliament to visit the UK for a series of meetings. The appeal was ultimately successful on the basis that their – as opposed to the appellant's – right to freedom of expression was disproportionately interfered with by a refusal to grant him entry clearance.

[4] *Sehewerert, R (on the application of) v Entry Clearance Officer and Others* [2015] EWCA Civ 1141.

### Non-discrimination

**7.123** *[At the end of this section, add:]*

In *Biao v Denmark*[33] the Grand Chamber concluded Denmark's family reunion provisions were discriminatory. Citizens who resided in Denmark for less than 28 years had to meet an 'attachment requirement' to secure entry clearance for their partners. The requirement entailed showing the couple did not have stronger ties with a country other than Denmark. Unsurprisingly the requirement disproportionately affected those who naturalised as Danish citizens, ie those with an ethnic origin other than Danish. Bearing in mind the very narrow margin of appreciation afforded in the circumstances, the government failed to show there were compelling or very weighty reasons unrelated to ethnic origin that justified the indirect discrimination arising from the requirement.

[33] Application no 38590/10, 24 May 2016 (GC).

### Effective remedy

**7.125** *[At the end of footnote 2, add:]*

Whilst the protection under Article 13 is less stringent than that offered by Article 6, there is a degree of overlap between the two, not least with 'access to court' protections under the latter being of relevance to the former: *GR v The Netherlands* (Application no 22251/07), 10 January 2012, at para 48. Similarly, the court also found a breach of Articles 3 and 13 in *VM and others v Belgium*, (Application no 60125/11), 7 July 2015 at paras 213–220 for a number of interrelated reasons including the possibility a stay on removal being wrongly refused; the difficultly in practice, and the complexity of securing, a stay; procedural delay; vulnerability of the persons concerned (especially with families); and being without notice of state decision making.

*[In the main text after footnote reference 3, insert:]*

In *De Souza Ribeiro v France*,[3a] Mr Ribeiro was removed from French Guiana to Brazil less than 36 hours after his arrest,[3b] 49 minutes after lodging his application to the authorities,[3c] and contrary to a French law protecting him from expulsion.[3d] The Grand Chamber held that although Article 8 was clearly engaged, the applicant ' . . . had no chance of having the lawfulness of the removal order examined sufficiently thoroughly by a national authority offering the requisite procedural guarantees'[3e] observing ' . . . speed should not go so far as to constitute an obstacle or unjustified hindrance to making use of it, or take priority over its practical effectiveness'. The haste with which the removal order was executed rendered the available remedies ineffective in practice and therefore inaccessible in violation of Article 13 in conjunction with Article 8.

*[In the main text at the end of the fifth sentence after footnote reference 4, insert:]*

In *De Souza Ribeiro v France*,[3a] Mr Ribeiro was removed from French Guiana to Brazil less than 36 hours after his arrest,[3b] 49 minutes after lodging his application to the authorities,[3c] and contrary to a French law protecting him from expulsion.[3d] The Grand Chamber held that although Article 8 was clearly engaged, the applicant ' . . . had no chance of having the lawfulness of the removal order examined sufficiently thoroughly by a national authority offering the requisite procedural guarantees'[3e] observing ' . . . speed should not go so far as to constitute an obstacle or unjustified hindrance to making use of it, or take priority over its practical effectiveness'. The haste with which the removal order was executed rendered the available remedies ineffective in practice and therefore inaccessible in violation of Article 13 in conjunction with Article 8.

[3a] Application no 22689/07, 13 December 2012 (GC).

[3b] Ibid, see para 88.

[3c] Ibid: '94. In the present case the file submitted to the competent 'national authority' cannot be said to have been particularly complex. The Court would reiterate that the applications lodged by the applicant contained clearly explained legal reasoning. In challenging the removal order the applicant alleged that it was both contrary to the Convention and illegal under French law. He referred, inter alia, to Article L. 511–4 of the CESEDA and presented detailed proof that most of his private and family life had been spent in French Guiana (see paragraph 18 above), thereby demonstrating that his case was sufficiently meritorious to warrant proper examination (see, mutatis mutandis, *IM v France*, cited above, § 155)'.

[3d] See para 90.

[3e] See paras 95–96:' . . . the manner in which the applicant's removal was effected was extremely rapid, even perfunctory'.

[3a] Application no 22689/07, 13 December 2012 (GC).

[3b] Ibid, see para 88.

[3c] Ibid: '94. In the present case the file submitted to the competent 'national authority' cannot be said to have been particularly complex. The Court would reiterate that the applications lodged by the applicant contained clearly explained legal reasoning. In challenging the removal order the applicant alleged that it was both contrary to the Convention and illegal under French law. He referred, inter alia, to Article L. 511–4 of the CESEDA and presented detailed proof that most of his private and family life had been spent in French Guiana (see paragraph 18 above), thereby demonstrating that his case was sufficiently meritorious to warrant proper examination (see, mutatis mutandis, *IM v France*, cited above, § 155)'.

<sup>3d</sup> See para 90.
<sup>3e</sup> See paras 95–96:' . . . the manner in which the applicant's removal was effected was extremely rapid, even perfunctory'.


## GOING TO EUROPE

### ECtHR

**7.127** *[In footnote 12 delete the sentence 'In 2013 the Grand Chamber gave only 13 judgments.']*

**7.128** *[Insert new footnote reference 3a at the end of the fourth sentence after ' . . . Rules of Court.']*

*[In the footnotes insert new footnote 3a text:]*

Rules of the European Court of Human Rights, 14 November 2016 (as amended by the Court on 17 June and 8 July 2002, 11 December 2007, 22 September 2008, 6 May 2013 and 1 June and 5 October 2015).

*[In footnote 8 delete the second and third sentences (after 'r 54(2)'.]*

*[In footnote 9 delete 'r 54(3)' and replace with 'r 54(5)'.]*

*[In the main text after the sentence ending 'pursuing merits of the case.' insert:]*

Where an applicant refuses the terms of a friendly-settlement proposal the respondent party may request to strike the application out.[10a] Such a request must be accompanied by a declaration clearly acknowledging that there has been a violation of the Convention in the applicant's case together with an undertaking to provide adequate redress and, as appropriate, to take necessary remedial measures.[10b] Prior to any attempt to reach a friendly settlement, a request may be made where exceptional circumstances justify it.[10c] The Court may strike out the application, in whole or in part, even if the applicant wishes the examination of the application to be continued.[10d]

*[In the main text, after footnote reference 11, insert:]*

Once an application made under Article 34 of the Convention has been declared admissible the parties may be invited to submit further evidence and written observations,[11a] and unless decided otherwise, the parties shall be allowed the same time for submission of their observations.[11b]

*[Insert new footnotes and text in the correct sequential order.]*

[10a] Rules of the European Court of Human Rights, r 62.A.1(a).
[10b] Rules of the European Court of Human Rights, r 62.A.1(b).
[10c] Rules of the European Court of Human Rights, r 62.A.2.
[10d] Rules of the European Court of Human Rights, r 62.A.2.
[11a] Rules of the European Court of Human Rights, r 59.1.
[11b] Rules of the European Court of Human Rights, r 59.1.


### Pilot procedure

**7.128A** *[Add new heading and paragraph:]*

The Court may initiate a pilot-judgment procedure and adopt a pilot judgment where 'the facts of an application reveal the existence of a structural or systemic problem or other similar dysfunction which has given rise, or may give rise, to similar applications'.[1] Before initiating a pilot-judgment procedure, the Court shall first seek the views of the parties.[2] A pilot-judgment procedure may be initiated by the Court of its own motion or at the request of one or both parties.[3] Any application selected for pilot-judgment treatment shall be processed as a matter of priority.[4] The Court shall in its pilot judgment identify both the nature of the structural or systemic problem or other dysfunction as established, the type of remedial measures to be taken,[5] and a specified time within which to make them.[6] Any similar applications may be adjourned pending the adoption of the measures in question.[7] Subject to any decision to the contrary, in the event of a failure to comply with the operative provisions of a pilot judgment, the Court shall resume its examination of the adjourned applications.[8] Friendly settlement must include a declaration to implement the measures and the redress to actual or potential applicants.[9] Information about the initiation of pilot-judgment procedures, the adoption of pilot judgments and their execution as well as the closure of such procedures shall be published on the Court's website.[10]

[1]  Rules of the European Court of Human Rights, r 61. Where this is done then per r 61.9: 'The Committee of Ministers, the Parliamentary Assembly of the Council of Europe, the Secretary General of the Council of Europe, and the Council of Europe Commissioner for Human Rights shall be informed of the adoption of a pilot judgment as well as of any other judgment in which the Court draws attention to the existence of a structural or systemic problem in a Contracting Party'.
[2]  Rules of the European Court of Human Rights, r 61.2(a).
[3]  Rules of the European Court of Human Rights, r 61.2(b).
[4]  Rules of the European Court of Human Rights, rr 61.2(c) and 41.
[5]  Rules of the European Court of Human Rights, r 61.3.
[6]  Rules of the European Court of Human Rights, r 61.4.
[7]  Rules of the European Court of Human Rights, r 61.6(a).
[8]  Rules of the European Court of Human Rights, r 61.8.
[9]  Rules of the European Court of Human Rights, r 61.7.
[10]  Rules of the European Court of Human Rights, r 61.10.

### Interim measures

**7.129** *[In footnote 3 delete text and replace with:]*

In 2015 there were 1,458 requests for interim measures; 161 were granted. European Court of Human Rights: Thematical Statistics, Interim Measures 2012-2015.

*[At the end of footnote 5, before the full stop, add:]*

and *Kondrulin v Russia* (Application no 12987/15), 20 September 2016, in which Russia failed to comply with the Court's Rule 39 request to obtain an independent medical examination of the applicant

*[In footnote 8, before the full stop, add:]*

; *WH v Sweden* (Application no 49341/10), 8 April 2015 (religious minority)

Chapter 8

# VISITS, STUDY AND TEMPORARY PURPOSES

## INTRODUCTION

**8.1** *[Existing 8.1 is deleted except for the extract on Designated Travel Bans, which is moved to new paragraph 8.3C (see below). Insert:]*

In 2015 the various rules on visitors in the main text of HC 359 were transferred to a new Appendix V by HC 1025, para 448. The changes set out in this paragraph took effect from 24 April 2015 and replaced Part 2 of the Immigration Rules. Any applications for entry clearance or leave to enter or remain made on or after 24 April 2015 are now decided in accordance with the new Visitor Rules in force from 24 April 2015.[1] According to the explanatory statement, the superceded rules contained 15 different visitor routes, which, to some degree, limited the individual to a single purpose.[2] These have now been redesigned so that there are only four:[3]

- visitor (standard);
- visitor for marriage or civil partnerships;
- visitor for permitted paid engagements; and
- transit visitor.

The visitor (standard) route consolidates the following existing routes: general, business, child, sport, entertainer, visitors for private medical treatment, visitors under the Approved Destination Status (ADS) Agreement with China, prospective entrepreneur, and visitors undertaking clinical attachments – the Professional and Linguistic Assessment Board (PLAB) test and the Objective Structured Clinical Examination (OSCE). In practice, this means that individuals will be able to undertake a range of activities if entering under the visitor (standard) route, without the risk of having to make separate applications for each different activity.

Two of the previous routes have now been rebranded and are no longer part of the visitor rules. These are:

(i) the student visitor and extended student visitor routes have been modified and now sit in Part 3 of the Immigration Rules alongside other study provisions;[4] and

(ii) 7.8. The 'Parent of a child at school' route which has been rebranded as 'Parent of a Tier 4 (child) student' to clarify the purpose of the route, and now sits in Part 7 of the Immigration Rules making it clear that these parents are not visitors.[5]

1    HC 1025, Implementation.
2    HC 1025, Explanatory Statement, para 7.4.
3    HC 1025, Explanatory Statement, para 7.5.
4    HC 395, Part 2, para 2, as amended by HC 1025.
5    HC 395, Part 2, para 2, as amended by HC 1025.

### 8.1A *[Insert new paragraph:]*

The new rules came into force on 24 April 2015. Appendix 1 of Appendix V sets out all the definitions and interpretations as relevant to the Visitor section.[1] Part 2 of the Immigration Rules used to contain all the main rules for visitors from paras 40–56Z. They have all been deleted. Part 2 now only contains transitional provisions for Part 2 and Appendix V, and confirms that any interpretations set out: (a) in the Immigration Rules, Introduction, para 6; (b) Part 1 of the rules; (c) Part 9; (d) Appendix 1; and (e) Appendix R, do not apply to visitors except where specifically provided for in Appendix V.[2] The new Part 2 also makes clear that applications made before 24 April 2015, but decided after that date will be determined under Appendix V. It is the date of decision which counts. This may be beneficial. For example, those who hold multi-entry visit visas will be treated as visitors (standard) after 24 April 2015 and can use that visa to do permitted activities as set out in Visitors Appendix 3. The only exception to this is where a child holds a long-term visit visa and they want to study a course, they will need to apply for a short-term student visa after 24 April 2015 as they will only be allowed to do incidental study on their existing visit visa.[3]

1    Paragraph 6 now defines a 'visitor' as a person granted leave to enter or remain in the UK under paras 40–56Z, 75A–75M or 82–87 of these Rules before 24 April 2015 or under Appendix V: Immigration Rules for Visitors on or after 24 April 2015. All the other 'Visitor' definitions in para 6 have been removed to Appendix 1. See HC 1025, paras 13–20.
2    The old Part 2 was deleted and replaced with four short paragraphs by HC 1025, para 49.
3    We are grateful to the authors of the Lexis PSL *Immigration Visitor Rules Analysis* for the last examples and have used this very helpful Analysis of Appendix P in our updating of this chapter.

### Visa and non-visa nationals

### 8.2 *[Insert new heading and delete existing paragraph 8.2 and substitute:]*

Non-visa nationals coming for a period of less than six months for a visit or other purpose, for which an entry clearance is not needed, do not need prior entry clearance,[1] unless they are visiting the UK to marry or form a civil partnership or to give notice of this, or are seeking to visit the UK for more than six months.[2] On the other hand, all visa nationals require a visa for a visit unless they are exempted. Appendix 2 to the Immigration Rules for visitors is an update of the old Appendix 1, which has been deleted. Appendix 2 lists the visa national countries, indicating the exceptions for nationals of certain countries.

- It is not necessary for a transit visitor to hold a visa before they travel to the UK if they are travelling on an emergency travel document and the purpose of their transit visit is to travel to the state in which they are ordinarily resident and the purpose of their transit visit is to travel to the state in which they are ordinarily resident.[3]
- The following visa nationals are exempted, except if they are visiting the UK to marry or to form a civil partnership or to give notice of this; or are seeking to visit the UK for more than 6 months:[4]

    (a) nationals or citizens of the People's Republic of China who hold a passport issued by the Hong Kong Special Administrative Region; or

    (b) nationals or citizens of the People's Republic of China who hold a passport issued by the Macao Special Administrative Region; or

    (c) nationals or citizens of Taiwan who hold a passport issued by Taiwan that includes in it the number of the identification card issued by the competent authority in Taiwan; or

    (d) people who hold a Service, Temporary Service or Diplomatic passport issued by the Holy See; or

    (e) nationals or citizens of Oman who hold a diplomatic or special passport issued by Oman; or

    (f) nationals or citizens of Qatar who hold a diplomatic or special passport issued by Qatar; or

    (g) nationals or citizens of the United Arab Emirates who hold a diplomatic or special passport issued by the United Arab Emirates; or

    (h) nationals or citizens of Turkey who hold a diplomatic passport issued by Turkey; or

    (i) nationals or citizens of Kuwait who hold a diplomatic or special passport issued by Kuwait; or

    (j) nationals or citizens of Bahrain who hold a diplomatic or special passport issued by Bahrain; or

    (k) nationals or citizens of South Africa who hold a diplomatic passport issued by South Africa; or

    (l) nationals or citizens of Vietnam who hold a diplomatic passport issued by Vietnam; or

    (m) nationals or citizens of Indonesia who hold a diplomatic passport issued by Indonesia.

- Passport holders from Kuwait, Oman, Qatar and the UAE who hold of electronic visa waiver (EVW) documents do not need to apply for a visit visa to enter for six months or less if they hold an EVW document.[5]

[1] HC 395, para 23A, inserted by HC 645. Also note para 23B which deals with British Nationals (Overseas) (BN(O)s), British Overseas Territories citizens (BOTCs), British Overseas citizens (BOCs), British Protected Persons (BPPs) and persons who under the British Nationality Act 1981 are British subjects. They need no visa even if they wish to stay longer than 6 months, but they may only be given up to 6 months on arrival. So far as Canada is concerned UK nationals need an electronic travel authorisation (eTA) as from 30 September 2016. With the USA there are mutual visa waiver requirements for visitors under the visa waiver programme (VWP). The EU allows Canadian and US citizens free travel throughout the EU, but this right, we understand, is not reciprocated for Bulgaria, Cyprus, Poland and Romania.

[2] Appendix V, V1.3(a) and (b).

[3] Appendix 2, para A2 of Appendix V.

⁴   Appendix 2, para A2.2 of Appendix V.
⁵   See Appendix 2, paras 4–19. for details of who may apply, how they do so and what documents they need to produce.

## Making the application

### 8.2A  *[Insert new heading and paragraph:]*

Practically, very little has changed. Applications must still be made overseas via the online form unless one is not available which, currently, only applies to North Korea. The new rules require only that an application for a visit visa is made while the applicant is outside the UK. Fees must still be paid, biometrics provided and valid travel documents presented.[1] When an application is deemed to have been made is a key question. This is normally when the fee is paid, but it may be when the form is submitted online if a fee is not required or when the paper form is received by the application centre if no online application is available and there is no fee. It should be noted that previously the amount and basis of fees for visits were set by the Consular Fees Act 1980 (CFA 1980) or by regulations or orders made under it. However, the CFA 1980 is no longer the legislation used for authorising immigration fee payment. See CHAPTER 3 above.

An application may be withdrawn by the applicant at any time before a decision is made by letter or email to the visa post or application centre where the applicant submitted their application. If an applicant requests the return of their travel document in writing or by email to the relevant visa post or application centre before a decision is made, this will also have the effect of withdrawing the application unless the procedures of the visa post state otherwise. Many visa application centres – for example in India, Sri Lanka, the Russian Federation and Thailand – operate official Passport Passback services whereby applicants can retain their passports while the Home Office processes the visa application. While not confirmed, it is a fair assumption that using these paid-for services will not have the effect of withdrawing the application.[2]

1   Visitors Appendix 1 defines 'fee' as being the fee payable under regulations made exercising the powers set out in the Immigration Act 2014, ss 68, 69.
2   See Tom Marsom, *Making initial applications*, Lexis PSL Immigration Visitor Rules Analysis.

## SUITABILITY REQUIREMENTS FOR ALL VISITORS

### 8.3  *[Existing paragraph 8.3 on best interests of children is moved to 8.19. Insert new heading and new paragraph 8.3:]*

This chapter deals with the formal requirements of the Immigration Rules relating to visits. It should be noted, however, that, in common with all other entry and remain applications, compliance with the eligibility Rules in Appendix V may not be sufficient to gain entry and the general requirements for refusal of entry may apply. In Appendix V these are now referred to as 'suitability requirements'. Travellers who qualify formally for admission may be refused entry because of their restricted returnability, their past immigration or criminal record, for medical reasons or for the other general reasons already dealt with in Part 9 of the Rules.[1] Similarly, a visa may be cancelled on or before arrival in the UK and existing leave may be curtailed and extensions of leave may be refused on any of the general grounds, even though the formal requirements for an extension are satisfied.[2] All suitability requirements are now included in Appendix V. Parts 3 and 9 of the Visitor Rules cover the suitability requirements for all visitors, the grounds for cancellation of a visa or leave, before or on arrival at the UK border, and curtailment. The suitability Part V3 of Appendix V reproduces paras 320, 321, 321A and relevant provisions of 322 and 323 from Part 9 of the Immigration Rules but Part 9 is no longer applicable to visitors,[3] Appendix V, Parts 3 and 9 are directed only to visitor situations. They are structured differently, but, according to the Explanatory Memorandum to HC 1025 (para 7.15), the tests that apply have not changed except in a few instances:

- the failure to provide biometrics, information or medical reports, if these have been required and if the applicant does not have a reasonable excuse has been made a mandatory ground for refusal;[4]
- a current visit visa or leave to enter or remain as a visitor may be cancelled whilst the person is outside the UK or on arrival in the UK, if the visitor holds a visit visa and their purpose in arriving in the United Kingdom is different from the purpose specified in the visit visa.[5]

Some of grounds call for mandatory refusal and others there is a clear discretion as the following Table indicates.

| Duration of re entry ban from date they left the UK (or date of refusal of entry clearance under paragraph (f) | This applies where the applicant | and | and |
|---|---|---|---|
| (a) 12 months | left voluntarily | at their own expense | — |
| (b) 2 years | left voluntarily | at public expense | Within 6 months of being given notice of liability for removal or when they no longer had a pending appeal or administrative review, whichever is later. |
| (c) 5 years | left voluntarily | at public expense | more than 6 months after being given notice of liability for removal or when they no longer had a pending appeal or administrative review, whichever is later. |

| Duration of re entry ban from date they left the UK (or date of refusal of entry clearance under paragraph (f) | This applies where the applicant | and | and |
|---|---|---|---|
| (d) 5 years | left or was removed from the UK | as a condition of a caution issued in accordance with section 22 of the Criminal Justice Act 2003 (and providing that any condition prohibiting their return to the UK has itself expired) | — |
| (e) 10 years | was deported from the UK or was re-moved from the UK | at public expense | — |
| (f) 10 years | used deception in an application for entry clearance (including a visit visa). | | — |

Where more than one breach of the UK's immigration laws has occurred, only the breach which leads to the longest period of absence from the UK will be relevant (para V3.11).

1   HC 395, para 320. Grounds (1) to (7D) specify circumstances in which entry clearance or leave to enter is to be refused and (8) to (22) where it *should normally* be refused. See **3.136** ff above.
2   HC 395, para 322(1)–(1A) where leave *is to* be refused, and (2)–(12) where leave *should normally* be refused. See **3.92** ff above.
3   HC 395, Part 2, para 4(c).
4   Appendix V, V3.7(b). This change is to make these Rules consistent with the mandatory requirement to refuse leave after a failure to attend an interview and to bring the Visitor Rules in line with the requirements in Appendix FM (Explanatory Memorandum, para 7.15).
5   Appendix V, paras V9.1 and V9.3. The Rules have been amended to better reflect the existing test which is set out in s 2A(2A) of Sch 2 to the Immigration Act 1971: see Explanatory Memorandum to HC 1025, para 7.15.

## Cancellation

### 8.3A *[Insert heading and new paragraph:]*

A current visit visa or leave to enter or remain as a visitor may be cancelled whilst the person is outside the UK or on arrival in the UK, if any of paragraphs V9.2–V 9.7 apply.[1] Under Appendix V, cancellation of leave may be for any one or a combination of the following reasons:

• *Change of circumstances.* Where the change in the circumstances since the visit visa or leave to enter or remain was granted is such that the basis of the visitor's claim to admission or stay has been removed (V9.2).

- *Change of purpose.* Where the visitor holds a visit visa and their purpose in arriving in the United Kingdom is different from the purpose specified in the visit visa (V9.3).
- *False information.* Where false representations were made or false documents or information submitted (whether or not material to the application, and whether or not to the applicant's knowledge) (V9.2(a)).
- *Failure to disclose a material fact.* Where material facts were not disclosed, in relation to the application for a visit visa or leave to enter or remain as a visitor, or in order to obtain documents from the Secretary of State or a third party provided in support of their application (V9.2(b)).
- *Medical.* Where it is undesirable to admit the visitor to the UK for medical reasons, unless there are strong compassionate reasons justifying admission (V9.5).
- *Not conducive to the public good.* Where the criteria in paras V3.2–V3.5 (as set out in the Table above) apply (V9.6).
- Failure to supply information. Where the person is outside the UK and there is a failure to supply any information, documents, or medical reports requested by a decision maker (V9.7). In our view this is an unclear ground in that it fails to make clear the timescale for production of these documents.

[1] Appendix V, para V9.1. The power to cancel is dealt in more detail at **3.126**.

## Curtailment

**8.3B** *[Insert new heading and paragraph:]*

A visit visa or leave to enter or remain as a visitor may be curtailed while the person is in the UK in any of the following circumstances:[1]

- *False information.* Where false representations were made or false documents or information were submitted (whether or not material to the application, and whether or not to the applicant's knowledge) (V9.9(a)).
- *Failure to disclose a material fact.* Material facts were not disclosed, in relation to any application for an entry clearance or leave to enter or remain, or for the purpose of obtaining relevant documents from the Secretary of State or third party, as specified in the rule (V9.9(b)).
- *Requirements of the Rules.* If the visitor ceases to meet the requirements of the Visitor Rules (V9.10).
- *Failure to comply with conditions.* If the visitor fails to comply with any conditions of their leave to enter or remain (V9.11).
- *Not conducive to the public good.* Where either:
  - (a) the visitor has committed an offence for which they are subsequently sentenced to a period of imprisonment within the first 6 months of getting a visit visa or leave to enter; or
  - (b) in the view of the Secretary of State the applicant's offending has caused serious harm; or
  - (c) in the view of the Secretary of State the applicant is a persistent offender who shows a particular disregard for the law; or

(d)     it would be undesirable to permit the visitor to remain in the UK in light of their conduct, character, associations, or the fact that they represent a threat to national security.

¹  Appendix V, para V9.8). More details of the use of curtailment is at **3.127**.

### Designated ban orders

**8.3C** *[The following paragraph is the deleted paragraph 8.1 minus the first sentence and is moved and renumbered as paragraph 8.3C:]*

Passengers who qualify formally for admission may be refused entry because of their restricted returnability, their past immigration or criminal record, for medical reasons or for the other general reasons already referred to.¹ Similarly, extensions of leave may be refused on any of the general grounds contained in the Immigration Rules, even though the formal requirements for an extension are satisfied.² In addition, section 8B of the Immigration Act 1971³ provides for Designated Travel Ban Orders requiring the mandatory exclusion of 'excluded persons' named or described in a designated UN Security Council Resolution or an instrument of the EU Council.⁴ The effect of including these travel bans in the Order is that, unless subject to one of the exemptions set out in Article 3 of the Immigration (Designation of Travel Bans) Order 2000, a person named by or described in a designated travel ban is an excluded person and must be refused leave to enter or remain in the UK, including transit through the UK. Any existing leave is automatically cancelled, and any exemption from immigration control, for example, as a diplomat, ceases.

¹  HC 395, para 320. Grounds (1) to (7D) specify circumstances in which entry clearance or leave to enter *is* to be refused and (8) to (22) where it *should normally* be refused. See **3.136** ff above.
²  HC 395, para 322(1)–(1A) where leave *is to* be refused, and (2)–(12) where leave *should normally* be refused. See **3.92** ff above.
³  Inserted by Immigration and Asylum Act 1999, s 8.
⁴  The Schedule to the Immigration (Designation of Travel Bans) Order 2000, SI 2000/2724 has been regularly updated and is currently replaced by Schedule 1 to the Immigration (Designation of Travel Bans) (Amendment) Order 2014/1849, which came into force on 21 July 2014. Part 1 of Schedule 1 specifies various UN Resolutions, and Part 2 of Schedule 1 specifies Common EU Positions and/or Council Decisions; they are now too numerous to set out here.

### CATEGORIES OF VISITOR

**8.4**  *[Delete paragraph and substitute:]*

From 15 categories of visit, Appendix V has shrunk them down to four – visitor (standard); visitor for marriage or civil partnerships; visitor for permitted paid engagements and transit visitor. The visitor (standard) route consolidates the following existing routes: general, business, child, sport, entertainer, visitors for private medical treatment, visitors under the Approved Destination Status (ADS) Agreement with China, prospective entrepreneur, and visitors undertaking clinical attachments – the Professional and Linguistic Assessment Board (PLAB) test and the Objective Structured Clinical Examination (OSCE). In practice, this means that individuals will be able to undertake a range of activities if entering under the visitor (standard) route, without the risk of having to make separate applications for each different activity.

The following Table taken from the Appendix V at para V1.5 shows what visitors in each category can do, and the maximum length of stay each type of visitor can be granted.

| Types of visit visa/Leave to enter or remain | Visitors of this type can: | The maximum length of stay that can be granted for each type of visitor: |
|---|---|---|
| (a) Visit (standard) | Do the permitted activities in Appendix 3 except visitors entering under the Approved Destination Status agreement who may only do the activities in paragraph 3 of Appendix 3 to these Rules; | Up to 6 months, except: (i) a visitor who is coming to the UK for private medical treatment may be granted a visit visa of up to 11 months; or (ii) an academic, who is employed by an overseas institution and is carrying out the specific permitted activities paragraph 12 of Appendix 3, of these Rules, along with their spouse or partner and children, may be granted a visit visa of up to 12 months; or (iii) a visitor under the Approved Destination Status Agreement (ADS Agreement) may be granted a visit visa for a period of up to 30 days. |
| (b) Marriage/civil partnership visit | Visit to marry or to form a civil partnership, or to give notice of this, in the UK, and do the permitted activities in Appendix 3; | Up to 6 months. |
| (c) Permitted Paid Engagements (PPE) visit | Do the paid engagements in Appendix 4 and do the permitted activities in Appendix 3; | Up to 1 month. |
| (d) Transit visit | Transit the UK. | Up to 48 hours, except for leave to enter as a transit visitor under the Transit Without Visa Scheme which may be granted until 23:59 hours on the next day after the day the applicant arrived. |

Within the period for which the visit visa is valid, a visitor may enter and leave the UK multiple times, unless the visit visa is endorsed as a single- or dual-entry visa (V1.6).

**8.5** *[Delete whole of 8.5 and paragraph 8.6 is now renumbered as 8.5.]*

*[In the main text after footnote reference 7, delete the last sentence and insert:]*

Overseas graduates from medical, dental or nursing schools may take the Professional and Linguistic Assessment Board (PLAB) test, or other specified tests.[8]

*[In footnote 2 delete the last sentence.]*

*[In footnote 7, after the word 'partnership', delete remaining text and replace with: .']*

– see 8.33 below.

[8]  Overseas graduates from medical, dental or nursing schools may take the Professional and Linguistic Assessment Board (PLAB) test or other specified tests. See Appendix 3 of Appendix V, para 22.


## ELIGIBILITY REQUIREMENTS FOR VISITORS (STANDARD)

**8.6** *[Insert new heading and new paragraph 8.6:]*

The decision maker must be satisfied that the applicant meets all of the eligibility requirements in paragraphs V4.2–V4.10, such as having a genuine intention to visit, having funds, maintenance and accommodation which may be provided by a third party, and does not intend to do any of the prohibited activities listed in V4.5–V4.10 (see below). The decision maker must also be satisfied that the applicant meets any of the additional eligibility requirements where the applicant is a child, someone coming for private medical treatment or as an organ donor, is a Chinese national travelling under the ADS agreement, or an academic seeking a 12-month stay in the UK. Each of these is dealt with in turn.

(a)  **Children.** Adequate arrangements must have been made for their travel to, reception and care in, the UK (V4.11). If they are not applying or travelling with a parent or guardian based in their home country or country of ordinary residence who is responsible for their care, they must have the written consent, if requested, of that parent or guardian with regard to the arrangements for the child's travel to, and reception and care in the UK (V4.12). If they require a visit visa it must state that they are travelling with an adult identified on the visa; if they are unaccompanied they may be refused entry (V4.13).

(b)  **Private medical patients** coming to the UK to receive private medical treatment must show that they have satisfied the medical inspector that if they are suffering from a communicable disease (V4.14), they must show that they have arranged their private medical treatment before they travel to the UK, and have a letter from their doctor or consultant giving details of their medical condition, the cost and likely finite duration of treatment and where the consultation or treatment will take place (V4.15). In addition, if the applicant is applying for an 11-month visit visa for the purposes of private medical treatment they must also provide evidence from their UK doctor that the proposed treatment is likely to exceed 6 months but not more than 11 months; and, if required to do so under the Rules, have undergone screening for active pulmonary tuberculosis and given the all-clear (V4.16).

(c)     **An organ donor,** coming to the UK to donate an organ must show that they genuinely intend to donate an organ, or be assessed as a potential organ donor, to an identified recipient in the UK with whom they have a genetic or close personal relationship (V4.17); they must provide written confirmation of medical tests to show that they are a donor match to the identified recipient, or that they are undergoing further tests to be assessed as a potential donor to the identified recipient (V4.18). Then they must provide a letter, dated no more than three months prior to the applicant's intended date of arrival in the UK from either: (a) the lead nurse or coordinator of the UK's NHS Trust's Living Donor Kidney Transplant team; or (b) a UK registered medical practitioner who holds an NHS consultant post or who appears in the Specialist Register of the General Medical Council, which confirms that the visitor is a donor match for an identified recipient and confirms when and where the planned organ transplant or medical tests will take place (V4.19). If required, the donor may need to demonstrate that the donee is legally present in the UK (V4.20), although normally that will be the task of the immigration authorities (see Visit Guidance, p 23). Individuals donating to patients receiving NHS treatment, can be reimbursed for expenses incurred which are directly attributable to being a donor. These can include travel costs and loss of earnings and are usually paid by the NHS after the treatment (Visit Guidance, p 23). Where a family member, friend or nurse is accompanying the visitor, they must apply as a visitor. Bringing the donor's children with them is discouraged, but not forbidden (Visit Guidance, p 23).

(d)     **The ADS agreement with China.** A visitor coming to the UK under the ADS agreement, must: (a) be a national of the People's Republic of China; and (b) intend to enter, leave and travel within the UK as a member of a tourist group under the ADS agreement (V4.21).

(e)     **Academics** seeking a 12-month visit visa, must be highly qualified within their own field of expertise; must currently be working in that field at an academic institution or institution of higher education overseas; and must, if required to do so under the Rules, have undergone screening for active pulmonary tuberculosis and got the all-clear (V4.22). See further **8.23** below.

**Genuine intention to visit**

**8.7** *[Insert new heading, delete existing paragraph and substitute:]*

The applicant must satisfy the decision maker that they are a genuine visitor (V4.2). This means that the applicant:

(a)     will leave the UK at the end of their visit; and

(b)     will not live in the UK for extended periods through frequent or successive visits, or make the UK their main home; and

(c)     is genuinely seeking entry for a purpose that is permitted by the visitor routes (these are listed in Appendices 3, 4 and 5); and

(d)     will not undertake any prohibited activities set out in V4.5–V4.10; and

(e)     must have sufficient funds to cover all reasonable costs in relation to their visit without working or accessing public funds.

For further discussion, see existing paragraphs **8.11–8.14.**

## Maintenance and accommodation

**8.8** *[Delete and substitute new heading and paragraph:]*

The need to have sufficient funds to cover all reasonable costs in relation to their visit without working or accessing public funds has already been included as an element going to the genuineness of the visit This includes the cost of the return or onward journey, any costs relating to dependants, and the cost of planned activities such as private medical treatment (V4.2). In addition, Appendix V puts third party funding, which may be from friends, relatives, business partners and employers in the spotlight for the first time in the Rules. See existing paragraph 8.15. Appendix V, para V4.3 provides that a visitor's travel, maintenance and accommodation may be provided by a third party where the decision maker is satisfied that they:

(a)    have a genuine professional or personal relationship with the visitor; and

(b)    are not, or will not be, in breach of UK immigration laws at the time of decision or the visitor's entry to the UK; and

(c)    can and will provide support to the visitor for the intended duration of their stay.

The third party may be asked to give an undertaking in writing to be responsible for the applicant's maintenance and accommodation. In this case HC 395, para 35, which deals in detail with sponsor undertakings, will also apply to Visitors. An applicant will normally be refused where, having been requested to do so, the applicant fails to provide a valid written undertaking from a third party to be responsible for their maintenance and accommodation for the period of any visit (V4.4).

## PROHIBITED ACTIVITIES

**8.8A** *[Insert new heading and new paragraph:]*

**Work.** The applicant as a standard visitor must not intend to work in the UK, which includes the following (V4.5):

(a)    taking employment in the UK;
(b)    doing work for an organisation or business in the UK;
(c)    establishing or running a business as a self-employed person;
(d)    doing a work placement or internship;
(e)    direct selling to the public;
(f)    providing goods and services;

unless expressly allowed by the permitted activities in Appendices 3, 4 or 5.

Permitted activities must not amount to the applicant taking employment, or doing work which amounts to them filling a role or providing short-term cover for a role within a UK based organisation (V4.6). In addition, where the applicant is already paid and employed outside of the UK, they must remain so. Payment may only be allowed in specific circumstances set out in V4.7 and Visitors Appendix 4.

**Payment.** The applicant must not receive payment from a UK source for any activities undertaken in the UK, except for the following (V4.7):

(a)  reasonable expenses to cover the cost of their travel and subsistence, including fees for directors attending board-level meetings; or

(b)  prize money; or

(c)  billing a UK client for their time in the UK, where the applicant's overseas employer is contracted to provide services to a UK company, and the majority of the contract work is carried out overseas. Payment must be lower than the amount of the applicant's salary; or

(d)  multi-national companies who, for administrative reasons, handle payment of their employees' salaries from the UK; or

(e)  where the applicant is engaged in Permitted Paid Engagements (PPE) as listed at Appendix 4, provided the applicant holds a visa or leave to enter as a PPE visitor; or

(f)  paid performances at a permit free festival as listed in Appendix 5.

**Study.** The applicant must not intend to study in the UK, except as permitted by para 25 of Appendix 3 (V4.8).

**Medical.** The applicant must not intend to access medical treatment other than private medical treatment or to donate an organ (for either of these activities they must meet the relevant additional requirements) (V4.9). This provision does not deal with unintended situations where medical help is needed and the visitor attends an NHS doctor or hospital, not necessarily in an emergency. Nor does this provision deal with those nationals who are by right entitled to NHS treatment because of a reciprocal agreement with their country.[1] However, the situation is dealt with in the Visitor Guidance at pp 22-23). See **8.29–8.30**, below.

**Marriage or civil partnership.** The applicant must not intend to marry or form a civil partnership, or to give notice of this, in the UK, except where they have a visit visa endorsed for marriage or civil partnership (V4.10). See **8.33** below.

[1]  Visitors are not eligible for free of charge treatment on the National Health Service (NHS), unless an exemption from charge applies in law, and therefore may be billed for any NHS treatment received in the UK. Further details are in the Department of Health guidance on overseas visitors. The UK has reciprocal healthcare agreements (RHCAs) with a number of countries. RHCAs generally provide equivalent access to immediately necessary healthcare for the citizens of the contracting countries, where they are present in the other's country for a limited period. Treatment is provided on the same terms as for a local resident (free of charge in the UK). The majority of these RHCAs apply only to short-term visitors. RHCAs cater for treatment that arises during a migrant's stay. RHCAs do not usually allow migrants to come to the UK for the specific purpose of seeking medical care.

### Permitted activities

**8.8B** *[Insert new heading and paragraph:]*

Permitted activities are set out in Appendix 3 of Appendix V. The following are a list of these activities:

(a)  **Tourism and volunteering.** Volunteering is not voluntary work, but is permitted as part of a visit, if is not the main purpose of the visit, it is for a registered charity and will be no longer than 30 days in total (Appendix 3, paras 1 and 3 apply).

(b)     **Business and other work related visits.** Permitted activities are catego-
rised as general business activities (Appendix 3, para 5 applies) and
intra-corporate activities (Appendix 3, paras 6 and 7 apply). These are
set out at **8.21** below. The tenor of the Visit Guidance is quite negative.
The permitted activities are being kept to a strict minimum. The bona
fides of every business visitor is being scrutinised. It is as if the Officials'
main role is to look for faults. For example, they must be sure that
business activities are not work or are being used to turn the UK into
the visitor's main place of work. If the visitors go to conferences the
official has to be sure they are not undertaking work experience. If they
are more than a couple of weeks attending conferences the officials
should check their activity does not amount to a course of studies. In
intra-company visits the concern is that the applicant may be coming to
fill a role in the UK company. Can a business visitor spend two days at
a conference and then drive up to visit the West coast of Scotland and
then follow it with a series of business meetings, without raising the
suspicions of the immigration officials? That surely is what the opening
up of the visitor routes is all about. Welcome to Britain.

(c)     **Prospective entrepreneurs.** (Appendix 3, para 8 applies.) See **8.37**
below.

(d)     **Manufacturing and supply of goods to the UK.** An employee of a
foreign manufacturer or supplier may install, dismantle, repair, service
or advise on equipment, computer software or hardware where it has a
contract of purchase or supply or lease with a UK company or
organisation. (Appendix 3, para applies). If the employee request a stay
of more than a month, it will not be automatic refusal but officials must
look carefully and be sure they are not filling a role (Visit Guidance, p
17).

(e)     **Clients of UK export companies.** This involves a UK export company
which has contracted to sell goods and services to an overseas company
(not in the same group) and employees of the oversees company are
seconded to the UK to supervise delivery of the contract (Appendix 3,
para 5 applies).

(f)     **Science and research.** This allows researchers and scientists who are
employed and paid overseas to come to the UK and take part in specific
projects directly related to their employment abroad and to participate
in international projects being led from the UK (Appendix 3, para 11
applies).

(g)     **Other academia.** Overseas academics can take part in formal exchange
arrangements with UK counterparts (including doctors) and, if they are
on sabbaticals, they can come to the UK to carry out research. Eminent
and experienced senior doctors or dentists may come to take part in
research, teaching or clinical practice as long as this remains incidental
to their employment overseas (Appendix 3, para 12 and Visit Guidance
p18 applies).

(h)     **Legal.** An expert witness may visit the UK to give evidence in a UK
court. Other witnesses may visit the UK to attend a court hearing in the
UK if summoned in person by a UK court. Officials, however, should
not let them in, if there are doubts about their intentions or if their
evidence could be given by video link (Visit Guidance, p 18). An
overseas lawyer has a relatively limited role to play. He or she is

restricted to advise a UK-based client on specific international litigation and/or an international transaction (Appendix 3, paras 13 and 14 apply). But lawyers from overseas may come to the UK and be paid for arbitration work in the UK if invited by a client. See **8.8C** below.

(i) **Religion.** Religious workers may visit the UK to preach or do pastoral work (Appendix 3, para 15 applies). This includes one-off engagements such as conducting wedding ceremonies or funerals, provided they are not receiving payment and they continue to be in employment overseas (Visit Guidance, p 18).

(j) **Creative.** An artist, entertainer, or musician may give performances; take part in competitions; make personal appearances; appear in promotional activities; and take part in cultural events or festivals on the list of permit-free festivals in Appendix 5 (where payment is permitted). Personal or technical staff or members of the production team can also visit; so too can film crews (actor, producer, director or technician) making a film or programme on location in the UK provided these are produced and financed overseas (Appendix 3, paras 5 and 16–18 apply).

(k) **Sport.** There is a difference here between amateurs and professionals. Appendix 3 only deals with amateur sports. Professionals need to apply for a work visa under Tier 2 or 5 of the Points Based System (PSB). However, there is also a let-out. A professional artist, entertainer, musician or sports person may carry out an activity directly relating to their profession, if they have been invited by a creative (arts or entertainment) or sports organisation, agent or broadcaster based in the UK (Appendix 4). Amateurs can take part in tournaments and other sporting events, do promotions, have unpaid trials and training and can join an amateur team or club to get experience. Some amateur sports are not without officials and support staff and they too can come to the UK provided they remain employed overseas (Appendix 3, paras 19 and 20 apply).

(l) **Work related training.** Overseas graduates from medical, dental or nursing schools may undertake clinical attachments or dental observer posts provided these are unpaid, and involve no treatment of patients. They may also take (i) the Professional and Linguistic Assessment Board (PLAB) test, or (ii) the Objective Structured Clinical Examinations (OSCE) for overseas, provided they can provide written evidence of this from the General Medical council for the PLABS trial or the Nursing and Midwifery Council for the OSCE (Appendix 3, para 22 applies).

(m) **Company training.** Short-term training is available to employees of an overseas company or organisation and may receive training from a UK-based company or organisation in work practices and techniques which are required for the visitor's employment overseas and not available in their home country (Appendix 3, para 23 applies). Similarly, an employee of an overseas-based training company contracted to deliver global training to the international corporate group to which the UK-based company belongs may come to the UK to deliver a short series of training to employees of a UK branch (Appendix 3, para 24 applies).

(n) **Study.** Educational exchanges or visits with a UK state or independent school are permitted, as is a maximum of 30 days' study, provided that the main purpose of the visit is not to study (i) recreational courses (not English language training), or (ii) a short-course (which includes English language training) at an accredited institution (Appendix 3, para 25 applies).

(o) **Medical treatment.** An individual may receive private medical treatment provided they meet the additional eligibility requirements at V4.14–V4.16, described at **8.6**, above or can be an organ donor, provided they meet the additional eligibility requirements at V4.17–V4.20, as described in **8.6**, above (Appendix 3, paras 26 and 27 apply).

**Permitted paid engagements**

**8.8C** *[Insert heading and new paragraph:]*

Visitors may only receive payment from a UK source in specific circumstances as set out in the visitor rules – this must not equate to a salary. Where this is the case, the application will be refused. See Appendix V, para V4.7 and Appendices 4 and 5 of the Visitor Rules. The following are permitted paid engagements:

(a) a highly-qualified academic within his or her field of expertise may, if invited by a UK Higher Education Institution or a UK-based research or arts organisation, examine students and/or participate in or chair selection panels as part of the organisation's quality assurance processes;

(b) an expert may give lectures in their subject area, if they have been invited by a UK Higher Education Institution; or a UK-based research or arts organisation provided this does not amount to filling a teaching position for the host organisation;

(c) a UK-based training organisation that is regulated by the UK Civil Aviation Authority may invite an overseas designated pilot examiner to assess UK-based pilots to ensure they meet the national aviation regulatory requirements of other countries;

(d) a qualified lawyer may, if invited by a client, provide advocacy for a court or tribunal hearing, arbitration or other form of dispute resolution for legal proceedings within the UK;

(e) a professional artist, entertainer, musician or sports person may carry out an activity directly relating to their profession, if they have been invited by a creative (arts or entertainment) or sports organisation, agent or broadcaster based in the UK.

## TIME LIMITS AND OTHER CONDITIONS OF STAY

**8.9** *[At the beginning of the paragraph, insert:]*

The maximum periods of stay are set out in the Table at Appendix V1.5 and they vary from 48 hours for transit passengers, one month for permitted paid engagements (PPE), 30 days for Chinese ADS visitors, 11 months for medical treatment and 12 months for academics carrying out specific permitted activities. But the most usual time limit is six months. One notable feature of Appendix V and the new visit regime is for officials to estimate how long a person needs to complete the purpose of their visit and to refuse entry if the applicant asks for more. This is particularly the case for business visitors. See 8.6, above.

Visas are either granted as single entry or multiple visit visas. Multiple entry visas allow visits of up to six months at a time for a standard visitor visa over a period of two years, five years or ten years. The Visit Guidance has full details of when a single visit visa should apply and what happens: (i) when a visitor comes for a six-month stay but his or her multiple entry visa runs out after one month; or (ii) what long-term visa can be given to a child. The answer to (i) is that the visitor will be allowed to extend his or her visa to let him or her to complete six months in the UK as a visitor. In the case of a child, a multiple visa can be given to expire no later than six months after the 18th birthday. See Visit Guidance, at pp 25–27.

As regards conditions of leave, visit visas, leave to enter or an extension of stay as a visitor will be subject to the following conditions (V4.23): (a) no recourse to public funds; and (b) no study, except as permitted by para 25 of Appendix 3; and (c) no work (which does not prohibit the permitted activities in Appendices 3, 4 or 5 as set out in V1.5 for 'permitted paid engagements' (PPE)). There are other conditions which could be imposed under s 3(1)(c) of the Immigration Act 1971 but there is no indication that they are to be used under the current visitor regime.

*[At the end of footnote 1, add:]*

It is now necessary to replace the HC 395 references and the Modernised Guidance reference. Appendix V, para V1.5 has the Table containing the maximum period of leave for different kinds of leave. See also Visit Guidance under the heading 'Visit: period of stay granted' at pp 25–27.

*[In footnote 9 delete the reference to 'Modernised Guidance' and substitute:]*

Visit Guidance under the heading 'Visit period of stay granted' at pp 25–27.

**Frequency of visits**

**8.10** *[At the beginning of the paragraph, insert:]*

There is no specified maximum period which an individual can spend in the UK in any period such as '6 months in 12 months'. However, in assessing whether there is a genuine intention to visit, the applicant must satisfy the decision maker that they will not live in the UK for extended periods through frequent or successive visits, or make the UK their main home by the use of frequent visits.[0] So although there is no legal bar on frequency of visits, the current thinking of the Home Office is set out in more detail in the Visit Guidance.[0a] First officials are advised that they should check the applicant's travel history: how long are they spending in the UK and how frequently are they returning? To assess if they are, in effect, making the UK their main home, the official should look at the purpose of the visit and intended length of stay stated and the number of visits made over the past 12 months and should then go through a whole list of checks, some of them very intrusive, such as where the visitor is registered for tax purposes, some of them obviously pertinent, such as whether they have registered with a general practitioner (GP) or sent their children to UK schools.

If it is clear to the official from the person's travel history that they are making the UK their home their application should be refused.

⁰ See Appendix V, para V4.2(b).

⁰ᵃ Visit Guidance: 'Frequent or successive visits: how to assess if an applicant is making the UK their main home or place of work', at pp 10–11.

**Genuine visit**

**8.11** *[N.B.]*

For the provisions on genuineness in Appendix V, see **8.7**, above.

**8.12** *[In footnote 3 delete the first sentence and insert:]*

The Modernised Guidance referred to has been discontinued. See now Visit Guidance, Version 4.0, 8 January 2016, pp 8-11.

**8.13** *[At the end of footnote 5, add:]*

However, a visitor (standard) who is successful in the PLAB Test may be granted an extension of stay as a visitor to undertake an unpaid clinical attachment, provided they meet the requirements of Appendix 3, para 22(a) (which allows overseas graduates to undertake unpaid clinical or dental posts) so that the total period they can remain in the UK (including both the original grant and the extension of stay) does not exceed 18 months.

**8.14** *[In footnote 2, delete 'See general grounds for refusal of entry clearance in HC 395, eg para 320(7A) (mandatory) and substitute:]*

See now the Suitability Requirements in Appendix V, Part V3, paras V3.6 and V3.8

*[In the main text, delete the final sentence before footnote reference 4 and substitute:]*

Appendix V makes it appropriate and acceptable to ask the third party to provide an undertaking regarding the applicant's maintenance and/or accommodation.

*[Delete the text of footnote 4 and substitute:]*

See Appendix V, para V4.4: 'The third party may be asked to give an undertaking in writing to be responsible for the applicant's maintenance and accommodation. In this case paragraph 35 of Part 1 of these Rules applies also to Visitors (the rule deals with undertakings). An applicant will normally be refused where, having been requested to do so, the applicant fails to provide a valid written undertaking from a third party to be responsible for their maintenance and accommodation for the period of any visit.'

## Maintenance and accommodation

**8.15** The provisions relating to maintenance and accommodation have been dealt with at **8.8**. The existing paragraph is dated and should be read with care.

## EXTENSION OF STAY AS A VISITOR

**8.16** *[At the beginning of the paragraph, insert:]*

Apart from the changes made by Appendix V there have also been a number of administrative changes set out in the *Visit Guidance*[0] which have taken place since this paragraph was written.

[0] Visit Guidance, Version 4.0, 8 January 2016.

## Concessions for Syrian nationals

**8.16A** *[Insert new heading and paragraph:]*

New Concessions for Syrian visitors seeking to extend their leave as visitors have superseded previous concessions as from 1 March 2017. They are as follows:[1]

- Syrian visitors, who have submitted applications before 24 April 2015 will be decided under the old Part 2 of the Immigration Rules as in force at the date of the application:
  - (i) under paragraph 44 (requirements for an extension of stay as a general visitor), subparagraph (ii) and (iv) shall not apply;
  - (ii) under paragraph 46D (requirements for an extension of stay as a child visitor), subparagraph (v) and (vii) shall not apply;
  - (iii) under paragraph 44 (requirements for an extension of stay as a general visitor), subparagraph (i) so far as it refers to paragraph 41(xi) and subparagraphs (ii)–(iv) do not apply.
- Visitors whose applications are submitted on or after 24 April 2015 will be decided under Appendix V of the Immigration Rules:
  - (i) under Part V8 (extension of stay as a visitor), paragraph V8.4 shall not apply;
  - (ii) under Part V8 (extension of stay as a visitor), paragraph V8.7 shall not apply to a visitor (standard), including a child, who is in the UK visiting family, friends or on holiday;
  - (iii) under Part V8 (extension of stay as a visitor), paragraph V8.8 shall not apply to a visitor (standard) who is in the UK for private medical treatment and is seeking an extension of stay for more than six months.

[1] *Concessions to the Immigration Rules for Syrian Nationals*, Version 3.0, authorised under the Equality (Syria) Authorisation 2017 which came into force on 1 March 2017. These concessions apply to other categories of Syrian nationals, but do not apply to anyone who is seeking indefinite leave, refugee status, humanitarian protection or discretionary leave under ECHR.

**Particular visits**

**8.18** *[Delete entire paragraph.]*

## CHILD VISITORS

**8.19** *[Existing para 8.3 is now moved below and renumbered as para 8.19:]*

Section 55 of the Borders, Citizenship and Immigration Act 2009[1] requires the UK Border Agency to carry out its existing functions in a way that takes into account the need to safeguard and promote the welfare of children in the UK. It does not impose any new functions, or override existing functions. Entry Clearance and Immigration Officers considering applications for entry clearance/leave to enter must make decisions affecting children with due regard to section 55.

There has been a wealth of decided cases on the best interests of children and the extent of the Secretary of State's duties under section 55 of the 2009 Act, following the Supreme Court decision in *ZH (Tanzania) v Secretary of State for the Home Department*,[2] see, for example, *Omotunde (best interests – Zambrano applied – Razgar) Nigeria*,[3] *Mundeba* (s 55 and para 297(i)(f))[4] and, *R (on the application of T) v Secretary of State for the Home Department.*[5] These are dealt with in more detail in CHAPTER 11 below.

[1]  In force from 2 November 2009; Borders, Citizenship and Immigration Act 2009 (Commencement No 1) Order 2009, SI 2009/2731.
[2]  [2011] UKSC 4, [2011] 2 All ER 783, [2011] 2 WLR 148.
[3]  [2011] UKUT 247 (IAC).
[4]  [2013] UKUT 88(IAC).
[5]  [2011] EWHC 1850 (Admin), [2011] All ER (D) 224 (Oct).

**Child best interests**

**8.19A** *[Insert new heading. Delete the whole of existing para 8.19 and insert as new para 8.19A:]*

The Home Office recognise that they have a statutory duty to have regard to the need to safeguard and promote the welfare of children in the UK under section 55 of the Borders, Citizenship and Immigration Act 2009 ( Visit Guidance, p 29). This means that all decision makers and/or immigration officers must make sure that the child's best interests are a primary consideration. In practical terms, they must be satisfied that the child will be adequately accommodated and looked after.

Adequate arrangements must have been made for made for their travel to, reception and care in the UK (V 4.11). If they are not applying or travelling with a parent or guardian based in their home country or country of ordinary residence who is responsible for their care; they must have the written consent, if requested, of that parent or guardian with regard to the arrangements for the child's travel to, and reception and care in the UK (V4.12). If they require a visit visa it must state that they are travelling with an adult identified on the visa; if they are unaccompanied they may be refused entry (V 4.13);

As set out in the deleted paragraph **8.19**, the intention of these rules is that in the case of a child, who subsequently comes to the attention of the caring or educational services, there will be a record of their family or carers, both prior to, and immediately after, their arrival. If the provision of these gives cause for concern, then entry to the UK may be refused or further investigation will need to take place. Children who are accompanied by an adult, whether a family member or not, and seeking entry as visitors, will have to give details of the accompanying adult so that the nature of the journey and the relationship can be established. If the provisions of this information or the information itself gives cause for concern, either when provided or at the point of entry, then entry to the UK may be refused and further investigation may have to take place. The information and identities provided will be a record that may be assessed, if the child subsequently comes to the attention of the caring or educational services.

The concern which has prompted these rules is the concern that minors are brought to the UK for trafficking purposes or that the accompanying adult disappears and the children then claim asylum.

**8.19B** *[Insert new paragraph:]*

If a parent or guardian is making the application for a visa on behalf of the child this will usually satisfy the requirement for parental consent. If the applicant's parents are divorced, the consent must come from the parent who holds legal custody or sole responsibility. If the application is not made by the parent or guardian, and there are no other factors which give cause for concern, a letter from the parent or guardian confirming their relationship to the child and consenting to the child's application will be sufficient to establish that this requirement has been met. If a child is travelling in the company of an adult, the adult's name and passport number must be included on the child's visa. If the child intends to travel with two adults one after another during the validity of the visa (for example, the child may arrive with one parent and then travel for a day trip to France with the other), each of the adult's passport numbers must be entered on the vignette (Visit Guidance, pp 30 and 33).

However, If the legal authorities (meaning the police or judiciary, not a legal representative of one parent) in the child's country of residence have indicated that they are at risk of being moved out of the country without consent the entry clearance officer should seek consent from both parents. If an application is made by someone other than the parent or guardian, unless that person is a social worker who holds parental rights and cares for the child, enquiries should be made about the identities of accompanying adults (Visit Guidance, p 30).

Where a child who is not residing with his or her parent, parents or guardian, and is travelling, there should be a letter of consent from the parent or guardian. If not, and there concerns about the child's welfare, inquiries should be made to confirm the identity and residence of the host and make sure the child is expected. If there are still concerns at the border, the immigration officer should contact the local authority children's services department and/or the police where appropriate. Children's Services will advise on the suitability of the sponsor and will take the child into their care, if they agree that the sponsor is unsuitable or if there is no responsible sponsor (Visit Guidance, p 29).

### Private foster care

**8.19C** *[Insert new heading and paragraph:]*

A visitor under the age of 18 is considered to be in private foster care when they are: under 16 years old or under 18 years old for those who have a disability; being cared for on a full-time basis for more than 28 days; and not being cared for by parents or close relatives. The child visitor will not be regarded as under foster care if a close relative, parent or legal guardian is looking after them or the child is part of a group travelling and staying together and accompanied by an adult, for example, a school group.

If a foster carer or relative who is not a parent or guardian will have responsibility for the child's care whilst in the UK, the applicant must be able to produce specified documents to satisfy the immigration authorities that that reception and care arrangements are adequate. These include identity documents of the foster carers, a letter of authority from parents or guardian for the foster care arrangements and confirmation that the parents have or will notify the relevant UK local authority of these arrangements. If the child is on an educational exchange visit that lasts longer than 28 days and they are not accompanied by their parent or guardian, a letter is needed from the school to include details of the foster care arrangements. Where a child's visit exceeds 28 days, under child foster care arrangements the host family must present evidence to satisfy you that they have contacted their local Social Services for a home assessment. Where a home assessment has been completed and approved, evidence of this must be provided (Visit Guidance, pp 31–32).

**8.19D** *[Insert new paragraph:]*

Two other situations for a child visitor are addressed in the Visit Guidance:

- **Child visiting to stay with a host family.** Here the necessary checks will vary and depend on whether the child is accompanied or unaccompanied. In all cases a clear record of who is responsible for the child's welfare in their home country and whilst in the UK is imperative. For host families it is necessary to establish the identity and address of the hosts and to make sure that the care arrangements are adequate, as required by paragraph V4.11. In routine cases this could mean seeing a letter from the host family. If care arrangements are not adequate the application should be refused.
- **Child visit organised by a charity.** Charities need to be registered to enable them to facilitate child visits to UK host families. They should renew this registration every 12 months. They must provide full details of the hosts allocated to accommodate the children whilst in the UK and the checks they have carried out on the hosts. These checks must be in line with the charity's own child protection policy. They must also state whether this is the first or a subsequent visit sponsored by the charity for the child. Where the stay will be for longer than 28 days, they will need to follow the private foster care guidance.

## STUDY VISITS

**8.20** *[Delete the heading 'Student Visitors' and replace with the above heading. Delete paragraph and insert:]*

At one stage, visitors could study during their stay provided it was not at a maintained school. Then the rules were changed to prohibit general visitors to study at any institution, unless they sought entry either in the new student visitor category or under the old student route and later under Tier 4.[1] This was changed by HC 628, which applied to applications made from 1 October 2013. A general visitor was allowed to study on a course which did not exceed 30 days in duration and was recreational but not an English language course.[2] Academic study could also be undertaken at recognised educational institutions provided it was a short course, no longer than 30 days.[3] This is still the case. Meanwhile the student visitor and extended student visitor routes have been rebranded as short-term study routes which are now set out in Part 3 of the Immigration Rules at paras A57A–A57H and apply only to English language courses.[4]

[1] Changes introduced on 1 September 2007. See Explanatory Memorandum to Cm 7074, para 7. In *CT (Rule 60(i), student entry clearance?) Cameroon* [2008] UKAIT 00010 (12 February 2008): the Tribunal held that a person who entered the United Kingdom with entry clearance as a short-term student prior to 1 September 2007, although subject to a condition prohibiting work, was admitted to the UK in possession of a valid entry clearance in accordance with para 57 of HC 395 and as a student not as a visitor.

[2] HC 395, para 43A, inserted by HC 628, para 8 to apply to all applications decided on or after 1 October 2013.

[3] HC 395, para 43A inserted by HC 628, para 8.

[4] The reason for this change is to make the system clearer for those whose main purpose for coming to the UK is to study a short course up to six months, or 11 months in the case of adults studying longer English language courses: see HC 1025, Explanatory Statement, paras 7.2 and 7.7.

## BUSINESS VISITS

**8.21** *[At the beginning of the paragraph, insert:]*

The Immigration Rules referred to in this paragraph are now superceded. Under Appendix 3 of Appendix V, business visits are divided into (i) general activities and (ii) corporate and intra-corporate activities. The new rules in Appendix V do not give all possible activities a visitor may wish to carry out on a visit and it is not a finite list. In our view the proper approach is to consider what is prohibited and then apply Sir Robert Megarry's famous quote about the difference between directly enforceable nominate rights and liberties: 'England . . . is a country where everything is permitted except what is expressly forbidden'.[0]

Business – general activities states a visitor may:

(a)     attend meetings, conferences, seminars, interviews;

(b)     give a one-off or short series of talks and speeches provided these are not organised as commercial events and will not make a profit for the organiser;

(c)     negotiate and sign deals and contracts;

(d)     attend trade fairs, for promotional work only, provided the visitor is not directly selling;

(e)     carry out site visits and inspections;

(f)     gather information for their employment overseas;

(g)     be briefed on the requirements of a UK based customer, provided any work for the customer is done outside of the UK.

Business corporate states – an employee of an overseas based company may:

(a)     advise and consult;

(b)     trouble-shoot;

(c)     provide training;

(d)     share skills and knowledge; on a specific internal project with UK employees of the same corporate group, provided no work is carried out directly with clients.

An internal auditor may carry out regulatory or financial audits at a UK branch of the same group of companies as the visitor's employer overseas.

[0]     *Malone v the Metropolitan Police Commissioner* [1979] Ch 344, at 366.

**8.22** *[At the beginning of the paragraph, insert:]*

For the provisions in Appendix V setting out the list of prohibited activities, see V4.5–V4.6, reproduced at **8.8A**, above. Existing paragraph **8.22** is a precursor of the Appendix V provisions and the Visit Guidance. It is dated and should only be used with care.


## ACADEMIC VISITORS

**8.23** *[At the beginning of the paragraph, insert:]*

For details of Appendix V provisions, see the changes to **8.6** above. They must also meet the additional eligibility requirements of Part V4 of Appendix V. Permitted activities are to be found in Appendix 3 of Appendix V and explained in the Visit Guidance, 8 January 2016, at p 42. See **8.6** and **8.8B** above. Given the short-term nature of this route, visiting lecturers must be employed at least part-time outside the UK and intend to return to this employment on completion of their engagement. Where a lecturer is fully retired and only does one-off lectures, the application should be refused. However, an individual who is semi-retired will qualify under this route, if they are carrying out regular lectures and earning income from them. If an academic is invited to give a lecture at a Higher Education Institution (HEI) as part of a course this is acceptable, providing that person is not replacing the formal role of the course teacher.[0]

[0]     See, further, Visit Guidance, 8 January 2016, at p 40.


## ENTERTAINERS AND SPORTSPERSONS

**8.24** *[At the beginning of the paragraph insert:]*

As already indicated at **8.6**, above, entertainers and sportspersons can only come to the UK as a visitor if they meet all the eligibility requirements in

Appendix V, paras V4.2–V4.10 and meet the additional eligibility requirements of Parts V4 and V5 of Appendix V. Permitted activities are to be found in Appendix 4 (permitted paid engagements) of Appendix V and permitted paid engagements (PPE) are in Part V5 and Appendix 4 and are explained in the Visit Guidance of 8 January 2016, at pp 18, 19 and 42. See **8.8B** and **8.8C** above. Existing paragraphs **8.24–8.26** are dated and should be read with care.

### Artist and Entertainer visitors

**8.25** *[The heading 'Entertainer visitors' is replaced with the above new heading. At the beginning of the paragraph insert:]*

An artist can include anyone coming to the UK to undertake an activity that is connected to the arts. There is no restriction on amateur or professional artists doing permitted activities. Examples include: poets, film crew, photographers, designers and artists. Entertainers can include dancers, comedians, members of circus acts or members of a film crew. Personal or technical staff can accompany the artist, entertainer or musician to the UK. Under Appendix 4 of Appendix V, a professional artist, entertainer, musician or sports person may carry out an activity directly relating to their profession, if they have been invited by a creative (arts or entertainment) or sports organisation, agent or broadcaster based in the UK. For details, see Appendix 3, paras 16–18 and Appendix 4, para 1(e). They must also meet the additional eligibility requirements of Parts V4 and V5 of Appendix V. More detail, see Visit Guidance, 8 January 2016, at pp 18, 19 and 42. See also **8.6B** and **8.6C**.

*[N.B.]*

The original paragraph is dated and should be read with care.

### Sports visitors

**8.26** *[At the beginning of the paragraph insert:]*

**Sport.** There is difference here between amateurs and professionals. Appendix 3 only deals with amateur sports. Professionals need to apply for a work visa under Tier 2 or 5 of the Points Based System (PSB). However, there is also a let-out. A professional sports person may carry out an activity directly relating to their profession, if they have been invited by a creative (arts or entertainment) or sports organisation, agent or broadcaster based in the UK (Appendix 4). A sports organisation includes any organisation involved in organising or staging sporting events or matches. So professional sports persons coming to the UK as part of an international or club rugby or football team to play in an international match or a European cup tie or a tennis player coming to play in a tournament organised by the Tennis Federation will qualify under Part V5 and Appendix 4.

*[N.B.]*

The original paragraph is dated and should be read with care.

## MEDICAL TREATMENT

### 8.27 *[N.B.]*

As already indicated at **8.6**, those seeking to come to the UK for private medical treatment must meet all the eligibility requirements in Appendix V, paras V4.2–V4.10 and meet the additional eligibility requirements in paras V4.14–V4.16 of Appendix V. Existing paragraphs **8.27** and **8.28** are dated and should be read with care.

The Visit Guidance (p 37) indicates that there no provision in the Rules for a woman to be allowed into the UK for the purpose of being a surrogate mother. Admission for private medical treatment is not appropriate since the applicant would not be suffering from any medical condition. Applications should normally be refused on the grounds that there is no provision in the Rules. But there may be exceptional circumstances.

### NHS treatment

### 8.29 *[At the beginning of the paragraph insert:]*

We have already dealt summarily with NHS treatment at **8.8A**.

## PARENT OF A CHILD AT SCHOOL

### 8.31 *[At the beginning of the paragraph insert:]*

With the introduction of Appendix V, para V7.8, the 'Parent of a child at school' route was being rebranded as 'Parent of a Tier 4 (child) student' to clarify the purpose of the route, and will now sit in Part 7 of the Immigration Rules as these individuals are not visitors.[0]

*[In the main text, after footnote reference 4, delete the text starting 'Under the rule . . . ' up to and including footnote reference 5, and insert:]*

With the coming into force of Appendix V for visitors, the 'parent of a child at school' rules have been moved to new rules at paras 276BT1–276BV1.[5] These new rules are the same in substance but not in form. The changes set out in para 199 of HC 1025 took effect from 24 April 2015 and replaced Part 2 of the Immigration Rules, including HC 395, paras 56A–56C. Any applications for entry clearance or leave to enter or remain made on or after 24 April 2015 will be decided in accordance with the new Rules in force from 24 April 2015. The material rules provide as follows:

'Parent of a Tier 4 (child) student

Requirements for leave to enter or remain as the parent of a Tier 4 (child) student

276BT1 The requirements to be met by a person seeking leave to enter or remain in the United Kingdom as the parent of a Tier 4 (child) student is that the parent is over 18 years old and:
(i)     is genuinely seeking leave to enter or remain for a period of up to 12 months to be the sole carer for their child who is under 12 years of age and attending or seeking to attend an independent fee paying day school in the United Kingdom, provided the child:
     (a)    meets the requirements of paragraph 245ZZA if seeking leave to enter as a Tier 4 (Child) Student,[6] or

(b)    meets the requirements of paragraph 245ZZC if seeking leave to remain as a Tier 4 (Child) Student;[7]

(ii)    will maintain and accommodate himself, the child and any other dependants adequately out of resources available to him without recourse to public funds or taking employment;

(iii)    can provide satisfactory evidence of adequate and reliable funds for maintaining a second home in the United Kingdom;

(iv)    is not seeking to make the United Kingdom their main home;

(v)    does not intend to take employment, to produce goods or provide services within the United Kingdom including the selling of goods or services direct to members of the public;

(vi)    does not intend to study in the UK;

(vii)    the parent was not last admitted to the United Kingdom under the Approved Destination Status Agreement with China;

(viii)    if seeking leave to remain must not be in the UK in breach of immigration laws except that any period of overstaying for a period of 28 days or less will be disregarded.'

To obtain leave the parent must meet each of the requirements of para 276BT1 and may then be granted leave to enter or remain, as the case may be, for a maximum period of 12 months, subject to a condition prohibiting employment, study and recourse to public funds.[8] Leave will be refused if the Immigration Officer or, in the case of an application for limited leave to remain, the Secretary of State is not satisfied that each of the requirements of para 276BT1 is met.[9]

*[In the main text footnote reference 6 is renumbered as 10. In the footnotes, existing footnote 5 is deleted and footnote 6 is renumbered as 10. Insert the new footnotes in the correct sequential order.]*

[0]    HC 1025, Explanatory Memorandum, para 7.8.

[5]    Inserted by HC 1025, para 199.

[6]    Where a child is under the age of 16, the sponsoring school must be an independent fee-paying school: see HC 395, App A, para 124(a).

[7]    Ibid.

[8]    HC 395, para 276BU1.

[9]    HC 395, para 276BV1.

## CARERS

**8.32** *[Delete existing paragraph and related footnotes from the beginning up to 'In TR (reg 8(3) EEA Regs 2006) . . . ' and insert:]*

The switch of visitor rules to Appendix V has not changed the rules for short term carers. Everything remains much as before. The new Operational Guidance – 'Visits' – states:

'Where a family member is coming to look after a child in the UK, this is permitted provided it is for a short visit and does not amount to the relative being employed as a child-minder. You must be satisfied that the visit is of a short duration and the relative is a genuine visitor. At the border, you will need to ask the applicant to explain what they are coming to do and for how long.'

This deals with a visit to care for a child and is a more narrow provision than what is said in the current IDI,[1] which makes it clear that, although there is no express provision in the rules for carers, a person who wishes to visit the UK to provide short-term care or make alternative arrangements for the long-term care of a friend/relative may do so under the Rules relating to general visitors. This means they must satisfy the requirements of the Immigration Rules relating to general visitors.[2]

Where the prospective carer cannot qualify under the general visitor rules, provision is made for exceptional grants of leave to enter or remain outside the rules. This policy stems from case law and in particular is based upon the case of *Ex parte Zackrocki*[3] in which a Polish couple were refused an extension of their visitor visa to care for a desperately sick close relative on a full-time basis. After considering the facts, Carnwath J concluded that the decision was unreasonable in the *Wednesburv* sense and should therefore be quashed. On the basis of this case, it can be inferred that while short-term care can be provided through the general visitor route, as we have indicated above, the carer concession is concerned with long-term care by someone who is already in the UK in temporary capacity. This may explain why entry under the concession after failing to meet the visitor requirements will only be for a period of three months, whereas, if the person already in the UK seeks an extension of leave and succeeds, the period of leave is twelve months.(see below).

The main plank of Home Office policy on the concession, stated at the start of the IDI,[4] is that:

> 'UKBA and the Department of Health have consistently argued that the care in the community policy is not designed to enable people to stay in the UK who would otherwise not have leave to do so. Rather, leave should only be granted where it is warranted by particularly compelling and compassionate circumstances.'

Where an ECO thinks that there are compelling and compassionate circumstances, the case can be referred to the UK's Referred Cases Unit to be considered outside the Immigration Rules.[5] In considering whether an exception can be made, the IDI set out key points which should be taken into account for prospective carers. These are:

- the type of illness/condition (this must be supported by a consultant's letter);
- the type of care required;
- the care which is available (eg from the social services or other relatives/friends);
- the long-term prognosis.[6]

If leave is refused it will be refused under HC 395, para 320(1) on the basis that the applicant is not seeking entry for a purpose that is covered by the Immigration Rules. Where leave is to be granted outside the Rules a distinction is made between sick and disabled relatives and sick and disabled friends.

Where the application is to care for a sick or disabled *relative* it will normally be appropriate to grant leave to remain for three months with no recourse to employment or public funds).[7] The applicant must be informed that leave has been granted on the strict understanding that during this period arrangements will be made for the future care of the patient by a person who is not subject to the Immigration Rules and that It is unlikely that any further leave will be granted on this basis.[8]

Where it is appropriate for entry clearance and leave to enter to be granted, leave may be granted for a period of three months (with no recourse to employment or public funds) outside the Immigration Rules. An extension of further leave should not be given unless there are wholly exceptional circumstances. Such circumstances could include where the sponsor is terminally ill and has no social services or family support available. If there are sufficient exceptional compassionate circumstances to continue the exercise of discretion, leave to remain may be granted for up to 12 months at a time.[9]

The IDI is much more strict about sick and disabled *friends*.[10] Leave should normally be refused. However, in an emergency (eg where the friend has suddenly fallen ill and there is insufficient time to arrange permanent care or where there is nobody else in the United Kingdom to whom the patient can turn), it may be appropriate to grant leave outside the rules for a period of three months with no recourse to employment or public funds. An extension of leave should not be given unless there are wholly exceptional circumstances. Such circumstances could include where the sponsor is terminally ill and has no Social Services or family support available.

EU law deals with carers in a number of different ways:

(i)   The primary carer and parent of a child under 18, who is an EU citizen resident in the Member State, of which he or she is a national, will be allowed to remain as carer of the child, if being forced to leave would compel the child to leave his or her own state and the territory of the whole EU.[11] The case law has not yet dealt with those taking care of sick or disabled relatives, living in the Member State of their own nationality.

(ii)  In our view the same reasoning should apply as in the case of children. Take the example of a disabled partner or child over 18 who has to be cared for full time by their third country national partner or parent, who would be compelled to leave if their carer partner or carer parent had to leave. It is highly arguable that the primary carer would be allowed to stay in these particular circumstances.

(iii) The same would apply if a child or sick relative (both EU citizens) had moved from one EU Member State to another. The carer relative, depending on the precise circumstances, would be entitled under applicable parts of the Citizen's Directive to remain to reside in the same EU Member State.

(iv)  Where EU citizens, nationals of one Member State, have moved to another Member State, sick or disabled or child family members of whatever nationality can join them 'where serious health grounds strictly require the personal care of the family member by the union citizen'.[12]

*[In the existing text, footnote 4 is renumbered as 13.]*

1   IDI 'Employment outside the rules', Chapter 17, Section 2: Carers, para 17.1 (first published 4 December 2013).
2   See, ibid, para 17.2.
3   *Secretary of State for the Home Department, ex p Zackrocki* [1996] EWCA Civ 1326 (29 March 1996).
4   IDI, as above, para 17, Introduction.
5   Ibid, paras 17.1.1.

6  Ibid, para 17.1.2. Further information on entry clearance and carers can be found in Chapter 18, section 18.21(ii), of the Entry Clearance Guidance, vol 1, General Instructions.
7  Ibid, para 17.3.1.
8  Ibid, paras 17.3.
9  Ibid, para 17.4.1.
10  Ibid, para 17.9.
11  See the *Zambrano* line of cases at **6.77**; *Ruiz Zambrano v Office National de l'Emploi (ONEm)*: C-34/09 (2011) C-34/09, [2012] QB 265, [2011] ECR I-1177, [2012] 2 WLR 866.
12  Citizens Directive, Directive 2004/38/EC, Art 3(2)(a).

## VISITS FOR MARRIAGE AND CIVIL PARTNERSHIP

**8.33** *[Delete the entire paragraph and substitute:]*

Appendix V, paras V4.10 and V6.1–V6.3 apply. See above **8.8**. According to the Explanatory Memorandum, the Appendix V Rules reproduce the policies in the superceded paras 56D–56F of HC 359.[1] A visitor seeking entry for the purpose of marriage or civil partnership ceremonies must show that he or she:

(i)    meets the requirements at V4.2–V4.10 (general requirements applicable to all visitors (V6.1). This includes the requirement (V4.10) that standard visitors must not intend to marry or form civil partnerships or give notice of this. Instead they must meet the additional eligibility requirements for a marriage or civil partnership visa;

(ii)   must be aged 18 or at over (V6.1);

(iii)  on arrival in the UK must have a valid visit visa endorsed with this purpose and the name of the holder's fiancé(e) or proposed civil partner (V 6.2);

(iv)   must satisfy the decision maker that during their visit to the UK they:
(a)    intend to give notice of marriage or civil partnership; or
(b)    intend to marry or form a civil partnership; and
(c)    do not intend to give notice of, or enter into, a sham marriage or sham civil partnership, within the validity period covered by their visit visa (V6.3).

A couple seeking to marry or enter into a civil partnership in the UK need not have any connection with the country, and neither spouse needs to be British or settled here. But even if one prospective spouse is British or settled, entry as a visitor for the purpose of marriage does not entitle a person to remain in the UK as a spouse after the marriage; for that, a fiancé(e) visa would be required. The prohibition on a person coming to the UK for the purpose of entering into a sham marriage or sham civil partnership introduced into the Rules on 20 October 2014,[2] is reproduced in Appendix V as set out above.

1  HC 1025, Explanatory Memorandum, para 7.19.
2  HC 395, para 56D(iv).

## VISITING RELIGIOUS WORKERS

**8.34** *[Note that the existing paragraph is dated and should be read with care. At the end of the paragraph add:]*

Since the visitor rules were moved to Appendix V, it is made clear that religious workers may visit the UK to preach or do pastoral work.[5] In the Visit Guidance published in 2016, which supercedes the Modernised Guidance referred to above, it is said that religious workers can undertake pastoral duties which can include one-off engagements such as conducting wedding ceremonies or funerals, provided these are one-off engagements for which they are not receiving payment and they continue to be in employment overseas. So, visits must still not be confused with Tier 2 or Tier 5 employment.

[5]   Paragraph 15 of App 3 of HC 359, App V.

## VISITORS FROM CHINA

**8.35** *[Delete the existing paragraph and insert:]*

In 2005 the change in rules, HC 486, created a new category of 'ADS visitor'[1] meaning someone seeking to enter the UK under the terms of the Memorandum of Understanding (MoU) on visa and related issues concerning tourist groups from the People's Republic of China to the UK. The requirements are now contained in the Visitor Rules at Appendix V of the Immigration Rules.[2] These are intended to regulate outward tourism from China to the UK by providing a mechanism for issuing visas for groups of Chinese tourists to authorised travel agents. The category is necessary because the terms of the MoU differ from the existing requirements for visitors under the Immigration Rules. ADS visitors will have to meet the requirements for ordinary visitors in HC 395, Appendix V, but in addition, applicants must be Chinese nationals; must be genuinely seeking entry as a visitor for a maximum period of 30 days; must intend to enter, travel and leave the UK as part of a group and will not be permitted to extend their stay beyond the maximum 30-day period.[3] When travelling in the UK under the ADS agreement they may only visit friends and family and/or come to the UK for a holiday.[4]

In conjunction with these rules changes, the Immigration (Leave to Enter and Remain) (Amendment) Order 2005, which came into force on 5 April 2005, provides that visas issued pursuant to the MoU shall have effect as single entry visas and have effect as leave to enter on one occasion unless endorsed as dual entry visas; in which case, they shall have effect as leave to enter on two occasions.[5]

The ADS is limited in scope. It relates to group tourism. A much wider scheme is currently being piloted. From 11 January 2016, a two-year visit visa pilot scheme will be launched in China. Under this, Chinese citizens applying for a six-month visit visa in mainland China may be granted a two-year multiple entry visa. These applicants are not required to demonstrate a frequent and ongoing need to visit the UK and the requirement to issue the visa applied should be disregarded (other than where there are reasons to issue a shorter/single entry visa).[6]

[1]   Approved Destination Status, created by the UK/China ADS Memorandum of Understanding which was signed on 21 January 2005. The 'ADS Agreement' is now defined in Appendix 1 of Appendix V at para 1.
[2]   Appendix V, paras V1.5(a)(iii) and V4.21 and the Guidance on applications under the ADS agreement in China, Visit Guidance, Version 4, 8 January 2016.

3   HC 395, Appendix V, paras V1.5(a)(iii) and V4.21. ADS tourists will be unable to extend their stay by applying for an extension in another visitor category; visitors under the ADS with China cannot switch to a general visit or a medical visit during their stay.
4   Paragraph 3 of Appendix 3 of Appendix V.
5   SI 2000/1161, arts 1(3) (definition of 'ADS Agreement with China') and 4(2A) and (2B) as inserted by SI 2005/1159.
6   Visit Guidance, Version 4.0, 8 January 2016, p 25. These changes were heralded by a Home Office Press Release by the Immigration Minister on 6 January 2016. In the year ending September 2015, the UK issued 484,065 visas in China, a 20% increase on the previous year, of which 404,084 were visit visas – a 22% increase.

## VISITORS IN TRANSIT

**8.36** *[Delete entire paragraph and insert:]*

Part 7 of the Visitor Rules sets out the eligibility requirements for visitors transiting the UK. These Rules reproduce the policies set out in the old rules at paras 47ZA–50F. See also the Modernised Guidance, Visitors in Transit.[1] A transit visitor is a person who seeks to travel via the UK en route to another destination country outside the common travel area.[2] Different rules apply to different categories of visitor in transit:

- Visa nationals from 55 countries listed in Schedule 1 to the Passenger Transit Visa Order 2014, as amended,[3] and those from the Palestinian Territories, who are seeking to transit the UK without passing through the UK border and entering the UK, need a Direct Airside Transit Visa (DATV),[4] unless they come under one of the exemptions in the Order.[5]
- A visa national (see the list of 111 visa countries in Appendix 2 of Appendix V) must either hold a transit visit visa or, if they meet the requirements for admission under the transit without visa (TWOV) scheme in paragraphs V7.6–V7.8, they may arrive at the Border and seek leave to enter.[6]
- Non-visa nationals are not mentioned in either the Immigration Rules at Part V7 of Appendix V or in the Passenger Transit Visa Order and are not required to obtain a transit visit visa, but will need to meet the requirements for leave to enter in para V7.5, if they need to leave airside and enter the UK, unless they are travelling under a visit waiver system.
- The transit visa requirements do not apply to crew members who are employed in the working or service of their ship, aircraft, hovercraft, hydrofoil or train who fall under section 8(1) of the Immigration Act 1971.[7]

1   HC 395, App V, Part V7; Transit Visitor, Modernised Guidance, Transiting, issued 24 April 2015.
2   HC 395, App V, para V7.1.
3   Immigration (Passenger Transit Visa) Order 2014, SI 2014/2702, which has revoked and replaced all previous Orders and is further amended by SIs 2015/657 and 1534.
4   HC 395, App V, para V7.1.
5   SI 2015/2702, as amended, art 4.
6   HC 395, App V, para V7.4.
7   HC 395, App V, para V7.3.

**8.36A** *[Insert new paragraph 8.36A:]*

The requirements of the TWOV scheme are set out in the Modernised Guidance 'Transit without visa scheme' (TWOV) – Version 3.0, 24 April 2015. In short, the scheme allows visa nationals who meet the requirements of paras V7.5 and V7.7 and hold one of the documents specified in para V7.8 of the Immigration Rules to transit the UK without a visa. The TWOV does not apply to nationals of the countries specified in the Immigration (Passenger Transit Visa) Order 2003. As set out above, these nationals require a UK Direct Airside Transit Visa (DATV) even when transiting airside without passing through the immigration control. The TWOV scheme requires that an applicant must:

- arrive and depart by air;
- be genuinely in transit to another country and their journey through the UK is part of a reasonable transit route;
- intend to, and be able to, leave the UK before 23:59 hours on the day after the day when they arrived;
- have a confirmed booking on a flight departing the UK before 23:59 hours on the day after the day when they arrived;
- be assured entry to their country of destination and any other countries they are transiting through on their way there.

The applicant must also comply with one of the following requirements:

- be travelling to or from (or on part of a reasonable journey to or from) Australia, Canada, New Zealand or the USA and have a valid visa for that country;[1]
- be travelling from (or on part of a reasonable journey from) Australia, Canada, New Zealand or the USA, having last entered that country with a valid entry visa less than six months ago;
- hold a valid residence permit issued by: Australia. Canada, New Zealand or USA with specified issue dates or other specified alternative US entry and residence documents;
- hold a valid common format residence permit issued by an EEA state or Switzerland or a valid uniform format category D visa for entry to an EEA state or Switzerland;
- be travelling on to the Republic of Ireland and have a valid Irish biometric visa;
- be travelling from the Republic of Ireland and it is less than three months since they were last given permission to land or be in the Republic by the Irish authorities with a valid Irish biometric visa.

E-visas or e-residence permits are not acceptable for landside transit.

[1] Syrian nationals or citizens cannot benefit from a landside or airside transit visa exemption where they hold a US issued B1 or B2 category visit visa.

### 8.36B *[Insert new paragraph 8.36B:]*

The eligibility requirements for a transit visa or leave to enter for transit are contained in Appendix V at para V7.5. An applicant must satisfy the decision maker that they:

(a) are genuinely in transit to another country outside the common travel area, meaning the main purpose of their visit is to transit the UK and that the applicant is taking a reasonable transit route; and

(b)      will not access public funds or medical treatment, work or study in the UK; and

(c)      genuinely intend and are able to leave the UK within 48 hours after their arrival; and

(d)      are assured entry to their country of destination and any other countries they are transiting on their way there.

Passengers meeting these conditions will be given a leave not exceeding 48 hours with a prohibition on employment, study and recourse to public funds.[1] Otherwise leave is to be refused.[2] Forty-eight hours is the maximum permitted leave and any application for an extension beyond this period is to be refused.[3] Where a woman on a tour party was given 48 hours by an immigration officer who wished to treat her as a transit passenger, but did not make this clear in the leave stamp, the Tribunal held that she was to be treated as an ordinary visitor with a right to apply for an extension.[4]

[1]   Modernised Guidance, Transiting, 24 April 2015, pp 4 and 12.
[2]   Ibid.
[3]   Ibid, p 12.
[4]   *Low v Secretary of State for the Home Department* [1995] Imm AR 435.

## PROSPECTIVE ENTREPRENUERS

**8.37** *[At the beginning of the paragraph, insert:]*

Under Appendix 3 of Appendix V, a prospective entrepreneur is permitted to carry out identical activities as before, they are spelt out at paragraph 8 of Appendix 3.

## VISITORS – SWITCHING CATEGORIES

**8.38** *[At the beginning of the paragraph, insert:]*

The move to Appendix V has changed little. According to the Explanatory Memorandum to HC 1025 (para 7.21), Part 8 of Appendix V sets out who can extend their stay in the UK as a visitor, how long for and the eligibility requirements they must meet. This reproduces Rules from across the now superceded Part 2 of HC 395. However, Appendix V, para V8.1 states that it is not possible to switch to become a visitor while in the UK where a person is in the UK in breach of immigration laws or has entry clearance or leave to enter or remain for another purpose. Other parts of the Immigration Rules make it clear that, as a general rule, visitors cannot switch into other categories. In the existing paragraph some of the possible switches no longer apply. The rules on overseas qualified nurses or midwives (paras 69M–69R) and those on post graduate doctors or dentists (paras 70–75 and 75A–75M) have all been deleted. Instead provision is made in the new visitor rules for those persons to sit such exams as the PL ABS and so there is now no need for a switch. The statement to the contrary in the existing paragraph should be ignored.

*[N.B. Footnote 2 and the sentence that goes with it no longer apply, since the prospective student visitor category no longer exists.]*

*[Medical visitors can no longer switch because rules 54 and 55 have been deleted and the reference to 'except medical visitor under HC 395, paragraphs 54 and 55;' in the second sub-paragraph is deleted including footnote reference 3 and the corresponding footnote text.]*

## APPEALS BY VISITORS

**8.40** *[This paragraph is deleted – of historical interest only.]*

# Chapter 9
# STUDENTS

## ENGLISH LANGUAGE REQUIREMENTS

### Proficiency in English language for Tier 4 (General) Students

**9.13** *[N.B.]*

Between 2013 and 2015 around 33,000 students a year had their leave curtailed. One major cause of this was the assumption by the Home Office that overseas students who had passed the Test of English for International Communication (TOEIC) administered by the American company Educational Testing Services (ETS) had obtained their English language certificates by fraud, following an *exposé* by BBC's Panorama in February 2014. This view was at first widely shared by both the public and the judiciary.

The trend has been reversed, however, since the promulgation of *SM & Qadir (ETS – Evidence – Burden of Proof)*.[1] The President of the Upper Tribunal, McCloskey J, was here very critical of the Home Office, concluding that the evidence adduced by the Secretary of State was insufficient to discharge the legal burden of proving that the TOEIC certificates awarded to the two appellants were procured by dishonesty (though he did not go so far as to say that the evidence did not prove that TOEIC certificates in general were procured by dishonesty). However, the generic evidence relied on by the Home Office in all ETS cases was shown to suffer from 'multiple shortcomings and frailties'.

The Secretary of State appealed against the Upper Tribunal's decision, but in *Majumder and another (Qadir) v Secretary of State for the Home Office*,[2] she informed the Court of Appeal shortly before the hearing that she was content to have her appeal dismissed without determination of the merits. The Court was not having that, as there were some 315 other cases lined up behind what was meant to be a test case. In the end, it was agreed that the pending cases fell into four categories, and that most of the cases would either be remitted to the Tribunal or conceded altogether by the Secretary of State. The Home Affairs Committee of the House of Commons has now written to the Home Secretary, asking why the *Qadir* case was conceded and what she will do about all the other ETS cases that are still pending.

Meanwhile, the President of the Immigration and Asylum Chamber of the Upper Tribunal has lambasted the Home Office even more severely in *R (on the application of Mohibullah) v Secretary of State for the Home Department (TOEIC – ETS – judicial review principles)*[3] In this case, a Bangladeshi student used a TOEIC certificate issued by ETS to obtain a place at a private college, but in August 2014 he was expelled on suspicion that the certificate had been obtained by fraud. He subsequently had his leave to remain curtailed without a right of appeal, so that his only remedy was to seek judicial review.

At the hearing before the Upper Tribunal, oral evidence was given by two witnesses. One, the principal of the private college, was found to be truthful; the other, a senior Home Office official, was found to be utterly unconvincing. The Tribunal concluded that, acting on no more than suspicion, the Home Office had exerted improper pressure on the college to expel Mr Mohibullah and a whole cohort of other students, threatening the principal with the revocation of his sponsor licence if he did not comply. Subsequently, the Home Office curtailed Mr Mohibullah's Tier 4 leave under para 323A of HC 395, which is mandatory if 'the Sponsor has excluded or withdrawn the mi-grant . . . from the course of studies'.

McCloskey J also held that the Home Office had 'acted with singular and manifest unfairness' in choosing this method of bringing the student's leave to an end, which left him with no right of appeal at all, whereas (at that time) curtailment of his leave under para 323 would have given him an in-country appeal, while a decision to remove him under s 10 of the Immigration and Asylum Act 1999 would have given him an out of country appeal.

The Upper Tribunal concluded that the Secretary of State's decision 'was so unfair and unreasonable as to amount to an abuse of power'. The decision was quashed, with an order to pay the applicant's costs.

1   [2016] UKUT 225 (IAC).
2   [2016] EWCA Civ 1167.
3   [2016] UKUT 561 (IAC).


## MAINTENANCE – 10 POINTS

### Maintenance requirements for Tier 4 (General) Students

#### 9.17 *[N.B.]*

Two significant changes have been made to the funding requirements for overseas students. First, the area within which the higher level of maintenance funds must be shown has expanded beyond certain Inner London boroughs to embrace the whole of Greater London, including far-flung outposts of London University such as Royal Holloway. The higher level of maintenance has gone up to £1,265 per month but, owing apparently to an oversight in the drafting of HC 297, which introduced these changes, the maintenance funds outside London initially remained unchanged at £820 per month. This was later rectified, and the amount was increased to £1,015 per month.

Second, if the applicant already had an 'established presence' as a student in the UK, he used to need only two months' worth of maintenance funds in his bank account for 28 days, rather than nine months' worth, in order to get further leave to remain. This reduction is now only available to PhD students on the Doctorate Extension Scheme, who must have £1,265 per month for a two-month period if studying in London, and £1,015 if studying outside London. All other Tier 4 (General) Migrants must now have nine months' worth of funds in their account when they apply for leave to study for a course of one year's duration or more, regardless of whether they have already been studying here. The need to show altogether £11,385 in their account when applying for further study in London may be a further deterrent to some overseas students.

## WORKING AS A STUDENT

### 9.27 [N.B.]

While they are studying, Tier 4 (General) Migrants can work for 20 hours per week during term time, and full-time during the vacations, if they are attending a publicly funded institution of higher education. This used to drop to 10 hours per week for a publicly funded institution of further education. But no work at all is now allowed for students at such an institution, and in this respect they are treated the same as students at private colleges – many of which have closed down because of the prohibition on work.

## EXTENSION OF LEAVE AS A TIER 4 STUDENT

### Leave to remain for Tier 4 (General) students

### 9.28 [N.B.]

The election of a Conservative government in May 2015 has spurred the Home Office to a more determined effort to reduce the number of inter-national students coming to the United Kingdom, save for the 'brightest and best' whose attendance at British universities is so vital to their finances. This aim is explicitly declared in HC 297, which introduced a further tightening of the rules for students from July 2015.

This Statement of Changes opens up a gulf between, on the one hand, 'UK recognised bodies' and higher education institutions in receipt of public funding (essentially, universities) and, on the other hand, publicly funded colleges of further education, offering courses at levels 3-5 of the National Qualifications Framework. Because of perceived abuse, from 12 November 2015 students at the latter can no longer work, spend more than two years on their course, or switch in-country to anything else at the end. Publicly-funded further education colleges, like private colleges before them, will no doubt see a sharp fall in overseas student numbers.

Tier 4 (General) Students can now spend no more than two years (reduced from three by HC 297) on courses below degree level, and five on courses at Bachelor's and Master's level, unless the subject of study is one which traditionally takes longer, such as Medicine or Architecture. Another new move to reduce the amount of time that students can spend here under Tier 4 is to include periods of leave granted before and after a particular course in the calculation. Leave to enter or remain is normally granted for a longer period than the actual course itself, and the extra bit used to be disregarded when working out whether a student had reached his maximum time in the UK. By including it in the total, the Home Office has made it more difficult for students to achieve settlement after ten years under the Long Residence Rule just by studying.

Some significant new restrictions have been introduced from 6 April 2016 by HC 877. Tier 4 (General) students may not extend their leave in order to study a course at a lower level than the previous one, and the new course must be at or above degree level. It should also represent 'academic progress'. So, if it is at the same level, the sponsoring Higher Education Institution must confirm that it is related to the previous course, or that the previous course and the new course in combination support the applicant's 'genuine career aspirations'. The idea of study for its own sake does not wash with the Home Office!

Nor does the Home Office smile upon the 'eternal student'. An overseas student cannot normally spend more than eight years here in tertiary education, so he is unlikely to achieve settlement through ten years' lawful residence solely through the Tier 4 (General) route. A student will now reach his maximum time here sooner, thanks to a change in the way the time limits are calculated. Rather than totalling up the actual time spent on a course, the official period of leave granted in respect of that course will be used, which may be considerably longer.

On the topic of maximum periods of study, the Upper Tribunal has reported a case which takes account of the modular nature of many degree courses nowadays. Tier 4 migrants are not normally allowed to spend more than five years on courses leading to the award of Bachelor's and Master's degrees (with the exception of subjects that do take longer, such as Medicine and Architecture). In *Luu (Periods of study: degree level)*,[1] the migrant had been refused further leave to undertake another Master's course, because she had already used up her five years on degree-level courses. On appeal, it was argued that her earlier years were not spent on degree-level study at all. The first year of her course had led to the award of a qualification at level 3 of the National Qualifications Framework (NQF), and the second year to a qualification at level 4. It was not until her third year that she achieved a qualification at level 6, ie a degree.

Upper Tribunal Judge Chalkley had little trouble rejecting that argument. The years spent on a course leading to the award of a degree, he concluded, all count as degree-level study. It may be remarked that, rather than let students who fail their final exams or who drop out before they get that far go away with nothing, many colleges and universities have adopted a modular framework in which the successful completion of each year of study is rewarded with something. The fact that this award is not a degree does not mean that their students are not pursuing degree-level study. In fact, exactly this point was made several years ago by Lord Carlile of Berriew in *R (on the application of De Oliveira) v Secretary of State for the Home Department*,[2] a case which was not cited to the Upper Tribunal.

[1]   [2016] UKUT 181.
[2]   [2009] EWHC 347 (Admin).

Concessions for Syrian national students extending leave

**9.28A** *[Insert new heading and paragraph:]*

New Concessions for Syrian nationals seeking to extend their leave as Tier 4 students have superseded previous concessions as from 1 March 2017. They are as follows:[1]

(i)     Tier 4 General (Student): under para 245ZX (requirements for leave to remain), the three-year time period stated in sub-paras (f)(iii) and (f)(iv), the two-year time period stated in sub-para (h) and the five-year time period stated in sub-para (ha) shall not apply.

(ii)    Short term students: Syrian nationals who entered the UK under paras A57A to A57H (short term student) of the Immigration Rules on or after 24 April 2015, who apply for further leave to remain in that category must have their application considered as an application for leave outside of the Immigration Rules.

[1]     *Concessions to the Immigration Rules for Syrian Nationals*, Version 3.0, authorised under the Equality (Syria) Authorisation 2017 which came into force on 1 March 2017.

## CHANGING SPONSORS AND COURSES

### Switching course

**9.33** *[N.B.]*

In-country 'switching' to Tier 4 is allowed from any of the previous study categories and from Tier 2, while graduates of British universities can switch to Tier 2 (General) or Tier 1 (Graduate Entrepreneur), but not any longer to the Tier 1 (Entrepreneur) route, except where funding of £50,000 is coming from a government department or an entrepreneurial seed-funding competition. As for Tier 4 (General) students at colleges rather than higher education institutions, thanks to HC 297 they cannot switch into any other Points Based route, or even into another course on Tier 4. If they want to do the latter, they must go home and apply for entry clearance again. There is an exception if they are studying at an 'embedded college offering pathway courses'. This would be a private college linked to a university and offering 'pathway' programmes designed to prepare students for entry to a higher education course at that university. (Such programmes are not to be confused with 'foundation' degrees, which are at level 5 of the National Qualifications Framework but are awarded by universities.)

In order to move from one course to another, whether by 'switching' or by going back and applying for entry clearance, Tier 4 students have to show that their new course represents 'academic progress', by moving up to a higher level on the NQF. An exception is now made for students at higher education institutions, if their new course is related to their previous one, or their sponsor confirms that the new course supports the student's genuine career aspirations.

## SWITCHING TO EMPLOYMENT AND OTHER CATEGORIES OUTSIDE TIER 4

**9.34** See paragraph 9.33 to this supplement.

## PROSPECTIVE STUDENTS

*9.68 [N.B.]*

The rules for admission of prospective students were deleted from Part 3 of HC395 from 1 October 2013. This route is no longer available. On the other hand, short-term students coming for six months (or up to 11 months for English language courses) still fall outside the Points Based System, having been transferred from the Visitor category to Part 3 of the Immigration Rules. But like students in Tier 4, they too are now subject to a 'genuineness' test.

Chapter 10

# WORKING, BUSINESS, INVESTMENT AND RETIREMENT IN THE UK

## INTRODUCTION

**10.1** *[After end of the second sentence delete from 'The whole scheme . . . '*
*to ' . . . divided into five tiers,' including footnote reference 3, and insert:]*

The intention was to introduce a 'transparent points system for all those who come to the UK to work, to carry out training, to start a business or join an existing one or simply to invest money into the UK economy. The aim was to have five tiers. Tier 3 has never happened and Tier 4 was for students (see CHAPTER 9 above).

*[Delete footnote 3.]*

**10.1A** *[Insert new paragraph:]*

This Supplement is dealing with updates since the publication of the 9th edition. Let us warn readers that we are wandering into a labyrinth. The 'transparent points system' has become a nightmare of obfuscation and indigestible complication. That is not just our view of things. The following remarks of senior Court of Appeal judges seem to be sending out a similar message. In *Pokhriyal*[1] Jackson LJ stated that:

> 'the provisions have now achieved a degree of complexity which even the Byzantine emperors would have envied'.

In *Singh*[2] Underhill LJ said:

> 'I fully recognise that the Immigration Rules, which have to deal with a wide variety of circumstances and may have as regards some issues to make very detailed provision, will never be "easy, plain and short" (to use the language of the law reformers of the Commonwealth period); and it is no doubt unrealistic to hope that every provision will be understandable by lay-people, let alone would-be immigrants. But the aim should be that the Rules should be readily understandable by ordinary lawyers and other advisers. **That is not the case at present.** I hope that the Secretary of State may give consideration as to how their drafting and presentation may be made more accessible.'

The latest criticism comes in the case of *SI (India)*[3] from Lady Justice Rafferty. The case turned on the meaning of 'nominee' in Indian banking law as regards the maintenance requirement for Tier 1 (Post Study Work) migrants, a category that was abolished in The Great Student Crackdown in 2014. She said:

'17. The SSHD's decision is set out in a letter of 5th November 2013. Although this is a PBS case, there are five pages of fairly dense typescript which recite the standard relevant paragraphs. One page shows in tabular form the points awarded. The reasoning supporting the decision is confined to two sentences in a box on page three. The first sentence does no more than recite the policy that parental sponsorship is not permitted for Tier 1 applications. It is silent as to any reasoning for the decision maker's reliance on that policy and in particular does not apply the policy to the evidence. The Applicant, and the tribunal, are left to navigate to their own conclusions about whether the evidence submitted is rejected and if so why. The second sentence – "parental sponsorship is not permitted . . . in addition the evidence submitted is post-dated the date you made the application . . . ' – reads as if the decision maker considered the additional evidence and rejected it as not submitted at the time the application was made. Both members of this court so construed it. So too did the Upper Tribunal judge and the Applicant. We were told in submissions that we are all wrong and that the sentence intended to convey that some of the additional evidence relates to a time period which is irrelevant.

18. . . . It is inappropriate to expect an applicant who may not enjoy publicly funded legal representation to construe such poor drafting. Nor should the administration of justice oblige a tribunal to expend public time and money itself attempting that task. Decision letters should set out with clarity (a) the facts determinative of the application, (b) why the applicant's evidence has been rejected and (c) the reasons for coming to the conclusion reached.

19. In our view a reader of the decision letter would struggle to understand (b) and (c) above. Three judges and one barrister certainly did. That is enough to dispose of this appeal, which we allow.'

[1] *Pokhriyal v Secretary of State for the Home Department* [2013] EWCA Civ 1568, [2014] PTSR D4, [2013] All ER (D) 52 (Dec).
[2] *Singh v Secretary of State for the Home Department* [2015] EWCA Civ 74.
[3] *SI (India) v Secretary of State for the Home Department* [2016] EWCA Civ 1255, paras 17–19.

### Managed migration and rules versus schemes

**10.2** *[After the words ' . . . these are normally considered by Home Office staff in Sheffield.' delete the text to the end of the paragraph.]*

**10.4** *[After the quotation and above the second paragraph starting 'As we shall see . . . ', insert the heading 'POINTS BASED SYSTEM (PBS)' taken from paragraph 10.5 below and insert paragraph number 10.5 below the moved heading.]*

*[The accompanying footnote 1 to the quotation should now appear at the end of the text for revised para 10.4.]*

**10.5** *[In the same paragraph, which is now paragraph 10.5, after the third sentence ending ' . . . the concept of one decision', delete the remaining text to the end of the paragraph and insert:]*

Secondly, the requirements to be fulfilled by an applicant are contained in the Immigration Rules rather than hidden in a scheme. Thirdly the rules are unbelievably detailed, especially with regard to the documents which must be provided. The applicants either meets or fails to meet the requirements; so that decision making should become a tick box exercise, leading to greater consistency of decisions. So there was little, if any, room for discretion under the PBS, until the government decided to introduce a genuineness test. This was aimed at stopping bogus applications, first in relation to students and then Entrepreneurs and then extending to varying degrees to a whole range of PBS applications. In practice, it is these alterations that have given case workers such a wide and loose discretion to label an application as not genuine that the main characteristic of the PBS is undermined. Fourth, the only appeal remedy available to failed applications is an administrative review, which is a very limited and unsatisfactory substitute for an appeal.[1]

*[In the original para 10.5 delete the footnote reference 1 attached to the first sentence of the last paragraph and delete the footnote text.]*

1    In the post Immigration Act 2014 world, recent Immigration Rules, starting with HC 693 have made administrative review available for persons refused leave to remain where they do not have a right of appeal. The rules now have their own Appendix AR. See further CHAPTER **19**.

**10.7** *[In the second sentence of this paragraph delete 'three rounds of criteria' and substitute 'four rounds of criteria'.]*

*[At the end of the paragraph, add:]*

The last sentence of this paragraph can no longer apply because the requirement to show funds for the 90-day period for Tier 1, Tier 2 and Tier 3 applicants cannot be by way of an overdraft.[3]

3    HC 395, Appendix C, para 1A(b), (f) and (l), as amended.

**10.8** *[Delete the paragraph and replace with:]*

The third round of criteria is that the main rules and Appendices A, B and C rely to a greater or lesser extent, depending on the particular Tier (ie Tier 2 and 5), on the existence of sponsors, who are regulated not by the Immigration Rules, but by administrative Guidance, whose legality was affirmed by the Supreme Court in the *New London College* case.[1] It is also the fact that since the decisions of the Court of Appeal in *Pankina*[2] and the Supreme Court in *Alvi*[3] a whole list of rules previously contained in Guidance have been made part of the Immigration Rules in accordance with the ruling in *Alvi*. The result has meant that the Immigration Rules have bulked up in a sometimes spectacular fashion and require frequent change[4] as does the increasingly bulky Sponsorship Guidance, which is also subject to similarly frequent amendment, entirely unsupervised by Parliament.

1    *R (on the application of New London College Limited) v Secretary of State for the Home Department* [2013] UKSC 51.
2    *Secretary of State for the Home Department v Pankina.* [2010] EWCA Civ 719, (2010) Times, 20 July, [2010] RTR 208, [2010] All ER (D) 140 (Feb). Following *Pankina* the Secretary of State has in fact chosen not to appeal (but has kept her options open) and has 'for the avoidance of doubt' brought various existing PBS requirements from Guidance into the Immigration Rules. These first batch were set out in the amendments in HC 863. It is a long, thorough and overdue list. Further transfers into the rules have followed in successive rule changes, following the revised test set out in *Alvi*.
3    *R (on the application of Alvi) v Secretary of State for the Home Department* [2012] UKSC 33, [2012] 4 All ER 1041, [2012] 1 WLR 2208.
4    See, for example, Appendix J and P.

## Genuineness tests

### 10.8A [Insert new heading and paragraph:]

The fourth category of requirements is the more recently inserted tests of genuineness, which give a discretion to the immigration authorities to require an applicant to send in additional information relating to the application and the applicant's immigration history and/or attend an interview to be questioned about the credibility and viability of the application, particularly that of a Tier 1 (Entrepreneur).[1] The test also applies to Tier 2 (Religious Workers) and Tier 5 (Temporary Workers).[2] A genuineness test was first introduced for students under the Tier 4 route in 2012.[3] The 'genuine entrepreneur' test was introduced for initial applications in Tier 1 in January 2013 (HC 943) and was then expanded to applications for extensions and indefinite leave to remain by rule change HC 1025 as from 6 April 2015.[4]

In Tier 2 (General) and Tier 2 (Intra Company) an assessment of whether a *genuine vacancy* exists was added to Tier 2 (Intra-Company Transfer) and Tier 2 (General). See further new paragraph **10.55A**, below. This change empowers Entry Clearance Officers and caseworkers to refuse applications where there are reasonable grounds to believe that the job described by the sponsor does not genuinely exist, has been exaggerated to meet the Tier 2 skills threshold,[5] or (in respect of Tier 2 (General)) has been tailored to exclude resident workers from being recruited, or where there are reasonable grounds to believe that the applicant is not qualified to do the job.[6]

---

[1] HC 395, para 245DB (f)–(j), of which (g)–(m) were inserted by HC 1025, para 101.

[2] Tier 5 (Temporary Workers), HC 395, para 245ZO ((i)–(l) and to Tier 2 (Religious Workers), HC 395, para 245HB (m)–(p).

[3] The Home Office explained that the genuineness approach 'has worked well on Tier 4 (the student route) since its introduction on 30 July 2012 as a result of HC 514. The test avoids having to keep tightening the rules on specified documents and evidence in ways which are burdensome for genuine applicants but not effective against bogus ones': see Explanatory Memorandum, HC 943, para 7.3.

[4] HC 395, paras 245DB(g)–(n), replacing 245DB(g)–(j) (substituted by HC 1025, para 101) and 245F(f), inserted by HC 1025, paras 109. As regards budding business persons the test, according to the Home Office, is 'to give the UK Border Agency the ability to test the credibility of suspicious applicants and to use their discretion, while leaving the basic requirements in Appendix A unchanged. It can also be said that it introduces a subjective element into the PBS, thus subverting its original aim. See further **10.25A** below.

[5] HC 395, Appendix A, paras 74H and 74I (intra company transfers) and paras77H, 77I and 77J (Tier 2 General).

[6] Appendix A, para 77H(ii) and (iii).

### 10.8B [Insert new paragraph:]

The case law so far has dealt with weak cases and has only clarified the obvious.[1] The problem is that no adverse decision can be appealed to a fact-finding tribunal. Administrative review is a bit of a 'rubber stamping' process in that it has a limited ambit and has neither the necessary independence nor procedures of the established immigration tribunal system. Judicial review has obvious limitations and whatever the judges might think of the facts, it is not within their jurisdiction to do anything about them in normal circumstances. *Singh and Another*[2] is a good illustration of these limitations; it was a case under paragraph 245ZO(i) of Tier 5 (Temporary Workers), where the Entry Clearance Officer was not satisfied that either of two religious workers was someone who 'genuinely intends to undertake, and is capable of undertaking, the role recorded in the Certificate of Sponsorship Checking Service'. They were otherworldly and pretty clueless, but hardly bogus. The Upper Tribunal, not unexpectedly, held that the refusal of entry clearance was within a reasonable range of responses, given that in interview neither could explain the nature of the work they were to do, the wages they would receive or where they would be staying. As drafted, the rules do not distinguish between the bogus and the incompetent applicant, but speak of a business plan as being both credible and viable. In practice, the tests, as worded, have moved a long way from the original purpose of seeking out the bogus applicant in order to safeguard the genuine one.

1   See *Sabir* [2015] EWHC 264 (Admin) and *Zang* [2015] UKUT 138.
2   *Singh and Another, R (on the application of) v Secretary of State for the Home Department (IJR)* [2015] UKUT 538 (IAC).

*Strict compliance and evidential flexibility*

**10.9A** *[After paragraph 10.9 Insert new heading and paragraph:]*

Paragraph 245AA deals with issues of strict compliance with the Immigration Rules and evidential flexibility. Under the Points-Based System applications are normally decided on the basis of documents provided by the applicant before the case is considered. Paragraph 245AA of the Immigration Rules sets out the limited circumstances in which a decision maker may write to an applicant to give them an opportunity to provide further or missing documents. Prior to September 2012, there was a flexibility policy contained in Guidance but nothing in the Immigration Rules. An evidential policy was inserted into the rules by HC 565, para 56 as from 6 September 2012. Further amendments were made by HC 760, paras 117–120 as from 13 December 2012 and by HC 628, paras 74, 75 which applied to all applications decided on or after 1 October 2013. New rules[1] and a new Guidance, version 8, came into force on 24 November 2016.

*In Mandalia*[2] a foreign national student made an application for an extension of his leave to remain under Tier 4 (general). Under the Tier 4 rules he was required to demonstrate that he had sufficient funds to support himself by enclosing bank statements. He failed to meet these requirements and his application was refused because the statement sent in covered only a 22-day period, albeit showing that there was a preceding statement in existence with sufficient funds. The Supreme Court held that UKBA should have given him an opportunity to supply the necessary additional statement before dismissing his application. Caseworkers dealing with such applications at the time were given a 'process instruction: evidential flexibility' document whereby, in the case of an application liable for refusal solely because of the absence of a piece of information which they had reason to believe existed – 'including . . . bank statements missing from a series' – they were to ask the applicant for that information before determining the application. According to judgment of Lord Wilson, agreed to by the other members of the Court, the process instruction, read as a whole, rightly stressed the need for flexibility by stating that: (a) there was no limit on the amount of information which could be requested, provided that the request was not speculative; (b) bank statements missing from a series represented only an example of the further evidence which should be requested; and (c) where there was uncertainty as to whether evidence existed, the applicant should be given the benefit of the doubt and it should be requested. The agency's decision to reject the application was therefore unlawful because, properly interpreted, the process instruction had obliged it first to have invited the applicant to repair the deficit in his evidence.

The wording of some of the rules are not always set in rigid imperatives but provide a modicum of flexibility. For example, in Tier 1 (Entrepreneur), para 41-SD(c) gives a long list of specified documents needed to show evidence of the funding available to invest, but states that 'the specified documents to show evidence of the funding available to invest . . . are one or more of the following specified documents'. In some cases it may also be acceptable to insert the words 'if appropriate' into the rule. These examples are small concessions to flexibility.

1  HC 395, para 245AA, as substituted by HC 667, para 6A.3.
2  *Mandalia v Secretary of State for the Home Department* [2015] UKSC 59, [2016] 4 All ER 189, [2015] 1 WLR 4546, overruling the Court of Appeal at [2014] EWCA Civ 2, [2014] Imm AR 588 (sub nom *Rodriguez v Secretary of State for the Home Department*). In the new Guidance, version 8 (see para **10.9B**, below), the Home Office still say that *Rodrigues* is the case to follow, not *Mandalia* as regards a case worker making speculative requests for information. See Guidance, version 8, p 16. See also *SH (Pakistan) v Secretary of State for the Home Department* [2016] EWCA Civ 426. The appellant was not in a position to submit an original degree certificate because although he had by then been awarded the degree, he had not at that point received his degree certificate. Accordingly, he had to provide the academic transcript from the awarding institution. He had to make his application before 29 October and therefore could not wait until his degree certificate was provided to him. The Court ruled that where there was a policy set in wider terms than the rules, the policy should be followed.

*New rules and guidance on flexibility*

**10.9B**  *[Insert new heading and paragraph:]*

In November 2016 the rules were changed. The new version of the Guidance followed suit.[1] It replaces previous instructions and Guidance on evidential flexibility. The Guidance makes a distinction between applications made on or after 24 November 2016 and those made before this date. It gives guidance to case workers on how to deal with *Mandalia* and *SH (Pakistan)* (see **10.9A** above). More importantly, it mirrors the new rules which are a complete substitute for the previous rules in HC 395, para 245AA.[2] Under para 245AA(a), the final day for the receipt of documents is the date on which the application is considered. This sounds fine but there is no way an applicant will know when his or her application is to be considered; so they will not know how much of a leeway they have or, if they have sent them, whether they will be considered – all a bit of a lottery. Under subparagraph (b) an unnecessary, petty, and possibly unfair, change has been made with regard to applications made on or after 24 November 2016. The rules and guidance reverse the decision in *Mandalia* by changing the circumstances, in which a document will be considered to be missing from a sequence. The change seeks to reinstate the decision of the Court of Appeal in *Rodrigues*. So a document will only be considered to be missing from a sequence where the documents at the beginning and the end of a sequence have both been provided and the missing document is within that sequence (sub-para (b)(i)). When further documents have been requested by the Home Office under these new rules, the time period the applicant has to provide the required document has been changed from seven working days to ten working days (sub-para (b)(iv)). In *SH (Pakistan)* (see **10.9A** above), Beatson LJ raised the issue of the common law duty of fairness imposing additional obligations on the Secretary of State in these cases. In his judgment he said:

'29. I would like to make a brief observation on what in argument was described as the "tailpiece argument", that based on the public duty of fairness of common law. It is common ground that this may impose obligations on the Secretary of State in addition to those under the Rules concerning the points-based system (see *Alam v Secretary of State for the Home Department* [2002] EWCA Civ 960 at 44). *EK (Ivory Coast) v Secretary of State for the Home Department* [2015] EWCA Civ 1517 is to the same effect although in a much more constrained way. That case establishes that the context of the points-based system informs the way in which the general public duty of fairness operates, as does *Rahman v Secretary of State for the Home Department* [2014] EWCA Civ 1640 . . .

30. . . . Given that a Secretary of State may act unfairly (see the authorities I have cited) notwithstanding her compliance with the Rule and the terms of the majority judgments in *EK (Ivory Coast)*, that case should not be taken as excluding the common law duty of fairness in such cases or confining it to cases in which the problem is caused by the Secretary of State's conduct.'

[1]    Evidential flexibility: points-based system, version 8, in force 24 November 2016.
[2]    Substituted by HC 667, para 6A.3, as from 24 November 2016.

*Indefinite leave – some general measures*

**10.10** *[N.B.]*

Under HC 395, para 245AAA, Tier 1 and Tier 2 migrants who apply for settlement must not have had more than 180 days absent from the UK per year during the qualifying period (usually five years). A change is being made to discount any absences from the UK from counting towards the 180-day limit, where the absence was due to the applicant assisting with the Ebola crisis which began in West Africa in 2014 (HC 1025, explanatory Memorandum para 7.28).

**10.11** *[At the end of sub-paragraph (a)(i), insert:]*

An exception to the 180-day (absence from the UK) rule has been added by rule change HC 1025 for those who have been assisting with the Ebola crisis which began in West Africa in 2014. Their absence shall not count towards the 180 days, if applicants provide evidence that this was the purpose of the absence(s) and that their Sponsor has agreed to the absence(s) (HC 1025, para 90).

*Appendix C – Maintenance (funds)*

**10.13** *[After sub-paragraph (f) add new sub-paragraph (ff):]*

(ff) An amendment was made by HC 535 (presented on 29 October 2015) to the maintenance rules for family members of Tier 2 migrants, so that where the Tier 2 migrant is exempt from having to show maintenance funds by virtue of applying to extend their stay in the same category, their dependants are also exempt, even if they apply at a later date. Previously the exemption only extended to dependants who applied at the same time as the main applicant.

**Changes relating to Tier 1 of the Points-Based System**

**10.17A** *[After paragraph 10.17, insert new heading and new paragraph:]*

Tier 1 of the Points-Based System caters for high value migrants, and currently consists of four categories: Tier 1 (Exceptional Talent), Tier 1 (Entrepreneur), Tier 1 (Investor) and Tier 1 (Graduate Entrepreneur). It also includes the Tier 1 (General) category, which was closed to new applicants in April 2011 but remains open for extension applications until April 2015 and indefinite leave to remain applications until April 2018. A further category, Tier 1 (Post-Study Work), was closed in April 2012. We deal with these changes below.

**Tier 1 (General)**

**10.19A** *[After paragraph 10.19 insert new paragraph:]*

Because of the closure of all leave to remain applications under the Tier 1 (General) category, a change was made in HC 693 to adjust the grant periods for Tier 1 (General) extensions to either three years (as at present) or the balance the applicant needs to take their time in the category to five years, whichever is longer.[1] This allows for applicants to accrue five years in the category before the closing date, even if their original grant was delayed due to a refusal and appeal. Then, in HC 1025, further changes were made in relation to the closure of leave to remain by deleting paras 245CA and 245CB.[2]

A further change was made in rule change HC 1025 to restrict the ability of Tier 1 (General) Migrants to switch into Tier 1 (Entrepreneur), unless they have already established a UK business before the date these changes take effect (6 April 2015), or they have funding from a government department or endorsed seed funding competition.[3] This change was made due to the closure of Tier 1 (General) extension applications and concerns that similar areas of abuse have been identified in both these two categories but only affects switching into the Tier 1 (Entrepreneur) route, which has been identified as a target for abuse.[4] Switching arrangements from Tier 1 (General) into other categories, for example Tier 2, remain unchanged. Tier 1 (General) Migrants can also still apply for indefinite leave to remain without changing category, until 2018.

Another change was made to those students who could switch into Tier 1 (Entrepreneur) category or a Tier 1 (Investor) category after finishing their studies. Paragraphs 245DD (e)(xxi) and 245ED (c)(xvi) were amended to limit a Tier 4 (General) student, who could switch to a business or investor visa, to someone whose last sponsor is or was:

(1)     a UK recognised body or a body in receipt of public funding as a higher education institution from the Department of Employment and Learning in Northern Ireland, the Higher Education Funding Council for England, the Higher Education Funding Council for Wales or the Scottish Funding Council; or

(2)     an overseas higher education institution sponsoring the student to undertake a short-term study abroad programme in the UK; or

(3)     an Embedded College offering Pathway Courses;[5] or

(4)     an independent school.[6]

A Tier 4 (Child) Student is not affected and can switch to Entrepreneur status from the age of 16.

[1]     See HC 395, para 245CB(a)(i) and (ii).
[2]     HC 1025, para 95, effective from 6 April 2015.
[3]     See HC 395, Appendix A, Table 4.
[4]     The change is the same as the arrangements put in place for Tier 1 (Post-Study Work) applicants in July 2014 (HC 532). See Table 4, above.
[5]     The definition of a 'UK Recognised Body'; an 'Independent School'; an 'Embedded College Offering Pathway Courses' and 'Pathway Courses' are now part of HC 359, para 6 definitions; see rule change HC 297 (13 July 2015), paras 11–13 and 15 and rule change HC 877, para Intro 2.
[6]     Added by rule change HC 877, paras 6A.1 and 6A.2, as from 6 April 2016.

**10.20–10.22** *Note that paragraphs 10.20, 10.21 and 10.22 are no longer operative due to the closure of leave to remain in this category on 6 April 2015.*

### Tier 1 (Entrepreneur)

**10.25** *[At the end of the paragraph delete the last sentence and footnote 3 and insert:]*

According to the Home Office, this category has been plagued by abuse. The rule changes in HC 693 (October 2014) complained that it had the potential to benefit the UK economy but had been heavily abused in recent years. In rule change HC 1025 (February 2015) this complaint was repeated. This has led to a recast of the genuineness test in the main body of the rules. Investing in a property business has been banned, but most of the changes are about detail – which documents must be produced, when the money must be available, where it must be kept, what needs to be proved and so forth. It is the most amended of the Tier 1 categories.

*[At the end of footnote 1, insert:]*

See 245DB(p) and (q).

*[In footnote 2 delete '(g)–(j)' and insert: '(f) to (m)'.]*

### The genuine entrepreneur

**10.25A** *[Insert new heading and paragraph:]*

The rules for testing the genuineness of an application were changed by HC 1025, as from 6 April 2015, to expand the use of the 'genuineness' test in Tier

1 (Entrepreneur) to applications for extensions and indefinite leave to remain.[1] This change is a more detailed version of the 'genuine entrepreneur' test introduced for initial applications in January 2013 (HC 943). Two major differences is that: (i) the rule now makes it a requirement that an applicant produces a business plan; and (ii) the test no longer ceases to operate, if within the twelve months immediately before the date of the application the applicant has had entry clearance, leave to enter or leave to remain under Tier 1 (Entrepreneur) and his or her application is being considered under Table 5.[2] For more detail of this cross-cutting change see **10.8A** above.

[1]   HC 395, paras 245DB (g)–(m); 245DD (i)–(o); and 245DF (f)–(k), substituted or inserted by HC 1025 paras 101, 106 and 109. The purpose, according to the Explanatory Memorandum, was 'to better protect the route against abuse without disadvantaging genuine applicants'. The problem is that it effectively introduces a two-track system. The applicant frequently scores all the points needed under Appendix A, B and C but then fails the genuineness test; the first being the objective tick box PBS scheme and the second opening up the decision making to the risk of subjective judgment by the case worker. Clearly the Home Office has great doubts about the efficacy of the PBS, which, notwithstanding all the detailed paperwork, it still cannot catch the bogus and/or incompetent applicants. Our view is that the genuineness test mixes up the rogues and cheats with the incompetent; it may weed out a few bogus applicants, but is more likely to refuse on the basis of incompetence than fraud and it does not ensure a lack of inconsistency and, most importantly, there is no right of appeal to an independent fact finding tribunal.

[2]   The exception in HC 395, para 2, 45DB(f) now deleted and replaced by the new provisions of para 245(d)(i). The deleted rule also applied to those who had leave in the now defunct categories of Businesspersons and Innovators.

## The attributes – Appendix A

**10.28** *[Delete the last sentence of this paragraph and insert the following paragraphs and Table 4:]*

An applicant who is applying for leave to remain as a Tier 1 (Entrepreneur) and has, or was last granted, entry clearance, leave to enter or leave to remain as a Tier 1 (Post-Study Work) Migrant will only be awarded points under the provisions in (b)(ii), (b)(iii) or (d) in Table 4 (36B).

For applications made in the UK, a new provision was added that the funds to be invested in the business must also be in the UK[1] A further change is about the evidence to be provided of business funding from a UK or Devolved Government Department. The rule change is to make it clear that government funding by way of an intermediary public body may be accepted, providing that body confirms that the funds were made available by a UK or Devolved Government Department for the specific purpose of establishing or expanding a UK business.[2]

**Table 4: Applications for entry clearance or leave to remain referred to in paragraph 36**

| Investment and business activity | Points |
|---|---|
| The applicant has access to not less than £200,000, or | 25 |
| (b) The applicant has access to not less than £50,000 from:) | |
| (i) one or more registered venture capital firms regulated by the Financial Conduct Authority (FCA), | |

| Investment and business activity | Points |
|---|---|
| (ii) one or more UK Entrepreneurial seed funding competitions which is listed as endorsed on the UK Trade & Investment website, or | |
| (iii) one or more UK Government Departments, or Devolved Government Departments in Scotland, Wales or Northern Ireland, and made available by the Department(s) for the specific purpose of establishing or expanding a UK business, or | |
| (c) The applicant: | |
| (i) is applying for leave to remain, | |
| (ii) has, or was last granted, leave as a Tier 1 (Graduate Entrepreneur) Migrant, and | |
| (iii) has access to not less than £50,000, | |
| or | |
| ([d] The applicant: | |
| (i) is applying for leave to remain, | |
| (ii) has, or was lasted granted, leave as a Tier 1 (Post-Study Work) Migrant, and | |
| (iii) has access to not less than £50,000. | |
| An applicant who is applying for leave to remain and has, or was last granted leave as a Tier 1 (General) Migrant will be awarded no points under (a) or (b)(i) above, unless he meets the additional requirements in (1) and (2) below. | |
| An applicant who is applying for leave to remain and has, or was last granted leave as a Tier 1 (Post-Study Work) Migrant will be awarded no points under (d) above, unless he meets the additional requirements in (1) and (2) below. | |
| (1) Since before the specified date below and up to the date of his application, the applicant must have been continuously engaged in business activity which was not, or did not amount to, activity pursuant to a contract of service with a business other than his own and, during such period, has been continuously: | |
| * registered with HM Revenue & Customs as self-employed, or | |
| * registered with Companies House as a director of a new or an existing business. Directors who are on the list of disqualified directors provided by Companies House will not be awarded points. | |
| (2) Since before the specified date below and up to the date of his application, has continuously been working in an occupation which appears on the list of occupations skilled to National Qualifications Framework level 4 or above, as stated in the Codes of Practice in Appendix J, and provides the specified evidence in paragraph 41-SD. 'Working' in this context means that the core service his business provides to its customers or clients involves the business delivering a service in an occupation at this level. It excludes any work involved in administration, marketing or website functions for the business, and. | |
| The specified date in (1) and (2) above is: | |
| * 11 July 2014 if the applicant has, or was lasted granted, leave as a Tier 1 (Post-Study Work) Migrant, or | |

| Investment and business activity | Points |
|---|---|
| * 6 April 2015 if the applicant has, or was last granted, leave as a Tier 1 (General) Migrant.] | |
| The money is held in one or more regulated financial institutions | 25 |
| The money is disposable in the UK If the applicant is applying for leave to remain, the money must be held in the UK. | 25 |

[1]  See Table 4, last row, inserted by rule change HC 693, para113. This was to assist in verifying that the funds are genuine: HC 693, para 7.26, Explanatory statement.

[2]  See amended para 41-SD(c)(iii), as amended by HC 1025, para 249.

### 10.28A *[Insert new paragraph:]*

Paragraph 41-SD deals with evidence required by Tier 1 (Entrepreneur) applicants. It has gone through multiple changes since its inception; none more so than the original sub-para 41-SD(a) (now metamorphosed into sub-para (c)). It lays down the documents needed from a bank and others to prove that the required funding is available to the applicant to invest. The main problem was that many banks would not write letters in the format required by what was then subparagraph (a), giving information relating to the involvement of third parties in funding. Challenges to decisions in these cases in the FTT led to contradictory findings. In three linked cases – *Fayyaz, Durrani* and *Akhter*[1] the Upper Tribunal rejected the argument that a literal interpretation of requirements (6), (9) and (10) in subparagraph 41-SD(a)(i) would produce absurd results. In *Fayyaz* (para 27) the UT commented that there was no evidence that any provision of Pakistani banking law or internal bank rule on regulation or bank/customer contract precludes disclosure of the information required by the Rules or prevents the production of a fully compliant bank letter. In *Durrani*(see paras 12 and 13) the Tribunal said they were not persuaded that there is any principle of United Kingdom banking law precluding the construction of the relevant provisions of the Rules. In *Iqbal and Tank*[2] the Court of Appeal agreed with the Upper Tribunal in these decisions. The Court said that there could be no conceivable difficulty in the third-party bank expressing its understanding, based on the customer's in-structions, that the use of specified funds in the customer's bank account/s is there to finance the applicant's proposed business venture. The Court rejected the argument that where applicants were relying entirely upon funds being made available to them by a third party did *not* have to comply with the requirements in para 41-SD(a)(i), because the requirements 'did not work in practice' in such cases, banks being unable or unwilling to provide the necessary information. Sullivan LJ said:

> 'The fatal flaw in Mr Macdonald's submission is that there is no satisfactory evidence that the financial institutions referred to in paragraph 41-SD(a)(i) would be unable or unwilling to provide the information required by that paragraph.'

Subsequent to these decisions, paras 41 and 41-SD have been further amended, no doubt to overcome the possibility that the evidence missing from each of the above cases was found. Whatever the reason the rules have been amended to provide a stricter but more flexible arrangement of the requirements to show the availability of the cash sums needed to meet the investment requirements and the specified documents for third party funding listed in 41-SD(d)(i)-(ii).

We deal with these changes in the next paragraph.

¹   *Fayyaz (Entrepreneurs: paragraph 41-SD(a)(i) –'provided to')* [2014] UKUT 296 (IAC);
*Durrani (Entrepreneurs: bank letters; evidential flexibility)* [2014] UKUT 295 (IAC); and
*Akhter and Another (paragraph 245AA: wrong format)* [2014] UKUT 297 (IAC).
²   *Iqbal and Others v Secretary of State for the Home Department; Tank and Another v
Secretary of State for the Home Department* [2015] EWCA Civ 169.

**10.28B** *[Insert new paragraph:]*

Paragraph 41 of Appendix A was deleted and a new paragraph was substituted by rule change HC 535, para A4 with effect from 19 November 2015.[1] Substituted para 41 confirms existing requirements and makes further changes. First, it makes it clear, as before, that applicants will only be considered to have access to funds in the form of cash money and they must show that they have permission to use the funds, by providing the specified documents in para 41-SD. They must still show that the money is held in a UK regulated financial institution[2] or is transferable to the UK and that it will remain available to the applicant until such time as it is spent for the purposes of the applicant's business or businesses.[3] Further amendments were made in March 2016, to come into force on 6 April 2016. We deal with these amendments separately in new paragraph **10.34C** below.

Second, it provides in para 41(a)(ii) for a new 90-day period of time, ending no earlier than 31 days before the date of application, during which an applicant must have held the money. Evidence for this is set out in para 41-SD(c)(ii). But if this cannot be met, a period of less than 90 days will be enough if applicants can provide the following specified documents:

(a)   those in either paras 41-SD(c)(i) or 41-SD(c) (ii) to demonstrate funding is available to them at the time of their application; and

(b)   documents for private third party funding listed in 41-SD (d)(i)-(ii); or

(c)   a letter as specified in para 41-SD(c)(iii) as evidence of the source of those funds where funding is to be provided by UK Seed Funding Competitions or one or more UK Government Departments, or Devolved Government Departments in Scotland, Wales or Northern Ireland.[4]

Third, a new subparagraph 41(b) has been added to deal with cases, such as those of applicants applying from the Post Study Work or Graduate Entrepreneur category, who have already started their business before making a Tier 1 (Entrepreneur) application under Table 4. Subparagraph 41(b) provides that points will be awarded for funds available as if the applicant had not yet invested the funds, providing:

(i)   the investment was made no more than 24 months before the date of the application in the case of Graduate Entrepreneurs and no more than 12 months for all the rest; and

(ii)   all of the specified documents required by para 46-SD (a)–(g) to show the amount of money invested and the fact that they have invested their money to start a new business in the UK or to take over an existing business.

¹   Earlier amendments attempting to make the same changes by adding a new para 41(c), as from
6 April 2015 were ditched under the new November 2015 changes. This chop and change

shows how careful practitioners must be in checking that they have got the updated version of the rules.

2   See also Appendix A paras 43-45. Funds held in a financial institution that is on the Home Office's unsatisfactory list in Appendix P will not count and no points will be awarded.

3   As before, the Secretary of State still reserves the right to request further evidence or otherwise verify that the money will remain available, and to refuse the application if this evidence is not provided or it is unable to satisfactorily verify: para 41(a)(iv).

4   This provision was added by rule change HC 877, para A10, effective from 6 April 2016.

## 10.28C   *[Insert new paragraph:]*

In *Arshad and Others*[1] the Upper Tribunal held that:

(a)   the Rules stipulate that every Tier 1 Entrepreneurial applicant have available £50,000 [or £200,000] to invest in the proposed business venture and that 'available' in this context denotes that the applicant must be in a position to invest this money in his or her business consequential upon a positive decision of the Secretary of State. The Tribunal then added that the clear import of the Rules is that the investment must be capable of being made almost immediately thereafter;[2]

(b)   a mere intention on the part of a Tier 1 Entrepreneurial applicant to invest £25,000 at the outset of the business venture, coupled with a further intention to invest the balance of £25,000 at some unspecified future date from some unspecified source, does not satisfy the Rules.

1   *Arshad and Others (Tier 1 applicants – funding – 'availability')* [2016] UKUT 00334 (IAC).
2   This remark may be based upon para 41(a), which states that the specified documents in para 41-SD must show the total amount required is available on the same date. But there is nothing about investing it all in one go. Indeed, in para 41(a)(iv), it is provided that the applicant only has to show that the 'money will remain available to the applicant until such time as it is spent for the purposes of the applicant's business or businesses'. The President did, however, say that the Rules should be clearer on this point.

## 10.28D   *[Insert new paragraph:]*

Paragraph 41-SD, which is very long and runs to five pages, deals with documents which need to submitted in order to evidence all the requirements of Table 4. We do not go into detail, except as above, because the evidential requirements are subject to frequent change[1] and need to be read in full by anyone seeking to check that an application has been correctly put together before it is submitted.

A summary of the evidential list is as follows:

•   Companies House documents where the funds are available to the applicant's business, which must be a company of which the applicant is a director (sub-para (b));
•   evidence of available funding (sub-para(c));
•   documents evidencing money from a third party other than from public funding as specified on Table 4 (sub-para (d));
•   evidence of business activity if previous leave has been as Tier 1 (General) or Tier 1 (Post Study Work) Migrant (sub-para (e));
•   if claiming points for being self-employed, evidence to show the applicant's compliance with National Insurance and tax requirements (sub-para (e)(v));

- if claiming points as director of a UK company, specified Companies house, tax and bank documents.

[1] Extensive changes since the publication of the 9th edition of this work have been made by a combination of HC 1025, paras 245–260, effective from 6 April 2015; HC 535, paras A5-A21, effective from 19 November 2015; and HC 877, paras A11-A14, effective from 6 April 2016.

## 10.29 *[N.B.]*

Table 5 deals with applications for entry clearance or leave to remain referred to in para 37 of Appendix A. The Table remains the same as that printed in Volume 2 of the 9th edition of this work and is not, therefore, reproduced here.

### Indefinite leave – Tier 1 (Entrepreneurs)

**10.34** *[At the end of this paragraph insert Table 6, as amended by rule change HC 1025, para 242 as from 6 April 2015 in Row 1; by rule change HC 877 as from 6 April 2016.]*

| Row | Investment and business activity | Points |
|-----|----------------------------------|--------|
| 1 | The applicant has spent the specified continuous period lawfully in the UK, with absences from the UK of no more than 180 days in any 12 calendar months during that period. | 20 |
| | The specified period must have been spent with leave as a Tier 1 (Entrepreneur) Migrant, as a Businessperson and/or as an Innovator, of which the most recent period must have been spent with leave as a Tier (1) (Entrepreneur) Migrant. | |
| | The specified continuous period is: | |
| | (a) 3 years if the number of new full time jobs, X, referred to in row 3 above is at least 10, or | |
| | (b) 3 years if the applicant has: | |
| | (i) established a new UK business that has had an income from business activity of at least £5 million during a 3 year period in which the applicant has had leave as a Tier 1 (Entrepreneur) Migrant, or | |
| | (ii) taken over or invested in an existing UK business and his services or investment have resulted in a net increase in income from business activity to that business of £5 million during a 3 year period in which the applicant has had leave as a Tier 1 (Entrepreneur) Migrant, when compared to the immediately preceding 3 year period, or | |
| | (c) 5 years in all other cases. | |

| Row | Investment and business activity | Points |
|---|---|---|
| | Time spent with valid leave in the Bailiwick of Guernsey, the Bailiwick of Jersey or the Isle of Man in a category equivalent to the categories set out above may be included in the continuous period of lawful residence, provided the most recent period of leave was as a Tier 1 (Entrepreneur) Migrant in the UK. In any such case, the applicant must have absences from the Bailiwick of Guernsey, the Bailiwick of Jersey or the Isle of Man (as the case may be) of no more than 180 days in any 12 calendar months during the specified continuous period. | |
| 2 | [The applicant meets the following conditions:] <br><br> (i) on a date no earlier than three months prior to the date of application was: <br><br> (a) registered with HM Revenue and Customs as self-employed, or <br><br> (b) registered with Companies House as a director of a new or an existing business, and <br><br> [(ii) where the applicant's last grant of entry clearance, leave to enter or leave to remain was as a Tier 1 (Entrepreneur) Migrant, on a date within six months of his entry to the UK (if he was granted entry clearance as a Tier 1 (Entrepreneur Migrant) and there is evidence to establish his date of arrival in the UK), or in any other case the date of the grant of leave to remain, the applicant was: <br><br> (a) registered with HM Revenue and Customs as self-employed, or <br><br> (a) registered with HM Revenue and Customs as self-employed, or <br><br> (b) registered with Companies House as a director of a new or an existing business. ] <br><br> Directors who are on the list of disqualified directors provided by Companies House will not be awarded points. <br><br> [The applicant will not need to provide the evidence of registration for condition (ii) if he was awarded points from row 2 of Table 5 in his previous grant of entry clearance or leave to remain as a Tier 1 (Entrepreneur) Migrant.] | 20 |
| 3 | The applicant has: <br><br> (a) established a new UK business or businesses that has or have created the equivalent of X new full time jobs for persons settled in the UK, or <br><br> (b) taken over or invested in an existing UK business or businesses and his services or investment have resulted in a net increase in the employment provided by the business or businesses for persons settled in the UK by creating the equivalent of X new full time jobs where X is at least 2. <br><br> Where the applicant's last grant of entry clearance or leave to enter or remain was as a Tier 1 (Entrepreneur) Migrant, the jobs must have existed for at least 12 months during that last grant of leave. | 20 |

| Row | Investment and business activity | Points |
|-----|----------------------------------|--------|
| 4 | The applicant has spent the specified continuous period lawfully in the UK, with absences from the UK of no more than 180 days in any 12 calendar months during that period. | 15 |
| | The specified period must have been spent with leave as a Tier 1 (Entrepreneur) Migrant, as a Businessperson and/or as an Innovator, of which the most recent period must have been spent with leave as a Tier (1) (Entrepreneur) Migrant. | |
| | The specified continuous period is: | |
| | (a) 3 years if the number of new full time jobs, X, referred to in row 3 above is at least 10, or | |
| | (b) 3 years if the applicant has: | |
| | (i) established a new UK business that has had an income from business activity of at least £5 million during a 3 year period in which the applicant has had leave as a Tier 1 (Entrepreneur) Migrant, or | |
| | (ii) taken over or invested in an existing UK business and his services or investment have resulted in a net increase in income from business activity to that business of £5 million during a 3 year period in which the applicant has had leave as a Tier 1 (Entrepreneur) Migrant, when compared to the immediately preceding 3 year period, | |
| | or | |
| | (c) 5 years in all other cases. | |
| | Time spent with valid leave in the Bailiwick of Guernsey, the Bailiwick of Jersey or the Isle of Man in a category equivalent to the categories set out above may be included in the continuous period of lawful residence, provided the most recent period of leave was as a Tier 1 (Entrepreneur) Migrant in the UK. In any such case, the applicant must have absences from the Bailiwick of Guernsey, the Bailiwick of Jersey or the Isle of Man (as the case may be) of no more than 180 days in any 12 calendar months during the specified continuous period. | |

**10.34A** *[Insert new paragraph:]*

Paragraph 46 requires that the specified documents in para 46-SD must be provided as evidence of any investment and business activity that took place during an earlier business leave. It is unchanged. Paragraph 46-SD deals with documents which need to be provided as evidence of any investment and business activity that predates the date of the application in respect of applicants during their leave as a Tier 1 (Entrepreneur) Migrant or a Tier 1 (Post-Study Work), and any investment made no more than 12 months before the date of the application (or 24 months for an applicant last granted leave as a Tier 1 (Graduate Entrepreneur)). We do not go into detail, except as above, because the evidential requirements are subject to frequent change and need to be read in full by anyone seeking to check that an application has been correctly put together before it is submitted. A summary of the evidential requirement list is as follows:

- Appropriate specified documents to establish how much money has been invested (taken from a six-part list (46-SD (a)(i)-(vi)).
- Audited or unaudited accounts to show the amount of money invested by the applicant directly in his own name or on his behalf (46-SD(b)).
- Documents to show that the applicant has established a UK business (46-SD (c)). Points will only be awarded in respect of a UK business or businesses, as defined in paragraph 48. A business will only be considered as a 'new' business for the purposes of Tables 5 or 6, if the requirements of paragraph 48(c) and (d).
- Documents to deal with residential property bought by the applicant but also used for his or her business (46-SD(d)).
- Where Table 4 applies and only some of the money has been invested into a business in the UK prior, appropriate documents to demonstrate that the balance of the funds is held in a regulated financial institution and disposable in the UK (46-SD(e)).
- Evidence of the applicant's registration as self-employed or as a director, where Tables 5 or 6 apply and he or she was awarded points under Table 4 on his or her last application (46-SD(f)).
- Evidence of current registration as self-employed or as a director (46-SD(g)).
- Evidence of job creation in Table 5 or 6 (46-SD(h)).

### No investment in property

**10.34B** *[Insert new heading and new paragraph:]*

Paragraph 47 provides that Tables 4, 5 and 6, 'investment and business activity' does not include investment in any residential accommodation, property development or property management, and must not be in the form of a director's loan unless it is unsecured and subordinated in favour of the business. 'Property development or property management' in this context means any development of property owned by the applicant or his business to increase the value of the property with a view to earning a return either through rent or a future sale or both, or management of property (whether or not it is owned by the applicant or his business) for the purposes of renting it out or resale. The principle is that the business income must be generated from the supply of goods and/or services, and not derived from the increased value of property or any income generated from property, such as rent.

### The April 2016 amendments

**10.34C** *[Insert new heading and new paragraph:]*

In HC 877, according to the Explanatory Memorandum, paras 7.8–7.12, the latest list of amendments include some good news and some bad news. The good news is that applicants who have access to investment funds from a trusted source can cut down on the number of documents they must provide with their applications. In particular:

- Applicants will be allowed to apply with funding from one or more UK Seed Funding Competitions or one or more UK Government Departments, or Devolved Government Departments in Scotland, Wales or Northern Ireland to supply a letter, confirming that the money was transferred to them less than 90 days before the date of the application.[1] This removes the need for the applicant to supply a third-party declaration and legal confirmation if they have not held the funds for this duration.[1]

- Applicants who have received investment from a UK Seed Funding Competition or UK Government Department will be able to produce financial accounts which show that the investment was made in the name of the source of funds, providing that source supplies a supplementary letter confirming that this investment was on their behalf.[2] This removes the need for the specified financial accounts evidence to confirm that the investment was made on the applicant's behalf.[2]

- Additionally, applicants will be allowed to provide financial accounts which show that the qualifying investment in their businesses was made in the name of an investing entity, different from UK Seed Funding Competitions or Government Departments, provided they supply a letter from UK Trade and Investment (UKTI) confirming their investment.[3]

The bad news is that, to address concerns about abuse, the evidential requirements for applicants who get funding from venture capital firms are being expanded.[4]

Further amendments are made to the rules relating to job creation (Appendix A, para 49, as amended by HC 877, para A23) and on indefinite leave to remain (ILR). The ILR changes to encourage applicants seeking accelerated ILR, because of the size of their investment (at least £5m). They will only have to demonstrate that:

- they have registered their business within six months of their specified date;[5] and

- having taken over and invested in an existing UK company and his or her input has resulted in a net increase of at least £5m (should they be applying for accelerated ILR on this basis).[6]

---

[1] Appendix A, para 41(a)(ii)(c), as amended by HC 877 A10.
[2] Appendix A, para 46-SD (b)(2), substituted by HC 877 A20.
[3] Appendix A, para 46-SD (b)(3), substituted by HC 877 A20. This done in order to better reflect normal business practice.
[4] See Appendix A, paras 41-SD (a)(v) and 41-SD(a)(iv), inserted and amended by HC 877 A14 and A18.
[5] Appendix A, para 46-SD(a)(v), inserted by HC 877 A19.
[6] Appendix A, para 46-SD(a)(vi), inserted by HC 877 A19.

## TIER 1 (POST-STUDY WORK)

### Tier 1 (Graduate Entrepreneur) Migrants

*Entry and stay in the UK*

**10.45A** *[After paragraph 10.45 insert new paragraphs 10.45A and 10.45B:]*

Entry clearance or leave to remain will be granted for a period of one year (HC 395, para 245FC) and will be subject to the following conditions:

(i)      no recourse to public funds;

(ii)      registration with the police, if this is required by paragraph 326 of these Rules;

(iii)      no employment as a Doctor or Dentist in Training;

(iv)      no employment as a professional sportsperson (including as a sports coach); and

(v)      study subject to the condition set out in Part 15 of these Rules where the applicant is 18 years of age or over at the time their leave is granted, or will be aged 18 before their period of limited leave expires.[1]

Provision is made in the rules for Graduate Entrepreneurs to switch into Tier 1 (Entrepreneur).[2]

[1]    Subparagraph inserted by HC 1025, Para 118, as from 6 April 2015. The stay is normally for one year, but may be extended for one further year - no more: HC 395, para 245FB(h).

[2]    HC 395, para 245DD(e)(v) and Appendix A, paras 45 and 46.

**10.45B** A change was made in 2015 by HC 1025 to restrict applicants in this category from engaging in businesses principally concerned with property development or property management and the full test of the change is now contained in in Row 3, subparagraph (c) in Table 10, below. This was done for consistency with the Tier 1 (Entrepreneur) category.[1]

A key requirement set out in set out in Table 10 is that a Tier 1 (Graduate Entrepreneur) applicant must have endorsement from a UK Higher Education Institution or UK Trade and Investment in order to qualify for the necessary points. A rule change in 2016 now requires that the prescribed content of the endorsement letter required from the applicant's endorsing body be expanded to request a telephone contact number from the authorising official at the endorsing body, and to also request the name and contact details of a person in an administrative role at the institution.[2]

**Table 10**

| Criterion | Points |
| --- | --- |
| (a) The applicant has been endorsed by a UK Higher Education Institution which: | 25 |
| (i) is a sponsor with Tier 4 Sponsor status, | |
| (ii) is an A-rated Sponsor under Tier 2 of the Points-Based System if a Tier 2 licence is held, | |
| (iii) an A-rated Sponsor under Tier 5 of the Points-Based System if a Tier 5 licence is held, | |

| Criterion | Points |
|---|---|
| (iv) has degree-awarding powers, and (v) has established processes and competence for identifying, nurturing and developing entrepreneurs among its undergraduate and postgraduate population; or | |
| (b) The applicant has been endorsed by the Department for International Trade. | |
| The applicant has been awarded a degree qualification (not a qualification of equivalent level which is not a degree) which meets or exceeds the recognised standard of a Bachelor's degree in the UK. For overseas qualifications, the standard must be confirmed by UK NARIC. | 25 |
| The endorsement must confirm that the endorsing body has assessed the applicant and considers that: | 25 |
| (a) the applicant has a genuine and credible business idea, and | |
| (b) the applicant will spend the majority of his working time on developing business ventures, and | |
| (c) if the applicant is applying for leave to remain and his last grant of leave was as a Tier 1 (Graduate Entrepreneur), he has made satisfactory progress in developing his business since that leave was granted. The endorsement must also confirm the applicant's intended business sector or business intention. Points will not be awarded if this business will be mainly engaged in property development or property management. 'Property development or property management' in this context means any development of property owned by the applicant or his business to increase the value of the property with a view to earning a return either through rent or a future sale or both, or management of property (whether or not it is owned by the applicant or his business) for the purposes of renting it out or resale. The principle is that business income must be generated from the supply of goods and/or services and not derived from the increased value of property or any income generated through property, such as rent. | |

[1] See Explanatory Memorandum to HC 1025, para 7.36.

[2] HC 395, Appendix A, para70(c)(ix), as amended by rule change HC 877, para A29, as from 6 April 2016.

## Tier 1 (Exceptional Talent) Migrants

**10.48** *[Delete the paragraph starting 'Entry clearance will be granted for a period of three years and four months . . . ' and footnote reference 4 and insert:]*

Entry clearance will be granted for a period of (i) 1 year, (ii) 2 years, (iii) 3 years, (iv) 4 years, or (v) 5 years and 4 months, as requested by the applicant, and will be granted subject to the following conditions:

(i)     no recourse to public funds;

(ii)    registration with the police, if this is required by para 326;

(iii)   no employment as a Doctor or Dentist in Training;

(iv)   no employment as a professional sportsperson (including as a sports coach);

(v)     study subject to the condition set out in Part 15 of these Rules, where the applicant is 18 years of age or over at the time their leave is granted, or will be aged 18 before their period of limited leave expires.[4]

*[Delete the final bullet point starting 'Leave to remain will be granted . . . ' and footnote reference 6 and insert as new paragraph:]*

Leave to remain will be granted for a period of (i) 1year, (ii) 2 years, (iii) 3 years, (iv) 4 years, or (v) 5 years, as indicated by the applicant and will be subject to the same conditions as set out above for entry clearance.[6]

[4]     HC 395, para 245BC, as amended by HC 1025, para 91. A reason for these changes and those applying for leave to remain is that this change is being made alongside the introduction of NHS surcharge payments, and means that Tier 1 (Exceptional Talent) applicants who only wish to come to the UK for a shorter time in this category will not need to stump up with the maximum leave period surcharge payment: HC 1025 Explanatory Memorandum, para 7.34.

[6]     HC 395, para 245BD, as amended by HC 1025, para 93 and 94.

### 10.50 *[N.B.]*

Changes, now well ensconced in Appendix L, have been made to the criteria applied by Designated Competent Bodies when considering endorsements for applicants. In general, to be considered for endorsement by a Designated body, applicants must meet a whole set of requirements. There are three groups of designated bodies:

(i)     The Royal Society, The Royal Academy of Engineering or The British Academy;
(ii)    The Arts Council; and
(iii)   Tech City UK.

In the case of group (i) these are in paras 1 to 4A of Appendix L; in the case of the Arts Council these are either within the fields of the arts (encompassing dance, music, theatre, visual arts and literature), museums or galleries in paragraphs 5 to 7; or within the film, television, animation, post-production and visual effects industry in paragraphs 8 and 9; and in the case of Tech City UK, in paras 10 to 12, including changes made in October 2015 (HC 535, para L1) in the criteria for digital technology applicants.

## TIER 1 – TRANSITIONAL ARRANGEMENTS

**10.51–10.53** *Note that paragraphs 10.51 to 10.53 are no longer operative because of the passage of time but are of historical interest.*

## TIER 1 (INVESTORS)

**10.53A** *[After paragraph 10.53 insert new heading and new paragraph:]*

**The Tier 1 (Investor) category** caters for high net worth individuals making a substantial financial investment to the UK. This category was reviewed by the Migration Advisory Committee in a report published on 28 February 2014. Changes, partially in response to that report,[1] were then made by rule change HC 693 to take effect as from 6 November 2014 and rule change HC 1025 as from 6 April 2015. The November changes were as follows:

- The current £1m minimum investment threshold was raised to £2m.[2]
- New Tables 8A and 9A and 8B and 9B were inserted. Tables 8B and 9B are transitional provisions.[3]
- A change was made to require **the full investment sum** to be invested in prescribed forms of investments (share or loan capital in active and trading UK companies, or UK Government bonds), rather than 75% of the sum as in pre-November 6 applications as set out in the new transitional Table B.[4]
- The then operative requirement that the migrant's investment must be 'topped up' if its market value fell was removed; instead Tier 1 Investors are only required to purchase new qualifying investments if they sell part of their portfolios and need to replace them in order to maintain the investment threshold.[5]
- The existing provision under which the required investment sum can be sourced as a loan was removed.[6]
- Transitional arrangements were put in place, so that Tier 1 (Investor) Migrants who have already entered the route before the above changes were introduced will not be subject to these changes when they apply for extensions or for indefinite leave to remain. See New Tables 8B and 9B.
- Entry Clearance Officers and UK Visas & Immigration caseworkers were empowered to refuse a Tier 1 (Investor) application if they have reasonable grounds to believe that:
  - the applicant is not in control of the investment funds;
  - the funds were obtained unlawfully (or by means which would be unlawful if they happened in the UK); or
  - the character, conduct or associations of a party providing the funds mean that approving the application is not conducive to the public good.[7]

[1] See Explanatory Memorandum HC 693, para 7.25, which we have drawn on in the above paragraph.
[2] Tables 7 and 8A as inserted by HC 693, paras 129-130, as from November 6 2014.
[3] See further Appendix A, paras 55–58.
[4] Tables 8A and 8B, as inserted by HC 693, para 130, as from November 6 2014.
[5] See Appendix A, para 65C (a), inserted by HC 693, para 150, as from November 6 2014, in respect of applicants under Tables 8A and 8B and contrast those using the transitional Tables 8B and 9B to whom para 65C(b) applies.
[6] Appendix A, para 61A, subject to an exception if the loan money is part of an application made before 13 December 2012.
[7] HC 395, paras 245EB(g) and 245ED(i), inserted by HC 693, paras 48 and 50.

**10.53B** *[Insert new paragraph:]*

The April 2015 changes were as follows:

- A requirement was added requiring prospective investors to open a UK regulated investment account before making an initial application.[1]
- The minimum age of applicants in this category was increased from 16 to 18.[2]
- Changes were made with regard to the maintenance of investors' investments.[3] Applicants will no longer need to invest additional capital if they sell part of their investments at a loss, but they will be required

to maintain all their capital within their investment portfolios. Buying and selling investments will continue to be permitted, providing the investor does not withdraw any capital.

- The restriction on investing in companies principally concerned with property investment, property development or property management have been amended to achieve consistency with the Rules for the Tier 1 (Entrepreneur) category.[4] Investing in property or property development is not allowed, but a business which is set up to lend money to property development is permitted.

[1]  HC 395, Appendix A, substituted Table 7(b). This change was intended to ensure that UK banks would carry out due diligence checks on investors before they apply for entry clearance or leave to remain, not after: HC 1025, Explanatory Memorandum, para 7.37.

[2]  HC 395, para 245EB(d) and 245ED(e). This change is being made to reflect the fact that it is not normally possible for 16- and 17-year old applicants to be wholly in control of their own funds and investments: HC 1025, Explanatory Memorandum, para 7.37.

[3]  HC 395, Appendix A, paras 65C(a) and 65C(b). This change is intended to remove an unintended incentive for investors to invest in UK government bonds rather than to invest in UK companies: HC 1025, Explanatory Memorandum, para 7.37.

[4]  Appendix A, para 65(c), as substituted by HC 1025, para 277.

### 10.53C *[Insert new paragraph:]*

Later changes limited the switch from student to investor category in line with similar changes made to those now applicable to Tier 1 (Entrepreneur).[1] Prior to July 2015, Tier 4 (General Students) could switch straight into Tier 1 (Investors). After 11 November 2015 the switch could still be made by a Tier 4 (Child) Student, but Tier 4 (General Students) could only switch if the student is or was last sponsored by either: (1) a UK recognised body or a body in receipt of public funding as a higher education institution from specified departments or Councils in England, Scotland and Northern Ireland; or (2) an overseas higher education institution to undertake a short-term study abroad programme in the United Kingdom; or (3) an Embedded College offering Pathway Courses.[2]

Minor changes followed in HC 535: (i) an amendment to Appendix A, sub-para 65-SD(b) to make it clear that it only applied to those who had previously had leave pre-PBS as an investor; (ii) a provision that when property is used as evidence for balance of funds, it can only be jointly owned with the spouse or partner of applicant;[3] and (iii) a provision that investment by way of share or loan capital in investment syndicate companies is not acceptable.[4]

[1]  See HC 395, paras 245DD(e)(xxi) and (xxii), as amended by HC 297, paras 6A.1 and 6A.2.

[2]  HC 395, para 245ED (c) (xvi) and (xvii), as amended by rule change HC 297, paras 6A.5 and 6A.6.

[3]  Appendix A, para 65-SD (c) (i), as amended by HC 535, para A34 as from 19 November 2015.

[4]  HC 395, Appendix A, para 65 (b) as amended by HC 535, para A29 as from 19 November 2015.

## TIER 2 – EMPLOYEES

The following abbreviations are used in this section:

| Cos | Certificate of Sponsorship |
|---|---|
| Tier 2 (ICT) | Tier 2 (Intra-Company Transfer) |
| Sponsor Guidance | Tier 2 and 5 Guidance for Sponsors, Version 11/16 |

### English language requirements for public sector workers

**10.53D** *[After the heading 'TIER 2 – EMPLOYEES' and before paragraph 10.54, insert new heading and new paragraph:]*

Part 7 of the Immigration Act 2016 places a duty on public authorities to ensure that anyone who works for them in a customer-facing role speaks fluent English, or in Wales, Welsh or English.[1] The definition of 'work' in section 77 of the Act includes those working under a contract of employment, apprenticeship or to do work personally, an agency worker, a constable and those in Crown employment. The Act defines fluent as having 'a command of spoken English which is sufficient to enable the effective performance of the person's role'. A code of practice has now been brought into being.[2] In the code, public sector workers are said to be 'public-facing' if, as a regular and intrinsic part of their role, they are required to speak to members of the public in English. This is described in Part 7 of the Act as a 'customer-facing role' and defined in section 77(7) of the Act. The policy objective is to ensure that citizens are able to interact with all public services. It intends to improve the quality, efficiency and safety of public service provision and ensure taxpayers' confidence that they are receiving value for money. It also intends to deliver consistency with existing language standards.[3] Section 80 of the Immigration Act 2016 provides that the Code of Practice, applicable to each public authority who must comply with the duty in Section 77, must include provision about four specific matters:[4]

- the standard of spoken English required to be met by a person working for a public authority to which the code applies in a public-facing role;
- the action available to such a public authority where such a person does not meet that standard;
- the procedure to be operated by a public authority to enable complaints to be made about breaches of the duty and for consideration of such complaints; and
- how the public authority is to comply with its other legal obligations as well as the duty.

[1] Immigration Act 2016, ss 77–84. A person who works for a public authority is defined in s 77(5) and (6).
[2] The Code of Practice (English Language Requirements for Public Sector Workers) Regulation 2016, SI 2016/1157.
[3] Code of Practice, Explanatory Statement, para 7.2.
[4] See Code of Practice, Explanatory Statement, para 4.3.

## Introduction

**10.55A** *[After paragraph 10.55 insert new heading and paragraph:]*

Since the publication of the 9th edition of this work, the basic categories of Tier 2 still exist, but one subcategory has been deleted (Skills Transfer) and the categories in Tier 5 have been added to. The regulation of these employment Tiers is far reaching and is continuously expanding. The two main sources of regulation are (i) the Sponsor Guidance now in its umpteenth edition[1] and (ii) the Immigration Rules. Since the 9th edition, paragraphs 245G, 245H, 245ZI and 245ZM and Appendix A of the rules have been subjected to frequent change.

There are three new Appendices. Appendix M only applies to Tiers 2 and 5 (Sportspersons) and contains a list of the governing bodies of a wide variety of sports. They play an important role in granting or refusing applications for entry clearance for non-EEA foreign players. It can be critical. Then there the other two Appendices. Tier 2 could not function without the input of these two underpinning Appendices and the work that goes into keeping them up to date. They are: (i) Appendix J, entitled 'Codes of Practice for Tier 2 Sponsors, Tier 5 Sponsors and Employers of Work Permit Holders', which deals with job skills and salaries and consists of nine Tables dealing with nine different levels of skill and setting out appropriate salary rates for each job; and (ii) Appendix K, entitled 'Shortage Occupation List', which deals with jobs where there is a labour shortage and creates lists of shortage occupations.

The policy behind the recruitment of foreign workers is longstanding. In the reconstruction period in post 1945 Britain, work permits could only be obtained for alien workers. The backbone of the permit scheme was the condition, which was tightened up over the years, that the employer must have made adequate efforts to find a suitable worker among the resident labour force.[2] A permit would only be issued where there was no suitable resident labour available to fill the post offered and the employer had made adequate efforts to find a worker from that source. Another important condition was that the wages and other conditions of employment offered were not under-cutting local wage rates and conditions. From acorns grow oaks. The fundamentals of Tier 2 regulation are not difficult to understand when seen against this background. The devil, however, is in the detail to which we now turn.

[1]  The current Guidance is Tier 2 and 5 Guidance for Sponsors, Version 11/16, and is to be used for all Tier 2 and Tier 5 sponsor licence applications made on or after 24 November 2016.

[2]  See the 2nd edition of this work, pp 194–197; Daniel Duysens, 'Work permits – Department of Employment Control of the Labour Market' (1997) 6 Ind LJ.85.

## Cross-cutting changes in Tier 2

**10.55B** *[Insert new heading and paragraph:]*

A number of cross-cutting changes to Tier 2 have been put in place between the end of 2014 and the start of 2016. These include the following:

- *Genuine vacancy test.* An assessment of whether a genuine vacancy exists was added to Tier 2 (Intra-Company Transfer) and Tier 2 (General) by rule change HC 693 as from November 2014.[1] This change was part of an ongoing introduction of 'genuineness' test throughout the different Tiers of the PBS. It empowered Entry Clearance Officers and caseworkers in this case to refuse applications where there are reasonable grounds to believe that the job described by the sponsor does not genuinely exist, has been exaggerated to meet the Tier 2 skills threshold, or (in respect of Tier 2 (General)) has been tailored to exclude resident workers from being recruited, or where there are reasonable grounds to believe that the applicant is not qualified to do the job. It operates notwithstanding that the applicant has provided the evidence required under the relevant provisions of Appendix A.[2]

- *Shortened response time.* A further change in November 2016 was made to the response time given to applicants and sponsors to respond to Home Office requests for further information in relation to genuineness, assessments in both categories was reduced from 28 calendar days to 10 working days.[3]

- *The 12-month gap or 'cooling off period'.* The 12-month gap is now applicable to both Tier 2 (ICT) and the remainder of Tier 2, (General), (Sportspersons) and (Ministers of religion) as regards entry clearance. But it does not apply to leave to remain for Tier (ICT) but does for the remainder of Tier 2.[4] The gap does not apply, due to amendments made for all 4 subcategories, where the previous period of engagement recorded by the CoS, used in support of the application, was granted for a period of three months or less.[5] The exceptions in para 245GB(e)(i) and (ii) and 245HB(g)(i) and (ii) remain the same except that for high earners, where the salary level has been raised to £155,300, up from £153,500 from the earlier position.[6] See further **10.58A**, below.

- *Hiring out applicants to third parties.* An existing rule in the published Guidance regarding the hiring out of employees to third parties has now become a rule under rule change HC 693 which disallows a job which amounts to: (a) the hire of the applicant to a third party who is not the sponsor; or (b) contract work to undertake an ongoing routine role or an ongoing routine service for a third party. No points will be awarded regardless of the nature or length of any arrangement between the sponsor and the third party.[7]

- *Absence from work without pay.* The rule that Tiers 2 and 5 Migrants may not be absent from work without pay for 30 days or more in total during any calendar year has now been amended from 30 days per year to four weeks per year, except where the absence from work is solely due to maternity, paternity, or shared parental leave or long-term sick leave of one calendar month or more during any one period.[8]

- *Dating entry clearance.* A change has been made to enable entry clearance grants to be post-dated in line with the applicant's stated date of travel to the UK, providing the travel date is not more than 14 days after the start date given by the applicant's Tier 2 Sponsor.[9] According to the Home Office, this change will give more flexibility to applicants and is designed to make it easier for them to collect their Biometric Residence Permits within the required timescale.[10]

- Throughout Tier 2 the rules used to say that any period of overstaying would be disregarded, which meant that submitting late applications for an extension leave could be disregarded for up to 28 days. This has now been changed wherever it appears in the rules and now the rules state: 'where paragraph 39E of these Rules applies, any current period of overstaying will be disregarded'. This new rule allows a 14-day delay in making an application for leave to remain, but only after scrutiny by the Home Office, who have to be satisfied that there is a good reason beyond the control of the applicant or their representative, given with the application, why an in-time application could not have been submitted within 14 days of the expiry of the leave.[11]

- Amendments are being made to reflect the closing down of the 'points based calculator' tool on the gov.uk website, which applicants may currently use if they would like to use an overseas qualification to demonstrate a requirement of the rules. From 6 April 2016, applicants should instead obtain an official statement from UK NARIC.[12]

[1] HC 395, Appendix A, paras 74H–74I (intra-company transfers in the short and long-term staff categories) and 77H–74J (Tier 2 (General)). Examples of non-genuine vacancies are given in Tiers 2 and 5: Guidance for Sponsors (version 11/16) at para 15.14 are: (i) one which contains an exaggerated or incorrect job description to deliberately make it appear to meet the requirements of the tier and category when it does not; (ii) for a job or role that does not exist in order to enable a migrant to come to, or stay in, the UK; (iii) advertisements with requirements that are inappropriate for the job on offer, and have been tailored to exclude resident workers from being recruited.

[2] HC 395, Appendix A, paras 74H and 77H.

[3] HC 667 contains a change to the time given to applicants and sponsors to respond to requests for further information in relation to genuineness assessments from 28 calendar days to 10 working days: see HC 395, paras 74I and 77J, amended by HC 667, paras A41 and A46. See also Explanatory Memorandum, para 7.23.

[4] HC 395, para 245HD(k).

[5] HC 395, paras 345GB(d) (Tier 2 (ICT)); paras 245HB, 245HB(g) and 245HD(k) (Tier2 (General), (Sportsperson) and (Minister of Religion)).

[6] See HC 395, para 245GB(e)(ii) (Tier 2 (ICT)) and 245HB(g)(ii) and 245H (k)(ii) (Tier 2 (General), (Sportsperson) and (Minister of Religion)).

[7] HC 395, Appendix A, paras 74G and 77G, inserted by HC 693, paras 161 and 163.

[8] HC 535, Explanatory Memorandum, para 17.16, as from 19 November 2015. This is being done due to continuing requests for clarification.

[9] HC 395, para 245GC (a)–(c) and 245HC(a)–(c), inserted by HC 535, paras 6A.9 and 6A.12, as from 18 November 2015.

[10] HC 535, Explanatory Memorandum, para 7.17.

[11] HC 395, para 39E, inserted by HC 667, para 1.13 and all parts of Part 6A, where a 28-day overstay has been disregarded. The new paragraph only operates on and after 24 November 2016.

[12] See HC 395, Appendix A, para 72(e) as amended by HC 877; see Explanatory Memorandum, paras 7.20 and 7.21.

### 10.55C *[Insert new paragraph:]*

The government announced changes to Tier 2 (General) and Tier 2 (ICT) on 24 March 2016 following a review published by the independent Migration Advisory Committee (MAC) on 19 January 2016. The government announced that the changes would be introduced in two stages, in autumn 2016 and April 2017. Rule change HC 667 contains the changes for autumn 2016, and additional minor changes. We deal with these below.

## Concessions for Syrian national workers in the UK

**10.55D** *[Insert new heading and paragraph:]*

New Concessions for Syrian visitors seeking to extend their leave under Tier 2 (Intra Company Transfer), Tier 2 (General), Tier 2 (Minister of Religion) or Tier 2 (Sportsperson) have superseded previous concessions as from 1 March 2017. They are as follows:[1]

(i)     Tier 2 (Intra Company Transfer): under paras 245GE(a)(iii) and 245GE(b)(ii)-(iii), the maximum five-year and nine-year periods shall not apply; so an applicant in this category can extend their total continuous leave in the Tier 2 (Intra-Company Transfer) Long Term Staff subcategory beyond five or nine years.

(ii)    Tier 2 (General), Tier 2 (Minister of Religion) or Tier 2 (Sportsperson): under para 245HE(a)(iv), the maximum six-year period shall not apply therefore an applicant can extend their total continuous leave in the relevant Tier 2 category specified beyond six years.

(iii)   There is no provision extending the Concessions to indefinite leave to remain (ILR), but someone who is eligible for ILR may apply in the usual way under the rules.

[1]   *Concessions to the Immigration Rules for Syrian Nationals*, Version 3.0, authorised under the Equality (Syria) Authorisation 2017 which came into force on 1 March 2017.

## Tier 2 (Intra company transfer)

**10.57** *[N.B.]*

The four sub-categories in Tier 2 (Intra-Company Transfer) are now three. The Skills Transfer sub-category is now closed to new applicants.[1] This means that there are now only two maximum periods of leave: twelve months for those applying in either of the Graduate Trainee or Short Term Staff sub-categories and five years and one month, if the applicant is applying in the Long Term Staff sub-category.[2]

[1]   HC 359, deleted paras 245GB(iv) and 245GD(e), and Appendix A, para 75(iii)(1), as amended by HC 667, as from 14 November 2016.
[2]   HC 395, para 245GE(i) and (ii)(c).

## Getting the points

**10.58** *[Delete the whole of the text from footnote reference 4 to the end of the paragraph, including footnotes 5 and 6, and insert:]*

Where an applicant is seeking entry clearance, they must still score 50 points for attributes and 10 for maintenance under Appendix C, but none will be awarded:

•       if the applicant's salary is less than the minimum amount shown in Table 11AA;[5]

- unless the job appears on the list of occupations skilled to NQF level 6 or above in Appendix J, or to NQF level 4 in one of the creative occupations referred to in para 74B(a)(ii) or meets the requirements of sub-paras 74B(b)–(d);
- unless the applicant meets the requirements of the 12-month gap for entry clearance rule as set out in 245GB(d) and (e);
- unless an applicant who is applying as a Tier 2 (Intra-Company Transfer) Migrant in the Graduate Trainee sub-category meets the requirements of para 74D;
- if the CoS Checking Service has him or her down as a sports person or a Minister of Religion;[6]
- if the CoS Checking Service has the applicant down as someone who is going to be hired out to a third party or is being employed to undertake routine contract work for a third party;[7]
- if the vacancy is not regarded as a genuine vacancy,[8] or the applicant is not appropriately qualified to do the job in question;[9]
- if the salary referred to in para 75 above is less than the minimum amount shown in Table 11AA.[10]

[5]  HC 395, Appendix A para 74A, inserted by HC 667 as from 24 November 2016. See below for details of Table 11AA.
[6]  Ibid, para 74F.
[7]  Ibid, para 74G, inserted by HC 395, Appendix A, paras 74G and 77G.
[8]  Ibid, para 74H(a). For more detail see 10.55B above.
[9]  Ibid, para 74H(b).
[10]  Ibid, para 75A, inserted by HC 667 as from 24 November 2016. See below 10.60 for details of appropriate salary and Table 11AA.

### 10.58A *[Insert new paragraph:]*

The requirements for entry clearance are contained in para 245GB. Currently the applicant must have a minimum of 50 points under paras 73–75E of Appendix A and a minimum of 10 points under paras 4 and 5 of Appendix C. This is still the case, but in the past the requirement in sub-para (d) was that employees seeking to come to the UK under the long-term or short-term sub-categories of Tier 2 (ICT) must have been working for the sponsor, for at least 12 months outside the UK, subject to exceptions in sub-para (e).[1] Sub-paragraph (d) is now amended and says that the applicant must not have had entry clearance or leave to remain as a Tier 2 Migrant at any time during the 12 months immediately before the date of the application, 'except where the period of engagement recorded by the Certificate of Sponsorship used in support of such entry clearance or leave to remain was granted for a period of three months or less'.[2] Subparagraph (e)(iii) has also been amended; high earners will now only be exempted from the gap year rule, if their gross earnings are £155,300, up from £153,500.[3]

Appendix A, para 74C gives more detail about the 12-month gap. It too has been amended. Firstly, an applicant is not confined solely to working with the Sponsor during the 12-month gap, as before, but his employer can be a business established outside the territory of the UK which is linked by common ownership or control to the Sponsor.[4] The purpose here is to reflect that the category is for internationally established companies, and the experience overseas may have been with a business established which is linked by common ownership or control to the Sponsor.[5]

Secondly, the circumstances where an aggregated 12 months is permitted by para 74C(c)(ii) have been changed. As now amended, an aggregated period of at least 12 months within the 24-month period immediately before the date of application, is allowed for specified kinds of leave taken by the applicant at some point within the 12 months preceding the date of application. This leave is now extended from maternity or paternity leave to shared parental leave.[6]

Thirdly, there were also problems as to the other circumstances in which the 12-month period did not need to be continuous. HC 1025 and HC 667 have amended Appendix A, para 74C(c)(iii) by deleting an obscure and unworkable subparagraph and replaced it with an aggregated 12-month period in less obscure text as follows:

'(iii) an aggregated period of at least 12 months overseas within any timeframe, providing the applicant has been working continuously and lawfully (either overseas or in the UK) for the Sponsor or the linked overseas business since the start of that aggregated 12-month period.'[7]

---

[1]   HC 395, para 245GB(e) (unamended) provided that sub-para (d) did *not apply* to an applicant who: (i) was not in the UK with leave as a Tier 2 migrant at any time during the above 12-month period, and provides evidence to show this; (ii) was applying under the Long Term Staff sub-category and who had, or last had leave under Tier 2 (ICT) in the Short Term Staff, Graduate Trainee or Skills Transfer sub-categories, or under the Rules in place before 6 April 2011; or (iii) would be a high earner with a gross annual salary of £153,500 or higher.
[2]   HC 395, para 245GB(d), as amended by HC 1025, para 119 as from 6 April 2015.
[3]   HC 395, para 245GB(e)(iii), as amended by HC 1025, para 120, as from 6 April 2015.
[4]   HC 395, Appendix A, para 74C(c) (iii) as amended by HC 353, para A39, effective from 19 November 2015. See also para 74C(b), as amended by HC 667, para A32, effective from 24 November 2016.
[5]   See HC 535, Explanatory Memorandum, para 7.16.
[6]   See HC 395, Appendix A, para 74C(c)(iii), as amended by HC 1025, para289, which confined the amended paragraph for employees who worked for the sponsor. HC 535 extended this to work carried out for a linked overseas business.
[7]   Ibid.

---

*Appropriate salary*

**10.60** *[Delete and replace with:]*

Twenty points need to be achieved for 'appropriate salary'. What is meant by this is set out at paras 75 to 75E of Appendix A. The appropriate salary levels quoted in this paragraph have been updated. Where the applicant was applying in the Long Term Staff sub-category, the position previously was that no points would be awarded if the salary referred to in Appendix A, para 75 above was less than £41,000 per year unless the applicant's last leave was under the rules in place before 6 April 2011 for an intra-company transfer under this category or the old work permit rules and the applicant has not been granted entry clearance in this or any other route since that grant of leave (para 75A). Similarly, where the applicant was applying in the Short Term Staff, Graduate Trainee or Skills Transfer sub-categories, the minimum salary had to be no less than £24,500 per year. All that has gone. Now the minimum salary in both these cases is set out in a new Table – Table 11AA, as follows:

**Table 11AA**

| Circumstance | Minimum salary |
|---|---|
| The applicant is applying in the Long Term Staff sub-category (and the exception below does not apply). | £41,500 per year or the appropriate rate for the job as stated in Appendix J, whichever is higher. |
| The applicant is applying for leave to remain in the Long Term Staff sub-category and:<br><br>(i) previously had leave as a Qualifying Work Permit Holder or a Tier 2 (Intra-Company Transfer) Migrant under the rules in place before 6 April 2011; and<br><br>(ii) has not been granted entry clearance in this or any other route since the grant of leave in (i). | The appropriate rate for the job as stated in Appendix J. |
| The applicant is applying in the Short Term Staff sub-category (and the exception below does not apply). | £30,000 per year or the appropriate rate for the job as stated in Appendix J, whichever is higher. |
| The applicant is applying for leave to remain in the Short Term Staff sub-category and:<br><br>(i) previously had leave in the Short Term Staff sub-category granted on the basis of a Certificate of Sponsorship which was assigned to the applicant before 24 November 2016; and<br><br>(ii) has not been granted entry clearance in this or any other route since the grant of leave in (i). | £24,800 per year or the appropriate rate for the job as stated in Appendix J, whichever is higher. |
| The applicant is applying in the Graduate Trainee sub-category. | £23,000 per year or the appropriate rate for the job as stated in Appendix J, whichever is higher. |

So far as the Graduate Trainee sub-category is concerned, the salary threshold has been reduced from £24,800 to £23,000 or the appropriate rate for the job as stated in Appendix J, whichever is the higher. and the number of places a sponsor can use has been increased from 5 to 20 per year.

**Tier 2 (General) Migrants, Tier 2 (Minister of Religion) Migrants and Tier 2 (Sportsperson) Migrants**

*245HA. Entry clearance Requirements*

Tier 2 (General)

**10.65** *[N.B.]*

To escape the 12-month cooling-off period, which is dealt with in HC 395, paras 245HB(g) for entry clearance and 245HD(k) for leave to remain, high earners now need a minimum salary level £155,300 up from £153,500 (paras 245HB(g)(iii) and 245HD(k)(iii)). A new exception is made in the same subparagraphs, where the previous period of engagement recorded by the Certificate of Sponsorship used in support of such entry clearance or leave to remain was three months or less, the 12-month cooling off period immediately before the date of the application does not apply. This applies to Tier 2 (General), (Sportspersons) and (Ministers of Religion) and is identical to the provision for Intra-Company transferees, seeking entry clearance.

*245HD. Requirements for leave to remain*

**10.66** *[N.B.]*

The 28-day overstaying rule in HC 395, para 245HD(p) has been replaced by the insertion of new rule 39E (see **10.55B** above).

**10.67** *[Delete the final sentence in the paragraph and substitute:]*

Recruitment can still take place outside the cap allocation and without having to pass the Resident Labour Market test, where the incoming employee is to be paid a salary of £155,300 (or £153,500, if the recruitment took place before 6 April 2015) or higher. High earners may also own more than 10% of the shares in the sponsor company but the minimum earnings have risen to £155,300 up from £153,500 (see HC 245HD(o)).[1]

[1] See HC 395, Appendix A, paras 77B(c) and 78C(a), as amended by HC 667, as from 16 November 2016. The salary figures in the last sentence of this paragraph have been amended. For £153,500 read £155,300 and for £152,100 read £153,500.

*Resident labour market test – Tier 2 (General)*

**10.68** *[N.B.]*

There are references to the Tier 2 and 5 Guidance for Sponsors, version 09/14 in this paragraph. This has now been replaced by version 11/16.

It should also be noted that normally inclusion of a job on the Job Shortage List in Appendix K exempts that job from the Resident Market Labour Test, provided the hours of work are 30 or more but a recent amendment to the rules makes it clear that nurses, although on the shortage list at occupation code '2231 Nurses' the Resident Market Labour Test must be met.[1]

[1] HC 395, Appendix A, para 78A(a), amended by HC 667, para A49, with effect from 16 November 2016.

**10.68A** *[Insert new paragraph:]*

In the advertising world, a 'milkround' is an annual recruitment programme where employers from a range of sectors visit universities to give presentations and/or interview students, usually as part of university careers fairs. If a sponsor uses a milkround to recruit new graduates or interns, they must visit a minimum of three UK universities, or all UK universities which provide the relevant course, whichever is the lower number.[1] From April 2017, a change to the rules around advertising via a milkround will be introduced to close a loophole in which a sponsor can offer a job to a migrant four years after carrying out a milkround, without the need for a further recruitment search. Sponsors can continue to rely on a milkround which ended up to four years prior to assigning a Certificate of Sponsorship, but only providing the migrant was offered the job within six months of that milkround taking place.[2]

[1] See Guidance for Sponsors Tiers 2 and 5, November 2016, para 28.35.
[2] See HC 667, Explanatory Memorandum, para 7.26.

*Tier 2 (General) skills and appropriate salary*

**10.69 [N.B.]**

The minimum salary rates set out in this paragraph are no longer correct. Paragraph 79A has been amended and para 79B has been deleted by rule changes in HC 667 as from 23 November 2016. The salary threshold for the majority of Tier 2 (General) applicants has been increased to £25,000 or the appropriate rate for the job as stated in Appendix J, whichever is higher. However, three groups as set out in Table 11CA, below, are exempted from the increase and the salary threshold has been held at £20,800 or the appropriate rate for the job as stated in Appendix J, whichever is higher. The middle group benefitting from this exemption are nurses, medical radiographers, paramedics and secondary school teachers in mathematics, physics, chemistry, computer science, and Mandarin. For them the exemption will continue until July 2019. For the third group of applicants in the Table, this is a transitional arrangement and they will only be exempted from the £25,000 threshold if they were issued a Certificate of Sponsorship before 24 November 2016 to extend their stay in Tier 2 (General).[1] Amended para 79A now states that no points will be awarded if the salary referred to in para 79 of Appendix A is less than the minimum amount shown in the Table 11CA below:

**Table 11CA**

| Circumstance | Minimum salary |
| --- | --- |
| None of the exceptions below apply. | £25,000 per year or the appropriate rate for the job as stated in Appendix J, whichever is higher |
| The applicant is considered to be a 'new entrant' due to one of the following:<br><br>(i) he is exempt from the Resident Labour Market Test due to the post-study work provisions in paragraph 78B above,<br><br>(ii) his Sponsor satisfied the Resident Labour Market Test under the provisions for 'new graduate jobs or internships' in the first row of Table 11B above, or | £20,800 per year or the appropriate rate for the job as stated in Appendix J, whichever is higher. |

| Circumstance | Minimum salary |
|---|---|
| (iii) he was under the age of 26 on the date the application was made and, in all cases, the applicant is not applying for a grant of leave that would extend his total stay in Tier 2 and/or as a Work Permit Holder beyond 3 years and 1 month. | |
| The job is one of the following public service occupations: 2217 Medical radiographers 2231 Nurses 2314 Secondary education teaching professionals – subject teachers in maths, physics, chemistry, computer science and Mandarin only 3213 Paramedics and the Certificate of Sponsorship was assigned to the applicant before 1 July 2019. | £20,800 per year or the appropriate rate for the job as stated in Appendix J, whichever is higher. |
| The applicant is applying for leave to remain and:<br><br>(i) previously had leave as a Tier 2 (General) migrant on the basis of a Certificate of Sponsorship which was assigned to the applicant before 24 November 2016; and<br><br>(ii) has not been granted entry clearance in this or any other route since the grant of leave in (i). | £20,800 per year or the appropriate rate for the job as stated in Appendix J, whichever is higher. |
| The applicant is applying for leave to remain and:<br>(i) previously had leave as:<br>a Qualifying Work Permit Holder,<br>(2) a Representative of an Overseas Newspaper, News Agency or Broadcasting Organisation,<br>(3) a Member of the operational Ground Staff of an Overseas-owned Airline,<br>(4) a Jewish Agency Employee, or<br>(5) a Tier 2 (General) Migrant under the Rules in place before 6 April 2011; and<br>(ii) has not been granted entry clearance in this or any other route since the grant of leave in (i). | The appropriate rate for the job as stated in Appendix J |

---

1   The government has also stated its intention to increase the threshold to £30,000 in April 2017; there will be no such transitional arrangement for workers sponsored in Tier 2 (General) between 24 November 2016 and April 2017 – they will need to satisfy the £30,000 threshold in any future application: see HC 667, Explanatory Statement, para 7.25.

*Appendix J and K*

**10.69A** *[Insert new heading and paragraph:]*

**Appendix J**. This Appendix sets out the skill level and appropriate salary rate for jobs, as referred to elsewhere in the Immigration Rules. The Standard Occupational Classification (SOC) codes are based on the SOC 2010 system designed by the Office for National Statistics. This system is designed to cover all possible jobs. The related job titles listed in Tables 1 to 7 of Appendix J are taken from guidance published by the Office for National Statistics. One difficulty with the Table is identifying which job title in Appendix J which matches the job the employer wants the new recruit to carry out. The drafters of Appendix J are aware of this and accept that references to 'job' refer to the *most appropriate match* for the job in question, as it appears in the tables in this Appendix. The job description must correlate with the most appropriate match according to further guidance on the SOC 2010 system published by the Office for National Statistics.[1] The most appropriate match may be applied based on the job description in an application, even if this is not the match stated by applicants or their Sponsor. In the Upper Tribunal case of *Tukhas*[2] the appellant's Certificate of Sponsorship identified that she would be paid a gross annual salary of £22,600. There was no admissible evidence she was contracted to work weekly hours or be paid an hourly rate. Consequently her 'appropriate salary' for the purposes of consideration under para 79 of Appendix A was to be taken as being £22,600 per annum. The 'appropriate rate for the job' (Appendix A, para 79B) was that set out in Table 2 of Appendix J at £22,600, the same figure as that of the appellant. The Upper Tribunal made it clear that the effect of para 14 of Appendix J is that, other than where an applicant has contracted weekly hours or is paid an hourly rate, the appropriate salary for the purposes of para 79 of Appendix A is an applicant's gross annual salary paid by the sponsor employer, subject to the conditions set out in paras 79(i)-(iii) of Appendix A.

Table 8 of this Appendix also sets out advertising and evidential requirements for creative sector jobs, as referred to elsewhere in the Immigration Rules. The rule change HC 1025 deleted Tables 1–5 and replaced them with five new Tables to take effect from 6 April 2015. Tables 6–9 remained. Minor changes were made by HC 535 in November 2015, affecting nurses and midwives.

[1] This guidance is reproduced in codes of practice for Sponsors published by the UK Border Agency.
[2] *Tukhas (para 245HD(f): 'appropriate salary')* [2016] UKUT 183.

*Shortage occupations*

**10.69B** *[Insert new heading and paragraph:]*

**Appendix K** lists shortage occupations; one for the UK and another exclusively for jobs in Scotland. In April 2015, HC 1025, para 435, deleted Table 2 and replaced it with a new Table 2 headed 'Scotland Only'. So jobs which appear on the United Kingdom Shortage Occupation List are set out in Table 1 and jobs which appear on the Scotland Only Shortage Occupation List are set out in Table 2. All these jobs which appear on the Shortage Occupation List mean only those specific jobs within each Standard Occupational Classification code stated in Tables 1 and 2 and, where stated, where further specified criteria are met. Companies which seek to use the list are called 'qualifying companies' and are subject to conditions,[1] which include the following:

- The company must hold a sponsorship licence for the purpose of Tier 2, which allows them to issue a CoS for a job on the Shortage Occupation List.
- The company should normally be employing between 20 and 250 employees (inclusive), but can have less employees if, having worked with the Department for International Trade, they get a letter of support from them.
- The company will not qualify if they are owned by a bigger company, having more than a 25% stake in it and which employs more than 250 employees.
- The company must not have been established in the UK for the purpose of supplying services exclusively to a single company or company group in the UK.
- If the company's CoSs are for jobs which lead to a grant of leave as a Tier 2 (General) Migrant, the company must have no more than ten Tier 2 (General) Migrants already working for it in shortage occupations.

For the purposes of Appendix K, where the job is one to which a requirement for specified experience applies, the sponsor must retain and provide to the Home Office on request:

(a)   references from the individual's past employer(s) detailing the required experience, as set out in Tables 1 and 2; and
(b)   relevant evidence enabling it to demonstrate:
  (i)    the job requires someone with the required experience;
  (ii)   why the job could not be carried out to the required standard by someone with less experience; and
  (iii)  how it would expect a settled worker to gain this experience before being appointed to the post.

Jobs which previously appeared on the United Kingdom and Scotland Only Shortage Occupation Lists are set out in Tables 3 and 4. These jobs set out Tables 3 and 4 for the purpose of informing indefinite leave to remain applications only.

[1]   Inserted by rule change HC 535, para K1, with effect from 19 November 2015.

*Nurses and other medical workers*

**10.69C** *[Insert new heading and paragraph:]*

Nurses were added to the Shortage Occupation List (SOL) in 2015.[1] The Home Office said that this change was made in view of the potential risks associated with high nursing vacancy rates while the NHS was experiencing winter pressures. The addition meant that nurses would not be subject to the Resident Labour Market Test, they would be given higher priority when allocating places in the Tier 2 limit, and they would be exempt from the earnings threshold when they applied for settlement (nurses who are currently sponsored in Tier 2 would continue to be exempt from this threshold, even if nurses are removed from the SOL in future).[2]

Following a separate review by the MAC on nursing shortages, the rules on nurses were changed. Nurses are still being retained on the Shortage Occupation List, but the 2015 changes are being amended. Nurses and midwives will require a Resident Labour Market Test to have been carried out before they can be assigned a Certificate of Sponsorship.[3] They have become such an important sector that the rules regarding pre-registration nurses are also being consolidated into a new para 77K(a)–(c) in Appendix A.[4] This provides that no points will be awarded to nurses or midwives unless the applicant can show that he or she has:

(a)(i) obtained full registration with the Nursing and Midwifery Council (NMC); or
(a)(ii) passed the Nursing and Midwifery Council's Computer Based Test of competence, or
(a)(iii) obtained the permission of the NMC before 30 April 2015 to undertake an overseas nurses training programme approved by them,

and, in the case where (a)(ii) or (iii) above applies, will, after obtaining registration, continue to be sponsored by the NMC and will be paid at least the appropriate rate for a Band 5 and equivalent nurse or midwife, as stated in Appendix J.[5]

In the case where (a)(ii) applies, the applicant:

(i)   must pass an Observed Structured Clinical Examination (OSCE), needed to obtain registration, no later than three months after the stated employment start date; and
(ii)  must achieve full registration within eight months of the stated employment start date or lose the sponsorship of the Nursing and Midwifery Council.[6] If the applicant is applying for leave to remain and was last granted leave as a Tier 2 Migrant to work as a nurse or midwife, registration must be achieved within eight months of the start date of that previous employment.

For a fuller account of employment process for non-EEA trained nurses and midwives, see Tiers 2 and 5: guidance for sponsors, version 11/16, para 15.19.

[1]  HC 535, para K3 with effect from 19 November 2015.
[2]  HC 535, Explanatory Memorandum, para 7.16.
[3]  HC 359, Appendix A, para 78A(a), amended by HC 667, para A49, with effect from 16 November 2016.
[4]  HC 395, Appendix A, para 77K, inserted by HC 667, para A47, with effect from 16 November 2016.
[5]  Ibid, para 77K(a) and (b).
[6]  Ibid, para 77K(c).

*The annual cap*

**10.71** *[Insert new heading above.]*

*[N.B.]*

The figure for the annual cap of 20,700 CoS has not changed but there have been many changes to the monthly distribution of CoS as a result of periodic reviews. The amounts of monthly applications are now set out in Table 11E.[1]

Recruitment can still take place outside the cap allocation and without having to pass the Resident Labour Market test if the worker is a high earner. The salary figures have been amended. For £153,500, now read £155,300, and for £152,100, read £153,500.[2] The salary of £153,500, only applies if the recruitment took place before 6 April 2015.

[1]  HC 395, Appendix A, para 80A(iii), as inserted by HC 877, para A32, for applications decided on or after 6 April 2016.
[2]  Appendix A, para 77B(c).

### 10.71A  *[Insert new paragraph:]*

The process by which Certificates of Sponsorship are allocated to Sponsors under the Tier 2 (General) limit is set out in paras 80C to 84A and a new Table 11D of Appendix A.[1] A sponsor's allocation of CoSs is now worked out by way of a points scheme, as follows. Available points are shown in a new Table 11D. No application will be granted unless it scores a minimum of 20 points under the heading 'Type of Job' and a minimum of 1 point under the heading 'Salary on offer'.[2] A further change is being made to the operation of the limit, to enable the Secretary of State to reclaim Certificates of Sponsorship which are unused by Sponsors before the certificates expire (after three months), and return those unused places to the limit.[3]

[1]  Appendix A, para 80B.
[2]  Appendix A, para 80D and Tables 11D substituted by rule change HC 437, paras A1 and A2, as from 12 October 2015.
[3]  HC 359, para 83, as substituted by rule change HC 437, para A6, as from 12 October 2015.

### Tier 2 (Minister of Religion) or Tier 2 (Sportsperson) categories

*Sportsperson under Tier 2 and Tier 5 – Attributes*

### 10.78  *[N.B.]*

There are a variety of changes to these Tier 2 and Tier 5 categories. They are:

* A definition of 'Professional Sportsperson' has been inserted[1] and a change has been made to the definition of 'Amateur' so as to include a person playing or coaching in a charity game.[2] According to the Home Office, this will provide clarity as to who is considered to be a 'Professional Sportsperson'. It will help customers differentiate more easily between a 'Professional Sportsperson' and an 'Amateur'.[3]
* A change is being made to apply a condition on all children of a Relevant Points Based System Migrant who are under the age of 18 when they apply, prohibiting them from being employed as a professional sportsperson (including as a sports coach).[4]

- Appendix M contains the list of sports governing bodies who may endorse Tier 2 (Sportsperson) and Tier 5 (Temporary Worker – Creative and Sporting) applications. These endorsements that can now be issued by the National Ice Skating Association of Great Britain and Northern Ireland to include Tier 2 applications in addition to Tier 5 applications.[5]

- Appendix A, paras 100 and 111 deal with the requirements of endorsement by the Governing Body for the applicant's sport – 100 for Tier 2 (Sportsperson) and 111 for Tier 5 (Temporary Worker – Creative and Sporting). Both have been amended in November 2015. A Government Body endorsement letter is now essential in either case, confirming that the player or coach is internationally established at the highest level and/or will make a significant contribution to the development of his sport at the highest level in the UK, and that the post could not be filled by a suitable settled worker. When a valid Governing Body endorsement letter is not provided as part of that application the application for entry clearance or leave to remain can be refused.[6]

- A change is being made to permit sportspersons applying for entry clearance or leave to remain under Tier 2 (Sportsperson) or Tier 5 (Temporary Worker – Creative and Sporting) to play for their national team when it is in the UK competing in British University and College Sport (BUCS) competitions. They may also take a temporary engagement as a Sports Broadcaster.[7]

[1]   HC 359, para 6 inserted by rule change HC 353, para Intro4, as from 19 November 2015.
[2]   HC 359, para 6 inserted by rule change HC 353, para Intro3, as from 19 November 2015.
[3]   See HC 353 Explanatory Memorandum, para 7.19.
[4]   HC 359, para 3191 (b) (iv) (2) inserted by rule change HC 353, para 8.4, as from 19 November 2015.
[5]   HC 395 Appendix M as amended by rule change HC 353, para M2, as from 19 November 2015. There have been other changes to the list since 2014, but it should be noted that the only needed port of call is Appendix M. Given that several governing bodies do not issue endorsements for both Tier 2 and Tier 5 routes, a change was made at the endo 2014 to the Table of governing bodies to include information on which Tier(s) each body may endorse applicants in. Hence the upgrading of the National Ice Skating Association.
[6]   HC 395, Appendix A paras 100 (b) and 111(a)(ii), as substituted by rule change HC 353, paras A45 and A46.
[7]   HC 395 para 245HC (c)(iii)(4), inserted by rule change HC 353, para 6A.13, as from 19 November 2015.

### English and maintenance requirements

10.80 *[N.B.]*

Amendments are being made to clarify that applicants relying on an approved English language test at level A1 of the Council of Europe's Common European Framework for Language Learning are only required to pass the speaking and listening components (and not the reading and writing components which are additionally required for higher levels).[1]

An amendment is being made to the maintenance rules for family members of Tier 2 migrants, so that where the Tier 2 migrant is exempt from having to show maintenance funds by virtue of applying to extend their stay in the same category, their dependants are also exempt, even if they apply at a later date. Previously the exemption only extended to dependants who applied at the same time as the main applicant.[2]

[1] HC 395, Appendix B, para 10A, inserted by HC 535, para B2, as from 18 November 2015.
[2] See Appendix E, para (p), inserted by rule change HC 535, para E1, as from 19 November 2015.

### Requirements for indefinite leave to remain as a Tier 2 (General) Migrant or Tier 2 (Sportsperson) Migrant

*Tier 2 (General) Migrant or Tier 2 (Sportsperson) Migrant*

**10.85** *[Delete the existing heading and replace with the above headings. Delete the whole paragraph and substitute:]*

Appendix A, paragraph 245HF has now been substituted by a more up-to-date version.[1] There are one set of requirements for Tier 2 (General) and Tier 2 (Sportsperson) and another for Ministers of Religion. In both cases the applicants for indefinite leave to remain must provide the documents specified in para 245HH, which is the new name for para 245HF–SD. The requirements for indefinite leave for Tier 2 (General) and Tier 2 (Sportsperson) migrants are as follows:

- The applicant must not fall for refusal under the general grounds for refusal, must not be an illegal entrant and must not be in the UK in breach of immigration laws except that, where paragraph 39E of these Rules applies, any current 14-day period of overstaying will be disregarded (para 245HF(a) and (j)).
- The applicant must have spent a continuous period of five years lawfully in the UK, of which the most recent period must have been spent with leave as a Tier 2 (General) Migrant or Tier 2 (Sportsperson) Migrant, in any combination of a list of categories set out in para 245HF(b)(i)–(x).[2]
- One of the categories in the above list is as a Tier 2 (Intra-Company Transfer) Migrant. Here the continuous period of five years spent lawfully in the UK must include a period of leave as a Tier 2 (ICT) Migrant granted under the Rules in place before 6 April 2010, or a Qualifying Work Permit Holder, who got the work permit as the subject of an Intra-Company Transfer para 245HF(b)(iii)).
- The Sponsor who obtained the applicant's last grant of leave must: (i) still hold a Tier 2 Sponsor licence in the relevant category, or be in the process of renewing it; and (ii) must certify that he or she still requires the applicant for the employment in question for the foreseeable future; and (iii) must certify the details of the employee's salary, including the gross annual amount and that they will pay it for the foreseeable future (para 245HF(c)(1)–(4)).
- Pay is an important element in the requirements for indefinite leave to remain in these two Tiers. The gross annual salary and any salary calculated because of the employee's absence for reasons of maternity, paternity, shared parental or adoption leave must be the basic pay (excluding overtime), plus allowances set out in para 245HF(d)(ii) and (iii) and should be at least equal to the appropriate rate for the job as

stated in Appendix J and must be at least £35,000 on or after 6 April 2016 going up each year to at least £36,200 on or after 6 April 2020 (para 245HF(d)(v) and (vi)).

- The requirement to attain these hefty minimum salaries, above, does not apply if the continuous five-year period in sub-para (b) includes a period of leave as (i) a Qualifying Work Permit Holder, or (ii) a Tier 2 Migrant, where a CoS which led to that grant of leave was assigned to the applicant by his Sponsor before 6 April 2011 (para 245HF(e)).
- The requirement to attain these hefty minimum salaries, above, does not apply (1) where the applicant's most recent job was on the PhD list in Appendix J or was, or had been, on the shortage occupation List at any time when he or she had leave or was granted leave as a Tier 2 (General) Migrant, either with the same or a different employer, during the continuous six-year period ending on the date of application for indefinite leave to remain (para 245HF(f)).
- Where the applicant is paid hourly, only earnings up to a maximum of 48 hours a week will be considered in para 245HF(d)(vi) above, even if the applicant works for longer than this (para 245HF(g)).
- The applicant must provide the specified documents in para 245HH as evidence of the salary in para 245HF(c)(ii)(2) or (3) above and the reasons for the absences set out in para 245AAA (para 245HF(h)).[3]
- The applicant must have sufficient knowledge of the English language and sufficient knowledge about life in the United Kingdom, in accordance with Appendix KoLL (para 245HF(i)).

[1]   HC 395, para 245HF was inserted by rule change HC535, para 6A.16, as from 19 November 2015. The new clause also provides that valid leave in the Bailiwick of Guernsey, the Bailiwick of Jersey or the Isle of Man in a category equivalent to any of the categories set out in para 245HF(b)(i) to (x), may be included in the continuous period of five years' lawful residence, provided that the requirements of para 245HF(k)(i) and (ii) are met.

[2]   One of the categories in the above list is as Tier 1 migrant but this does not include Tier 1 (Post Study Work) or Tier 1 (Graduate Entrepreneur).

[3]   See further 10.10 in the main text.


*Requirements for indefinite leave to remain as a Tier 2 (Minister of Religion) Migrant*

**10.85A** *[Insert new heading and new paragraph:]*

The requirements in new substituted paragraph 245HG to qualify for indefinite leave to remain as a Tier 2 (Minister of Religion) Migrant are:

- The applicant must not fall for refusal under the general grounds for refusal, must not be an illegal entrant and (f) must not be in the UK in breach of immigration laws except that, where para 39E of these Rules applies, any current period of overstaying will be disregarded (sub-para (a) and (f)).
- The applicant must have spent a continuous period of five years lawfully in the UK, of which the most recent period must have been spent with leave as a Tier 2 (Minister of Religion) Migrant, in any combination of the ten categories set out in sub-paras (b)(i)–(ix).[1]

- The Sponsor who obtained the applicant's last grant of leave must (i) still hold a Tier 2 Sponsor licence in the relevant category, or be in the process of renewing it and (ii) must certify that he or she still requires the applicant for the employment in question for the foreseeable future (sub-para (c)).
- The applicant must provide the specified documents in para 245HH as evidence of the reasons for the absences set out in para 245AAA (sub-para (d)).[2]
- The applicant must have sufficient knowledge of the English language and sufficient knowledge about life in the United Kingdom, in accordance with Appendix KoLL (sub-para (e)).
- For the purposes of (b), time spent with valid leave in the Bailiwick of Guernsey, the Bailiwick of Jersey or the Isle of Man in a category equivalent to any of the categories set out in (b)(i)–(x), may be included in the continuous period of five years' lawful residence, provided that the most recent period of leave was granted in the UK as a Tier 2 (Minister of Religion) Migrant (sub-para (g)).

[1]  One of the categories in the above list is as Tier 1 migrant but this does not include Tier 1 (Post Study Work) or Tier 1 (Graduate Entrepreneur). Another category is as a Tier 2 (ITC) HC as set out in 245HG (b)(iii) and the comments made in 10.85 on para245HF (b)(iii) apply.

[2]  See further **10.10**.

## TIER 5

### Tier 5 (Youth Mobility Scheme)

**10.87** *[N.B.]*

The annual allocations for participating countries on the scheme are set for each new year. These are contained in rule changes – for example, HC693 set 2015 allocations, HC 535 set those for 2016, and HC 667 set those for 2017. The allocations are based on previous levels of take-up by British citizens of equivalent schemes offered by participating countries. This scheme has extended to Japan, where demand is expected to significantly increase and to Taiwan, on whom deemed sponsorship status has been conferred, even although it is a territory and not a country.

*[Footnote 8 is deleted.]*

### Tier 5 (Temporary workers)

**10.88** *[N.B.]*

The Temporary Workers category consists of five sub-categories: Creative and Sporting, Charity Workers, Religious Workers, Government Authorised Exchange, and International Agreement. Changes in these are:

- Creative and Sporting: Some of the changes in this subcategory have been referred to at **10.78** above.
- Charity workers: A CoS may now be issued in the Charity Workers subcategory, if the work the applicant is being sponsored to do is: (i) voluntary fieldwork which contributes directly to the achievement or

advancement of the sponsor's charitable purpose; (ii) not paid or otherwise remunerated except for reasonable expenses; and (iii) is not filling a permanent position, including on a temporary basis.[1] The rules now define 'voluntary fieldwork' as above to clarify the type of work activities which may be undertaken by users of this category. The rules concerning remuneration of Tier 5 (Charity Worker) migrants have also been amended to clarify that charity workers are not permitted to receive any form of remuneration, including benefits in kind, other than reasonable expenses as outlined in section 44 of the National Minimum Wage Act. The aim of the changes is to prevent permanent vacancies being filled by temporary charity workers on a recurring basis and to prevent it being used to undertake low skilled work ancillary to the sponsors charitable purpose.

- Religious: No change.
- Government Authorised Exchange: All the current government exchange schemes are to be found in Appendix N. Over 50 schemes are listed, for example, both the bar Council and the Law Society are sponsors for creating opportunities for overseas law students and lawyers to do a pupillage at Bar or an internship at Solicitor's office. The scheme is constantly changed. Since the end of 2014, a number of bodies have been deleted from the scheme because they are either no longer in existence or are not providing the particular service; other new bodies are being recognised and are listed in Appendix N.
- International Agreement: The most active category under International Agreements has been domestic servants in diplomatic households. There have been extensive changes, which we have dealt with together with domestic servants in private households at **10.109A – 10.111E** below.

[1]  HC 395, Appendix A, para 111(c), inserted by HC 353, para 111(c), inserted by rule change HC 353, para A47, as from 19 November 2015.

*Maintenance – Tier 5 (Temporary Worker)*

**10.90** *[Insert new heading above.]*

*[N.B.]*

The maintenance requirements under all the Tier 5 (Temporary Worker) routes are being amended to clarify that, when a sponsor certifies maintenance, they are confirming that the applicant will not claim public funds during their period of leave.[1] Six months later the April amendment was further amended to provide A-Rated Tier 5 sponsors with the option of certifying maintenance in respect of a Tier 5 migrant by confirming that they will maintain and accommodate the migrant for the first month of their stay.[2]

[1]  HC 395, Appendix C, para 9 and the Table accompanying it, as amended by rule change HC 877, para C1, as from 6 April 2016.
[2]  HC 395, Appendix C, para 9 and the Table accompanying it, as amended by rule change HC 667, para C4, as from 24 November 2016.

**10.92** *[Note that this paragraph has been moved and renumbered as paragraph 10.111B below.]*

# DEFUNCT CATEGORIES

## Fully operational categories

*Representatives of overseas businesses*

### 10.106 *[N.B.]*

Changes have been made to the rules relating to sole representatives. Amended paras 144(iii) and 147(ii) and (iii) of the rules are substituted for the previous paragraphs, but merely add further requirements to the existing ones which are reproduced. Paragraph 144 deals with leave to enter. It now requires the sole representative to obtain various documents from the overseas employer, including a full description of the company's activities, their assets, accounts and share distribution for the previous year; a letter which confirms the overseas company will establish their business in the UK and the applicant will be employed full time as their sole representative in the UK.[1]

[1] New para 144(iii)(5) requires a notarised statement which confirms the applicant will be their sole representative in the UK; the company has no other branch, subsidiary or representative in the UK; its operations will remain centred overseas; and the applicant will not engage in business of their own nor represent any other company's interest.

### 10.107A *[After paragraph 10.107, insert new paragraph 107A:]*

The requirements for leave to remain have been amended and new para 147(ii)–(iii) inserted. Subparagraph (ii) deals with the business side of things. The previous rules are repeated to the effect that the overseas business still has its headquarters and principal place of business outside the UK and the applicant is still employed full time as a sole representative and is still required for the employment in question. The changes add three extra requirements: (d) details of the salary paid in the previous 12 months to the sole representative; (e) evidence that he or she has generated business in the UK, showing accounts and details of business transactions with firms in the UK; and (f) evidence from Company House documents of the registration of new branches or incorporation of a new subsidiary. Subparagraph (iii) deals with new requirements relating to the situation of the sole representative, to show that he is still employed in in the employment for which the entry clearance was granted and is still required for this employment; and has evidence to show what type of pay he receives (basic salary or commission), his hours, and how much he has earned in the previous 12 months.

## Overseas domestic workers

### 10.109A *[After paragraph 10.109, insert new heading and paragraph:]*

Overseas domestic workers (whether in private or diplomatic households) are now subject to three sets of rules: (i) transitional provisions for those who got leave before 6 April 2012, who can still qualify for indefinite leave to remain; (ii) those in private or diplomatic service who are not victims of slavery or human trafficking; and (iii) those who are such victims.[1] Three important differences between private and diplomatic service are: (i) that diplomatic service is part of the International Agreement category of Tier 5 (Temporary workers) and needs a sponsor and points to obtain entry and leave to remain; (ii) a period of leave for diplomatic service may be anything up to two years; whereas in private service leave is never more than six months, unless the first leave in this category was granted under the pre-6 April 2012 rules and the transitional provisions apply. We deal with both these categories together, because diplomatic workers can change jobs and become private domestic workers and because the Modern Slavery Act 2015 brings the two categories into closer alignment.

1   For further information see Modernised Guidance – Domestic workers in private households, Published for Home Office staff on 14 June 2016: https://www.gov.uk/government/uploads/system/uploads/attachment_data/file/529329/Domestic-workers-in-private-households-v16.0.pdf.

## Overseas Domestic Workers in a private household

**10.110A** *[After paragraph 10.110, insert new heading and paragraph:]*

The Overseas Domestic Worker in a private household route exists to allow employers resident overseas to be accompanied by their household staff on visits to the UK. As set out in **10.110**, their position is dealt with under paras 159A–159H. Four important changes have been made to the rules, as follows:

(a)   The Upper age limit of 65 has been abolished. Now it is only necessary that the servant is over 18.[1]

(b)   There is already a requirement in the General Visitor Rules that prevents visitors from effectively living in the UK through making repeated or successive visits to the UK. A similar change now applies to Overseas Domestic Workers who must only come to the UK with a visitor.[2]

(c)   Domestic workers are free to change employment but must remain in domestic work (see further below).

(d)   As from 6 April 2015, further changes were made by HC 1025. The requirement to pay domestic workers the National Minimum Wage in leave to enter and leave to remain applications was strengthened:

   (i)   ECOs and immigration officers must be satisfied that the employer is going to pay the national minimum wage;[3]

   (ii)   to avoid employers bypassing this rule a new requirement was made[4] to prevent employers using an exemption in the National Minimum Wage Regulations, that was designed for au pairs by allowing employers to decline to pay the Minimum Wage to those living as part of the family;

   (iii)   in both leave to enter and remain, employers must sign a statement confirming that the work that will be carried out by the employee will not constitute work within the meaning of reg 57 of the National Minimum Wage Regulations 2015[5] This means that the applicant cannot be treated as if he or she was an au pair, who would not fall within the National Minimum Wage legislation;

(iv)   the two parties must have entered into a contract in accordance with the statement of the terms and conditions of employment in the format specified in Appendix 7 of the Immigration Rules;[6]

(v)   the new template now in force is more detailed than before and it replaces not only the old template for domestic workers in private households but also those in diplomatic households. It is compliant with employment law and is designed to ensure that both employers and employees are aware of their rights and responsibilities. The upshot is that the terms and conditions of employment is in a common format for all Overseas Domestic Workers working in both the private and diplomatic households.

[1]   HC 395, Part 4, para 159A (i), as amended by HC 667, with effect from 24 November 2016.
[2]   HC 395, para 159A(iv), as amended by HC 693, para 39, as from 6 November 2014.
[3]   HC 395, paras 159A(va) and 159D(iva), inserted by HC 1025, paras 76 and 77.
[4]   HC 395, paras 159A(vb) and 159D(ivb), inserted by HC 1025, paras 76 and 77.
[5]   National Minimum Wage Regulations 2015, SI 2015/621 (as amended from time to time) These Regulations remake the National Minimum Wage Regulations 1999, SI 1999/584, and consolidate the amendments made to those Regulations: changes made by HC 437, paras 5.1–5.3.
[6]   HC 395, Appendix 7 states: 'Two copies of this form must be completed and signed by the employer and the overseas domestic worker and signed originals must be submitted with the entry clearance application or with the leave to remain application as required by HC 395, paras 159A(v), 159D(iv), 159EA(iii), 245ZO(f)(ii), and 245ZQ(e)(ii).'

*Concessions for Syrian domestic workers in a private household*

**10.110B**   *[Insert new heading and paragraph:]*

New Concessions for Syrian nationals in the UK apply to nationals who are overseas Domestic Workers in a private household: in their case the 6 months period of stay imposed under paragraph 159E (extension of stay as a domestic worker in a private household) shall not apply.[1]

[1]   *Concessions to the Immigration Rules for Syrian Nationals*, Version 3.0, authorised under the Equality (Syria) Authorisation 2017 which came into force on 1 March 2017.

*Domestic servants working in a diplomatic household*

**10.111A**   *[After paragraph 10.111, insert new paragraph:]*

The old rules still apply, in that applicants who entered the United Kingdom under the Rules in place before 6 April 2012 can still apply for extensions of stay for up to 12 months and for indefinite leave after they have been in the UK for five years. An amendment in HC 667 clarifies the meaning of full-time employment in the context of extension applications made in respect of those admitted under the Rules in force prior to April 2012. It is now 30 hours.[1]

[1]   HC 395, para 159EA(iii), as amended by HC 667, para 5.12, as from 24 November 2016.

**10.111B**   *[This paragraph 10.92 is renumbered as 10.111B. The final paragraph after the bullet list has been added.]*

Private servants in diplomatic households if their last grant of entry clearance was made before 6 April 2012 may qualify for indefinite leave under this category. The applicant must meet the requirements of paragraph 245ZS of the Immigration Rules:

- None of the general grounds for refusal in paragraphs 320 to 324 of the Immigration Rules apply and the applicant is not in breach of immigration laws, except that any period of overstaying for a 28-day period or less shall be disregarded.
- The applicant has spent a continuous period of five years in the UK lawfully with leave in the Tier 5 (International agreement) category, working as a private servant in a diplomatic household.
- The applicant has sufficient knowledge of the English language and about life in the UK, with reference to Appendix KoLL (knowledge of language and life) This is unless the applicant is under the age of 18, or aged 65 or over at the time the application is made.
- The applicant provides a letter from the employer detailing any absences from employment, including periods of annual leave. Where the absence was due to a serious or compelling reason, the applicant must provide a personal letter which includes full details of the reason for the absences with all original supporting documents, such as medical certificates, birth or death certificates, and the reasons which led to the absence from the UK.

Paragraph 245ZS limits the grant of indefinite leave to remain to those in diplomatic service who were last granted entry clearance in this capacity under the pre-6 April 2012 rules, and this is backed up in the Modern Guidance,[1] but no such limitation is to be found in para 158 of the rules. Under this paragraph, diplomatic domestic workers can qualify for indefinite leave to remain, if they have spent a continuous period of five years lawfully in the UK in that capacity and meet the other requirements of HC 395, para 158. However, this provision could only apply to cases where leave to remain had been given in this capacity before this particular route was brought to an end by HC 1113 in 2008, about the time when the PBS came into operation.

[1]   Modern Guidance, Tier 5 (Temporary Worker) of the points-based system, Version 16.0, at p 24. See https://www.gov.uk/government/uploads/system/uploads/attachment_data/file/515557 /Tier-_5-Temporary-Worker-of-the-points-based-system-v16_0.pdf.

### 10.111C *[Insert new heading and new paragraph:]*

Domestic servants working in a diplomatic household still need to be sponsored as a private servant under Tier 5 (International Agreement) category and gain 30 points under Appendix A and 10 points under Appendix C, paras 8 and 9 to qualify for entry.[1] Their employer must be either a diplomat, or an employee of a recognised international organisation, who enjoys certain privileges or immunity under UK or international law.[2] The requirements for entry clearance or leave to enter have now been tightened up. Not only is it necessary to provide evidence that the applicant will be paid in accordance with the National Minimum Wage Act 1998 and regulations made under that Act,[3] but the applicant must also satisfy the Entry Clearance Officer or Immigration Officer that:

(a)   throughout their employment in the UK, the employer intends to pay them at least the National Minimum Wage rate to which they are entitled by the law in force at the relevant time;

(b)      there is provided a written and signed statement from the employer confirming that the applicant is an employee; and

(c)      the work that will be carried out by the applicant will not constitute work within the meaning of reg 57 of the National Minimum Wage Regulations 2015 (as amended from time to time). This, as with domestic servants in a private household, is to prevent employers using an exemption in the National Minimum Wage Regulations, that was designed for au pairs by allowing employers to decline to pay the minimum wage to those living as part of the family;

(d)      the applicant may now leave their employment and take a new job in a different household and will not be prevented from doing so by any conditions attached to their leave. Alternative employment was subject to a maximum period of six months, or the period of extant leave remaining to the person (whichever was the lesser), but this time limit has been deleted from the rules by rule change HC 667 as from 24 November 2016.[4]

Extensions of leave are subject to the provisions in paras 245ZQ and 245ZR and the length of the leave is calculated according to the formula in para 245ZR(d) in the case of someone who entered the UK with entry clearance before 6 April 2012 and by the formula in para 245ZR(e) for someone who entered with entry clearance under the rules in place from 6 April 2012. Indefinite leave is only available to someone who has been working as a private servant in a diplomatic household lawfully for a continuous period of five years and who was last granted entry clearance in this capacity under the rules in place before 6 April 2012.[5]

1    Paragraph 245ZO(b) and (c).
2    See HC 395, paras 245ZO(f)–(g), 245ZQ(e)(ii), 245ZR(d)–(e) and Appendix A, para 111(g).
3    These are now the National Minimum Wage Regulations 2015, SI 2015/621 which have remade the National Minimum Wage Regulations 1999, SI 1999/584 and its later amendments. See also the contract form in Appendix 7.
4    HC 395, para 245ZP(f)(iii)(5), as amended by HC 667, para 6A.32.
5    HC 395, para 245ZS.

## Domestic workers as victims of slavery or human trafficking

**10.111D** *[Insert new heading and paragraph:]*

Section 53(1) of the Modern Slavery Act 2015 ('the 2015 Act')[1] provides that the Immigration Rules must make provision for leave to remain in the United Kingdom to be granted to an overseas domestic worker in a private or diplomatic household who has been determined to be a victim of slavery or human trafficking and meets such other requirements as may be provided for by the rules (s 53(1)). Secondly, the conditions on which such leave is to be granted must in particular provide that the leave is to be for the purpose of working as a domestic worker in a private household, with the ability to change employer, but working in the same capacity (s 53(2)). The rules may specify a maximum period of leave but it must not be less than six months (s 53(3)). The section also sets out the means by which an overseas domestic worker is to recognised as a victim of slavery or human trafficking (s 53(4)) and makes the issue of Guidance by the Home Secretary a 'must' (s 53(5)). The Guidance must provide for a period during which no enforcement action should be taken against overseas domestic workers in respect of their becoming overstayers or breaching a condition of their leave relating to their employment, if they did so because of the matters relied on as slavery or human trafficking (s 53(6)). The section also makes it clear that, although the suggested leave to be granted to victims is as a domestic worker in a private household, the provisions of the section include in the term 'overseas domestic worker' a domestic worker in both private and diplomatic households (s 53(7)).

[1]  Section 53 came into force on 15 October 2015 by SI 2015/1690, reg. 2(c).

### 10.111E  *[Insert new paragraph:]*

Changes were made by HC 437 as from 6 November 2015 with further changes in HC 667, as from 24 November 2016, to implement the 2015 Act. New paras 159I–151K have been inserted into the rules, setting out the requirements for a special leave. No-one will get special leave, unless she or he is the subject of a 'positive conclusive grounds decision' made by a competent authority under the National Referral Mechanism.[1] The applicant's most recent grant of leave must have been as a domestic worker in either private or diplomatic households or as a domestic worker who has been granted leave as the victim of slavery or human trafficking or has previously been granted leave as a domestic worker in either a private or diplomatic household outside the rules following a 'positive conclusive grounds decision' made by a competent authority under the National Referral Mechanism.[2] This leave will be for a period not exceeding a total of two years, taking into account earlier leave,[3] and the new leave is to be granted only for the purpose of working as a domestic worker in a private or diplomatic household.[4] It is specified that, where the employment is in a diplomatic setting, a Certificate of Sponsorship should be issued in the normal way before the employment commences.[5] Further rule changes, as we have described above, have been introduced in all domestic worker cases to ensure that the statement of the terms and conditions of employment in the format specified in Appendix 7 of the Immigration Rules is submitted in respect of any employment as a domestic worker.

The upshot of these provisions in the 2015 Act is, according to the Home Office, to enable overseas domestic workers who have been determined to be a victim of slavery or human trafficking to continue to work as a domestic worker, to change employer, and for a period of time in order to be able to earn some money.[6] However, it is doubtful if these high hopes will greatly ameliorate the position of victims of this type of human trafficking or encourage those who are too hidden and too afraid to escape and challenge their mistreatment, when they are faced with a too rigorous and inflexible immigration control, an inability to have recourse to public funds and a period of leave which sounds more generous than it really is, once previous leave periods are subtracted from the offered 'not exceeding two years'.[7]

[1]  HC 395, para 159I(ii). National Referral Mechanism is a multi-agency victim identification and support process (see 'Review of the National Referral Mechanism for victims of human trafficking', Home Office, June 2014; Home Office Guidance, 15 October 2015; 'Victims of modern slavery – Competent Authority guidance', Version 3.0, 21 March 2016. See further **13.22**, below.
[2]  HC 395, para 159I(i).
[3]  Ibid, paras 159J and 159JA.

4   Ibid, para 159J (i)(a) and (b).
5   Ibid, para159J(ii)(b).
6   HC 437, Explanatory Memorandum, para 7.2.
7   See further 'The Impact of the 2012 Domestic Workers in a Private Household Visa on Human Trafficking for Domestic Servitude' by Amy Weatherburn and Julia Muraszkiewicz, *Immigration, Asylum and Nationality Law*, Vol 30, No 3, 2016. See further CHAPTER 13.

# Chapter 11

# FAMILIES, PARTNERS AND CHILDREN

## CHANGES CONCERNING CHILDREN

**11.2** *[At the end footnote 6 add:]*

See on the application of the section 55 welfare principles: *AT and Another (Article 8 ECHR – Child Refugee – Family Reunification: Eritrea)* [2016] UKUT 227 (IAC); *PD and Others (Article 8 : conjoined family claims) Sri Lanka* [2016] UKUT 108 (IAC); *Abdul (Section 55 – Article 24(3) Charter : Nigeria)* [2016] UKUT 106 (IAC).

## FAMILY AND IMMIGRATION LITIGATION – THE COMMON AND DIVERGING ISSUES

**11.5** *[At the end of footnote 1 add:]*

*KB & RJ v RT (Rev 1)* [2016] EWHC 760 (Fam); *Z (Foreign Surrogacy: Allocation of Work: Guidance on Parental Order Reports) (Rev 1), Re* [2015] EWFC 90, [2016] Fam Law 314, [2015] All ER (D) 230 (Dec).

*[At the end of footnote 3, before the full stop, add:]*

, *N (A Child), Re* [2016] EWHC 3085 (Fam)

*[At the beginning of footnote 4, insert:]*

*Bi v Mohammed* [2016] EWHC 506 (Fam),

**11.10** *[At the end of footnote 3 add:]*

See also, *GS v SS* [2016] EWHC 3085 (Fam).

**11.11** *[At end of footnote1, before the full stop, add:]*

; *Treebhawon and Others (Section 117B(6))* [2015] UKUT 674 (IAC); *AM (Section 117B)* [2015] UKUT 260 (IAC); *Miah (Section 117B NIAA 2002 – Children)* [2016] UKUT 131 (IAC); *E (Female Genital Mutilation and Permission to Remove)* [2016] EWHC 1052 (Fam)

*[In footnote 6, delete the sentences: 'Such prospective adopters must first get an order from the High Court giving them parental responsibility for the purposes of adopting abroad. In order to be eligible to apply for parental responsibility for this purpose the child must have had his/her home with the*

*proposed adopter/adopters at all times during the preceding ten weeks.' At the end of footnote 6, insert:]*

, *Kent County Council v PA-K and IA (a child)* [2013] EWHC 578 (Fam), [2013] 2 FLR 541, [2013] All ER (D) 226 (Mar), sub nom *A (a child) (adoption: placement outside jurisdiction), Re* [2014] Fam 1, [2013] 3 WLR 1454.

**11.12** *[At the end of footnote 3, before the full stop, insert:]*

; *GS v SS* [2016] EWHC 3085 (Fam)

**11.13** *[At the end of footnote 2, before the full stop, insert:]*

, *GS v SS* [2016] EWHC 3085 (Fam)

**11.14** *[At the end of footnote 7, add:]*

See: *N (Children), Re* [2016] UKSC 15, [2016] 2 WLR 1103, [2016] 1 FLR 1082 concerning EU citizen children in public law care proceedings whose cases fall within the scope of the Council Regulation (EC) No 2201/2003, on jurisdiction and the recognition and enforcement of judgments in matrimonial matters and the matters of parental responsibility, Brussels II revised Regulation. In every case with such European/Regulation dimension UK courts have to ask themselves whether they have jurisdiction to determine such case and, if they have jurisdiction, whether, by reference to Article 15 it is in the child's best interests for the case to be determined in another jurisdiction and the case should be transferred to the relevant court in another Member State. See also *In Re E (A Child) (Care Proceedings: European Dimension): Practice Note* [2014] EWHC 6 (Fam), [2014] EWHC 6 (Fam), [2014] 1 WLR 2670, [2014] 2 FCR 264; *Merton London Borough Council v B (Central Authority of the Republic of Latvia intervening)* [2015] EWCA Civ 888, [2016] 2 WLR 410. See also: *T v K* [2016] EWHC 2963 (Fam), [2016] All ER (D) 41 (Dec).

**11.15** *[At the end of the para insert:]*

The converse also applies. Family courts have rejected submissions advanced by the Secretary of State that judges should decline to grant permission to commence adoption proceedings, to recognise a foreign adoption or grant an adoption order where the parties could have complied with relevant adoption and immigration rules but have not done so or their application under the relevant adoption and immigration rules has failed. In the recent case of *GS v SS*,[4] the President of the Family Division held that in such submissions 'The Secretary of State was seeking in effect to introduce additional criteria in the form of a further filter limiting the family court's discretion'.

*[At the end of footnote 3, before the full stop, insert:]*

; *S v Bradford Metropolitan District Council and Another* [2015] EWCA Civ 951, [2016] 1 WLR 407; *T v K* [2016] EWHC 2963 (Fam); *GS v SS* [2016] EWHC 3085 (Fam)

4  [2016] EWHC 3085 (Fam)

**11.18** *[At the end of footnote1, before the full stop, insert:]*

; *FAS v Secretary of State for the Home Department* [2015] EWCA Civ 951, [2016] 1 WLR 407, [2016] 2 All ER 251, [2016] 1 FCR 191; *GS v SS* [2016] EWHC 3085 (Fam)

## DOMICILE

**11.21** *[At the end of footnote 3, add:]*

In *Awuku v Secretary of State for the Home Department* [2016] EWCA Civ 1303, the Ghanaian applicant challenged the refusal to issue him with a residence card as a spouse of an EU national. They were married by proxy in Ghana and their marriage was registered in accordance with the Ghanaian Marriage and Divorce (Registration) Law 1985. The marriage was recognised in Ghana, was properly executed and satisfied Ghanaian law and there was nothing in the law of either party's country of domicile that restricted freedom to enter into the marriage. The Upper Tribunal upheld the refusal of a residence card applying the case of *Kareem* [2014] UKUT 24, which held such EU marriage must be shown to be recognised in the EEA national's home state, in this case Germany. On appeal to the Court of Appeal, both the appellant and the Secretary of State submitted that *Kareem* was wrong. At the request of both parties the Court agreed to hear the case on its merits and adjourned the hearing so that the Attorney General could be invited to appoint an advocate to the court and the important private international law issue could be fully argued on both sides. The appeal is pending.

## MARRIAGE AND CIVIL PARTNERSHIP ISSUES CONCERNING VALIDITY AND RECOGNITION

### Validity of marriage or civil partnerships

**11.28** *[In the second sentence of the first paragraph, after the word 'Tribunal' and before 'held', insert:]*

in the *Kareem* case

*[At the end of the first paragraph ending with footnote reference 2, insert:]*

However, in *Awuku* both the applicant spouse and the Secretary of State submitted that this Tribunal decision was wrong and the *Kareem* tribunal finding is to be considered by the Court of Appeal with the Attorney General as Advocate for the Court.[2a]

*[At the end of footnote 3 insert:]*

See also *Southwark, The London Borough of v KA (Capacity to Marry) (rev 1)* [2016] EWCOP 20.

*[In footnote 5 – insert before the CB citation:]*

*Khan v Ahmad* [2014] EWHC 3850 (Fam), [2015] 2 FLR 461, [2015] Fam Law 137;

*[In footnote 12, after the Kareem citation, before the word 'and', insert:]*

, however, this decision is doubted, see: *Awuku v Secretary of State for the Home Department* [2016] EWCA Civ 1303

*[In footnote 12, after the CB citation, insert:]*

; *Cudjoe (Proxy marriages: burden of proof) (rev 1) Ghana* [2016] UKUT 180 (IAC)

2a *Awuku v Secretary of State for the Home Department* [2016] EWCA Civ 1303.


## POLYGAMOUS MARRIAGES

**11.29** *[In footnote 2, after the Ali v Ali citation and before the full stop, insert:]*

; *Adepoju v Akinola* [2016] EWHC 3160 (Ch)


## MARRIAGE/CIVIL PARTNERSHIP — THE FORMALITIES AND PROCEDURES

**11.37** *[In the main text, insert a new footnote reference 0 at the end of the first sentence.]*

*[In the footnotes, insert new footnote 0 text:]*

To be valid in the UK, a marriage must be monogamous and have no other impediments. It must be 'accomplished in accordance with' the requirements of the Marriage Acts 1949 to 1994, the Marriage (Scotland) Act 1977 and the Marriage (Northern Ireland) Order 2003, as amended by any subsequent legislation.

*[In footnote 6, add:]*

The provisions in Part 4 are now all in force. Sections 56, 59, 60–61 came into force on 14 July 2014; sections 49, 51–54 on 20 October 2014 and sections 48, 50, 55, 57, 58 and 62 on 1 March 2015. See also: Referral of proposed marriages and Civil Partnerships Regulations 2015, SI 2015/123; Proposed Marriages and Civil Partnership (Meaning of Exempt Persons and Notice) Regulations 2015, SI 2015/122, The Registration of Births, Deaths and Marriages and registration of Civil partnerships (Fees) Amendment Order 2015/117; Referral and Investigation of Proposed Marriages and Civil Partnerships (Scotland) Order 2015, SI 2015/396; and Referral and Investigation of Proposed Marriages and Civil Partnerships (Northern Ireland and Miscellaneous Provisions) Order 2015, SI 2015/395. Note these changes allowing referral of proposed marriages and partnerships to the Secretary of State to decide whether to investigate the relationship have been the subject of investigation by David Bolt, Independent Chief Inspector of Borders and Immigration, in his recent report, 'The implementation of the 2014 "hostile environment" provisions for tackling sham marriage, August to September 2016', Presented to Parliament pursuant to s 50(2) of the UK Borders Act 2007, December 2016. This report found, at 3.8, that a high proportion of couples complied with the investigation and were determined by interviewers not to be sham relationships. The Chief Inspector recommended changes in practice, including that where a marriage is determined to be sham but is allowed to proceed because the couple has been compliant with an investigation, the Home Office should ensure that the couple is informed in writing of the determination to act as a deterrent.

**11.40** *[In footnote 4 delete the text 'Form (VAF4A Dec 2008)' and substitute:]*

Forms (VAF4A Dec 2013, FLR(M)(2016), SET(M)(2016))

## MARRIAGE AND PARTNERSHIPS IN PART 8 AND THE IMMIGRATION RULES

### The Arrangement and Transitional Operation of the Rules

**11.41** *[In footnote 2 delete 'November 2014' and substitute 'August 2015'.]*

### 'Sham' Marriages/Partnerships and 'Marriages of Convenience'

**11.47** *[In the first paragraph, at the end of the first sentence insert new footnote reference 0.]*

*[In the second paragraph beginning 'This definition . . . ', delete the phrase 'in terms which . . . into force' and substitute 'in force from 1 March 2015'.]*

*[In the footnotes, insert new footnote 0 text:]*

See: *IS, R (on the application of) v Secretary of State for the Home Department* [2016] EWHC 1623 (Admin); *Ait-Rabah, R (on the application of) v The Secretary of State for the Home Department* [2016] EWHC 1099.

*[At the end of footnote 3, insertinsert:]*

*Agho v The Secretary of State for the Home Department* [2015] EWCA Civ 1198.

## PERMISSION TO MARRY OR ENTER INTO CIVIL PARTNERSHIPS

**11.48** *[In the main text, in the sentence 'The new (and at the time of writing, partially implement) . . . ', delete the words in brackets.]*

*[In the main text, after footnote reference 12, delete the sentence 'At the time of writing, IA 2014, s 57 implementing this arrangement is not yet in force' and insert:]*

IA 2014, s 57, implementing this arrangement is now in force.

*[In the main text after footnote reference 18, delete the sentences beginning: 'The consequences of non-compliance . . . ' and 'It is expected that if the Secretary of State . . . ' and insert:]*

The consequences of non-compliance with an investigation or of a finding that the marriage/civil partnership is a 'sham' is not spelt out in the legislation but is included in regulations. If the Secretary of State decides that one or both of the parties have failed to comply with the investigation the registrar cannot proceed to marry the couple.

*[At the end of footnote 13 insert:]*

See also Referral of Proposed Marriages and Civil Partnerships Regulations 2015, SI 2015/123, Part 4.

*[At the end of footnote 14 insert:]*

See also Referral of Proposed Marriages and Civil Partnerships Regulations 2015, SI 2015/123, Part 4.

*[At the end of footnote 15 insert:]*

See also Referral of Proposed Marriages and Civil Partnerships Regulations 2015, SI 2015/123, Part 5.

*[At the end of footnote 17 insert:]*

See also Referral of Proposed Marriages and Civil Partnerships Regulations 2015, SI 2015/123, Part 5.

*[At the end of footnote 19 insert:]*

Referral of Proposed Marriages and Civil Partnerships Regulations 2015, SI 2015/123; the Proposed Marriages and Civil Partnership (meaning of Exempt persons and Notice) Regulations 2015, SI 2015/122, the Registration of Births, Deaths and Marriages and Registration of Civil partnerships (Fees) Amendment Order 2015, SI 2015/117; the Referral and Investigation of Proposed Marriages and Civil Partnerships (Scotland) Order 2015, SI 2015/396); and the Referral and Investigation of Proposed Marriages and Civil Partnerships (Northern Ireland and Miscellaneous Provisions) Order 2015, SI 2015/395. See on implementation of this regulatory scheme, David Bolt, Independent Chief Inspector of Borders and Immigration, 'The implementation of the 2014 "hostile environment" provisions for tackling sham marriage, August to September 2016', Presented to Parliament pursuant to s 50(2) of the UK Borders Act 2007, December 2016.

## ENTRY CLEARANCE FOR PARTNERS AND SPOUSES UNDER THE PART 8 TRANSITIONAL RULES

**11.52** *[At the end of footnote 3 insert:]*

For recent applications of the *Chikwamba* guidance see: *Agyarko and Others, R (on the application of) v The Secretary of State for the Home Department* [2015] EWCA Civ 440, Times, 09 June, [2015] All ER (D) 50 (May); *Dulagan, R (on the application of) v Secretary of State for the Home Department (IJR)* [2016] UKUT 136 (IAC); *R (on the application of ZAT and Others) v Secretary of State for the Home Department (Article 8 ECHR – Dublin Regulation – interface – proportionality) (IJR)* [2016] UKUT 61 (IAC).

## THE PART 8 TRANSITIONAL RULES — LIMITED AND INDEFINITE LEAVE TO ENTER AND REMAIN FOR SPOUSE/PARTNERS

**11.53** *[Delete the sentence 'Spouses or partners could be granted . . . prior to the application).' Retain footnote reference 3 which is now attached to the previous sentence ending with 'prohibition'.]*

*[In the main text, after footnote reference 6 in the sentence beginning 'Rule 284 – in addition to status, language . . . ', after 'language' insert new footnote reference 6a.]*

*[Insert text for new footnote 6a:]*

Strict language requirements apply to partner applicants seeking entry or stay in the UK. Save for those who are nationals of exempt countries (Antigua and Barbuda; Australia; the Bahamas; Barbados; Belize; Canada; Dominica; Grenada; Guyana; Jamaica; New Zealand; St Kitts and Nevis; St Lucia; St Vincent and the Grenadines; Trinidad and Tobago; United States of America) or who have documents showing they have obtained a Bachelors or postgraduate qualifications from a UK or exempt country university and that the qualification was taught or researched in English – the applicant must provide an original English language test certificate in speaking and listening from an English language test provider approved by the Secretary of State for these purposes, which clearly shows the applicant's name and the qualification obtained (which must meet or exceed level A1 of the Common European Framework of Reference). There are further exemptions from this requirement for applicants aged 65 or over at the time they make their application; or applicants who have a physical or mental condition that would prevent them from meeting the requirement; or where there are exceptional compassionate circumstances that would prevent the applicant from meeting the requirement. Note there are 2 key approved level A1 tests from 6 April 2015 for new partner and parent test candidates: Graded Examinations in Spoken English (GESE) offered by Trinity College London (available in the UK); and IELTS Life Skills offered by the IELTS SELT Consortium (available in the UK and overseas). There are also security features in booking, administration and invigilation testing procedures in approved secure test centres. See HC395 Appendix O which reflects the changes to approved tests and providers. Note: In *Ali and Bibi, R (on the application of) v Secretary of State for the Home Department (Rev 1)* [2015] UKSC 68 (18 November 2015), the Court unanimously held that the rule concerning the pre-entry English Language test did not breach Article 8 or Article 14. However, the Court expressed concerns that within certain countries with which many UK citizens have a close connection, there are areas, including rural areas, from which it may not be reasonably practicable for the incoming spouse or partner to obtain the needed tuition without incurring inordinate cost, for example by having to travel long distances repeatedly or to reside for a prolonged period in an urban centre in order to complete the relevant language course. The Court suggested that the appropriate solution would be to recast the Guidance, to cater for those cases and grant an exemption where it is simply impracticable for a person to learn English, or to take the test, in the country of origin, whether because the facilities are non-existent or inaccessible because of the distance and expense involved. The current IDI Guidance Appendix FM 1.21 English Language Requirement – Family Members under Part 8, Appendix FM and Appendix Armed Forces – November 2015, pp 18–21 does not deal with the Court's concerns. The Court envisaged at [60] and [101] that the operation of the Rule, in the light of the present Guidance, is likely to be incompatible with the convention rights of a significant number of sponsors.

**11.55** *[At the end of footnote 7 insert:]*

At the time of writing this Supplement, this guidance was no longer on the UKVI website.

## PART 8 TRANSITIONAL RULES AND VICTIMS OF DOMESTIC VIOLENCE

**11.56** *[In footnote 3 delete 'Jan 2014, p 9' and substitute:]*

May 2015, p 10

*[In footnote 5 delete 'Jan 2014, p 23' and substitute:]*

May 2015, pp 22–27

*[In footnote 6 delete 'Jan 2014, pp 26–27' and substitute:]*

May 2015, pp 29–30

*[In footnote 8 delete 'Jan 2014, p 28' and substitute:]*

May 2015, p 31

*[In footnote 10 delete 'Jan 2014, pp 40–42' and substitute:]*

May 2015, pp 44–47

## PART 8 TRANSITIONAL RULES – UNMARRIED AND SAME SEX PARTNERS

**11.58** *[In the main text, delete the following sentence 'However, where an unmarried partner . . . knowledge of life criteria.' and attach footnote reference 2 to the previous sentence ending in 'satisfied'.]*

## PART 8 TRANSITIONAL RULES – MAINTENANCE AND ACCOMMODATION FOR SPOUSE AND CIVIL PARTNER

**11.61** *[At the end of footnote 9 insert:]*

However, the Immigration Act 2014, sections 38 and 39 allowed for the introduction of an immigration health surcharge for all immigration applicants seeking leave to enter or remain for more than 6 months. The charge applies to all relevant applications for leave to enter or remain made on or after 6 April 2015. The charge is to cover National Health Service (NHS) healthcare in the UK and applicants are entitled to receive the same cover as a permanent UK resident.

### Part 8 Transitional Rules and third-party support

**11.65** *[In the main text after footnote reference 3, in the sentence 'The current IDI states that a partner's prospective earnings do not count . . . ', delete the words 'do not count' and substitute 'can count'.]*

*[In footnote 3 delete '(April 2013)' and substitute '(August 2015)'. Delete 'Section FM 1.7A' and substitute:]*

Section 1, Annex F, p 13

*[In footnote 4 delete '(April 2013)' and substitute '(August 2015)'. Delete Section FM 1.7A and substitute:]*

Section 1, Annex F, p 13

*[In footnote 5 delete '(April 2013)' and substitute '(August 2015)'. Delete 'Section FM 1.9A' and substitute:]*

Section 1, Annex F, p 7

## APPENDIX FM AND FM-SE – THE RULES FOR SPOUSES, PARTNERS AND PARENTS

### Appendix FM rules

**11.69** *[Delete the entire text of footnote 3 and insert:]*

IDI Family Migration, Appendix FM, Section 1.0a Family Life as a partner or parent – five year routes PPs 47–49 and P52 which states:

> 'Where an applicant does not meet the requirements of the Rules under Appendix FM and paragraph 276ADE(1)-DH, the decision maker must go on in every case to consider whether there are exceptional circumstances which warrant a grant of leave outside the Rules on Article 8 grounds . . .

> "Exceptional" does not mean "unusual" or "unique". Whilst all cases are to some extent unique, those unique factors do not generally render them exceptional. For example, a case is not exceptional just because the criteria set out in EX.1 of Appendix FM have been missed by a small margin. Instead, "exceptional" means circumstances in which refusal would result Appendix FM 1.0 Family Life (as a Partner or Parent) and Private Life: 10-Year Routes August 2015 48 in unjustifiably harsh consequences for the individual or their family such that refusal of the application would not be proportionate under Article 8. If the family could all go to the country of return together but they choose to separate, this will not in itself constitute exceptional circumstances. However, the decision maker should not usually make a decision that forces a family to split if there is no criminality to add weight to the public interest in removal. Cases that raise exceptional circumstances that warrant a grant of leave outside the rules are likely to be rare.

> . . .

> Compassionate factors are compelling compassionate reasons on a basis other than family or private life under Article 8, which might justify a grant of leave to remain outside the Immigration Rules, even though the applicant has failed to meet the requirements of the Rules and there are no exceptional circumstances in their case. While exceptional circumstances on the basis of Article 8 must be considered in every case falling for refusal under the Rules, compassionate factors only need to be considered if they are specifically raised by the applicant. Compassionate factors are, broadly speaking, exceptional circumstances, e.g. relating to serious ill health, which might mean that a refusal of leave to remain would result in unjustifiably harsh consequences for the applicant or their family, but not constitute a breach of Article 8. In considering compassionate factors, the decision maker must consider all relevant factors raised by the applicant.'

## RELATIONSHIP REQUIREMENTS — PARTNERS

### Family life with a partner

**11.71** *[At the end of the first paragraph 'the EC1 exception' should read 'the EX1 exception'.]*

*[In sub-para (d), after 'in the UK', add:]*

with refugee leave or with humanitarian protection

*[In footnote 2, replace 'In R (on the application of Bibi) . . . the Court of Appeal held' and accompanying text to the end of the footnote with:]*

In *Ali and Bibi, R (on the application of) v Secretary of State for the Home Department (Rev 1)* [2015] UKSC 68 (18 November 2015) the Court unanimously held that the rule concerning the pre-entry English Language test did not breach Article 8 or Article 14. However, the Court expressed concerns that within certain countries with which many UK citizens have a close connection, there are areas, including rural areas, from which it may not be reasonably practicable for the incoming spouse or partner to obtain the needed tuition without incurring inordinate cost, for example, by having to travel long distances repeatedly or to reside for a prolonged period in an urban centre in order to complete the relevant language course. The Court suggested that the appropriate solution would be to recast the Guidance, to cater for those cases and grant an exemption where it is simply impracticable for a person to learn English, or to take the test, in the country of origin, whether because the facilities are non-existent or inaccessible because of the distance and expense involved. The current IDI Guidance, Appendix FM 1.21 English Language Requirement – Family Members under Part 8, Appendix FM and Appendix Armed Forces – November 2015, pp 18–21 does not deal with the Court's concerns. The Court envisaged at [60] and [101] that the operation of the Rule, in the light of the present Guidance, is likely to be incompatible with the convention rights of a significant number of sponsors.

**11.72** *[At end of first paragraph add:]*

In *Sultana and Others (rules: waiver/further enquiry; discretion)*,[0] President McCloskey held that whether applicants wished to invoke discretionary powers of waiver and further enquiry in the Immigration rules in respect of specified evidence they should do so when making the relevant application, highlighting the specific provision of the Rules invoked and the grounds upon which the exercise of discretion is requested.

*[In the first line of the second paragraph, replace 'the IDI' with:]*

FM 1.7 Financial Requirement Guidance

*[In the third paragraph referencing 'IDI, Annex FM, Section FM 1.7' replace 'July 2014 at p 15' with:]*

May 2016 at p 17

*[In the fourth paragraph, replace '26 pages' with:]*

23 pages

[0]   [2014] UKUT 00540 (IAC).

## Appendix FM – Bereaved partners and victims of domestic violence

**11.73** *[At the end of the paragraph add:]*

In *A v Secretary of State for the Home Department* [2016] CSIH 38, the Inner House of the Court of Session held that excluding the spouses of refugees from the domestic violence concession in DVILR of the Immigration Rules discriminated against such spouse in violation of Article 14.

## Appendix FM – Family life as a parent of a child in the UK

**11.74** *[In the third paragraph beginning 'The applicant parent', delete sub-para (c)(ii) and (iii) and insert:]*

(ii) direct access (in person) to the child,[2] as agreed with the parent or carer with whom the child normally lives or as ordered by a court in the UK; and (iii) the applicant must provide evidence that they are taking, and intend to continue to take, an active role in the child's upbringing;

[2] In order to prove access rights, the Secretary of State's guidance requires applicants to provide either a residence or contact (now a child arrangement) order made by a court in the UK or a sworn affidavit from the UK resident parent, or carer of the child confirming that the applicant parent can have access to the child, describe 'in detail' the arrangements for this and if the contact is supervised any supervisor must endorse the statement: IDI, Appendix FM 1.0, Family Life (as a Partner or Parent): 5-Year Routes (August 2015) pp 35–36. in *JA (meaning of 'access rights') India* [2015] UKUT 00225 (IAC) the Tribunal noted that where the Immigration Rules are silent as to interpretation, it may be necessary to refer to the Children Act 1989 (as amended) and other family legislation in order to construe those parts of the Rules which provide a route to entry clearance or leave to remain as a parent. 'Access' in the latest version of the Immigration Rules means the same as 'contact' in the previous paragraph 284A. Neither term is now used in the Family Court where Child Arrangements Orders are made to regulate '(a) with whom a child is to live, spend time or otherwise have contact; and (b) where a child is to live, spend time or otherwise have contact with any person'. The expression 'access rights' previously in paragraph E-LTRPT.2.4(a)(i) may refer equally to parents who have 'indirect' access to a child by means of letters, telephone calls, etc as well as to those who spend time with a child ('direct' access). A parent may also have 'access rights' where there is no court order at all, for example, where parents agree access arrangements (the 'no order' principle; section 1(5) of the Children Act 1989 (as amended)). Having satisfied the requirements of paragraph E-LTRPT.2.4(a)(i), an appellant must still prove that he/she 'is taking and intend to continue to take an active role in the child's upbringing' (paragraph E-LTRPT.2.4(a)(ii)). Whether he/she will be able to do so will depend upon the evidence rather than the nature of the 'access rights'. However, it is likely to be unusual that a person having only 'indirect' access rights will be able to satisfy this provision. In some cases, Tribunals may need to examine the reasons why the Family Court has ordered 'indirect' rather than 'direct' access. Note the Appendix FM rule is now changed to require the parent to have 'direct access in person' to their child.

## PART 8 AND APPENDIX FM RULES – ADMISSION AND STAY OF CHILDREN

### Children under 18 with UK-settled parent, parents or relative

**11.85** *[N.B. There is no footnote 2 reference or text. Footnotes will be renumbered accordingly.]*

## The sole responsibility rule

**11.87** *[In footnote 2 in the reference to 'Appendix FM 1.0' replace '(July 2014) at page 31' with:]*

(August 2015) at p 33

## The rule that family or other considerations make exclusion undesirable

**11.94–11.98** *[At the end of the paragraph, add:]*

Children or young adults who do not qualify under these rules may succeed in showing that the refusal of entry clearance or leave to remain is in breach of their Article 8 rights.[7]

---

[7] See on the importance of a child or young adult's family life rights: *AT and Another (Article 8 ECHR – Child Refugee – Family Reunification: Eritrea)* [2016] UKUT 227 (IAC) and *AP (India) v The Secretary of State for the Home Department* [2015] EWCA Civ 89 where at [45] Mc Combe LJ stated:

'45. It seems to me that adult children (male or female) who are young students, from most backgrounds, usually continue to form an important part of the family in which they have grown up. They attend their courses and gravitate to their homes during the holidays, and upon graduation, while (as the FTT put it) they seek to "make their own way" in the world. Such a child is very much part of the on-going family unit and, until such a child does fly the nest, his or her belonging to the family is as strong as ever. The proportionality of interference with the family rights of the various family members should receive, I think, careful consideration in individual cases where this type of issue arises.'

## INTER-COUNTRY ADOPTION AND SURROGACY ARRANGEMENTS

### The assessment and approval of adoptive parents

**11.102** *[In the fourth paragraph, second sentence, amend 'There are . . . ' to 'There have been . . . '.]*

*[In the fifth paragraph, 'Rule 309B states' should be amended to read:]*

With respect to applications made before 24 November 2016 (HC 667), Rule 309B states:

*[At the end of the penultimate paragraph ending 'the 2002 Act', insert new paragraphs:]*

The Changes to Immigration Rules HC 667 amended Rule 309B and the new version of this rule applies to all applications made on or after 24 November 2016. The new Rule states:

'309B. Inter-country adoptions may be subject to section 83 of the Adoption and Children Act 2002 or the equivalent legislation in Scotland or Northern Ireland if the adopter's habitual residence is there. Where this is the case, a letter obtained from the Department for Education (England and Wales habitual residents) or the equivalent from the relevant central authority (Scotland or Northern Ireland habitual residents) confirming the issue of a Certificate of Eligibility must be provided with any entry clearance adoption application under paragraphs 310–316C.'

This is a modest improvement. The new version clearly notes that section 83 applies to those adopters who are habitually resident in the British islands but does not make clear that section 83 is engaged only when the child is also habitually resident outside the British islands. The Rule also fails to note that for children adopted abroad whose adoptions are recognised in UK law (and thus will not be brought here for adoption) the section 83 stricture applies only for 12 months after the 'overseas adoption'. It therefore will not apply to applications under para 310 where the recognised adoption is more than 12 months old. It follows that the Rule continues to be inconsistent with section 83 and if strictly applied without reference to the section 83 provision it purports to apply – the new Rule will also result in wrongful refusals.

**11.103** *[In footnote 5 after 'Lord Denning' insert:]*

*N (A Child), Re* [2016] EWHC 3085 (Fam) (1 December 2016),

*[In footnote 14 delete 'The Adoption and Children Act 2002' and replace with:]*

The Children Act 1989

## ENTRY AND STAY FOR ADOPTED CHILDREN

### Legal but unrecognised adoptions

**11.109** *[At the end of footnote 2, add:]*

*N (A Child), Re* [2016] EWHC 3085 (Fam) (1 December 2016). This judgment by the President of the Family Division Sir James Munby is important. It involves the recognition of an Indian customary religious adoption. The Secretary of State intervened to object to the Court's recognition of the Indian adoption and the making of an adoption order. The Court rejected the Home Secretary's submissions that 'where an adoption application relates to a non-British citizen and either (a) the relevant adoption and immigration rules could have been complied with but have not been or (b) an application has been made under the relevant adoption and immigration rules and has failed, then the court should ordinarily refuse leave for and/or dismiss an alternative application such as for recognition or for an adoption order' and that 'something exceptional is likely to be necessary to persuade the court that it is appropriate for all of these detailed rules to be circumvented in this way and the application instead to be determined by the court in accordance with directions it makes'. The President held at [176–177]:

> '176. . . . the key point is that the Secretary of State (or the FTT judge) and the family court are performing different functions; that they are applying different tests arising under different legal regimes; and that the perspective of the family court is a narrow focus on the welfare of the individual child, whereas the perspective of the Secretary of State is different and much wider, having to balance the child's private interest against the public interest in a proper system of immigration control, so that the child's interests whilst a "primary consideration" in the immigration context are not, as in the family court, "paramount": *ZH (Tanzania) v Secretary of State for the Home Department* [2011] UKSC 4, [2011] 2 AC 166.

> 177. Plainly, as I said in *Re A*, paras 66, 71, although the family court "does not act as a policeman for the Secretary of State", it must be alert to the possibility that in cases such as this it is "being used by desperate parents for ulterior purposes". And where the proceedings are being used for some impermissible purpose amounting to

an abuse of process they will be struck out: *S v S* [2008] EWHC 2288 (Fam), [2009] 1 FLR 241. But that is simply not this case.'

## De facto adoptions

**11.111** *[In the last sentence of the third paragraph beginning 'Rule 309B', substitute:]*

Rule 309B, in its pre-November 2016 form,

*[At the end of footnote 4, before the full stop, insert:]*

in its pre-November 2016 form

## Adoptions recognised at common law

**11.112** *[In footnote 1 for 'The recognition procedure is in two stages', substitute:]*

The recognition procedure is often in two stages

*[At the end of footnote 2 before the full stop, insert:]*

, N (A Child), Re [2016] EWHC 3085 (Fam) (1 December 2016)

## Adoptions by relatives

**11.113** *[In the final paragraph, after the first sentence, delete the text 'Providing one of the adoptive parents . . . ' to the end of the paragraph, and insert:]*

The President of the Family Division, in *N (A Child)* made an order recognising the customary religious adoption of N by her maternal aunt. Sir James Munby held:

> 'The reasoning in *Re Valentine's Settlement* indicates the existence of four, and only four, criteria:
> (i)     The adoptive parents must have been domiciled in the foreign country at the time of the foreign adoption.
> (ii)    The child must have been legally adopted in accordance with the requirements of the foreign law.
> (iii)   The foreign adoption must in substance have the same essential characteristics as an English adoption. Did the concept of adoption in the foreign jurisdiction substantially conform with the English concept of a full adoption?
> (iv)    There must be no reason in public policy for refusing recognition.'[3]

[3]   N (A Child), Re [2016] EWHC 3085 (Fam) (1 December 2016).

## Adoptions in the UK conferring an immigration benefit

**11.114** *[After the final paragraph, insert new paragraph:]*

The *Re B* and *ASB* principles have been further confirmed by the Court of Appeal in *S v Bradford Metropolitan District Council and Another*[8] , and by the President of the Family Division in *N (A Child), Re.*[9] In S, Lord Justice Sales, having considered the *Re B* principles and the Adoption and Children Act provisions, held:

> '42. The result of this is that if, after taking account of the practical benefits of adoption for a child throughout his life, it can be seen that it best promotes the child's welfare that he be adopted by a British citizen so as automatically to acquire British citizenship under section 1(5) of the 1981 Act, the court should ordinarily make the adoption order which is sought. Just as for the first of the periods considered by Lord Hoffmann in the context of applying section 6 of the 1976 Act in *Re B*, the state's interest in maintaining effective immigration controls will have very little significance. It will not be appropriate for a court to refuse to make the order as some sort of indirect means of reinforcing immigration controls.'

[8]   [2015] EWCA Civ 951, [2016] 1 WLR 407.
[9]   [2016] EWHC 3085 (Fam) (1 December 2016).

**11.117**  *[In the first paragraph, after footnote reference 2, delete 'The Act does not allow' and substitute:]*

The Act does not make provision for

*[At the end of footnote 3, insert:]*

In *X (A Child)*, the President of the Family Division held that section 54(3) of the Human Fertilisation and Embryology Act 2008 does not have the effect of preventing the court making an order merely because the application is made after the expiration of the six-month period both because Parliament could not have intended the gate to such an important family order should be barred forever if the application for a parental order was delayed and that such result is justified by reference to the Human Rights Convention.

**11.119**  *[In the main text, at the end of the second paragraph, after footnote reference 3, insert:]*

In *Z, Re (Foreign Surrogacy: Allocation of Work: Guidance on Parental Order Reports) (Rev 1)*, [3a], Ms Justice Russell considered a case where the surrogate born children were stranded abroad as the Passport Office had unreasonably delayed making a decision on the passport and citizenship registration applications submitted for the children. Russell J gave guidance in such cases, directing that such cases should be transferred to the Royal Courts of Justice and assigned to one of the specialist judges dealing with surrogacy applications. She directed the Foreign and Commonwealth and Passport Offices to explain the reasons for their delay. The Court's intervention secured a timely decision on the citizenship registration applications and the children were admitted to the UK. Russell J held, at [86]:

> 'It is the view and guidance of this court that the parental order reporter's investigation in any case must include the child being seen with the applicants unless there are compelling and exceptional reasons based on the child's welfare why such observations cannot take place or where there is sufficient independent evidence pertaining to the child's welfare from an alternative source.'

In one such exceptional case, *Re A (Foreign Surrogacy: South Africa)*,[3b] the Court made the parental order for a child who remained in South Africa with the commissioning parents. The parental order reporter did not see the child but Russell J noted (at [87]) that he had the benefit of a comprehensive independent report from a South African social worker on which both he and the court could rely and South Africa's surrogacy arrangements were well regulated, overseen by the South African High Court under their Children Act 2005 and South African surrogacy legislation is framed to ensure that there is no exploitation of the surrogate.

In a similar case, *KB and RJ v RT (Rev 1)*,[3c] where the surrogate born child was stranded in India, Mrs Justice Pauffley invited the Secretary of State to intervene in the case and arranged a preliminary hearing to resolve issues in contention concerning whether the applicant parents could be expected to be granted a parental order. The hearing concerned a number of issues in HFEA 2008, section 54, namely – the intended parents' domicile, the status of their 'out of time' application, whether or not J can be said to have his 'home' with them, whether the surrogate mother's estranged husband is to be treated as J's father for the purposes of section 35 of the 2008 Act and whether the court in its discretion should retrospectively authorise the payments made to the surrogate in so far as they did not constitute reasonable expenses. In the light of the Court's positive findings on these section 54 issues, the Secretary of State reconsidered the child's application for entry clearance and the child was granted entry clearance under the terms of the surrogate child policy. Pauffley J noted in advance of the Secretary of State's reconsideration:

> 'I am though anxious about the potential for unconscionable delay. To that end, I will direct that the application must be restored for further hearing by no later than 1 June 2016. In the event that the immigration impasse persists, I will consider whether in the circumstances I should proceed to make a Parental Order. The effect of so doing would be to circumvent the entry clearance difficulties at one stroke.'

If the applicant parents had been granted a parental order while their child was stranded abroad and refused entry clearance, the child would have acquired British citizenship on the making of the parental order[3d] – and it is in that circumstance that the entry clearance difficulty would have been circumvented.

3a   [2015] EWFC 90, [2016] Fam Law 314, [2015] All ER (D) 230 (Dec)
3b   [2015] EWHC 1756, [2015] Fam Law 1050, [2015] All ER (D) 238 (Jun).
3c   [2016] EWHC 760 (Fam) (07 April 2016).
3d   See on a child's acquisition of British citizenship when their British citizen 'parent' is granted a parental order – Human Fertilisation and Embryology (Parental Orders) Regulations 2010. SI 2010/985. Schedule 4 References in Enactments to be read as References to Parental Orders etc, para 1, reg 5.

### Proposal for British resident child to be adopted abroad

**11.120** *[At the end of footnote 6, insert:]*

; *LA (A Child), Re* [2013] EWHC 578 (Fam) [2013] 2 FLR 541.

## PARENTS, GRANDPARENTS AND OTHER DEPENDENT RELATIVES

### The classes of admissible dependent relatives

**11.122** *[At the end of the paragraph insert new paragraphs:]*

The rule was challenged as ultra vires in *Britcits, R (on the application of) v Secretary of State for the Home Department* .[2] Mr Justice Mitting held that the right to apply for indefinite leave to enter the UK contained in sections E-ECDR 2.1 to 2.5 of Appendix FM to the new Immigration Rules was not ultra vires the rule-making power in the Immigration Act 1971 s 1(4), nor was it arbitrary or unreasonable. While it appeared to have had a much heavier impact on families than was acknowledged when approved by Parliament, the court was bound by the authority of *R (on the application of MM) v Lebanon and the Secretary of State for the Home Department*[3] to determine that it was not incompatible with Article 89 of the ECHR. Mitting J noted that it was 'unsurprising' that dependent relative applicants have succeeded on appeal on Article 8 grounds and 'these conclusions are likely to be replicated in many cases' as the issue under Article 8 is always whether the interference is justified; in other words, proportionate.

Mitting J further noted that in this measure 'adopted mainly for financial reasons, estimates of the outcome have proved hopelessly amiss and do not take into account the potential loss to the UK Exchequer of sponsors who might leave the United Kingdom to avoid the hardship and loss imposed on their family members by the refusal of leave to enter for their elderly parents' nor alternative methods of avoiding a burden on the NHS and social care. At [1.43] he stated:

> 'Free of authority, therefore, I would not have hesitated to consider the lawfulness on the ground of proportionality of the rule and, if I had found it to be disproportionate and so unlawful, to declare it so.'

Mitting J granted leave to appeal and the case is pending appeal in the Court of Appeal.

[2]   [2016] EWHC 956 (Admin) (20 April 2016).
[3]   [2015] 1 WLR 1073.

Chapter 12

# REFUGEES, ASYLUM, HUMANITARIAN PROTECTION AND DISCRETIONARY LEAVE

## THE DEFINITION OF REFUGEE

### 'Owing to a well-founded fear'

*Well-founded*

**12.26** *[At the end of the paragraph, add:]*

There has been controversy over time as to whether the *Ravichandran* principle was strictly applicable where there was a breach of duty by the Secretary of State in assessing an asylum claim. It has now been authoritatively confirmed that the principle is generally applicable, the Supreme Court deciding the issue in the context of tracing duties regarding family members of minor asylum seekers: *MA and AA (Afghanistan) v Secretary of State for the Home Department.*[5]

[5]   [2015] UKSC 40.

### The burden and standard of proof

**12.30** *[At the end of footnote 3, add:]*

*MA (Bangladesh) v Secretary of State for the Home Department* [2016] EWCA Civ 175 holds that the first question is whether a disputed document is at the centre of the request for protection, the second is whether a simple process of inquiry will conclusively resolve its authenticity and reliability, bearing in mind the evidence available as a whole and the principle of anxious scrutiny.

### Refraining from acts exacerbating risk

**12.34** *[At the end of footnote 4, add:]*

*MSM (journalists; political opinion; risk)* [2015] UKUT 413 (IAC).

'Outside the country of nationality . . . residence'

**12.36** *[At the end of footnote 6, , before the full stop, add:]*

; *RM (Sierra Leone) v The Secretary of State for the Home Department* [2015] EWCA Civ 541 and *MW (Nationality; Art 4 QD; duty to substantiate)* [2016] UKUT 453 (IAC).

### Persecution for Convention reasons

*Persecution by non-state actors*

**12.55** *[In the second paragraph of the main text, after footnote reference 7, delete from 'The implementing Regulations . . . ' to the end of the paragraph, and substitute:]*

Protection as envisaged by the Directive could, in principle, embrace a broad array of measures, ranging from an efficacious witness protection model to home security, enhanced police protection, simple warnings and security advice to the person concerned, the grant of a firearms licence, or, as a comprehensive relocation package, which may involve a change of identity, accompanied by appropriate financial and logistical support.[8]

*[Footnote 8 is replaced. Delete footnote 9.]*

[8] *NA and VA (protection: Article 7(2) Qualification Directive) India* [2015] UKUT 432 (IAC).

### Refusal to perform military service

**12.79** *[At the end of the paragraph, insert new paragraphs:]*

In *Shepherd*[10] the CJEU examined the claims of for military service evaders in context of internationally condemned conflicts. International protection should be available for all military personnel, including logistical or support personnel who might be participating only indirectly in the commission of such crimes where it was reasonably likely that tasks expected of them would provide indispensable support to the preparation or execution of those crimes. Conflicts that might give rise to viable claims included those where it was highly likely that such crimes would be committed, not just those where crimes had already eventuated. Relevant considerations would be whether refusal of military service was the only alternative to committing such crimes, and the fact that the state of origin was one that prosecuted international crimes or was engaged in a military intervention engaged upon pursuant to a mandate of the United Nations Security Council, would be relevant considerations.

When assessing whether punishment was disproportionate, it was relevant to have regard to the legitimacy of the state's right to maintain an armed force having regard to the laws and regulations of the country in question and whether the penalties imposed on military service objectors was clearly discriminatory. The risk of a custodial sentence of up to five years did not of itself suggest that the measure was unnecessary in maintaining an armed force; nor could the social ostracism that might follow legitimate prosecution or punishment be regarded as an act of persecution.

[10] *Shepherd v Bundesrepublik Deutschland* C-472/13 (26 February 2015), ECLI:EU:C:2015:117, [2015] QB 799, [2015] 3 WLR 611.

## Exclusion

**12.90** *[At the end of the first sentence, add a new footnote reference 0 and new footnote text:]*

HC 395, para 339AA provides for a person to be excluded in accordance with the Refugee or Person in Need of International Protection (Qualification) Regulations 2006, SI 2006/2525, reg 7 which in turn provides that a person is not a refugee, if he falls within the scope of Article 1D, 1E or 1F of the Convention.

**12.91** *[In footnote 2, after the first sentence, add:]*

In *Gekhang (Interaction of Directives and Rules)* [2016] UKUT 374, the Secretary of State, with the Tribunal's approval, conceded that a Chinese national Tibetan previously resident in India could not be properly excluded from protection under Refugee Convention, Article 1E/Qualification Directive, Article 12(1)(b), because the background evidence does not show that a Tibetan in China has the 'rights and obligations which are attached to the possession of the nationality' of India, or equivalent.

### Exclusion for criminal activity

**12.92** *[In the text, after footnote reference 12, add:]*

Perhaps having been alerted to this omission by this work, the Immigration Rules now make clear that as regards the application of Article 1F as a whole, exclusion applies where the Secretary of State is satisfied that the person has instigated or otherwise participated in the crimes or acts mentioned therein.[12a]

*[In footnote 13, delete: 'para 339A(vii) . . . ' to the end of the sentence and substitute:]*

para 339AA, as inserted by HC 535.

[12a] HC 395, para 339AA, as inserted by HC 535 from 19 November 2015.

**12.93** *[In the text after the close of quotation marks and before the sentence commencing 'Legislation and the authorities . . . ' insert:]*

On remittal, the Tribunal held in *Al-Sirri*[6a] that in every case involving exclusion of protection under Article 1F, the onus of proof is on the Secretary of State, a detailed and individualised examination of the facts is required, there must be clear and credible evidence of the offending conduct, and the overall evaluative judgment involves the application of a standard higher than suspicion or belief.

*[At the end of footnote 8, add:]*

See also Advocate-General Sharpston's opinion in *Commissaire général aux réfugiés et aux apatrides v Mostafa* (Case C-573/14), 31 May 2016.

[6a] *Al-Sirri (Asylum-Exclusion-Article 1F(c))* [2016] UKUT 448. See also *AN (Afghanistan) v Secretary of State for the Home Department* [2015] EWCA Civ 684: the Supreme Court in *Al-Sirri* had found that the UT in *Gurung* [2002] UKIAT 04870, [2003] Imm AR 115, had laid down a standard of proof that was insufficiently demanding on the Secretary of State's case for excluding a person.

**12.94** *[In footnote 1, after the first sentence add:]*

See also *Al – Sirri (Asylum-Exclusion-Article 1F(c))* [2016] UKUT 448.

*[In the main text, after footnote reference 11, insert:]*

At least in the context of Article 1F(a), there is an initial evidential burden on an appellant to raise a ground for excluding criminal responsibility such as duress; though the overall burden remains on the Secretary of State to establish that there are serious reasons for considering that the appellant did not act under duress.[11a]

[11a] *AB (Article 1F(a)-defence-duress) Iran* [2016] UKUT 376.

## War crimes, crimes against humanity and crimes against the purposes and principles of the UN

**12.95** *[In footnote 26, at the end add:]*

In *Commissaire général aux réfugiés et aux apatrides v Mostafa* (Case C-573/14, 31 May 2016) AG Sharpston, in her Opinion, considered it unnecessary to demonstrate that an asylum applicant has previously been convicted of a terrorist offence in order to be refused refugee status on the ground laid down in the Qualification Directive, Art 12(2)(c) (Refugee Convention, Art 1F(c)); but that a previous conviction for being part of a terrorist organisation may not automatically lead to the exclusion from international protection. A final conviction for a terrorist offence by the Courts of a Member State should, however, be given significant weight in the individual assessment of, whether the grounds for exclusion in Art 12(2)(c). She considered that the assessment should include an examination of whether the applicant shared personal responsibility and the implications of the group's activities for international peace and security. In order to invoke grounds for exclusion it is not necessary to establish that the applicant himself has instigated or participated in terrorist acts.

*[In footnote 28, at the end add:]*

See also *Shepherd v Bundesrepublik Deutschland* [2015] QB 799, ECJ, in the context of interpreting Art 9(2)(e) of the Qualification Directive regarding prosecution or punishment for refusal to perform military service in a conflict, where performing military service would include acts that would lead to exclusion under Art 12(2) (or under Refugee Convention, Art 1F) (see **12.50**, fn 13 above): acts that could lead to such exclusion covered all military personnel, including logistical or support personnel; and concerned the situation in which the military service performed would itself include, in a particular conflict, the commission of war crimes, including situations in which the applicant for refugee status would participate only indirectly in the commission of such crimes if it was reasonably likely that, by the performance of his tasks, he would provide indispensable support to the preparation or execution of those crimes.

### Serious non-political crime

**12.96** *[In the text after footnote reference 5, insert:]*

The Court of Appeal held, on appeal in the same case, that to justify exclusion under Article 1F(b), the offence had to be of the stipulated gravity and that the phrase 'serious crime' denoted especially grave offending but that the word 'serious' needed no further qualification.[5a]

[5a] *AH (Algeria) v Secretary of State for the Home Department* [2015] EWCA Civ 1003, [2016] 1 WLR 2071, [2016] 3 All ER 453, [2016] 1 WLR 2071. In particular, the word 'serious' in Article 1F(b) is not to be qualified by the adverb 'particularly'.

**12.97** *[In the text after footnote reference 1, insert:]*

In *AH (Algeria)*[1a] the Court of Appeal firmly rejected the appellant's and the UNHCR's submissions to the effect that in determining whether a person should be excluded under Article 1F(b) the determining body should take account of expiating events occurring after the commission of the offence. The Court considered that the construction favoured by the UNHCR would involve the decision maker exercising a power retained by the Refugee Convention itself, namely judging whether the asylum seeker should obtain protection. The Convention did not authorise an inquiry into the asylum seeker's character, rather, it presumed that to give refugee status to anybody who had committed a crime of the stipulated gravity posed a risk to the systemic integrity and viability of refugee law.

*[At the end of footnote 1, add:]*

See now, *AH (Algeria) v Secretary of State for the Home Department* [2015] EWCA Civ 1003, [2016] 1 WLR 2071 – above.

[1a] *AH (Algeria) v Secretary of State for the Home Department* [2015] EWCA Civ 1003, [2016] 1 WLR 2071: the Court of Appeal agreed with the approach of the majority in the Supreme Court of Canada in *Febles v Canada (Citizenship and Immigration)* [2014] 3 SCR 431.

## EXPULSION OF REFUGEES

### National security

**12.102** *[In the text, after the sentence ending ' . . . see CHAPTER 16 below', insert:]*

The European Court of Justice held in *HT v Land Baden-Württemberg*[1a] that support for a terrorist organisation[1b] may constitute one of the 'compelling reasons of national security or public order' within the meaning of the Qualification Directive, Article 24(1) (relating to the issue or refusal to issue residence permits for refugees), even if the conditions set out in Article 21(2) of the that Directive, which mirror the provisions of Refugee Convention,

Article 33(2) (see above) are not met. In order to be able to revoke, on the basis of the Qualification Directive, Article 24(1), a residence permit granted to a refugee on the ground that that refugee supports such a terrorist organisation, the competent authorities are nevertheless obliged to carry out, under the supervision of the national courts, an individual assessment of the specific facts concerning the actions of both the organisation and the refugee in question.[1c]

[1a]  *HT v Land Baden-Württemberg* (C-373/13) ECLI:EU:C:2015:413, [2016] 1 WLR 109, [2016] 1 CMLR 187.

[1b]  The ECJ was considering a case involving support for the 'Kurdistan Workers' Party' ('the PKK') which at the relevant time was included on the list annexed to the Council Common Position 2001/931/CFSP of 27 December 2001 on the application of specific measures to combat terrorism.

[1c]  The ECJ held however that where a Member State decides to expel a refugee whose residence permit has been revoked, but suspends the implementation of that decision, it is incompatible with the Qualification Directive to deny access to the benefits guaranteed by Chapter VII of the Directive – 'content of international protection' – unless an exception expressly laid down in the Directive applies.


## CONSEQUENCES OF RECOGNITION

### Refugees in the EU

**12.108**  *[In the text, delete the last sentence and footnote 4 and substitute:]*

The presumption in Protocol 24 therefore applies to asylum claims made by nationals of all EU states, and in practice, in the UK such asylum claims will be declared inadmissible and will not be considered unless the applicant satisfies the Secretary of State that there are exceptional circumstances which require the application to be admitted for full consideration and such exceptional circumstances may include in particular those set out in the text above as provided for in Protocol 24.[4]

[4]  HC 395, paras 326E and 326F. Paragraph 326C defines an EU asylum applicant as a national of a Member State of the EU who either makes a request to be recognised a refugee under the Refugee Convention or otherwise makes a request for international protection. Paragraphs 326C to 326F added by HC 535 with effect from 19 November 2015.


## UK PRACTICE ON ASYLUM

### The application

**12.109A**  *[After paragraph 12.109, insert new paragraph:]*

Somewhat belatedly, immigration rules have been introduced so as to specifically provide for an asylum claim, made by a non-EU national, to be declared inadmissible, such that it will not be substantively considered, in accordance with the provisions of the Procedures Directive, Articles 25 to 27.[1] An asylum claim will be declared inadmissible and will not be substantively considered if the Secretary of State determines that one of the following conditions are met: (i) another Member State has granted refugee status; (ii) a country which is not a Member State is considered to be a first country of asylum for the applicant (see further below); (iii) a country which is not a Member State is considered to be a safe third country for the applicant (see further below); (iv) the applicant is allowed to remain in the UK on some other grounds and as a result of this has been granted a status equivalent to the rights and benefits of refugee status; (v) the applicant is allowed to remain in the UK on some other grounds which protect them against *refoulement* pending the outcome of a procedure for determining their status in accordance with (iii) above.[2] Further to (ii), a country is a 'first country of asylum', for a particular applicant, if: the applicant has been recognised in that country as a refugee and they can still avail themselves of that protection; or the applicant otherwise enjoys sufficient protection in that country, including benefiting from the principle of *non-refoulement*; and the applicant will be readmitted to that country in either case.[3] Further to (iii), a country is a 'safe third country' for a particular applicant if: the applicant's life and liberty will not be threatened on account of race, religion, nationality, membership of a particular social group or political opinion in that country; the principle of *non-refoulement* will be respected in that country in accordance with the Refugee Convention; the prohibition of removal, in violation of the right to freedom from torture and cruel, inhuman or degrading treatment as laid down in international law, is respected in that country; the possibility exists to request refugee status and, if found to be a refugee, to receive protection in accordance with the Refugee Convention in that country; there is a sufficient degree of connection between the person seeking asylum and that country on the basis of which it would be reasonable for them to go there; and the applicant will be admitted to that country.[4] In order to determine whether it is reasonable for an individual to be removed to a safe third country (as above), the Secretary of State may have regard to, but is not limited to: any time the applicant has spent in the third country; any relationship with persons in the third country which may include: nationals of the third country; non-citizens who are habitually resident in the third country; family members seeking status in the third country; family lineage, regardless of whether close family are present in the third country; or any cultural or ethnic connections.[5] It will be observed that in respect to both a 'first country of asylum' and a 'safe third country' it is a necessary requirement, for an asylum claim to be declared inadmissible, that the applicant will be admitted to the country in question. It is suggested that the onus of establishing such admissibility to the country lies on the Secretary of State to the balance of probabilities standard.[6] Finally, with respect to inadmissible asylum claims, the Secretary of State shall decline to substantively consider an asylum claim if the applicant is transferable to another country in accordance with the Dublin Regulation.[7]

[1]  HC 395, paras 345A to 345E as inserted by HC 667 with effect from 24 November 2016 and applicable to all asylum claims made on or after that date. For the Procedures Directive, see **12.107** above – it entered into force on 2 January 2006. See *Gekhang (Interaction of Directives and Rules)* [2016] UKUT 374 for the possible impetus for these new rules: the Tribunal held at [33] that the Qualification and Procedures Directives impact on the interpretation of the Refugee Convention and that para 334 of the rules (see **12.109** above) must be read in line with the Directives. For asylum claims made by EU nationals being declared inadmissible, see **12.108** above.

[2]  HC 395, para 345A (see fn 1 above). See Procedures Directive, Art 25.

[3]  HC 395, para 345B (see fn 1 above). See Procedures Directive, Art 26.

[4]  HC 395, para 345C (see fn 1 above). See Procedures Directive, Art 27.

[5]  HC 395, para 345D (see fn 1 above).

[6]  See *Gekhang* (above) at [30] at least with regard to a 'first country of asylum.'

[7]  HC 395, para 345E. For the Dublin Regulation, see **12.107** and **12.157ff**.

*Applications at the port*

**12.112A** *[After paragraph 12.112, insert new paragraph:]*

Note that paragraph **12.112** in the main text is to be read in light of the developments described below.

The Asylum and Immigration Tribunal (Fast Track Procedure Rules 2005[1] were superseded from 20 October 2014 by the Fast Track Rules contained in the Schedule to the Tribunal Procedure Rules 2014.[2] These Fast Track Rules provided for a speeded-up appeals process in cases where the asylum determination had been processed through the DFT (see **12.112**). However, by judgment in a further case brought by Detention Action,[3] Nicol J held, in June 2015, that the 2014 fast track procedure rules were *ultra vires*[4] having incorporated structural unfairness in putting an appellant at a serious procedural disadvantage, in asylum cases, where only the highest standards of fairness would suffice, because of their abbreviated timetable and curtailed case management powers imposed by the respondent to the appeal – being the Secretary of State-without sufficient judicial supervision. In July 2015, the Court of Appeal dismissed the Secretary of State's appeal[5] holding that the DFT system was systemically unfair because the complex and difficult nature of the issues that are often raised, given that instructions had to be obtained from individuals in detention and the varied and numerous tasks that had to be performed in preparing an appeal, could not be adequately addressed by the limited power to adjourn, bearing in mind that it would be difficult to persuade the Tribunal that the appeal cannot be justly determined within the proscribed evidence as there may not have been time to complete the relevant enquiries into the possible corroborative evidence, and bearing in mind the tension between having to argue that the available evidence was insufficient whilst being aware that such evidence would be all that could be used to support the case if an adjournment was refused; in practice, First-tier Tribunal judges would consider the time limits set out in the DFT Rules to be the default position bearing in mind the need to ensure that proceedings are handled quickly and efficiently; the time limits were too tight to permit a fair hearing in a significant number of cases, and the safeguards did not provide a sufficient answer, meaning the system was structurally unfair and unjust. However, following the High Court judgment, in July 2015, the Secretary of State suspended the DFT policy and in its place implemented the Detention Interim Instruction (or DII). In rejecting a challenge to the overall fairness of the DII, Cranston J[6] considered that on its face the DII policy was fundamentally different from the DFT: the DFT policy was to detain asylum seekers on the sole criterion that their claims for asylum could be determined speedily, even when there was no risk of absconding; under the DII, Chapter 55 of the Enforcement Instructions and Guidance (EIG), governs detention and there is a presumption in favour of release unless, for example, there is the specified risk of absconding; the timescales ensure that detention is kept to a minimum; DII makes clear on its face that Home Office caseworkers should consider requests for more time, for example to obtain documents or translations, which means that if the asylum claim really needs more than the 28 days set down in the 'Process map' (in the DII) for valid reasons, this will be granted and the officials managing detention will reconsider whether detention remains appropriate under *Hardial Singh*[7] principles and Chapter 55 of the EIG;

individually and cumulatively the DII mechanisms ensured that asylum-seekers are released from detention where fairness demands, because their own vulnerabilities make detention inappropriate, or where it is apparent that their asylum claim is complex and that it would not be proportionate to detain them during its determination.

1. See **12.112**, fn 5.
2. Tribunal Procedure (First-tier Tribunal) (Immigration and Asylum Chamber) Rules 2014, SI 2014/2604. These rules came into on 20 October 2014: r 1(1). The Schedule of Fast Track Rules has effect in the circumstances and in the manner specified in that Schedule: r 1(3).
3. *R (Detention Action) v First-tier Tribunal (Immigration and Asylum Chamber)*, sub nom *Detention Action v First-tier Tribunal (Immigration and Asylum Chamber; Lord Chancellor v Detention Action* [2015] EWHC 1689 (Admin): affd [2015] EWCA Civ 840; [2015] 1 WLR 5341.
4. *Ultra vires* that is of the enabling provision in Tribunals, Courts and Enforcement Act 2007, s 22.
5. *R (Detention Action) v First-tier Tribunal (Immigration and Asylum Chamber)* [2015] EWCA Civ 840, [2015] 1 WLR 5341, [2015] Imm AR 1349, [2016] INLR 79. The Supreme Court refused the Secretary of State permission to appeal on 3 December 2015.
6. In *R (Hossain and others) v Secretary of State for the Home Department* [2016] EWHC 1331 (Admin). Cranston J did hold that the Secretary of State had failed to have due regard, in all aspects, to her public sector equality duty, under the Equality Act 2010, s 149, in considering asylum claims in detention, when implementing the DII policy. The Court of Appeal, in a detailed judgment, refused the claimants' permission to appeal: see *R (TH (Bangladesh)) v Secretary of State for the Home Department* [2016] EWCA Civ 815.
7. See *R v Governor of Durham Prison, ex p Singh* [1984] 1 WLR 704, [1984] 1 All ER 983, [1983] Imm AR 198.

### Asylum interviews

**12.128** *[At the end of the paragraph, add:]*

The Immigration Rules now provide that the Secretary of State may require an audio recording to be made of the personal interview and where an audio recording is considered necessary for the processing of a claim for asylum, the Secretary of State shall inform the applicant in advance that the interview will be recorded.[16]

16. HC 395, para 339NE, as added by HC 667 from 24 November 2016.

## REMOVAL TO SAFE THIRD COUNTRIES

### Introduction

*Certification of human rights claims under the 2002 Act*

**12.145** *[In the main text after footnote reference 11, delete the sentence: 'There have to date been no successful challenges to certification on refoulement grounds.' and substitute:]*

Until *Ibrahimi* and the recognition that legislative changes in Hungary led to the possibility of chain *refoulement* onwards to unsafe destinations, there had been no successful challenges to certification on *refoulement* grounds.[11a] There is no requirement to seek a declaration of incompatibility of the statutory regime with the Human Rights Act 1998 in *refoulement* challenges: because the prospect of *refoulement* will infringe not only ECHR, Article 3 (which is caught by the statutory provisions deeming a third country to be safe for *refoulement* purposes), but additionally Article 4 of the Charter of Fundamental Rights which is not).[11b]

[11a] *Ibrahimi and Another v The Secretary of State for the Home Department* [2016] EWHC 2049 (Admin).
[11b] *R (on the application of Dudaev v Secretary of State for the Home Department* [2015] EWHC 1641 (Admin), [2015] 3 CMLR 1063, [2015] All ER (D) 151 (Jun).

## Asylum and Immigration (Treatment of Claimants, etc) Act 2004

**12.147** *[At the end of the final paragraph, add:]*

The Immigration Rules make specific provision for treating asylum claims as inadmissible where there are certain degrees of connection with a particular third country (see **12.109A** above).

### Opportunity to claim in the third state

**12.153** *[Paragraph 12.153 and the above heading are both deleted.]*

### Clear evidence of admissibility

**12.154** *[Paragraph 12.154 is deleted.]*

### The Dublin II and Dublin III Regulations

#### General principles

**12.158** *[At the end of footnote 3, add:]*

The temporary admission granted to a person who received a positive 'reasonable grounds' decision as a potential trafficking victim did not qualify as a residence document for the purposes of Dublin 3 such as to make the UK the responsible country for considering the asylum claim: *B, R (on the application of) v The Secretary of State for the Home Department* [2016] EWHC 786 (Admin).

**12.160** *[At the end of the paragraph, add:]*

Vulnerable asylum seekers may be returnable only in the light of specific assurances[21] at least where they are not simply vulnerable *qua* asylum seeker but are peculiarly vulnerable due to some additional characteristic such as being a victim of torture or suffering mental health problems.[22] It cannot be presumed that the same problems that afflict the external borders of the European Union will necessarily affect asylum seekers returning under Dublin arrangements.[23]

*[At the end of footnote 13, delete the final sentence and substitute:]*

Save for those Italian returns involving families with children (*Tarakhel v Switzerland* [2014] ECHR 1185); the UK High Court is one of the Member States which has found Hungary returns incompatible with the ECHR, see *Ibrahimi and Another v The Secretary of State for the Home Department* [2016] EWHC 2049 (Admin).

*[In footnote 19, add:]*

*Pour and Others v The Secretary of State for the Home Department* [2016] EWHC 401 (Admin), [2016] 2 CMLR 1362, [2016] All ER (D) 06 (Mar).

21 NA *(Sudan) v The Secretary of State for the Home Department* [2016] EWCA Civ 1060
22 NA *(Sudan)*, above.
23 NA *(Sudan)*. above.

## THE HUMANITARIAN CLAUSES

**12.163** *[In the final sentence of the paragraph after footnote reference 13, and before the full stop, insert:]*

; however, an especially compelling case under Article 8 would have to be demonstrated to deny removal of the affected persons following a Dublin 2 decision.[14]

14 CK *(Afghanistan) and Others, R (on the application of) v The Secretary of State for the Home Department* [2016] EWCA Civ 166.

## TAKING CHARGE AND TAKING BACK

**12.165** *[At the end of footnote 9, add:]*

Subject to suspensive judicial review proceedings: hence the need to ensure that there is a judicially ordered stay of any proceedings challenging third country removal to avoid the Secretary of State being precluded from return: *R (WK(Eritrea)) v Secretary of State for the Home Department* [2016] EWCA Civ 502.

## ADMINISTRATIVE COOPERATION AND CONCILIATION

**12.171** *[At the end of the paragraph, add:]*

Challenges to the decision making in third countries have so far run aground because of the principle that it is only disagreements as to the *interpretation* rather than the *application* of the Refugee Convention which are amenable to review, and the presumption that EU Member States will comply with international law responsibilities, particularly where they have developed judicial systems of their own.[8]

8 *Dudaev and Others v The Secretary of State for the Home Department* [2015] EWHC 1641 (Admin), [2015] 3 CMLR 1063, [2015] All ER (D) 151 (Jun); *Pour and Others v The Secretary of State for the Home Department* [2016] EWHC 401 (Admin), [2016] 2 CMLR 1362, [2016] All ER (D) 06 (Mar).

## APPLICATION OF DUBLIN REGULATIONS BETWEEN MEMBER STATES AND INDIVIDUALS

**12.172** *[At the end of the paragraph, add:]*

This view was confirmed by decisions of the CJEU finding that disputes as to the responsible Member States applying the Dublin 3 hierarchy, including the question of lapse of responsibility following a person's departure from the European Union, were justiciable at the instance of the asylum seeker.[13]

13  *Ghezelbash* [2016] EUECJ C-63/15, ECLI:EU:C:2016:409, [2016] 1 WLR 3969, [2016] All ER (D) 58 (Jun) and *Karim* [2016] EUECJ C-155/15.

## ASYLUM APPEALS

**12.174** *[In footnote 2, add at the end:]*

The Supreme Court dismissed the appellant's appeal in *MS (Uganda) v Secretary of State for the Home Department* [2016] UKSC 33, [2016] 1 WLR 2615, [2016] 1 WLR 2615, [2016] All ER (D) 128 (Jun), holding that a claimant could only avail himself of the right of appeal in s 83 (pre-amendment) if he had limited leave totalling more than 12 months counting from the day of refusal of his asylum claim, whether his leave was the result of a single grant or more than one.

**12.174A** *[Insert new paragraph:]*

Note that the significant amendments to the appeals regime brought by the Immigration Act 2014 are now fully in force. See for details in CHAPTER 19. In relevant summary, for asylum purposes, a person, 'P', may appeal to the First-tier Tribunal where the Secretary of State has decided to refuse a protection claim made by P[1] or where the Secretary of State has decided to revoke P's protection status.[2] A 'protection claim' means a claim made by a person ('P') that P's removal from the UK: (i) would breach the UK's obligations under the Refugee Convention; or (ii) would breach the UK's obligations in relation to persons eligible for a grant of humanitarian protection.[3] Thus, the Court of Appeal's judgment in *FA (Iraq)*[4] is given effect with full 'equivalence' given to refugee status[5] and humanitarian protection[6] for appeal rights purposes. P's protection claim is refused if the Secretary of State makes one or more of the following decisions: (i) that removal of P from the UK would not breach the UK's obligations under the Refugee Convention; (ii) that removal of P from the UK would not breach the UK's obligations in relation to persons eligible for a grant of humanitarian protection.[7] A person has 'protection status' if the person has been granted leave to enter or remain in the UK as a refugee or as a person eligible for a grant of humanitarian protection.[8] An appeal against the refusal of protection claim must be brought on one or more of the following grounds: (a) that removal of the appellant from the UK would breach the UK's obligations under the Refugee Convention; (b) that removal of the appellant from the UK would breach the UK's obligations in relation to persons eligible for a grant of humanitarian protection; (c) that removal of the appellant from the UK would be unlawful under Human Rights Act 1998, s 6 (public authority not to act contrary to Human Rights Convention).[9] An appeal against revocation of protection status must be brought on one or more of the following grounds: (a) that the decision to revoke the appellant's protection status breaches the UK's obligations under the Refugee Convention; (b) that the decision to revoke the appellant's protection status breaches the UK's obligations in relation to persons eligible for a grant of humanitarian protection.[10]

1   Nationality, Immigration and Asylum Act 2002, s 82(1)(a) as substituted by Immigration Act 2014, s 15(2) from 20 October 2014 (though with transitional provisions, as to which see Chapter 19).
2   NIAA 2002, s 82(1)(c), as substituted.
3   NIAA 2002, s 82(2)(a), as substituted.
4   *FA (Iraq) v Secretary of State for the Home Department* [2010] EWCA Civ 696, [2010] 1 WLR 2545. See **12.174**, fn 5.
5   'Refugee' has the same meaning as in the Refugee Convention: NIAA 2002, s 82(2)(e), as substituted.
6   'Humanitarian protection' is to be construed in accordance with the Immigration Rules: NIAA 2002, s 82(2)(d), as substituted. See especially HC 395, paras 339C–339H.
7   NIAA 2002, s 82(2)(b), as substituted.
8   NIAA 2002, s 82(2)(c), as substituted.
9   NIAA 2002, s 84(1), as substituted by IA 2014, s 15(4) from 20 October 2014: see above.
10   NIAA 2002, s 84(3), as so substituted.

## Credibility

### Fresh claims for asylum

**12.185A** *[Following paragraph 12.185, insert new paragraph:]*

With the coming into full effect of the new appeal provisions as brought in by the Immigration Act 2014 (see **12.174A** above), the Tribunal has held, in a series of decisions, that the effect of the 'fresh claims' provisions in the Immigration Rules still applies with full force.[1] This is because the right of appeal now arises against the Secretary of State's decision to refuse a protection claim (refugee asylum or humanitarian protection: see **12.174A** above) and accordingly, where a person has previously been refused asylum or 'protection' in the UK and then makes further submissions to the Secretary of State, purporting to constitute a fresh protection claim, but the Secretary of State on rejecting the further submissions also refuses to accept that they constitute a fresh protection claim, no right of appeal to the FTT arises as there has not been – according to the Tribunal – a refusal of a protection claim.[2] Instead any remedy is, as previously, by way of judicial review to the Upper Tribunal challenging, on rationality grounds, the decision to refuse to accept that a fresh claim has been made.[3]

1   *See R (Waqar) v Secretary of State for the Home Department (statutory appeals/paragraph 353) IJR* [2015] UKUT 169 (IAC), [2015] All ER (D) 78 (Apr); *R (Robinson) v Secretary of State for the Home Department (paragraph 353-Waqar applied) IJR* [2016] UKUT 133 (IAC); *R (MG) v First-tier Tribunal (Immigration and Asylum Chamber) ('fresh claim'; para 353: no appeal) IJR* [2016] UKUT 283 (IAC); *R (Sharif Hussein) v First-Tier Tribunal (para 353: present scope and effect) IJR* [2016] UKUT 409 (IAC). However, the Secretary of State has to be careful not to give any indication in the refusal notice that she is refusing a protection claim: see *Sheidu (Further submissions; appealable decision)* [2016] UKUT 412 (IAC), per the Tribunal: 'If the SSHD makes a decision that is one of those specified in s 82(1), it carries a right of appeal even if the intention was not to treat the submissions as a fresh claim'.
2   In accordance with HC 395, para 353 and the case law referenced in **12.185**, fns 2 and 7.
3   See further, **12.185**, fns 8 to 19.

Chapter 13

# VICTIMS OF TRAFFICKING IN HUMAN BEINGS

## INTRODUCTION

**13.2** *[Delete the text of footnote 7 and substitute:]*

UKVI Enforcement and Instructions and Guidance, Ch 55b – Adults at risk in immigration detention.

**Trafficking Texts**

**13.3** *[At the end of the bullet list add:]*

- The Modern Slavery Act 2015.
- Human Trafficking and Exploitation (Criminal Justice and Support for Victims) Act (Northern Ireland) 2015.

**13.4** *[In the text after the second sentence add:]*

The Modern Slavery Act received royal assent on 26 March 2015.

## THE DEFINITION OF TRAFFICKING IN HUMAN BEINGS

**Overview of definition**

**13.5** *[Delete the first sentence and substitute:]*

The offences 'Slavery Servitude and forced or compulsory labour' and 'Human Trafficking' are defined in The Modern Slavery Act 2015 in sections 1 and 2. The Home Office's guidance now refers to victims of modern slavery which encompasses victims of human trafficking and victims of slavery, servitude, or forced or compulsory labour.[0]

*[Delete text of footnote 4 and substitute:]*

Home Office: Victims of Modern Slavery – Frontline Staff Guidance, 18 March 2016, p 23; Home Office: Victims of Modern Slavery – Competent Authority Guidance, 21 March 2016, p 29.

[0]  Home Office: Victims of Modern Slavery – Competent Authority Guidance, 21 March 2016, p 1.

### 13.6 *Victims of Trafficking in Human Beings*

**13.6** *[At the end of footnote 1 add:]*

See also the country guidance case *HD (Trafficked women) Nigeria CG* [2016] UKUT 00454 (IAC), at para 164.

**13.7** *[At the end of footnote 6 add:]*

See also *Nguyen (Anti-Trafficking Convention: respondent's duties)* [2015] UKUT 00170 (IAC). The Upper Tribunal found that on a proper reading of ECAT, the Secretary of State's obligations extended to a person who had not been trafficked into the UK but had been the victim of historical trafficking into the country from which he later travelled into the UK.

### The Means

**13.14** *[Delete the following text in the third sentence ' . . . or anger or displeasure from the person considered by the victim to be his or her partner'.]*

*[After the third sentence and footnote reference 3, add:]*

The Competent Authority Guidance includes 'anger or displeasure from the person considered by the victim to be his or her partner' for Modern Slavery, but not for Trafficking. In all other respects the section on coercion is the same.

*[Delete text of footnote 1 and substitute:]*

Home Office: Victims of Modern Slavery – Competent Authority Guidance, 21 March 2016, at p 32.

*[Delete text of footnote 2 and substitute:]*

Home Office: Victims of Modern Slavery – Competent Authority Guidance, 21 March 2016, at p 33.

**13.15** *[Delete text of footnote 2 and substitute:]*

Home Office: Victims of Modern Slavery – Competent Authority Guidance, 21 March 2016, at p 32.

### Victims of slavery, servitude and forced or compulsory labour

*Overview of definition*

**13.19A** *[Insert new heading and paragraph:]*

There is now provision for victims of slavery, servitude and forced or compulsory labour where the victims have not been trafficked in the Competent Authority Guidance.[1]

The definition of Modern Slavery, forced or compulsory labour has two constituent elements:

- *Means* – threat of a penalty, eg threat or use of force, coercion, abduction, fraud, deception, abuse of power or vulnerability.
- *Service* – as a result of the means an individual provides a service for benefit, eg begging, sexual services, manual labour and domestic service.

Servitude is an aggravated form for forced or compulsory labour.

The concept of ownership is what makes slavery distinct. It is a form of servitude with the additional concept of ownership.[2]

The Means:

- *Coercion:*
  The Competent Authority Guidance notes that physical coercion refers to the threat or use of force against a victim or a victim's family members but that it may also entail more subtle measures of control such as withholding travel or immigration documents (as it does for trafficking). The guidance gives the same examples of psychological coercion as it does for trafficking, but in addition includes 'anger or displeasure from the person to considered by the victim to be his or her partner'.[3]
- *Threat of a penalty:*
  The Competent Authority Guidance acknowledges that 'penalty' may go as far as physical violence or restraint, but it can also take subtler forms of a psychological nature, such as threats to denounce victims to the police or immigration authorities when their employment status is illegal. Consent is a factor in forced and compulsory labour, but a victim may have given consent in a situation where they felt they had no viable alternative, in which case they could still be subject to forced or compulsory labour.[4]

[1]  Home Office: Victims of Modern Slavery – Competent Authority Guidance, 21 March 2016.
[2]  Ibid, at p 41
[3]  Ibid, at pp 41–42.
[4]  Ibid, at p 41.

## DETERMINATION OF THE STATUS OF A VICTIM OF TRAFFICKING

### A positive obligation to identify a victim of trafficking

**13.21** *[At the end of footnote 3 add:]*

See also Home Office: Victims of Modern Slavery – Competent Authority Guidance, 21 Marchc2016, p 108. See also *R (on the application of SF) v Secretary of State for the Home Department* [2015] EWHC 2705 (Admin), [2016] 1 WLR 1439, 165 NLJ 7671, paras 133–137. It was held that it would be wrong for the Competent Authority to rely on police investigations in identification because (1) it is not known what the purpose of the police investigations was, given that it could have been whether to decide the Claimant was a victim of trafficking or whether to prosecute the traffickers (2) if it was the former then it would be of no value as the standard of proof would have been very different and (3) if it was the latter then it does not assist in determining whether or not the claimant was a victim of trafficking.

*[Delete text of footnote 4 and substitute:]*

Home Office: Victims of Modern Slavery – Frontline Staff Guidance, 18 March 2016, p 20.

*[Delete text of footnote 5 and substitute:]*

Ibid.

*[Delete text of footnote 6 and substitute:]*

Home Office: Victims of Modern Slavery – Competent Authority Guidance, 21 March 2016, p 105.

**National Referral Mechanism ('NRM')**

*Duty to notify*

**13.22A** *[Insert new heading and paragraph:]*

From 1 November 2015, specified public authorities have a duty to notify the Secretary of State of any individual encountered in England and Wales who they believe is a suspected victim of slavery or human trafficking. The 'duty to notify' provision is set out in section 52 of the Modern Slavery Act 2015 and currently applies to:

(a)  a chief officer of police for a police area;
(b)  the chief constable of the British Transport Police Force;
(c)  the National Crime Agency;
(d)  a county council;
(e)  a county borough council;
(f)  a district council;
(g)  a London borough council;
(h)  the Greater London Authority;
(i)  the Common Council of the City of London;
(j)  the Council of the Isles of Scilly;
(k)  the Gangmasters Licensing Authority.

The government's guidance states that the duty is intended to gather statistics and help build a more comprehensive picture of the nature and scale of modern slavery.[1]

[1]  Home Office: Guidance – Duty to Notify the Home Office of Potential Victim of Modern Slavery, 18 March 2016.

*First Responders*

**13.23** *[In the text after 'These are (currently):' delete the list of First Responders and substitute:]*

• The Home Office;
• Local authorities;
• Health and Social Care Trusts (HSC Trusts);
• Police;
• POPPY Project;
• National Crime Agency (NCA);
• Trafficking Awareness Raising Alliance (TARA);
• Migrant Help;
• Kalayaan;
• Gangmasters Licensing Agency;
• Medaille Trust;

- Salvation Army;
- Barnardo's;
- National Society for the Prevention of Cruelty to Children (NSPCC);
- Unseen UK;
- New Pathways;
- BAWSO;
- Refugee Council.[0]

*[In the text after 'although the Home Office recognise in their own guidance that children . . . ' delete 'may provide very few indicators' including footnote reference 1, and substitute:]*

may find it additionally hard to disclose as the traffickers may have given them inaccurate information about the role of authorities, they may have had bad experiences with corrupt authorities in their home country or during their journey.[1] The guidance also acknowledges that children may not be familiar with the words 'slavery' or 'trafficking' or be able to label their experience as abuse.[1a]

*[Delete text of footnote 2 and substitute:]*

Home Office: Victims of Modern Slavery – Frontline Staff Guidance, 18 March 2016, p 17.

[0]   Home Office: Victims of Modern Slavery – Competent Authority Guidance, 21 March 2016, p 22.
[1]   Ibid, p 17.
[1a]  Ibid, p 39.

**13.24** *[In the text after footnote reference 2, delete the sentence beginning: 'Where a potential victim claims . . . an age assessment is carried out' including footnote reference 3, and substitute:]*

On 15 October 2015, the Government commenced the 'Presumption about Age' provision (section 51) in the Modern Slavery Act 2015 for child victims of trafficking in England and Wales. The provision ensures that in cases where there is uncertainty over the age of a victim, but whom authorities believe to be under 18, that authorities should assume that the victim is under 18, until an age assessment takes place by the local authority.

*[Delete text of footnote 1 and substitute:]*

Home Office: Victims of Modern Slavery – Competent Authority Guidance, 21 March 2016, p 44; Home Office: Victims of Modern Slavery – Frontline Staff Guidance, 18 March 2016, p 39.

*[Delete text of footnote 2 and substitute:]*

Home Office: National Referral Mechanism – Guidance for First Responders, 21 March 2016, p 16

*[Delete footnote 3 and renumber accordingly.]*

### Decision making by the Competent Authority

**13.25** *[Delete text of footnote 1 and substitute:]*

Home Office: Victims of Modern Slavery – Competent Authority Guidance, 21 March 2016, p 19.

*[Delete text of footnote 2 and substitute:]*

Home Office: Victims of Modern Slavery – Competent Authority Guidance, 21 March 2016, pp 53 and 69.

*[Delete text of footnote 3 and substitute:]*

Home Office: Victims of Modern Slavery – Competent Authority Guidance, 21 March 2016, p 54.

*[At end of main text add:]*

If it is a Home Office case the second caseworker or manager must not be directly involved in the case's asylum decision.[4]

[4]    Home Office: Victims of Modern Slavery – Competent Authority Guidance, 21 March 2016, p 54.


### Interviewing

**13.26** *[In the text, delete the first sentence and substitute:]*

The Competent Authority Guidance states that interviews are more likely to be relevant to a conclusive grounds decision rather than a reasonable grounds decision.

*[In the text after footnote reference 1, delete 'For the purpose of making a conclusive grounds decision,' and capitalise 't' in the following word 'the'.]*

*[Delete the text of footnote 1 and substitute:]*

Home Office: Victims of Modern Slavery – Competent Authority Guidance, 21 March 2016, p 66.

*[Delete the text of footnote 2 and substitute:]*

Ibid, pp 66 and 67.

*[Delete the text of footnote 3 and substitute:]*

Ibid, p 68.


### Credibility

**13.27** *[Delete the text of footnote 1 and substitute:]*

Home Office: Victims of Modern Slavery – Competent Authority Guidance, 21 March 2016, pp 98 and 99.

*[Delete the text of footnote 4 and substitute:]*

Home Office: Victims of Modern Slavery – Frontline Staff Guidance, 18 March 2016, p 20.

*[Delete the text of footnote 5 and substitute:]*

Home Office: Victims of Modern Slavery – Competent Authority Guidance, 21 March 2016, p 99.

## Reasonable grounds decision

**13.28** *[In the text, before the full stop and footnote reference 3, add:]*

and whether a reasonable person having regard to the information in the mind of the decision maker, would think there are reasonable grounds to believe the individual had been a victim of human trafficking or modern slavery

*[In current text after footnote 3 delete 'The decision maker is required 'to make every effort to secure all relevant information that could prove useful in establishing if there are reasonable grounds' including from the police, the local authority and support provider' and substitute:]*

The Competent Authority Guidance no longer requires the decision maker to make every effort to secure all relevant information that could prove useful in establishing if there are reasonable grounds. Instead they must make a positive decision as soon as they have sufficient information.

*[At end of main text before the full stop and footnote reference 5 add:]*

and make reasonable enquiries in a collaborative manner with agencies involved in the case

*[Delete the text of footnote 1 and substitute:]*

Home Office: Victims of Modern Slavery – Competent Authority Guidance, 21 March 2016.

*[Delete the text of footnote 2 and substitute:]*

Ibid, pp 20 and 50.

*[Delete the text of footnote 3 and substitute:]*

Ibid, pp 50 and 51.

*[Delete the text of footnote 4 and substitute:]*

Ibid, 21 March 2016, p 52.

*[Delete the text of footnote 5 and substitute:]*

Ibid, 21 March 2016, p 52.

**13.29** *[In the main text, delete the second sentence including footnote reference 1 and substitute:]*

The Secretary of State has a discretion to extend this period where the circumstances warrant it and will consider representations for more time. Where it is extended the Competent Authority, first responder and support provider must keep the extension under review. The Competent Authority must review the extension every 28 calendar days and/or when there is a change in the victim's circumstances.[1]

*[Delete the text of footnote 3 and substitute:]*

Home Office: Victims of Modern Slavery – Competent Authority Guidance,

21 March 2016, p 57.

1   Home Office: Victims of Modern Slavery – Competent Authority Guidance, 21 March 2016, pp 93 and 94.

## Conclusive grounds decision

**13.30** *[In the text, delete the first sentence and footnote 1 and substitute:]*

If a positive reasonable grounds decision has been made a further 'conclusive grounds' decision has to be made. The expectation is that it should be made as soon as possible following day 45 of the recovery and reflection period.[1]

*[Delete the last sentence in the text and substitute:]*

In November 2014, the government published a review of the NRM, which concluded that changes should be made.[5]

*[Delete the text of footnote 2 and substitute:]*

Home Office: Victims of Modern Slavery – Competent Authority Guidance, 21 March 2016, p 65.

*[Delete the text of footnote 3 and substitute:]*

Ibid.

*[Insert new footnotes in correct sequential order.]*

1   Home Office: Victims of Modern Slavery – Competent Authority Guidance 21 March 2016, p 64.
5   https://www.gov.uk/government/uploads/system/uploads/attachment_data/file/467434/Revie w_of_the_National_Referral_Mechanism_for_victims_of_human_trafficking.pdf

**13.31** *[Delete the text of footnote 1 and substitute:]*

Home Office: Victims of Modern Slavery – Competent Authority Guidance, 21 March 2016, p 74.

*[Delete the last sentence of the text of footnote 3 and substitute:]*

Home Office: Victims of Modern Slavery – Competent Authority Guidance, 21 March 2016, p 122.

## THE REFUGEE CONVENTION AND TRAFFICKING VICTIMS

## Persecution

**13.34** *[Delete the text of footnote 2 and substitute:]*

See, for example, *TD and AD (Trafficked women)* CG [2016] UKUT 00092 (IAC), para 119(h) and *HD (Trafficked women) Nigeria* CG [2016] UKUT 00454 (IAC), para 190.

*[At the end of footnote 6 before the full stop, add:]*

and *TD and AD (Trafficked women)* CG [2016] UKUT 00092 (IAC)

## Sufficiency of protection

**13.36** *[At end of main text add:]*

Where the state is making significant efforts to combat trafficking it does not necessarily mean that there is a sufficiency of protection if those measures are not having an effect on the numbers of victims being trafficked.[6]

[6]    *HD (Trafficked women) Nigeria CG* [2016] UKUT 00454 (IAC), para 141.

## TRAFFICKING AND THE EUROPEAN CONVENTION ON HUMAN RIGHTS

### Article 4 of the European Convention on Human Rights

*Slavery*

**13.40** *[At the end of main text add:]*

The Competent Authority Guidance, refers to slavery in the following terms:

> '1926 Slavery Convention defines slavery as "the status or condition of a person over whom any or all of the powers attaching to the right of ownership are exercised".'
>
> This concept of ownership is what makes slavery distinct – for example a situation where an individual was being controlled by another would not meet this threshold, unless there was clear evidence the person was being used as a commodity. It is a form of servitude with the additional concept of ownership.'[5]

[5]    Home Office: Victims of Modern Slavery – Competent Authority Guidance, 21 March 2016, p 40.

*Servitude*

**13.41** *[At end of main text add:]*

The Competent Authority Guidance refers to slavery in the following terms:

> '"Servitude"' means an obligation to provide a service that is imposed by the use of coercion.
>
> Servitude is an "aggravated" form of forced or compulsory labour. The fundamental distinguishing feature between servitude and forced or compulsory labour is in the victim feeling that their condition is permanent and that the situation is unlikely to change.'[11]

[11]    Home Office: Victims of Modern Slavery – Competent Authority Guidance, 21 March 2016, p 40.

*Forced or compulsory labour*

**13.42** *[At end of main text add:]*

The Competent Authority Guidance refers to slavery in the following terms:

'UN Convention No. 29 concerning forced or compulsory labour defines "forced or compulsory labour" as "all work or service which is exacted from any person under the menace of any penalty and for which the said person has not offered himself voluntarily".

Labour is the provision of any service, not just manual labour. "Penalty" may go as far as physical violence or restraint, but it can also take subtler forms of a psychological nature, such as threats to denounce victims to the police or immigration authorities when their employment status is illegal. Consent is a factor in forced and compulsory labour, but a victim may have given consent in a situation where they felt they had no viable alternative, in which case they could still be subject to forced or compulsory labour.'

For a person to be a victim of forced or compulsory labour there must have been two basic components:

(a)    means; and
(b)    service.

### Positive Obligations under Article 4 of the ECHR

**13.45** *[In the text after footnote reference 6 add:]*

The Immigration Rules have now been amended to address this.[6a]

*[At end of main text add:]*

In *MS (Trafficking–Tribunal's Powers–Art 4 ECHR) Pakistan*,[13] the Upper Tribunal confirmed that Article 4 of ECHR is justiciable before the tribunal as it is one of the Convention rights and that the procedural obligations inherent in Article 4 of ECHR are linked to those enshrined in the Trafficking Convention, Articles 10(2) and 18 in particular (see paras 45 and 41).

In *Secretary of State for the Home Department v Minh*,[14] the Court of Appeal held that a failure by the Competent Authority to follow her policy guidance was not capable of amounting to a breach of Article 4 of ECHR because the application of the guidance was not the mechanism by which the UK satisfied those obligations. The Court highlighted that the procedural obligation under Article 4 was identified in *Rantsev v Cyprus* and in *CN v United Kingdom*[15] as a duty arising where there was a 'credible suspicion' of trafficking and that states were not obliged to investigate matters outside their own jurisdiction. Accordingly, the Court found that the focus of Article 4 was on the investigation of trafficking and the identification of those responsible, and on the provision of immediate relief for those who were suffering. The Court held that ECAT was wider in scope because it was concerned, not only with immediate relief for victims, but also with their medium-term treatment for immigration purposes, and with the criminalisation and prosecution of behaviour associated with trafficking. The Court concluded that as the Competent Authority's guidance was not the mechanism by which the UK satisfied procedural obligations under Article 4 of ECHR and as such a failure to follow that guidance could not result in a breach (See paras 29–31 and 33–34).

Both parties in *MS* have applied for and been granted permission to appeal to the Court of Appeal. The Secretary of State is challenging the Tribunal's jurisdiction concerning the Trafficking Convention and the State's non-immigration related duties under Article 4 of ECHR. The Court of Appeal will therefore be required to revisit this issue.

*[At end of the text of footnote 2 add:]*

The Modern Slavery Act now provides for this.

*[Insert new footnotes in correct sequential order.]*

6a Statement of Changes HC877.
13 [2016] UKUT 226 (IAC).
14 [2016] EWCA Civ 565.
15 Application No 4239/08, [2012] NLJR 1465, 34 BHRC 1, [2012] ECHR 4239/08.,

## DEPORTATION OF VICTIMS AND POTENTIAL VICTIMS OF TRAFFICKING

**13.47** *[At end of the text of footnote 1 add:]*

The Modern Slavery Act introduced a new statutory defence for victims of Modern Slavery (including trafficking). See CPS guidance on human trafficking and smuggling at http://www.cps.gov.uk/legal/h_to_k/human_trafficking_and_smuggling/.

## DETENTION OF TRAFFICKING VICTIMS

**13.50** *[Delete text of footnote 1 and substitute:]*

Home Office: Victims of Modern Slavery – Competent Authority Guidance, 21 March 2016, p 118.

## CHALLENGING DECISIONS RELATED TO TRAFFICKING

**13.51** *[At the end of the main text add:]*

In *MS (Trafficking–Tribunal's Powers–Art 4 ECHR) Pakistan*,[8] the Upper Tribunal found that tribunals must take into account, where relevant, a decision of the Competent Authority that an appellant had been a victim of trafficking, but that they had jurisdiction to review those decisions and, if perverse or reached in breach of the Competent Authority guidance, come to their own conclusion. The Upper Tribunal acknowledged that in some cases the tribunal may be better equipped to make those findings and remarked that they had had the benefit of hearing live evidence from the appellant.

8 [2016] UKUT 226 (IAC).

Chapter 14
# WELFARE PROVISION FOR MIGRANTS AND ASYLUM SEEKERS

## MIGRANTS FROM NON-EEA COUNTRIES

### The public funds condition

**14.8** *[At the end of the paragraph add:]*

On 6 April 2016, the Home Office amended the Immigration Rules by adding a 'discretionary welfare support payment' administered by a local authority to the list of public funds (para 6(i)) which migrants with no recourse to public funds are prohibited from claiming. Local welfare assistance schemes have replaced Crisis Loans and Community Care Grants paid under the discretionary Social Fund, which were abolished in April 2013 by the Welfare Reform Act 2012.

### Persons subject to immigration control (PSIC)

*Exemption based on 'living with a family member of an EEA national'*

**14.17** *[At the end of the paragraph add:]*

*MS v Secretary of State for Work and Pensions (DLA) (DLA, AA, MA: general: other)*[6] concerned a claim for Disability Living Allowance by a child who was an Israeli national whose mother and appointee had dual Israeli/British nationality. The claim for DLA was refused because the claimant did not meet the condition of being ordinarily resident in Great Britain (see **14.78**). In the course of the judgment, the Judge said that the claimant did not fall within the exemption of 'living with a family member of an EEA national' contained in reg 2(1) and Part II of the Schedule to the Social Security (Immigration and Asylum) Consequential Amendments Regulations 2000.[7] The Judge said that if he had needed to decide the issue, he would have preferred the purposive approach adopted in CDLA/708/2007, which held that the exemption only applied if the EEA national was exercising an EU right (which excluded most UK citizens), to the literal approach adopted by the Northern Ireland Commissioner in *JFP v Department for Social Development (DLA)*,[8] which concluded that under the 2002 Regulations, EEA nationals included UK nationals.

In April 2016, the Home Office revised its official guidance (Modernised Guidance Public Funds) to clarify that a parent who has leave to remain with a no recourse to public funds condition may claim Child Benefit for a British Citizen child. Note that this does not apply to parents who have an EU-derived right to reside as the primary carer of a British Citizen child (*Zambrano* carer) because they are excluded from claiming Child Benefit by the regulations governing eligibility to that benefit: see **14.73**.

6   [2016] UKUT 42 (AAC) (25 January 2016).
7   SI 2000/636.
8   [2012] NICom 267.

## Couples with a mixed immigration status

**14.20** *[At the end of footnote 2 add:]*

The Child Benefit rules provide that someone can be treated as 'responsible for a child' if he or she contributes towards the cost of providing for them 'at a weekly rate which is not less than the weekly rate of child benefit payable in respect of the child for that week': section 143(1)(b) of Social Security Contributions and Benefits Act 1992. *RK v Revenue and Customs (CHB) (Benefits for children: child benefit)* [2015] UKUT 357 (AAC) (24 June 2015) reported as [2016] AACR 4 held that a Polish national working in the UK met this test, notwithstanding the fact that the payments were being made by the claimant on a monthly basis, rather than weekly. The Upper Tribunal held that the contribution did not need to be made weekly so long as the contribution by the claimant was made at a rate that was not less than the applicable rate of Child Benefit. Note that where claims for family benefits are being made under the EU coordination rules then, as a general rule, a step-child cannot be included in the claim. The Upper Tribunal has ruled that a claim for ChB made by a Polish national working in the UK in respect of two children who were described as his niece and nephew and who lived in Poland must be rejected because the children did not come within the definition of a 'member of the family' in Article 1(i)(2) of Regulation (EC) 883/2004 (*KT v HMRC* [2013] UKUT 151 (AAC) (15 March 2013)).

## EEA NATIONALS

### The right to reside requirement

*The United Kingdom's withdrawal from the European Union–Brexit*

**14.32A** *[After paragraph 14.32, Insert new heading and paragraph:]*

A referendum held on 23 June 2016 resulted in a decision to leave the European Union based on 51.89% of the total votes. It remains unclear what kind of future relationship the UK will have with the EU and EEA/Swiss States after the UK leaves the EU. A Briefing Paper published by the House of Commons Library in August 2016 gave the following summary of the possible impact of Brexit on social security:

'Entitlement to welfare benefits for people moving between EU Member States is closely linked to free movement rights. Brexit could have significant implications both for EU/EEA nationals living in or wishing to move to the UK, and for UK expatriates elsewhere in the EU/EEA, and those considering moving abroad.

If Brexit means the end of free movement rights, the UK will be able to impose restrictions on access to many social security benefits via immigration law. Entitlement to contributory social security benefits could be limited by limiting access to employment. It will also be possible to restrict the ability of EU nationals to apply for social housing.

The UK could seek to secure bilateral social security agreements on reciprocal rights with individual EU/EEA states, but negotiations could be difficult and protracted. Alternatively, the UK could seek a single agreement with the EU/EEA as a whole. Such an arrangement could, however, end up closely resembling existing provisions in EU law. Whatever the solution, decisions would have to be made on how to protect social security rights already accrued at the point of withdrawal from the EU.'[1]

[1] 'Brexit: impact across policy areas – Briefing Paper Number 07213', House of Commons Library, Edited by Vaughne Miller, 26 August 2016, pp 14–15.

## The Rights of Residence Directive

**14.34** *[At the end of the paragraph add:]*

The Immigration (European Economic Area) Regulations 2006, SI 2006/1003 have been revoked and are to be replaced with the Immigration (European Economic Area) Regulations 2016, SI 2016/1052, with effect from 1 February 2017 with the exemption of regulation 9, which came into effect on 25 November 2016, (see regs 1, 44 and Sch 5), which deals with the circumstances in which a British citizen can be treated as an EEA national (see **14.52**). Schedule 7 contains a table of equivalences outlining the way in which the provisions of the 2006 Regulations which have changed position correspond to the provisions of the 2016 Regulations.

## EXTENDED RIGHT OF RESIDENCE

### Jobseekers

*New measures aimed at restricting EEA migrants' access to out-of-work benefits*

**14.37** *[At the end of the paragraph, add:]*

The Upper Tribunal has considered the 2014 amendments to reg 6 of the EEA Regulations 2006 applicable to EEA jobseekers in *Secretary of State for Work and Pensions v MB (JSA) and Others (European Union law: free movement)*;[8] see **14.39** and **14.57**.

[8] [2016] UKUT 372 (AAC) (05 August 2016).

THE REQUIREMENT FOR 'COMPELLING EVIDENCE'

**14.39A** *[After paragraph 14.39 insert new heading and new paragraph:]*

In *KS v Secretary of State for Work and Pensions (Jobseekers allowance: other)*[1] the Upper Tribunal considered the qualifying conditions for jobseekers in reg 6 of the Immigration (European Economic Area) Regulations 2006, as amended by SI 2013/3032, which provides that an EEA national may not retain the status of a worker for longer than six months unless he or she provides 'compelling evidence' that they have 'a genuine chance of being engaged' (reg 6(7)). The Upper Tribunal rejected a submission that the 'compelling evidence' requirement imposed a higher standard of proof where the EEA jobseeker had been unsuccessful in obtaining work in the last six months. The judge said that this did not accord with Scottish or English law which provided that in civil proceedings there was a requirement for evidence to be established on a balance of probabilities.

In *Secretary of State for Work and Pensions v MB (JSA) and Others (European Union law: free movement)*[2] the Upper Tribunal held that given the ruling in *R v Immigration Appeal Tribunal, ex p Antonissen*,[3] a national court or tribunal is required to take a period of six months (or longer) of unsuccessful jobseeking into account when assessing whether a person has a genuine chance of finding work. The Upper Tribunal gave the following guidance on the correct construction to be given to reg 6 of the Immigration (European Economic Area) Regulations 2006 following the 2014 amendments and the application of the Genuine Prospect of Work ('GPOW') test to EEA jobseekers:

- 'Genuine' is an everyday word which implies that the chance is founded on something objective, as opposed to illusory or speculative.
- The 'genuine chance' has to be of something coming to fruition within a reasonable period of time. What is a 'reasonable period of time' is to be determined in the light of *Antonissen*, which held that a period of six months was sufficient to enable jobseekers to 'apprise themselves . . . of offers of employment corresponding to their occupational qualifications and to take, where appropriate, the necessary steps in order to be engaged'.
- The test is to be decided on the civil standard of proof. That is proof that the fact more probably occurred than not and common sense, not law, requires that in deciding the question, regard should be given to inherent probabilities.[4]
- The reference to 'compelling evidence' in reg 6(7) does not raise the bar any higher than that required under the *Antonissen* test:

  'A right under Antonissen will subsist as long as the conditions for it are met. It applies therefore from the start of jobseeking, even if a Member State is free to decide not to check for an initial period whether the conditions attaching to the right are fulfilled, as appears to be the Secretary of State's position. Applying the concept of the "reasonable period" after increasing periods of unsuccessful jobseeking may mean that the conditions become ever harder to satisfy, but there is no indication in anything I have seen that under EU law there is an absolute time limit on the right. Indeed, the decision in Antonissen itself indicates the opposite. It may be that a Member State wishes to provide for a review at frequent intervals after an initial period in order to satisfy itself that the Antonissen conditions continue to be met, but that must be distinguished from only granting the right for a set period of time. There is nothing to stop a Member State conducting a review after 6 months but nor is there anything in EU law which permits any kind of step change in what has to be proved at that (or any other) point. If Ms Smyth's [counsel for the DWP] submission that "It is for Member States to prescribe the temporal limitation, ie the permitted period of job seeking" goes beyond this, it is inconsistent with Antonissen.'

- Compliance with the domestic law requirements for Jobseeker's Allowance (ie following a jobseeker's agreement) cannot be relied upon to satisfy the GPOW test as EEA nationals face an additional hurdle as jobseekers compared to UK citizens ((*R(IS) 8/08* considered).
- In short, the GPOW test required the following enquiry of a claimant:

'Given that you have had six months of unsuccessful jobseeking, a period appearing to the Court of Justice to be in principle not insufficient to take the steps which Article 45 requires you to be allowed to take, on what basis do you say you nevertheless have a genuine chance of being engaged?' (para 51).

The official guidance, which was described as too restrictive in *Secretary of State for Work and Pensions v MB*, has been updated, as from 27 October 2016, see DMG, Vol 2, Ch 7, Part 3. This gives the following guidance on what type of evidence could count for the GPOW test (at paragraph 073100):

'Examples of genuine evidence which may be taken into account in assessing whether, on the balance of probability, there is a genuine chance of being engaged may include:

1    length of the period of unsuccessfully seeking work;
2    a definite job offer of genuine and effective work;
3    awaiting the outcome of a job interview;
4    completion of a training course which offers real prospects of success in obtaining genuine and effective work;
5    previous genuine and effective work history;
6    acquisition of qualifications which enhances the claimant's employment prospects;
7    relocation to an area where there are improved chances in obtaining genuine and effective work;
8    steps taken by the claimant to improve their prospects of being offered genuine and effective work within a reasonable period.'

These examples are not exhaustive. It is open to the DM to obtain other evidence which is considered to be 'compelling'.

1    [2016] UKUT 269 (AAC) (20 May 2016).
2    [2016] UKUT 372 (AAC) (05 August 2016).
3    C-292/89, [1989] 2 CMLR 957.
4    *Re B (Children)* [2008] UKHL 35, [2009] AC 11, [2008] 4 All ER 1.

Exclusion of certain EEA Jobseekers from Housing Benefit

**14.40** *[At the end of the paragraph, add:]*

In *EP v Secretary of State for Work and Pensions (JSA) (European Union law: free movement)*[5] the Upper Tribunal said that notwithstanding the amendments made to the Housing Benefit regulations by SI 2013/539, a decision on the right to reside for the purposes of a Jobseeker's Allowance claim by the DWP is *not* determinative for Housing Benefit purposes made by the local authority

> 'The parties are not the same (DWP in one, local authority in the other). The statutory provisions applicable are (in the case of DWP benefits) section 17 of the Social Security Act 1998 and (in the case of housing benefit) para 11 "of schedule 7 of the Child Support, Pensions and Social Security Act 2000. Neither has the effect of fixing a local authority with a decision already taken on the point by the DWP or prevents a claimant from arguing the point afresh" [at 24].'

> 'Whether a claimant has a right to reside other than as a jobseeker is, like most other decisions on housing benefit, a decision for the "relevant authority" ie, in this context, the local authority . . . It may well wish to seek to explore the evidence on which the DWP decided what it did, but the DWP's view, or indeed that of a tribunal on appeal from the DWP, is not conclusive [at 25].'

5    [2016] UKUT 445 (AAC) (11 October 2016).

*Workers*

### Self-Employed Persons

**14.46** *[At the end of the paragraph, add:]*

In *Revenue and Customs v IT (CTC) (European Union law: workers)*[9] concerned a Romanian national who was selling the *Big Issue* to support himself, his wife and their seven children. He claimed, and was awarded, Working Tax and Child Tax Credits in May 2009. A decision was subsequently made to terminate the award on the basis that the claimant's self-employed work was not 'genuine and effective'. That decision was upheld by the Upper Tribunal having regard to the following findings of fact:[10]

> 'The basis for self-employed work as a *Big Issue* seller was that the claimant paid £1 for each copy of the magazine he sold at £2 a magazine. He thus made a gross profit of £1 per magazine sold. For the period for which invoices had been supplied, the gross profit was £1066. Once travel expenses are deducted this become a net profit of £890, which translates to £37.83 per week or £2.36 per hour. This . . . was the sole work during this period and was being done to support the claimant, his wife and their seven children.'

The outcome in this case can be contrasted with Bristol *City Council v FV (HB)*,[11] which also involved a *Big Issue* vendor, where it was held that the claimant was in genuine and effective self-employment, based on a different set of facts.

In *Secretary of State for Work and Pensions v HH (SPC) (European Union law: Council regulations 1408/71/EEC and (EC) 883/2004)*,[12] the Upper Tribunal upheld a decision to refuse to award State Pension Credit to a retired claimant who argued that he had a right to reside based on the self-employed activity involved in writing a book. In reaching this decision, the Upper Tribunal had regard to a number of factors including: the substantial sum the claimant had paid in order to publish the book; the fact that between 1998 and 2003 he received no money back from the first edition; that between 2008 and 2014 he was working on the second edition without a contract in place; that even if the second edition were to sell as many copies as had been produced, this would only result in a return of £3,050, which the judge said was 'minimal recompense' for working 14 hours a week between 2008 and 2010 and that minimal efforts were being made to promote the book.

⁹ [2016] UKUT 252 (AAC) (24 May 2016).
¹⁰ Ibid, at para 27.
¹¹ [2011] UKUT 494 (AAC).
¹² [2015] UKUT 583 (AAC) (22 October 2015).

SELF-SUFFICIENT PERSONS

**14.47** *[At the end of the paragraph, add:]*

In Case C-218/14 *Singh and Others v Minister for Justice and Equality*¹⁰ the CJEU held that an EU citizen could rely on the earnings of a non-EEA national spouse/civil partner when showing that they had sufficient resources for themselves under Article 7(1)(b) of Directive 2004/38/EC.

The Immigration (European Economic Area) Regulations 2006, SI 2006/1003 have been revoked and replaced with the Immigration (European Economic Area) Regulations 2016, SI 2016/1052, with effect from 1 February 2017.

¹⁰ [2016] CMLR 12, [2015] 3 WLR 1311 (16 July 2015).

WHETHER A EUROPEAN HEALTH INSURANCE CARD CAN BE RELIED UPON AS COMPREHENSIVE SICKNESS INSURANCE COVER

**14.48A** *[After paragraph 14.48 insert new heading and paragraph:]*

In *Secretary of State for Work and Pensions v GS (PC) (European Union law: free movement)*¹ the Upper Tribunal considered a claim for State Pension Credit made by an Italian national, who had lived and worked in the UK between 1970 and 1984, but left when he separated from his wife. He then worked in the catering trade in Spain, Switzerland and Italy. He returned to the UK in or around January 2004 with savings of around £20,000. He hoped to set up a coffee shop but it did not come to fruition. He had a European Health Insurance Card ('EHIC') issued by the Italian authorities. When he turned 65 in October 2012 he claimed State Pension Credit; on the relevant form he indicated he planned to stay in the UK 'indefinitely'. His claim was rejected but a First-tier Tribunal allowed his appeal holding that he had acquired a right of permanent residence based on the period of 4 years 10 months from January 2004 onwards of residing in the UK as a self-sufficient person and a further two months of residing as a jobseeker when he had claimed Jobseeker's Allowance. The Tribunal said that the claimant could rely on the possession of the EHIC to meet the requirement for comprehensive sickness insurance cover ('CSIC') under Article 7 of the Citizenship Directive 2004/38/EC.

The Upper Tribunal said at the outset that it was bound by *Ahmad v Secretary of State for the Home Department*² to hold that the ability to access free NHS treatment did not of itself amount to CSIC. The question the Upper Tribunal was considering in this appeal was whether holding an EHIC medical card could make a difference. After referring to *I v Health Service Executive*

(C-255/130) the judge noted that if the claimant's residence in the UK only amounted to a 'stay' then it would be possible for the UK government to seek reimbursement of NHS treatment costs from Italy and consequently the claimant would be accepted as having CSIC. If, however, the claimant was 'habitually resident' in the UK, then the UK would be the competent state for paying the medical costs and the EHIC medical card would have no effect. The Upper Tribunal concluded that in the instant case the evidence showed that the claimant was habitually resident in the UK and he could not rely on the EHIC medical card. Judge Ward added:

> 'It does not however follow from what I have said that there are no circumstances in which reliance could be placed on an EHIC as amounting to CSIC. The conditions governing the scope of the coverage must be considered and applied to the circumstances of the case. While, as C-255/13 – with its exceptional facts – demonstrates, very lengthy periods would not necessarily always be precluded from constituting a "stay", it will be for temporary – and so, in practice though not as a matter of law, probably shorter – periods that such reliance is most likely to be possible' (at [40]).

The judge also rejected an argument that it would be disproportionate to enforce the requirement for CSIC against the claimant so as to deprive him of a right of permanent residence, noting that since the case of *Mirga v Secretary of State for Work and Pensions*,[3] that 'the window through which a claimant has to squeeze is a very narrow one'.

1  [2016] UKUT 394 (AAC) (16 August 2016).
2  [2014] EWCA Civ 988, [2015] 1 All ER 933, [2015] 1 WLR 593.
3  *Mirga v Secretary of State for Work and Pensions; Samin v Westminster City Council* [2016] UKSC 1.


DEPENDENCY WHERE THE CLAIMANT IS IN RECEIPT OF
SUBSISTENCE BENEFITS

**14.51A**  *[After paragraph 14.51 insert new heading and paragraph:]*

In *Secretary of State for Work and Pensions v MB (JSA) and Others (European Union law: free movement)*[1] the claimant (MB) was in receipt of Housing Benefit and Jobseeker's Allowance. MB claimed to be dependent on her adult daughter on the basis that over a period of eight months, her daughter had put money on the top-up keys for gas and electricity, and would give her mother £5 for food, if asked. Judge Ward said that he accepted, on the authority of *Lebon*,[2] that receipt of a subsistence benefit did not preclude the possibility that support from other sources may give rise to a situation of dependency, but this did not alter the need to produce evidence of actual dependency. The judge also accepted that the rates of Jobseeker's Allowance were such that, being in receipt of it, especially for a prolonged period, was liable to result in a degree of financial pressure. Nevertheless, the judge concluded that on the facts of this case that the contribution from her daughter of approximately £10 fortnightly to help with utility costs did not amount to a 'situation of real dependence' as envisaged by EU case law.

1  [2016] UKUT 372 (AAC) (05 August 2016).
2  C-316/85.

Family members of British citizens

**14.52** *[At the end of the paragraph, add:]*

The Immigration (European Economic Area) Regulations 2006, SI 2006/1003 have been revoked and are to be replaced with the Immigration (European Economic Area) Regulations 2016, SI 2016/1052, with effect from 1 February 2017, with the exemption of reg 9, which came into effect on 25 November 2016 (see regs 1, 44 and Sch 5). The new reg 9 is more restrictive than the old provision and includes a provision (reg 9(4)) that the regulation does not apply: 'in circumstances where the purpose of the residence of the British citizen in the other EEA State was as a route to circumvent any applicable requirement for any non-EEA family members to have leave to enter or remain in the UK under the Immigration Act 1971' (Explanatory Memorandum, paras. 4.6).

EEA nationals who acquire British citizenship and become dual nationals

**14.52A** *[Insert new heading and paragraph:]*

In *R (Lounes) v Secretary of State for the Home Department*[1] the High Court considered whether the exclusion of dual nationals under the 2012 amendment to the EEA Regulations was justified in EU law. The facts concerned a Spanish national who worked in the UK and then acquired British citizenship, which she held in addition to her Spanish nationality (a dual national). Several years after acquiring British citizenship, she married a third country national (TCN) with whom she lived with in the UK. When the TCN applied for a residence card as a family member of a Spanish national exercising Treaty rights in the UK, this was refused on the basis that the definition of 'EEA national' in reg 2 of the Immigration (EEA) Regulations 2006 had been amended on 16 July 2012 to preclude dual British citizens/EEA nationals from benefiting from the Directive. The TCN (Mr Lounes) brought judicial review proceedings against that decision. The Court (Lang J) made a reference to the CJEU on whether the 2012 amendment to the definition of 'EEA citizen' unlawfully restricts the right to free movement under TFEU, Article 21 and Directive 2004/38/EC. The reference C-165/16 was lodged with the CJEU for a preliminary ruling on 21 March 2016.[2]

[1]  [2016] EWHC 436 (Admin), [2016] 2 CMLR 1263, [2016] All ER (D) 80 (Mar).
[2]  Official Journal, C 191, 30 May 2016.

## RETAINED RIGHT OF RESIDENCE

### Retaining worker status

**14.53** *[At the end of the paragraph, add:]*

The Immigration (European Economic Area) Regulations 2006, SI 2006/1003 have been revoked and replaced with the Immigration (European Economic Area) Regulations 2016, SI 2016/1052, with effect from 1 February 2017.

In *EP v Secretary of State for Work and Pensions (JSA) (European Union law: free movement)*[7] Upper Tribunal Judge Ward said that despite having the option of applying for discretionary leave, a trafficked person was not precluded from arguing that they were a worker or have retained worker status. For it is not the case that only lawful work is relevant to establishing whether a person has 'worker' status.[8] Further, although it was unlikely there would be documentary evidence in many trafficking cases, this would not be fatal to the chance of establishing, and hence retaining 'worker' status, as there is no rule that a claimant's evidence requires corroboration.

[7] [2016] UKUT 445 (AAC) (11 October 2016).
[8] See *JA v Secretary of State for Work and Pensions (ESA)* [2012] UKUT 122 (AAC).

### Retained worker status as a jobseeker

**14.54** *[After the first paragraph, add new paragraph:]*

Case law has established that the proper approach to the issue of retaining worker status when there was a delay between the end of a period of employment and claiming benefit is to ask whether, having regard to all the circumstances of the case, there has been 'undue delay' in meeting the requirements of the Citizenship Directive 2004/38/EC.[4] This test was applied[5] where there was a period of five weeks between the claimant's employment at an agency ending and her making a claim for Jobseeker's Allowance. The Upper Tribunal found that the claimant acted promptly after it became apparent that there was no further work for her from the agency. See also *FT v London Borough of Islington and Secretary of State for Work and Pensions (HB) (European Union law: free movement)*[6] in which the claimant, a Greek national, left her employment on 10 June 2012 but did not claim Jobseeker's Allowance until 24 August 2012. It was nevertheless accepted that she retained her worker status between those dates because there had not been undue delay having regard to: (a) the claimant's history of looking for, and speedily obtaining, jobs previously; (b) the availability of existing savings to tide her over; and (c) the details of the steps which she had taken at the time to look for work.

[4] *Secretary of State for Work and Pensions v MK (IS)* [2013] UKUT 163 (AAC).
[5] *Secretary of State for Work and Pensions v MM (IS)* [2015] UKUT 128 (AAC) (18 March 2015), at [51].
[6] [2015] UKUT 121 (AAC) (06 March 2015).

### Are the new conditions for jobseekers in the EEA Regulations compatible with EU law?

**14.57** *[At the end of the paragraph, add:]*

In *Secretary of State for Work and Pensions v MB (JSA) and Others*[3] the Upper Tribunal confirmed that the UK was entitled to require an individual EEA jobseeker to demonstrate a more compelling case at the conclusion of a six-month period of unsuccessful jobseeking, and that this was compatible with the *Antonissen* test. Judge Ward, however, said that the six-month period was not to be seen as a 'trump card', rather it was a factor that the national court or tribunal had to take into account; see also **14.39** above.

In *Secretary of State for Work and Pensions (IS) v MM (Residence and presence conditions: other)*,[4] a case decided prior to the amendments to the provisions on retaining worker status as a jobseeker in reg 6 of the EEA Regulations 2006, Judge White opined that where an EU citizen had been employed for at least one year in the host State, the right to retain worker status under Article 7(3)(b) of the Citizenship Directive was 'open-ended'.

> 'Under Article 7(3)(b) of the Citizenship Directive, there is no indication of the duration for which a person continues to be treated as a worker. My interpretation is that the period of retention of the status is open-ended though not forever more. I justify this in part by the provision in Article 7(3)(c) of the Citizenship Directive which limits the period of retention of the status to "no less than six months" where the period of employment is less than a year.' (at [53]).

The treatment of jobseekers who have been employed for at least one year under the terms of Article 7(3)(b) of the Citizenship Directive, as interpreted by *Secretary of State for Work and Pensions v MM* can be contrasted with reg 6 of the EEA Regulations, which provides that the GPOW test will apply after six months to such jobseekers (reg 6(2)(b), (5) and (6)) and to the official guidance, which advises decision makers that any extension under the GPOW test should be limited to a maximum period of three months (para 073009).

In *Alhashem v The Secretary of State for Work and Pensions*,[5] the claimant, was a Dutch citizen living in the UK but who had not worked here. She had been awarded Jobseeker's Allowance solely on the basis that she was a jobseeker. She later became unable to sign on for work due to ill-health. Her subsequent application for Employment and Support Allowance ('ESA') was refused on the basis that she did not have the right to reside in the UK. She appealed to the First-tier Tribunal on the basis that it was not permissible under EU law to deny access to benefits intended to facilitate access to the labour market to someone who had the right to reside as a jobseeker.[6] The Court of Appeal dismissed the claimant's appeal from the Upper Tribunal saying that EU case law had taken a narrow approach to what is a labour market-related benefit and that this did not include a subsistence benefit.[7] ESA's primary function was the welfare of claimants who cannot work or who are on the borderlines due to some disability or past episode in their lives, and it could not properly be described as intended to facilitate access to the labour market for the purposes of EU law but rather was social assistance. The fact that it was a condition of receiving ESA that claimants might have to undertake work-related activity in order to help them get fit for work did not make ESA a benefit that was intended to facilitate access to the labour market in the sense of EU law. As ESA was social assistance and the clamant was a jobseeker under EU law (without a retained worker status), this meant she could not apply for ESA.

---

3    [2016] UKUT 372 (AAC) (05 August 2016).
4    [2015] UKUT 128 (AAC) (18 March 2015).
5    [2016] EWCA Civ 395, [2016] 3 CMLR 20, [2016] 3 WLR 853.
6    *Vatsouras and another v Arbeitsgemeinschaft (ARGE) Nürnberg 900* (C-22/08 and C-23/08), [2009] ECR I-4585, [2009] All ER (EC) 747, [2009] All ER (D) 51 (Jun), ECJ.
7    *Jobcenter Berlin Neukolln v Alimanovic* (C-67/14), at [42]–[46] considered.

*Retaining worker status after ceasing work due to pregnancy*

**14.60** *[At the end of the paragraph, add:]*

The scope of the decision in *Saint Prix* [7], was considered by the Upper Tribunal in three linked cases: *Secretary of State for Work and Pensions and Others v SFF and Others (European Union law: workers)*.[8] The decision confirmed that *Saint Prix* rights are available to those EEA nationals who have been employed in the UK, and to those who have retained worker status under Article 7(3) of the Directive. The question of whether *Saint Prix* rights are available to those who at the beginning of the maternity period are jobseekers only was expressly left open (at [25]). Otherwise, *Secretary of State for Work and Pensions v SFF and Others* established the following:

(a) A *Saint Prix* right may be established prospectively. This means that a woman will continue to be protected by her worker status until such time, not exceeding the end of the 'reasonable period' contemplated by *Saint Prix*, that she, by her words or actions, shows an intention not to be part of the employment market (at [20]–[24]).

(b) The *Saint Prix* right starts, ordinarily, 11 weeks prior to the expected date of birth, but this starting point is fact-specific and may be displaced in particular cases (at [26]).

(c) The 'reasonable period' is to be determined by taking into account the 52 weeks maternity leave available to an employed woman under the Employment Rights Act 1996, ss 71 and 73, and the circumstances of a particular case. In practice, the reasonable period will be 52 weeks in most cases (at [27]-[37]).

(d) A woman who had already retained worker status (as a former worker who was jobseeking *before* she became pregnant), may enjoy the *Saint Prix* right during her maternity period, and exit that period by becoming a jobseeker who retains worker status again (at [40]–[41]).

(e) A *Saint Prix* right counts towards the period of time needed to acquire a right of permanent residence under Article 16 of the Citizenship Directive (at [44]).

A panel of three Upper Tribunal judges came to effectively the same conclusion in *Weldemichael and Another (St Prix C-507/12; effect)*.[9]

The official DWP guidance issued to decision makers was updated to incorporate these changes.[10]

Note: The DWP Guidance at 073216 it states: 'Self-employed persons do not fall within the scope of the *Saint Prix* judgment. The CJEU only considered the retention of "worker" status under Article 45 TFEU'. The question of whether the *Saint Prix* principle applies to self-employed women who take time off due to pregnancy and childbirth was stayed by the Upper Tribunal in *Revenue and Customs v HD and GP (CHB)*[11] pending the outcome in *Florea Gusa*, a referral to the CJEU made by the Court of Appeal (Ireland) in *Florea Gusa v Minister for Social Protection, Attorney General*.[12] The Upper Tribunal did, however, give guidance on the circumstances in which a self-employed person's right to reside could continue during a period of 'maternity leave' if the claimant took steps which showed that they were continuing to trade until they resumed the activities of a self-employed person, such that they did not need to rely on *Saint Prix*.

7   *Saint Prix v Secretary of State for Work and Pensions,*C-507/12 (2014) C-507/12, ECLI-:EU:C:2014:2007, [2014] All ER (EC) 987, [2015] 1 CMLR 118.
8   [2015] UKUT 502 (AAC) (10 September 2015).
9   [2015] UKUT 540 (IAC) (23 September 2015).
10  See DMG, Vol 2, Ch 7, Part 3, at paras 071180–071379.
11  [2017] UKUT 11 (AAC).
12  C-442/16 [2016] IECA 237.

*Family members who retain their right to reside*

**14.62** *[N.B.]*

The Immigration (European Economic Area) Regulations 2006, SI 2006/1003 have been revoked and replaced with the Immigration (European Economic Area) Regulations 2016, SI 2016/1052, with effect from 1 February 2017.

## PERMANENT RIGHT OF RESIDENCE

### Five years residence

**14.63** *[N.B.]*

The Immigration (European Economic Area) Regulations 2006, SI 2006/1003 have been revoked and replaced with the Immigration (European Economic Area) Regulations 2016, SI 2016/1052, with effect from 1 February 2017.

*Effect of absences*

**14.65** *[At the end of the paragraph, add:]*

The Immigration (European Economic Area) Regulations 2006, SI 2006/1003 have been revoked and replaced with the Immigration (European Economic Area) Regulations 2016, SI 2016/1052, with effect from 25 November 2016. Regulation 3 of the 2016 Regulations provides that continuity of residence is broken when a person serves a sentence of imprisonment. The Explanatory Memorandum states that this gives effect to the CJEU judgments in C-378/12 *Onuekwere* and in C-400/12 *MG*.[4]

An argument that when considering the acquisition of a permanent right to reside under Article 16(1) of the Citizenship Directive 2004/38/EC, the 'gaps' in an EEA national's work record could be treated in the same way as the exemptions for a temporary absence from the UK under Article 16(2) was rejected by the Court of Appeal in *Secretary of State for the Home Department v Ojo*.[5]

The DWP in its official guidance on establishing a permanent residence says that the Department was prepared to ignore gaps of up to 30 days in any one year between two periods where they are different residence rights, for example, between a student to a worker or from an employed to a self-employed person.[6]

4   *Secretary of State for the Home Department v MG* C-400/12 (2014) C-400/12, ECLI-:EU:C:2014:9, [2014] 1 WLR 2441, [2014] 2 CMLR 1172,

5    [2015] EWCA Civ 1301.
6    See DMG, Vol 2, Ch 7, Part 3, para 073433–34.

*Retaining permanent residence where a worker or self-employed person has 'ceased activity'*

**14.66** *[N.B.]*

The Immigration (European Economic Area) Regulations 2006, SI 2006/1003 have been revoked and replaced with the Immigration (European Economic Area) Regulations 2016, SI 2016/1052, with effect from 1 February 2017.

*Family members who can retain a permanent right of residence*

**14.67** *[N.B.]*

The Immigration (European Economic Area) Regulations 2006, SI 2006/1003 have been revoked and replaced with the Immigration (European Economic Area) Regulations 2016, SI 2016/1052, with effect from 1 February 2017.

## DERIVATIVE RIGHT TO RESIDE OF A PRIMARY CARER

**14.68** *[N.B.]*

The derivative right to reside in reg 15A of the Immigration (European Economic Area) Regulations 2006, SI 2006/1003 appears in reg 16 of the Immigration (European Economic Area) Regulations 2016, SI 2016/1052, in force with effect from 1 February 2016.

### Based on a child of a migrant worker being in general education

**14.69** *[At the end of the paragraph, add:]*

*The primary carer cannot rely on an unmarried partner who is not the child's biological parent*

*IP v Secretary of State for Work and Pensions (IS)*[10] concerned a claimant and her partner, both of whom were Latvian. They were not married. They came to the UK in 2007. The claimant had three children by former partners but she had not worked in the UK. The youngest child, S, had entered education in 2008. In September 2010, the claimant made a claim for Income Support on the basis that she was a primary carer of a child admitted into general education and therefore had a derived right to reside under Article 12 of Regulation 1612/68 (in force at the time). The claim was refused and her appeal dismissed. The Upper Tribunal said the claimant's case differed from *Harrow London Borough Council v Ibrahim*[11] and *Teixeira v Lambeth London Borough Council,*[12] as neither of S's parents had ever been a worker in this country. Whilst the claimant's current partner had been a worker in the UK the claimant could not benefit from this as a child of a cohabiting partner could not be regarded as the child of the spouse of a migrant worker or former migrant worker for the purposes of the derivative right under Article 12; the reasoning in *ONAFTS v Ahmed* (Case C-45/12) applied:

'The key point is that S can only benefit from Article 12 if she is the child of someone who is or has been a worker. The only person who has been a worker is the claimant's partner and she is not his child as he has no formal legal relationship with her mother.'[13]

The Upper Tribunal added that in terms of the EEA Regulations, the claimant's partner was not a 'family member' as defined by Article 2 of the Citizenship Directive as he was not her spouse or in a registered partnership with her. He could apply to be issued with residence documentation as an 'extended family member' under Article 3 on the basis that he was in a durable relationship with the claimant. However, this did not make S his child for the purposes of the derivative right of a primary carer under reg 15A.

*Derivative right to reside can arise even when the EU worker parent has left the Member State*

*Secretary of State for the Home Department v NA (Aire Centre intervening)*[14] concerned NA, a national of Pakistan, who married KA, a German national. The couple moved to the UK in March 2004. The marital relationship deteriorated and NA was the victim of domestic violence. KA left the matrimonial home, and in December 2006 he left the UK. While resident in the UK, KA had been a worker. The couple had two daughters who were born in the UK and had German nationality. After divorce proceedings became final in 2009, NA was granted sole custody of her two daughters who were attending schools in the UK. The CJEU confirmed that Article 12 of Regulation (EEC) No 1612/68 (in force at the time) would still apply in this situation – namely where the child of a worker started education *after* the EU worker parent had left the Member State.

*Grandparent may be the primary carer of a child but the parent must have also worked in the UK*

In *JS v Secretary of State for Work and Pensions (ESA) (Residence and presence conditions: right to reside)*[15] the claimant and his wife were Slovakian nationals acting as primary carers of their two grandchildren who were in education in the UK. The grandmother had been in registered employment under the Accession State Worker Registration Scheme for over a year. The children's parents, however, were not resident in the UK, and there was no evidence that they had ever worked in the UK. The Upper Tribunal accepted that it was possible for grandparents to be primary carers because they are the direct relatives of their grandchildren under reg 15A(7) of the EEA Regulations. However, there was a clear requirement for an EEA parent to have been employed in the UK at the same time their child was resident in the UK (reg 15A(4) when read with 15A(3)), and this condition was consistent with the terms of Article 10 of Regulation (EU) No 492/2011, which uses the wording the 'children of a national of a Member State who is or has been employed [in that State]'. As this condition had not been satisfied in the instant case, the fact that the claimant and his wife were the primary carers was not sufficient as that of itself did not establish a derivative right to reside under regulation 15A.

*Guardianship order did not have the effect that a sister became a direct descendant of her brother under Directive 2004/38/EC*

In *MS v Secretary of State for Work and Pensions (IS)*[16] the claimant was a Polish national. After her mother's death, her brother was appointed as her legal guardian by a court order in Poland. She came to the UK in June 2008 to join him. In June 2015, she claimed Income Support as a lone parent. It was argued that as she was under 21 and her brother was a worker, she had a right to reside as a 'direct descendant' under Article 2(2)(c) of Directive 2004/38/EC. The claimant's appeal was dismissed. The Upper Tribunal said the effect of the guardianship order was to confer rights and responsibilities, not to change relationships. Consequently, the claimant was not a direct descendant of her brother with an automatic right to reside as a 'family member' under Article 2 of Directive 2004/38/EC. Instead she continued to be his sister and was 'another family member' within the terms of Article 3(2)(a). However, any right to reside under that provision could not arise until the Secretary of State for the Home Department issued the appropriate documentation; see **14.84**.[17]

The guidance memo for DWP decision makers[18] has been amended and contains the following summary of the criteria for a derived right to reside for a person in general education:

'13 The derivative rights in regulation 16 of the Imm (EEA) Regs 2016 now state that such a right arises where the dependant "would be unable to remain in the United Kingdom if the [primary carer] left the United Kingdom for an indefinite period." From 1.2.17, guidance at DMG 073387 is amended to read:

"**Person in general education**

2. where

2.1 any of the child's parents is an EEA national who resides or has resided in the UK and

2.2 both the child and EEA national parent reside or have resided in the UK at the same time and during such a period of residence, the EEA national parent has been a worker in the UK and

2.3 the child is in general education in the UK.

Note 1: The EEA national who has worked or been a worker must be the parent of the child(ren) (see 2.2 above).

Note 2: From 1.2.17, where a child of an EEA national has a derivative right to reside because they are in education in the UK, the EEA national parent does not have to have been resident when the child first entered education (see 2.3 above)."'

*Shared care and derivative rights as a primary carer*

*Secretary of State for Work and Pensions v MH (IS) (European Union law: free movement)*[19] concerned a claim for Income Support by a Slovakian national which had been refused on the basis that he did not have a right to reside. The claimant had stopped working in order to care for his mother-in-law. A First-tier Tribunal found that the claimant was not the primary carer of his children despite the fact that the DWP had conceded that he shared responsibility for their care with his wife equally. The Upper Tribunal said that the DWP's concession only got the claimant part of the way, for in order to meet the terms of reg 15A(7)(b)(ii) he needed to establish that his wife was not an 'exempt person'. Further evidence showed that the wife, a Slovakian national, did not have a right to reside and, given her level of disability, reflected in an award of Personal Independence Payment, she had little realistic prospect of getting one. As a result, she fell outside the definition of 'exempt person' in para 6(c), which in turn meant the claimant qualified as a primary carer under para (7). The Upper Tribunal remade the decision holding that the claimant had a right, pursuant to reg 15A of the Immigration (European Economic Area) Regulations 2006 as the primary carer of his daughter, who had entered education.

10   [2015] UKUT 691 (AAC) (17 December 2015).
11   C-310/08 (2010) C-310/08, [2010] ECR I-1065, [2010] ICR 1118, [2010] PTSR 1913.
12   C-480/08 (2010) C-480/08, [2010] ECR I-1107, [2010] ICR 1118, [2010] PTSR 1913.
13   Ibid, at para 8.
14   C-115/15 (30 June 2016).
15   [2016] UKUT 314 (AAC) (05 July 2016).
16   [2016] UKUT 348 (AAC) (21 July 2016).
17   *Cf Alarape and Another (Article 12, EC Reg 1612/68) Nigeria* [2011] UKUT 413 (IAC) which confirmed that the term 'child' includes a 'step-child' for the purposes of Article 12.
18   Memo DMG/24/16 – Right to Reside – Immigration (EEA) Regulations 2016 – IS, JSA(IB), ESA(IR) & SPC).
19   [2016] UKUT 526 (AAC) (22 November 2016).

### The meaning of 'employed'

**14.71** *[At the end of the paragraph, add:]*

In *Revenue and Customs v IT (CTC) (European Union law: workers)*[5] the Upper Tribunal rejected an argument advanced on behalf of a claimant from Romania that Article 12 of Regulation (EEC) No 1612/68 is not affected by the derogations made by the Treaty of Accession to Arts 1–6 of Regulation No 1612/68, such that unregistered employed work would bring an A2 national within Article 12 even though that employment was not authorised under the Worker Authorisation Scheme. The Upper Tribunal said that the argument could not succeed because in order to be 'employed' for the purposes of Article 12, a person has to have been admitted to the UK employment market in the first place under Article 1.1 of the Regulation, and in order to do that, the claimant had to meet the conditions of the UK's derogations from Arts 1–6 of the Regulation as set out in the Worker Authorisation Scheme.

5   [2016] UKUT 252 (AAC) (24 May 2016).

### Derived right based on being a primary carer of a British citizen child

**14.73** *[At the end of the paragraph, add:]*

The Court of Appeal considered the position of *Zambrano* carers in the UK and the provision of social welfare in *Sanneh and Others v Secretary of State for Work and Pensions*.[8] The Court made the following rulings:

(a)   it held that the *Zambrano* right raises as soon as the conditions are satisfied, and not only at the point where the EU child's removal from the country is imminent. This means that there would be no need for the decision-maker to wait until the carer was threatened with actual removal;

(b)　the Court held that Member States must make social assistance available to *Zambrano* carers to make that right effective. However, as third country nationals do not have any right to social assistance as a matter of EU law, a Member State could decide on the level of support it grants to *Zambrano* carers. In the UK, the payment of adequate social assistance was achieved through the availability of section 17 of the Children Act 1989. This provided a 'back-stop provision' which was designed to save the carer and child from homelessness and destitution; and

(c)　the Court dismissed a challenge to the Amending Regulations 2012: SI 2012/2587 brought forward by the Department for Work and Pensions; SI 2012/2588, brought forward by the Department for Communities and Local Government; and SI 2012/2612 brought forward by HM Treasury, which excluded *Zambrano* carers from mainstream benefits and social housing, saying that these were not precluded by the non-discrimination principle in EU law or the ECHR.

On 7 March 2016, the Supreme Court granted permission to *HC* (one of the appellants in *Sanneh*) on the question of whether the blanket denial of social welfare assistance to *Zambrano* carers is unlawful because it is discriminatory under EU law or the ECHR. The case is due to be heard in sometime in 2017 under the case reference: UKSC/2015/0215.

[8]　[2015] EWCA Civ 49, [2015] 3 WLR 1867 (10 February 2015).


# SPECIAL RULES FOR ACCESSION NATIONALS

## A8 nationals

**14.74** *[At the end of the paragraph, add:]*

The question of whether the extension of the A8 restrictions in the Worker Registration Scheme effected by the Accession (Immigration and Worker Registration) (Amendment) Regulations 2009, SI 2009/892 from 1 May 2009 to 30 April 2011 was incompatible with EU law, is due to be considered by the Court of Appeal in *Secretary of State for Work and Pensions v Gubeladze*[5] sometime in 2017, which is the Secretary of State's appeal against *TG v Secretary of State for Work and Pensions.*[6] The case concerned an A8 national who, but for the extension of the WRS, could have relied on having a permanent right to reside as a worker who had ceased activity under regs 5(2) and 15(1)(c) of the EEA Regulations 2006 when she made a claim for State Pension Credit in November 2012.

In *RP v Secretary of State for Work and Pensions (ESA) (European Union law: free movement)*[7] the Upper Tribunal made a reference to the CJEU on the question of whether an A8 national who had not completed 12 months' registered work could nonetheless retain their worker status as a jobseeker from 1 May 2009, on condition that the decision in *TG v Secretary of State for Work and Pensions* will be upheld by the Court of Appeal in *Secretary of State for Work and Pensions v Gubeladze* (above).

[5]　C3/2015/1796.
[6]　[2015] UKUT 50 AAC (30 January 2015).

## FURTHER RESIDENCE REQUIREMENTS

**14.78** *[After paragraph 14.78, insert new headings and paragraphs below.]*

### Ordinary residence

*Ordinary residence must be lawful*

**14.78A** *MS v Secretary of State for Work and Pensions (DLA) (DLA, AA, MA: general: other)*[1] concerned a child who was an Israeli national, whose mother and appointee had dual Israeli/British nationality. A claim for Disability Living Allowance ('DLA') for the child was made. The child had entered the UK on a visitor's visa and was thus an overstayer on the expiry of that visa (no attempt had been made to obtain further leave). The claim was refused on the basis that the conditions relating to ordinary residence in Great Britain were not satisfied.[2] A tribunal dismissed the appeal on the basis that the child was a person subject to immigration control under section 115 of the Immigration and Asylum Act 1999. The Upper Tribunal upheld this decision, holding the child could not meet the –ordinarily resident' requirement for DLA as he was not lawfully present in the UK, even though his mother was.[3] The Upper Tribunal also found that the claimant could not be treated as a person not subject to immigration control within the exception of being a 'family member of an EEA national' in the Social Security (Immigration and Asylum) Consequential Amendments Regulations 2000,[4] as his mother was not exercising any EEA rights of residence. The judge said that if he had needed to decide the issue, he would have said that the purposive interpretation of the Agreement on the European Economic Area of 2 May 1992 adopted in CDLA/708/2007 was to be preferred to the literal interpretation adopted in *JFP v Department for Social Development (DLA):*[5] but see also **14:17** above.

[1] [2016] UKUT 42 (AAC) (25 January 2016).
[2] SSCBA 1992, s 71(6) and the Social Security (DLA) Regulations 1991, SI 1991/2890, reg 2(1)(a).
[3] *R v LBC, ex p Shah* [1983] 2 WLR 16 considered.
[4] SI 2000/636.
[5] [2012] NICom 267.

### *'Genuine and sufficient link' to the UK*

**14.78B** *PB v Secretary of State for Work and Pensions (DLA) (Residence and presence conditions: presence)*[1] involved a claim for DLA made by a Czech national, who was 13 years of age. He had ADHD, autism and a learning disability. He came to the UK with his mother in March 2014 to live with his sister. The sister had been working in the UK for a number of years. The claim for DLA was refused on the mistaken basis that the claimant had arrived in the UK accompanied by his mother and his sister, such that the claimant did not have a genuine and sufficient link to the UK pursuant to reg 2A of the Social Security (DLA) Regulations 1991,[2] because neither he nor his sister had previously lived or worked in the UK. The Secretary of State later admitted that he had been wrong to argue that the sister had arrived in the UK in March

2014 when she had in fact been living and working in the UK for the last six years, and so conceded the appeal on the basis that the claimant had a 'genuine and sufficient link' with the UK's social security system through his sister. The Upper Tribunal set the First-tier Tribunal's decision aside, saying that while it had been correct to hold that the sister did not come within the definition of 'member of a family' in Article 1(i) of Regulation (EC) No 883/2004, it should have had regard to the sister's ties with the UK (in terms of her working here and paying tax and national insurance for some five years, and providing care and support for the claimant and being in receipt of Child Tax Credit and Child Benefit for him) when assessing her brother's links with the UK.

Judge Wright also raised the possibility that consideration should have been given to aggregating the claimant's periods of qualifying residence in the Czech Republic, where he was in receipt of disability benefits, with his period of residence in the UK, pursuant to Article 6 of Regulation No 883/2004 but, given the Secretary of State's concession, this issue was left undecided. However, in *Secretary of State for Work and Pensions v MM (AA) (European Union law-Council regulations 1408/71/EEC and (EC) 883/2004)*,[3] the Upper Tribunal rejected an argument that mere residence in another Member State on its own (without evidence of residence that equates to insurance in the Member State) can be aggregated with presence in the UK in order to pass the past presence test under Article 6 and paragraph 2 of Annex XI of Regulation 883/2004. The Upper Tribunal held that if a claimant's residence in another state could be aggregated under Article 6 in this way it would render the need for a genuine and sufficient link test 'completely irrelevant' and the decision in *Stewart v Secretary of State for Work and Pensions*[4] nugatory.

[1]   [2016] UKUT 280 (AAC) (15 June 2016).
[2]   SI 1991/2890.
[3]   [2016] UKUT 547 (AAC) (12 December 2016).
[4]   C-503/09.

*Past presence test unlawfully discriminates against family members of refugees*

**14.78C** In *MM and SI v Secretary of State for Work and Pensions (DLA) (European Union law: other)*,[1] MM was a Ugandan national whose mother had been granted refugee status in the UK in March 2012. He joined his mother in April 2013 with entry clearance on the basis of family reunion. SI was a Somali national who arrived in the UK with her mother and sister in August 2013. On arrival, they were given indefinite leave to remain. Both children had substantial disabilities, and claims for DLA were made in August 2013. The claims were refused because neither had been present in the UK for the 104 weeks required under the past presence test ('PPT'), pursuant to reg 2(1)(iii) of the Social Security (DLA) Regulations 1991. The claimants argued that the application of the PPT amounted to unlawful and indirect discrimination, contrary to Article 28 of EU Directive 2004/83/EC (the Qualification Directive), which provides that Member States 'shall ensure that beneficiaries of refugee or subsidiary protection status receive . . . the necessary social assistance, as provided to nationals of that Member State'. The Upper Tribunal concluded that: (i) Article 28 had direct effect; (ii) DLA was 'social assistance' for the purposes of the Qualification Directive; and that

(iii) refugees were intrinsically less likely to satisfy the PPT than UK nationals as a whole. The Upper Tribunal then went on to consider the question of justification and held that the rationale for the PPT did not apply to refugees in the way that it did to other migrants. This was because refugees were not voluntary migrants exercising a choice of where to live; they were people who had been compelled to leave their country of nationality and reside in a host state with which they may have no prior connection. In general, refugees would have established their genuine link with the UK by applying for, and obtaining, refugee status, and severing their links with their home countries. Against this context, the Upper Tribunal decided that the Secretary of State had not given sufficient justification for not exempting refugees and their family members from the PPT. The Upper Tribunal also found that the application of the PPT to refugees was not justified under Article 14 of the ECHR for the same reasons.

In September 2016, the DWP issued new guidance to decision-makers–'The Past Presence Test and Refugees' in DMG Memo 20/16 and ADM Memo 21/16–advising decision-makers that the past presence test was no longer to be applied to claims for Disability Living Allowance, Attendance Allowance, Personal independence Allowance and Carer's Allowance submitted by refugees and their families.

1    [2016] UKUT 149 (AAC) (30 March 2016).

## ADDITIONAL WELFARE BENEFIT RIGHTS FOR EEA NATIONALS

### The social security coordination rules

*Disputes over which European state is responsible for payment of certain 'cash sickness benefits'*

**14.80A** *[After paragraph 14.80 Insert new heading and paragraph:]*

In *Commission of the European Communities v European Parliament and Council of the European Union* (C-299/05) the CJEU held that Attendance Allowance, the care component of Disability Living Allowance or Carer's Allowance are to be classified as a 'sickness benefit' under the coordination regulations which could be exported to other states within the EEA so long as the UK remained the competent state and this was incorporated into the UK legislation governing entitlement to those benefits by the Social Security (Disability Living Allowance, Attendance Allowance and Carer's Allowance) Regulations 2011.[1] Consequently, the DWP could refuse to pay any of these benefits to an EEA national where some other EEA State was responsible for payment of 'sickness benefit' to that individual. The following cases illustrate this principle and what should happen when the other EEA State does not agree with the UK's view as to who is the competent state.

*Secretary of State for Work and Pensions (AA) v AK (European Union law: Council regulations 1408/71/EEC and (EC) 883/2004)*[2] concerned a Greek national, born in 1938, who had neither worked nor been self-employed in the UK, or paid national insurance; he received a Greek pension. He claimed Attendance Allowance under the 'special rules' for terminally ill claimants as he had lung cancer. His claim was refused on the grounds that the UK was not the competent state to pay sickness benefits. When the matter came before the Upper Tribunal it made the following rulings on the issues raised by the case:

(a)     As Greece was already paying the claimant a pension in this case, then it was the competent state ultimately responsible for the costs of the claimant's sickness benefits in kind (ie NHS treatment) and therefore for cash sickness benefits, including Attendance Allowance.

(b)     In cases where the UK is not the competent state for the benefit claimed and there is no evidence of a difference of view between the competing States, Article 81 of Regulation No 883/2004 requires that the UK as the authority which has received the application must then pass it on to the competent authority 'without delay'.

(c)     The rules for a terminally ill claimant did not override the rule that a sickness benefit cannot be paid by the UK if another EEA State is responsible for paying it.

(d)     The fact that a claimant has a permanent residence under the Citizenship Directive 2004/38/EC does not make any difference as the Directive is concerned with the right to move and reside whereas the coordination rules are concerned with a different issue, namely which Member State has responsibility for meeting the cost of the claimant's care by way of sickness benefits.

(e)     The Upper Tribunal rejected the contention that Attendance Allowance should be reclassified as an 'invalidity benefit' in the light of Stewart (C-503/09). It is awarded only to those over pensionable age and may be awarded either for short periods, for example, while a claimant waits for, and recovers from, a hip replacement and in some cases for the rest of the person's life. Stewart was therefore distinguishable as Incapacity Benefit in Youth which is awarded to young people who will probably never be able to function independently or productively in the labour market.

In *Secretary of State for Work and Pensions v HR (AA) (European Union law: Council regulations 1408/71/EEC and (EC) 883/2004),*[3] the claimant was Swedish and in receipt of a Swedish state pension. She came to live in the UK with her daughter and claimed Attendance Allowance which was refused on the grounds that the UK was not the competent state to pay sickness benefits because the claimant was receiving a pension from another EEA State. The claimant appealed, submitting a document from the Swedish authorities which was a declaration that it did not consider itself competent, even though it was paying the claimant a pension. To resolve this, UT Judge Jacobs made reference to Regulation (EC) 987/2009 which requires the 'competent institutions' to co-operate and to sort out such a dispute between them. If they cannot agree, it can be arbitrated by the Administrative Commission. In the meantime, they also require that the claimant is not left without benefit, as ultimately one of the States will be competent to pay it. Therefore, provided all the other conditions of entitlement are met, it is usually either the State of residence or the State in which the claimant is employed which pays the benefit on a provisional basis.

In *Secretary of State for Work and Pensions v FF (CA) (Bereavement and death benefits: widows pension)*[4] the claimant, who was Italian, had a pension from France. He came to the United Kingdom in 2009 and, in June 2013, made a claim for Carer's Allowance. The DWP refused the claim on the ground that France was the competent state to pay such benefits. The claimant appealed against that decision, stating that he had contacted the French social security office but they had been told him that they would never pay a carers allowance for a disabled person living in the UK. The Secretary of State had also contacted the French authorities but received no response, even when the matter was escalated to policy official level. The Secretary of State argued that there was no sufficient evidence of a difference of view, so that Article 6(2) did not apply; further, it was clear on the legislation that the UK was not the competent state. The Upper Tribunal gave guidance on what amounted to a 'dispute' under Article 6(2) saying that it did not need to take the form of a formally expressed in a decision and that the claimant's evidence could be sufficient to show that there was a difference of view. The Upper Tribunal remitted the case to the Secretary of State to determine whether Carer's Allowance should be paid to the claimant on a provisional basis until the difference of view with France is settled by the Administrative Commission, whose decision would be determinative.

The Secretary of State for Work and Pensions has been granted permission to appeal against this decision by the Court of Appeal. The appeal is listed to be heard in May 2017 under the case name *Fileccia v The Secretary of State for Work and Pensions* (C3/2016/0358).

In *IG v Secretary of State for Work and Pensions (European Union law: Council regulations 1408/71/EEC and (EC) 883/2004)*,[5] the claimant was a Lithuanian national who came to the UK in August 2011, following her husband's death. She had Alzheimer's and came to join her son who would care for her. The claimant received a pension from Lithuania of somewhere between £80 and £100 a month. But she did not receive a retirement pension from Great Britain. When she claimed Attendance Allowance in July 2012, it was refused on the ground that, being classified as a 'sickness benefit' under EU law, Lithuania was the competent state for the purposes of Regulation 883/2004 (Social Security Contributions and Benefits Act 1992, s 65(7)). The Upper Tribunal rejected the claimant's argument based on the possibility of an award being made, even if the UK was not the competent state, saying that the approach adopted in *Hudzinski*[6] did not apply to a 'sickness benefit' as this was subject to the overlapping rules.

The Supreme Court raised the possibility that Attendance Allowance should be reclassified as an 'invalidity benefit' by analogy with *Stewart* (C-503/09) in *Secretary of State for Work and Pensions v Tolley (Deceased acting by her personal representative)*:[7]

> 'In this court's view, although the matter was not argued before us, the principled solution to a case such as this would be to treat the care component of DLA as an invalidity benefit for the purpose of the Regulation, and thus freely exportable under article 10, leaving the detailed provisions of Chapter 1 of Title III to deal with sickness benefits *stricto sensu*. Then none of the current issues would have arisen: see *Stewart* (Case C-503/09) [2012] 1 CMLR 13. The broad characteristic of the benefits listed in article 10 is that they are long-term or one-off payments in respect of permanent conditions, such as disability, old age or death, rather than short-term benefits in respect of potentially temporary conditions, such as sickness, maternity or unemployment. Income replacement cannot be an essential feature of an

invalidity benefit, because they include "those intended for the maintenance or improvement of earning capacity" (article 4(1)(b)).'

The Advocate General's Opinion on *Secretary of State for Work and Pensions v Tolley*,[8] however, rejected this suggestion and advised the CJEU that there is no reason for the court to depart from its classification of the care component of DLA as a 'sickness benefit' in the earlier decision of *Commission of the European Communities v European Parliament and Council of the European Union*.[9] The CJEU has subsequently upheld its view that the care component of DLA is a 'sickness benefit' for the purposes of Council Regulation (EEC) No 1408/71, in *Tolley (Judgment)*.[10] The Court said the fact that the grant of the care component of DLA can relate to a substantial period of time did not change its underlying purpose, which was to improve the quality of life of persons reliant on care.[11]

1   SI 2011/2426.
2   [2015] UKUT 110 (AAC) (04 March 2015).
3   [2014] UKUT 571 (AAC) (18 December 2014) reported as [2015] AACR 26.
4   [2015] UKUT 488 (AAC) (03 September 2015).
5   [2016] UKUT 176 (AAC) (08 April 2016).
6   (C-611/10) [2012] 3 CMLR 23.
7   [2015] UKSC 55, at 24.
8   Cases C-430/15 and C-430/15 (5 October 2016).
9   C-299/05.
10  [2017] EUECJ C-430/15 [2017] WLR(D) 65 (01 February 2017).
11  *Commission v Parliament and Council* (C 299/05) and *da Silva Martins* (C 388/09) followed.

## THE CROSS-OVER BETWEEN SOCIAL SECURITY AND IMMIGRATION LAW

### The jurisdictional divide between social security and immigration law

*Non-EEA nationals*

EEA Nationals

**14.84** *[At the end of the paragraph, add:]*

In *MD v Secretary of State for Work and Pensions (SPC) (Residence and presence conditions: right to reside)*[4] the claimant was a Cypriot national who had been in the UK since 2000. He had never worked in the UK and in 2004 he had been awarded Income Support in error, ie without the right to reside test being applied. In 2013, he was issued with a document by the Home Office certifying that he had a permanent right of residence (also in error). When he claimed state pension credit two months later, however, the claim was rejected as he did not in fact have a permanent right of residence. The Upper Tribunal said that where there was clear and uncontested evidence that a person did not have a right of permanent residence, then the Secretary of State for Work and Pensions should be able to determine entitlement to social security benefits on that basis, notwithstanding the existence of a Home Office document certifying permanent residence that has been issued in error. The Upper Tribunal added that a document certifying permanent residence was only evidence and did not in itself create a right to reside (CPC/3588/2006 followed).

4    [2016] UKUT 319 (AAC) (07 July 2016).


PROCEEDINGS BROUGHT BY THE EUROPEAN COMMISSION

**14.92** *[At the end of the paragraph, add:]*

In *Commission v United Kingdom of Great Britain and Northern Ireland*[6] the Commission argued that by requiring a claimant to have a right to reside as a condition of claiming Child Benefit ('ChB') and Child Tax Credit ('CTC'), the UK was applying the wrong legal test. Under Article 11(3)(e) of Regulation No 883/2004 a person is subject to the legislation of the Member State of residence, and 'residence' is defined as the place where a person habitually resides (Article 1(j)); which is to be determined in the light of the factual circumstances of the person concerned rather than the EU citizen's legal status. In the alternative, the Commission argued that imposing the right to reside test a condition of entitlement to ChB and CTC which is automatically met by its own nationals, the UK created a situation of direct, or at least indirect, discrimination against nationals of other Member States and thus breached the anti-discrimination provision in Article 4 of the Regulation. The CJEU rejected the Commission's case. Having decided that ChB and CTC are 'social security benefits' rather than 'social assistance' on the Commission's first argument the Court said that Article 11(3)(e) did not lay down a condition creating the right to social security benefits. Rather it was a conflict rule used to determine the national legislation applicable to the payment of the social security benefits listed under the Coordination Regulations. The Court therefore rejected the Commission's argument that Article 11(3)(e) was distorted by the right to reside test. As for the Commission's second argument, the CJEU acknowledged that the right to reside test in UK national legislation gave rise to indirect discrimination,[7] but held that the difference in treatment was justified by the need to protect the finances of the host Member State.[8]

6    C-308/14 (14 June 2016).
7    *Bressol and Others* (C-73/08).
8    *Dano* (C-333/13) at [63] applied.


*The need for a proportionality assessment*

NO NEED FOR AN INDIVIDUAL ASSESSMENT

**14.94A** *[After paragraph 14.94 insert new headings and paragraphs:]*

In *Jobcenter Berlin Neukölln v Alimanovic*[1] the applicant was a Swedish national who had worked in Germany in temporary jobs lasting less than a year. After she became unemployed, she and her three children had been paid benefit under the German Social Code but these benefits were withdrawn after she had been unemployed for more than six months. Adopting the analysis in *Dano* (C-333/13), the CJEU held that social assistance could be refused to Ms Alimanovic after six months as she only retained worker status under Article 7(3)(c) of the Citizenship Directive for that period. The CJEU said this could be done without the need for an individual assessment. The Directive had established a 'gradual system' for the retention of worker status and the legislation itself could be regarded as having taken the relevant factors into account. While a single applicant could not in reality be regarded as an 'unreasonable burden' for a Member State, the accumulation of all the individual claims would. According to the court, this approach had the advantage of 'legal certainty and transparency' as it enabled those who wish to access social assistance to know, without any ambiguity, what their rights and obligations were.

This same approach was subsequently applied by the CJEU in *Vestische Arbeit Jobcenter Kreis Recklinghausen v Garcia-Nieto and Others*[2] in which the CJEU confirmed that social benefits may be refused to EEA migrants in the first three months of residence in a host state, including those who were job-seeking.

[1] C-67/14, [2016] 1 CMLR 29, [2016] 2 WLR 208, [2016] QB 308.
[2] C-299/14, [2016] 1 WLR 3089.

## ECONOMICALLY INACTIVE EEA NATIONALS AND PROPORTIONALITY

**14.94B** In *Mirga and Another v Secretary of State for Work and Pensions*[1] the Supreme Court ruled that EU migrants who are economically inactive and do not have a legal right of residence in the UK, can be refused social assistance, regardless of their personal circumstances.

**The facts:** *Mirga* concerned the refusal of Income Support to a 17-year-old Polish national in the late stages of pregnancy. Ms Mirga was born in 1988 in Poland. She first came to the UK with her parents and three siblings in 1998, but they returned to Poland in 2002 after being refused asylum. Two years later, in June 2004, on Poland's accession to the EU, the family returned to the UK. Her mother died four months later, and her father, who had been working, gave up his job due to depression. He received Income Support based on incapacity for work until late 2007, when it was decided that he should not have been receiving it, on the ground that he did not have a right of residence in the UK. (This meant that his daughter did not acquire any rights under the Directive as a family member of a worker who retained their worker status.) When Ms Mirga finished her education in April 2005, she began registered work as an A8 national, but this was for less than one year. In February 2006, she became pregnant and started to do unregistered work. In June 2006, she left home for rented accommodation, having become estranged from her father. In August 2006, she claimed Income Support on the grounds of her pregnancy. This was refused on the ground that she could not claim to be a 'worker' as she was an A8 national who had not completed 12 months' registered employment, and thus could not be a 'qualifying person' for the purpose of the EEA Regulations.

*Samin*, which was heard together with *Mirga*, concerned an Iraqi national who successfully sought asylum in Austria in 1992, together with his wife and children, and was accorded Austrian citizenship. He became estranged from his wife and children and he came to the UK in December 2005. During the ten months following his entry into the UK, he had some paid employment on occasions but had not worked since 2006, and had not been looking for work since 2007. Mr Samin became socially isolated and suffered from clinical depression and post-traumatic stress disorder. In June 2010, he applied to Westminster City Council for housing under the homelessness provisions in Part VII of the Housing Act 1996. After making inquiries, the Council decided that he was not eligible for housing assistance because he did not have the right of residence in the UK.

**The issues:** The first issue raised in the appeal was whether the domestic regulations infringed the appellants' Treaty rights to non-discrimination and 'the right to move and reside freely within the territory of the member states'. On this first issue, the court held that as neither of the appellants could claim to be a 'worker', the granting of social assistance could be made subject to a right of residence condition. The court said this conclusion was consistent with recent decisions of the CJEU, including *Brey* (C-140/12), *Dano* (C-333/13) (see **14.91** above) and *Alimanovic* (C-67/14) (see **14.94A** above). The court also rejected the contention that the refusal of social assistance amounted to a form of 'constructive expulsion' of Ms Mirga from the UK. The second issue raised by the appeal was based on the need for a proportionality assessment where reliance was placed on certain passages in the *Brey* judgment and the observations of the Advocate General in *Alimanovic* which indicated that the EEA national's links with the host state needed to be taken into account when considering whether to refuse social assistance to someone who was economically inactive. On this issue, the Supreme Court adopted the CJEU's analysis in *Alimanovic* (which did not follow the Advocate General's Opinion on this issue) that benefit could be refused to someone who did not satisfy the right to reside test without the need for an individual assessment (see **14.94A** above).

**The outcome:** The dismissal of Ms Mirga and Mr Samin's appeals indicates that the Supreme Court is prepared to contemplate a situation where any EU citizen who does not meet the right to reside condition can automatically be refused benefits, regardless of their personal circumstances. However, the judgment does leave some room for the concept of proportionality albeit that the threshold that needs to be met is a high one:

'69. Where a national of another member state is not a worker, self-employed or a student, and has no, or very limited, means of support and no medical insurance (as is sadly the position of Ms Mirga and Mr Samin), it would severely undermine the whole thrust and purpose of the 2004 Directive if proportionality could be invoked to entitle that person to have the right of residence and social assistance in another member state, save perhaps in extreme circumstances. It would also place a substantial burden on a host member state if it had to carry out a proportionality exercise in every case where the right of residence (or indeed the right against discrimination) was invoked.

70. Even if there is a category of exceptional cases where proportionality could come into play, I do not consider that either Ms Mirga or Mr Samin could possibly satisfy it. They were in a wholly different position from Mr Baumbast: he was not seeking social assistance, he fell short of the self-sufficiency criteria to a very small extent indeed, and he had worked in this country for many years. By contrast Ms Mirga and Mr Samin were seeking social assistance, neither of them had any significant means of support or any medical insurance, and neither had worked for sustained periods in this country. The whole point of their appeals was to enable them to receive social assistance, and at least the main point of the self-sufficiency test is to assist applicants who would be very unlikely to need social assistance.

71. Whatever sympathy one may naturally feel for Ms Mirga and Mr Samin, their respective applications for income support and housing assistance represent precisely what was said by the Grand Chamber in *Dano*, para 75 (supported by its later reasoning in *Alimanovic*) to be the aim of the 2004 Directive to stop, namely "economically inactive Union citizens using the host member state's welfare system to fund their means of subsistence".'

¹   [2016] UKSC 1, [2016] 1 WLR 481, [2016] 2 CMLR 31, (27 January 2016).

PROPORTIONALITY ARGUMENTS FOLLOWING THE SUPREME COURT DECISION IN MIRGA

**14.94C**  The decision in *Secretary of State for Work and Pensions v PS-B (IS)*¹ concerned a Portuguese claimant who had been born in the UK in June 1997. She was brought up and educated in the UK and had not been absent for any significant length of time. Her father had always lived in Angola. At the age of 16, the appellant was abandoned by her mother, who returned to Angola. After this, she lived first with her aunt and then with her godmother. She then went to live in a hostel. In September 2013, she claimed Income Support, but this was refused on the basis that she did not have a right to reside in the UK. A First-tier Tribunal allowed the appellant's appeal. While it accepted that the appellant did not fit into any established category of right to reside, it found that there was a gap in the scope of EU law, given her circumstances. The Secretary of State appealed. In response, the appellant argued that the Supreme Court in *Mirga v Secretary of State for Work and Pensions*² does not rule out the possibility of it being disproportionate to deny a right to reside to someone who is claiming an income-related benefit. The Upper Tribunal allowed the Secretary of State's appeal and the decision refusing Income Support was restored. UT Judge Jacobs said he was bound by *Mirga* and had to decide what the decision means and how it should be applied. The Court in *Mirga* held that where a national of another Member State is not a worker, self-employed, a student, or a self-sufficient person, it would severely undermine the purpose of the 2004 Citizenship Directive if proportionality could be invoked to accord that person a right to reside and social assistance, save perhaps in extreme circumstances. In Ms Mirga's case, it was held that she did not have a right to reside, even though she had worked in the UK. Turning to the instant case the judge said:

> 'On the facts, the claimant's case is not as strong as Ms Mirga's. She has spent more of her life in this country than Ms Mirga had, but she has never worked or been self-employed, she has never been a student, and she has never had sufficient resources or the necessary sickness insurance to be self-sufficient. She has not come close to satisfying any accepted category of right to reside. This is not a case in which the conditions for a category are so close to being met that it would be disproportionate to insist on strict compliance.'³

The Upper Tribunal also rejected the argument that there was a gap in EU provision, holding that it follows from *Mirga* that the rejection of a general policy of proportionality was a good indication that the absence of a category allowing easier access to a right to reside was not an omission that the courts should fill. Judge Jacobs concluded with the following observation, which appears to cast doubt on proportionality having *any* role to play in social security cases:

'The facts of Ms Mirga's case . . . show the uncertain, and certainly limited, scope for proportionality in a social security case. Lord Neuberger did not even acknowledge that there definitely was any possibility. In [69], he only said 'save perhaps in extreme circumstances'; and he began [70] with the words: "Even if there is a category of exceptional cases".'[4]

1   [2016] UKUT 511 (AAC).
2   [2016] UKSC 1.
3   At para 11.
4   At para 10.

## BACKDATING OF BENEFIT UPON BEING GRANTED REFUGEE STATUS

### Backdating for means-tested benefits – abolished

**14.96** *[At the end of the paragraph, add:]*

The challenge to the government's decision to abolish regulation 21ZB was dismissed in *Blakesley v Secretary of State for Work and Pensions.*[8] The Court of Appeal held that the former statutory regime which provided backdated payments of income support to persons who were found to be refugees went further than Article 23 of the Geneva Convention required. While international law required that successful asylum seekers were paid the same welfare benefits as UK citizens from the date their refugee status was established, Article 23 did not have any retrospective effect. The Court referred to Lord Hope's judgment in *R (ST) v Secretary of State for the Home Department*[9] on the Geneva Convention and the distinction he drew between asylum seekers who are lawfully present in the UK, and those determined to be refugees whose presence is lawful under domestic law. A refugee was only 'lawfully staying in' the United Kingdom once it was established that he/she was indeed a refugee. The Court concluded that if it was intended that all welfare benefits should be backdated for genuine refugees, Article 23 would have referred to 'refugees', not 'refugees lawfully staying in their territory'. Thus, while the current regime (of basic asylum plus the availability of integration loans) was less generous to refugees than the pre-June 2007 regime, it was still compliant with international law. The Court also rejected the appellant's case based on Article 28 of the Qualification Directive (2004/83/EC), saying that the text did not go beyond the requirements of the Geneva Convention

8   [2015] EWCA Civ 141, [2015] 1 WLR 3150, [2015] AACR 17 (26 February 2015)
9   [2012] UKSC12.

## CLAIM FOR ASYLUM HAS BEEN 'RECORDED BY THE SECRETARY OF STATE'

**14.101** *[At the end of the paragraph, add:]*

In circumstances where an individual makes a subsequent claim for asylum under Rule 353 of the Immigration Rules, there had been in the past debate as to when those further submissions are deemed to be recorded.[5] This has largely resolved when the Secretary of State introduced a process requiring further submissions to be made in person at the Liverpool Further Submissions Unit. As the submissions are made in person, they will be recorded and the individual provided with a receipt of this so disputes over whether a claim has been recorded has reduced significantly. From February 2016 onward, individuals wishing to make further submissions on asylum or human rights grounds have had to first make an appointment with the Further Submissions Unit by telephone and attend on the date allocated to submit the further submissions.

5     *R (Nigatu) v Secretary of State for the Home Department* [2004] EWHC 1806 (Admin).

## CLAIM FOR ASYLUM HAS BEEN DETERMINED

**14.102** *[At the end of the paragraph, add:]*

On 12 May 2016, the Immigration Act 2016 received Royal Assent. Failed asylum seekers with dependents who were previously in receipt of asylum support under section 95 of the Immigration Act by operation of section 94(5) notwithstanding having had their asylum or humanitarian protection claims refused will no longer be entitled to stay on section 95 support when that part of the Immigration Act 2016 comes into force[10] on a date yet to be determined. Their section 95 support will stop 90 days after they become appeal rights exhausted.

A new provision, section 95A, will be inserted into Part VI of the Immigration and Asylum Act 1999 to address the eligibility of failed asylum seekers to asylum support. By this new provision, the previous concession permitting certain failed asylum seeking families with dependents to remain on section 95 support will be withdrawn. Support will still be available to such families under section 95A where it appears to the Secretary of State that the failed asylum seeker and his dependents are destitute or likely to become destitute within a prescribed period of time and they face a genuine obstacle to leaving the United Kingdom.[11] 'Destitute' bears the same meaning as under section 95(3)–(8) of the Immigration and Asylum Act 1999. There is no definition in section 95A as to what constitutes a 'genuine obstacle to leaving the United Kingdom'. This falls to be defined by regulations to be made by the Secretary of State. In the course of the debates to the Immigration Bill (which has now become the Immigration Act 2016), the government agreed that regulations laid before Parliament will be subject to affirmative resolution. At the time of writing, the government has not publicly provided an indicative timescale for when the regulations will be laid before Parliament.

Pending consideration of an application for section 95A support, the Secretary of State will have a power to provide or arrange for the provision of temporary support for failed asylum-seekers under a new section 98A, which will also be inserted into Part VI of the Immigration and Asylum Act 1999 when it is brought into force under the Immigration Act 2016.[12] This operates similarly to the existing power under section 98 to provide or arrange temporary accommodation for those applicants awaiting a decision on their application for asylum support under section 95.

Sections 99 and 100 of the Immigration and Asylum Act 1999 will also be amended to include those families eligible for sections 95A or 98A in the categories of persons not eligible for support under section 17 of the Children Act 1989.[13] New powers have been created under the Immigration Act 2016 to allow local authorities to provide support to these families in certain prescribed circumstances. This is known as paragraph 10A support, outlined in Schedule 12 to the Immigration Act 2016 and to be inserted in Schedule 3 to the NIAA 2002. The details of how this type of support will operate will largely be fleshed out in regulations which have yet to be laid before Parliament. Paragraph 10A has not yet come into force at the time of writing. It is understood that it is unlikely to come into force until after April 2017.

[10]  Immigration Act 2016, Sch 11, para 7.
[11]  Immigration Act 2016, Sch 11, para 9.
[12]  Immigration Act 2016, Sch 11, para 13.
[13]  Immigration Act 2016, Sch 11, paras 14 and 15.

## THE DETAIL OF THE SCHEME FOR ASYLUM SUPPORT

### Applications for asylum support

**14.110** *[At the end of the paragraph, add:]*

If the Secretary of State is not satisfied that information provided on the asylum support application is complete or accurate or considers that the applicant is not cooperating with enquiries, the Secretary of State may decide that the application shall not be entertained.[9] There is no right of appeal against a decision to not entertain an application. Chapter 10 of the Secretary of State's Asylum Support Policy Bulletin Instructions sets out how the Secretary of State considers what is accurate or complete information.

[9]  Section 57 of the Nationality Immigration and Asylum Act 200; Asylum Support (Amendment) (No 3) Regulations 2002, reg 2 amending reg 3(4) of the Asylum Support Regulations 2000.

### Domestic violence

**14.124** *[Delete the first two sentences and substitute:]*

The definition of domestic violence and abuse as defined in the Home Office *Policy Bulletin* is as follows:

> 'Any incident or pattern of incidents controlling, coercive or threatening behaviour, violence or abuse between those aged 16 or over who are or have been intimate partners or family members regardless of gender or sexuality. This can include, but is not limited to, psychological, physical, sexual, financial or emotional abuse. The policy bulletin further elaborates on what constitutes controlling or coercive behaviour.'

*[At the end of footnote 1, add:]*

On 21 December 2015, the Secretary of State published further consolidated asylum support policies, *Home Office Asylum Support Policy Bulletin Instructions*, version 7. Chapter 23 addresses domestic violence cases.

## EXCLUSION FROM SUPPORT

**14.126** *[At the end of the paragraph, add:]*

The Immigration Act 2016 will insert two new categories of ineligible persons under Schedule 3 to the Nationality Immigration and Asylum Act 2002 who are also not eligible for asylum support. These include:

(a)   persons in England who require leave to enter or remain in the United Kingdom pursuant to the Immigration Act 1971 and are not asylum-seekers;[14]

(b)   a person who is the primary carer of a British citizen residing in the UK, is not an asylum-seeker, and would otherwise require leave to enter or remain in the UK and who, if required to leave the UK, would cause the relevant British citizen to be unable to reside in the UK or in another EEA state. This provision is directed at dealing with *Zambrano* carers.

These categories of persons are additional to categories (6)–(9) and are dealt with under the rubric of community care provision.

[14]   Paragraph 7B as inserted into Sch 3 to the Nationality Immigration and Asylum Act 2002 by the Immigration Act 2016, Sch 12, para 9.

## PROVISION OF SUPPORT

### The EC Reception Directive

*Amounts provided*

**14.151** *[At the end of the paragraph, add:]*

On 11 August 2014, four months after the judgment in *Refugee Action*, the Secretary of State decided to maintain the level of support payable to single adult asylum seekers at £36.62 per week although the Secretary of State stated that the decision was reached using a different method to that employed in 2013, of which Popplewell J in *Refugee Action* had been critical. On 8 April 2015, the Secretary of State increased the single adult rate to £36.95 per week with effect from 6 April 2015.[8] On 16 July 2015, the Secretary of State announced that the level of support payable with respect of child dependents of asylum seekers would be reduced from £52.96 to £26.95 per week, the same rate as for adults.[9] All three of these decisions were challenged by judicial review.[10] The challenges were not successful and the changes to the level of support for single adults and child dependants were upheld.

[8]   Asylum Support (Amendment No 2) Regulations 2015 (SI 2015/944).
[9]   Asylum Support (Amendment No 3) Regulations 2015 (SI 2015/1501).
[10]   The judicial review challenge was brought in three conjoined cases of *R (SG, K, YT & RG) v Secretary of State for the Home Department* [2016] EWHC 2639 (Admin).

### Providing accommodation

**14.153** *[At the end of the paragraph, add:]*

In asylum support cases involving dependent children, the Secretary of State is required to have due regard to the need to safeguard and promote the welfare of children in line with section 55 of the Borders Citizenship and Immigration Act 2009. This requires the Secretary of State to evidence how a dispersal decision has been made having regard to the children's welfare, including considerations around disruption to schooling particularly where the children receive additional input including special educational needs provisions as well as disruptions to medical or psychological treatment.[8]

[8] See *Nzolameso v Westminster City Council* [2015] UKSC 22, [2015] PTSR 549 in the context of section 11 of the Children Act 2004 as applied to the context of statutory homelessness decisions. Section 11 is a mirror image of section 55 of BCIA 2009. See also *R (C, T, M, U) v London Borough of Southwark* [2016] EWCA Civ 707.

*National Health Service prescriptions/dental treatment/sight tests*

**14.160** *[In footnote 1, add:]*

NHS entitlements: migrant health guide https://www.gov.uk/guidance/nhs-entitlements-migrant-health-guide.

## HARD CASES

**14.174T** *[At the end of the paragraph, add:]*

There have been heavy criticisms of the delay in arranging section 4(1)(c) bail addresses for detainees who wish to make an application for immigration bail to the First-tier Tribunal (Immigration and Asylum Chambers), particularly where the individual has a criminal conviction and is under the supervision of probation services and deemed unsuitable for a grant of initial accommodation. Research carried out by Bail for Immigration Detainees[12] in September 2014 found that the average time taken to get a grant of section 4 bail accommodation in initial accommodation took on average nine days whereas the average time taken to get a grant of complex dispersal bail accommodation was 158 days in cases where probation services were required to approve the address. It was on average 60 days where licence address checks were not required.

In three conjoined cases, *R (Sathanantham and Others) v Secretary of State for the Home Department*,[13] the High Court considered the use of the power to provide bail accommodation under section 4(1)(c) in the context of complaints regarding a systemic failure to deal with bail application within a reasonable period of time. The claimants were each detained at the time of their applications for section 4 bail accommodation. Each was a high-risk application which limited the type of accommodation which could be offered. No accommodation was found after a considerable period of time in each case. Two of the applicants were subsequently released because it was acknowledged that their continued detention risked becoming unlawful but they were released without accommodation. The principal issue in the judicial review was whether the Secretary of State owed high risk detainees: (i) a duty to provide bail accommodation on request, if satisfied that the claimant would have nowhere to go unless that was done if bail was granted; (ii) a duty to make reasonable efforts to provide bail accommodation on request, if satisfied that the claimant would have nowhere to go unless that was done if bail was granted; (iii) a duty to determine any application for such accommodation fairly and rationally; (iv) no duty in respect of the section 4(1)(c) power at all. The Court held that the power under section 4(1) was coupled with a duty to operate the policy on bail accommodation fairly and rationally. That involved a duty to determine applications fairly and rationally and to apply the relevant published policy. This duty extends to all parts of the process for which the Secretary of State was responsible. Having regard to the evidence before the Court, the judge observed that the section 4 bail system did not work for high-risk offenders. The timescales set by the Secretary of State in accordance with the published bail accommodation policies were not routinely met and missed by substantial margins. Although the judge did not find that the section 4 bail system operated unlawfully because it permitted significant delays in a significant proportion of high-risk bail cases, the judge found that a failure to determine an individual application at all within a reasonable period of time did breach the duty to determine applications fairly and rationally. So the system was not itself unlawful but the way it operated was. Thus, in each of the claimant's cases the time taken to resolve the application amounted to a breach by the Secretary of State of her duty to deal with the applications fairly and rationally. It was essential that the system was overhauled.

By the Immigration Act 2016, section 4 support, whether in respect of bail or in respect of refused asylum seekers, will be completely abolished and replaced with a new form of support called 'section 95A support'. Although the Home Office has presented this as the new section 4 support, this is misleading as a large proportion of people who currently qualify for section 4 support will not qualify for section 95A support.

Section 95A support will be available to refused asylum seekers who are destitute and have a 'genuine obstacle' to leaving the UK. What is meant by a genuine obstacle is yet to be defined and will only be so defined through regulations to be made by the Secretary of State. It is expected that this will be limited to people with medical conditions that prevent them from travelling and people who are taking all reasonable steps to leave the UK. Unlike with section 4, there will be no right of appeal against the refusal of an application for section 95A support.

The most radical and restrictive element of section 95A support is that it will only be possible to apply for it within a 'grace period' after appeal rights become exhausted. For single people this will be 21 days, for those with children it will be 90 days. In practice, this means that most people who have a genuine obstacle to leaving the UK will be made destitute, since this obstacle is unlikely to occur and be evidenced within the grace period. As an example, according to the Asylum Support Appeals Project, of the 105 applications for support made in 2015 for 'genuine obstacle' reasons (ie medical or voluntary return), only six were made within the grace period.

In the context of immigration bail, section 4 is replaced by section 61 and Sch 10 to the Immigration Act 2016. By paragraph 9 of Sch 10, the Secretary of State may provide or arrange for the provision of facilities for accommodation to enable a person to meet bail conditions imposed. This provision is not yet in force.

*[In footnote 3, add:]*

See also *R (Sathanantham) v Secretary of State for the Home Department* [2016] EWHC 1781 (Admin).

¹² 'No place to go: delays in Home Office provision of Section 4(1)(c) bail accommodation', Bail for Immigration Detainees, September 2014.
¹³ [2016] EWHC 1781 (Admin), [2016] 4 WLR 128.

## COMMUNITY CARE PROVISION FOR THOSE SUBJECT TO IMMIGRATION CONTROL

### Asylum seekers

**14.175** *[At the end of the paragraph, add:]*

Sections 21 and 21A of the National Assistance Act 1948 were repealed by the coming into force of Part 1 of the Care Act 2014 on 1 April 2015. The purpose of the Care Act 2014 was to reform the law relating to care and support for adults and their carers. The old language of 'care and attention' under section 21 is no longer used or referred to in the Care Act. The Care Act 2014 introduced a new concept of need for 'care and support' which includes objectives such as promoting the well-being of the adult and the prevention of the development of needs.⁶ By the Care Act 2014, a new national eligibility criteria was also introduced for the purposes of determining an adult's needs for care and support.⁷ This has largely been seen as a positive development in the law, moving away from the varying eligibility criteria that used to be determined by individual local authorities, creating what was perceived to be a post code lottery situation.

Residential care is still available under the Care Act 2014 where an adult's needs for care and support and is included in the non-exhaustive list of ways in which needs for care and support can be met under the act.⁸ There have been very few reported judgments since Part 1 of the Care Act 2014 came into force on 1 April 2015. It is widely believed that the case law developed under the National Assistance Act 1948 (and set out at **14.176–14.179** below) remain good law and applicable to residential care provisioning under the Care Act 2014.⁹

Section 21 of the Care Act 2014 operates in the same way as the repealed section 21A of the NAA 1948 so that a local authority may not meet the needs for care and support of an adult who is excluded from benefits and whose needs for care and support have arisen solely because he is destitute or because of the physical effects or anticipated physical effects of being destitute.

⁶ Care Act 2014, ss 1 and 2.
⁷ Care Act 2014, s 13. See also Care and Support (Eligibility Criteria) Regulations 2015 and Chapter 6 of the Care and Support Statutory Guidance.
⁸ Section 8 of the Care Act 2014, s 8.
⁹ In *R (GS) v London Borough of Camden* [2016] EWHC 1762 (Admin), it was confirmed that s 8 of the Care Act 2014 did not provide for a need for accommodation alone to constitute a need for care and support. The need for accommodation must still, like under the NAA 1948, be related to a need for care and support.

## Exclusion from support

**14.181** *[At the end of the paragraph, add:]*

The Immigration Act 2016 introduces two further categories of persons excluded from support. See amendment to **14.126** above.

*[In footnote 12, add:]*

The repeal of section 21 of the NAA 1948 will unlikely alter the relevance of *AA v Lambeth* as the old case law on section 21 residential care has been applied in the context of the Care Act. See *R (GS) v London Borough of Camden* [2016] EWHC 1762 (Admin), above.

## Provision of support

**14.184** *[At the end of the paragraph, add:]*

This remains the case under the Care Act 2014.

## Accommodation and support under section 17 of the Children Act 1989

**14.186** *[At the end of the paragraph, add:]*

Since *PO v Newham*[9] there have been two further reported judgments examining the way in which local authorities set levels of support for families subject to immigration control. In *R (Mensah and Another) v Salford City Council*,[10] the claimants, two single-parent families applied for judicial review of the policy that the local authority used for calculating financial support payments to families ineligible for mainstream benefits as a result of their immigration status. The local authority's policy was to provide each family with accommodation and to pay the utility bills and council tax for the property. In addition, each family received financial assistance calculated by reference to the amount that was provided to failed asylum seekers pursuant to section 4 of the Immigration and Asylum Act 1999. The policy had some flexibility and the local authority could provide additional assistance if needed, for example for school uniforms. It was argued by the claimants that it was unlawful, or alternatively, irrational, to use a level of support calculated for the statutory purpose of supporting failed asylum seekers for the different purpose of safeguarding and promoting the welfare of children in need under section 17 of the Children Act 1989. The court dismissed the judicial review finding that the local authority's policy was rational and it was not for the court to determine the appropriate level of payments. The claimants in *Mensah* appealed the decision to the Court of Appeal, and were granted permission, but prior to the substantive appeal hearing had to withdraw after the claimants each were able to obtain employment and become self-sufficient.

In *R (C, T, M, U) v London Borough of Southwark*,[11] the claimants, three children and their mother, brought a challenge to the local authority's use of bed and breakfast accommodation to accommodate them under section 17of the Children Act 1989 and also contended that the local authority's provision of subsistence support was inadequate. The judicial review claim was dismissed with the judge observing on the facts of the claim that several needs assessments had been undertaken over a long period of time and the conclusions were not reached through any unfair or irrational process. The claimants appealed against the judgment to the Court of Appeal. Before the Court of Appeal, the claimants obtained disclosure from the local authority which showed that a policy was operated which pegged subsistence levels to section 4 of the Immigration and Asylum Act 1999 in a similar manner as the *Mensah* case. However, the policy was not applied in that way in the context of the claimants' case and they received subsistence levels above the section 4 level. Permission was granted to appeal to the Court of Appeal[12] but the appeal was ultimately dismissed. The Court of Appeal held on the facts of the appeal that the local authority had not followed a flawed policy or practice thereby fettering its discretion in its provision of accommodation and financial support to the claimants. Although the appeal failed on its facts, the Court of Appeal found, accepting the submissions of the Intervener, Coram Children's Legal Centre, that the legislative purpose of section 17 of the Children Act 1989 is different from that of sections 4 and 95 of the Immigration and Asylum Act 1999.[13] It would thus be difficult for a local authority to demonstrate that it had paid regard to the former by adopting a practice or internal guidance for subsistence that described as its starting point either of the asylum support rates. The starting point for a decision to support under the Children Act 1989 has to be an analysis of all appropriate evidential factors and any cross-checking that there may be must not constrain the decision-maker's obligations to have regard to the impact on the individual child's welfare and the proportionality of the same. In this way, albeit obiter, the Court of Appeal cast doubt on the analysis in *Mensah*.

9   See fn 3 above.
10   [2014] EWHC 3537 (Admin), [2015] PTSR 157.
11   [2014] EWHC 3983.
12   [2016] EWCA Civ 707, [2016] HLR 36.
13   See, in particular, paras 21–23 of the Court of Appeal's judgment.

**14.187** *[At the end of the paragraph, add:]*

Schedule 12 to the Immigration Act 2016 introduces significant amendments to Sch 3 to the NIAA 2002 which has in essence created a new support scheme for those families subject to immigration control who are not asylum-seekers and who may otherwise fall within a category of eligible persons under Sch 3 to the NIAA 2002. Instead of being able to access support under section 17 of the Children Act 1989 if it can be shown that to withhold or withdraw support would breach their rights under the European Convention on Human Rights, Sch 12 inserts into Sch 3 of NIAA 2002 a new scheme of support for these families under paras 3A and 10A.

When it comes into force, para 3A, which is the linchpin of the new support regime, will impose a complete prohibition on the provision of certain types of support under s 17 of the Children Act 1989 to a person who falls within its ambit.[2] It does not preclude the provision of section 17 support to a child, only 'to a person in respect of a child', most likely a parent, relative or carer. It still operates subject to NIAA 2002, Sch 3, para 2, which states that the exclusions do not 'prevent the provision of support or assistance . . . (b) to a child'.

Paragraph 10A, to which para 3A refers, creates a new scheme of support for certain categories of persons who are prima facie ineligible for support under

Sch 3 to NIAA 2002 but who are not either asylum seekers or failed asylum seekers. A failed asylum seeker in this context bears the same meaning as a failed asylum seeker within the meaning of s 95A of the Immigration and Asylum Act 1999 as amended by the Immigration Act 2016. By the stipulation that para 10A support via local authority will not be available to those who are failed asylum seekers and their dependants, paras 3A and 10A will have the significant effect of reversing the principles laid down in *R (VC and K) v Newcastle City Council*[3] which states that there is no hierarchy between s 4 of the Immigration and Asylum Act 1999 and s 17 of the Children Act 1989. Where the two powers arise, a local authority is not able to refuse support without assessing the needs of the child under s 17 of the Children Act 1989. When the new scheme comes into force, there will be a hierarchy whereby if a family is eligible for s 95A support, they will be precluded from seeking support via para 10A.

In order to qualify for support under the scheme, an application must be destitute (which bears the same meaning as s 95(3)–(8) of the Immigration and Asylum Act 1999), have a dependent child with him or her, not be a relevant failed asylum seeker and satisfy one of five conditions. The precise requirements of the conditions are set out at para 10A(3)–(7). In broad terms, these cover cases where: the applicant is pursuing an application for leave to remain on non-asylum grounds; the applicant is or could be pursuing an in-country appeal; the applicant's appeal rights are exhausted but has not failed to cooperate with arrangements that would enable him to leave the UK. There is a fall-back provision under condition E which allows for other categories of persons to be included where the provision of support is necessary to safeguard and promote the welfare of a dependent child. The circumstances in which this may arise are to be dealt with in regulations to be made by the Secretary of State.[4]

An applicant who is eligible for support under paragraph 10A is not completely barred from accessing support under s 17 of the Children Act 1989. The exclusion from support under s 17, introduced by the new para 3A, only prevents the application from accessing 'support or assistance . . . of a type that could be provided to the person by virtue of paragraph 10A' and does not preclude the provision of support to a child. The rationale underpinning this is that the main social care need of families without immigration status is accommodation and support to prevent destitution.[5] Hence it is only accommodation and support to prevent destitution which will be available under para 10A. Other support under s 17 of the Children Act 1989 will remain available (either to the child or to the parent) where the child has other more complex needs over and above this.

[2]   Paragraph 3A is inserted into Sch 3 to NIAA 2002 by the Immigration Act 2016, Sch 12, para 6.
[3]   [2011] EWHC 2673 (Admin,) [2011] 43 LS Gaz R 22.
[4]   Paragraph 10A(7) as inserted into Sch 3 to NIAA 2002 by Immigration Act 2016, Sch 12, para 10.
[5]   See Reforming support for migrants without immigration status (Home Office, January 2016) at [59]: https://www.gov.uk/government/uploads/system/uploads/attachment_data/file/494240/Support.pdf.

## Accommodation under section 20 of the Children Act 1989

*Transfer scheme for unaccompanied children*

**14.188A** *[After paragraph 14.188, insert new heading and paragraph:]*

Sections 69 to 73 of the Immigration Act 2016 created a new mechanism under which responsibility for an unaccompanied child may be transferred from one local authority to another, either on a voluntary basis or under a compulsory scheme enforced by the Home Office.

Under the voluntary scheme, a local authority may make arrangements with another local authority in England to transfer an unaccompanied child and the responsibility for their care. The child then becomes the responsibility of the second local authority at the point of actual transfer, and is treated in law as if they had always been cared for by that local authority. An *Interim National Transfer Protocol for UASC* has been published and implemented to set out a procedure for voluntary transfer.

The Immigration Act 2016 also makes provision for a compulsory scheme under which the Home Office may order local authorities to take responsibility for children if they do not come forward voluntarily to offer assistance. Local authorities are placed under a duty to provide information to the Home Office if requested to do so, for example about the number of available foster carers in their area. The Home Office may direct that the local authority comply with the scheme but must give 14 days' written notice during which time the local authority may make representations for the Home Office to change or withdraw its direction. The government states that its aim is to use the voluntary scheme as far as possible and only use the compulsory powers if these become necessary.

At the present time, the relevant provisions have only come into force in England on 31 May 2016. There is a power to extend the provisions to Wales, Scotland and Northern Ireland. Some of the local authorities in those regions have volunteered to participate.

*Children who may be transferred to another local authority*

**14.188B** *[Insert new heading and paragraph:]*

The Immigration Act 2016 defines 'relevant children' who may be transferred to another local authority under the scheme. They include unaccompanied children who make a claim for asylum or for protection under Articles 2 or 3 of the European Convention on Human Rights (protecting the right to life and prohibiting torture and ill-treatment). The legislation also allows for regulations to be made at a later date permitting the transfer of other unaccompanied children who do not have leave to remain (which could include, for example, trafficked children making other types of application) and the transfer of children who have been granted leave to enter or remain. The government stated that it included this last category to enable children to be transferred under the scheme where they were brought to the UK under a resettlement scheme.

*When children may be transferred to another local authority*

**14.188C**  *[Insert new heading and paragraph:]*

Local authorities in which the numbers of unaccompanied asylum seeking children are higher than 0.07% of the population of children in the area (currently Kent and some London boroughs) will be able to use the transfer scheme to refer children to another local authority. The intention behind the scheme is to make provision for newly arrived children but there are no time limits in the legislation itself to prevent children being transferred at a later stage or to prevent children being left in limbo where delays arise in the process. Statutory guidance on safeguarding and promoting the welfare of children issued by the Department for Education, however, requires local authorities to promote permanence and stability in their care of looked after children and to ensure that changes to a child's placement do not disrupt their education or training.[1] The *Interim Transfer Protocol* gives guidance on the transfer process which states that the transfer decision should be made as soon as practicable, and ideally within 48 hours of the arrival of the child into care, unless it would be in the child's best interests to defer that decision. It also states that where children are settled and established in a local authority area, the local authority may make the decision that it is not in the best interests of the child for them to be moved.

[1]  'Care of Unaccompanied Asylum-Seeking and Trafficked Children: Statutory guidance for local authorities on the care of unaccompanied asylum seeking and trafficked children', July 2014. See also 'The Children Act 1989 guidance and regulations, Volume 2: Care Planning, Placement and Case Review', June 2015, Department of Education.

*How the best interests to the child will be considered*

**14.188D**  *[Insert new heading and paragraph:]*

The protocol states that a decision to transfer a child under the scheme must take into account their best interests and provides guidance on assessing the best interests of the child. The assessment includes the need to take into account the child's wishes and feelings in the decision about the transfer to another local authority, and their welfare. Other considerations include matters relating to their personal identity, their care, protection and safety, their health needs and education as well as access to legal representation. The decision on the child's transfer must be recorded in writing.

*Children whose age is disputed*

**14.188E**  *[Insert new heading and paragraph:]*

The protocol makes clear that age assessments should not be a routine part of a local authority's assessment of unaccompanied children but, where age is disputed, it is the local authority to which they are transferred that is responsible for the age assessment process.[1]

[1]  See 14.190–14.192.

**14.192**  *[At the end of the paragraph, add:]*

Fact-finding hearings to determine age have now been going on for five years since the Supreme Court handed down judgment in *A v Croydon*. The bulk of age assessment challenges by judicial review are now transferred to the Upper Tribunal (Immigration and Asylum Chamber). In March 2012, the Home Office sought to introduce the use of dental x-rays in a pilot in conjunction with the London Borough of Croydon as a means of determining the age of those unaccompanied young people whose age is disputed. This was halted before it could proceed because of objections from professional bodies and civil society. The controversy flared up again in 2015 when the London Borough of Croydon sought to require an age disputed child to submit to a dental age assessment because the local authority contended that it required such evidence to be able to fairly defend judicial review proceedings in respect of the age dispute. When the putative child refused to submit to a dental age assessment, Croydon applied to strike out his judicial review claim, which had at that point been granted permission to proceed and trial was about to commence. Croydon's strike-out application was dismissed by the Upper Tribunal but on appeal, the Court of Appeal overturned the decision of the Upper Tribunal.[17] The Court of Appeal held that there was no basis to refuse Croydon's application. Although the local authority had failed to comply with certain procedural obligations, these could not justify a decision to refuse the application unless at least it caused the claimant to suffer significant prejudice. As the complaint made on behalf of the putative child that dental x-rays are unreliable, the Court of Appeal held that the weight and reliability of x-rays can be investigated at the hearing and are a matter of weight to be placed by the trial judge.

Following judgment in *Y v Croydon*, there was a noticeable dramatic increase in applications made by local authorities for young people to be required to undergo dental age assessments or have their claims struck out. The Vice President of the Upper Tribunal made directions for two cases to proceed at a preliminary hearing for the purposes of considering the methodology of using dental x-rays to determine the age of unaccompanied children. In a judgment handed down in November 2016, the Upper Tribunal provided guidance on the use of dental evidence.[18] The effect of the judgment appears to be to reverse the position following the Court of Appeal's judgment in *Y v Croydon* that any unaccompanied child could be asked to undergo a dental assessment and were they to refuse have their case struck out. It would be inappropriate for dental assessments to be requested in cases other than those in which it could be satisfied that the taking of a dental x-ray might be of assistance in showing the existence of immature teeth which the Upper Tribunal stated might be useful at the 10- and 13-year old boundaries' when immature teeth would be fully expected to still be present and that the absence of immature teeth might serve as a 'warning' against which other evidence can be considered in cases where a young person presented with the existence of mature molars. As a result of this guidance, requests for dental assessments must only be made in cases where the local authority can set out proper justification for its request which is likely to be limited to cases where a young person is claiming to fall within the age range of 10–13. There is little or no value in requesting dental examination in cases involving young people in the 15–17 age bracket because of the lack of immature teeth and the 'unreliability' of an estimate of age for young people falling within this age group. The judgment highlighted the need to scrutinise any requests by a local authority to adduce dental evidence from a dental expert.

17  *London Borough of Croydon v Y* [2016] EWCA Civ 398. The facts of the case are summarised at paras 1–8 of the judgment.
18  *R (ZM and Another) v London Borough of Croydon* (JR/2567/2016; JR/3413/2016).

*Accommodation and support for children leaving care*

**14.195**  *[At the end of the paragraph, add:]*

Since the case of *Nfuni*,[13] there has been further litigation around the approach to be taken in respect of pathway planning for care leavers where their immigration status has yet to be finally determined. Chapter 6 of the statutory guidance to the Children Act states that pathway planning should adopt a dual and triple-planning approach which envisages a transitional plan during the period of uncertainty when a young person is in the UK without permanent immigration status.[14] Although the guidance acknowledges that funding arrangements may be limited by uncertainty of immigration status, the guidance stresses that during the period of uncertainty, the local authority is to base planning around 'short term achievable goals whilst entitlement to remain in the UK is being determined'. The guidance positively requires active support to be provided to the young person and does not sanction inaction. The High Court has granted permission on successive judicial review challenges to the failure of local authorities to consider the 'short term achievable goal' a care leaver with uncertain immigration status may have, acknowledging that the statutory consideration that local authorities must address in discharging their pathway planning and support duties toward care leavers irrespective of their immigration status.[15]

When Sch 12 to the Immigration Act 2016 comes into force, it will significantly impact on certain categories of care leavers accessing continued support under ss 23C or 23CA of the Children Act 1989 as well as the type of support that they can access. This will depend on the care leavers' relevant immigration status. Those care leavers who are asylum seekers, including those who have further qualifying submissions,[16] will by and large not be affected by the changes to Sch 12 to the Immigration Act 2016 save as to their eligibility for grants to meet expenses connected with education or training where that grant is made to enable them to meet all or part of their tuition fees.[17] Care leavers who have been granted limited leave to remain or have made an application for leave to enter or remain in the UK which has not been withdrawn or determined will also remain eligible for leaving care support but be excluded from grants to meet all or part of their tuition fees.[18] Unless these care leavers are able to access scholarships and bursaries from alternative sources, able to fund themselves without support from the local authority or access a course which does not charge tuition fees, they will unlikely be able to continue with their education or training whilst they do not have settled immigration status. The rationale of this amendment to Sch 3 by the Immigration Act 2016 is to relieve local authorities in England of the burden that is said to have been created by case law[19] requiring local authorities to fund tuition fees where care leavers are not eligible for student finance.[20] The analysis in the 'Reforming support' document pays little if any regard to the principle statutory purpose of the leaving care duties, that is for the local authority to act as a corporate parent to those young adults who otherwise have no one with parental responsibility, or family members to look out for them.[21]

For all other care leavers who fall within a category of ineligible persons under Sch 3 to the NIAA 2002, including the new categories under paras 7B and 7C,[22] a new support scheme has been created under para 10B, Sch 3 to the NIAA 2002, as inserted by the Immigration Act 2016, operated on similar principles to the para 10A scheme referred to above for families. Instead of being able to access support under ss 23C, 23CA, 24A or 24B of the Children Act 1989, if it can be shown that to withhold or withdraw support would breach their rights under the European Convention on Human Rights, Sch 12 inserts into Sch 3 to NIAA 2002 a new scheme of support for these families under paras 3B and 10B.

When it comes into force, para 3B, which is the linchpin of the new support regime, will impose a complete prohibition on the provision of leaving care support to a person who falls within its ambit.[23]

Paragraph 10B, to which para 3B refers, creates a new scheme of support for certain categories of care leavers who are prima facie ineligible for support under Sch 3 to NIAA 2002, but who are not either asylum seekers or failed asylum seekers. By the stipulation that para 10B support via local authority will not be available to failed asylum seekers who are care leavers, paras 3B and 10B will have the significant effect of reversing the principles laid down in *R (SO) v Barking and Dagenham London Borough Council*[24] that the duties owed to care leavers under the Children Act 1989 take precedent over the power to provide support under the asylum support scheme, whether for asylum seekers or failed asylum seekers.

In order to qualify for support under the scheme, an applicant must be otherwise eligible for leaving care support, destitute (which bears the same meaning as s 95(3)–(8) of the Immigration and Asylum Act 1999), and satisfy one of four conditions. The precise requirements of the conditions are set out at para 10B(2)–10B(5). In broad terms, these cover cases where: the applicant is pursuing an application for leave to remain on non-asylum grounds; the applicant is, or could be, pursuing an in-country appeal; the applicant's appeal rights are exhausted and the provision of support appears to a specified person to be necessary. The circumstances in which this may arise and who the specified person is will be dealt with in regulations to be made by the Secretary of State.[25] It is clear from the 'Reforming Support for Migrants without Immigration Status' paper, the government's approach to these care leavers are not to treat them as young adults who have had to spend their formative childhood years in the care of the local authority because they have no family member able and willing to look after them, but to treat them simply as adults who have failed to establish any right to remain in the UK. The introduction of the para 10B scheme, like the introduction of para 1A referred to above, will fundamentally change the nature of the corporate parenting duty and which young adults can continue to benefit from this protection.

[13] See fn 12 above.

14 See statutory guidance, 'The Children Act 1989 guidance and Regulations: Volume 3 planning transition to adulthood for care leavers' (Revised January 2015).

15 See the cases of *Nluta* (CO/3477/2015) and *Salih* (CO/963/2016). Permission was granted by Goss J in the first case and by Karon Monaghan QC in the second case. Neither case proceeded to trial and were settled in favour of the claimant by consent.

16 This bears the same meaning as that s 94(2C) of the Immigration and Asylum Act 1999 as amended by the Immigration Act 2016, Sch 11, para 3(3).

17 The provision of grant to meet expenses connected with education or training is under the Children Act 1989, ss 23C(4)(b), 23CA(4) and 24B(2)(b). Tuition fees are defined under the Education Reform Act 1988, Sch 6.

18 Immigration Act 2016, Sch 12, para 3 amending NIAA 2002, Sch 3 to insert para 1A. See also the Immigration Act 2016, Sch 12, para 5 amending NIAA 2002, Sch 3 to insert para 2A.

19 *R (Kebede) v Newcastle City Council* [2013] EWHC 355 (Admin) upheld by the Court of Appeal ([2013] EWCA Civ 960).

20 See Reforming support for migrants without immigration status at para 68: https://www.gov.uk/government/uploads/system/uploads/attachment_data/file/494240/Support.pdf

21 The importance of the corporate parenting duty and the explanation of why, by the Leaving Care Act 2000, it was extended to young adults leaving care, and up to the age of 25 is explained by Lady Hale in *R (M) v London Borough of Hammersmith and Fulham* [2008] UKHL 14 [2008] 1 WLR 535 at paras 4, 16-24, confirmed in *R (G) v London Borough of Southwark* [2009] UKHL 26, [2009] 1 WLR 1299 at paras 4–6.

22 See 14.126 above.

23 Paragraph 3B is inserted into NIAA 2002, Sch 3 by the Immigration Act 2016, Sch 12, para 6.

24 [2010] EWCA Civ 1101.

25 Paragraph 10B(5) as inserted into NIAA 2002, Sch 3 by the Immigration Act 2016, Sch 12, para 10.

## ACCESS TO HOUSING UNDER THE HOUSING ACTS

**Asylum seekers, refugees and persons granted humanitarian protection and forms of discretionary leave**

14.203 *[At the end of the paragraph, add:]*

In 2015, judicial review challenges[11] were brought to challenge regs 3 and 5 of the Allocation of Housing and Homelessness (Eligibility) (England) Regulations 2006[12] in respect of its exclusion of those with Appendix FM leave with recourse to public funds from eligibility for an allocation of social housing and homelessness assistance. Under reg 3, those with exceptional leave to enter or remain in the UK granted outside the provisions of the Immigration Rules; and have recourse to public funds are eligible for allocation of social housing and homelessness assistance. Until the codification of most Article 8 claims under Appendix FM, this provision covered the eligibility of most, if not all, who were granted limited leave to remain outside the Rules under Article 8 of ECHR. The introduction of Appendix FM had what appeared to have been the unintentional consequence of exclusion of those falling within that regime. The Department for Communities and Local Government agreed to consider the amendment of the 2006 Regulations to address the claimants' concern as to the vires of such an exclusion. On 30 October 2016, the Allocation of Housing and Homelessness (Eligibility) (England) (Amendment) Regulations 2016[13] came into force amending regs 3 and 5 of the 2006 Regulations, inserting a new class of persons subject to immigration control who are eligible for allocation of social housing and homelessness assistance, namely those who have limited leave to enter or remain in the UK with recourse to public funds on family or private life grounds under Article 8 of ECHR where the leave has been granted under Immigration Rules, para 276BE(1), 276DG or Appendix FM.

11    *Alabi* (CO/12312016) and *Romans* (CO/1921/2016).
12    SI 2006/1294.
13    SI 2016/965.

## ACCESS TO EDUCATIONAL PROVISION

### Higher education

**14.213** *[At the end of the paragraph, add:]*

The 2011 Regulations came under challenge in its exclusion of those with discretionary leave from being eligible for tuition fees in the case of *R (Tigere) v Secretary of State for Business, Innovation and Skills*.[4] There, a young woman had spent the best part of her childhood in the UK with periods of discretionary leave and with no condition preventing her from having recourse to public funds. She was on track to becoming eligible to obtain indefinite leave to remain in 2018. She obtained a university place in April 2013 and applied for a student loan under the 2011 Regulations. She satisfied all criteria save for having indefinite leave to remain. She sought judicial review of the Secretary of State's exclusionary policy which had rendered her ineligible to receive a loan because of her immigration status on the grounds that it was incompatible with her right to education under Article 2 Protocol 1 of the ECHR read with Article 14 of ECHR. The Supreme Court held that although the court would treat the judgments of the Secretary of State as primary decision-maker regarding the distribution of finite resources at some cost to the taxpayer with appropriate respect, there was no evidence that he had addressed his mind to the particular issue or that Parliament had actively considered the matter. The Court further noted that, since the claimant and those in her position had lived in the UK for most of their lives, been educated here, could not be removed save for grave misconduct, and were treated throughout as members of UK society, there were the same reasonable prospects of society benefitting from the contribution which university education would equip them to make, and of obtaining repayments of loans, as applied to applicants who were normally resident in the UK. The exclusion in the Regulations was thus not rationally connected to its objectives and, in any event, even if a bright-line rule were justified in the particular context, the particular rule chosen had itself to be rationally connected to its aim and proportionate in its achievement. The Court found that a rule which fitted more closely the legitimate objectives could have been chosen; that, having regard to the effect on the claimant, and those in her position, of the denial or delay of university education and to the harm to the community and the economy, the settlement rule did not represent a fair balance between the effect on those whose rights were engaged and the interests of the community; and that, accordingly, application of the settlement rule to the claimant could not be justified and violated her Convention rights.

Following the Supreme Court judgment, on 2 December 2015, the Department of Business Innovation and Skills published a consultation 'New Eligibility Category for Higher Education Student Support'. The proposal was to create a new long residency eligibility category to sit alongside existing categories. This was introduced by the Education (Student Fees, Awards and Support) (Amendment) Regulations 2016[5] which came into force on 6 June 2016. It requires the person to be continuously and lawfully ordinarily resident in the UK for three years prior to starting the course. If the applicant is a child (defined as under 18), he or she must have lived in the UK continuously for seven years prior to the first day of the first academic year of the course. If the applicant is a young adult aged 18 years or above, he or she must have lived in the UK continuously for either half their life or a period of 20 years. Ordinary residence means habitual, normal and lawful residence. Thus, if an applicant came to the UK with no immigration status, he or she would only start accruing ordinary residence from when immigration status was first regularised. Similarly, if the applicant subsequently becomes unlawfully present in the UK, ordinary residence is then calculated from when he or she next gains lawful status.

[4]    [2015] UKSC 57, [2015] 1 WLR 3820.
[5]    SI 2016/584.

## ACCESS TO THE NATIONAL HEALTH SERVICE

**14.214** *[At the end of the paragraph, add:]*

On 6 April 2015, the National Health Service (Charges to Overseas Visitors) Regulations 2015[7] ('the Charging Regulations') came into force. It applies to all course of treatment commenced on or after that date. The Regulations were subsequently amended with further changes coming into effect on 1 February 2016. The Charging Regulations place a legal obligation on NHS trusts, NHS foundation trusts and local authorities in the exercise of public health functions in England, to establish whether a person is an overseas visitor to whom charges apply, or whether they are exempt from charges. When charges apply, a relevant NHS body must make and recover charges from the person liable to pay for the NHS services provided to the overseas visitor. Significant changes have been made to the exemption categories by these Charging Regulations. An exemption for temporary migrants coming to the UK for six months or more from outside the EEA has been introduced because such visitors are now required to pay the immigration health charge (referred to as the health surcharge). Certain temporary migrants may also be exempt from paying the health surcharge or will have payment waived; these individuals will generally also be exempt from NHS charges. Payment of, or exemption or waiver from, the health surcharge entitles the person to free NHS hospital services on the same basis as an ordinarily resident patient while their visa remains valid, which means they must not be charged for NHS services. Overseas visitors who are visiting the UK for six months or less, including on a multiple entry visa, or who are in the UK without permission, must be charged for services they receive at the point of accessing care, unless exempt from charges under other categories of the Charging Regulations. Overseas visitors who reside in an EEA state (including non-EEA nationals) may be insured under the public healthcare insurance system in their resident member state, or country of work for frontier workers. They will consequently be exempt from charges for any medically necessary treatment they receive under the Charging Regulations, as long as they present the appropriate EEA healthcare document. This is because the UK can recover the cost of their care from the relevant insuring Member State, if the details of their healthcare form are recorded. The way in which a person qualifies as insured varies depending on their country of residence (or country of work if they are a posted worker). However, in every case where someone is insured under the public system they will have, or should be entitled to hold, a European Health Insurance Card ('EHIC') or Provisional Replacement Certificate ('PRC') from the EEA state in which they are insured. Each family member, including children, will have their own EHIC or PRC. EEA residents may also be issued an S2 form if they wish to seek pre-planned treatment abroad. They may instead produce a PRC to prove entitlement to free healthcare in the UK under the EU Regulations. It should be for the patient or their representative to arrange the issue of the PRC from the EEA state/Switzerland that would issue their EHIC, but the OVM may assist with this if needed. EEA residents who are visiting the UK on a temporary basis or to pursue a course of study, and who are insured by their resident state, should present a valid EHIC or PRC from that country to access free medically necessary treatment. This includes British nationals who are insured in another EEA state. The EHIC/PRC is issued by the country of residence or work, not country of citizenship. The UK will recover the cost of that healthcare from the relevant Member State. Those visitors from the EEA to the UK who do not have a valid EHIC, PRC or S2 and who are not covered under another exemption category under the Charging Regulations, must be charged for services they receive at the point of accessing care. The precise position as to the categories of persons subject to charge or exempt from charge are detailed in the regulations and in the guidance issued in January 2016 by the Department of Health, 'Guidance on implementing the overseas visitor hospital charging regulations 2015'.[8]

*[At the end of footnote 3, add:]*

The 2011 Regulations were repealed on 6 April 2015. They are replaced by the National Health Service (Charges to Overseas Visitors) Regulations 2015 (SI 2015/238).

*[At the end of footnote 4, add:]*

The 2011 Regulations were repealed on 6 April 2015. They are replaced by the National Health Service (Charges to Overseas Visitors) Regulations 2015 (SI 2015/238).

*[At the end of footnote 5, add:]*

The 2011 Regulations were repealed on 6 April 2015. They are replaced by the National Health Service (Charges to Overseas Visitors) Regulations 2015 (SI 2015/238).

*[At end of footnote 6, add:]*

On 16 March 2015, the Immigration (Health Charge) Order 2015 (SI 2015/792) was made. It came into force on 6 April 2015. Schedule 2, paras 1 and 3 set out the list of circumstances in which a person is exempt from paying a charge.

[7]    SI 2015/2025.

8   https://www.gov.uk/government/uploads/system/uploads/attachment_data/file/496951/Overse
as_visitor_hospital_charging_accs.pdf.

## NHS hospital treatment

**14.216**  *[Delete the paragraph and replace with:]*

For an up-to-date list of persons entitled to free non-emergency NHS hospital treatment, see the National Health Service (Charges to Overseas Visitors) Regulations 2015 (SI 2015/238).

**14.218**  *[Delete the paragraph and replace with:]*

For an up-to-date list of other individuals who have a more limited entitlement to free NHS hospital treatment for conditions which arose during a visit, see the National Health Service (Charges to Overseas Visitors) Regulations 2015. EEA or Swiss nationals in possession of a Form S2 are eligible for treatment for the particular condition specified on the form and for which they have been referred to the UK.

**14.219**  *[At the end of footnote 1, add:]*

The 2011 regulations were repealed on 6 April 2015. They are replaced by the National Health Service (Charges to Overseas Visitors) Regulations 2015 (SI 2015/238).

*[At the end of each of footnotes 2–7, add:]*

The 2011 Regulations were repealed on 6 April 2015. They are replaced by the National Health Service (Charges to Overseas Visitors) Regulations 2015 (SI 2015/238).

## Primary care

**14.220**  *[At the end of footnote 2, add:]*

The 2004 Regulations were repealed on 7 December 2015 and replaced by the National Health Service (General Medical Services Contracts) Regulations 2015 (SI 2015/1862).

**14.221**  *[At the end of footnote 4, add:]*

The 2011 Regulations were repealed on 6 April 2015. They are replaced by the National Health Service (Charges to Overseas Visitors) Regulations 2015 (SI 2015/238).

# Chapter 15

# PENAL AND CARRIER SANCTIONS

## INTRODUCTION

**15.1** *[In the text after footnote reference 8, add:]*

The 'right to rent' scheme was piloted in a number of English midlands local authorities from 1 December 2014[8a] and then extended throughout the whole of England from 1 February 2016.[8b] The Immigration Act 2016 (IA 2016) made the scheme even more draconian by adding criminal sanctions of up to five years' imprisonment for landlords renting to or permitting occupation of premises by those without a 'right to rent' and by creating new powers to evict summarily those without the right to rent.[8c] The 2014 Act instituted other features of a hostile environment for those without a requisite immigration status and the 2016 Act made them even more hostile as well as making further innovations. The Immigration Act 2014 introduced a requirement of lawful residence as a qualification for obtaining a driving licence and gave the Secretary of State power to revoke a licence held by a person not meeting that requirement.[8d] The Immigration Act 2016 gave immigration officers new powers to enter premises to search for and seize driving licences held by persons not lawfully in the UK.[8e] It also created a new criminal offence of driving whilst unlawfully in the UK[8f] and gave immigration officers powers to seize vehicles used for committing the offence.[8g] The Immigration Act 2014 prohibited banks and building societies from opening accounts for persons who require but do not have leave to remain in the UK[8h] whilst the 2016 Act required them to check the immigration status of account holders and to close accounts held by those without requisite immigrations status.[8i] The 2016 Act made it a criminal offence for a person to work in the UK if he or she does not have an immigration status that permits the person to work[8j] and it made it a criminal offence to employ such a person if the employer has 'reasonable cause to believe' that the person is disqualified by immigration status from working;[8k] previously the employer committed the offence only if he or she knew that the person was prohibited from working.[8l] The 2016 Act also gave immigration officers extensive new powers to close or regulate the use of premises that had been used for the employment of those working illegally.[8m] The regimes for issuing licences to drive private hire vehicles and for the sale of alcohol and food were amended by the 2016 so as to include an immigration status requirement for obtaining and retaining a licence.[8n]

[8a] SI 2014/2771, art 6.
[8b] SI 2016/11, art 2.
[8c] IA 2016, ss 39–42.

[8d] IA 2014, ss 46, 47, amending the Road Traffic Act 1988.
[8e] IA 2016, s 43, inserting new paras 25CA, 25CB and 25CC into Sch 2 to IA 1971.
[8f] IA 2016, s 44, inserting new s 24C into IA 1971.
[8g] IA 2016, s 44.
[8h] IA 2014, s 40.
[8i] IA 2016, s 45 and Sch 7.
[8j] IA 2016, s 34, introducing s 24B into the IA 1971.
[8k] IA 2016, s 35, amending IANA 2006, s 21.
[8l] IANA 2006, s 21 prior to its amendment by IA 2016, s 35.
[8m] IA 2016, s 38 and Sch 6.
[8n] IA 2016, ss 36, 37.

## ARREST AND DETENTION

### Arrest without warrant

**15.4** *[In the text after footnote reference 1, add:]*

the Immigration Act 2016 added the offences of illegal working,[1a] employing an illegal worker,[1b] driving whilst unlawfully in the UK[1c] and obstructing an officer in the performance of 'maritime enforcement' functions or failing to comply with a requirement made by an officer in the performance of those functions[1d] to the offences carrying a power of arrest without warrant

[1a] IA 2016, s 34 (4), amending IA 1971, s 28A(3)(a).
[1b] IA 2016, s 35(9), amending IA 1971, s 28A.
[1c] IA 2016, s 44(3), amending IA 1971, s 28A.
[1d] IA 2016, Sch 14, adding new Sch 4A, paras 11, 22 and 33 to IA 1971.

### Arrest with a warrant

**15.6** *[In the text, delete the full stop at the end of the first sentence and after footnote reference 2, and add:]*

or of renting property or permitting occupation by a person not having the right to rent.[2a]

[2a] IA 2016, s 39(6), amending IA 1971, s 28A.

## SEARCH AND SEIZURE OF EVIDENCE

### Search for evidence of crime

**15.13** *[At the end of the paragraph, add:]*

The Immigration Act 2016 provides new powers to enter and search premises for evidence of offences of illegal working[19] and renting premises to or permitting their occupation by persons without a right to rent.[20] An immigration officer lawfully on any premises may seize anything found in the course of exercising his or her functions under the Immigration Acts that the officer reasonably believes was obtained in consequence of the commission of an offence or is evidence relating to an offence.[21] The immigration officer is obliged then to notify a person who has functions in relation to the investigation of the offence with a view to passing on the seized materials.[22]

[19]   IA 2016, s 34(7), amending IA 1971, s 28D.
[20]   IA 2016, s 39(2), inserting new s 33C(6) into IA 2014.
[21]   IA 2016, s 48.
[22]   IA 2016, s 49.

## Search for evidence to support a civil penalty

**15.13A** *[Insert new heading and new paragraph:]*

An immigration officer lawfully on any premises may search for and seize documents that may assist in determining liability for a civil penalty for employing an illegal worker or leasing premises to a person without a right to rent.[1]

[1]   IA 2016, s 47.

## Search for evidence to assist nationality and immigration control

**15.14** *[In the text after footnote reference 2, add:]*

An immigration officer may search premises for evidence supporting a ground for curtailing a person's leave to enter or remain. For such a search to be carried out, the person has to be on the premises and be liable to detention as a person in respect of whom there are reasonable grounds to be believe that removal directions may be given.[2a]

*[In the text after footnote reference 3, add:]*

The Secretary of State may direct a detainee custody officer, prison officer or prisoner custody officer to search a detainee, his or her property and accommodation for documents that might establish the person's identity, nationality or citizenship or might indicate where the person embarked from or intended to go.[3a]

*[Insert footnotes in correct sequential order:]*

[2a]   IA 2016, s 46(3), introducing a new para 15A into IA 1971, Sch 25.
[3a]   IA 2016, s 51.

**15.15** *[At the end of the paragraph add:]*

An immigration officer who has reasonable grounds to believe that a person has a driving licence but is not lawfully present in the UK may enter and search premises occupied or controlled by the person or in which the person was encountered in order to look for the driving licence.[8] The immigration officer may also search the person for a driving licence.[9]

[8]   IA 2016, s 43, adding new para 25CA to IA 1971, Sch 2.
[9]   IA 2016, s 43(2), adding new para 25CB to IA 1971, Sch 2.

## Maritime control and enforcement

**15.15A**  *[Insert new heading and new paragraph:]*

The Immigration Act 2016 confers an array of new powers[1] upon 'relevant officers', who are immigration officers, constables and 'enforcement officers', ie commissioned officers of any naval ship or persons in command of any naval, army or RAF aircraft or hovercraft.[2] The same powers are also conferred on 'assistants' who are persons accompanying relevant officers and as such, may perform any of the relevant officers' functions under a relevant officer's supervision.[3] The purpose of the new powers is to prevent, detect and investigate the facilitation of: breaches or attempted breaches of immigration law; the arrival or attempted arrival or entry into the UK of asylum seekers or entry or attempted entry in breach of a deportation order.[4] The powers may be exercised in the territorial seas adjacent to England and Wales, Scotland and Northern Ireland and separate provisions are made for each of the three jurisdictions. If a relevant officer has reasonable grounds to believe that one of the offences enumerated above is being committed on a ship in territorial waters, the relevant officer may:

- stop and board the ship and require the ship to be taken to a port in the UK;
- search the ship and anyone or anything in the ship;
- require a person on the ship to give information about him or herself or anything on the ship;
- arrest without warrant anyone suspected of committing one of the enumerated offences;
- seize and retain anything appearing to be evidence of the offence and require the production of or search for nationality documents.

Reasonable force may be used and it is an offence to obstruct a relevant officer or to fail to comply with a requirement made by a relevant officer for which a person may be arrested without warrant and sentenced to up to 51 weeks' imprisonment.

[1]  In Sch 14, which amends Immigration Act 1971, including by adding a new Sch 4A.
[2]  IA 1971, s 28Q, as inserted.
[3]  IA 1971, Sch 4A, para 7, as inserted.
[4]  IA 1971, ss 25, 25A and 25B, as amended by IA 2016, Sch 14, paras 2–4 and IA 1971, s 28M(2), as inserted.

## Forfeiture of detained property

**15.18**  *[At the end of the paragraph add:]*

Immigration officers or constables may detain vehicles used to commit the offence of driving whilst unlawfully in the United Kingdom and may enter and search premises to that end.[2] If a person is convicted of driving whilst unlawfully in the UK, the court may order the forfeiture of the vehicle used to commit the offence.[3]

[2]  IA 2016, s 44(2), inserting new ss 24D and 24E into IA 1971.
[3]  IA 2016, s 44(2), inserting new s 24F into IA 1971.

## BIOMETRIC INFORMATION AND DOCUMENTS

**15.23** *[The paragraph lists those whose fingerprints may be taken. In place of '(vi) dependents of any of the above' substitute:]*

(vi) members of the family of any of the above.

*[In footnote 7, at the beginning of the first sentence in front of 'IAA 1999, s 141', insert:]*

IA 2016, s 57, amending

## GETTING AND EXCHANGING INFORMATION

### Other information-gathering powers

**15.29** *[At the end of the paragraph add:]*

The Immigration Act 2016 amends the IAA 1999 so that public authorities[10] generally, rather than a list of specifically identified persons, are given a power to supply information to the Secretary of State.[11] The Act also gives the Secretary of State a power to require listed bodies to provide her with nationality documents that she believes they hold in relation to a person who may be liable to removal from the UK.[12] The listed bodies include law enforcement agencies, local authorities, regulatory bodies, health bodies, educational institutions and registration officials.[13] A nationality document is very broadly defined as one which might establish a person's identity, nationality or citizenship or place from which the person travelled to the UK or intends to go to.[14]

[10] Ie persons with functions of a public nature, but not including HMRC, Parliament, the Scottish Parliament or the Welsh or Northern Irish Assemblies.
[11] IA 2016, s 55.
[12] IA 2016, s 55(11), introducing a new s 20A to the Immigration and Asylum Act 1999.
[13] IA 2016, Sch 9, containing a new Sch A1 to IAA 1999.
[14] IAA 1999, s 20A(14), as inserted.

## CRIMINAL OFFENCES

### Facilitating unlawful immigration and assisting asylum seekers

**15.49** *[In footnote 2, add:]*

Section 25(3) permits other evidence to prove the breach of law in another state, such as expert evidence or admissions: *R v Bina* [2014] EWCA Crim 1444, [2015] Crim LR 287, [2014] 2 Cr App R 30, CA.

**15.50** *[In footnote 1, add:]*

On a prosecution under section 25(1), it is not necessary for the Crown to prove that any actual breach of immigration law occurred; and the word 'facilitates' in section 25 requires no elaboration as to its meaning by the judge when summing up: *R v Ali (Nazakat)* [2015] 1 Cr App R 32, CA (considering *Javaherifard* and *Miller*).

### Trafficking offences

**15.55** *[In footnote 3, add:]*

In *R v Ali* ; *R v Ashraf* [2015] EWCA Crim 1279, 2015] 2 Cr App Rep 457, [2015] All ER (D) 202 (Jul) (relating to the offence of trafficking within the UK in section 58(1) of the Sexual Offences Act 2003), the court considered the distances required for the element of 'travel within' the UK to be made out and held that the legislation did not specify a minimum distance or duration of travel; whist walking between adjacent rooms may well be outside the ambit of the provision because the offence had a clear geographic element, substantive journeys 'involving a number of miles' would fall within the provision.

**15.56** *[Delete the text from the start of the paragraph until the end of footnote reference 9 and replace with the following text:]*

The trafficking offences in sections 57–59 of the Sexual Offences Act 2003 remain in force. However, the offence of trafficking for exploitation in section 4 of the Asylum and Immigration (Treatment of Claimants) Act 2004 has been repealed by the Modern Slavery Act 2015[1] which has introduced new trafficking offences in force as of 31 July 2015.[2] Section 1 creates a new offence of slavery, servitude and forced or compulsory labour. An offence is committed if either: (i) a person holds another person in slavery or servitude and the circumstances are such that the person knows or ought to know that the other person is held in slavery or servitude; or (ii) the person requires another person to perform forced or compulsory labour and the circumstances are such that the person knows or ought to know that the other person is being required to perform such labour.[3] The offence is required to be interpreted in accordance with Article 4 of ECHR.[4] In determining whether the offence is committed all the circumstances are to be considered, including personal circumstances which may make the victim more vulnerable (including the person being a child, or any mental or physical illness).[5] Subsection 5 provides that the victim's consent does not preclude a finding by the court that the elements of the offences are made out by the perpetrator.

Section 2 of the Act creates a general offence of human trafficking. A person commits the offence if they arrange or facilitate the travel of another person with a view to the other person being exploited.[6] Travel is defined as arriving in, entering, departing or travelling within any country.[7] Consent is irrelevant to whether or not the offence is made out.[8] Examples are given in subsection (3) of what may amount to arranging or facilitating travel, and include recruiting, transporting, transferring, harbouring, receiving or exchanging control of the system. The language reflects the definitions of trafficking set out in the Convention on Action against Trafficking and the Palermo Protocol. The *mens rea* is made out if the perpetrator either intends to exploit the victim, or knows or ought to know that any other person is likely to exploit them.[9] For UK nationals the offence is extra-territorial in reach: the offence is committed regardless of where the arranging or facilitating takes place or the country of travel, entry and departure. For non-UK nationals, the offence is only made out if any part of the arranging or facilitating, or the travel, involves the UK.[9a]

The definition of exploitation is set out in more detail in section 3, to include not only slavery, servitude and forced labour with reference to the section 1 offence, but also any conduct amounting to an offence under the Sexual

Offences Act 2003 or taking indecent images of a child (sexual exploitation); the removal of organs; and securing services or benefits by force, threats or deception, including where a person is used to do something for the purpose of securing services or benefits on the grounds that they are a child, ill or disabled.

The maximum penalties for the offences under sections 1 and 2 are life imprisonment on indictment; and on summary conviction imprisonment for six months, or a fine, or both.[9b]

*[In the next paragraph, starting 'In R v SK . . . ', insert at the beginning:]*

The case law relating to the now repealed trafficking offence under AI(TC)A 2004 remains relevant to the new offences in the Modern Slavery Act 2015.

[1]   Modern Slavery Act 2015, s 57(1), Sch 5, Pt 1, para 6(1) and (2) in relation to England and Wales.
[2]   SI 2015/1476, reg 2(a).
[3]   Modern Slavery Act 2015, s1(1).
[4]   Ibid, s1(2).
[5]   Ibid, s 1(3) and (4).
[6]   Ibid, s2(1).
[7]   Ibid, s 2(5).
[8]   Ibid, s 2(2).
[9]   Ibid, s 2(4).
[9a]  Ibid, s 2(6) and (7).
[9b]  Ibid, s 5(1). On the coming into force of s 154(1) of the Criminal Justice Act 2003, the maximum sentence on summary conviction will be 12 months: s 5(4).

## Breach of conditions and overstaying

**15.58** *[In footnote 1, add:]*

Where the condition is a prohibition on working, there is now a new, separate, criminal offence of illegal working by virtue of section 34 of the Immigration Act 2016, see **15.65A** below.

## New offence of illegal working

**15.65A** *[Insert new heading and new paragraph:]*

Section 34 of the Immigration Act 2016, which inserts a new section 24B into IA 1971 and came into force on 12 July 2016, creates a new criminal offence of illegal working.[1] The offence is committed where a person subject to immigration control works at a time when they are disqualified from doing so by reason of their immigration status and knows or has reasonable cause to believe that they are so disqualified.[2] A person is disqualified from working if they do not have leave to enter or remain in the UK, or their leave is either invalid, has ceased to have effect (by reason of curtailment, revocation, cancellation, passage of time or otherwise) or is subject to a condition preventing them from working.[3] The new offence is summary only and the maximum penalty is six months' imprisonment or an unlimited fine, or both[4] (in England and Wales); or (in Scotland or Northern Ireland) six months' imprisonment or a fine not exceeding the statutory maximum (currently £5,000), or both.[5] Those living under the UK under the new form of immigration bail (not yet in force but replacing current bail and temporary admission)[6] will not be disqualified from working if they have been granted permission to work, since they are treated as if they have been granted leave to enter or remain for the purposes of section 24B(2).

'Work' is broadly defined in this provision, to include not only contracts of employment (whether agreed orally or in writing, by express or implied terms), but also apprenticeships and contracts to undertake work on a self-employed basis.[7] Section 45 of the Modern Slavery Act 2015 provides a defence for those who commit this new offence if they are compelled to do so as a result of their exploitation.

Prior to the coming into force of this provision it was, of course, already an offence under section 24 of the IA 1971 to work when a condition of leave prohibited it.[8] However, the government has emphasised the importance of creating an offence of illegal working 'in its own right', as part of its policy aim 'to make it harder for people to live and work illegally in the UK'.[9] In addition, wages paid for illegal working under this provision may now be subject to confiscation orders under the Proceeds of Crime Act 2002.[10]

1   See SI 2016/603, reg 3(e).
2   IA 1971, s 24B(1).
3   IA 1971, s 24B(2).
4   To be increased to 51 weeks' imprisonment if and when s 281(5) of the Criminal Justice Act 2003 comes into force.
5   IA 1971, s 24B(3).
6   See Sch 10 to the IA 2016 and see further **18.66A** et seq.
7   IA 1971, s 24B(10).
8   See **15.58** and **15.64**.
9   See 'Immigration Act 2016 Factsheet – Illegal Working', Home Office, July 2016.
10   IA 1971, s 24B(5)°C(7).

### New driving offence

**15.93A** *[Insert new heading and new paragraph:]*

Section 44(2) of the Immigration Act 2016 inserts a new section 24C into IA 1971 to create a new offence of driving whilst unlawfully in the UK. The offence is committed if a person drives a vehicle on a road or other public place and at the time knows or has reasonable cause to believe that they are not lawfully resident.[1] A person guilty of this offence will be liable on summary conviction to imprisonment of up to six months[2] and/or a fine of up to the statutory maximum, or an unlimited fine in England and Wales. After conviction, the court may order forfeiture of the vehicle.[3] These provisions are not yet in force at the time of writing.

1   IA 1971, s 24C(1).
2   Or, in England and Wales, 51 weeks on the coming into force of s 281(5) of the Criminal Justice Act 2003.
3   See **15.18**.

## EMPLOYER SANCTIONS

### Introduction

**15.95** *[Delete the text between footnote references 2 and 3 and substitute:]*

and (2) a criminal offence of employing someone where the employer knew or ought to have known that their employee was disqualified from working.

*[Delete the text of footnote 3 and insert:]*

See below at **15.100–15.101**.

### Criminal offence

**15.100** *[Delete text of whole paragraph and substitute:]*

The second sanction is a criminal offence contained in section 21 of IAN 2006. Prior to its amendment by section 35 of the Immigration Act 2016, which came into force on 12 July 2016,[1] the offence required knowledge on the part of the employer that the employee was subject to immigration control. Now an employer is caught by the offence not only if they know that their employee is disqualified from working by reason of their immigration status, but also if they have reasonable cause to believe their employee is so disqualified.[2] In other words, it is enough that an employer ought to have known that their employee did not have the right to work. The government rationale was to target employers who deliberately 'turn a blind eye' to employing illegal migrants, who risked a fine under the civil penalty but escaped criminal sanctions where it was necessary to prove knowledge of the employee's immigration status.[3] As with the new offence of illegal working,[4] a person is disqualified from working if they do not have leave to enter or remain in the UK, or their leave is either invalid, has ceased to have effect (by reason of curtailment, revocation, cancellation, passage of time or otherwise) or is subject to a condition preventing them from working.[5]

The maximum penalty for this offence on indictment is now five years' imprisonment, or a fine, or both; and on summary conviction imprisonment for six months or a fine of £5000, or both.

[1] See SI 2016/603, reg 3(f).
[2] IAN 2006, s 21(1A).
[3] See 'Immigration Act 2016 Factsheet – Illegal Working', Home Office, July 2016.
[4] See **15.65A**.
[5] IAN 2006, s 21(1B).

**15.101** *[After the words ' . . . is imputed to the body' and before the words 'Section 22(2) provides . . . ' insert:]*

A new section 22(1A), inserted by section 35 of the Immigration Act 2016, provides that such a person is also criminally liable if they had reasonable cause to believe relevant facts about the employee, to mirror the *mens rea* in section 21(1A). Hence, the 2016 Act significantly widens the criminal liability of directors, trustees and partners, who are caught by this provision where the person within their organisation with responsibility for conducting right to work checks ought to have known that an employee did not have permission to work.

### Illegal working notices and closure orders

**15.101A** *[Insert new heading and new paragraph:]*

Schedule 6 to the Immigration Act 2016, which came into force on 1 December 2016,[1] grants a new power to chief immigration officers to issue a notice to close premises where they are satisfied on reasonable grounds that an employer operating at the premises is employing an illegal worker and one of the following conditions is met: the employer has either been required to pay a fine within the last three years for employing an illegal worker, has a fine as yet unpaid, or has been convicted of the offence of employing an illegal worker under section 21 of IAN 2006.[2] There is a duty for the officer to make reasonable efforts to inform people who live on the premises and consult others as appropriate before issuing a notice.[3] The notice enables the chief immigration officer to close and prohibit entry to the premises for a period of up to 48 hours.[4] The notice may be cancelled if the conditions for issuing the notice are not in fact met.[5] If the closure notice is not cancelled, the chief immigration officer must apply to the magistrates' court for an illegal working compliance order. The court may adjourn the hearing of the application for up to 14 days to enable any person who has an interest in the premises to show why an order should not be made.[6] The court may issue an order if satisfied on the balance of probabilities that an illegal worker is being employed on the premises, the employer meets one of the aforementioned conditions and the order is necessary to prevent illegal working.[7]

Breach of an illegal working closure notice or illegal working compliance order is a criminal offence. The maximum penalty is six months' imprisonment, an unlimited fine, or both.[8] There is a right of appeal against an illegal working compliance order, or an order that an illegal working closure notice remains in force, to the Crown Court.

[1]  SI 2016/1037, reg 5(j).
[2]  IA 2016, Sch 6, para 1(6).
[3]  Ibid, para 1(11) and (12).
[4]  Ibid, para 3.
[5]  Ibid, para 5(1).
[6]  Ibid, para 6(2).
[7]  Ibid, para 5(5).
[8]  In England and Wales (or 51 weeks if, and when, s 281(5) of the Criminal Justice Act 2003 comes into force). In Scotland and Northern Ireland, the maximum penalties are imprisonment for 12 and 6 months respectively, or a fine not exceeding the statutory maximum (currently £5,000). See Para 11(4).

## LANDLORD SANCTIONS

**5.118** *[In the main text, after footnote reference 2, delete 'both of which come into force on 1 December 2014' and substitute:]*

both of which came into force on 1 December 2016

*[Delete the next sentence 'Given our publication deadlines it is too late to comment on the new Orders.']*

*[In footnote 3, delete the text and substitute:]*

IA 2014, ss 20–33. Following a pilot in the West Midlands, this scheme was extended to the whole of England on 1 February 2016.

## New offence of leasing premises

**15.121** *[Insert new heading and new paragraph:]*

Section 39 of the Immigration Act 2016, which came into force in full on 1 December 2016,[1] inserts new sections 33A–33C into IA 2014, creating new offences relating to letting private residential premises to adults disqualified from renting as a result of their immigration status. Section 33A creates two new offences. The first is committed by a landlord under a residential tenancy agreement if premises are occupied by a person disqualified from doing so as a result of their immigration status[2] and the landlord knows or has reasonable cause to believe this to be the case.[3] The offence applies where any adult is occupying the premises, regardless of whether they are named in the tenancy agreement, so long as the landlord knew or had reason to believe they were present. There is a defence under section 33A(6) where the landlord has taken reasonable steps to terminate the tenancy within a reasonable period of time. In determining whether the defence applies, the court must have regard to guidance issued by the Secretary of State.[4] The second offence is committed only if a tenant's leave to remain expires during the course of a tenancy, the tenant's eligibility period[5] has expired, the tenant continues to occupy the property and the landlord knows or has reasonable cause to believe this has happened but does not notify the Secretary of State as soon as reasonably practicable.[6]

Section 33B creates two analogous offences for agents responsible for carrying out right to rent checks on behalf of a landlord. The offences are triable either way and carry a maximum penalty of five years' imprisonment, or a fine, or both, on indictment; or on summary conviction six months' imprisonment,[7] or a fine, or both.

[1] See SI 2016/1037, reg 5(c).
[2] Ie the persons defined by IA 2014, s 21. See above at **15.118**, fn 4.
[3] IA 2014, s 33A(1)–(3).
[4] IA 2014, s 33A(7).
[5] As defined in IA 2014, s 27.
[6] IA 2014, s 33A(10).
[7] Or twelve months when section 154(1) of the Criminal Justice Act 2003 comes into force.

## New eviction powers

**15.122** *[Insert new heading and new paragraph:]*

The Immigration Act 2016 also introduces new powers for landlords and agents to evict persons occupying premises who are disqualified from renting as the result of their immigration status.[1] These powers came into force on 1 December 2016.[2] Under the new section 33D of IA 2014, a landlord may terminate a residential tenancy agreement where they have been notified by the Secretary of State that a person occupying their property does not have the right to rent.[3] The power applies not only to tenants and other persons named in the tenancy agreement, but also to any person the landlord knows is occupying the premises.[4] There is a 28-day notice period, and a notice to terminate must be given by delivering it to the tenant(s); leaving it at the premises; sending it by post to the tenant(s) at the address of the premises; or in any other prescribed manner.[5] Under the new section 33E of IA 2014 there is provision for landlords to evict in other circumstances where an occupant is a disqualified person. Under subsections (1) and (2), there is an implied term in any residential tenancy agreement that is not a protected, statutory or assured tenancy[6] that allows for the termination of the agreement when an adult occupant does not have the right to rent. For these purposes the agreement is excluded from the safeguards in the Protection from Eviction Act 1977.[7]

[1]   IA 2016, s 40, inserting new ss 33D and 33E into IA 2014.
[2]   SI 2016/1037, reg 5(d).
[3]   Or to put it in the words of this and the similar provisions surveyed in this section, the person is disqualified as a result of their immigration status from entering into a residential tenancy agreement.
[4]   IA 2014, s 33D(8).
[5]   IA 2014, s 33D(4) and (5).
[6]   Within the meaning of the Rent Act 1977 and the Housing Act 1988.
[7]   IA 2014, s 33E(5).

## NEW LICENSING PROVISIONS

### Taxis and private hire vehicles

**15.123**  *[Insert new two new headings and new paragraph:]*

Schedule 5 of the Immigration Act 2016, in force as of 1 December 2016, amends the licensing regime for taxis and private hire vehicles to prevent those who do not have permission to work in the UK from holding taxi operator or driver licences. The stated aim of this provision is to make immigration checks compulsory in this area, since most drivers and operators are self-employed and hence not subject to the right to work checks carried out by employers.[1] The detailed provisions insert amendments to various legislation determining the licencing of private hire vehicles.[2] They prohibit the issue of driver and operator licences to applicants who are disqualified by their immigration status from driving a licenced vehicle or taxi, and require that the licencing authority has regard to guidance issued by the Secretary of State when determining whether an applicant is so disqualified.[3] Where a person's immigration leave is time-limited to less than the statutory length for a driver's licence, the licence will be issued for a duration which does not exceed the applicant's period of leave, and where leave has been extended via section 3C of IA 1971, any and licence granted will be limited to a period not exceeding three months.[4] Where a licence holder's leave comes to an end (for example as the result of curtailment), their licence automatically lapses, and the holder must return their licence and driver's badge to the licensing authority. Any failure to do so within seven days, without reasonable cause, amounts to a criminal offence liable to a fine not exceeding level 3 on the standard scale (currently £1,000) on summary conviction, or a daily fine for each day of failure to return the documents after conviction.[5]

For the purpose of these provisions, a person is disqualified from driving or operating a private hire vehicle or taxi by reason of their immigration status if they not have leave to enter or remain in the UK, or their leave is either invalid, has ceased to have effect (by reason of curtailment, revocation, cancellation, passage of time or otherwise) or is subject to a condition preventing them from driving or operating a private hire vehicle or taxi.[6] Hence the definition mirrors that contained in the new offence of illegal working.[7]

[1]  See 'Immigration Act 2016 Factsheet – Illegal Working', Home Office, July 2016.
[2]  Including the Metropolitan Public Carriage Act 1989 (for London), the Local Government (Miscellaneous Provisions) Act 1976, the Plymouth City Council Act 1975 and the Civic Government (Scotland) Act 1982.
[3]  IA 2016, Sch 5, paras 18, 21, 23, 30, 36, 38. 'Guidance for Licensing Authorities to prevent illegal working in the taxi and private hire sector in England and Wales', Home Office, 1 December 2016.
[4]  IA 2016, Sch 5, paras 20, 32, 37, 47.
[5]  IA 2016, Sch 5, paras 20, 32, 37, 47.
[6]  See, eg paras 4 and 6.
[7]  See **15.65A** above.

## Licenses for the sale of alcohol and food

**15.124** *[Insert new heading and new paragraph:]*

Schedule 4 to the Immigration Act 2016 introduces similar restrictions, not yet in force at the time of writing, on the licencing regime for personal or premises licences (for the sale of alcohol or for the sale of hot food or drink between 11pm and 5am) so that the licence holder must have the right to work in the UK.

## BANK ACCOUNTS

**15.125** *[Insert new heading and new paragraph:]*

Under section 40 of IA 2014, in force since 12 December 2014,[1] banks and building societies are required to undertake immigration status checks and are prohibited from opening current accounts for people without leave to enter in the UK. Schedule 7 to the Immigration Act 2016 inserts new sections 40A–40H which go further and facilitate the closure of accounts in the majority of cases. The provisions impose new requirements for banks and building societies to carry out periodic checks, and where such checks identify that the account holder requires leave to enter or remain in the UK but does not have it, and the Secretary of State considers that the person should not be provided with a current account, the bank or building society is required to notify the Secretary of State.[2] The Secretary of State may then apply to the magistrates' court for an order to freeze the disqualified person's account or accounts, or notify the bank or building society that it is under a duty to close the account as soon as reasonably practicable.[3] These provisions are not yet in force at the time of writing.

1   SI 2014/1943, art 2.
2   IA 2016, Sch 7, para 2; IA 2014, ss 40A and 40B.
3   IA 2016, Sch 7, para 2; IA 2014, ss 40C and 40G.

Chapter 16

# DEPORTATION AND REPATRIATION

## DEPORTATION

### Introduction

**16.1** *[Delete footnote 3 and substitute:]*

*R (on the application of George (Fitzroy)) v Secretary of State for the Home Department* [2014] UKSC 28. However, only deportation orders pursuant to s 32 of the UK Borders Act 2007 may be made whilst an appeal is pending under s 82 (s 79(3)). However, where an appeal is pending against such a deportation order, leave is not invalidated where there is an in-country appeal pending (s 79(4) read with s 78 of Nationality Immigration and Asylum Act 2002). Where such ILR remains extant the Secretary of State can revoke it under section 76 Nationality Immigration and Asylum Act 2002. See below for the effect of s 94B of the Nationality Immigration and Asylum Act 2002 in force from 28 July 2014 in respect of deportees and whether appeals can be brought or continued in-country. (See also **CHAPTER 19** as to the extension of section 94B to other Article 8 appeals under section 82 of the Nationality Asylum Immigration Act 2002 from 1 December 2016 by section 63 of the Immigration Act 2016.)

**16.2** *[Delete the paragraph and substitute:]*

In 2006, populist agitation in the media led to a public outcry over foreign national prisoners being released from prison at the end of their sentences without being considered for deportation. This led initially to amendment of the Immigration Rules and thousands of people being considered for deportation in circumstances where prior to that date such consideration would have been unlikely. It also led to foreign nationals (or in some instances those with 'foreign sounding' names) being refused release from prison on their release date or being recategorised from open prison conditions to closed conditions. By the end of 2007, radical statutory changes had been enacted by Parliament requiring the Secretary of State to make an 'automatic deportation order' in prescribed circumstances and introducing a presumption of detention.[1] The incremental tightening of deportation processes continued with the introduction into the Immigration Rules on 9 July 2012 of new provisions introducing for the first time a set of criteria by reference to which the impact of Article 8 in criminal deportation cases was to be assessed.[2] It culminated in the Immigration Act 2014 incorporation into primary legislation a series of 'considerations' designed to dictate the approach to Article 8 assessment by decision makers[3] and further by the introduction of a new certification process rendering non-suspensive the appeal rights of deportees absent demonstration of serious and irreparable harm.[4]

1 UK Borders Act 2007, ss 32–39.
2 Statement of Changes to the Immigration Rules HC 194, paras 390–399A. These paragraphs were further amended by Statement of Changes HC 532, 10 July 2014, to come into effect at the same time as the Immigration Act 2014, from 28 July 2014. (See *YM (Uganda v Secretary of State for the Home Department* [2014] EWCA Civ 1292, [2015] INLR 405, as to the relevance of the rules in force at the date of the appeal).
3 Immigration Act 2014, ss 17A–17C.
4 Immigration Act 2014, s 19.

### History of the power to deport

**16.3** *[In the final sentence of the paragraph, retain footnote reference 6, and substitute the words: 'or on a recommendation in a criminal case' with:]*

or by the sentencing judge in a criminal case

*[In footnote 1, delete the text and substitute:]*

Ie not Commonwealth citizens. Defined in the British Nationality Act 1981, s 50(1).

*[In footnote 2, delete the text and substitute:]*

SI 1953/1671, made under the Aliens Restriction Act 1914 and the Aliens Restriction (Amendment) Act 1919, which were temporary laws renewed each year under the Expiring Laws Continuance Acts. For arguments about the Prerogative, see CHAPTER 1, above (and see now the Supreme Court in *Miller and Others v Secretary of State for Exiting the European Union* [2017] UKSC 5 to the exercise of prerogative powers).

### DEPORTATION – LIABILITY AND EXEMPTION

### Non-British citizens

**16.5** *[Delete paragraph and substitute:]*

A British citizen cannot be deported.[1] If someone becomes a citizen (or acquires the right of abode and is therefore deemed to be a citizen for the purposes of the Immigration Acts) any deportation order ceases to have effect.[2] The term 'British citizen' includes a Commonwealth citizen who had the right of abode in the UK before 1983.[3] Thus a Commonwealth woman married to a British citizen before 1983 is not liable to be deported.[4] Section 65 of the Immigration Act 2014, inserts sections 4E to 4J into the British Nationality Act 1981, to allow certain citizens of the UK and colonies to register by entitlement, where there was no acquisition of citizenship by birth, as a consequence of the father not being married to the mother. Where the deportee was historically denied citizenship as a result of discriminatory legislation, deportation may amount to a breach of Articles 8 and 14 of ECHR.[5] There is no legal bar in UK domestic law to deporting a British Overseas Territories citizen or a British Overseas citizen,[6] and in the case of British Overseas citizen visitors there can be no legitimate expectation that they will not be deported[7] unless they are otherwise stateless.[8] In practice, however, it is extremely difficult as there appears to be little obligation on the country of former residence to receive them back.[9] Equally, there is no bar on the deportation of EEA nationals or Turkish nationals and their dependants who have rights to reside as employed or self-employed persons under the Turkey-EC Association Agreement, but special rules apply.[10] There is no statutory bar on the deportation of Convention refugees, although the Immigration Rules preclude the making of a deportation order against anyone whose removal would breach the UK's obligations under the Refugee Convention or the ECHR.[11] There are provisions for revoking both citizenship and the right of abode. See Chapters 2 and 4, above. If this action was taken successfully such people would become liable for deportation. Similarly, where citizenship was obtained by deception or other means rendering the person liable to deprivation, a person would become liable for deportation.[12] Importantly, however, a deprivation of nationality order and deportation order can be made at the same time. Further, the Secretary of State may argue that citizenship obtained by deception is a nullity, and thus does not require the deprivation mechanism to be invoked at all and rendering a person liable to deportation.[13] Where British Citizenship is in dispute, the onus is on the person facing deportation, who asserts their entitlement, to prove it.[14]

1    Immigration Act 1971, ss 3(5), 6(2).
2    Immigration Act 1971, s 5(2). This contrasts with the position under the old law of an alien who became a British subject after the making of a deportation order: see *C v E* (1946) 62 TLR 326.
3    Immigration Act 1971, s 2, as amended by British Nationality Act 1981.
4    Immigration Act 1971, ss 2(2) and 5(2). But if the marriage took place after a deportation order had been signed, then she would not be deemed to be a British citizen.
5    The Supreme Court in *R (on the application of Johnson) v Secretary of State for the Home Department* [2016] UKSC 56, [2016] 3 WLR 1267 (upheld the earlier judgment at first instance of Dingemans J, and overturned the Court of Appeal in a challenge to a clearly unfounded certification of an ECHR, Article 8 claim against deportation and declared that the imposition of a good character requirement (by s 41A of the British Nationality Act 1981 (as amended from 6 April 2015) for the acquisition of British nationality for such a person (now adult) who have otherwise acquired citizenship by right at birth but for his illegitimacy was incompatible with the ECHR). The Court held that whilst the ECHR did not guarantee the right to acquire a particular citizenship, the denial of citizenship, which had such an important effect upon a person's social identity, was sufficiently within the ambit of Article 8 to trigger Article 14 and very weighty reasons were required to justify discrimination in circumstances resulting in liability for deportation and where, but for the accident of birth outside wedlock (for which he was not responsible), he would otherwise have been a British citizen by birth in the UK (and no justification was posited for the distinction).
6    See *R v Immigration Appeal Tribunal, ex p Sunsara* [1995] Imm AR 15.
7    *Patel v Secretary of State for the Home Department* [1993] Imm AR 392, CA.
8    See Chapter 2 on nationality: re: registration under s 4B of the Nationality Immigration and Asylum Act 2002 in such circumstances.
9    See *R v Chief Immigration Officer, Gatwick Airport, ex p Singh (Harjendar)* [1987] Imm AR 346, QBD. The absence of evidence that the country specified in the removal direction would accept a person did not remove the Secretary of State's power to deport: *Sunsara*, above.
10   See further Chapter 6 above.
11   See *Raziastaraie v Secretary of State for the Home Department* [1995] Imm AR 459, CA. See also *Gurung v Secretary of State for the Home Department* [2002] UKIAT 4870, [2003] Imm AR 115, [2003] INLR 133.
12   An appeal against deprivation under s 40A of the British Nationality Act 1981 is no longer suspensive (following the repeal of s 40A(6) of the 1981 Act by the Asylum and Immigration (Treatment of Claimants etc) Act 2004 from 3 April 2005. See also the Nationality Instructions, Chapter 55, as to the timing of the making of a deprivation order. The earlier

provision that no order would be made unless, or until, a decision to grant leave to remain or take a decision to remove at Chapter 55.7.7.1 has now been removed. It is the Secretary of State's position that a person on deprivation of citizenship has no leave to remain unless granted at that point.

13 *Hysaj v Secretary of State* [2015] EWCA Civ 1195, [2016] 1 WLR 673. At the time of writing, this case is seeking permission to appeal to the Supreme Court. In that case the Secretary of State conceded that ILR obtained by deception in such circumstances was however valid.

14 Nationality, Immigration and Asylum Act 2002, s 117D(5) inserted by s 19 of the Immigration Act 2014, where a person seeks to rely on that status for themselves or any other relevant person in the context of an Article 8 appeal under section 82 of the Nationality Immigration and Asylum Act 2002.

## Exemption from deportation

### Five-year rule for Irish and Commonwealth citizens

**16.8** *[Delete the text for footnote 1 and substitute:]*

Immigration Act 1971, s 7(1)b) (substituted by the Nationality, Immigration and Asylum Act 2002, s 75), and (c). Section 7(1)(a) (which exempted Commonwealth and Irish citizens from deportation on public good grounds if they were ordinarily resident on 1 January 1973 and at all times until the date of the decision) was repealed as redundant (NIAA 2002, s 75). See *R v Secretary of State for the Home Department, ex p Oladehinde* [1992] Imm AR 443, QBD.

### Special circumstances of Irish nationals

**16.10** *[In sub-paragraph (ii), for ' . . . the exceptional circumstances' substitute 'the most exceptional circumstances.]*

*[In footnote 2, delete 'v3,0' and substitute with:]*

, Version 4.0, 6 October 2015

## AUTOMATIC DEPORTATION OF FOREIGN CRIMINALS

**16.18** *[Replace paragraph:]*

Section 34 of the 2007 Act governs the timing of the making of the deportation order. Apart from precluding the making of an order under section 32 while any timely[1] criminal conviction or sentence is under appeal or could be brought,[2] the section gives the Secretary of State complete discretion as to timing. There is no restriction on the making of an order under section 32 whilst any appeal against that process is before the IAC.[3] The timing of the deportation order is important in the justification for the operation of the statutory power to certify an appeal to be heard out of country under section 94B of the Nationality Immigration and Asylum Act 2002. (See **16.90** below.)

1 UK Borders Act 2007, s 34(3).
2 UK Borders Act 2007, s 34(2).
3 UK Borders Act 2007, s 35 modifies s 79 of the Nationality, Immigration and Asylum Act 2002, which is the section which normally prevents a deportation order being made while an appeal is brought, so that the section does not apply in cases of automatic deportation

orders made under s 32 of the 2007 Act. However, see above for the impact of section 78 of the Nationality, Immigration and Asylum Act 2002 which suspends the invalidation of any leave by the making of such an order pending the outcome of an in-country appeal.

**16.21** *[Replace paragraph:]*

In most contested cases of automatic deportation, the most common defence is Article 8 of ECHR. Comments on new case law are at **16.44**. However, para A362 of the Immigration Rules states that:

> 'where Article 8 is raised in the context of deportation under Part 13 of these Rules, the claim under Article 8 will only succeed where the requirements of these rules as at 28 July 2014 are met, regardless of when the notice of intention to deport or the deportation order, as appropriate, was served'.

Thus, for the majority of appeals on Article 8 grounds to be successful, they must engage the more limited interpretation of Article 8 contained within section 117C of the Nationality Immigration and Asylum Act 2002[1] and in the Immigration Rules at paras A398 to 399A.[2] The proportionality of the earlier version of those rules was examined by the Court of Appeal in *MF (Nigeria)*[3] and then very recently by the Supreme Court in *Ali* – see **16.28A** below.

[1]  As amended by Immigration Act 2014, s 19.
[2]  HC 395, as amended by Statement of Changes to the Immigration Rules, HC 532.
[3]  [2014] 2 All ER 543, [2014] 1 WLR 544.

**16.26** *[Delete the first two words of the text.]*

**16.27** *[At the end of the first sentence and the beginning of the second, amend the words ' . . . Statement of Changes HC194. Under . . . ' to read as follows:]*

. . . Statement of Changes HC 194 with a statement of intent by the Home Office that under . . .

**16.28** *[Delete and substitute:]*

The exigencies of the new Immigration Rules scheme were explained, and to a material extent, tempered by decisions of the courts, in particular, *MF (Nigeria) v Secretary of State for the Home Department*[1] in which the Court of Appeal held *inter alia* that whilst the Immigration Rules contained in Part 13 constituted a 'complete code' for the purposes of an Article 8 assessment such that 'very compelling' reasons would be required to outweigh the public interest in deportation where an individual fell outwith the criteria laid down in paras 398–399A of the Immigration Rules. Those compelling reasons were encapsulated in the 'exceptional circumstances' threshold specified in the rules, the determination of which would be the product of an application of the proportionality test required by the Strasbourg jurisprudence.

> 'The word "exceptional" is often used to denote a departure from a general rule. The general rule in the present context is that, in the case of a foreign prisoner to whom paras 399 and 399A do not apply, very compelling reasons will be required to outweigh the public interest in deportation. These compelling reasons are the "exceptional circumstances".[2] Therefore that the new rules are a complete code and that the exceptional circumstances to be considered in the balancing exercise involve

the application of a proportionality test as required by the Strasbourg jurisprudence.'[3]

Importantly the Court in *MF (Nigeria)*[4] recognised that where paras 399 and 399A did apply, determination of the issues arising within them would likely involve questions of evaluation as well as hard-edged fact, such as whether it would be 'reasonable' to expect a child to leave the UK or whether there are 'insurmountable obstacles'. In so finding, the Court held that, provided appropriate and substantial weight was given to the public interest as described by the rules, a Tribunal could properly undertake a reasoned evaluation of all of the issues in the case so as to record favourable findings on exceptional grounds, as in fact the Upper Tribunal had done effectively and lawfully in that instance.

[1]    [2013] EWCA Civ 1192, [2013] EWCA Civ 1192, [2014] 1 WLR 544.
[2]    At para 43.
[3]    At para 44.
[4]    [2013] EWCA Civ 1192, [2013] EWCA Civ 1192, [2014] 1 WLR 544


**16.28A** *[Insert new paragraph:]*

For the first time the Supreme Court gave consideration to a deportation appeal and the correct approach to appellate decision making in *Ali (Iraq) v Secretary of State for the Home Department* (referred to here as *Ali*).[1] Although the Supreme Court considered the Immigration Rules in operation before 28 July 2014, their guidance is equally applicable to decision making by reference to the statutory factors in s 117 of the Nationality Immigration and Asylum Act 2002 because: (a) s 117 mirrors the post 28 July 2014 Immigration Rules relating to deportation (paras 398–399A); (b) s 117C(6) ('very compelling circumstances') is an amendment motivated by the Court of Appeal's interpretation of 'exceptional circumstances' in the pre-July 2014 Immigration Rules: *MF (Nigeria) v Secretary of State for the Home Department;*[2] (c) their Lordships' guidance is not dependent upon the specific wording of the rules; and (d) the higher courts' interpretation of s 117 and its guidance (see below), coheres with the approach of the majority in *HA (Iraq)* the majority held:[3]

(i)     **The rules are not law.** The rules (paras 398–390) are not law and do not govern First-tier Tribunal decision-making: *HA (Iraq)* at paras 17 and 53. At para 36 the majority state: the rules ' . . . provide guidance to officials as to categories of case where it is accepted by the Secretary of State that deportation would be disproportionate'.

(ii)    **The rules are not a lens.** The Supreme Court held that since then the courts had 'mistakenly interpreted' *MF* as meaning that the Rules alone governed appellate decision-making. The rules were not a 'complete code' in the sense that they, and they alone, govern appellate decision-making. They are a 'relevant and important consideration' for tribunals (paras 52–53, 80).

(iii)   **The correct approach.** In essence, this requires the tribunal, not to 'look through the lens of the rules' but to conduct its 'own assessment': *HA (Iraq)* at paras 39–46. It is for tribunals to judge whether the countervailing factors led to the conclusion that deportation would be disproportionate: *HA (Iraq)* at paras 46, 49, 51–53. The rules do not (as the decision of the Court of Appeal might have indicated) determine the weight which tribunals must give to the public interest in all cases (paras 62–63).

(iv) **Strasbourg's guiding principles.** Those factors include the SSHD's policy as expressed in the rules but also Strasbourg's non-exhaustive guiding principles: *HA (Iraq)* at para 26 (and see below).

(v) **The Secretary of State's assessment is not to be disregarded.** Where appellate courts or tribunals reach their own decisions after hearing evidence, they should not disregard the decision under appeal. The 'critical issue' would generally be whether, giving due weight to the public interest, the Article 8 claim was sufficiently strong to outweigh it. Generally, only a very strong claim would succeed: *HA (Iraq)* at paras 14, 38 and 45–50.

(vi) **Fact specific.** It is necessary to feed into the analysis the facts of a particular case and the criteria which are appropriate to the context, which permits the relevant differences between lawfully settled migrants and those seeking to be admitted to be taken into account: *HA (Iraq)* at para 50.

(vii) **Structure.** At para 82 of *HA (Iraq)*, Lord Thomas wished to 'emphasise the importance of the structure of judgments of the First-tier Tribunal in decisions where Article 8 is engaged. Judges should, after making their factual determinations, set out in clear and succinct terms their reasoning for the conclusion arrived at through balancing the necessary considerations in the light of the matters set out by Lord Reed at paras 37–38, 46 and 50'. He went on at para 83 to say:

> 'One way of structuring such a judgment would be to follow what has become known as the "balance sheet" approach. After the judge has found the facts, the judge would set out each of the "pros" and "cons" in what has been described as a "balance sheet" and then set out reasoned conclusions as to whether the countervailing factors outweigh the importance attached to the public interest in the deportation of foreign offenders.'

(viii) **Proportionality.** There must be a structured approach to proportionality: *HA (Iraq)* at para 48. At para 161 Lord Kerr said:

> '[A]s Lord Reed has explained, the analytical structure by which the proportionality of a decision or measure should be assessed can, with modest modification, be applied to the present circumstances. That structure has been developed and refined through such cases as *Huang; R (Aguilar Quila) v SSHD (AIRE Centre intervening)* [2011] UKSC 45, [2012] 1 AC 621, and *Bank Mellat v HM Treasury (No 2)* [2013] UKSC 39, [2014] AC 700. It is now firmly established as the appropriate means by which the proportionality of an impugned decision should be determined and it comprehends the fair balance element.'

Incorporated in the judgment is the observation that, where a foreign offender has received a sentence of at least four years, their deportation would 'almost always' outweigh the private interest (para 46) and that successful cases, other than those specified in the conditions in the Rules, are likely to be a very small minority particularly in 'non-settled' cases (para 38). Significantly, however, the Court also held as follows:

(a) The Strasbourg jurisprudence (in particular *Boultif*, *Uner* and *Maslov* at paras 72–75) indicates the relevant factors to consider, including factors bearing on the weight of the public interest in the instant case and all the other factors relevant to the specific case (paras 26, 38, 50).

(b) Consistently with *Huang*, successful cases beyond those specified in the Rules do *not* need to show 'extraordinary' (para 38), or 'unusual' (para 77) circumstances; nor is the review before the tribunal akin to judicial review: the tribunal makes its own decision albeit with weight given to the SSHD's reasons (paras 42–45).

(c) The use of the phrase 'exceptional circumstances' must not distract the decision-maker from the requisite inquiry into the strength of the public interest and the gravity of the proposed interference judged in the light of all the relevant factors in the case. Thus, applying *Huang*, 'exceptionality' was not the legal test (paras 77–78).

(d) A wise approach to structuring a judgment in these cases is to set out a 'balance sheet' approach, listing the pros and cons (paras 83–84).

(e) Cases involving non-settled migrants in which the ties to the UK were established when the person's status rendered his ability to remain living in the UK precarious, are inherently weak (para 75).

It follows from *Ali* that:

(i) the weight to be attached to competing considerations under Article 8 fell within the margin of appreciation of the national authorities (subject to supervision by Strasbourg); the ECHR could, within limits, accommodate judgments made by the national legislatures and governments in that area; the Courts were to attach considerable weight to a general assessment by the SSHD contained in the Rules (paras 35, 46, 50). (Note: the Grand Chamber has been clear that the margin afforded in these cases is a 'certain' not a 'wide' one: *Maslov*, para 76; *Jeunesse v Netherlands*,[4] para 106);

(ii) where the circumstances did not fall within paras 399–399A, the public interest would generally only be outweighed by 'countervailing factors which are very compelling' (para 46).

Hence the factors regarded as relevant by Strasbourg remain of key importance, whether or not expressly referred to in the Rules. It also follows that, whatever expectations may be expressed about the numbers of 'serious' criminals who may succeed, there remains no legal test of 'exceptionality' and decision-takers are conscientiously to consider all the relevant circumstances, in a fact-sensitive exercise so as to strike the appropriate balance for themselves in the particular case. The guidance is of relevance to the post-28 July 2014 regime given the similarity of the provisions and with the inspiration for the amendments deriving from the pre-July 2014 case of *MF* (above).

Thus, it follows that in *LC (China) v Secretary of State for the Home Department*[5] Moore-Bick LJ incorrectly afforded primacy to the Rules. Moore-Bick LJ reasoned to the same effect in *Danso v Secretary of State for the Home Department*,[6] and Jackson LJ applied *LC (China)* in *NA (Pakistan)* at para 51 (see above). In *Secretary of State for the Home Department v AJ (Angola)*,[7] Sales LJ went further holding: 'a tribunal should seek to take account of any Convention rights of an appellant through the lens of the new rules themselves, rather than looking to apply Convention rights for themselves in a free-standing way outside the new rules'. A recent example of its application is *Suckoo v Secretary of State for the Home Department*[8] and *LW (Jamaica) v Secretary of State for the Home Department*[9] (a case involving a 'home grown offender'. See also *Secretary of State v MA (Somalia)*.[10] This was another case where the court of appeal directed itself to *AJ (Angola)* at paras 39–40) (see *MA (Somalia)* at para 20), and held at para 25(ii) that the principle of Maslov should be considered within the framework of the new rules and asking itself whether there were very compelling reasons to outweigh the public interest in deportation. The Supreme Court was categorical; this is not the correct approach.

1   [2016] UKSC 60, [2016] 1 WLR 4799, 166 NLJ 7724.
2   [2013] EWCA Civ 1192, [2013] EWCA Civ 1192, [2014] 1 WLR 544.
3   Lord Reed gave the majority judgment with whom Lord Neuberger, Lady Hale, Lord Wilson, Lord Hughes, and Lord Thomas agreed. Lord Kerr dissented, although much of what he said is more accurately described as animating the majority judgment rather than delivering a judgment at odds with the majority.
4   Application No 12738/10, [2014] ECHR 12738/10.
5   [2014] EWCA Civ 1310, at para 17. A case concerning deportation following a five-year sentence for a serious robbery.
6   [2015] EWCA Civ 596, at para 17.
7   [2014] EWCA Civ 1636, at para 39.
8   [2016] EWCA Civ 39, at para 39.
9   [2016] EWCA Civ 369, at para 30.
10  [2015] EWCA Civ 48. Note that the facts are striking and he was sentenced to 10 years' imprisonment.

## Additional statutory public interest considerations

**16.29** *[Insert new heading and replace paragraph:]*

The Secretary of State has now responded by further modifying her rules, substituting the 'exceptional circumstance' threshold for one of 'very compelling circumstances over and above those described in paragraphs 399 and 399A',[1] and further still by importing a range of considerations material to the disposal of ECHR, Article 8 applications and deportation cases by the court or tribunal charged with the responsibility for determining the question of proportionality into primary legislation ss 117A–117D of NIAA 2002, as inserted by s 19 of the Immigration Act 2014.[2] As noted above in respect of non-deportation cases, at the same time as the Immigration Rules were amended from 28 July 2014, section 117C introduced additional considerations to those applicable to 'ordinary' Article 8 ECHR cases to which the court must 'in particular' have regard when determining 'the public interest question', ie whether an interference with a person's right to respect for private and family life is justified under Article 8(2) in deportation cases:

'**117C Article 8: additional considerations in cases involving foreign criminals**
(1)    The deportation of foreign criminals is in the public interest.
(2)    The more serious the offence committed by a foreign criminal, the greater is the public interest in deportation of the criminal.
(3)    In the case of a foreign criminal ("C") who has not been sentenced to a period of imprisonment of four years or more, the public interest requires C's deportation unless Exception 1 or Exception 2 applies.
(4)    Exception 1 applies where—

(a)    C has been lawfully resident in the United Kingdom for most of C's life,

(b)    C is socially and culturally integrated in the United Kingdom, and

(c)    there would be very significant obstacles to C's integration into the country to which C is proposed to be deported.

(5)    Exception 2 applies where C has a genuine and subsisting relationship with a qualifying partner, or a genuine and subsisting parental relationship with a qualifying child, and the effect of C's deportation on the partner or child would be unduly harsh.

(6)    In the case of a foreign criminal who has been sentenced to a period of imprisonment of at least four years, the public interest requires deportation unless there are very compelling circumstances, over and above those described in Exceptions 1 and 2.

(7)    The considerations in subsections (1) to (6) are to be taken into account where a court or tribunal is considering a decision to deport a foreign criminal only to the extent that the reason for the decision was the offence or offences for which the criminal has been convicted.'

As noted above, the public interest in deportation as expressed in the rules arises through the will of Parliament, since it is rooted in primary statute (the 2007 Act) and now 117A–117D of NIAA 2002. However, section 117A requires courts or tribunals to 'have regard' to the public interest considerations when reaching their decision on proportionality under Article 8 ECHR. Similarly to the Immigration Rules, they are not determinative of the outcome of the proportionality assessment, albeit that the rules and section 117C set out clear statements of policy to which the court must 'have regard' in any appeal.

In cases concerning the deportation of 'foreign criminals' (those sentenced to at least 12 months, or are convicted of an offence causing 'serious harm', or who are 'persistent offenders': s 117D(2) of the 2002 Act), in considering the public interest, a 'court or tribunal', must 'have regard' and 'take into account' the considerations listed in section 117C of NIAA 2002 (ss 117A(2) and 117C(7)). These statutory provisions are also relevant to decisions taken by the SSHD.[3]

The relevant considerations are, first, that the deportation of foreign criminals is in the public interest and the more serious the offence, the greater is the public interest in deportation (s 117C(1), (2)). As to this, both the courts and tribunals are 'obliged to give due respect to the high level of importance which the legislature attaches to the deportation of foreign criminals'.[4] Second, in the case of a person sentenced to *less* than four years' imprisonment, the public interest requires their deportation unless one of two 'exceptions' applies (s 117C(3)).

The first exception applies to those lawfully resident in the UK for 'most of their life', who are 'socially and culturally integrated in the UK' and who face 'very significant obstacles' integrating into the country of return (s 117C(4)).

The second exception applies to those with family life connections to the UK, namely those with a 'genuine and subsisting relationship' with a 'qualifying' partner or child (as defined: s 117D(1)) and the effect of deportation would be 'unduly harsh' (s 117C5)).

Third, as to persons sentenced to at least four years' imprisonment, the public interest requires deportation 'unless there are very compelling circumstances, over and above' those described in the two exceptions (s 117C(6)). This also applies to those sentenced to less than four years who cannot satisfy either exception (see further below for the construction of the statute).

Separate considerations apply in relation to the ability to speak English, financial independence and the legality/ precariousness of immigration status when the Article 8 ties were formed (s 117B).

The first detailed consideration of section 117C was given by the Court of Appeal in *NA(Pakistan) v Secretary of State for the Home Department*[5] which held:

(a) **First, with regard to the relevance and weight of exceptions within s 117C:** at [para 31]: ' . . . the factors singled out for description in Exceptions 1 and 2 will apply with greater or lesser force depending on the specific facts of a particular case'; and where a factor 'of an especially compelling kind'[6] is identified, all factors are carried over into the proportionality assessment; at [para 32]: 'The decision maker, be it the Secretary of State or a tribunal, must look at all the matters relied upon collectively, in order to determine whether they are sufficiently compelling to outweigh the high public interest in deportation'.

(b) **Second, strong factors in s 117C(4) and (5) carry over to s 117C(6):** A foreign criminal seeking to satisfy s 117C(6) ('very compelling circumstances over and above') could rely on matters of the kind referred to in Exceptions 1 and 2 (as per s 117C(4) and (5)), but there would need to be features making the Article 8 claim very strong: *NA* at paras 19–21, 29 and 30–32. (See also: *JZ (Zambia) v Secretary of State for the Home Department*[7] where the Court held that factors *of the character* described in paras 399–399A, albeit not actually satisfying the conditions there specified, were not excluded from the assessment required under para 398.)

(c) **Third, great weight should be accorded to public interest:** Section 117C(1) re-states the deportation of foreign criminals is in the public interest. Both courts and tribunals are obliged to give due respect to the high level of importance which the legislature attaches to the deportation of foreign criminals: *NA (Pakistan) v Secretary of State for the Home Department*.[8]

The Court of Appeal's approach in *NA (Pakistan)* can be read consistently with the decision of the UKSC in *Ali* and does not require a different approach. Both *NA* (at paras 35–37) and *Rhuppiah v Secretary of State for the Home Department*[9] suggest that the Rules, and thus also ss 117A–117D, provide a 'complete code' and therefore specify what the outcome must be in cases concerning foreign criminals. The logic of this approach is, however, reversed by *Ali* (above) in which it was held that the Rules do not provide for such completeness.

(1) A failure to satisfy s 117C(4)–(5) and paras 399–399A cannot be negatively dispositive of the satisfaction of the criterion in s 117C(6) and para 398. The Court in *NA (Pakistan)* held that the criterion in s 117C(6) also applies to those offenders sentenced to under four years, despite the drafting error in s 117C(3) and (6).[10] Hence the interpretation of the wording in s 117C(6)/para 398 must be constant whether

applied to a medium or serious (over four-year sentence) offender, otherwise a medium offender (sentenced to less than four years) could never obtain the benefit of s 117C(6)/para 398, since such an offender does not require their protection *unless* they fail to satisfy s 117C(4)–(5)/paras 399–399A.

(2)     In *NA (Pakistan)*, the SSHD accepted, and the Court found, that the approach in *JZ* was correct (at paras 21, 29) and in order to succeed under s 117(6)/para 398, an applicant would need to point to 'features of his case of a kind' mentioned in s 117C(4)(5)/paras 399–399A, *or* to 'features falling outside' those criteria which made his claim 'especially strong' (at para 29).

The Court in *NA* further held that bare satisfaction of s 117C(4)(5)/paras 399–399A would not be sufficient. However, an applicant who could point to factors identified in those provisions of an 'especially compelling kind' could qualify under s 117C(6)/para 398, whether those factors were taken by themselves, or taken cumulatively 'in conjunction with other factors'. The factors singled out for description within s 117C(4)(5)/paras 399–399A would 'apply with greater or lesser force depending on the specific facts of the case' (at paras 30–32). The Strasbourg jurisprudence, in particular *Maslov* and *Uner*, would continue to have an 'important role' to play in applying the tests (at para 38).

Hence when a court or tribunal is considering s 117C(6), the issue is whether there is anything 'over and above' the circumstances outlined in Exceptions 1 and 2 (s 117C(4) and (5)). That can be shown by other factors, or by relying on the Exceptions, where on the facts one or both of them are met in an 'exceptionally compelling' way, per *NA (Pakistan)*. It is unlikely, according to *NA (Pakistan)*, that being able to show one of the Exceptions is only just met, will met the s 117C(6) threshold. There is, however, tension between that approach and the one outlined in *MM (Uganda)*.[11] There the court held 'unduly harsh' is 'an ordinary English expression' that 'requires regard to be had to all the circumstances including the criminal's immigration and criminal history'. Logically, if a court or tribunal funds deportation it would be unduly harsh on a partner or child (Exception 2), then it is difficult to see how a further search for something 'over and above' is compatible with Article 8 of ECHR, because all the circumstances have already been taken into account.

When section 19 of the Immigration Act 2014 was enacted introducing section 117 into NIAA 2002, the statute also provided at section 71 that the Borders, Citizenship and Immigration Act 2009, section 55 duty to have regard to the best interests of the child was not limited on the SSHD or the court by section 117 or at all.

Further, clearly the restriction in section 117D of 'qualifying child' to either a British citizen or a child who has lived in the United Kingdom for a continuous period of seven years or more is not exhaustive. Moreover, the assessment of proportionality must permit more weight to be given to (as here) a child who is a British citizen *and* who has lived in the UK for a period of over seven years (in this instance, the entire 13 years of her life).

[1]     Statement of Changes HC 532 amending paragraph 398; IDI's Chapter 13, version 5, Section 6.

² Amending Nationality, Immigration and Asylum Act 2002, s 117. The explanatory notes to the Immigration Act 2014 state:

'On 11 June 2012 the Government published its response to the consultation setting out that Immigration Rules would be made to reflect the Government's and Parliament's view of how the balance should be struck between the right to respect for private and family life under Article 8 of the ECHR and the public interest, including safeguarding the economic well-being of the UK, enforcing immigration controls and protecting the public from foreign criminals. New Immigration Rules came into force on 9 July 2012. The Act gives the force of primary legislation to the principles reflected in those rules by requiring a court or tribunal, when determining whether a decision is in breach of Article 8 ECHR, to have regard to the public interest considerations as set out in the Act.'

³ *NS (Sri Lanka) and Others v Secretary of State for the Home Department* [2016] EWCA Civ 705, at para 15.

⁴ *NA (Pakistan) v Secretary of State for the Home Department* [2016] EWCA Civ 662, at para 22.

⁵ [2016] EWCA Civ 662.

⁶ *NA (Pakistan)*, above, at para 30.

⁷ [2016] EWCA Civ 116, at paras 28–32.

⁸ [2016] EWCA Civ 662, at para 22.

⁹ [2016] 1 WLR 4203 (obiter in relation to NIAA 2002, s 117C, at para 50).

¹⁰ *NA (Pakistan)*, above, at paras 24–27.

¹¹ *MM (Uganda) and Another v Secretary of State for the Home Department* [2016] EWCA Civ 617.

**16.30** *[In front of the first sentence, insert 'Hence,' and in the next word, change first letter to lower case.]*

## DEPORTATION OF FAMILY MEMBERS

**16.40** *[At the end of footnote 4, add:]*

See also the Modernised Guidance: Deportation of family members of foreign national offenders, 14 November 2014.

*[In the main text after footnote reference 9 insert:]*

The family members of a person subject to automatic deportation orders under section 32 of the UK Borders Act 2007 may have ancillary orders made against them,⁹ᵃ but not more than 8 weeks⁹ᵇ after the principal order.

⁹ᵃ UK Borders Act 2007, s 37(1).

⁹ᵇ UK Borders Act 2007, s 37(2).

## THE DECISION TO DEPORT – CONSIDERATION OF MERITS

### The Rules post 9 July 2012 – Statement of Changes HC 194

**16.67** *[Delete paragraph and substitute:]*

In evaluating exceptional circumstances and whether they apply, the Court of Appeal accepted in *MF (Nigeria)*¹ that in the balancing exercise, great weight should be attached to the public interest for those who do not satisfy paragraphs 398, 399 or 399A. The Supreme Court in *Ali*² concurred with this view especially where the circumstances (in cases with more than a 4-year sentence) did not fall within paras 399–399A, the public interest would generally only be outweighed by 'countervailing factors which are very compelling' (at para 46). In 'precarious' family life cases, where family life was established when immigration status was uncertain, that it was likely to be only in the most exceptional of circumstances that the removal of the deportee would be likely to violate ECHR, Article 8. Exceptionality was considered to be a likely factual characteristic of a claim that properly succeeds rather than a legal test to be met. In this context, 'exceptional' has been held to mean circumstances in which deportation would result in unjustifiably harsh consequences for the individual or their family such that a deportation would not be proportionate.[3] The Court held that whether there are 'very compelling reasons' or exceptional circumstances in the assessment of Article 8 this is a proportionality test in accordance with Strasbourg jurisprudence. What amounts to exceptional circumstances or very compelling circumstances is very much fact dependent but must necessarily be seen in the context of the articulated will of Parliament in favour of deportation. Thus 'exceptional' or 'compelling' must describe the end result of the proportionality weighing exercise.[4]

[1]  [2013] EWCA Civ 1192, [2013] EWCA Civ 1192, [2014] 1 WLR 544
[2]  *Hesham Ali (Iraq) v Secretary of State for the Home Department* [2016] UKSC 60.
[3]  *MF (Nigeria)* ante; *Nagre* ante; *Kabia (MF: Para 298-Exceptional Circumstances)* [2013] UKUT 00569 IAC.
[4]  *McLarty (Deportation – proportionality balance)* [2014] UKUT 00315 (IAC).


## Settled migrant children

**16.68** *[Delete paragraph and substitute:]*

The Supreme Court in *Ali*[1] also held that deficiencies in the construction of paragraphs 399 and 399A, as amended by HC 194, were identified so as to admit of exceptionality in a number of cases. As noted in *Ogundimu*[2] by the tribunal the new rules made no attempt to reflect one of the most important Strasbourg decisions on deportation, that of *Maslov*[3] and that the ratio of that decision continued to apply, so that very serious reasons were required to justify expulsion of a settled migrant who had lawfully spent all or the majority of his or her childhood in the UK.[4] Even in such cases, however, deportation may be justified where offences perpetrated are very serious and where too they were committed during majority.

[1]  *Hesham Ali (Iraq) v Secretary of State for the Home Department* [2016] UKSC 60.
[2]  *Ogundimu (Article 8 – new rules) Nigeria* [2013] UKUT 60 (IAC).
[3]  *Maslov v Austria* [2008] ECHR 546. See also *JO (Uganda) v Secretary of State for the Home Department* [2010] 1 WLR 1607). Note that *Maslov* does not apply where the appellant has no right to be in the UK, as to which see: *Darko v Secretary of State for the Home Department* [2012] EWCA Civ 39; *Richards v Secretary of State for the Home Department* [2013] EWCA Civ 244.
[4]  *Balogun v United Kingdom* (Application 60286/09) [2012] ECHR 614. The ECtHR held that the possession of Class A drugs with intent to supply for which a sentence of three years was given was undoubtedly very serious, particularly in light of the fact that the majority of the applicant's offences were committed when he was already an adult, the Court proceeding to find that the applicant could not excuse his past criminal conduct by reference to his upbringing and that his removal would not be disproportionate. See also *AW Khan v UK* (Application 47486/06).

**Best interests considerations**

**16.69** *[At the beginning of text substitute the words 'The rules' with:]*

The Supreme Court in *Ali*[0] also held that the rules

[0]  *Hesham Ali (Iraq) v Secretary of State for the Home Department* [2016] UKSC 60.

**16.71** *[At the end of the paragraph add:]*

However, in the Supreme Court in *Makhlouf v Secretary of State for the Home Department*,[4] in which judgment was handed down at the same time as *Ali*[5] where Lord Kerr[6] held at para 40[7] that where a decision is taken about the deportation of a foreign criminal who has children residing in this country, separate consideration of their best interests is obviously required, especially if they do not converge with those of the parent to be deported, which where a child has a dual ethnic background, that factor requires close examination as a primary consideration.[8]

[4]  [2016] UKSC 59.
[5]  *Hesham Ali (Iraq) v Secretary of State for the Home Department* [2016] UKSC 60.
[6]  With whom the Court agreed unanimously here.
[7]  Baroness Hale concurring at para 46.
[8]  Per *ZH (Tanzania) v Secretary of State for the Home Department* [2011] 2 AC 166.

**16.73** *[In the first sentence delete the duplicated word 'to'.]*

**16.74** *[Delete the last sentence in the paragraph and substitute:]*

The Upper Tribunal considered the statutory public interest considerations relating to Article 8, set out in sections 117A–117D of NIAA 2002, meant that the appeal could not have succeeded under the old or new regimes.

**16.75** *[At the end of the paragraph, add:]*

The Supreme Court in *Makhlouf*[2] held that where a court with appropriate jurisdiction had made important decisions in relation to their welfare, the Secretary of State was under no further obligation to make further inquiries into the children's best interests.

[2]  *Makhlouf v Secretary of State for the Home Department* [2016] UKSC 59, at paras 44 and 49.

**16.76** *[Add new second paragraph:]*

The very recent decision of the Grand Chamber in *Paposhvili v Belgium*[3] clarifies, widens and provides guidance on the circumstances in which a person suffering from a serious illness can resist removal under ECHR, Article 3; and gives rise to serious questions as to whether the domestic jurisprudence is in step with the standards set in Strasbourg. It is now clear that non 'deathbed' health cases may be 'very exceptional'[4] where there is a risk of a decline of the quality described which either results in 'intense suffering' or a 'significant reduction in life expectancy'. The failure to assess and investigate conditions on return may breach Article 3[5] and give rise to a breach of procedural obligations under Article 8.[6] The Court of Appeal in *GS (India) v Secretary of State for the Home Department*[7] strictly adhered to the approach of the House of Lords in *N v Secretary of State for the Home Department*,[8] declaring that the 'D exception is confined to deathbed cases' (at para 66). It follows from *Paposhvili*, that the decision in *N* and its application in *GS (India)*) will need to be re-visited by the UK courts.

3  Application No 41738/10, 13 December 2016.
4  At para 183.
5  At para 205.
6  At para 224a.
7  [2015] 1 WLR 3312.
8  [2005] AC 296 (Lord Nicholls at para 15, Lord Hope at para 36, Baroness Hale at para 69).

### The Rules post 28 July 2014 – Statement of Changes HC 532

**16.77** *[Replace the penultimate sentence beginning 'Whilst the modified rules ' with:]*

The public interest in deportation will only be outweighed by other factors where there are 'very compelling circumstances over and above' those described in paragraphs 399 and 399A.

## THE IMMIGRATION ACT 2014

**16.82** *[In the sixth sentence, correct the typo for the word 'the':]*

In particular, no similar steer is given in the new Part 5A regarding the outcome of the judge's consideration of the factors stated to be relevant.

## PROCEDURE AND APPEALS

### Making and notifying a decision

**16.86** *[At the end of footnote 13, delete the citation '[2003] INLR 521' and substitute '[2003] IR 521'.]*

### Certification of Deportation appeals under the new regime

**16.88** *[Replace the existing heading with the above heading.]*

*[In first sentence, amend the word 'exiting' to 'existing'.]*

**16.89** *[In the second paragraph beginning 'It is apparent . . . ' delete the sentence and substitute:]*

Hence the new certification regime entered force in two stages.

**16.90** *[Replace entire paragraph:]*

For those cases in respect of which the appealable decision is generated post-28 July 2014, the language of section 94B provides that certification may be permissible at any stage in the course of the appeal process once the claim has been refused.[1] The section 94B certification provisions were subject to considerable criticism while passing onto the statute books, mainly suggesting that they violated the ECHR and laws of procedural fairness laid down in the common law. It is clear from the statement of the Home Secretary during the passage of the bill that the stated aims were *inter alia*:

(i)      Not to allow foreign criminals who should be deported time to remain here and build up a further claim to a settled life in the UK (Second reading, 22 Oct 2013, Hansard, Column 161);

(ii)     Not to permit the appeals system to be abused or manipulated to delay removal of those who do not have a good case when set against the new immigration rules and statutory public interest provisions which are a complete code (Second reading, 22 October 2013, Hansard, Column 162).

Concerns were raised by MPs regarding the certification process, particularly with regard to maladministration in the SSHD decision-making and appeals process, as well as potential breaches of Article 8 of ECHR, the Home Secretary confirmed that the appeals system would protect fundamental human rights (Column 62).

The legality of imposition of such a certificate post-decision, upon an appeal having been lodged would have to be appraised in the context of the Court of Appeal's decision in *AM (Somalia)*.[2] Such a step would likely falter on rationality grounds, absent some manifest change in circumstances, obliging substantial justification. It is likely with such considerations in mind that the Secretary of State signals in her casework instructions that post-decision certification will only be contemplated following on from an initial negative appeal determination, in circumstances where a linked element of the appeal relating to asylum or Article 3 protection which would ordinarily be amenable to certification under section 94B (see below) has not been pursued to the Upper Tribunal.[3]

Section 94B of the Nationality, Immigration and Asylum Act 2002 as it was enacted allowed a human rights claim to be certified where the appeals process has not yet begun or is not yet exhausted if the Secretary of State considered that removal pending the outcome of an appeal would not breach section 6 of the Human Rights Act 1998. One ground upon which the Secretary of State may certify a claim under section 94B is that the person liable to deportation would not, before the appeal process is exhausted, face a real risk of serious irreversible harm if removed to the country of return.

By section 92(3) of the amended 2002 Act, an appeal under section 82(1)(b) must be brought from within the UK unless a certificate has been made under section 94 or 94B of the 2002 Act. Hence now:

(i)      The decision-maker must consider (s 94B(2)) whether P's removal from the UK while his/her statutory appeal is pending would be unlawful under section 6 of the Human Rights Act 1998 ('the human rights question'). If it would be unlawful, then the section 94B certificate *must not be applied*.

(ii)     In so considering, the decision-maker should consider (s 94B(3)), as one facet of the human rights question, whether P's removal would cause him/her to face a real risk of serious irreversible harm ('the serious irreversible harm question'). If the answer to this question is yes, the s 94B certificate, again, *must not be applied*.

(iii)     If the answers to the human rights question and the serious irreversible
harm question are both negative, the decision-maker must then consider whether or not to exercise his/her discretionary power to certify
the claim ('the discretion question'), having regard to all relevant
considerations. This follows from the use of 'may' in both sub-paras (2)
and (3) of section 94B.

The result of section 94B certification is that the right of appeal against the
decision to refuse the human rights claim is non-suspensive, ie it is not a barrier
to removal. Any appeal can only be lodged and heard, or continued if the claim
is certified after the appeal is lodged, while the person is outside the UK.

The Home Office guidance provides that in criminal cases with indeterminate
sentences, where human rights claims are made from such persons where
release is at the discretion of the Parole Board, will not normally be suitable for
section 94B certification,[4] because applying section 94B to these cases may be
counterproductive. The Parole Board will have made a decision about release
based on the claimant's deportation rather than the possibility that they may
return to the UK if any appeal is successful. Consequently, there may be no
provision to recall to prison in the event of such return even if the Parole Board
would otherwise have deemed it to be appropriate, or to impose licence
conditions. These cases are not excluded from the scope of certification under
section 94B. Consideration must be given to all such cases on an individual
basis about whether or not it is appropriate to certify under section 94B.[5]

Importantly, however, the new guidance states that a case should only be
considered for certification if the claimant has been informed that the power
might apply and given the opportunity to provide reasons why their claim
should not be certified.

Regulations 24AA and 29AA were introduced into the Immigration (European
Economic Area) Regulations 2006 on 28 July 2014. Regulation 24AA allows
non-suspensive appeals in certain EEA deportation cases to reflect the provision in Article 31 of the Free Movement Directive. The Home Office has
separate guidance available for EEA cases: reg 24AA of the Immigration
(European Economic Area) Regulations 2006. Although it is primarily used in
non-EEA deportation cases, section 94B may also be used in certain EEA
deportation cases where the claim under the EEA Regulations is being
considered for certification under reg 24AA, but the claim also constitutes a
human rights claim which will give rise to a right of appeal under section 82
of the 2002 Act if refused.

[1]     Nationality, Immigration and Asylum Act 2002, s 94B(1)(a), (b).
[2]     *R (on the application of AM (Somalia)) v Secretary of State for the Home Department* [2009]
EWCA Civ 114.
[3]     Certification under section 94B of the Nationality, Immigration and Asylum Act 2002, version
8.0, 27 January 2017. The Home Office guidance 'Section 94B certification guidance for
Non-European Economic Area deportation cases' was substantially amended on 29 October
2015 after the Court of Appeal judgment in *Kiarie and Byndloss* on 15 October 2015 and
again from 1 December 2016 by the Immigration Act 2016 (Commencement No 2 and
Transitional Provisions) Regulations 2016 (SI 2016/1037). Section 63 of the Immigration Act
2016 extended section 94B certification of the NIAA 2002 from deportation cases to apply to
all refusals of human rights claims where such certification would not cause serious irreversible
harm or otherwise breach human rights.

4     This includes those who were: (i) sentenced in accordance with the Discretionary Conditional Release Scheme ('DCR') under the Criminal Justice Act 1991; (ii) given an Extended Sentence for Public Protection ('EPP'); (iii) given an Extended Determinate Sentence ('EDS').

5     Certification under section 94B of the Nationality, Immigration and Asylum Act 2002.

*Timing of certification*

**16.90A** *[Insert new heading and paragraph:]*

The Home Office guidance deals with when to certify under section 94B and provides that it is possible to certify under section 94B at any stage prior to the claimant exhausting their appeal rights. In practice, this means that if a claim is not certified at the initial decision stage, and either party challenges the decision of the First-tier Tribunal (or that of the Upper Tribunal), the case-worker must consider whether it is appropriate to certify the claim before it is heard by the Upper Tribunal (or the Court of Appeal). If it is decided to certify at any stage after the claimant has lodged an appeal, *the case-worker* must write to the claimant asking if there are any new reasons that certification should not apply and provide prompt written notification of any decision to certify to both the claimant and the relevant court.

**16.91** *[Replace entire paragraph:]*

Certification under section 94B is discretionary and not mandatory, as evidenced by the use of the term 'may' in section 94B(2) and (3) as opposed to 'shall'.[1]

The power thus created is discretionary and in common with any such provision which significantly restricts access to a tribunal; section 94B must be read restrictively. However, whilst the power is discretionary, the Home Office guidance in the deportation cases states that the Home Office will seek to use these powers in all cases: 'The Government's policy is that the deportation process should be as efficient and effective as possible and therefore case owners should seek to certify a case using the section 94B power in all cases meeting these criteria where doing so would not result in serious irreversible harm'.

In fact, the statutory test is whether there would be a breach of section 6 of HRA 1998 occasioned by the decision to certify, ie in the removal pending appeal. Hence in exercising the discretionary power to certify a claim pursuant to section 94B of the 2002 Act, the Secretary of State must therefore consider the impact of a temporary removal from the UK. Thus, in justifying such removal for the purposes of any qualified human right, the Secretary of State must therefore demonstrate that removal of a person before consideration of a person's ECHR rights has been completed, and for the period while that process is being completed (thereby requiring his/her absence from the jurisdiction during that process), is justified. In particular, she must demonstrate that there is no less intrusive means of achieving any legitimate aim pursued (see *Secretary of State for the Home Department v Huang*[2]). For the requirement that a person leave the United Kingdom pending the consideration of his/her human rights claim, see further by analogy the approach of the House of Lords in *Chikwamba v Secretary of State for the Home Department*.[3]

Hence the application of a certificate is subject only to the Secretary of State's being satisfied that enforcement action would be consistent with the Human Rights Act 1998[4] and would not result in the deportee 'facing a real risk of serious irreversible harm'.[5] Satisfaction of the former requirement is implicit in any decision the Secretary of State in which she authorises the commencement of deportation action. The Section 94B certification guidance also deals with dual certification. The instruction to caseholders is that 'If a protection claim is certified under sections 94 or 96, but it is not possible to certify a linked Article 8 claim (or other non-protection human rights claim) under either of those powers, then consideration must be given to certifying the Article 8 claim under section 94B as long as there is not a real risk of serious irreversible harm'.[6]

1    NIAA 2002, s 94B(2). Compare with s 94(3) of the 2002 Act.
2    [2007] UKHL 11, at 19.
3    [2008] UKHL 40.
4    NIAA 2002, s 94B(2).
5    NIAA 2002, s 94B(3). See section 94B certification guidance: Real risk of serious irreversible harm, at paras 3.3–3.8.
6    Certification under section 94B of the Nationality, Immigration and Asylum Act 2002.

**16.93** *[Delete the text of footnote 3 and substitute:]*

Home Office Guidance: Certification under section 94B of the Nationality, Immigration and Asylum Act 2002, version 8.0, 27 January 2017.

## Role of the Court

**16.94A** *[Insert new heading and paragraph:]*

The only challenge to a certification decision is by way of Judicial Review. Importantly because of the express terms of section 94B and the reference to a breach of section 6 of HRA 1998, the Court of Appeal in *Kiarie* held at [32]:[1]

'it follows from all this that the line of cases to the effect that, where a right of appeal exists against a removal decision, judicial review will not lie unless special or exceptional factors are in play . . . has no direct relevance in this context.'

As for the principles applicable to the judicial review: (i) the findings of fact made by the Secretary of State are amenable to judicial review on normal *Wednesbury* grounds; but (ii) for the assessment of proportionality, the Court must 'form its own view, while giving appropriate weight (which will depend on the context) to any balancing exercise carried out by the primary decision-maker' (at [33]).

The lawfulness of the decision must be assessed on the basis of the evidence before the Secretary of State at the time of that decision under challenge. The Court rejected the contention that the court should decide the matter for itself on the basis of all the evidence now before the court. That would go beyond the usual parameters if judicial review of the Secretary of State's decisions and would involve a usurpation of her role as the person entrusted by Parliament with the power to certify under section 94B (at [99]).

In order to assess whether there is a breach of section 6 of HRA 1998, the Court (and the SSHD) must address why and how the public interest in removal pending appeal requires this on the facts. The Court is a public authority for the purposes of the Human Rights Act 1998 and, accordingly, it must act compatibly with ECHR rights. It is clear from the decision of the Court of Appeal in *Kiarie* (at [33])[2] in an application for judicial review of the certification decision, the Court must assess for itself whether the interim removal of the applicant for the indeterminate duration of his appeal proceedings would constitute a disproportionate interference with his rights under Article 8 of ECHR (with appropriate weight to be given to the position adopted by the respondent, which will depend on the circumstances of the case).

> 'But as to the assessment of proportionality, the decision of the Supreme Court in *R (Lord Carlile of Berriew) v Secretary of State for the Home Department* [2014] UKSC 60, [2015] AC 945 shows that the court is obliged to form its own view, whilst giving appropriate weight (which will depend on context) to any balancing exercise carried out by the primary decision-maker.'

In order to undertake a lawful, fully informed proportionality assessment with the requisite anxious scrutiny the Court must consider this evidence for itself. One issue is whether it is on traditional judicial review principles restricted to the evidence that was before the Secretary of State, the role of further material and supplementary decisions (in *Kiarie* (see below) the Court considered the new material it was presented with *de bene esse*).

Inherent in a lawful section 94B certification must be a recognition that notwithstanding the SSHD's position on substantive deportation or removal (ie that she has taken a decision to deport or remove and concluded that no breach of Article 8 of ECHR would arise) that there is a right of appeal against that decision and it is open to an immigration judge to conclude differently. Hence the key issue is whether there is breach of section 6 of HRA 1998 occasioned by removal pending appeal on the facts by a breach of Article 8 ECHR.

Manifestly there is a different public interest in temporary removal pending appeal and permanent removal/deportation. Whilst it may be considered that less justification is required for temporary removal pending appeal because it is short-term and not permanent, in fact, and in particular in cases involving children, precisely temporary and unknown period of separation and/or disruption to education and housing by travel abroad go directly to the proportionality of such removal.

*Kiarie and Byndloss:* The current interpretation and application of section 94B in the context of deportation is the subject of the Court of Appeal's judgment in *R (Kiarie and Byndloss) v Secretary of State for the Home Department*[3] which is the subject of a pending appeal in the Supreme Court (which was heard on 15/16 February 2017). There the Court concluded:

(i)    That the statutory precondition for certification under s 94B is that set out at s 94B(2): the Secretary of State 'cannot lawfully certify unless she considers that removal pending the outcome of an appeal would not be in breach of any of the person's *Convention rights* . . . ' (*Kiarie and Byndloss* at 34);

(ii)     That while one 'ground' for certification is that a person would not, before the appeals process is exhausted, face a real risk of serious, irreversible harm (if removed), that ground 'does not, however, displace the statutory condition in subsection (2), or does it constitute a surrogate for that condition'. This means that, even if the Secretary of State is satisfied that removal would not give rise to such risk, 'that is not a sufficient basis for certification' (at 35).

(iii)    It follows that the [originally] published guidance on s 94B is 'inaccurate and misleading' in focusing as it does on the criterion of serious, irreversible harm (at 36).

(iv)    In deciding whether a s 94B certificate can be made, (i) consideration must be given 'to whether removal pending determination of an appeal would interfere with the person's rights under article 8'; (ii) if so, consideration must be given to whether 'the interim period would meet the requirements of proportionality'. If the answer to the first question is 'yes' and the second 'no', then certification is unlawful (at 38).

(v)     In considering proportionality in para [44]: (i) 'it may be thought that less weight attaches to the public interest in removal [of foreign national criminals] in the context of section 94B, when the only question is whether the person should be allowed to remain in the United Kingdom for an interim period'; but (ii) 'the fact that Parliament has chosen to allow removal for that interim period, provided that it does not breach section 6 of the Human Rights Act, shows that substantial weight must be attached to that public interest in this context also' (NB this seems a very circular argument; also The Court of Appeal does not appear to have been directed to the judgment of the House of Lords in *Chikwamba v Secretary of State for the Home Department*];[4] so (iii) public interest is 'not a trump card' but is an 'important consideration in favour of removal'.

(vi)    Even if the statutory condition is met, the Secretary of State 'has a *discretion* whether to certify or not' (at 45).

In *Kiarie* the Court held:

(i)      The Secretary of State is entitled to 'proceed on the basis that an out of country appeal will meet the procedural requirements of article 8 *in the generality of criminal deportation cases*' (at 71); an out of country of appeal does not by its nature 'deprive [a claimant] of effective participation in the decision-making process' (at 69).[5]

(ii)     But, importantly, 'if particular reasons are advanced as to why an out of country appeal would fail to meet those requirements, they must be considered and assessed' (at 71).

(iii)    There is a clear requirement that a person should be 'informed in advance that consideration was being given to the certification of [his/her] claim under section 94B'. Absent that process, a person will not have been 'given a fair opportunity to make representations on the subject'. Such procedural failings 'have to be viewed with caution and they will often invalidate a decision' at 73(i) and 74.

The Court concluded (at 64) that although an out of country appeal will be less advantageous to the appellant than an in-country appeal, Article 8 does not require the appellant to have access to the best possible appellate procedure or even to the most advantageous procedure available, it requires access to a procedure that meets the essential requirements of effectiveness and fairness, and with specific comparison to entry clearance appeals.

The reality in practice of appellants from abroad seeking to collate evidence and give live evidence will only be seen when the system is operating in practice. The reasons that the appellant would be faced with significant practical difficulties in procuring, preparing and presenting evidence for his appeal were not regarded by the Court as insurmountable. Thus, the importance of the process of evidence gathering, including obtaining witness statements and documentary evidence to prove integration (school, social services) and rehabilitation (prison, probation) whilst in the UK making the initial claim. The largely illusory availability of a video link to the UK to give evidence needs to be tested in practice against the facilities available in the UK tribunals, let alone from the appellant who is out of country.

Hence the Home Office approach to the principles under which out of country appeals must be considered to have been taken from *Kiarie* and appear in the SSHD's guidance:

(1)　an out-of-country appeal is generally fair;
(2)　oral evidence from the appellant and/or attendance at the appeal by the appellant are not generally required for an appeal to be fair and effective; and
(3)　the SSHD is entitled to rely on the specialist immigration judges within the tribunal system to ensure that the person is given effective access to a remedy against the decision.

The person may make representations to the effect that, despite the powers of the Tribunal to secure a fair and effective appeal, his or her personal circumstances mean that he or she would not be able to access a fair and effective remedy. The SSHD cites examples of the steps the Tribunal could take to ensure a fair and effective appeal where the appellant is outside the UK are to: consider whether the appeal can be fairly determined without the appellant giving oral evidence including considering any written evidence submitted by the appellant, documentary evidence and oral or written evidence from family members, friends and others.

Importantly, the Supreme Court on 22 March 2016 granted permission to appeal in both *Kiarie* and *Byndloss* (those appeals were heard on 15 and 16 February 2017, judgment reserved). The issues in that appeal are:

(1)　The correct approach to cases where there is a dispute before the court or tribunal regarding the conclusions of fact reached by the Secretary of State in the course of determining whether to exercise her power to certify a human rights claim under section 94B of the 2002 Act; whether in resolving that dispute the court or tribunal should hear evidence, including evidence that post-dates the decision of the Secretary of State; and whether, in any case, the Court of Appeal was wrong to hold that the *Wednesbury* standard should be applied.
(2)　The correct approach to be taken to an assessment of the proportionality of, and in particular, the nature of the public interest in, the removal of a person liable to deportation under s 3(5)(a) of the

Immigration Act 1971, pursuant to certification under section 94B of the 2002 Act and pending the resolution of his human rights appeal against deportation, and in particular, as against, the protection to be given to children's best interests.

(3)     Whether the Court of Appeal was wrong in concluding that a requirement to pursue a human rights appeal against deportation from abroad will not, in the generality of criminal deportation cases, amount to a breach of the procedural guarantees provided by Article 8, including those guarantees arising from and under the Convention on the Rights of the Child.

(4)     The correct approach to the assessment of the best interests of any children affected by the removal of a person liable to deportation under section 3(5)(a) of the Immigration Act 1971, pursuant to certification under section 94B of the 2002 Act and pending the resolution of his human rights appeal against deportation. In particular, having regard to the Secretary of State's own policies, the nature and extent of any duty on her to conduct inquiries as to the best interests of any affected children before taking the decision to certify and or maintain certification.

This judgment will have far-reaching effects beyond deportation given the recent extension of the section 94B powers to all ECHR, Article 8 appeals.

[1]     *R (on the application of Kiarie) v Secretary of State for the Home Department*; *R (on the application of Byndloss) v Secretary of State for the Home Department* [2015] EWCA Civ 1020. The Secretary of State had argued that the existence of an out of country appeal was presumptively an adequate remedy, not only for the deportation decision, but for the section 94B certificate. The Court did not accept that approach.

[2]     Applying the decision of the Supreme Court in *R (Lord Carlile of Berriew QC and Others) v Secretary of State for the Home Department* [2014] UKSC 60, [2014] 3 WLR 1404).

[3]     *R (on the application of Kiarie) v Secretary of State for the Home Department*; *R (on the application of Byndloss) v Secretary of State for the Home Department* [2015] EWCA Civ 1020.

[4]     [2008] UKHL 40.

[5]     For reasons for this conclusion, see paras 64–70 of the Judgment. It is, however, plain that the Court had very limited evidence to suggest that there might be any difficulties in requiring the Tribunal to comply (in practice) with its obligations of fairness.

## 16.95 *[Replace the paragraph:]*

The Supreme Court will have to examine the impact of such certification on the Article 8 interests of third parties, particularly minor children, invoking the ratio of the House of Lords in *Beoku-Betts v Secretary of State for the Home Department*,[1] and will examine the procedural protections required under Article 8 (following *inter alia* will prove a central platform from which to challenge certification, given that on a section 94B(3) certification the Secretary of State will be concerned only with ruling on whether the deportee would face a 'real risk of serious irreversible harm'. The term 'real risk' is a relatively low threshold and has the same meaning as when used to ascertain whether removal would breach ECHR, Article 3. However, the terms 'serious' and 'irreversible' must be given their ordinary meanings. 'Serious' indicates that the harm must meet a minimum level of severity, and 'irreversible' means that the harm would have a permanent or very long-lasting effect. If the human rights claim is based on Article 8, case owners must consider not only the impact on the foreign criminal's rights, but also those of any partner or child.[2]

Moreover, if the appellant's out of country appeal is successful, the deportation order will normally be revoked and the appellant may apply to return to the UK. However, the Home Office guidance only requires consideration to be given to whether they should pay for the appellant's journey back to the UK.

[1] *Beoku-Betts v Secretary of State for the Home Department* [2008] UKHL 39, [2009] AC 115, [2008] 4 All ER 1146, [2008] 3 WLR 166. The children of Byndloss have been given permission to intervene in the appeal in the Supreme Court and are separately represented.

[2] The amended post-1 December 2016 section 94B guidance 'Certification under section 94B of the Nationality, Immigration and Asylum Act 2002' (now version 8.0, 27 January 2016) distinguishes between deportation and removal cases on this issue and provides in the implementation phase that in non-deportation cases the cases will not be certified where the person has extant leave or where the appellant does not rely on their relationship with a British national family member. Note that section 3C leave will come to an end on certification under section 94B.

**16.96** *[After the third sentence, delete the text from 'There then follows . . . ' to the end of the paragraph including the footnote and substitute:]*

On the one hand, the onus is on the Secretary of State to demonstrate that there is not a real risk of serious irreversible harm. On the other hand, if a person claims that a non-suspensive appeal would risk serious irreversible harm, the onus is on that person to substantiate the claim with documentary evidence, preferably from official sources.[1]

[1] Certification under section 94B of the Nationality, Immigration and Asylum Act 2002, version 8.0, 27 January 2017.

**16.97** *[Delete the paragraph and substitute:]*

Reference to earlier versions of the Secretary of States Guidance affords valuable indications as to how case holders are expected to assess whether to certify. It had previously indicated that those engaged in family proceedings would not be automatically excepted from certification[1] which has been quietly removed, because: (a) it is likely to prove controversial if put into practice; (b) it must have become clear that even a short break in residence could potentially prejudice the pursuit of litigation before the family courts; and (c) the practice would arguably be contrary to rulings of the European and domestic courts in cases such as *Ciliz v Netherlands*[2] and *MS (Ivory Coast) v Secretary of State* and now in light of the Supreme Court decision in *Makhlouf*.[3]

[1] Certification under section 94B of the Nationality, Immigration and Asylum Act 2002, version 8.0, 27 January 2017.
[2] *Ciliz v Netherlands* [2000] ECHR 365.
[3] *MS (Ivory Coast) v Secretary of State for the Home Department* [2007] EWCA Civ 133.

**16.98** *[Delete the penultimate sentence beginning 'The hurdle for deportees . . . ' to 'go unchallenged' and substitute:]*

The hurdle for deportees, of course, will primarily be a financial one unless they are eligible for legal aid, with the effect that many certification decisions may well go unchallenged. The statistical evidence available shows that where the certificates are unchallenged and persons are removed, few appeals proceed and even fewer succeed. However, it is not clear how many certificates have been successfully challenged or withdrawn, but this is clearly likely to be many more.

## Deportation of EEA nationals

**16.100** *[In the final sentence of the first paragraph, correct the spelling of 'provisions'.]*

## Burden of proof on residence

**16.104** *[After the first paragraph add new paragraph:]*

In *Secretary of State for the Home Department v Vassallo*,[2] the Secretary of State appealed against a decision preventing deportation of a foreign criminal, an Italian national, under the Immigration (European Economic Area) Regulations 2006, reg 19(3)(b), on public policy or public security grounds. The issues for consideration by the Court included: whether V's period of residence in the UK prior to 1963, before the UK's accession to the EU, could be taken into account in determining whether V had acquired a right of permanent residence, and if so, whether the character of V's residence thereafter was such as to prevent the acquisition of a right of permanent residence. The Court dismissed the appeal. It held that the character of V's residence from 1963 onwards was plainly such as to prevent the acquisition of a right of permanent residence on the basis of the period between 1952 and 1963.

[2]   [2016] EWCA Civ 13.

**16.105** *[Replace the entire paragraph:]*

A comparable certification regime to section 94B was also introduced on 28 July 2014 for EEA deportation cases by the Immigration (European Economic Area) (Amendment) (No 2) Regulations 2014, by introducing reg 24AA.[1]

The new Regulations amend the Immigration (European Economic Area) Regulations 2006 so that an appeal against a deportation decision under reg 19(3)(b) can still be lodged in the UK but no longer suspends removal proceedings, except where:

- the Secretary of State has not certified under reg 24AA that the person would not face a real risk of serious irreversible harm if removed to the country of return before the appeal is finally determined;
- the person has made an application to the courts for an interim order to suspend removal proceedings (eg judicial review) and that application has not yet been determined, or a court has made an interim order to suspend removal;
- the application of a reg 24AA certificate does not prevent a person from lodging an appeal from within the UK; but by amending reg 29 of the EEA Regulations, it limits the suspensive effect of that appeal. So,

whilst a person may lodge an appeal in-country, the lodging of such an appeal does not suspend removal from the UK, if the Secretary of State has exercised her discretion to certify.

Where an interim order to suspend removal proceedings is initiated (eg by way of judicial review and that application is outstanding) the Secretary of State's guidance indicates that removal will be suspended, however this will not be the case where such an order is made in cases where the order is made where:

- the notice of a decision to make a deportation order is based on a previous judicial decision; or
- the person has had previous access to judicial review; or
- the removal decision is based on imperative grounds of public security.

The Secretary of State's 'Regulation 24AA of the Immigration (European Economic Area) Regulations 2006' guidance, version 4.0, 9 May 2016,[2] sets the same general test and criteria as apply in non-EEA cases to this category of deportation. However, there are specific exceptions for EEA nationals, eg where the person has a permanent right to reside, and the person has not been sentenced to a period of imprisonment of at least four years, will not normally be suitable for regulation 24AA certification. Consideration of whether or not it is appropriate to certify must be given to all cases on an individual basis. Moreover, this guidance emphasises that regulation 24AA is a discretionary power, meaning that it does not have to be applied in all cases even where removal pending the outcome of any appeal would not breach the ECHR.

[1] SI 2014/1976.
[2] www.gov.uk/government/uploads/system/uploads/attachment_data/file/521818/Regulation _24AA_guidance-v4.pdf.

**16.106** *[Delete the final paragraph and footnotes and substitute:]*

Regulation 29AA of the EEA Regulations 2006 provides for the general duty on the Secretary of State to grant temporary admission to the UK to attend an appeal hearing, subject to the public policy exception.

The guidance purports to limit this provision to cases where the appeal was lodged in time, an appeal hearing date has been set and the person wants to make 'submissions' in person.[1] The Upper Tribunal has interpreted this[2] as permitting a person to 'appear' at their appeal hearing, as opposed to being permitted to re-enter the UK generally and concluded that the presumption operates in respect of a person's re-admission to make submissions in person before a tribunal hearing his appeal.

Further, the guidance states that permission for entry must be sought in advance: simply turning up at the border will lead to refusal of admission.[3]

[1] Regulation 24AA of the Immigration (European Economic Area) Regulations 2006 at www.gov.uk/government/uploads/system/uploads/attachment_data/file/521818/Regulation _24AA_guidance-v4.pdf.
[2] *Kasicky (Reg 29AA: Interpretation)* [2016] UKUT 107 (IAC), [2016] Imm AR 576; and applied by the Northern Ireland High Court in MB's [2016] NIQB 75.
[3] Regulation 24AA of the Immigration (European Economic Area) Regulations 2006.

## SUCCESSFUL APPEALS

*(ii)* Under the new appeal regime

**16.108** *[At the start of the paragraph, delete 'version 2' and replace with 'current'.]*

*[Delete 'I' in the last sentence of first paragraph before 'considering'.]*


## REVOCATION OF DEPORTATION ORDERS

**16.113** *[Replace the first sentence and footnote 1:]*

The effect of a deportation order is to invalidate any leave to enter or remain in the UK (including ILR) given before the order is made or while it is in force.[1]

1    Immigration Act 1971, s 5(1), see also *R (on the application of George (Fitzroy)) v Secretary of State for the Home Department* [2014] UKSC 28 re: invalidation of ILR.


**16.114** *[Delete the text in footnote 1 and substitute:]*

Where requests are made from abroad, see policy document: ECB04: Deportees, 24 April 2015, *inter alia* as to the effect of delay prior to deportation as to the length of the exclusion period.

**16.115** *[At the end of the last sentence before the full stop, insert:]*

under section 94B (see above)


### Returned deportees

**16.117** *[At the end of the paragraph, add:]*

Those provisions must also now be seen in light of the power under section 94B of the 2002 Act for the Secretary of State to certify appeals to be heard out of country (see above).

**16.118** *[Footnote 5 is deleted.]*

**16.120** *[In sub-paragraph (3) after the word 'programme', add footnote reference 1 and insert new footnote text:]*

See now the Home Office evaluation of the new family returns process (December 2013) at https://www.gov.uk/government/uploads/system/uploads/attachment_data/file/264658/horr78.pdf.


### Facilitated Returns Scheme

**16.122A** *[After paragraph 16.122, insert new heading and paragraph:]*

The main aim of the Facilitated Return Scheme (FRS) is to promote and assist early removals by encouraging eligible foreign national offenders (FNOs) willing to return to their country of origin voluntarily.[1] Since July 2014, the FRS covers the following categories of FNO who have received a custodial sentence of up to 4 years, (although this does not guarantee eligibility in every individual case):

- time-served prisoners;
- prisoners subject to the Early Removal Scheme (ERS);
- prisoners, including mentally-disordered offenders, who are not already subject to removal directions;
- FNOs under the age of 18 detained for example at youth offender institutes, subject to certain conditions.

The terms on offer under FRS are different for FNOs still serving their sentence and those who are time-served, but the scheme continues to provide financial support for reintegration to encourage FNOs to cooperate with their early removal.

The subsidiary intention of the scheme is to support early removal where possible under ERS.[2] If an FNO leaves early under ERS, the amount of assistance offered under FRS is higher than if an application for FRS is made after they complete the custodial part of their sentence.

Where a deportation decision has been certified under section 94B, and the deportee subsequently indicates via an FRS application that they would be willing to return home voluntarily, then the issue of any appeal or other legal challenge against deportation should not arise. If a deportee who has made a FRS application later challenges a section 94B certificate, the application for FRS will be rejected, and any prior acceptance withdrawn.

[1]    Modernised Guidance, dated 3 October 2016, as to the operation of the FRS for foreign national offenders (FNOs).
[2]    See below, ERS allows FNOs serving determinate sentences to be removed up to 270 days (9 months) before their release date, in turn allowing the removal of FNOs from prisons sooner than otherwise possible.

Chapter 17

# REMOVAL AND OTHER EXPULSION

## INTRODUCTION

**17.1** *[Delete the second paragraph and corresponding footnotes and substitute:]*

Substantial changes to the power of administrative removal have been passed into law by section 1 of the Immigration Act 2014 (IA 2014).[1] This section was brought into effect gradually but with general effect from 6 April 2015 with some saving provisions. This has the effect of entirely replacing section 10 of the Immigration and Asylum Act 1999 (IAA 1999, as amended), which was the principal means by which administrative removals were carried out. IA 2014 also repeals section 47 of the Immigration and Nationality Act 2006 (IAN 2006), a source of considerable litigation on the issue of administrative removal.[2] This text addresses the old powers and the new ones.

[1]   The Immigration Act 2014 (Commencement No 3, Transitional and Saving Provisions) Order 2014, SI 2014/2711, brought into effect s 1 of IA 2014, along with some other provisions of IA 2014, but only in respect of two groups of migrants: foreign criminals and students who make Tier 4 applications on or after 20 October 2014. The Immigration Act 2014 (Commencement No 4, Transitional and Saving Provisions and Amendment) Order 2015, SI 2015/371 brings into effect all relevant provisions as of 6 April 2015. Saving provisions apply.

[2]   IA 2014, Sch 9, para 5.

**17.8** *[Delete footnote 1.]*

## OVERSTAYERS, BREACHERS OF CONDITIONS OF STAY AND OTHERS

### Overstaying and breach of conditions

**17.45** *[Delete final sentence and substitute:]*

The apparent date of expiry of leave is not conclusive on the issue of overstaying, since if a valid in-time application for a variation was made prior to the expiry of limited leave, that leave is extended by statute while the decision on the variation application is pending and, if the decision is negative and is received before leave would otherwise expire, while an in-time appeal could be brought and, while any appeal is pending,[3] an application for

Administrative Review.

3    Immigration Act 1971, s 3C, as amended.

**17.47** *[Delete the final sentence and footnote 2.]*

**17.49** *[Delete the first sentence to the end of '. . . about residence' including footnote reference 1 and substitute:]*

In cases of breach of conditions, the Home Office must show that the conditions are ones which may be lawfully imposed – there are only six conditions which may be lawfully imposed on a grant of leave: restrictions on work or occupation; restriction on studies; no recourse to public funds; registration with police; reporting to an immigration officer or the Secretary of State; or being subject to a condition about residence[1]

1    Immigration Act 1971, s 3(1)(c), as amended by the UK Borders Act 2007, s 16, Borders, Citizenship and Immigration Act 2009, s 50 and Immigration Act 2016, s 34(2). Before the 2009 Act amendment, failure by a student to maintain 15 hours a week attendance on a course would not place him or her in breach of a condition attached to the leave to enter, so as to render that person liable to removal under s 10 of IAA 1999, although it could give rise to curtailment of student leave under the Immigration Act 1971, s 3(3)(a), or refusal of an extension (HC 395, para 323): *R (on the application of Zhou) v Secretary of State for the Home Department* [2003] EWCA Civ 51, [2003] 12 LS Gaz R 30(2003) Times, 7 February.

**17.50** *[In the main text delete the sentence beginning after footnote reference 3 ('However, Home Office policy . . . ' to the end of the paragraph.]*

*[In footnote 1 delete the final two sentences from 'Home Office instructions' to 'ibid 10.6.3.']*

*[Delete footnotes 4 and 5.]*

### Use of deception in seeking leave to remain

**17.51** *[Delete the sentence 'Leave granted on the basis of such deception would be invalidated by the issue of removal directions, but deception must be proved to a high degree of probability.' including the footnote references 4 and 5 and substitute:]*

Leave granted on the basis of such deception is invalidated by the issue of removal directions[4] and deception must be proven by the Secretary of State on the balance of probabilities.[5]

*[Delete the following sentences: 'Removal for practising deception only applies to persons who have practised deception from 1 October 1996. If it appears that leave to remain was obtained by deception prior to that date this does not stop the case being referred for possible deportation action on non-conducive grounds under s 3(5)(a) of the Immigration Act 1971.' including footnote references.]*

*[Delete footnotes 6 and 7 and footnote 8 is renumbered as 6.]*

4    IAA 1999, s 10(8). See also *R (on the application of Mehmood and Another) v Secretary of State for the Home Department* [2015] EWCA Civ 744, [2016] 3 All ER 398, [2016] 1 WLR 461.

⁵ *Secretary of State for the Home Department v Shehzad and Another* [2016] EWCA Civ 615 applying *Re B (Children)* [2009] 1 AC 11, [2016] All ER (D) 12 (Jul).

## THE LONG RESIDENCE RULE

**17.59** *[Delete final two sentences of the paragraph from 'A person who . . . ' to ' . . . with the law.'*

*[Delete footnote 4.]*

**17.60** *[Delete the paragraph and footnotes.]*

**17.62** *[At the end of the second paragraph, add:]*

This approach to spent convictions has probably not survived the change from 1 October 2012 onwards to disapply the 1974 Act in immigration and nationality applications.⁵

⁵ UK Borders Act 2007, s 56A as inserted by s 140 of the Legal Aid, Sentencing and Punishment of Offenders Act 2012 which came into force on 1 October 2012. It exempts certain immigration and nationality decisions from the scope of s 4(1), (2) and (3) of the Rehabilitation of Offenders Act 1974.

## REMOVAL DIRECTIONS

**17.63** *[In the main text, line 19, after ' . . . as amended by the Immigration Act 2014' add:]*

and the Immigration Act 2016

### Removal under section 10 of the Immigration and Asylum Act 1999

**17.67** *[Add final sentence:]*

Under the Immigration Act 2014 version of section 10, the power to remove applies to a migrant who does not have leave so invalidation no longer arises. However, where a family member is served with removal directions under the new section 10 and the family member has extant leave, that leave is invalidated.⁹

⁹ IAA 1999, s 10(6) as amended by IA 2014, s 1.

## CARRYING OUT REMOVAL

**17.73** *[At the end of footnote 5, add:]*

In *R (on the application of JM (Zimbabwe)) v Secretary of State for the Home Department* [2016] EWHC 1773 (Admin) it was held that section 35 does not empower prosecution of a person for refusing to lie to a receiving state in order to facilitate their own removal.

**17.74** *[Delete footnote 7. Footnotes 8–10 are renumbered accordingly.]*

# Chapter 18
# DETENTION AND BAIL

## INTRODUCTION

**18.1** *[In the first paragraph delete the text from 'Claimants in the DFT . . . '*
*to ' . . . families with children' and replace with:]*

The old DFT process was suspended in July 2015 following the successful challenge in *Detention Action v Secretary of State for the Home Department.*[6] However, the government did not take the opportunity to stop considering asylum claims in detention but maintained its commitment to fast-track processing of some asylum claims, forming the Detained Asylum Casework team operating under a new policy, Detention: Interim Instruction (DII). That policy was then held to be lawful, save for a breach of the public sector equality duty, in *Hossain v Secretary of State for the Home Department.*[6a] Since the autumn of 2006, Yarl's Wood has also dealt with female detained non-suspensive appeal cases (NSA) as well as female DAC cases. Yarl's Wood and Dungavel have been used to detain families with children.

*[in the second paragraph delete the last two sentences from 'The cur-*
*rent . . . ' to 'Barnardos' and replace with:]*

The government has announced that the controversial 'pre-departure accommodation' centre Cedars is to close and families will now be accommodated at Tinsley House. Barnardo's has stated that it will not supply services there as it cannot support the move because it is not in the best interests of the children affected.

*[In the third paragraph delete first sentence and footnote reference 9 and*
*replace with:]*

There are currently 11 removal/detention centres, nine of which are in private hands.

*[In footnote 2 delete the last sentence and replace with:]*

The previous policy which included continuing detention during the appeals process was held to be unlawful in respect of the delays in facilitating access to legal representation, carrying an 'unacceptably high risk of unfairness' in *Detention Action v Secretary of State for the Home Department (Equality Human Rights Commission intervening)* [2014] EWHC 2245 (Admin). It was then suspended. However, the policy that replaced it continues to allow for asylum claims to be considered while a person is detained and that was upheld in *Hossain v Secretary of State for the Home Department* [2016] EWHC 1331

(Admin) and then T *H (Bangladesh) v Secretary of State for the Home Department* [2016] EWCA Civ 815.

*[At the end of footnote 5 delete full stop and add:]*

and now *Hossain v Secretary of State for the Home Department* [2016] EWHC 1331 (Admin).

*[Footnote 9 is deleted.]*

*[Delete the text for footnote 10 and substitute:]*

Brook House, near Gatwick Airport. Contractors G4S. Capacity of 426 men, soon to be expanded to 486. Tinsley House, near Gatwick Airport. This will shortly reopen with an expanded capacity of 194 men and families. Contractors G4S. Campsfield House, Kidlington. Opened 1993. Contractors Mitie. Capacity of 276 men. Cedars is still currently open although soon to close, and has a capacity of 9 families. When it closes, families will be sent to Tinsley House. Contractors are G4S. Dungavel, Strathaven, South Lanarkshire. Capacity of 249 men. Contractors GEO. Colnbrook near Heathrow Airport. Opened August 2004. Capacity of 396 men and 27 women. Contractors Mitie. Harmondsworth, near Heathrow Airport (treated by contractors as part of a single 'Heathrow Immigration Removal Centre' with Colnbrook). Capacity of 661 men. Contractors Mitie. Larne House. Capacity for 19 men and women for short stay. Pennine House, second of two residential short-term holding facilities with Larne House (max 7 days). Capacity 43 men and women. Contractor: Tascor. The Verne, a former prison now converted to an IRC. Capacity 580 men. Run by HM Prison Service. Yarl's Wood, Bedford. Opened November 2001. Capacity of 410 women and families with a small short-term holding facility for men. Contractor: Serco. Oakington is now closed.

*[At the end of footnote 13 add:]*

The number of people entering detention in year ending June 2016 decreased by 1% to 31,596 from 32,053 in the previous year (Home Office figures). The Migration Observatory at the University of Oxford is an excellent source of up-to-date facts and statistics on immigration detention.

6   [2014] EWHC 2245 (Admin), [2014] All ER (D) 113 (Jul).
6a   [2016] EWHC 1331 (Admin), 166 NLJ 7703, [2016] All ER (D) 40 (Jun).

**18.2** *[At the end of footnote 1 add:]*

In the year ending June 2015 the number of people detained was 32,053 according to official statistics.

**18.6** *[In footnote 1 replace the citation '(1990) 13 EHRR 157' with '(1991) 13 EHRR 157'.]*

**18.7** *[In the text, before footnote reference 1, replace the words 'Detained Fast-track' with 'Detained Asylum Casework'.]*

*[After footnote reference 5 in the text add:]*

In January 2016, Stephen Shaw published his Review into the Welfare in Detention of Vulnerable Persons which was severely critical of the Secretary of State's detention of vulnerable migrants and the mechanisms used to identify them as such. As a result, a statutory limitation on the detention of pregnant women was introduced in the Immigration Act 2016 (s 60) as well as provision at section 59 for the Adults at Risk policy which is designed to improve identification of those whose vulnerabilities are such that they should not be detained. The Policy is in its infancy but *prima facie* leaves much to be desired in terms of providing protections to migrants, and may even provide less protection than Chapter 55.10.

*[In footnote 1 delete text and substitute:]*

The 'target time' for cases under the old Fast-track was 14 days: see 'Fast track asylum and detention policy', Parliamentary Written Answer of Desmond Browne MP, Minister for Citizenship and Immigration (Hansard, 16 September 2004, Column 157WS). It is unclear whether there is a similar target in the new Detained Asylum Casework system.

**18.8** *[In the first paragraph after footnote reference 9, insert:]*

The introduction of apparent further limitations on the power to detain in the Dublin III Regulation (Council Regulation 604/2013) has been entirely ignored by the government, which made no alterations to either law or policy to reflect it. The question of whether or not the failure to make relevant changes affects the lawfulness of detention is currently before the Court of Justice of the European Union in *Al Chodor* (Case C-528/15) following a reference by the Czech Courts.

*[In final paragraph delete 'UKBA' and replace with 'UKVI'.]*

*[Delete final sentence and replace with:]*

The government recently completed consultation on draft new Rules for Short-Term Holding Facilities modelled on the Detention Centre Rules 2001.

## IMMIGRATION OFFICERS' POWERS TO DETAIN

**18.9** *[In the text in the first sentence replace '2014' with '2016'.]*

*[In the numbered list add a further category between (11) and (12):]*

(11A) A person whose admission to the UK in accordance with EEA rights has been revoked because that person was not entitled to be admitted.[13a]

*[In the second paragraph delete the text from beginning until after footnote reference 24. Delete footnotes 19–24.]*

[13a] SI 2006/2003, reg 23A.

## TEMPORARY ADMISSION

**18.11** *[At the beginning of the paragraph insert:]*

The provisions in respect of temporary admission remain in force pending the coming into force of the provisions in respect of bail in section 61(1)–(2) of the Immigration Act 2016.

*[After footnote reference 9 in the text add:]*

However, section 36 of the 2004 Act does not provide legislative authority for the imposition of a curfew.[9a]

*[In the text after footnote reference 16, delete 'Reporting to the police . . . ' to ' . . . should be lifted' and replace with:]*

Reporting to a police station (as opposed to a reporting centre) should not normally be required more than once a month, and if a non-Criminal Casework Directorate (CCD) case remains unresolved for three years, reporting requirements should be lifted.

*[Delete footnote 16 and renumber footnotes 17 to 19 accordingly.]*

[9a]   *R (Gedi) v Secretary of State for the Home Department* [2016] EWCA Civ 409, [2016] 4 WLR 93, [2016] All ER (D) 140 (May).


## SPECIAL IMMIGRATION STATUS

**18.14**  *[Delete footnote 10 and replace with:]*

https://www.gov.uk/government/uploads/system/uploads/attachment_data/file /575522/Restricted-leave-v2.pdf. Note that limiting discretionary leave to six-month periods is not now limited to criminals but is used as a means of making life difficult for many migrants who cannot lawfully be removed: https://www.gov.uk/government/uploads/system/uploads/attachment_data/file /460712/Discretionary_Leave_2__v7_0.pdf.


## SECRETARY OF STATE'S POWERS TO DETAIN

**18.15**  *[At the end of footnote 1 insert:]*

The power itself is contained in paragraph 16 of Schedule 2.

*[In the second paragraph in sub-para (3) delete final sentence beginning 'Which provision . . . '. including the footnote reference.]*

*[In the final paragraph delete the text from 'A person admitted . . . ' to end of the paragraph and substitute:]*

A person admitted to or residing in the UK under the EEA Regulations may be detained under the powers contained in the IA 1971, Sch 3 if a decision is taken to remove the person on the grounds that the person's removal is justified on public policy, public security or public health grounds.[16] Such a person may also be detained where the Secretary of State has reasonable grounds for suspecting that he is a person who may be removed under the power in regulation 19(3).[17]

*[Footnote 13 is deleted and remaining footnotes renumbered accordingly.]*

[16]   Immigration (European Economic Area) Regulations 2006, SI 2006/1003, reg 24(3).
[17]   Immigration (European Economic Area) Regulations 2006, SI 2006/1003, reg 24(1); reg 19(3).


**18.16**  *[At the end of footnote 8 add:]*

This is no longer an issue of significance following the decision of the Supreme Court in *R (O) v Secretary of State for the Home Department* [2014]

EWCA Civ 990, [2015] 1 WLR 641 disapproving the decision in R *(on the application of Francis) v Secretary of State for the Home Department* [2014] EWCA Civ 718.

### Restriction orders

**18.17** *[N.B.]*

Following the decision of the Court of Appeal in R *(Gedi) v Secretary of State for the Home Department* [2016] 4 WLR 93, it is clear that the Secretary of State has no power to impose a curfew via a Restriction Order.

**18.18** *[Delete heading 'Accommodation centres' and delete paragraph 18.18.]*

### Prisoners recommended for deportation

**18.19** *[In the main text, after footnote reference 6, delete from 'Following the decision . . . ' to ' . . . false imprisonment and damages' and replace with:]*

Following the decision of the Supreme Court in R *(O) v Secretary of State for the Home Department*,[7] it is clear that there is no difference in effect between those detention powers couched in 'shall' rather than 'may' terms.

*[Footnote 8 is deleted and footnote 9 renumbered as 8.]*

[7]   [2016] WLR 1717.

### Foreign national prisoners – treatment in detention

**18.20** *[At the end of the paragraph insert:]*

This figure increased to 1,000 for a period in 2012. This SLA formally expired in March 2015 and it is unclear whether it has been replaced, although the Secretary of State's policy continues to refer to it. The Court of Appeal held in R *(on the application of Richards) v Teeside Magistrates Court* [12] that the practice of keeping individuals in prisons pending deportation was not arbitrary for the purposes of Article 5 of ECHR unless the conditions were 'seriously inappropriate', which will depend both on the conditions and the individual in question. The Court did not interfere with the decision at first instance that the policy was an unlawful blanket policy that eschewed consideration of individual circumstances and so was irrational, as the Administrative Court had granted no relief.[13]

*[In footnote 10 delete the last two sentences from 'The blanket . . . ' to ' . . . 2012'.]*

[12]   [2014] EWCA Civ 1187, [2016] 1 WLR 1694.
[13]   R *(on the application of Idira) v Secretary of State for Home Department* [2014] EWHC 4299 (Admin), 165 NLJ 7637, [2014] All ER (D) 241 (Dec).

**Power of arrest**

**18.22** *[At the end of the paragraph add:]*

Following the introduction of the Immigration Act 2014, Immigration Officers have a power to use 'reasonable force' when carrying out any function under the Immigration Acts.[3]

[3] Immigration and Asylum Act 1999, s 146, as amended.

## WHY, WHERE AND HOW DETAINED

**Place of detention**

**18.23** *[At the end of the fourth paragraph add:]*

In *R (on the Application of Idira) v The Secretary of State for the Home Department*[6] the Court of Appeal held that it is generally lawful to detain immigration detainees in prisons and that this does not breach Article 5(1) of ECHR. However, the Master of Rolls acknowledged that 'detention in an IRC is generally more appropriate for immigrant detainees than detention in prison'.

*[In footnote 4 add:]*

However, see *R (on the Application of Idira) v The Secretary of State for the Home Department* [2015] EWCA Civ 1187 above.

*[Delete footnote reference 5 and the footnote text. Renumber existing footnote 6 as footnote 5]*

[6] [2015] EWCA Civ 1187

**18.24** *[In the sentence ending with footnote reference 4, correct the typographical error 'detained in eparture accommodation' with 'detained in pre-departure accommodation'.]*

*[In the main text, after footnote reference 7, insert:]*

The government has announced that the controversial 'pre-departure accommodation' centre Cedars is to close due to its expense and families will now be accommodated at Tinsley House. Barnardo's has stated that it will not supply services there as it cannot support the move because it is not in the best interests of the children affected.

*[At the end of footnote 6 insert:]*

However, Cedars is shortly to close, and will be replaced by pre-departure accommodation at Tinsley House.

*[At the end of the paragraph add:]*

With the introduction of section 60 of the Immigration Act 2016, a pregnant woman may only be detained if the Secretary of State is satisfied that she will shortly be removed from the United Kingdom, or there are exceptional circumstances which justify the detention. In any event, a pregnant woman may only be detained for 72 hours or for 7 days maximum if the period of detention is authorised personally by a Minister of the Crown (see s 60(4)).[12]

[12] Chapter 55A for the Enforcement Instructions and Guidance Detention of Pregnant Women, published 12 July 2016, provides guidance on the detention of pregnant women for the purpose of removal and on the duration of their detention: https://www.gov.uk/government/uploads/system/uploads/attachment_data/file/537066/Chapter_55a_Detention_of_pregnant_women_v1.pdf. See also: Detention Services Order 05/2016 – Care and management of pregnant women, in force Nov 2016: https://www.gov.uk/government/uploads/system/uploads/attachment_data/file/564431/DSO_05_2016_-_Pregnant_Women_In_Detention.pdf.

**18.27** *[At the end of the paragraph, add:]*

The Court of Appeal held in *R (Idira) v Secretary of State for the Home Department* [2016] 1 WLR 1694 that the practice of keeping individuals in prisons pending deportation was not arbitrary for the purposes of Article 5 of ECHR unless the conditions were 'seriously inappropriate', which will depend both on the conditions and the individual in question.

*[Delete footnote 4.]*

**Reasons for detention**

**18.28** *[Delete footnote 8.]*

**POLICY AND CRITERIA FOR DETENTION**

**18.29** *[In the main text, after footnote reference 3, add:]*

The policy in respect of pregnant women and vulnerable adults has been put on a statutory footing following the coming into force of the Immigration Act 2016.

*[Delete the list items (i)–(iv) and replace with:]*

(i) wherever possible alternatives to detention are used;
(ii) detention is most usually appropriate to effect removal, establish a person's identity or basis of claim, or where there is a risk that they will fail to comply with conditions of release;
(iii) people should not be detained for lengthy periods if it would be practical to effect detention later in the process when the appeals process has been exhausted;
(iv) detention should be used sparingly and for the shortest period necessary.

*[Footnote 6 is renumbered as 4 and at the end of the footnote add:]*

They must also be read with the Adults at Risk policy produced in accordance with s 59 of the Immigration Act 2016, and the policy at Chapter 55b of the EIG in respect of pregnant women.

**18.31** *[In the main text, after footnote reference 2 and before the closing bracket, add:]*

and removal falls to be cancelled applying the policy in paragraph 4.1 of Chapter 60

*[At the end of footnote 2 add:]*

However, the circumstances in which removal will be deferred upon the bringing of judicial review proceedings are much reduced in the latest version of Chapter 60, see in particular paragraph 4.1.

### Special categories of detainee

**18.32** *[In the first paragraph delete final sentence and replace with:]*

It identified certain categories as follows:

*[Delete first category and replace with:]*

*Pregnant women* could normally be detained only in very exceptional circumstances. Exceptions to that were cases where there was a clear prospect of early removal and medical advice did not suggest that confinement before removal, or women who were less than 24 weeks' pregnant who could be detained at Yarl's Wood as part of the fast-track process.[3] Following the introduction of s 60 of the Immigration Act 2016 there are also statutory limitations on the power to detain pregnant women. In particular, pregnant women may only be detained where she will 'shortly' be removed or in exceptional circumstances. Detention may not be for more than 72 hours without Ministerial authorisation and for no more than 7 days in total, starting from the point at which the Secretary of State is aware that a person in detention is pregnant. Any decision to detain must have regard to the woman's welfare.

*[In category 5 delete the word 'OR' at the end of sub-para (c) and delete sub-para (d).]*

*[In category 6 delete 'and support of Bernardo's' and add:]*

Notwithstanding the current terms of the policy, the government has announced that the controversial 'pre-departure accommodation' centre Cedars is to close and families will now be accommodated at Tinsley House. Barnardo's has stated that it will not supply services there as it cannot support the move because it is not in the best interests of the children affected.

*[In footnote 12 delete from 'It was held . . . ' to ' . . . subject to appeal' and replace with:]*

In *Home Office v VS* [2015] EWCA Civ 1142, the Court of Appeal declined to reach a conclusion as to whether a *Merton*-compliant assessment would have to have been actually seen by the Secretary of State in order for the obligation to establish that one existed to be discharged, but considered that the available *pro forma* was insufficient.

*[In footnote 13 add:]*

See also *Home Office v VS* [2015] EWCA Civ 1142, [2015] All ER (D) 92 (Nov).

[3] EIG, para 55.9.1. For the experiences of women in detention, see for example, Sarah Culter and Sophia Ceneda, 'They took me away: women's experiences of immigration detention in the UK' (BID and Refugee Women's Project, 2004).

**18.33** *[Delete the first line but retain the footnote reference, and replace with:]*

Until relatively recently, the EIG set out groups considered unsuitable for detention, who should be detained only in very exceptional circumstances; they were:

*[Delete existing footnote reference 5 and footnote text.]*

*[Add additional new paragraph:]*

There have been concerns for many years that the above categories provide insufficient protection to vulnerable people who are detained. In January 2016, the Shaw Review[5] was highly critical of the detention of vulnerable people, and concluded, among other things, that further categories should be added to Chapter 55.10 including in relation to victims of gender-based violence, transsexuals, those suffering from PTSD, those with learning difficulties, or those more generally vulnerable.[6] It was identified that Rule 35 of the Detention Centre Rules 2001 was not doing 'what it was intended to' in providing adequate protection to vulnerable people, and recommended that an alternative mechanism be devised.[7]

As a result of the findings of the Shaw Review, the government[8] undertook to make significant changes to its policies in respect of the detention of vulnerable people. It was said that these changes would introduce a new 'adult at risk' policy with a 'clear presumption' that vulnerable people would not be detained.[9] Those changes came in the Immigration Act 2016.[10]

Section 59 of the Immigration Act 2016 obliges the Secretary of State to issue and lay before Parliament guidance specifying matters to be taken into account in determining whether a person would be particularly vulnerable to harm in detention. On 12 September 2016, the Secretary of State issued Statutory Guidance in the form of the Adults at Risk in Immigration Detention policy. At the same time, DSO 17/2012 was withdrawn and replaced with DSO 09/2016. The Detention Centre Rule 35 Process Policy was also withdrawn. On 15 September 2016, the Secretary of State issued Chapter 55b of the Enforcement Instructions and Guidance on Adults at Risk, which gives further guidance on the application of the statutory guidance. Chapter 55.10 EIG, by which the various categories therein were protected from detention save in very exceptional circumstances, was deleted.

The new policy includes the following.

The Statutory Guidance and DSO 09/2016 both substitute the restrictive definition of torture in Article 1 of the United Nations Convention Against Torture and Other Cruel, Inhuman and Degrading Treatment or Punishment (UNCAT) rejected by Burnett J in *R (EO and others) v Secretary of State for the Home Department*.[11] By that definition, an act can only amount to torture if it is 'inflicted by or at the instigation of or with the consent or acquiescence of a public official or other persons acting in an official capacity'. A rider was added to the definition, which means that an act will constitute torture where it consists of an act 'carried out by terrorist groups exploiting instability and civil war to hold territory'. The wholly bizarre nature of this definition is perhaps best illustrated by the fact that whether a person seriously ill-treated by, eg the LTTE was 'tortured' or not for the terms of the policy will depend on whether that ill-treatment took place during a period in which that organisation held territory. That is currently the subject of legal challenge by

Medical Justice, and following a grant of interim relief the 'EO' definition remains in place.

The remainder of the Adults at Risk policy is equally controversial. Rather than an express provision that vulnerable people are only to be detained in 'exceptional circumstances', the guidance introduces a system in which 'levels' of evidence are to be balanced against 'immigration factors'. The guidance has yet to be the subject of definitive interpretation. However, if it is to be interpreted consistently with the information provided to Parliament it must have the effect that an Adult at Risk is only to be detained in 'very exceptional circumstances'.

5    'Review into the Welfare in Detention of Vulnerable Persons- A report to the Home Office by Stephen Shaw', Cm 9186, January 2016 ('the Shaw Review'). An overall conclusion of the Shaw Review was that *'there is too much detention; detention is not a particularly effective means of ensuring that those with no right to remain do in fact leave the UK; and many practices and processes associated with detention are in urgent need of reform.'* He identified *'shortcomings in both the identification of vulnerability and in the policies designed to maintain wellbeing.'* Shaw Review, S11. He relied on evidence from Professor Mary Bosworth which he considered *'demonstrates incontrovertibly that detention in and of itself undermines welfare and contributes to vulnerability.'* Shaw Review, S11. This report was immediately preceded, in January 2015, by the Tavistock Review of mental health issues in immigration removal centres.
6    Shaw Review, Section 4.
7    Shaw Review, recommendation 21.
8    Statement of James Brokenshire, 14 January 2016. HCWS470: 'The Government is grateful to Mr Shaw for his review, welcomes this important contribution to the debate about effective detention, and accepts the broad thrust of his recommendations. Consistent with our policies, we will now take forward three key reforms, working across Government and the National Health Service and with private sector providers . . . The Government expects these reforms, and broader changes in legislation, policy and operational approaches, to lead to a reduction in the number of those detained, and the duration of detention before removal, in turn improving the welfare of those detained'.
9    Statement of James Brokenshire, 14 January 2016. HCWS470.
10   During the passage of the bill the government repeatedly emphasised that the Adults at Risk Statutory Guidance would 'build on' the protections already present in Chapter 55.10 of the Enforcement Instructions and Guidance, including strengthening the existing presumption. See, eg Immigration Minister James Brokenshire MP on 25 April 2016, Hansard 608/1189.
11   [2013] EWHC 1236 (Admin), [2013] All ER (D) 248 (May).

## Detainees with mental health problems

18.34 *[At the beginning of the paragraph add:]*

The policy in respect of detaining those with mental health problems has now been altered by the Adults at Risk Policy as set out in the preceding paragraph. However, the old case law remains relevant to those pursuing damages claims in relation to detention under that policy, as well as to the interpretation of the new policy.

*[in the third paragraph, after footnote reference 14, add:]*

In *BA (Eritrea) v Secretary of State for the Home Department*,[14a] the Court of Appeal gave guidance on the circumstances in which a Rule 35 report would amount to independent evidence of torture for the application of the old policy in Chapter 55.10.

[14a] [2016] EWCA Civ 458, [2016] 4 WLR 101, [2016] All ER (D) 119 (May).

## Detention of foreign national prisoners

**18.35** *[In the text delete from 'The Court of Appeal in 'R (on the application of Francis) . . . ' to ' . . . was not undermined by such a breach'. Delete footnote 4.]*

*[In the text, after footnote reference 5, delete 'In the case of EEA nationals, the criteria for deportation are a sentence of at least 24 months' imprisonment.']*

*[In footnote 2 delete the sentence beginning 'For further consideration . . . '. Footnotes 5 to 8 are renumbered 4 to 7.*

**18.36** *[At the end of the paragraph add:]*

The Detention Centre Rules and, in particular, the mechanism in Rule 35, was seriously criticised in the Shaw Review (see **18.33** above). However, those Rules remain in place as the means by which the Adults at Risk policy is to be enforced.

*[At the end of Footnote 2 add:]*

These criticisms were again made by Stephen Shaw whose Recommendation 21 was that the Home Office should 'immediately consider an alternative to the current rule 35 mechanism'.

## Fast track detention

**18.37** *[In the first paragraph, after footnote reference 5, add:]*

The Detained Fast Track Process instruction is currently 'suspended' although the guidance is still available online. It requires as follows.

*[At the end of the final paragraph add:]*

The old DFT process was suspended in July 2015 following the successful challenge in *Detention Action v Secretary of State for the Home Department*.[10] It remains suspended. However, the government did not take the opportunity to stop considering asylum claims in detention but maintained its commitment to fast-track processing of some asylum claims, forming the Detained Asylum Casework team operating under a new policy Detention: Interim Instruction (DII). That policy was then held to be lawful, save for a breach of the public sector equality duty, in *Hossain v Secretary of State for the Home Department*.[11] Since the autumn of 2006, Yarl's Wood has also dealt with female detained non-suspensive appeal cases (NSA) as well as female DAC cases.

[10] [2014] EWHC 2245 (Admin).
[11] [2016] EWHC 1331 (Admin), 166 NLJ 7703, [2016] All ER (D) 40 (Jun). That decision was itself upheld in *TH (Bangladesh) v Secretary of State for the Home Department* [2016] EWCA Civ 815.

**18.38** *[At the end of footnote 4 add:]*

This policy remains suspended, and replaced by the *Detention: Interim Instruction* policy (DII).

**18.39** *[Delete paragraph and footnotes and substitute:]*

The difficulty with the (currently suspended) detained Fast Track Processes system in practice was that, prior to detention, there was no effective screening (apart from determining the person's nationality), to find out if fast tracking was suitable or if any of the general policy considerations militating against detention applied. The DFT List made it clear that screening staff were not expected to engage in any analysis of asylum claims or to question claimants and when screened applicants were expressly told that they would not be asked any questions about the substance of their asylum claims. Furthermore, there was normally no effective screening to see whether the person was a torture victim, had mental health problems or other special medical needs such that they were otherwise unsuitable for the DFT (see eg *Detention Action v Secretary of State for the Home Department*[1]). The Detention Centre Rules provide for new arrivals to a detention centre to be medically examined within 24 hours of arrival and for the medical practitioner conducting the examination to report any concern that the detainee may have been the victim of torture to the Secretary of State.[2] The objective is in part to ensure that victims of torture are identified and so not subject to the fast-track procedure and to being detained in breach of the policy. However, deliberately and in breach of the statutory obligation under the Detention Centre Rules, medical examinations at Oakington detention centre were routinely delayed beyond 24 hours. Continued detention beyond the point at which a person should have been identified, by a timely medical examination, as a victim of torture and so released in accordance with the detention and fast-track policies was held to be unlawful.[3] The case of *Renford Johnson*[4] was indicative. Mr Johnson, a Jamaican national in his sixties, was detained at Oakington in circumstances where his claim could not be determined within the seven-day period but nevertheless, and despite the requirement for reviews, remained detained at Oakington pending a decision on his claim for over five weeks. Jack J held that the detention became unlawful after six days, when it was clear that the claim could not be determined speedily, and roundly rejected the surprising submission on behalf of the Secretary of State that seven days 'was merely a target' on the basis that it was 'wholly contrary' to the Department's submissions in *Saadi* and the basis on which the lawfulness of such detention was upheld by the House of Lords in that case.[5] He also held unlawful the period of Oakington detention after the decision on the claim, as it was contrary to the general policy, there being no basis for concluding that Mr Johnson would not co-operate or that he might abscond.[6] Following *Renford Johnson* the Home Office revised the fast-track detention policy, stating that the timetable for processing claims was only a guide and that if the timetable could not be adhered to, detention would continue beyond the 10- to 14-day timescale which was the subject of the litigation in *Saadi*, provided 'the indications are that we can make and serve a decision within a reasonable timescale'. The revised policy also stated that detention may be prolonged, if merited according to the general detention criteria, and could continue after service of a decision.[7] Application of the fast-track procedures proved particularly controversial in disputed minors cases, where expert reports necessary to displace assumptions of adulthood[8] cannot normally be performed within the usual seven-day period, leading to delays and/or the reconsideration of cases where interviews have taken place, during which period claimants remain in detention. Detention and fast-tracking is patently unsuitable in such cases.[9] The change in the age dispute policy[10] has substantially reduced the number of disputed children in the fast-track system.

The new Detention: Interim Instruction policy is less prescriptive than the old DFT policy and simply permits detention of asylum seekers where that detention would be permissible applying Chapter 55 of the Enforcement Instructions and Guidance, and, in particular, whether removal appears likely within a reasonable period of time.

1   [2014] EWHC 2245 (Admin).
2   SI 2001/238, rr 34 and 35.
3   *R (on the application of D) v Secretary of State for the Home Department; R (on the application of K) v Secretary of State for the Home Department* [2006] EWHC 980 (Admin), 150 Sol Jo LB 743, [2006] All ER (D) 300 (May). However, where an asylum seeker claimed to have been tortured, there was no obligation on the Secretary of State to carry out an earlier medical examination than required by the Detention Centre Rules in order to determine whether, by reason of being a torture victim, the person was unsuitable for the fast-track – *HK (Turkey) v Secretary of State for the Home Department* [2007] EWCA Civ 1357, [2007] All ER (D) 310 (Dec). Where an allegation of past torture is made, this cannot simply be ignored by the decision maker *E v Home Office* (Claim No (CL01651) (10 June 2010, unreported).
4   *R (on the application of Johnson (Renford)) v Secretary of State for the Home Department* [2004] EWHC 1550 (Admin).
5   *R (Johnson)*, above, at para 32.
6   *R (Johnson)*, above, at para 34.
7   Desmond Browne (Minister for Citizenship and Immigration) Hansard HC, 16 Sept 2004, Column 157–158 WS.
8   See **17.32** above.
9   For a challenge to the practice of detention while age disputes are resolved, see *R (on the application of I) v Secretary of State for the Home Department* [2005] EWHC 1025 (Admin), [2015] 1 WLR 567.
10  See **18.33** above.

## UNHCR Guidelines for detention of asylum seekers

**18.40** *[At the end of footnote 1 add:]*

On 3 July 2014, UNHCR called for an end to the detention of asylum seekers and refugees, launching a five-year global strategy to support governments in achieving that goal.

*[At the end of footnote 6 add:]*

See also Chapter 55b of the EIG and the Adults at Risk policy.

## Children

**18.41** *[At end of footnote 1 add:]*

The ending of child detention is a key Goal of UNHCR's Global Strategy to support governments to end the detention of asylum-seekers and refugees – 2014–2019.

**18.42** *[At the end of the paragraph add:]*

Following the introduction of the Immigration Act 2014, an unaccompanied child may only be detained in a short-term holding facility and for a maximum period of 24 hours, and only where removal directions are already in place or directions and removal are imminent (para 18B of Sch 2 to the Immigration Act 1971, inserted by s 5 of the Immigration Act 2014). Interestingly, the definition of an unaccompanied child is by reference to that person's actual age rather than their assessed age.

## LIMITS TO THE POWER TO DETAIN

### General principles

**18.44** *[In final paragraph delete the text from 'It has since been held . . . ' to the end of the paragraph and substitute new text and footnotes:]*

It was held by the Court of Appeal in *R (on the application of Francis) v Secretary of State for the Home Department*[9] that where a person was detained under para 2(1) of Schedule 3 to the 1971 Act, that might provide authority for detention notwithstanding a public law error bearing on the decision to detain. The Supreme Court finally resolved this longstanding issue and emphatically held that this is not the case in *R (O) v Secretary of State for the Home Department*.[10]

[9]  [2014] EWCA Civ 718, [2015] All ER (D) 113 (Aug).
[10]  [2016] WLR 1717.

### The purpose and length of detention

**18.47** *[In the duplicated number footnote 8, renumber as 8a and delete the text from 'In Fardous . . . ' to the end of the footnote and replace with:]*

In *Fardous v Secretary of State for the Home Department* [2015] EWCA Civ 931, [2015] All ER (D) 113 (Aug), however, the Court of Appeal deprecated the practise of using case law to establish 'yardsticks' for lawful detention holding: 'There is no period of time which is considered long or short. There is no fixed period where particular factors may require special reasons to make continued detention reasonable'.

**18.50** *[Following the quotation from FTT bail guidance add:]*

In *Fardous v Secretary of State for the Home Department*,[14a] however, the Court of Appeal deprecated the practise of using case law to establish 'yardsticks' for lawful detention holding: 'There is no period of time which is considered long or short. There is no fixed period where particular factors may require special reasons to make continued detention reasonable'.

*[In footnote 14 delete from 'By contrast . . . ' to the end of the footnote.]*

*[In footnote 22 add:]*

See also the decision of Garnham J in *R (Babbage) v Secretary of State for the Home Department* [2016] EWHC 148 (Admin), in particular, dealing with the

Secretary of State's practice of redacting key documentation.

[14a] [2015] EWCA Civ 931, [2015] All ER (D) 113 (Aug).

**18.54** *[In the main text, after footnote reference 4, delete the words 'In the case of a person who is detained other than following a court order for deportation', including footnote reference 5, and amend the next word to 'There'.]*

*[In the main text, after footnote reference 9, delete the sentence beginning 'It follows from these . . . ' and replace with:]*

It follows from these cases that decisions to detain people in breach of the policies in Chapter 55 EIG and the Adults at Risk Statutory Guidance would normally be unlawful.

*[In footnote 3 delete 'R (on the application of Francis)'.]*

*[Footnote 5 is deleted.]*

*[In footnote 6 delete 'R (on the application of Francis)'.]*

## EUROPEAN CONVENTION ON HUMAN RIGHTS

**18.57** *[At the end of the paragraph, after footnote reference 15, add:]*

The Court of Appeal held in *R (Idira) v Secretary of State for the Home Department*[16] that the practice of keeping individuals in prisons pending deportation was not arbitrary for the purposes of Article 5 of ECHR unless the conditions were 'seriously inappropriate', which will depend both on the conditions and the individual in question.

[16] [2016] 1 WLR 1694.

## CHALLENGING DETENTION IN THE HIGH COURT

### Habeas corpus and judicial review

**18.59** *[At the end of the paragraph add:]*

Habeas Corpus is in principle available even to those who are on bail, as they remain detained in the eyes of the law.[5]

[5] *Mitchell v Mitchinham* (1823) 2 D & R. See discussion at para 32 of *R (B) v Secretary of State for the Home Department* [2015] EWCA Civ 445, [2015] 3 WLR 1031, [2015] All ER (D) 35 (May), in which the Court of Appeal accepted that a person could not be placed on bail if they could not be lawfully detained. The Immigration Act 2016 at s 61 essentially reveres that decision and with it, without much fanfare, hundreds of years of common law.

### Damages, judicial review and county court actions

**18.62** *[At the end of the paragraph add:]*

The Court of Appeal endorsed these statements in *R (SS) v Secretary of State for the Home Department*.[14] In *R (Ashraf) v Secretary of State for the Home Department*,[15] Mr Justice Cranston said that it might be considered abusive to bring a judicial review claim in the Administrative Court with a detention ground that had 'no obvious distinct merit' for the purposes of circumventing the Lord Chief Justice's Direction that immigration judicial reviews should generally be filed in the Upper Tribunal.

¹⁴ [2015] EWCA Civ 652, [2015] All ER (D) 277 (Jun).
¹⁵ [2013] EWHC 4028 (Admin).


## SOME DAMAGE AWARDS

**18.63** *[At the end of the list of bullet points insert:]*

- In *R (Supawan) v Secretary of State for the Home Department*²³ Blake J awarded £9,000 for 15 days' detention in a case with no initial shock or *Simmons v Castle* uplift.²⁴
- In *Tarakhil v The Home Office*²⁵ an Afghan national was awarded £14,250 for 24 days' detention as well as £2,000 for aggravated damages.
- In *AS v Secretary of State for the Home Office*²⁶ having reviewed the authorities in some detail (including the requirement for a *Simmons v Castle* uplift)²⁷ awarded £23,000 for 61 days' detention in addition to £5,000 aggravated damages and separate damages for psychiatric damage.
- In *R (Santos) v Secretary of State for the Home Department*²⁸ the claimant was awaiting consideration of his application for a residence card when he was detained as an overstayer and the Secretary of State attempted to remove him. Lang J awarded him *Frankovich* damages and special damages for loss of wages, in addition to £40,000 for 154 days' detention as well as £10,000 aggravated damages and £20,000 exemplary damages.
- In *AXD v Home Office*²⁹ the claimant suffered from paranoid schizophrenia. The judge somewhat surprisingly concluded that the fact of his illness did not affect the level of basic award, although the nature of the regimes to which he was subjected while detained in prison did. The claimant was victimised because of his sexuality in prison and assaulted. There was no initial shock. Unusually, the judge made three separate 'in the alternative' findings as to what basic damages should be awarded in case the matter went further: £80,000 for 20 months and 5 days; £62,000 for 13 months and 5 days; £58,000 for 11 months and 5 days. Aggravated damages were £25,000, £15,000 and £13,500 respectively.

²³ [2014] EWHC 3224 (Admin).
²⁴ [2012] EWCA Civ 1039, [2012] EWCA Civ 1288, [2013] 1 All ER 334, [2013] 1 WLR 1239.
²⁵ [2015] EWHC 2845 (QB), 165 NLJ 7675, [2015] All ER (D) 194 (Oct).
²⁶ [2015] EWHC 1331 (QB).
²⁷ [2012] EWCA Civ 1039, [2012] EWCA Civ 1288.
²⁸ [2016] EWHC 609 (Admin), [2016] 3 CMLR 251, 166 NLJ 7695.
²⁹ [2016] EWHC 1617 (QB), [2016] All ER (D) 88 (Jul).

## PAYING FOR DETENTION

**18.66** *[At the end of the paragraph add:]*

By late 2015 that figure had fallen to £91 per day according to Home Office quarterly statistics.

**18.66A** *[Add new paragraphs 18.66A to 18.66H as follows:]*

Schedule 10 of the Immigration Act 2016 sets out an entirely new bail regime, which replaces paras 22 and 29 of Sch 2 to the Immigration Act 1971, together with numerous consequential amendments, and sets out new provisions relating to the power to grant bail and as to its exercise; as to the conditions of bail, including electronic monitoring and restricted judicial control thereof; a limited right to automatic review of detention in non-deportation cases; and in relation to enforcement powers arising from breaches of bail. Schedule 10 is not in force at the time of writing and the editors are not aware of its proposed commencement date. It applies equally to bail proceedings in the Special Immigration Appeals Commission, by consequential amendments made via paras 22–25 of Sch 10 to the Special Immigration and Appeals Commission Act 1997 (SIACA 1977).

### The power to grant immigration bail

**18.66B** Schedule 10 creates the statutory concept of 'immigration bail', which is defined as the grant of bail by:

- the Secretary of State to a person who is being detained (para 1(1)) or is liable to detention (para 1(2))[1] on the basis of the following statutory provisions: (a) para 16(1), (1A) or (2) of Sch 2 to the Immigration Act 1971 (detention of persons liable to examination or removal); (b) para 2(1), (2) or (3) of Sch 3 to that Act (detention pending deportation); (c) s 62 of the Nationality, Immigration and Asylum Act 2002 (detention of persons liable to examination or removal); or (d) s 36(1) of the UK Borders Act 2007 (detention pending deportation);
- the FTT to a person who is being detained (para 1(3)) or is liable to detention (para 1(5)(a)), on the basis of the above listed statutory detention powers;
- the Secretary of State or the FTT, as appropriate, to a person who has been arrested for breach of bail conditions under para 10(12) of Sch 10.

Under para 1(5), a person may be granted and remain on immigration bail even if the person can no longer be detained, if: (a) the person is liable to detention under a provision mentioned in sub-para (1);[2] or (b) the Secretary of State is considering whether to make a deportation order against the person under s 5(1) of the Immigration Act 1971. By para 1(6), a grant of immigration bail to a person does not prevent the person's subsequent detention under a provision mentioned in sub-para (1) (ie the powers listed (a)–(d) in the first bullet point above). Under para 1(8), a grant of immigration bail to a person ends when: (a) para 1(5) no longer applies to the person, where it had previously applied; (b) the person is granted leave to enter or remain in the United Kingdom; (c) the person is detained under a provision mentioned in sub-para (1); or (d) the person is removed from or otherwise leaves the United

359

Kingdom.

1   The phrase 'liable to detention' was defined by the House of Lords in the context of Sch 2 to the 1971 Act as meaning that there is 'some prospect' of removal being achieved: *R (Khadir) v SSHD* [2005] UKHL 39, [2006] 1 AC 207, [2005] 4 All ER 114, at [32]. See, relatedly, s 67 of the Nationality Immigration and Asylum Act 2002.

2   This represents an attempt to reverse the historic common law position, under which a person who could no longer be detained lawfully could not be subjected to the bail powers of the Secretary of State and/or the immigration tribunals: see *R (B) v Special Immigration Appeals Commission* [2015] EWCA Civ 445, [2015] 3 WLR 1031 at [31] (which is under appeal to the Supreme Court, hearing in November 2017). This is a long-standing principle of the common law dating back many centuries and enshrined in cases such as *Mitchell v Mitchinham* (1823) 2 D & R ('When common bail is filed, still the party in the eye of the law is in custody'); *Foxall v Barnet* (1853) 2 E&B 928; see also Highmore, *Digest of the Doctrine of Bail* (1783), 'He who is bailed shall not be said by the law to be at large, or at his liberty'.

**18.66C** In determining whether to grant bail, and as to what conditions should be attached to it, para 3(1) of Sch 10 requires the Secretary of State and the FTT to have regard to a list of mandatory relevant factors listed in para 3(2), which are: (a) the likelihood of the person failing to comply with a bail condition; (b) whether the person has been convicted of an offence (whether in or outside the United Kingdom or before or after the coming into force of this paragraph); (c) the likelihood of a person committing an offence while on immigration bail; (d) the likelihood of the person's presence in the United Kingdom, while on immigration bail, causing a danger to public health or being a threat to the maintenance of public order; (e) whether the person's detention is necessary in that person's interests or for the protection of any other person; and (f) such other matters as the Secretary of State or the First-tier Tribunal thinks relevant.

Under para 3(3), a person who is being detained under para 16(1) of Sch 2 to the Immigration Act 1971 must not be granted immigration bail by the First-tier Tribunal until after 8 days has elapsed beginning with the date of the person's arrival in the United Kingdom. Under para 3(4), a person must not be granted immigration bail by the First-tier Tribunal without the consent of the Secretary of State if: (a) directions for the removal of the person from the United Kingdom are for the time being in force; and (b) the directions require the person to be removed from the United Kingdom within the period of 14 days beginning with the date of the decision on whether the person should be granted immigration bail. A notice granting or refusing bail must be set out in a notice and given to the bail applicant (para 3(5) and to the Secretary of State (para 3(6)). If bail is granted, the notice must state when the grant of bail commences and what are the bail conditions (para 3(7)). The commencement of a grant of immigration bail may be specified to be conditional on arrangements specified in the notice being in place to ensure that the person is able to comply with the bail conditions (para 3(8)).

## Conditions of immigration bail

**18.66D** In the case of a person who is not being detained, or liable to detention, under the detention pending deportation provisions, a grant of bail must (under para 2(1)) be granted subject to one or more of the following conditions: (a) a condition requiring the person to appear before the Secretary of State or the First-tier Tribunal at a specified time and place; (b) a condition restricting the person's work, occupation or studies in the United Kingdom; (c) a condition about the person's residence; (d) a condition requiring the person to report to the Secretary of State or such other person as may be specified; (e) an electronic monitoring condition; (f) such other conditions as the person granting the immigration bail thinks fit.

In relation to those who are being detained, or are liable to detention, under para 2(1), (2) or (3) of Sch 3 to the Immigration Act 1971, or s 36(1) of the UK Borders Act 2007 (detention pending deportation), the grant of bail must be subject to an electronic monitoring condition unless the Secretary of State considers that this would be 'impractical' or would be contrary to 'the person's Convention rights', in which case an electronic monitoring condition must not be imposed (para 2(2), (3), (5)–(11)). These exceptions apply, where bail is being decided by the FTT, if, 'the Secretary of State informs the Tribunal that the Secretary of State considers that', the impracticality or ECHR exception are made out (para 2(7)–(8)). 'Impractical' is not defined, but a list of factors to which the SSHD 'may in particular have regard' in deciding impracticality are set out in para 2(9)(a)–(d) of Sch 10 and include any obstacles to making arrangements as specified in para 4 of Sch 10 (see below); the resources that are available for imposing electronic monitoring conditions; the need to give priority to the use of those resources; and the matters listed in para 3(2). 'Convention rights' are as defined in s 1 of the Human Rights Act 1998. If an electronic monitoring condition is not imposed, bail must be imposed subject to one or more of the other conditions listed in para 2(1); and if an electronic monitoring condition is imposed, it may be imposed subject to one or more of the other conditions listed in para 2(1) (para 2(3)(c)).

Any electronic monitoring condition imposed is to be in accordance with para 4 of Sch 10. By para 4(1), an electronic monitoring condition means a condition requiring the person on whom it is imposed ('P') to co-operate with such arrangements as the Secretary of State may specify for detecting and recording by electronic means one or more of the following: (a) P's location at specified times, during specified periods of time or while the arrangements are in place; (b) P's presence in a location at specified times, during specified periods of time or while the arrangements are in place; (c) P's absence from a location at specified times, during specified periods of time or while the arrangements are in place. Under para 4(2), the arrangements may in particular require P to: (a) wear a device; (b) make specified use of a device; (c) communicate in a specified manner and at specified times or during specified periods; and (d) may involve the exercise of functions by persons other than the Secretary of State or the First-tier Tribunal. Under para 4(3), if the arrangements require P to wear, or make specified use of, a device they must: (a) prohibit P from causing or permitting damage to, or interference with the device; and (b) prohibit P from taking or permitting action that would or might prevent the effective operation of the device. An electronic monitoring condition may not be imposed on a person unless the person is at least 18 years old (para 4(5)). The subsequent removal or amendment of an electronic monitoring condition is regulated by paras 7 and 8 of Sch 10, addressed below.

Where there has been non-compliance with bail conditions, a financial condition may be imposed upon the grant of bail, under para 2(4) of Sch 10. Paragraph 5(1) states that a 'financial condition' means a condition requiring the payment of a sum of money by the person to whom immigration bail is granted ('P') or another person, in a case where P fails to comply with another condition to which P's immigration bail is subject. Paragraph 5(2) states that a financial condition may be imposed on P only if the person imposing the condition thinks that it would be appropriate to do so with a view to ensuring that P complies with the other bail conditions. Under para 5(3), the financial condition must specify: (a) the sum of money required to be paid; (b) when it is to be paid; and (c) the form and manner in which it is to be paid. Under para 5(4), a sum to be paid under a financial condition is to be paid to the person who granted the immigration bail, subject to sub-para (5), which provides that, if the First-tier Tribunal has directed that the power in paragraph 6(1) (power to vary bail conditions) is to be exercisable by the Secretary of State in relation to P, the sum is to be paid to the Secretary of State. Under para 5(6), no sum is required to be paid under a financial condition unless the person who is liable to make a payment under it has been given an opportunity to make representations to the person to whom it is to be paid. A sum payable under a financial condition is treated as a civil debt owed by the payee, and is enforceable in the County Court (England, Wales and Northern Ireland) and Sheriff Court (Scotland). Under para 5(10), where action is taken under for the recovery of a sum payable under a financial condition, the requirement to pay the sum is treated as a judgment entered in the county court or equivalent.

By para 9(4)–(5), the Secretary of State may make a payment to a person on immigration bail in respect of travelling expenses which the person has incurred or will incur for the purpose of complying with a bail condition, provided that the Secretary of State thinks that there are exceptional circumstances which justify the making of the payment. By para 9(1)–(3), the Secretary of State may provide, or arrange for the provision of, facilities for the accommodation of a person who is on immigration bail subject to a condition requiring them to reside at an address specified in the condition, where the person would not otherwise be able to support himself or herself at the address (para 9(1)–(2)). This power only applies 'to the extent that the Secretary of State thinks that there are exceptional circumstances which justify the exercise of the power' (para 9(3)). Consequent to this provision is the repeal of section 4(1)(c) of the Immigration and Asylum Act 1999, by which bail accommodation is provided to prospective bail applicants, which is dealt with within the main text at **14.174T** above, by section 66 of the 2016 Act, and Sch 11, para 1 thereof, which is not yet in force.

**Variation of bail**

**18.66E** Under para 6(1) of Sch 10, where a person is on immigration bail, any of the conditions to which it is subject may be amended or removed; or one or more new conditions of the kind mentioned in paragraph 2(1) or (4) may be imposed on the person. The amendment, removal or addition of bail conditions is exercisable by the person who granted immigration bail (para 6(2)), save that the Secretary of State may exercise those powers, where the FTT last granted immigration bail, 'if the Tribunal so directs' (para 6(3)). In this way, the FTT can assign to the Secretary of State the power to amend, remove or add bail conditions; and if the FTT does so, it may not itself exercise those powers in relation to the person (para 6(4)). However, the FTT may not exercise the power in para 6(1)(a) so as to amend or remove an electronic monitoring condition (para 6(5)). A notice must be given to the person who is on immigration bail whenever the Secretary of State, or the FTT, exercises or refuses to exercise the power to amend, vary or add conditions; the FTT must also provide a copy of the notice to the Secretary of State (para 6(6)–(7)).

In cases where a person is detained or liable to detention pending deportation (ie under a provision mentioned in para 1(1)(b) or (d)) and has been granted bail by the Secretary of State, or has been granted bail by the FTT and the FTT has made a direction under para 6(3) that the power in para 6(1) is exercisable by the Secretary of State, an existing electronic monitoring condition must not be removed by the Secretary of State unless it would be impractical, or it would be contrary to the person's Convention rights, for the person to continue to be subject to the condition: para 7(1)–(3). Provisions as to the 'impracticality' issue are set out in para 2(9) of Sch 10. 'Convention rights' are as defined in section 1 of the Human Rights Act 1998. Conversely, if the person is not subject to an electronic monitoring requirement, and the Secretary of State considers that it would not be 'impractical' and not contrary to the person's Convention rights to do so, the Secretary of State must impose an electronic monitoring requirement (para 7(4)–(5)).

Where the FTT retains its power to amend, remove or add bail conditions (ie the FTT has not made a direction under para 6(3)) in respect of a person who is detained or liable to detention pending deportation under para 1(1)(b) or (d), and that person is subject to an electronic monitoring requirement, the FTT must not remove that condition unless 'the Secretary of State notifies the First-tier Tribunal that the Secretary of State considers that' it would be impractical, or would be contrary to that person's Convention rights, for the person to continue to be subject to the condition (para 8(2)–(3)). Conversely, if such a person is not subject to an electronic monitoring requirement, whether by virtue of a previous decision by the Secretary of State or otherwise, the FTT can only impose an electronic monitoring requirement if the Secretary of State notifies the FTT that she does not consider that it would be impractical, or would be contrary to the person's Convention rights to impose such a condition. If such notification has occurred, the FTT must impose an electronic monitoring requirement condition: para 8(4) and (5). Given that the FTT is a public authority for the purposes of section 6 of the Human Rights Act 1998, it is difficult to see how the FTT could impose or authorise the continuance of an electronic monitoring requirement on a person if the FTT thinks that to do so would violate a person's Convention rights, even if the SSHD disagrees. In such a situation, there is unlikely to be, or to have been, a lawful 'notification' and/or 'consideration' of the ECHR issue by the Secretary of State under para 8(3) and (5).

## Automatic reference for FTT to review detention in non-deportation cases

**18.66F** Where a person is detained under a provision mentioned in para 1(1)(a) or (c),[1] the Secretary of State 'must' arrange a reference to the FTT for the Tribunal to decide whether to grant bail to a person, upon the expiry of four months beginning on the date on which the person's detention began (para 11(1) and (2)(a)); or upon the expiry of four months from a 'relevant event', namely (para 11(3)):

(a) consideration by the First-tier Tribunal of whether to grant immigration bail to the person (whether or not there was a hearing, and whether or not the FTT makes a determination in the case in question – para 11(4)); and includes the dismissal of an application by virtue of para 12(2) (bail application made within 28 days of a previous unsuccessful application where no material change of circumstances). The FTT has not considered bail for the purposes of para 11(3)(a) where the FTT is prevented from granting bail to the person by para 3(4) (requirement for Secretary of State's consent to bail);

(b) withdrawal by the person of an application for immigration bail treated as made by the person as the result of a reference under this paragraph. Under para 11(7), a reference to the First-tier Tribunal under this paragraph is to be treated for all purposes as an application by that person for the grant of bail under para 1(3);

(c) withdrawal by the person of a notice given under sub-para (6)(b); that is a written notice given to the Secretary of State by the person that the person does not wish the person's case to be referred to the First-tier Tribunal under this paragraph.

The duty in para 11(1) to arrange a reference does not apply if section 3(2) of the Special Immigration Appeals Commission Act 1997 (persons detained in interests of national security etc) applies to the person (para 11(6)(a)).

[1] That is, (a) under para 16(1), (1A) or (2) of Sch 2 to the Immigration Act 1971 (detention of persons liable to examination or removal); or (c) the person is being detained under s 62 of the Nationality, Immigration and Asylum Act 2002 (detention of persons liable to examination or removal).

### Powers of arrest for breach of immigration bail

**18.66G** Under para 10(1), an immigration officer or a constable may arrest without warrant a person on immigration bail if the immigration officer or constable: (a) has reasonable grounds for believing that the person is likely to fail to comply with a bail condition, or (b) has reasonable grounds for suspecting that the person is failing, or has failed, to comply with a bail condition. Under paras 10(2)–(3), if an appropriate judicial officer is satisfied that there are reasonable grounds for believing that a person liable to be arrested under this paragraph is to be found on any premises, they may issue a warrant authorising any immigration officer or constable to enter, by reasonable force if necessary, the premises named in the warrant for the purposes of searching for and arresting that person. By para 10(5)–(7), where such a warrant is issued, a detainee custody officer may enter the premises if need be by reasonable force, for the purpose of carrying out a search. Under para 10(8), the powers of entry and search of premises under paras 25A to 25C of Sch 2 to the Immigration Act 1971 are extended to persons arrested under Sch 10 to the 2016 Act. Under para 10(9)–(13), such a person must as soon as practicable after the person's arrest, be brought before the relevant authority, and may be detained under the authority of the Secretary of State in the meantime. The relevant authority is: (a) the Secretary of State, if the Secretary of State granted immigration bail to the arrested person or the First-tier Tribunal has directed that the power in para 6(1) is exercisable by the Secretary of State in relation to that person, or (b) otherwise, the First-tier Tribunal. The relevant authority must then decide whether the arrested person has broken or is likely to break any of the bail conditions. Under para 10(12), if the relevant authority decides the arrested person has broken or is likely to break any of the bail conditions, the relevant authority must: (a) direct that the person is to be detained under the provision mentioned in para 1(1) under which the person is liable to be detained, or (b) grant the person bail subject to the same or different conditions, subject to sub-para (14). Under para 10(13), if the relevant authority decides the person has not broken and is not likely to break any of the bail conditions, the relevant authority must grant the person bail subject to the same conditions (but this is subject to sub-para (14), and does not prevent the subsequent exercise of the powers in para 6). Under para 10(14), the power in sub-paragraph (12) to grant bail subject to the same conditions and the duty in sub-para (13) to do so do not affect the requirement for the grant of bail to comply with para 2.

### Transitional provisions

**18.66H** A significant difference between the existing regime and the new regime set out in the 2016 Act is that the concept of temporary admission is abolished and those to whom it is currently subject will, under the new regime, be placed on immigration bail, together with others who are liable to detention but not actually detained. Paragraph 13 of Sch 10 refers to transitional arrangements by way of regulations with a view to treating those who are at commencement on temporary admission or liable to detention (listed in para 13(2)) as being subject to immigration bail, and as to the conditions of such bail. Transitional regulations have not been published at the time of writing.

### PROVISIONS FOR RELEASE OR BAIL

**18.67** *[Delete fifth sentence starting 'The grant of bail . . . ' including footnotes 2 and 3 and replace with the following:]*

The grant of bail is distinct from the issue of lawfulness of detention. The likely unlawfulness of a person's detention is a relevant factor in the exercise of the tribunals' discretion whether to grant bail.[2] However, it is not the tribunals' job to decide the lawfulness of detention; that is a matter for the High Court.[3]

---

[2]   See for example, *R (Othman) v Special Immigration Appeals Commission* [2012] EWHC 2349 (Admin), [2012] All ER (D) 78 (Aug), per Hughes LJ (as he then was) at [18]: '[A]ny tribunal charged with considering bail is bound sometimes to have to ask, en route to its decision, whether the detention is still lawful or not . . . '. This principle is reflected in the *Bail Guidance for Immigration Judges* (implemented 11 June 2012) see [5], [17] and [18]. Historically, one reason for this was that the tribunals' bail jurisdiction assumed that the applicant was being detained lawfully; that is, if detention was unlawful, the tribunals' bail jurisdiction would be ousted: *R (B) v Special Immigration Appeals Commission* [2015] EWCA Civ 445, [2015] 3 WLR 1031 at [31] (which is under appeal to the Supreme Court, hearing in November 2017). This is a long-standing principle of the common law dating back many centuries: see further **18.66B**, fn 2, above. However, since 12 May 2016, section 61(3)–(5) of

the Immigration Act 2016 has been in force, with the effect that the tribunals' bail jurisdiction is unaffected by whether the applicant's detention is unlawful, or, were it to be exercised, would be unlawful. These provisions have retrospective effect, by section 61(5). Once the new bail provisions in Sch 10 to the 2016 Act come into force (see below), section 61(3)–(5) will be repealed and replaced by similar provisions under para 1(5) of that Schedule.

3  See the existing footnotes 2 and 3 in the 9th Edition; as well as *R (Lumba and Mighty) v Secretary of State for the Home Department* [2011] UKSC 12, [2011] 2 WLR 671, [2011] 4 All ER 1, at [118]; and *Bail Guidance for Immigration Judges* (2012), [5], [17] and [18].

## New arrivals and those detained for removal: bail under the Immigration Act 1971

**18.68** *[At the end of footnote 9, add:]*

The Court of Appeal has recently approved the provisions of the *Bail Guidance for Immigration Judges* (No 1 of 2012) at [32]–[35] as correctly representing the law, namely that, where there is no pending appeal, and the FTT releases a person on conditional bail, those conditions lapse upon the person's surrender to an immigration officer, who must then re-fix the bail if he or she considers it appropriate to do so, and to determine any appropriate conditions. Any conditions imposed, 'are to be treated in law as imposed by the immigration officer', who is 'likely to continue the terms' set by the FTT, although 'any departure from them to the prejudice of the bailed person would have to be justified and could be amenable to judicial review': see *R (Raza) v Secretary of State for the Home Department* [2016] EWCA Civ 807, at [23]–[28].

*[At the end of footnote 10, add:]*

The case of *R (Gedi) v SSHD* [2016] EWCA Civ 409, [2016] 4 WLR 93 may call into question whether para 22(2) authorises the imposition of a curfew. In *Gedi*, the Court of Appeal held at [38] that para 2(5) of Sch 3 to the Immigration Act 1971 (permitting the SSHD to impose a 'restriction as to residence') did 'not necessarily incorporate a right to impose a curfew'. It might be said that the broad wording of para 22(2) ('conditions appearing likely to result in the appearance of the person bailed . . . ') lacks the necessary specificity in a case where restriction of liberty is at stake (see *Gedi* at [36]).

*[At the end of footnote 16 add:]*

In *R (Cham) v Secretary of State for the Home Department* [2014] EWHC 4569 (Admin), Andrews J said at [23], 'If someone makes a bail application and it cannot be heard within the window [of 14 days before removal is executed], and there are genuine reasons for making the application and challenging the person's removal, then if the Secretary of State does not defer removal directions so that the bail application can be heard in time, she may get very short shrift coming back to this court and opposing an application for interim relief made on the same grounds . . . '.

*[At the end of footnotes 17, 18 and 19, add:]*

See the addition to footnote 9, above, concerning *R (Raza) v Secretary of State for the Home Department* [2016] EWCA Civ 807, at [23]–[28].

*[In footnote 20, delete 'To be achieved via procedure rules' and replace with:]*

FTT Procedure Rules 2014 (SI 2014/2604), rule 39(3), from 20 October 2014.

## Bail pending appeal

**18.69** *[At the end of footnote 5, add:]*

In *R (Lauzikas) v Secretary of State for the Home Department* [2016] EWHC 3215 (Admin) it was held at [55]–[61] that, where a person subject to deportation action is on bail pending appeal under para 29 of Sch 2, the Secretary of State was permitted to impose a restriction relating to the person's right to work under para 2(5) of Sch 3 to the 1971 Act since that did not cut across the bail conditions, which were to secure attendance at appeal.

*[At the end of footnote 6 add:]*

See the addition to fn 16 of **18.68**, above.

**18.70** *[After the first sentence, add the following:]*

However, paras 13.3–13.14 of the *Practice Directions of the Immigration and Asylum Chambers of the First-tier Tribunal and the Upper Tribunal* (13 November 2014) provide that an Upper Tribunal judge may exercise bail jurisdiction under the Immigration Act 1971 by reason of being also a First-tier judge. At the same time, it will usually be appropriate for a bail application to be made to an Upper Tribunal judge only where the appeal in question is being heard by the Upper Tribunal, or where a hearing before the Upper Tribunal is imminent. In case of doubt, a potential applicant should consult the bails section of the First-tier Tribunal.

**18.71** *[At the end of footnote 4, add:]*

The modified provisions conferring SIAC's bail powers are set out in *R (B) v Special Immigration Appeals Commission* [2015] EWCA Civ 445 at [21].

## Bail procedure before the First-tier Tribunal

**18.72** *[In the body of the paragraph, before footnote reference 7, and before the full stop preceding it, insert:]*

if practicable within three working days of receipt by the Tribunal of the notice of application (see paras 13.1–13.2 of the IAC Practice Direction cited by the addition to **18.70**, above.

*[At footnote 6, delete the first sentence, and replace with:]*

SI 2014/2604, r 40(2). See the addition to **18.68**, fn 16, above, for the view that bail hearings within the 14-day window may be expected before seeking release by way of interim relief from the Administrative Court.

## Bail guidance for judges

**18.73** *[At the end of the paragraph, insert a new footnote 15 as follows:]*

See the addition to **18.68**, fn 9, above.

**18.73** *Detention and Bail*

*[At footnote 2, after 'Para 5', add the following:]*
See **18.67**, and the additions made to it, above.

## Procedures before the Special Immigration Appeals Commission

**18.74** *[In the main text, after footnote reference 3, add the following:]*
Where the Commission has refused a bail application and a fresh application is made before 28 days has expired since that decision, the Commission must dismiss that further application unless there has been a material change in circumstances (and make so determine without a hearing): r 30A of the SIAC Rules 2003 (amended by SI 2015/867) from 12 April 2015.

## Bail pending judicial review or habeas corpus

**18.76** *In the second sentence, delete the words 'new arrivals' to the end of the sentence and replace with:]*
those detained under para 16(1) of Sch 2 pending examination before seven days has elapsed following their arrival in the UK.

**18.77** *[At the end of footnote 8, add:]*
But see fn 1 at **18.67** above.

# Chapter 19

# RIGHTS OF APPEAL AND ADMINISTRATIVE REVIEW

## BACKGROUND AND STRUCTURE OF THE APPEALS SYSTEM

### Background

**19.12** *[Replace the entire paragraph and footnotes with:]*

The amendments to the appeals provisions in Part 5 of the NIAA 2002 by IA 2014, substituting rights of appeal against refusals of asylum and human rights claims for appeals against immigration decisions have now been brought fully into force, subject to transitional provisions. The series of commencement orders[1] by which this was accomplished demonstrated once again the contemporary legislator's preference for complex and opaque drafting in the field of immigration. The first order in the series identified the new appeals provisions as being 'the relevant provisions' and the appeals provisions they were to replace as 'the saved provisions'.[2] It brought the relevant provisions into force on 20 October 2014 but subject to the saving provision in article 9 of the order.[3] The effect of the first in the series of orders was that the saved provisions continued to apply and the relevant provisions did not apply[4] other than in relation to:

(1) a person who becomes a 'foreign criminal' as defined in NIAA 2002, s 117D(2) on or after 20 October 2014;[5]
(2) a person liable to deportation as belonging to the family of a person in (1);[6]
(3) a person making an application for leave to remain as a Tier 4 migrant on or after 20 October 2014;[7]
(4) a person making an application for leave to remain as the partner or child of a person in (2).[8]

Those people would no longer have rights of appeal against an 'immigration decision' but would only have rights of appeal against refusals of protection and human rights claims and revocation of protection status. The second order brought the relevant provisions into effect in relation to deportation decisions made on or after 10 November 2014, deportation decisions being decisions to make a deportation order or to refuse to revoke a deportation order and decisions that the automatic deportation provisions of the UK Borders Act 2007 applied.[9] The third order amended the saving provision in article 9 of the first order so as to extend the range of circumstances in which the relevant provisions applied and the saved provisions did not apply.[10] First of all, the relevant provisions would also apply to any person making an application for leave to remain on or after 2 March 2015 as a Tier 1, 2 or 5 Migrant or as a partner or child of such a person.[11] Second, from 6 April 2015 the first order was amended so as to substitute a new article 9 saving provision. What that did was to apply the relevant provisions to all cases other than those specified to which the saved provisions were to apply.[12] Thus the saved provisions continue to apply to:

(1)    a decision made on or after 6 April 2015 refusing leave to remain to a person who applied before 20 October 2014 for leave to remain as a Tier 4 Migrant or family member of a Tier 4 Migrant;

(2)    a decision made on or after 6 April 2015 refusing leave to remain to a person who applied before 2 March 2015 for leave to remain as a Tier 1, 2 or 5 Migrant or family member of a Tier 1, 2 or 5 Migrant;

(3)    a decision made on or after 6 April 2015 to refuse an application made before 6 April 2015 for leave to enter, entry clearance, a certificate of entitlement to the right of abode or to refuse to vary a person's leave unless the decision is also a refusal of an asylum, protection or human rights claim;

(4)    a decision made before 6 April 2015 in relation to which, immediately before 6 April 2015 an appeal could have been brought or was pending under the saved provisions, including a decision where the right of appeal could only be exercised once the appellant had left the UK.[13]

Only in those circumstances does NIAA 2002, s 82 give a right of appeal against an 'immigration decision'. Otherwise, the only rights of appeal are against refusals of asylum and human rights claims and revocation of protection status.

1    Made under IA 2014, ss 73(1) and 75(3).
2    Immigration Act 2014 (Commencement No 3, Transitional and Saving Provision) Order 2014, SI 2014/2771.
3    By article 2.
4    By article 9.
5    By article 10(a).
6    By article 10(b).
7    By article 11(1)(a).
8    By article 11(1)(b) and (c).
9    Immigration Act 2014 (Transitional and Saving Provisions) Order 2014, SI 2014/2928, art 2.
10    Immigration Act 2014 (Commencement No 4, Transitional and Saving Provisions and Amendment) Order 2015, SI 2015/371.
11    SI 2015/371, art 7.
12    Article 8, substituting a new article 9 in SI 2014/2771.
13    *R (Roodi) v Secretary of State for the Home Department (2014 Act: saved appeal rights) IJR* [2015] UKUT 685 (IAC).

## REFUSAL OF ASYLUM AND PROTECTION CLAIMS

**19.17** *[At the end of the paragraph add:]*

However, thus far the tribunal has taken the view that where a person has previously made a protection claim or human rights claim, there is a right of appeal against refusal of a further claim only if the Secretary of State chooses to treat the 'further claim' as a 'fresh claim' within the meaning of paragraph 353 of the immigration rules.³ The tribunal's willingness thus to delegate to the Secretary of State the task of determining whether a decision on a claim is appealable is surprising in the light of *BA (Nigeria)* where the Supreme Court rejected the proposition that paragraph 353 had any part to play in deciding whether a claim was a claim within the meaning of NIAA 2002, s 113.⁴ The tribunal has acknowledged that 'despite the unanimity thus far, there is clearly room for a modest measure of doubt' on the question⁵ and the court of appeal has given permission to appeal on the issue.⁶ In the case of *Sheidu*, the tribunal accepted that there was a right of appeal against the decision purporting to be a refusal to accept a fresh claim under paragraph 353 of the Rules because on analysis of the terms of the decision, it was clear that in fact the Secretary of State had accepted that an asylum claim had been made and that she had decided to refuse a protection claim.⁷

³   *R (Waqar) v Secretary of State for the Home Department (Statutory Appeals / Paragraph 353) IJR* [2015] UKUT 169 (IAC), [2015] All ER (D) 78 (Apr); *R (Robinson) v Secretary of State for the Home Department (Para 353 – Waqar applied) IJR* [2016] UKUT 133 (IAC); *R (MG) v First-tier Tribunal (IAC) (fresh claim; para 353; no appeal) IJR* [2016] UKUT 283 (IAC), [2016] All ER (D) 108 (Jun); *R (Hussein) v First Tier Tribunal (Para 353; present scope and effect) IJR* [2016] UKUT 409 (IAC).
⁴   *R (BA (Nigeria)) v Secretary of State for the Home Department* [2009] UKSC 7.
⁵   *Sheidu (Further submissions; appealable decision)* [2016] UKUT 412 (IAC), Mr Ockelton VP and UTJ Dawson.
⁶   In the above-mentioned case of *Robinson*.
⁷   *Sheidu*, cited above.

**19.18** *[In the text delete the second sentence ending with footnote reference 2 and replace with:]*

In order for a person to have a right of appeal under NIAA 2002, s 83 (now repealed) it was not necessary that the grant of leave to remain for more than one year had to follow the refusal of asylum; it was sufficient that the person had leave extending for more than a year beyond the day on which asylum was refused.²

²   *MS (Uganda) v Secretary of State for the Home Department* [2016] UKSC 33, [2016] 1 WLR 2615, [2016] All ER (D) 128 (Jun).

## DECISION TO REFUSE A HUMAN RIGHTS CLAIM

**19.20A** *[Insert new heading and new paragraph:]*

Determining whether a human rights claim has been made is critically important for the purpose of establishing whether there is a right of appeal against a decision in response, but is not entirely straightforward. NIAA 2002, s 113 defines a 'human rights claim' as 'a claim made by a person to the Secretary of State at a place designated by the Secretary of State that to remove the person from or require him to leave the United Kingdom or to refuse him entry to the United Kingdom would be unlawful under section 6 of the Human Rights Act 1998'. The provision contains no procedural or formal requirements, save that the claim has to be made to the Secretary of State and at a place designated by the Secretary of State. No such place has been designated. Immigration Act 1971, s 3C contemplates that a human rights claim may take the form of an application to vary leave to enter or remain because s 3C(2)(b) refers to an appeal against 'the decision on the application for variation'. However, it is only possible for there to be an appeal against a 'decision on the application for variation' if a human rights claim and a protection claim are treated as being such applications because there is no longer any right of appeal against any other kind of application to vary leave. The Home Office Guidance[1] equates human rights claims with applications for leave to enter or remain. It identifies various categories of applications under the immigration rules as being 'human rights applications', refusal of which attracts a right of appeal under NIAA 2002. s 82. They are applications for leave to remain under the long residence and private life rules; applications for leave to remain under the rules for partners and children of members of the armed forces; applications as family members under Part 8 of the Rules, Appendix FM (other than as bereaved partners or victims of domestic violence), as dependents of PBS migrants and applications under the asylum rules.[2] Applications for entry clearance or leave to enter under the rules relating to family of members of the armed forces, as dependents of PBS migrants and as family members under Part 8 and Appendix FM are also treated as 'human rights applications'.[3] 'Applications for leave to remain outside the rules on human rights grounds' have to be made on forms FLR(O) or SET(O) and have to satisfy the requirements of paragraph 34 of the rules as to validity.[4] Applications for entry clearance 'based on a human rights claim outside the Immigration Rules must form part of a valid application for entry clearance' and a person making such an application should be told to do so by completing a visitor visa application form.[5] Decision makers are required by the Home Office Guidance to address three questions: does the application for leave to remain or for entry clearance say that it is a human rights claim? If not, does it raise matters that may amount to a human rights claim? And 'Are the matters raised capable of engaging human rights?'[6] Whilst the Secretary of State may be entitled to impose procedural requirements for making applications for leave to remain or entry clearance, such as requirements to complete particular forms, treating those same requirements as having to be satisfied in order to make a human rights claim is unwarranted by NIAA 2002, s 113. Nor does s 113 permit the Secretary of State to introduce into the definition of human rights claim a requirement that the claim must be 'capable of engaging human rights', thereby restricting access to the right of appeal against refusal of a claim by reference to the Secretary of State's view of the claim's merit. The legitimate place for the Secretary of State's views to play a part in Part 5 of the NIAA 2002 is in her exercise of the various powers to certify human rights claims.

1   Home Office 'Rights of Appeal', version 4.0, 15 January 2016 ('Home Office Guidance').
2   Home Office Guidance, p 8.
3   Home Office Guidance, p 12.
4   Home Office Guidance, p 9.
    Home Office Guidance, p 9.
5   Home Office Guidance, p 12f.
6   Home Office Guidance, pp 9f and 13.


## EEA decisions

**19.21** *[At the end of the paragraph add:]*

From 1 February 2017, the Immigration (European Economic Area) Regulations 2016[9] will take effect in place of the 2006 Regulations.[10] Regulation 36 makes similar provision for a right of appeal against 'an EEA decision' to that made by regulation 26 of the 2006 Regulations. The 2016 Regulations contain a similar definition of 'EEA decision' to the 2006 Regulations but the definition expressly excludes: refusal to issue an EEA family permit, registration certificate or registration card to an extended family member; refusal to set aside the 12-month prohibition on re-entry following removal as a person without a right of residence; a decision to certify that removal of a person with a pending appeal would not be in breach of the person's human rights; refusal of an interim order to suspend removal and refusal to grant temporary admission to enable a person who had been removed from the UK to make submissions at his or her appeal.[11] Exclusion of those decisions from the definition of 'EEA decision' means that they cannot be appealed to the tribunal.

[9]   SI 2016/1052.
[10]   SI 2006/1003.
[11]   SI 2016/1052, reg 2.

## VENUE

**19.24** *[At the end of the paragraph add:]*

The Immigration (European Economic Area) Regulations 2016, in force from 1 February 2017 make the same provision as did the 2006 Regulations for appeals against EEA decisions to be brought to the First-tier Tribunal unless excluded on political or national security grounds in which case the right of appeal is to the SIAC.[7]

[7]   Immigration (European Economic Area) Regulations 2016, SI 2016/1052, regs 36(9), 38 and 39.

## EEA DECISIONS: IN-COUNTRY OR OUT OF COUNTRY APPEALS

**19.29** *[Replace existing heading with amended heading above and at the end of the paragraph add:]*

The Immigration (European Economic Area) Regulations 2006 were amended so that the making of an asylum or human rights claim no longer brings an entitlement to appeal in-country when otherwise the right of appeal would be from abroad.[5] From 1 February 2017, the Immigration (European Economic Area) Regulations 2016[6] will take effect in place of the 2006 Regulations,[7] making the same provision about whether an appeal may be brought from within the UK or may only be brought from outside the UK.[8]

[5]   Immigration (European Economic Area) (Amendment) Regulations 2015 (SI 2015/694), Sch 1, para 13, revoking SI 2006/1003, reg 27(2)(c).
[6]   SI 2016/1052.
[7]   Immigration (European Economic Area) Regulations 2006, SI 2006/1003.
[8]   SI 2016/1052, reg 37(1).

## CERTIFICATION OF ASYLUM AND HUMAN RIGHTS CLAIMS AS CLEARLY UNFOUNDED

**19.30** *[Replace existing heading with amended heading above and note:]*

The paragraph in the main text refers to certification of asylum and human rights claims as clearly unfounded under the provisions in existence prior to amendment by the IA 2014.

## IN COUNTRY APPEALS: POST-IMMIGRATION ACT 2014

**19.31** *[N.B.]*

The paragraph in the main text discusses NIAA 2002, s 92 as substituted by IA 2014. That provision applies in accordance with the commencement orders referred to in **19.12** above. A certificate may be issued under NIAA 2002, s 94 or 94B whilst an appeal is pending and has the effect of requiring the appeal to be continued from outside the UK (NIAA 2002, s 92(6)).

## CERTIFICATION UNDER NIAA 2002, S 94B

**19.32** *[Insert new heading and at the end of the paragraph add:]*

The Court of Appeal considered the operation of NIAA 2002, s 94B in *Kiarie* and *Byndloss*;[4] the Supreme Court will be hearing an appeal, currently listed for February 2017, against its decision. The Court of Appeal held that the Secretary of State was obliged to give notice to a person if consideration was being given to certification of his or her human rights claim. It also held that the Secretary of State's guidance which suggested that a human rights claim could be certified if the Secretary of State was satisfied that removal pending determination of the appeal would not cause serious and irreversible harm. That was not a sufficient basis for certifying a claim; the Secretary of State also had to be satisfied that removal would not be unlawful under section 6 of the Human Rights Act 1998 as being incompatible with a person's ECHR rights. If a certificate was challenged on ECHR Article 8 grounds, an important consideration in favour of removal being found proportionate, albeit not a trump card, was the legislative policy, expressed in the automatic deportation provisions of the UK Borders Act 2007, s 32 in favour of deporting foreign criminals. That policy, so the court held, was carried through into s 94B. The Court acknowledged that a s 94B certificate might also breach the procedural rights inherent in Article 8. However, whilst the Court accepted that an out of country appeal would be 'less advantageous' than an in-country appeal, it went on to say that Article 8 did not entitle a person to the best possible appellate procedure or even the most advantageous procedure available. It required only a procedure that met the essential requirements of effectiveness and fairness and it concluded that an out of country appeal would meet those requirements in the absence of reasons specific to a particular case for concluding otherwise. The Court relied on the expertise of specialist immigration judges and their sensitivity to the gravity of deportation to ensure a process that was fair to the appellant and it relied on the flexibility of the system that could facilitate video conferencing, two-way electronic communication and even the issue of a witness summons to require the appellant's attendance.[5] Electronic means of communication, so the Court held, meant that an appellant's absence from the country would not be a serious obstacle to the preparation of witness statements, obtaining of relevant documents and instructing lawyers and experts. Those used to preparing and presenting appeals against deportation may be surprised by the Court's optimism and insouciance and may wonder whether it is a reflection of the pariah status accorded to deportees by the Court.

4   *R (Kiarie) v Secretary of State for the Home Department*; *R (Byndloss) v Secretary of State for the Home Department* [2015] EWCA Civ 1020.
5   The Secretary of State accepts that if such a summons is issued but she does not permit the appellant to return in order to give evidence, 'the tribunal may draw inferences in the appellant's favour', Home Office Guidance, 'Certification under section 94B of the Nationality, Immigration and Asylum Act 2002', version 7, 1 December 2016, p 23.

### 19.32A  *[Insert new paragraph:]*

Immigration Act 2016, s 63 amends NIAA 2002, s 94B so that it applies to a human rights claim made by any person, not just to a person who is liable to deportation. The amendments came into effect on 1 December 2016, without any transitional provision.[1] Whilst any human rights claim may be certified under s 94B, the Secretary of State's guidance[2] provides that certification should be considered in non-deportation cases unless the case falls outside the 'phased implementation' cohort comprised of claimants who both did not have extant leave when they made their human rights claims and do not rely on a relationship with a British national family member, ie a partner, parent or child where there is evidence of the relationship.[3] In addition, claims based on ECHR Articles 2 or 3 should not be certified under s 94B.[4] Other claims that are not normally considered suitable for certification under s 94B are those made by: a person serving an indeterminate length sentence; unaccompanied children and potential victims of trafficking where the question of whether the person is a victim of trafficking is yet to be resolved.[5] Before deciding to certify a claim under s 94B, the person must be informed that certification may be considered and invited to give reasons why certification would not be appropriate.[6] The Home Office guidance sets out in some detail the kind of considerations that may lead to a conclusion that a claim should or should not be certified.

1   The Immigration Act 2016 (Commencement No 2 and Transitional Provisions) Regulations 2016, SI 2016/1037, reg 5(h). The Home Office Guidance 'Certification under section 94B of the Nationality, Immigration and Asylum Act 2002', version 7, 1 December 2016, p 31, contemplates human rights claims refused before 1 December 2016 being considered for certification.
2   Home Office Guidance, 'Certification under section 94B of the Nationality, Immigration and Asylum Act 2002', version 7, 1 December 2016 (hereafter, 'Guidance').
3   Guidance, p 7.
4   Guidance, p 8.
5   Guidance, p 9.
6   Guidance, p 31.

## SUSPENSORY EFFECT OF AN APPEAL

**19.35** *[Delete the sentence beginning 'Appeals against EEA decisions . . . ' containing footnote references 6 and 7 and replace with:]*

If a person in the UK appeals against an EEA decision refusing admission to the UK or to remove the person from the UK any removal directions given cease to have effect unless the decision was made on grounds of public policy, public security or public health.[6] An appeal against refusal of a residence document does not have suspensive effect.[7] If the Secretary of State intends to make an EEA decision to remove a person on public policy, public security or public health grounds, she may not remove the person whilst the person is in time to bring an appeal or an appeal is pending unless the Secretary of State certifies that to remove the person would not be incompatible with ECHR protected rights.[7a] Notwithstanding that removal pending disposal of an appeal may be prohibited, the powers to detain may still be exercised.[7b] The 2006 Regulations prevent the making of a deportation order whilst an appeal against the EEA decision to remove is pending;[7c] the 2016 Regulations contain no such prohibition.

[6] Immigration (European Economic Area) Regulations 2006, SI 2006/1003, reg 29, as amended by SI 2014/1976 and Immigration (European Economic Area) Regulations 2016, SI 2016/1052, reg 40 with effect from 1 February 2017.
[7] *R (Ahmed) v Secretary of State for the Home Department* [2016] EWCA Civ 303.
[7a] SI 2006/1003, reg 24AA and SI 2016/1052, reg 33.
[7b] SI 2006/1003, reg 29(4) and SI 2016/1052, reg 40(4).
[7c] SI 2006/1003, reg 29(6).

## CERTIFICATION OF HUMAN RIGHTS CONSIDERATIONS IN EEA APPEALS

**19.35A** *[Insert new heading and new paragraph:]*

The Secretary of State may not remove a person with a right of appeal against a decision to remove on public policy, public security or public health grounds unless she certifies that removal pending the outcome of the appeal would not breach human rights.[1] Whilst such a certificate may be issued if the person would not face a real risk of serious and irreversible harm if removed pending the appeal,[2] by itself that is not a sufficient ground; the Secretary of State also has to be satisfied that there would be no breach of human rights.[3] In *Gheorghiu*,[4] the tribunal gave guidance about the factors relevant to assessment of the proportionality of removal prior to the hearing of an EEA appeal: first, removal of a person exercising a treaty right is significantly different to removal of a person with leave to enter or remain. Where a person has such a right the person's presence needs to be a sufficiently serious threat to the requirements of public policy if removal is to be justified. Considerations of general deterrence or the maintenance of effective immigration control will not suffice. Second, removal from the household of a worker providing support to a family will be a serious interference with rights protected by Article 8 of the ECHR, the Charter of Fundamental Rights and the EU right of residence. Third, even in cases of serious criminality, the case for expulsion may not be strong in the absence of continuing risk to the public. Fourth, where an important issue is whether the appellant has been sufficiently rehabilitated 'the experience of immigration judges has been that hearing and seeing the offender give live evidence and the enhanced ability to assess the sincerity of that evidence is an important part of the fact-finding process'.[5] If an application is made to the court or tribunal for an interim order to suspend enforcement of a removal decision, the person may not be removed until the application for the interim order has been decided unless the expulsion decision is based on a previous judicial decision; the person has had previous access to judicial review or the decision is based on imperative grounds of public security.[6] If a person is removed on public policy, security or health grounds whilst his or her appeal is pending, the person may apply for temporary admission in order to return to the UK to make submissions at the hearing of the appeal[7] and temporary admission must be granted unless the person's 'appearance may cause serious troubles to public policy or public security'.[8] The tribunal has adopted a narrow interpretation of 'appearance' as referring not to the person's appearance in the UK but his or her appearance at the hearing of the appeal.[9] That qualified right to be admitted to the UK to make submissions at an appeal hearing meant that removal pending the appeal could be compatible with the procedural protections provided by article 47 of the Charter of Fundamental Rights.[10] The right does not extend to returning to the UK in order to prepare the appeal.[11]

[1]   Immigration (European Economic Area) Regulations 2006, SI 2006/1003, reg 24AA(1) and (2) and, from 1 February 2017, Immigration (European Economic Area) Regulations 2016, SI 2016/1052, reg 33(1) and (2).
[2]   SI 2006/1003, reg 24AA(3); SI 2016/1052, reg 33(3).
[3]   *R (Masalskas) v Secretary of State for the Home Department (Regulations 24AA and 29AA EEA Regulations) IJR* [2015] UKUT 677 (IAC), applying *Kiarie v Secretary of State for the Home Department* [2015] EWCA Civ 1020; *R (X) v Secretary of State for the Home Department* [2016] EWHC 1997 (Admin).
[4]   *Gheorghiu (Regulation 24AA EEA Regulations – Relevant Factors)* [2016] UKUT 24 (IAC).
[5]   Blake J in *Gheorghiu.*
[6]   SI 2006/1003, reg 24AA(4); SI 2016/1053, reg 33(4).
[7]   SI 2006/1003, reg 29AA; SI 2016/1052, reg 41.
[8]   SI 2006/1003, reg 29AA(3); SI 2016/1052, reg 41(3).
[9]   *R (Kasicky) v Secretary of State for the Home Department (Regulation 29AA interpretation) IJR* [2016] UKUT 107 (IAC).
[10]   *R (Ahmed) v Secretary of State for the Home Department* [2015] UKUT 436, followed in *R (Masalskas)* and *R (X).*
[11]   *R (Masalskas).*

## CERTIFICATION UNDER SECTION 96

**19.56** *[in the text, after footnote reference 4, insert:]*

In *J*[4a] Stadlen J described a four-stage test that had to be applied if a certificate was to be issued. First, had the person been notified of an earlier right of appeal (or had the person received a one stop notice).[4b] Second, was the matter one that could have been raised in an earlier appeal (or statement in response to a one stop notice). Third, was there no satisfactory reason for the matter not having been raised in an earlier appeal (or statement in response to a one stop notice). Fourth, having regard to all the circumstances, was it appropriate to exercise the discretion to certify. Where the matter could not have been raised in a previous appeal or statement, the Secretary of State was not entitled to issue a certificate just because she regarded the new matter as unmeritorious.[4c]

[4a]   *J v Secretary of State for the Home Department* [2009] EWHC 705 (Admin).
[4b]   Where a one stop notice was brought to a person in prison but the person refused to accept the notice, the person was to be treated as having 'received' the notice for the purpose of s 96(2): *R (Yesafu) v Secretary of State for the Home Department* [2016] EWHC 2883 (Admin).

## ADMINISTRATIVE REVIEW

**19.58** *[in the text, after footnote reference 3, insert:]*

The list of decisions eligible for administrative review has been extended. It includes decisions on applications for leave to remain, either refusing the application or as to the period of leave or the conditions attached where the decision was made on an application made on or after 20 October 2014 for leave to remain as a Tier 4 migrant or the partner or child of such a person; a decision made on an application made on or after 2 March 2015 for leave to remain as a Tier 1, 2 or 5 migrant or as a partner or child of such a migrant; an application for leave to remain under the Turkey–EC association agreement; a decision made on or after 6 April 2015 on an application for leave to remain made under the Immigration Rules unless it is an application as a visitor or 'where an application or human rights claim is made under' the long residence or private life rules; rules relating to partners and children of members of the HM forces; under Part 8 of the Rules, the asylum rules or Appendix FM (though not as a bereaved partner or victim of domestic violence).[3a] The list of eligible decisions also includes a decision made on arrival in the UK on or after 6 April 2015 to cancel leave to enter or remain on the ground of a change of circumstances or that the leave was obtained as a result of false information or material non-disclosure.[3b] The list of eligible decisions also includes refusal of entry clearance, including an application under the Turkey-EC Association Agreement, where the application was made on or after 6 April 2015 unless it is an application as a short-term student or a visitor or where an application or human rights claim is made under the rules that are treated as being human rights claims, ie partners and children of members of the HM Forces; Part 8 and Appendix FM of the Rules or where the sponsor of an application as refugee status or humanitarian protection.[3c] A case-working error is made where the decision maker applies the immigration rules incorrectly or fails to apply the Secretary of State's published policy and guidance.[3d]

*[In the text, replace the sentence beginning 'The rules exhaustively list . . . ' ending with footnote reference 4 with:]*

In carrying out an administrative review, the reviewer will only consider evidence that was not before the original decision maker if it is submitted to demonstrate: that it was incorrect to refuse or cancel leave on various specified grounds relating to deception or misconduct; that it was incorrect to have treated an application as beyond a time limit or the decision maker was incorrect not to request specified documents under paragraph 245AA of the rules[4] or to show that a refusal under paragraph 322(2) of the rules (use of false representations or material non-disclosure to obtain leave) was incorrect.[4a]

⁴  Appendix AR, paragraph AR2.4.
⁴ᵃ  Appendix AR, paragraph AR2.4.

**19.59** *[Delete the paragraph and substitute:]*

The Immigration Rules make detailed provision as to the procedure to be followed in connection with an application for administrative review,[1] non-compliance with which will result in the application being treated as invalid.[2] Written notice must be given of an 'eligible decision' (unless it is a decision to grant leave to remain) with reasons for the decision and information about how and when to apply for administrative review.[3] Only one application for administrative review of an eligible decision may be made unless the outcome of the first application is to uphold the decision but giving different or additional reasons.[4] An application for administrative review may not be made if the person signs an administrative review waiver form[5] or, within the time during which an application may be made for administrative review, the person makes a further application for entry clearance, leave to enter or remain.[6] An application for administrative review of a decision to refuse leave to remain or to cancel leave which is in force must be made whilst the applicant is in the UK (unless the decision to cancel leave was made whilst the person was in a Control Zone).[7] An application for administrative review of refusal of entry clearance must be made from abroad.[8] Where the applicant is in the UK, the application must be made within 14 calendar days of receiving the decision unless the applicant is in detention in which case the time for making the application is 7 calendar days.[9] Where the applicant is outside the UK, the time limit is 28 calendar days after receiving notice of the decision[10] and where the decision is a grant of leave to remain the time limit is 14 days.[11] An application may be accepted out of time if the Secretary of State is satisfied that it would be unjust not to waive the time limit and the application was made as soon as reasonably practicable.[12] Applications may be made on-line or by post or courier, in each case, paying any specified fee, completing any part of the application designated as mandatory and providing documents specified as mandatory.[13] Applications for administrative review of entry clearance decisions may be made by post, courier, hand, fax or e mail.[14] A postal application for administrative review is made on the marked date of posting; an application by courier is made on the date of delivery; an application made on line is made on the date of submission.[15] Appendix SN to the rules makes provision about the service of notices concerned with administrative review.

1  Paragraph 34L–34Y.
2  Paragraph 34M.
3  Paragraph 34L.
4  Paragraph 34N.
5  Paragraph 34N(3).
6  Paragraph 34N(4).
7  Paragraph 34Q(1), (2).
8  Paragraph 34Q(3).
9  Paragraph 34R(1)(a), (b).
10  Paragraph 34R(1)(c).
11  Paragraph 34R(1)(d).
12  Paragraph 34R(3).
13  Paragraphs 34U and 34V.
14  Paragraph 34VA.
15  Paragraph 34W.

**19.60** *[Insert new paragraph:]*

Where an application for administrative review is pending, the Secretary of State will not seek to remove the applicant from the UK.[1] An application for administrative review is pending for the purpose of the Immigration Rules and for the purpose of the Immigration Act 1971, s 3C during the period whilst: an in-time application for administrative review may be made in accordance with the rules and whilst an in-time application has been made, until it is treated as invalid or is withdrawn or the notice of outcome is served.[2] Administrative review is not pending where the applicant has signed a waiver form or has made a further application for leave to enter or remain or for entry clearance.[3]

1   Immigration Rules, para AR2.8.
    Immigration Rules, para AR2.8.
2   Paragraph AR2.9.
3   Paragraph AR2.10.

Chapter 20

# APPEALS TO THE FIRST-TIER TRIBUNAL

## THE FIRST-TIER TRIBUNAL

**20.1** *[At the end of the paragraph, add:]*

The Senior President of Tribunals issued a Practice Statement delegating a number of the First-tier Tribunal's functions to caseworkers. The delegated functions include: case management powers (to extend or shorten time for complying with a rule, practice direction or direction; to permit or require a party to amend a document or to provide documentary evidence, information or submissions to the tribunal or to a party; to hold a hearing to consider any matter; to adjourn or postpone a hearing; to require a party to produce a bundle for a hearing; to transfer proceedings to another court or tribunal); powers to strike out an appeal for non-payment of a fee or to reinstate an appeal; to treat an appeal as abandoned or finally determined; to deal with withdrawal of an appeal (other than declining to treat an appeal a withdrawn); to deal with notices of appeal including late notices of appeal; to decide whether the tribunal will accept a notice of appeal; to issue directions in relation to respondents' response to notices of appeal; to deal with clerical mistakes and accidental slips and omissions and receiving and dealing with bail applications (prior to hearing of the bail application).[18] A party receiving notice of a decision made by a caseworker can, within 14 days, apply for the decision to be considered afresh by a judge.[19]

[18] Practice Statement: Senior President of Tribunals, 20 April 2016, 'Delegation of functions to tribunal caseworkers'.
[19] Practice Statement, para 3.

## PRE-IMMIGRATION ACT 2014 POWERS OF THE FIRST-TIER TRIBUNAL

### Scope of appeal

**20.8** *[in the text, after footnote reference 5, add:]*

The tribunal is obliged to determine appeals against all of the decisions against which the appellant has a right of appeal, even if the appellant does not wish to pursue all of the appeals.[5a]

[5a] *Hanson Olatunde v Secretary of State for the Home Department* [2015] EWCA Civ 670, [2015] 1 WLR 4602, (2015) Times, 16 July.

## THE TRIBUNAL AS PRIMARY DECISION MAKER

### The appellate jurisdiction in asylum and human rights appeals

**20.25** *[At the end of the paragraph, add:]*

Whilst a decision by the National Referral Mechanism that an appellant is not a victim of trafficking is not appealable to the tribunal, the tribunal nevertheless has to decide for itself whether an individual is a victim of trafficking in so far as that is relevant to the issues in the appeal.[21]

[21] *AS (Afghanistan) v Secretary of State for the Home Department* [2013] EWCA Civ 1469, [2013] All ER (D) 266 (Nov) and *XB v Secretary of State for the Home Department* [2015] EWHC 2557 (Admin), [2015] All ER (D) 61 (Sep) ,where Collins J said that it would be wrong to read *AS (Afghanistan)* as requiring the tribunal to adopt the NRM decision unless satisfied that it was perverse. He said 'it seems to me that if a tribunal is satisfied that the decision of the NRM was wrong it not only is entitled to but should decide to the contrary'. See also *MS (Trafficking – Tribunal's powers – Article 4 ECHR) Pakistan* [2016] UKUT 226 (IAC).

## COSTS

**20.40** *[In the text, after footnote reference 4, add:]*

There is a rebuttable presumption that a fee award will be made in favour of a successful appellant.[4a]

*[In the text, after footnote reference 9, add:]*

A Home Office Presenting Officer is a 'legal or other representative'.[9a] The conduct that may result in an order for wasted costs includes that of 'any employee' of a party's representative,[9b] so that liability cannot be avoided by attributing responsibility to, eg a representative's secretary or administrative support staff.[9c]

*[Insert new footnotes in correct sequential order.]*

[4a] *Cancino (Costs – First-tier Tribunal – New Powers)* [2015] UKFTT 0059 (IAC).
[9a] *Cancino,* para 11.
[9b] Tribunals, Courts and Enforcement Act 2007, s 29(5)(a).
[9c] *Cancino,* above.

**20.41** *[At the end of the paragraph, add:]*

The Presidents of the First-tier Tribunal and Upper Tribunal sat together to provide guidance as to the scope and exercise of the tribunal's costs jurisdiction in the case of *Cancino.*[9] They acknowledged that *Ridehalgh v Horesefield*[10] provides 'authoritative construction of the statutory terminology' and that the tribunal should adopt the approach to wasted costs described in that case.[11] The tribunal highlighted that it would be a rare case in which a legal representative could be held to have knowingly promoted or encouraged the pursuit of a hopeless case so as to warrant the making of a wasted costs order against him or her.[12] Conduct which constitutes abuse or misuse of process by the representative might attract liability for a wasted costs order but the tribunal must always be careful to distinguish between the conduct of the party and the representative and bear in mind that the burden of proving liability for wasted costs is on the applicant.[13] The power to make a wasted costs order is applicable to all aspects of the conduct of an appeal including interlocutory applications and case management review hearing. Concessions and withdrawals should not routinely attract wasted costs orders, but a late concession or withdrawal may do and will not satisfactorily be explained by the late receipt of advice or late involvement by a presenting officer.[14]

[9]    *Cancino (Costs – First-tier Tribunal – New Powers)* [2015] UKFTT 0059 (IAC).
[10]   [1994] EWCA Civ 40, [1994] Ch 205, [1994] 3 All ER 848, [1994] 3 WLR 462.
[11]   *Cancino*, para 19.
[12]   *Caninco*, para 20.
[13]   *Cancino*, para 21.
[14]   *Caninco*, para 25.

### 20.42 *[At the beginning of the paragraph insert:]*

The tribunal expects that its power to order wasted costs will be 'rarely exercised'.[0] Consideration to making a wasted costs order in relation to the breach of directions should not happen until the party in breach has been issued with a reminder.[0a] 'Even where a hearing has had to be adjourned because of an avoidable omission by one party, such as inadequate preparation, it would not normally be appropriate to make an order for costs. Not only has the paying party the right to offer an explanation but it should be remembered that representatives have many demands on their time and are subject to a multitude of pressures, which may lead, even in well-managed organisations, to occasional lapses. The making of an order for wasted or unreasonable costs should be a very rare event'.[0b]

*[In the text after footnote reference 2 add:]*

If an application for costs is made orally at a hearing, the judge should make a decision refusing the application straightaway if it appears to be without merit. Otherwise it should be referred to the Resident Judge. Directions will be issued requiring the filing of a written application, skeleton argument and schedule of the costs claimed and indicating that the matter will be decided on the papers unless either party requests an oral hearing.[2a] A post hearing written application will also be referred to the Resident Judge who will dispose of it summarily if apparently without merit but will otherwise make similar directions.[2b]

*[In the text after footnote reference 6 add:]*

'It is only when all allowance is made the conduct of the proceedings is quite plainly unjustifiable that it is appropriate to make a wasted costs order'.[7]

*[Insert new footnotes in correct sequential order.]*

[0]    Presidential Guidance Note No 1 of 2014, Mr Michael Clements, President of the First-tier Tribunal (IAC), 17 October 2014, para 27.
[0a]   Presidential Guidance Note No 1 of 2014, para 31.
[0b]   Presidential Guidance Note No 1 of 2014, para 31 and Presidential Guidance Note No 1 of 2015 'Wasted Costs and Unreasonable Costs', para 19.
[2a]   Presidential Guidance Note No 1 of 2015, para 27.

2b   Presidential Guidance Note No 1 of 2015, para 28.
7    Presidential Guidance Note No 1 of 2015, para 20.

## PROCEDURE ON APPEALS

### Normal and fast track appeals

**20.46** *[At the end of the paragraph insert:]*

The Fast Track Rules[6] were held to be *ultra vires* section 22(4) of the Tribunals, Courts and Enforcement Act 2007, the provision under which the rules were made, because they gave rise to systemic or structural unfairness; notwithstanding the various procedural safeguards provided by the Rules, there was an unacceptable risk of unfairness to asylum seekers.[7] The principal safeguard referred to was that appeals are heard by independent, impartial, expert judges. The court said: 'I have no doubt whatsoever about the independence and impartiality of tribunal judges who deal with the appeals. I accept that they are specialist judges who can readily be trusted to get the right answer on the basis of the material that is provided to them. I am also sure they do their best to comply with the overriding objective'. However, because of the complex and difficult nature of the issues; the difficulty of obtaining instructions from detained clients and the highly-abbreviated timetable, it was 'inevitable that significant numbers of appellants will be denied a fair opportunity to present their cases' under the Fast Track Rules.[8]

6    Schedule 1 to the Tribunal Procedure (First-tier Tribunal) (IAC) Rules 2014, SI 2014/2604.
7    *The Lord Chancellor v Detention Action, Secretary of State for the Home Department Intervening* [2015] EWCA Civ 840.
8    *Lord Chancellor v Detention Action*, para 38.

### Notices of decision or action

**20.54** *[At the end of the paragraph, add:]*

It was wrong for the tribunal to have concluded that because the notice of decision did not comply with the Notices Regulations[9] the recipient had no right of appeal.[10] Whilst such non-compliance would mean that the notice was not lawfully served (so that the time for appealing would not start to run) the recipient was entitled to waive his or her right to a decision in accordance with the Notices Regulations and give notice of appeal.[11]

9    Immigration Appeals (Notices) Regulations 2003, SI 2003/658.
10   *BJ (Singh explained) Sri Lanka* [2016] UKUT 184 (IAC).
11   *BJ (Singh explained) Sri Lanka*, referring to *R (Khan) v Secretary of State (right of appeal – alternative remedy) IJR* [2015] UKUT 353 (IAC); *Abiyat (Iran)* [2011] UKUT 314; *OI (Nigeria)* [2006] UKAIT 42.

### Fees for bringing an appeal

**20.60** *[N.B.]*

The fees for bringing an appeal against decisions made on or after 10 October 2016 were increased from £80 to £490 for an appeal to be determined without a hearing and from £140 to £800 for an appeal to be determined with a hearing.[1] However, the government quickly decided, in response to the representations made opposing the fee increases, to reinstate the original fees and to 'take stock and review the immigration and asylum fees'.[2] The exemptions from the requirement to pay a fee listed in the main text as (1) and (2) continue in relation to appeals where the pre-IA 2014 appeals provisions continue to apply[3] but otherwise have been replaced by the following:[4]

(1)     an appeal against deprivation of citizenship under the British Nationality Act 1981, s 40;
(2)     an appeal against a decision to exclude or remove from the UK under article 19(3) of the Immigration (European Economic Area) Regulations 2006, SI 2006/1003;
(3)     an appeal under NIAA 2002, s 82(1)(c) against revocation of protection status.

In addition to (1)–(3) above and (3)–(6) in the main text, fee exemptions also apply to the following:

(4)     an appeal against a decision made in response to an application for limited leave to enter where an exception to paying the application fee under the Fees Regulations applied as being a person in the UK and liable to detention, where requiring payment of the fee would be incompatible with the person's ECHR rights;[5]
(5)     an appeal against a decision in response to a 'specified human rights application' in respect of which an exception to the requirement to pay a fee applied on the ground that requiring payment of the fee would be incompatible with the ECHR;[6]
(6)     an appeal brought by a child supported under s 17 of the Children Act 1989 or equivalent provisions in Scotland, Northern Ireland and Wales;
(7)     an appeal brought by a person having parental responsibility for a child supported as in (6);
(8)     an appeal brought by a child accommodated by the local authority under Children Act 1989, s 20 or equivalent provision in Scotland, Northern Ireland and Wales.

[1]   The First-tier Tribunal (IAC) Fees (Amendment) Order 2016, SI 2016/928.
[2]   Hansard, HLWS287, 28 November 2016 and The First-tier Tribunal (IAC) Fees (Amendment) (No 2) Order 2016, SI 2016/1149.
[3]   SI 2016/928, reg 5(2).
[4]   SI 2016/928, reg 5.
[5]   SI 2016/928, reg 5, ie where an exception applied under table 4.5 in Schedule 1 to the Immigration and Nationality (Fees) Regulations 2016, SI 2016/226.
[6]   SI 2016/928, reg 5, ie where an exception applied under table 9.4 in SI 2016/226.

### Withdrawal of appeals

**20.76** *[At the end of the paragraph, add:]*

The tribunal has held that withdrawal of an appeal takes effect when the tribunal is notified, either orally or in writing, of the withdrawal.[13] However, that may not be correct because the procedure rules provide for the tribunal to decide whether it will treat the appeal as withdrawn once notice of withdrawal has been given[14] indicating that action by the tribunal is required before an appeal is withdrawn.

[13] R *(Patel) v Secretary of State for the Home Department (Section 3C(4); simultaneous application; withdrawal) IJR* [2015] UKUT 273 (IAC).
[14] Tribunal Procedure (First-tier Tribunal) (IAC) Rules 2014, SI 2014/2604, r 17(2).

## TRIBUNAL HEARINGS

### Procedure at the hearing

**20.100** *[In the text after footnote reference 10, add:]*

Bearing in mind the 'seminal importance that the fairness, impartiality and detached objectivity of the judicial officer holder are manifest from beginning to the end of proceedings', and 'the importance of appearance, impression and perception', improper conduct by an advocate that is not stopped by the judge may render a hearing unfair, for example, comment in the form of improper questioning by a presenting officer.[10a]

*[In the text after footnote reference 11, add:]*

However, statements by the judge during the course of a hearing as to his or her views on the merits of the case or the evidence, so long as they do not indicate a closed mind, are legitimate and even conducive to a fair hearing and may even be necessary to displace a party's or advocates misplaced presumption or misapprehension.[11a]

*[in the text after footnote reference 14, add:]*

Independent research by a judge is inappropriate, but looking at documents referred to in a refusal letter with a link to their internet address does not constitute independent research.[14a]

*[Insert new footnotes in correct sequential order.]*

[10a] *Wagner (Advocate's conduct – fair hearing)* [2015] UKUT 655 (IAC).
[11a] *Sarabjeet Singh v Secretary of State for the Home Department* [2016] EWCA Civ 492, [2016] All ER (D) 16 (Jun).
[14a] *AM (Fair Hearing) Sudan* [2015] UKUT 656 (IAC).

## EVIDENCE AND FINDINGS

**20.105A** *[After paragraph 20.105, insert new paragraph:]*

The Immigration Law Practitioners' Association brought a challenge to the lawfulness of rule 13(2) and (3) of the Procedure Rules[1] which permit the tribunal to consider evidence withheld from one of the parties.[2] Blake J accepted that the rules do contemplate a closed material procedure operating in the tribunal.[3] However, non-disclosure to a party would be permitted only if the tribunal was satisfied that disclosure would cause 'serious harm' to a person which would have to be significant physical or mental suffering; harm to commercial or privacy interests or distress and anxiety would not be sufficient.[4] Moreover, the risk of serious harm would have to be established by credible information, not mere assertion, and to a standard higher than a mere risk or possibility of harm. Even if the risk of serious harm was established, the tribunal would also have to be satisfied that non-disclosure is consistent with the interests of justice and is proportionate.[5] Blake J acknowledged that the introduction of a closed material procedure had the potential to conflict with common law standards of fairness[6] but that was insufficient to establish the systemic or inherent unfairness falling below the minimum standards of fairness necessary to hold the rule *ultra vires*.[7] Before permitting a closed material procedure, the tribunal would need to be satisfied that it was proportionate and consistent with the interests of justice[8] and he could not envisage circumstances where such a procedure could be justified:[9] provision for anonymisation of witnesses or for non-publication of the determination might obviate the need for such a procedure; the possibility of threats having been made to a witness would not be sufficient basis to authorise a secret trial.[10] Blake J acknowledged that 'the very existence of the power is troubling' as was the absence of provision in the rules (as there had been in previous tribunal procedure rules) prohibiting the tribunal from considering evidence not made available to all the parties.[11] In the event that the power was to be used, there would need to be notification of the fact to the party and a full account somewhere in the determination of what was done and why so that it could be reviewed by the Upper Tribunal or the court.[12]

1    Tribunal Procedure (First-tier Tribunal) (IAC) Rules 2014, SI 2014/2604.
2    *R (ILPA) v Tribunal Procedure Committee and Lord Chancellor* [2016] EWHC 216 Admin.
3    *R (ILPA)*, para 13.
4    *R (ILPA)*, para 15.
5    *R (ILPA)*, para 15.
6    *R (ILPA)*, para 16.
7    *R (ILPA)*, para 67.
8    *R (ILPA)*, para 70.
9    *R (ILPA)*, para 84.
10   *R (ILPA)*, para 83.
11   *R (ILPA)*, para 85.
12   *R (ILPA)*, para 85.

## Credibility of witnesses

**20.107**  *[In footnote 6 add:]*

In *R (G and H) v Upper Tribunal* [2016] EWHC 239 (Admin), [2016] 1 WLR 3417, 166 NLJ 7688, Walker J held that it was an error of law for the tribunal to have gone behind the concession made by the presenting officer that the appellant's historical account was accepted.

## Documentary evidence

**20.111**  *[In footnote 5, before the full stop, add:]*

; *MA (Bangladesh) v Secretary of State for the Home Department* [2016] EWCA Civ 175

*Evidence of like facts in other appeals and judgments*

**20.118** *[In the text after footnote reference 3, add:]*

Decisions following a substantive hearing of an application for judicial review will also be reported.[3a]

[3a] Upper Tribunal Immigration and Asylum Chamber, Guidance Note 2011 No 2: 'Reporting decisions of the Upper Tribunal Immigration and Asylum Chamber', as amended.

## Burden and standard of proof

**20.122** *[After sub-paragraph (14) insert:]*

(15) Where leave to remain is refused on the suitability ground that 'the applicant has failed without reasonable excuse to comply with a requirement to provide information' the burden is on the applicant to show there was a reasonable excuse; it is not for the Secretary of State to show there was no reasonable excuse.[23]

*[In footnote 7 add:]*

In *Collins Agho v Secretary of State for the Home Department* [2015] EWCA Civ 1198 and in *Rosa v Secretary of State for the Home Department* [2016] EWCA Civ 14, [2016] 2 CMLR 464, 166 NLJ 7684, the court of appeal approved *Papajorgi (Greece)* [2012] UKUT 38 (IAC). A person establishes a prima facie case to being a family member of an EEA national by producing a marriage certificate and the passport of the EEA spouse. The person does not additionally have to prove that the marriage is not a marriage of convenience; in relation to that issue, the legal burden is on the Secretary of State and the tribunal would have to be satisfied on the totality of the evidence that the marriage is more likely than not a marriage of convenience.

[23] *Muhandiramge (section S-LTR 1.7)* [2015] UKUT 675 (IAC).

*Standard of proof*

**20.124** *[In footnote 6 add:]*

In *R (Bijendra Giri) v Secretary of State for the Home Department* [2015] EWCA Civ 784, [2016] 1 WLR 4418, [2015] All ER (D) 323 (Jul), the Court of Appeal endorsed *NA (Cambridge College of Learning) Pakistan* [2009] UKAIT 31 where the tribunal had held that for the Secretary of State to discharge the burden on her of proving that a person had relied on deception in a previous application, she would need to furnish evidence of sufficient strength and quality commensurate with the context. Thus, in *R (Saimon) v Upper Tribunal* [2015] EWHC 2814 Admin, a document verification report produced by the Secretary of State which merely asserted that a document was false, but without explanation, was not sufficiently cogent to prove its falsity, having regard to the consequences of such a finding.

## MAKING A DETERMINATION

**20.132** *[In the text after footnote reference 7, add:]*

Judges are expected to provide written determinations within 14 days of the appeal being heard.[7a]

[7a] Presidential Guidance Note No 1 of 2014, Mr Michael Clements, President of the First-tier Tribunal (IAC), 17 October 2014.

## POST-DETERMINATION POWERS OF THE TRIBUNAL

**20.137** *[At the end of the paragraph, add:]*

The 'slip rule'[8] apparently confers a very broad power on the tribunal to 'correct any clerical mistake or other accidental slip or omission in a decision'. However, it may only be used to enable a misprint to be corrected or to make the judge's meaning clear; it cannot be used to change the substance of a judgment or order, eg by changing 'I allow the appeal' into 'I dismiss the appeal'.[9] In such circumstances, the decision would have to be set aside by review under rule 32 or by appeal to the Upper Tribunal.

[8] Tribunal Procedure (First-tier Tribunal) (IAC) Rules 2014, SI 2014/2604, r 31.
[9] *Katsonga ('Slip rule'; FT's general powers)* [2016] UKUT 228 (IAC).

Chapter 21

# APPEALS TO THE UPPER TRIBUNAL, THE COURT OF APPEAL AND APPLICATIONS FOR JUDICIAL REVIEW

## THE UPPER TRIBUNAL

### The right of appeal and excluded decisions

**21.2** *[At the end of the paragraph add:]*

An administrative decision, made without a hearing, that there was no right of appeal to the First-tier Tribunal was an excluded decision which did not attract a right of appeal to the Upper Tribunal.[13] The tribunal only has such power as the statute gives it to alter or review a decision once made; the judge-made rule that allows decisions by the court to be amended or reversed up until an order is drawn up does not apply to the tribunal because it is not provided for in the statute.[14] The statutory power to review decisions does not apply to excluded decisions[15] so that permission to appeal to the Upper Tribunal, once granted, may not be withdrawn.[16]

[13] *Bangura v The Upper Tribunal* [2016] EWCA Civ 279.
[14] *Manorama Patel v Secretary of State for the Home Department* [2015] EWCA Civ 1175.
[15] Tribunals, Courts and Enforcement Act 2007, s 10(1).
[16] *Manorama Patel*, above.

## CONSTITUTION OF THE UPPER TRIBUNAL

**21.4** *[In the text after footnote reference 7, add:]*

Although the presiding member has the casting vote where a panel hearing an appeal is divided, it would be unlawful to exercise that vote rather than transfer the appeal to a different constitution of the tribunal where the disagreement is fundamental.[7a]

[7a] *PF (Nigeria) v Secretary of State for the Home Department* [2015] EWCA Civ 251, [2015] 1 WLR 5235, [2015] All ER (D) 290 (Mar).

## POWERS OF THE UPPER TRIBUNAL

### Failure to give adequate reasons

**21.8** *[N.B.]*

The tribunal has expressed concern that the Secretary of State brings challenges to the FT's reasoning without applying the established legal principles to the judge's actual reasoning: in particular, the need to show that the matter was raised as a substantial issue between the parties that had to be determined and that it was not dealt with at all or adequately by the judge.[1]

¹   VV *(Grounds of appeal) Lithuania* [2016] UKUT 53 (IAC).

## APPLICATION TO THE FIRST-TIER TRIBUNAL FOR PERMISSION TO APPEAL

### Extending time for applying for permission to appeal

**21.16** *[At the end of the paragraph, add:]*

The tribunal has given guidance about the principles applicable to applications to extend time for applying for permission to appeal[13] adopting the approach to be taken by the courts to applications for relief from sanctions under the civil procedure rules.[14] First, account has to be taken of the seriousness of the breach of the rules, the more serious the breach, the less likely it is that relief will be granted. Second, account has to be taken of the reasons for the breach; if there is a good reason, it is more likely that relief will be granted. Third, all the circumstances of the case have to be considered, having particular regard to factors highlighted by the overriding objective. Particular care has to be taken in asylum and human rights cases to ensure that appeals are not frustrated by representatives' failures to comply with time limits. Inability to pay for legal representation, including inability resulting from delay on the part of the Legal Aid Agency in dealing with an application for public funding cannot be regarded as a good reason for delay.[15] In most cases, the merits of the case will not be relevant unless it can be seen without much investigation that the grounds are either very strong or very weak.

¹³   R *(Onowu) v First-tier Tribunal (IAC) (extension of time for appealing: principles) IJR* [2016] UKUT 185 (IAC).

¹⁴   In *Mitchell v News Group Newspapers* [2013] EWCA Civ 1537, [2014] 2 All ER 430, [2014] 1 WLR 795; *Denton v White* [2014] EWCA Civ 906 and R *(Hysaj) v Secretary of State for the Home Department* [2015] EWCA Civ 1195.

¹⁵   A series of cases discounted an applicant's funding difficulties as a good reason for delay: R *(Hysaj)*; ZP *(South Africa) v Secretary of State for the Home Department* [2015] EWCA Civ 1273; JA *(Ghana) v Secretary of State for the Home Department* [2015] EWCA Civ 1031: instead of simply waiting for a decision on public funding, the applicant should have filed the grounds relied on in applying to the Upper Tribunal for permission to appeal to the Court of Appeal together with an application for a stay pending the funding application; R *(Frank Kigen and Janet Cheruiyot) v Secretary of State for the Home Department* [2015] EWCA Civ 1286, [2016] 1 WLR 723, 166 NLJ 7683 (at most, delay in obtaining legal aid 'may still be a factor that can be taken into account'. The court indicated that where there were funding difficulties, representatives should take steps either to lodge an application on behalf their clients or advise them of the need to do so on their own behalf.

## The FT's decision on an application for permission to appeal

**21.18** *[In the main text after footnote reference 9, insert:]*

It is a 'fundamental requirement' that reasons be given for granting or refusing permission to appeal,[9a] including reasons for extending or refusing to extend time for a late application.[9b]

[9a] *MR (Permission to appeal: tribunal's approach) Brazil* [2015] UKUT 29 (IAC).
[9b] *R (Onowu) v First-tier Tribunal (IAC) (extension of time for appealing: principles) IJR* [2016] UKUT 185 (IAC).

## APPLICATION TO THE UT FOR PERMISSION TO APPEAL

### Time limits

**21.19** *[In the main text, delete the sentences containing footnote references 5–8 and substitute:]*

An application to the Upper Tribunal for permission to appeal must be received by the tribunal no later than 14 days after the First-tier Tribunal's decision refusing permission (on some or all of the grounds[5]) was sent to the appellant where he or she is in the UK.[6] In a fast-track case, the person has four working days from the date on which the First-tier Tribunal's notice of decision was sent.[7] Where the appellant is outside the UK, the person has one month from being sent the notice of the First-tier Tribunal's decision.[8] The time for making an application to the Upper Tribunal is no longer abbreviated if the notice of the First-tier Tribunal's decision is sent electronically or delivered personally.[8a]

[5] Tribunal Procedure (Upper Tribunal) Rules 2008, SI 2008/2698, r 21(8).
[6] SI 2008/2698, r 21(3)(aa)(i), as amended from 20 October 2014 by SI 2014/2128, r 8(b). Previously, the application had to be made within seven days.
[7] SI 2008/2698, r 21(3)(aa)(ii).
[8] SI 2008/2698, r 21(3)(b), the default period of one month applying following the revocation by SI 2014/2128, r 8(c) of r 21(3)(ab) which gave appellants outside the UK 56 days in which to apply to the Upper Tribunal.
[8a] As it was by SI 2008/2698, r 21(3A), revoked by SI 2014/2128, r 8(d).

## The UT's decision on an application for permission to appeal

**21.22** *[In the text after footnote reference 3, add:]*

However, in an asylum case where the appellant is in the UK and is not the Secretary of State, the tribunal must provide written notice of the refusal to the Secretary of State who must then send the notice to the applicant within 30 days and inform the tribunal of the date on which, and the means by which, the notice was sent. If the tribunal has not received that information from the Secretary of State within 31 days of providing her with the refusal of permission to appeal, the tribunal must send the notice directly to the appellant.[3a]

[3a] Tribunal Procedure (Upper Tribunal) Rules 2008, SI 2008/2698, r 22A inserted by SI 2014/2128.

## THE UPPER TRIBUNAL'S DECISION

### Remitting or remaking the decision

**21.50** *[In the main text, after footnote reference 2, insert:]*

The Upper Tribunal is likely to remake the decision itself unless satisfied that the effect of the error in the First-tier Tribunal's decision was to deprive a party of a fair hearing or other opportunity to have his or her case put to and considered by the First-tier Tribunal or that the nature or extent of any judicial fact finding which is necessary makes it appropriate, having regard to the overriding objective, to remit to the First-tier Tribunal.[2a]

[2a] Practice Statements: Immigration and Asylum Chambers of the First-tier Tribunal and Upper Tribunal, 13.11.2014, para. 7.2.

**21.51** *[At the end of the paragraph, add:]*

The tribunal has held that when it remits a case to the First-tier Tribunal 'with directions for its reconsideration' as required by the statute[4] the directions referred to encompass matters such as guidance on the law and the scope of the remitted appeal.[5] The statute also enables the tribunal to 'give procedural directions' when it remits a case and those concern the conduct of the remitted appeal.[6]

[4] Tribunals, Courts and Enforcement Act 2007, s 12(2)(b)(i).
[5] *ONM (Remittal to FTT with directions) Jamaica* [2015] UKUT 517 (IAC).
[6] *ONM*, above.

### Correcting, setting aside and review of decisions

**21.55** *[At the end of the paragraph, insert:]*

A grant of permission to appeal to the Upper Tribunal is an excluded decision and therefore one that cannot be reviewed by the tribunal.[6]

[6] Tribunals, Courts and Enforcement Act 2007, s 10(1); *Manorama Patel v Secretary of State for the Home Department* [2015] EWCA Civ 1175.

### Appeal to the Court of Appeal or Court of Session

**21.59** *[At the end of the paragraph, add:]*

For the purpose of applying the second appeals test, it is relevant to consider whether a finding of fact underpinning a key element of the First-tier Tribunal's reasoning was scrutinised by the Upper Tribunal.[17]

[17] *JA (Ghana) v Secretary of State for the Home Department* [2015] EWCA Civ 1031.

### Application to the Court of Appeal for permission to appeal

**21.62** *[At the end of the paragraph, add:]*

Permission to appeal, once granted, may be set aside[19] but only in 'exceptional circumstances;' inaccuracy or infelicity of expression in the application for permission to appeal would be insufficient but inaccurate or incomplete statements without which permission would not have been granted would suffice.[20]

19   CPR 52.9.
20   *R (Shahid Sabir and Asif Mehmood) v Secretary of State for the Home Department* [2015] EWCA Civ 1173.

## Scope of court's jurisdiction

**21.64** *[At the end of the paragraph, add:]*

Whilst an appellant should not assume that a new ground can be taken for the first time in the court of appeal[12] and doubt was expressed[13] about the extent to which *Bulale*[14] enabled the court to find an error of law by the tribunal in failing to deal with a point that was not *Robinson* obvious,[15] the court permitted the Secretary of State to raise a new ground given that it would not necessitate a further hearing and further fact finding and would not have resulted in the case having been conducted differently had the point been raised below.[16] In a 'historical injustice' case, the court had regard to the moral dimension of the argument not raised below as a reason to permit it to be advanced in the court of appeal.[17]

12   *Oswald Washington Thomas v Secretary of State for the Home Department* [2016] EWCA Civ 1151.
13   *AA (Nigeria) v Secretary of State for the Home Department* [2015] EWCA Civ 1249.
14   *Bulale v Secretary of State for the Home Department* [2008] EWCA Civ 806, [2009] QB 536, [2009] 2 WLR 992.
15   *Robinson v Secretary of State for the Home Department* [1997] Imm AR 568.
16   *Abdul Saleem Koori v Secretary of State for the Home Department* [2016] EWCA Civ 552.
17   *AP (India) v Secretary of State for the Home Department* [2015] EWCA Civ 89.

## Appeals from the Upper Tribunal to the Supreme Court

**21.66A** *[Insert new heading and new paragraph:]*

A party before the Upper Tribunal who has a right of appeal to the court of appeal in England and Wales or to the court of appeal in Northern Ireland may apply for permission to appeal directly to the Supreme Court if the Upper Tribunal has issued a certificate enabling the party to do that [1].[1] Before the Upper Tribunal may issue such a certificate, it has to be satisfied that there is a sufficient case to justify an application for permission to appeal to the Supreme Court and that: (a) the case involves a point of law concerned with the construction of a statute or enactment that was fully argued before the tribunal; or (b) the case involves a point of law that was fully considered by the Court of Appeal or Supreme Court in another case that binds the tribunal; or (c) the point of law is of general public importance; the proceedings relate to a matter of national importance and are so significant that a hearing by the Supreme Court is justified or the benefits of early consideration by the Supreme Court outweigh the benefits of consideration by the Court of Appeal.[2] If the Upper Tribunal issues a certificate, there is no right of appeal to the Court of Appeal during the period in which an application for permission to appeal to the Supreme Court may be made and whilst any such application is pending or has been granted.[3]

1   Tribunals, Courts and Enforcement Act 2007, s 14B, as inserted by the Criminal Justice and Courts Act 2015, s 64.
2   Tribunals, Courts and Enforcement Act 2007, s 14A.
3   Tribunals, Courts and Enforcement Act 2007, s 14B(4)–(6).

## Judicial review

**21.69**  *[At the end of the paragraph, add:]*

Historical maladministration as opposed to illegality would not give rise to the obligation on the Secretary of State to consider the exercise of her remedial powers,[8] nor would an erroneous but lawful decision as to the applicant's nationality resulting in his losing the benefit of a favourable policy.[9]

8   *Mousasaoui v Secretary of State for the Home Department* [2016] EWCA Civ 50.
9   *R (Zargul Safi) v Secretary of State for the Home Department* [2015] EWHC 95 (Admin).

## Statutory appeals and judicial review

**21.70**  *[In the main text, after footnote reference 3, insert:]*

In the absence of 'special or exceptional factors' the court or tribunal will not entertain an application for judicial review in respect of a decision against which there is a right of appeal, albeit exercisable only after departure from the UK. The existence of disputes of fact and matters of procedural unfairness are 'rarely likely to constitute special or exceptional circumstances' as they can be dealt with in an out of country appeal, nor is the inconvenience and detriment to a student having to leave the UK in the middle of a course.[3a] That a person was being detained pursuant to the decision was a 'special or exceptional circumstance' that would justify judicial review of the decision, notwithstanding the existence of an out of country appeal; so too would be 'compelling evidence that in the circumstances of the particular case, the issue could not properly or fairly be ventilated in an out of country appeal'.[3b] Where there is a dispute about whether or not there is a right of appeal, generally the remedy is to give notice of appeal to the tribunal, applying for judicial review of the tribunal if it refuses to accept the notice of appeal rather than bringing judicial review proceedings against the decision.[3c]

3a   *R (Sheraz Mehmood and Shahbaz Ali) v Secretary of State for the Home Department* [2015] EWCA Civ 744.
3b   *R (Sood) v Secretary of State for the Home Department* [2015] EWCA Civ 831.
3c   *R (Khan) v Secretary of State for the Home Department (right of appeal – alternative remedy) IJR* [2015] UKUT 353 (IAC).

## Procedure in the Administrative Court

**21.72**  *[At the end of the paragraph, add:]*

The court may not set aside a consent order that disposes of proceedings, bearing in mind that in public law proceedings, a consent order will only be made if judicially approved.[15]

If a grant of permission to apply for judicial review is ambiguous as to the grounds on which permission has been granted, any ambiguity should be resolved in favour of the applicant.[16]

[15]  R *(Muude Mohamud Gacal) v Secretary of State for the Home Department* [2015] EWHC 1437.

[16]  R *(Sandra Behary) v Secretary of State for the Home Department* [2016] EWCA Civ 702, [2016] 4 WLR 136, 166 NLJ 7707.

### Challenging removal directions, third country and non-suspensive appeal cases

**21.73** *[At the beginning of the paragraph, insert:]*

The Home Office policy 'Judicial Review and Injunctions'[o] has been changed since the 9th Edition, most recently on 25 November 2016. There are three different ways in which a person may be given notice of removal which are[0a]: (a) notice of a removal window, ie a period of up to three months, extendable for 28 days, during which the person may be removed without further notice; (b) notice of removal directions, specifying the date of departure; and (c) limited notice of removal where exact details of the flight are not given but the person is told that removal may take place within 21 days of the notice being given but not before expiry of the 'notice period'. A person must be given at least seven calendar days' notice of a removal window unless the person is detained.[0b] In other cases (including detained recipients of notice of a removal window and recipients of removal directions or limited notice of removal), the period of notice must be at least five working days in third country cases or where an asylum or human rights claim has been certified or 72 hours (including at least two working days, one of which must fall in the last 24 hours) in a normal enforcement case.[0c] Those being removed on charter flights or by other special arrangements (eg where complex medical needs require a significant number of medical escorts and special equipment)[0d] will be given a minimum of five working days' notice of removal.[0e] Exceptions to the foregoing are port cases where removal is to take place within seven days of refusal, 72 hours' notice is not required;[0f] cases where a non-suspensive appeal decision has previously been unsuccessfully challenged by judicial review require only 72 hours' notice.[0g] Removal will not be deferred if judicial review is merely threatened[0h] except in port cases where removal directions were set for a date within seven days of the refusal.[0i] Removal will normally be deferred if an application for judicial review has been lodged unless it has been less than six months since a previous judicial review or statutory appeal or the person is within the removal window or is being removed by charter flight or other special arrangements or there has been an order refusing an injunction to stop removal within the proceedings or permission has been refused with an order that renewal is no bar to removal.[0j] Removal will always be suspended if an injunction is granted; if the judicial review is the first challenge to a decision to certify an asylum or human rights claim resulting in there being no appeal or an out of country appeal only or permission to apply for judicial review has been granted.[0k]

*[In the text after footnote reference 11, add:]*

As an application for permission to appeal to the court of appeal following disposal of judicial review proceedings does not have suspensive effect, an applicant may ask for an order staying removal in the appellant's notice. In the ordinary course, a judge will decide whether to order a stay on the basis of whether the pleaded grounds disclose an arguable appeal; in other words, whether permission to appeal should be granted. However, where a stay behind a leading case is sought, the question for the judge will be whether the instant case is likely to be affected by the outcome of the lead case. The court of appeal indicated that where an appellant gave notice to the Secretary of State that an application for permission to appeal had been made, the Secretary of State should not set removal directions for 28 days following the appellant's notice being filed.[11a] Interim relief would not normally be granted on the application of an individual (as opposed to an NGO) for the benefit of a class of unidentified individuals who were not themselves party to proceedings, eg to stop removals to a particular country pending a lead case determining whether it was safe.[11b]

*[In the text after footnote reference 15, add:]*

The tribunal ordered return to the UK of a mother and child after deciding that the Secretary of State unlawfully concluded that the mother had not made a fresh claim: key considerations for the tribunal were that the case involved a child and the Secretary of State's failure to discharge her duties to the child; post-decision evidence about the circumstances of the mother and child and the possibility of delay whilst the asylum claim was further considered.[15a]

*[In footnote 15, before the full stop, add:]*

; *R (H) v Secretary of State for the Home Department* [2015] EWHC 377 (Admin)

*[Insert the new footnotes in the correct sequential order.]*

[0]  Enforcement Instructions and Guidance, Chapter 60, Judicial Review and Injunctions ('EIG Chapter 60').
[0a]  EIG Chapter 60, section 2.
[0b]  EIG Chapter 60, section 2.4.
[0c]  EIG Chapter 60, section 2.4.1.
[0d]  EIG Chapter 60, section 6A.
[0e]  EIG Chapter 60, section 2.5.
[0f]  EIG Chapter 60, section 3.1.1.
[0g]  EIG Chapter 60, section 3.1.3.
[0h]  EIG Chapter 60, section 4
[0i]  EIG Chapter 60, section 5.2.
[0j]  EIG Chapter 60, section 4.1 and 6.1.
[0k]  EIG Chapter 60, section 6.2.
[11a]  *R (EK) v Secretary of State for the Home Department* [2016] EWCA Civ 502.
[11b]  *R (Majit) v Secretary of State for the Home Department* [2016] EWHC 741 (Admin).
[15a]  *R (RA) v Secretary of State for the Home Department IJR* [2015] UKUT 292 (IAC).

**21.74** *[At the end of the paragraph, add:]*

The court of appeal has recently endorsed the approach taken in *Turgut* where the defendant responds to an application for judicial review and supporting evidence with a new decision: if the applicant has a properly arguable challenge to the new decision 'it will typically be just, proportionate and appropriate' to grant permission to amend the existing claim so as to deal with the new decision.[10] Requiring a new application for judicial review to be commenced in respect of the new decision[11] was an 'over-rigid' approach.[12] The administrative court has refused to stay judicial review proceedings when the defendant has agreed to remake the decision challenged with a view to the proceedings continuing as a challenge to the new decision,[13] but it may be that that too is 'over-rigid'.

[10] *R (Tanvir Hussain) v Secretary of State for the Home Department* [2016] EWCA Civ 1111, para 21.
[11] As in *R (Rathakrishnan) v Secretary of State for the Home Department* [2011] EWHC 1406 (Admin).
[12] *R (Tanvir Hussain)*, above, para 27.
[13] *R (Mohamed Asif) v Secretary of State for the Home Department* [2015] EWHC 1007 (Admin) and *R (Yousuf) v Secretary of State for the Home Department* [2016] EWHC 663 (Admin), citing *R (Bhatti) v Bury MBC* [2013] EWHC 3093 (Admin) and *R (P) v Essex County Council* [2004] EWHC 2027 (Admin).

### Evidence

**21.75** *[At the end of the paragraph, insert two new paragraphs:]*

The tribunal has emphasised that it is 'not an absolute rule or principle' that the material to be considered in judicial review proceedings is restricted to that considered by the original decision maker but may take a flexible approach to new evidence.[9] It also eschewed the rules that judicial review is an unsuitable vehicle for resolving factual disputes and that the defendant's evidence should be preferred to the applicant's where there is a conflict,[10] having regard to tribunal judges' familiarity with making findings of fact in the particular context.[11]

Precedent facts, ie those upon whose existence the exercise of statutory powers, eg to detain and remove a person depends, may be determined by the court or tribunal whereas facts upon which the exercise of a discretion depends are for determination by the Secretary of State, subject to *Wednesbury* review only: so, for example, whether deception had been used would be a precedent fact for the purpose of reviewing a decision to remove based on the use of deception but would not be a precedent fact when reviewing a refusal of leave to enter, based on the same fact.[12]

[9] *R (HN and others) v Secretary of State for the Home Department (JR – Scope – Evidence) IJR* [2015] UKUT 437 (IAC), para 76.
[10] *R (HN and others)*, above, para 77.
[11] *R (HN and others)*, above, para 78.
[12] *R (Bijendra Giri) v Secretary of State for the Home Department* [2015] EWCA Civ 784, [2016] 1 WLR 4418, [2015] All ER (D) 323 (Jul).

### Relief

**21.77** *[At the end of the paragraph, add:]*

The Upper Tribunal may grant a declaration where a coercive order may not be appropriate but a formal, judicial statement pronouncing on the existence or non-existence of a legal state of affairs would be; good reasons for granting a declaration include providing vindication for the applicant; avoiding the misleading impression that would be created by simply dismissing an application for judicial review following a finding of illegality and providing guiding for future decision making by the public authority.[8]

---

[8]  Under Tribunals, Courts and Enforcement Act 2007, s 15(1)(d); *R (SS) v Secretary of State for the Home Department (Declaratory Orders) IJR* [2015] UKUT 462 (IAC).

## JUDICIAL REVIEW IN THE UPPER TRIBUNAL

**21.80**  *[In the text after footnote reference 2, insert:]*

An application for permission to apply for judicial review must not be accepted by the tribunal unless it is accompanied by the requisite fee or the tribunal accepts an undertaking that the fee will be paid.[2a]

---

[2a]  Tribunal Procedure (Upper Tribunal) Rules 2008, SI 2008/2698, reg 28A(1).

**21.82**  *[In the text after footnote reference 2, insert:]*

If the tribunal refuses permission to apply for judicial review or refuses to admit a late application and records in the decision that the application is 'totally without merit', the applicant may not apply for the decision to be reconsidered at a hearing.[2a] A case should only be certified as 'totally without merit' if it is 'bound to fail' which means not only is the application 'not arguable' so as to warrant refusal of permission to apply for judicial review but it does not even identify a rational argument in support of the case.[2b] If a judge does decide to certify an application as 'totally without merit', particular care must be taken to address all of the arguments advanced for the applicant and to give specific reasons for certifying the application as well as refusing permission.[2c]

---

[2a]  Tribunal Procedure (Upper Tribunal) Rules 2008, SI 2008/2698, r 30(4A).
[2b]  *Samir Wasif v Secretary of State for the Home Department* [2016] EWCA Civ 82, para 15.
[2c]  *Samir Wasif*, above, paras [19]–[21].

### Conduct of judicial review proceedings

**21.83**  *[Insert new heading and new paragraph:]*

The court has repeatedly deprecated the bringing and conduct of judicial review applications in a way that is contrary to lawyers' duties to their clients and to the court.[1] Applications to the High Court should be made under the supervision of a qualified lawyer who is expected to make a statement of truth in relation to the matters relied on in support of the application.[2] Representatives have a duty to disclose all material facts in judicial review proceedings, including those adverse to the claimant.[3] It is not sufficient merely to disclose the documents containing the adverse material; it is necessary also to identify the significance of the material and the adverse points in the submissions supporting the application.[4]

1   For example, *R (Hamid) v Secretary of State for the Home Department* [2012] EWHC 3070 (Admin); *R (Butt) v Secretary of State for the Home Department* [2014] EWHC 264 (Admin); *In the matter of the conduct of Sandbrook Solicitors* [2015] EWHC 2473.

2   *R (Adil Akram and Amir Akram) v Secretary of State for the Home Department* [2015] EWHC 1359 (Admin).

3   *R (Mohammed Shazad Khan) v Secretary of State for the Home Department* [2016] EWCA Civ 416.

4   *R (Mohammed Shazad Khan)*, above.

# Chapter 22

# SPECIAL IMMIGRATION APPEALS COMMISSION

## BACKGROUND AND STRUCTURE OF THE SPECIAL IMMIGRATION APPEALS COMMISSION

**22.2** *[In footnote 2, third sentence, delete 'The current Chairman of the Commission is Mr Justice Irwin' and substitute:]*

The current Chair of the Commission is Mrs Justice Elisabeth Laing, appointed in January 2017 on the elevation to the Court of Appeal of the previous incumbent, Lord Justice Flaux.

## JURISDICTION

**22.3** *[At the end of the paragraph, add:]*

Reviewable decisions now also include certain deportation decisions excluded from the right of appeal following the coming into force of section 2E of SIACA 1997.[2]

[2]  Immigration Act 2014, Pt 2, s 18 (6 April 2015).

## REVIEW

**22.6** *[At the end of the last paragraph, insert new paragraph:]*

Section 18 of the Immigration Act 2014 has introduced s 2E of the Special Immigration Appeals Act 1997 with effect from 6 April 2015, which provides for a right of review in SIAC in respect of certain deportation decisions certified by the Secretary of State under s 97 of the Nationality Immigration and Asylum Act 2002 (see **22.4**) and where (i) no right of appeal lies or (ii) the decision gives rise to issues which may not be raised on appeal.

### Procedure on SIAC review

**22.7** *[At the end of the paragraph, add:]*

The Commission's approach to its review jurisdiction was further considered by the Divisional Court in R *(on the application of the Secretary of State for the Home Department) v Special Immigration Appeals Commission, AHK and others Interested Parties.*[2] While upholding the Commission's general approach, the Divisional court refined the Commission's approach to the extent of disclosure required to be provided to the Commission of material relied upon by the decision maker.

[2]   [2015] EWHC 681 (Admin), [2015] 1 WLR 4799, [2016] 2 All ER 620, [2015] INLR 670.

### Review of certain deportation decisions

**22.8** *[N.B.]*

See **22.6** above, section 2E of the Special Immigration Appeals Act 1997 now in force: see Immigration Act 2014 (Commencement No 4, Transitional and Saving Provisions and Amendment) Order 2015, SI 2015/371, Pt 1, art 4(a).

### PRESENCE OF APPELLANTS IN THE UK

**22.9** *[At the end of the paragraph, add:]*

Section 97(2G) of NIAA 2002 provides the Commission with power to set aside a certificate issued under s 97(2C) on application under subsection 97(2F). The power is exercisable on judicial review principles (ss 97(2G)) and 97(2H) provides, as yet untested by the courts that, the Commission's decision on a section 97(2F) application is final.

### PROCEDURE AND EVIDENCE BEFORE THE SPECIAL IMMIGRATION APPEALS COMMISSION

### Procedure on appeals

**22.11** *[At the end of the paragraph, add:]*

By s 2(2) of SIACA 1997, the Commission's appellate jurisdiction mirrors that of the First-tier Tribunal and thus is now limited to appeals on human rights, discrimination or Refugee Convention grounds. Similarly, the s 87 power to make directions on allowing an appeal has been repealed although it still appears in the list of applicable appeals provisions in s 2(2) of SIACA 1997.

**22.13** *[At the end of the paragraph, add:]*

Changes to the Commission's procedure rules introduced by the Special Immigration Appeals Commission (Procedure) (Amendment) Rules 2015, SI 2015/867 include primarily changes to the Rules' terminology to include references to the procedure on review under sections 2C–2E of SIACA 1997 and associated nomenclature.[13]

[13]   And see also the Commission's Practice Note in force from 11 January 2016 and downloadable in pdf form at https://www.gardencourtchambers.co.uk/wp-content/uploads/2016/01/SIAC-practice-note-2016.pdf. This important note is in the manner of a Practice Direction and indicates the procedural steps that will normally be taken by the Commission unless specific directions to the contrary are sought and obtained. An important lacuna appears to be any requirement for the Secretary of State to serve a defence in reviews brought under SIACA 1997, ss 2C–2E.

### The approach in cases engaging EU law and article 6

**22.15** *[At the end of the paragraph, add:]*

In *Pham v Secretary of State for the Home Department*,[4] the Supreme Court reviewed the applicability of EU law in the deprivation of citizenship context and considered that the Court of Appeal may have been wrong in *G1 v Secretary of State for the Home Department*,[5] when it rejected the argument based on *Rottmann v Freistaat Bayern*[6] that where deprivation of British citizenship meant loss of EU citizenship (as parasitic on British citizenship), EU law may be engaged. However, the Court held, EU law may make no practical difference if owing to the fundamental and 'radical' nature of the deprivation measure under challenge, common law intensity scrutiny was on a par with a proportionality test. On current practice, SIAC will normally undertake a fact-finding exercise in appeals or applications before it which may engage EU law in order to determine what difference EU law may have made to: (i) disclosure requirements; or (ii) proportionality.

4   [2015] UKSC 19, [2015] 1 WLR 1591, [2015] 3 All ER 1015, [2015] 2 CMLR 49.
5   [2012] EWCA Civ 867, [2013] QB 1008, [2013] 2 WLR 1277, [2012] 4 All ER 987, [2012] 3 CMLR 36.
6   [2010] QB 761, [2010] 3 WLR 1166, [2010] ECR I-1449, [2010] 3 CMLR 2, [2010] All ER (EC) 635, [2011] CEC 35, ECJ (Grand Chamber), 02 March 2010.

### 'National security' deportations

**22.17** *[At the end of the paragraph, add:]*

Following some 13 years of litigation, the Memoranda of Assurance agreed between the UK and the Algerian President were finally rejected by SIAC in allowing the appeals of *BB, U, Y, Z, W* and *PP* against deportation to Algeria in 2016.[8] The Court of Appeal[9] had rejected the judgment of an earlier constitution of the Commission which had wrongly imposed a requirement to show a systemic risk of Article 3 ill treatment and failed to apply the 'full, nuanced, and holistic approach of *Ahmad v United Kingdom* (24027/07) (2013) 56 EHRR 1 to the unusual circumstances of the case'.

8   SC/39/2005, SC/34/2005, SC/54/2005, SC/32/2005, SC/36/2005 and SC/37/2005 – judgment given 18 April 2016.
9   *BB and others v Secretary of State for the Home Department* [2015] EWCA Civ 9.

### Fairness of proceedings before the Special Immigration Appeals Commission

**22.20** *[At the end of the paragraph, add:]*

In a number of cases, the Commission has upheld the Secretary of State's approach to giving fair warning of the need to disclose matters which may raise doubts as to a person's character in a naturalisation case[10] which include guidance on application forms and accompanying notes which applicants should study carefully. The Court of Appeal has upheld the fairness of proceedings before SIAC in deprivation of citizenship cases.[11]

10   See, eg *MNY v Secretary of State for the Home Department* SN/53/2015

[11] See, eg *S1 and others v Secretary of State for the Home Department* [2016] EWCA Civ 560, [2016] 3 CMLR 37.

## Bail

**22.23** *[At the end of the paragraph, add:]*

A new rule 30A(1) introduced into the SIAC Procedure Rules by SI 2015/867[21] (in force from 12 April 2015) provides that the Commission must dismiss repeat applications for bail made during the period of 28 days since any decision made by the Commission to refuse bail unless there had been a 'material change of circumstances'. Rule 30A(2) provides that the Commission may determine whether there has been a material change of circumstances without a hearing. The Court of Appeal held in *B v Secretary of State for the Home Department*[22] that the Special Immigration Appeals Commission has no power to impose bail conditions where a person is not lawfully detained.

[21] Special Immigration Appeals Commission (Procedure) (Amendment) Rules 2015, SI 2015/867.
[22] [2015] EWCA Civ 445, [2016] QB 789, [2015] 3 WLR 1031.

# Index

# Index